Ocean Ships

Ocean Ships

David Hornsby

Ian Allan
PUBLISHING

Contents

First published 1964
This Edition 2006

ISBN (10) 0 7110 3141 X
ISBN (13) 978 0 7110 3141 8

© Ian Allan Publishing 2006

Published by Ian Allan Publishing

an imprint of Ian Allan Publishing Ltd, Hersham, Surrey KT12 4RG.
Printed by Ian Allan Printing Ltd, Hersham, Surrey KT12 4RG.

Code: 0605/B3

Visit the Ian Allan Publishing web site at:
www.ianallanpublishing.com

Front Cover: **Royal Caribbean's** NAVIGATOR OF THE
SEAS – the 4th of five 'Voyager' class vessels built
1999-2004 and until recently the largest cruise ships
ever built. *Royal Caribbean*

Back cover, top: **Costamare Shipping Co SA.**
MAERSK KOLKATA (on charter to Moller-Maersk).
Vandriessche Guido

Back cover, top: **Dampskib. Torm.** TORM MARY.
N. Kemps

Half title: **P&O Cruises's** AURORA. *Phil Kempsey*

Title page: **Teekay's** NORDIC TRYM and **Brostrom's**
BRO ATLAND. *Hans Kraijenbosch*

Royal Caribbean's recently delivered FREEDOM OF THE SEAS. The largest passenger ship ever built and the first
of three 'Ultra' class sisterships. *David Hornsby*

Preface

Just two years after the previous edition, this new edition of *Ocean Ships* once again records the ever changing scene within merchant shipping companies and services, based in or operating regular deep-sea services to the UK and northern Europe.

This edition again records over 250 passenger ships operating world-wide and the enlarged cargo section now includes some 6,300 vessels, together aggregating over 280 million gross tonnes, nearly 320 million tonnes deadweight and moored bow-to-stern would extend almost 900 miles (over 1,400 kilometres).

In the cruise ship sector, the forecast pressure on medium-sized companies became a really and this trend will no doubt continue with the continued ordering of even larger vessels by the major groups. Just prior to publication, the title of the world's largest ever passenger ship is due to be transferred to the 158,000 grt *Freedom of the Seas*, the first of three sister-ships. However, the same company has now ordered the even larger 220,000 grt *Project Genesis* for 2009 delivery, which will accommodate up to 5,400 passengers. Apart from the five cruise ships due for 2006 delivery, there are currently 25 other cruise ships on order averaging almost 110,000 grt each, so the realignment of the cruising industry will continue unabated.

Container shipping has seen significant changes during the past two years. The most notable events included the Moller-Maersk take-over of P&O Nedlloyd, giving the former some 17% of the world market share, followed by Hapag-Lloyd taking over CP Ships, which itself had not even completed the unification of its six former 'brands'. The delivery of 'post-panamax' vessels (too long and too wide to transit the Panama Canal) continues in large numbers, with the first 10,000 TEU (20-foot equivalent unit) vessels due for imminent delivery and even larger 12-15,000 TEU vessels being offered by Far Eastern builders.

The trend for many owners to charter newbuildings directly from management companies or German KG investment funds, rather than have direct ownership, has continued unabated and has expanded from container ships to include large numbers of bulk carriers, tankers and other types of ship.

The International Ship and Port Facility Security Code (ISPS) has had a marked affect on access for enthusiasts and photography to some ports, but new vantage points have been found at many to enable 'maritime twitchers' to continue enjoying the movements and activities of busy ports.

The world wide web continues to be a great source of information and misinformation. The best sites provide excellent user-friendly information on a number of levels, whilst others frustratingly seek to place a cloak over their shipping activities and do not even respond to straight-forward enquiries. Every effort has been taken to avoid minor errors, but these are bound to occur in a book of this complexity on a subject that is always 'on the move'.

Once again, I express my thanks to the photographers who have kindly provided more material than can possibly be included and to my many friends and acquaintances for their interest, comments and information.

Lastly, but most importantly, apologies to my wife, who somehow manages to put up with the household upheaval and unsocial hours caused by my efforts to ensure that *Ocean Ships* remains successful.

David Hornsby
Southampton, England
March 2006

Disclaimer

The publishers, the shipping companies and the Author accept no liability for any loss or damage caused by any error, inaccuracy or omission in the information published in this edition of *Ocean Ships*.

Glossary

The companies in each section are listed in alphabetical order under the main company name, followed by the country of origin. Individual 'one-ship' owning companies are not given, but in some cases subsidiary fleets are separately listed. Other variations in ownership, joint ownership, management or charter are generally covered by footnotes. Funnel and hull colours are those normally used by the companies, although these may vary when a vessel is operating on a particular service, or on charter to another operator.

Name registered name
Eng all vessels are diesel motorships with a single screw; unless indicated as having more than one screw or other types of main propulsive machinery as follows

as	sail with auxiliary engines		gt	gas turbine with electric drive
me	diesel with electric drive		st	steam turbine
gm	combined gas turbine and diesel with electric drive			

Flag

Ant	Netherlands Antilles	Cyp	Cyprus	Isr	Israel	Pmd	Madeira
Are	United Arab Emirates	Deu	Germany	Ita	Italy	Pol	Poland
		Dis	Danish International	Jpn	Japan	Qat	Qatar
Arg	Argentina	Dmk	Denmark	Kor	South Korea	Rus	Russia
Atf	Kerguelen Islands	Ecu	Ecuador	Kwt	Kuwait	Sau	Saudi Arabia
Atg	Antigua and Barbuda	Egy	Egypt	Lbr	Liberia	Sgp	Singapore
		Esp	Spain	Lka	Sri Lanka	Swe	Sweden
Aus	Australia	Est	Estonia	Lux	Luxembourg	Tha	Thailand
Bel	Belgium	Eth	Ethiopia	Lva	Latvia	Tur	Turkey
Bgr	Bulgaria	Fin	Finland	Mar	Morocco	Tuv	Tuvalu
Bhr	Bahrain	Fra	France	Mex	Mexico	Twn	Taiwan
Bhs	Bahamas	Fro	Faroe Islands	Mhl	Marshall Islands	Ukr	Ukraine
Bmu	Bermuda	Gbr	United Kingdom	Mlt	Malta	Usa	United States of America
Bra	Brazil	Gib	Gibraltar	Mmr	Myanmar (Burma)		
Brb	Barbados	Grc	Greece	Mys	Malaysia	Vct	St. Vincent and Grenadines
Can	Canada	Hkg	Hong Kong (China)	Nis	Norwegian International		
Che	Switzerland	Hrv	Croatia			Ven	Venezuela
Chl	Chile	Ind	India	Nld	Netherlands	Wlf	Wallis & Futura
Chn	China	Iom	Isle of Man (British)	Nor	Norway	Zaf	South Africa
Cni	Canary Islands	Irl	Ireland	Pan	Panama		
Cym	Cayman Islands	Irn	Iran	Phl	Philippines		

Year year of completion — not necessarily of launching or commissioning.
GRT gross registered tonnage — not weight, but volume of hull and enclosed space — one gross ton equals 100 cu. ft.
DWT deadweight tonnes — maximum weight of cargo, stores, fuel etc — one tonne (1000 kg) equals 0.984 ton (British)
LOA overall length (metres); (- -) length between perpendiculars
Bm overall breadth of hull (metres) - some vessels have greater width to superstructure/bridge etc.
Kts service speed in normal weather and at normal service draught — one knot equals 6,050ft per hour or 1.146 mph.
Type general description of type of vessel

B	bulk carrier	HL/hl	heavy-lift vessel	ROI	roll-on, roll-off/icebreaker
BC	bulk/container carrier	hls	heavy-lift / semi-submersible	Rr	refrigerated with roll-on, roll-off
Bcs	bulk/caustic soda	L	livestock carrier		
Bp	bulk/pitch carrier	LC	lighter/containers	T	tanker
Bu	bulk carrier - self discharging	Lgc	liquefied gas carrier	Tb	tanker-bitumen
		Lng	liquefied natural gas carrier	Tfj	tanker-fruit juice
Bw	bulk woodchip carrier	Lpg	liquefied petroleum gas carrier	Tm	tanker-molten sulphur
C	general cargo			Ts	storage tanker
CC	cellular container	O	ore carrier	V	vehicle carrier
Ce	cement carrier	Obo	ore/bulk/oil carrier		
Co	cargo/part container	R	refrigerated cargo		
Cp	cargo/pitch carrier	RO	roll-on, roll-off		

Pass maximum number of passengers in lower and upper berths or (——) in lower berths only
Remarks:

conv	date converted from other type		len	date hull lengthened
ex:	previous names followed by year of change to subsequent name		short	date hull shortened
			wid	date hull widened
l/a	name at launch or 'float-out'		NE	date re-engined
l/dn	name allocated when laid-down at commencement of construction.		teu	twenty-foot equivalent unit (one teu equals about 14 tonnes deadweight)
pt:	part of ship			

Right: The funnel of **Cunard's** QUEEN ELIZABETH 2. *Phil Kempsey*

PART ONE
Passenger Liners and Cruise Ships

Name	Eng	Flag	Year	GRT	Loa	Bm	Kts	Pass	Former names

Carnival Corporation

USA

Carnival Cruise Line Inc/USA

Funnel: *Red forward, blue aft, separated by white curved vertical band.*
Hull: *White with narrow red band, blue boot-topping.*

Name	Eng	Flag	Year	GRT	Loa	Bm	Kts	Pass	Former names
Carnival Conquest	(me2)	Pan	2002	110,239	290	36	19	3,700	
Carnival Destiny	(me2)	Bhs	1996	101,353	272	36	18	3,336	
Carnival Glory	(me2)	Pan	2003	110,239	290	36	22	3,700	
Carnival Legend	(me2)	Pan	2002	85,942	293	32	22	2,680	
Carnival Liberty	(me2)	Pan	2005	110,320	285	32	22	3,700	
Carnival Miracle	(me2)	Pan	2004	85,942	293	32	22	2,680	
Carnival Pride	(me2)	Pan	2001	85,920	293	32	22	2,680	
Carnival Spirit	(me2)	Pan	2001	85,920	293	32	22	2,680	
Carnival Triumph	(me2)	Bhs	1999	101,509	272	36	21	3,470	
Carnival Valor	(me2)	Pan	2004	110,239	290	36	22	3,710	
Carnival Victory	(me2)	Pan	2000	101,509	272	36	22	3,470	
Celebration	(2)	Pan	1987	47,262	223	28	19	1,896	
Ecstasy	(me2)	Bhs	1991	70,367	262	32	18	2,634	
Elation	(me2)	Pan	1998	70,390	262	32	20	2,634	
Fantasy	(me2)	Pan	1990	70,367	261	32	18	2,634	
Fascination	(me2)	Bhs	1994	70,367	262	32	18	2,624	
Holiday	(2)	Bhs	1985	46,052	222	28	22	1,794	
Imagination	(me2)	Bhs	1995	70,367	262	32	18	2,624	
Inspiration	(me2)	Bhs	1996	70,367	262	32	18	2,634	
Paradise	(me2)	Pan	1998	70,390	262	32	21	2,634	
Sensation	(me2)	Bhs	1993	70,367	262	32	20	2,634	
newbuildings									
Carnival Freedom	(me2)	Pan	2007	110,000	290	36	21	(2,974)	
Carnival Splendor	(me2)	Pan	2008	110,000	290	36	21	(3,006)	
Carnival un-named	(me2)	Pan	2009	130,000	-	-	-	(3,608)	

Costa Crociere SpA/Italy

Funnel: *Yellow with blue 'C' and narrow black top.*
Hull: *White with blue line and blue boot-topping.*

Name	Eng	Flag	Year	GRT	Loa	Bm	Kts	Pass	Former names
Costa Allegre	(2)	Ita	1969	28,430	188	26	20	1,066	ex Alexandra-90, Regent Moon-88, Annie Johnson-86 (len/conv CC-92)
Costa Atlantica	(me2)	Ita	2000	85,619	293	32	22	2,680	
Costa Classica	(2)	Ita	1991	52,926	221	31	19	1,766	
Costa Concordia	(me2)	Ita	2006	112,000	290	36	21	3,780	
Costa Europa	(2)	Ita	1986	53,872	243	29	19	1,773	ex Westerdam-02, Homeric-88 (len-90)
Costa Fortuna	(me2)	Ita	2003	102,587	272	36	20	3,470	
Costa Magica	(me2)	Ita	2004	102,600	272	36	20	3,470	
Costa Marina	(2)	Ita	1969	25,558	174	26	20	1,025	ex Italia-90, Regent Sun-86, Axel Johnson-86 (conv CC-90)
Costa Mediterranea	(me2)	Ita	2003	85,619	293	32	22	2,680	
Costa Romantica	(2)	Ita	1993	53,049	221	31	19	1,782	
Costa Victoria	(me2)	Ita	1996	75,166	253	32	23	2,200	
newbuildings									
Costa Serena	(me2)	Ita	2007	112,000	290	36	21	3,780	
Costa un-named	(me2)	Ita	2009	112,000	290	36	21	3,780	

Holland-America Line/Netherlands

Funnel: *White with black/white ship symbol within double black ring, narrow black top or vents.*
Hull: *Black with red boot-topping.*

Name	Eng	Flag	Year	GRT	Loa	Bm	Kts	Pass	Former names
Amsterdam	(me2)	Nld	2000	60,874	238	32	21	1,738	
Maasdam	(me2)	Nld	1993	55,451	219	31	20	1,629	
Noordam	(gm2)	Nld	2006	82,318	290	32	24	1,800	
Oosterdam	(gm2)	Nld	2003	81,769	285	32	22	2,388	
Prinsendam	(2)	Nld	1988	37,983	204	29	21	837	ex Seabourn Sun-02, Royal Viking Sun-99
Rotterdam	(me2)	Nld	1997	59,652	238	32	22	1,620	
Ryndam	(me2)	Nld	1994	55,819	219	31	20	1,629	
Statendam	(me2)	Nld	1993	55,819	219	31	20	1,629	
Veendam	(me2)	Bhs	1996	55,451	219	31	20	1,629	
Volendam	(me2)	Nld	1999	60,906	237	32	22	1,824	

Carnival Corp. (Costa Crociere S.p.A.). COSTA EUROPA. *Hans Kraijenbosch*

Carnival Corp. (Costa Crociere S.p.A.). COSTA FORTUNA. *M. D. J. Lennon*

Carnival Corp. (Holland-America Line). PRINSENDAM. *G. J. de Boer*

Name	Eng	Flag	Year	GRT	Loa	Bm	Kts	Pass	Former names
Westerdam	(gm2)	Nld	2004	81,811	285	32	22	1,800	
Zaandam	(me2)	Nld	2000	61,396	237	32	22	2,272	
Zuiderdam	(gm2)	Nld	2002	81,769	285	32	22	1,848	
newbuilding									
Cruise ship	(gm2)	Nld	2008	86,000	290	32	24	(2,044)	plus option for 2010 delivery.

Windstar Cruises Ltd

Funnel: *White with turquoise symbol.*
Hull: *White with turquoise band and blue boot-topping.*

Name	Eng	Flag	Year	GRT	Loa	Bm	Kts	Pass	Former names
Wind Spirit	(as/me)	Bhs	1988	5,736	134	16	11	150	
Wind Star	(as/me)	Bhs	1986	5,307	134	16	11	150	
Wind Surf	(as/me2)	Bhs	1989	14,745	187	20	15	453	ex Club Med 1-97, l/a La Fayette

Cunard Line Ltd/UK

Funnel: *Red with two narrow black rings and black top.*
Hull: *Black with white band above red boot-topping.*

Name	Eng	Flag	Year	GRT	Loa	Bm	Kts	Pass	Former names
Queen Elizabeth 2	(me2)	Gbr	1969	70,327	294	32	28	1,850	(NE-87)
Queen Mary 2	(gm4)	Gbr	2003	148,528	345	41	29	2,620	
newbuilding									
Queen Victoria	(gm3)	Gbr	2007	89,500	290	32	24	1,850	

Seabourn Cruises Inc/USA

Funnel: *White with three narrow white lines forming 'S' on blue shield and blue top.*
Hull: *White with pale blue band and blue boot-topping.*

Name	Eng	Flag	Year	GRT	Loa	Bm	Kts	Pass	Former names
Seabourn Legend	(2)	Bhs	1992	9,961	135	19	16	212	ex Queen Odyssey-96, Royal Viking Queen-94, l/dn Seabourn Legend
Seabourn Pride	(2)	Bhs	1988	9,975	134	19	16	212	
Seabourn Spirit	(2)	Bhs	1989	9,975	134	19	16	212	

Operates as subsidiary of Cunard Line.

Ocean Village/UK

Funnel: *Pink with multi-coloured 'ocean' on large white oval disc.*
Hull: *White with multi-coloured half-rings above waterline.*

Name	Eng	Flag	Year	GRT	Loa	Bm	Kts	Pass	Former names
Ocean Village	(me2)	Gbr	1989	63,524	246	32	19	1,692	ex Arcadia-03, Star Princess-97, Sitmar Fairmajesty-89

Also see AIDAblu being transferred from Aida Cruises in 2007.

P&O Cruises Ltd/UK

Funnel: *Yellow.*
Hull: *White with red boot-topping.*

Name	Eng	Flag	Year	GRT	Loa	Bm	Kts	Pass	Former names
Arcadia	(gm2)	Gbr	2005	82,972	285	32	22	2,556	l/dn Queen Victoria
Artemis	(2)	Gbr	1984	44,348	231	29	21	1,260	ex Royal Princess-05
Aurora	(me2)	Gbr	2000	76,152	270	32	24	1,878	
Oceana	(me2)	Gbr	1999	77,499	261	32	21	2,272	ex Ocean Princess-02
Oriana	(2)	Gbr	1995	69,153	260	32	24	2,108	
newbuilding									
Ventura	(me2)	Gbr	2008	116,000	290	36	22	3,100	

P&O Cruises Australia Ltd/Australia

Funnel: *Blue with small white 'Pacific' and large yellow 'Star or Sun'.*
Hull: *White with broad blue above narrow yellow bands.*

Name	Eng	Flag	Year	GRT	Loa	Bm	Kts	Pass	Former names
Pacific Star	(2)	Gbr	1981	33,250	205	26	19	1,411	ex Costa Tropicale-05, Tropicale-01
Pacific Sun	(2)	Bhs	1986	47,262	225	28	19	1,800	ex Jubilee-04

Princess Cruises Inc/USA

Funnel: *White funnel with blue 'Princess' insignia with flowing hair, dark green top.*
Hull: *White.*

Name	Eng	Flag	Year	GRT	Loa	Bm	Kts	Pass	Former names
Caribbean Princess *	(me2)	Bmu	2004	112,894	290	36	22	3,598	l/dn Crown Princess
Coral Princess	(gm2)	Bmu	2002	91,627	294	32	21	2,581	
Crown Princess		Bmu	2006	116,000	290	36	22	(3,100)	
Dawn Princess	(me2)	Bmu	1997	77,441	261	32	21	1,950	
Diamond Princess *	(gm2)	Bmu	2004	115,875	290	38	23	2,600	l/dn Sapphire Princess
Golden Princess	(me2)	Bmu	2001	108,865	290	36	22	3,300	
Grand Princess	(me2)	Bmu	1998	108,806	290	36	22	3,300	
Island Princess	(gm2)	Bmu	2003	91,627	294	32	24	2,581	
Pacific Princess	(me2)	Bmu	1999	30,277	181	25	18	688	ex R Three-02

Carnival Corp. (Cunard Line). QUEEN MARY 2. *C. J. Dornom*

Carnival Corp. (P&O Cruises). ARCADIA. *N. Kemps*

Carnival Corp. (P&O Cruises). ARTEMIS. *C. J. Dornom*

Name	Eng	Flag	Year	GRT	Loa	Bm	Kts	Pass	Former names
Regal Princess *	(me2)	Bmu	1991	70,285	245	32	19	1,900	
Sapphire Princess *	(gm2)	Bmu	2004	115,875	290	38	23	3,078	l/dn Diamond Princess
Sea Princess	(me2)	Bmu	1998	77,499	261	32	19	2,342	ex Adonia-05, Sea Princess-03
Star Princess	(me2)	Bmu	2002	108,977	290	36	22	3,211	
Sun Princess	(me2)	Bmu	1995	77,441	261	32	21	2,342	
Tahitian Princess	(me2)	Bmu	1999	30,277	181	25	18	688	ex R Four-02
newbuildings									
Emerald Princess	(me2)	Bmu	2007	116,000	290	36	22	(3,100)	
Un-named Princess	(me2)	Bmu	2009	116,000	290	36	22	(3,100)	

* owned by Princess Cruises Lines, Bermuda. ** to be transferred to P&O Cruises Australia Ltd later in 2006.

Swan Hellenic/UK

Funnel: *Dark blue with yellow swan symbol.*
Hull: *Dark blue with white band above red boot-topping.*

Minerva II	(me2)	Mhl	2001	30,277	181	25	18	777	ex R Eight-03

To be transferred to Princess Cruises in 2007 and renamed Royal Princess.

Aida Cruises/Germany

Funnel: *White with 'AIDA' (letters in blue, red, yellow and green respectively).*
Hull: *White with colourful 'eye' graphics and blue wave symbols.*

AIDAaura	(me2)	Ita	2003	42,289	203	28	19	1,582	
AIDAblu *	(me2)	Ita	1990	70,310	245	32	19	1,900	ex A'Rosa Blu-04, Crown Princess-02
AIDAcara	(2)	Ita	1996	38,557	193	28	18	1,186	ex Aida-01
AIDAvita	(me2)	Ita	2002	42,289	203	28	19	1,582	
newbuildings									
AIDAdiva	(me2)	Ita	2007	68,500	249	32	21	(2,030)	
Un-named	(me2)	Ita	2008	68,500	249	32	21	(2,030)	
Un-named	(me2)	Ita	2009	68,500	249	32	21	(2,030)	

Subsidiary of Princess Cruises. See also Transocean Tours.
* to be renamed and transferred to Ocean Village 2007.

Classic International Cruises   Portugal

Funnel: *Yellow with light blue band, black top*
Hull: *White with blue band, blue boot-topping.*

Arion	(m2)	Pmd	1965	5,888	117	17	18	312	ex Nautilus 2000-99, Astra I-99, Astra-96, Istra-91
Athena	(2)	Ita	1948	16,144	160	21	18	566	ex Caribe-05, Valtur Prima-03, Italia Prima-00, Italia I-93, Fridtjof Nansen-93, Volker-86, Volkerfreundschaft-85, Stockholm-60
Funchal	(m2)	Pmd	1961	9,563	153	19	14	442	
Princess Danae	(m2)	Pan	1955	16,531	162	21	17	497	ex Baltica-96, Starlight Princess-94, Anar-92, Danae-92, Therisos Express-74, Port Melbourne-72

Subsidiary of Arcalia Shipping Co. Ltd., Portugal, vessels often chartered out to other operators.

Peter Deilmann Reederei   Germany

Funnel: *White with red 'D' outline containing insignia.*
Hull: *White with red band.*

Deutschland	(2)	Deu	1998	22,496	175	23	20	600	

Disney Cruise Vacations   USA

Funnel: *Red with white 'Mickey Mouse' symbol over three black waves, black top.*
Hull: *Black with white band above red boot-topping.*

Disney Magic	(me2)	Bhs	1998	83,338	294	32	21	2,500	
Disney Wonder	(me2)	Bhs	1999	83,308	294	32	21	2,500	

Classic International Cruises. ATHENA. *G. J. de Boer*

Classic International Cruises. PRINCESS DANAE. *Phil Kempsey*

Disney Cruise Vacations. DISNEY MAGIC. *Hans Kraijenbosch*

Name	Eng	Flag	Year	GRT	Loa	Bm	Kts	Pass	Former names
Louis Cruise Lines Ltd									**Cyprus**

Funnel: White with red sun/wave symbol above dark blue 'L', black top
Hull: White with red or dark blue boot-topping.

Name	Eng	Flag	Year	GRT	Loa	Bm	Kts	Pass	Former names
Aegean 1 *	(2)	Grc	1973	11,563	141	21	-	682	ex Aegean Dolphin-96, Dolphin-90, Aegean Dolphin-89, Alkyon-86, Narcis-85
Ausonia	(st2)	Cyp	1957	12,609	160	21	20	690	
Birka Princess	(2)	Cyp	1986	22,712	143	25	17	1,537	
Coral *	(2)	Grc	1971	13,995	148	22	24	912	ex Triton-05, Sunward II-91, Cunard Adventurer-77
Perla *	(2)	Bhs	1971	16,710	163	23	21	750	ex Seawing-05, Southward-95
Princesa Marissa	(2)	Cyp	1966	10,487	134	20	18	583	ex Prinsessan-87, Finnhansa-77
Sapphire *	(2)	Cyp	1967	12,263	149	21	16	562	ex Princesa Oceanica-96, Sea Prince V-95, Sea Prince-95, Ocean Princess-93, Italia-83
Serenade	(2)	Bhs	1957	14,173	162	20	16	672	ex Mermoz-99, Jean Mermoz-70
The Calypso *	(2)	Bhs	1967	11,162	135	19	16	486	ex Calypso-05, Regent Jewel-94, Sun Fiesta-93, Ionian Harmony-90, Durr-89, Canguro Verde-81

* operated by Greek-based offshoot Louis Hellenic Cruises and ** on charter to Travelscope.
See also Thomson Cruises (under TUI), Transocean Tours and Holland America (under Carnival Corp.).

Mediterranean Shipping Cruises
Italy

Funnel: White or dark blue with white 'M' over 'SC' inside white 12-pointed compass rose.
Hull: White with narrow blue band, blue boot-topping.

Name	Eng	Flag	Year	GRT	Loa	Bm	Kts	Pass	Former names
Melody	(2)	Pan	1982	35,143	205	27	23	1,292	ex Starship Atlantic-97, Atlantic-88
Monterey	(st)	Pan	1952	20,046	172	23	16	661	ex Free State Mariner-56
MSC Armonia	(me2)	Pan	2001	58,625	251	29	21	1,566	ex European Vision-04
MSC Lirica	(me2)	Pan	2003	59,058	251	29	20	2,200	
MSC Musica	(me2)	Pan	2006	89,600	294	32	23	3,013	
MSC Opera	(me2)	Pan	2004	59,058	251	29	20	2,200	
MSC Sinfonia	(me2)	Pan	2002	58,625	251	29	21	1,566	ex European Stars-04, I/a European Dream
Rhapsody	(2)	Ita	1977	17,095	164	23	18	947	ex Cunard Princess-95, I/a Cunard Conquest
newbuildings									
MSC Orchestra		Pan	2007	89,600	294	32	23	3,013	
MSC Poesia		Pan	2008	89,600	294	32	23	3,000	
MSC Fantasia		Pan	2008	133,500	333	38	23	3,887	
MSC Seranata		Pan	2009	133,500	333	38	23	3,887	

Mitsui-OSK Lines KK
Japan

Funnel: Light red.
Hull: White.

Name	Eng	Flag	Year	GRT	Loa	Bm	Kts	Pass	Former names
Fuji Maru	(2)	Jpn	1989	23,235	167	27	20	603	
Nippon Maru	(2)	Jpn	1990	21,903	167	24	18	607	

Nippon Yusen Kaisha
Japan

Crystal Cruises Inc./USA

Funnel: Black, large white side panels with blue symbol.
Hull: White with narrow blue band.

Name	Eng	Flag	Year	GRT	Loa	Bm	Kts	Pass	Former names
Crystal Serenity	(me2)	Bhs	2003	68,870	250	34	23	1080	
Crystal Symphony	(me2)	Bhs	1995	51,044	238	31	21	975	

Yusen Cruise/Japan

Funnel: White with two red bands and black top.
Hull: White with blue boot-topping.

Name	Eng	Flag	Year	GRT	Loa	Bm	Kts	Pass	Former names
Asuka II	(me2)	Bhs	1990	48,621	241	30	22	960	ex Crystal Harmony-06

Jointly owned by Asuka Ship Co., Japan

Mediterranean Shipping Cruises. MELODY. *M. D. J. Lennon*

Mediterranean Shipping Cruises. MSC OPERA. *M. D. J. Lennon*

Nippon Yusen Kaisha (Crystal Cruises). CRYSTAL SERENITY. *Hans Kraijenbosch*

Name		Eng	Flag	Year	GRT	Loa	Bm	Kts	Pass	Former names

Oceania Cruises USA

Funnel: *White with 'O' symbol.*
Hull: *White.*

Name		Eng	Flag	Year	GRT	Loa	Bm	Kts	Pass	Former names
Insignia		(me2)	Mhl	1998	30,277	181	25	18	684	ex R One -03
Nautica		(me2)	Mhl	2000	30,277	181	25	18	684	ex Blue Star-05, R Five-04
Regatta		(me2)	Mhl	1998	30,277	181	25	18	684	ex Insignia-03, R Two-03

Managed by V. Ships Leisure SAM, Monaco

Fred Olsen & Co. Norway

Funnel: *White with red oval and white/blue houseflag.*
Hull: *White with green boot-topping.*

Name		Eng	Flag	Year	GRT	Loa	Bm	Kts	Pass	Former names
Black Prince		(2)	Bhs	1966	11,209	142	20	18	451	ex Black Prince/Venus-87
Black Watch		(2)	Bhs	1972	28,670	205	25	18	902	ex Star Odyssey-96, Westward-94, Royal Viking Star-91 (NE-05)
Boudicca		(2)	Pan	1973	28,388	205	25	18	1,022	ex Grand Latino-05, SuperStar Capricorn-04, Hyundai Kumgang-01, SuperStar Capricorn-98, Golden Princess-96, Sunward-93, Birka Queen-92, Sunward-92, Royal Viking Sky-91 (NE-06)
Braemar *		(2)	Pan	1993	19,089	164	23	18	916	ex Crown Dynasty-01, Norwegian Dynasty-99, Crown Majesty-97, Crown Dynasty-97, Cunard Dynasty-97, Crown Dynasty-95

* owned by Olsen Cruise Lines, UK.

Phoenix Seereisen Germany

Funnel: *Turquoise with white seagull in flight over yellow sun.*
Hull: *White with red or green boot-topping.*

Name		Eng	Flag	Year	GRT	Loa	Bm	Kts	Pass	Former names
Albatros *		(2)	Bhs	1973	29,518	205	25	18	812	ex Crown-04, Norwegian Star I-02, Norwegian Star-01, Royal Odyssey-97, Royal Viking Sea-91 (len-83)
Alexander von Humboldt †		(2)	Bhs	1996	12,331	133	20	16	428	ex Explorer II-05, Saga Pearl-05, Minerva-03, I/a Okean
Amadea		(2)	Jpn	1991	28,856	190	25	21	604	ex Asuka-06
Maxim Gorkiy **		(st2)	Bhs	1969	24,220	195	27	23	600	ex Maksim Gorkiy-92, Hanseatic-74, Hamburg-73

* on charter from Club Cruise, Netherlands or ** Sovcomflot (managed by Unicom Management Services (Cyprus) Ltd)
† on summer charter from Vlasov Group (V.Ships) until 2008 (remainder of year as Explorer II on charter to Abercrombie & Kent q.v.)

Pullmantur Cruises Spain

Funnel: *Blue or white with red striped globe symbol on white disc.*
Hull: *White or very dark blue with red or white 'Pullmantur Cruises', red boot-topping.*

Name		Eng	Flag	Year	GRT	Loa	Bm	Kts	Pass	Former names
Holiday Dream		(2)	Bhs	1981	37,301	200	29	21	758	ex SuperStar Aries-04, SuperStar Europe-99, Europa-99
Oceanic		(st2)	Bhs	1965	38,772	238	29	20	1,562	ex Starship Oceanic-98, Royale Oceanic-85, Oceanic-85
Pacific		(2)	Bhs	1970	20,186	169	25	19	723	ex Pacific Princess-02, Sea Venture-75
Blue Dream		(me2)	Mhl	2000	30,277	181	25	18	777	ex R Six
Blue Moon		(me2)	Mhl	2000	30,277	181	25	18	702	ex Delphin Renaissance-06, R Seven-03
Sky Wonder		(st2)	Gbr	1984	46,087	240	28	21	1,600	ex Pacific Sky-06, Sky Princess-00, Fairsky-88

Radisson Seven Seas Cruises USA

Funnel: *White with blue 'harp' symbol.*
Hull: *White with blue band and blue waterline above red boot-topping.*

Name		Eng	Flag	Year	GRT	Loa	Bm	Kts	Pass	Former names
Paul Gauguin *		(me2)	Fra	1997	19,170	156	22	18	320	
Seven Sea Mariner		(me2)	Wlf	2001	48,075	216	29	19	769	
Seven Seas Navigator		(2)	Bhs	1999	28,550	171	24	17	542	I/dn Akademik Nikolay Pilyugin (1991)

Oceania Cruises. INSIGNIA. *F. de Vries*

Fred Olsen & Co. BLACK WATCH. *Phil Kempsey*

Radisson Seven Seas Cruises. SEVEN SEAS VOYAGER. *Hans Kraijenbosch*

Name	Eng	Flag	Year	GRT	Loa	Bm	Kts	Pass	Former names
Seven Seas Voyager	(me2)	Bhs	2003	41,500	207	29	20	769	

Formed with Radisson Hotel Corp., Mitsui O.S.K. Lines with others and managed by V. Ships, Monaco.
*See also chartered vessel under Societe Services et Transports (Club Mediterranee), France. * on charter until 2008.*

Royal Caribbean International — Norway

Funnel: *White with blue crown and anchor symbol.*
Hull: *White with blue band and blue boot-topping.*

Name	Eng	Flag	Year	GRT	Loa	Bm	Kts	Pass	Former names
Adventure of the Seas	(me3)	Bhs	2001	137,276	311	39	23	3,840	
Brilliance of the Seas	(gt2)	Bhs	2002	90,090	294	32	24	2,500	
Empress of the Seas	(2)	Bhs	1990	48,563	211	31	19	2,020	ex Nordic Empress-04
Enchantment of the Seas	(me2)	Bhs	1997	82,910	301	32	22	2,730	(len-05)
Explorer of the Seas	(me3)	Bhs	2000	137,308	311	39	23	3,840	
Freedom of the Seas		Bhs	2006	158,000	339	39	22	4,375	
Grandeur of the Seas	(me2)	Bhs	1996	73,817	279	32	22	2,440	
Jewel of the Seas	(gt2)	Bhs	2004	90,090	293	32	24	2,500	
Legend of the Seas	(me2)	Bhs	1995	69,490	264	32	24	2,060	
Majesty of the Seas	(2)	Nis	1992	73,937	268	32	20	2,744	
Mariner of the Seas	(me3)	Bhs	2004	138,279	311	39	22	3,807	
Monarch of the Seas	(2)	Nis	1991	73,937	268	32	20	2,744	
Navigator of the Seas	(me3)	Bhs	2003	138,279	311	39	22	3,807	
Radiance of the Seas	(gt2)	Bhs	2001	90,090	293	32	24	2,500	
Rhapsody of the Seas	(me2)	Nis	1997	78,491	279	32	22	2,416	
Serenade of the Seas	(gt2)	Bhs	2003	90,090	293	32	24	2,501	
Sovereign of the Seas	(2)	Nis	1987	73,192	268	32	21	2,524	
Splendour of the Seas	(me2)	Nis	1996	69,130	264	32	24	2,066	
Vision of the Seas	(me2)	Bhs	1998	78,340	279	32	22	2,416	
Voyager of the Seas	(me3)	Bhs	1999	137,276	311	39	22	3,840	
Xpedition		Ecu	2001	2,842	89	14	13	96	ex Sun Bay-04
newbuildings.									
Liberty of the Seas		Bhs	2007	158,000	339	39	22	4,375	
Un-named		Bhs	2008	158,000	339	39	22	4,375	
Project Genesis		Bhs	2009	220,000	360	47	-	5,400	

Controlled by Anders Wilhelmsen & Co. AS q.v.

Celebrity Cruises/Greece

Funnel: *Black or black/white horizontal striped with large white diagonal cross (edged yellow on later vessels)*
Hull: *White with broad black band and black or blue boot-topping or dark blue with black boot-topping.*

Name	Eng	Flag	Year	GRT	Loa	Bm	Kts	Pass	Former names
Century	(2)	Bhs	1995	70,606	247	32	21	1,778	
Constellation	(gt2)	Bhs	2002	90,280	294	32	24	2,449	
Galaxy	(2)	Bhs	1996	76,522	264	32	21	1,896	
Infinity	(gt2)	Bhs	2001	90,228	294	32	24	2,449	
Mercury	(2)	Bhs	1997	76,522	264	32	21	1,896	
Millennium	(gt2)	Bhs	2000	90,228	294	32	24	2,449	
Summit	(gt2)	Bhs	2001	90,280	294	32	24	2,449	
Zenith	(2)	Bhs	1992	47,255	208	29	21	1,774	
newbuildings.									
Solstice		Bhs	2008	118,000	315	37		(2,850)	
Equinox		Bhs	2009	118,000	315	37		(2,850)	

Island Cruises/UK

Funnel: *White with green, red and yellow 'palm tree' symbol.*
Hull: *White with 'palm tree' symbol on five coloured squares (three shades of blue and yellow)*

Name	Eng	Flag	Year	GRT	Loa	Bm	Kts	Pass	Former names
Island Escape	(2)	Bhs	1982	40,132	185	27	18	1,863	ex Viking Serenade-02, Stardancer-90, Scandinavia-85
Island Star	(2)	Bhs	1990	46,811	208	29	19	1,798	ex Horizon-05

Managed by V. Ships Leisure for joint venture between RCCL and First Choice

Royal Caribbean International. LEGEND OF THE SEAS. *C. J. Dornom*

Royal Caribbean International. SERENADE OF THE SEAS. *Hans Kraijenbosch*

Name	Eng	Flag	Year	GRT	Loa	Bm	Kts	Pass	Former names

Saga Holidays Ltd UK

Funnel: *Yellow with narrow white band below narrow dark blue top.*
Hull: *Dark blue with red boot-topping.*

Name	Eng	Flag	Year	GRT	Loa	Bm	Kts	Pass	Former names
Saga Rose	(2)	Bhs	1965	24,528	189	24	20	587	ex Gripsholm-97, Sagafjord-96
Saga Ruby	(2)	Gbr	1973	24,492	191	25	21	670	ex Caronia-05, Vistafjord-99
Spirit of Adventure	(2)	Bhs	1980	9,570	139	18	17	352	ex Orange Melody-06, Berlin-05, Princess Mahsuri-85, Berlin-82 (len-86)

managed by Columbia Shipmanagement Ltd., Cyprus

Silversea Cruises Ltd. Italy

Funnel: *White with plain and striped blue flags.*
Hull: *White.*

Name	Eng	Flag	Year	GRT	Loa	Bm	Kts	Pass	Former names
Silver Cloud	(2)	Bhs	1994	16,927	156	21	17	314	
Silver Shadow	(2)	Bhs	2000	28,258	182	25	21	388	
Silver Whisper	(2)	Bhs	2001	28,258	182	25	21	388	I/dn Silver Mirage
Silver Wind	(2)	Bhs	1995	16,927	156	21	17	296	

managed by V. Ships (Vlasov Group) q.v.

Star Clippers Ltd. Monaco

Hull: *White*

Name	Eng	Flag	Year	GRT	Loa	Bm	Kts	Pass	Former names
Royal Clipper	(as)	Lux	2000	4,425	133	16	13	224	I/a Gwarek
Star Clipper	(as)	Lux	1992	2,298	112	15	12	194	
Star Flyer	(as)	Lux	1991	2,298	112	15	12	194	I/a Star Clipper

Star Cruise AS Sendirian Berhad Singapore

Funnel: *Dark blue with yellow eight-pointed star on broad red band.*
Hull: *White with red band and blue boot-topping.*

Name	Eng	Flag	Year	GRT	Loa	Bm	Kts	Pass	Former names
MegaStar Aries	(2)	Pan	1991	3,264	82	14	16	82	ex Aurora II-94, I/a Lady Sarah
MegaStar Taurus	(2)	Pan	1991	3,341	82	14	16	82	ex Aurora I-94, Lady D-91, I/a Lady Diana
Star Pisces	(2)	Pan	1990	40,053	177	30	22	2,165	ex Kalypso-93
SuperStar Gemini *	(2)	Pan	1992	19,093	164	23	19	916	ex Crown Jewel-95
SuperStar Libra	(2)	Bhs	1988	42,276	216	32	20	1,798	ex Norwegian Sea-05, Seaward-97
SuperStar Virgo	(me2)	Pan	1999	75,338	269	32	24	(1,960)	

* chartered from Neptun Maritime (51% controlled by Sea Containers group).

Norwegian Cruise Line/Norway

Funnel: *Dark blue with gold 'NCL' within gold square outline.*
Hull: *White with red stripe (Norwegian Dawn with multi-coloured artwork), or dark blue, blue boot-topping.*

Name	Eng	Flag	Year	GRT	Loa	Bm	Kts	Pass	Former names
Blue Lady **	(st2)	Bhs	1961	76,049	316	34	18	2,548	ex Norway-06, France-79
Independence *	(st2)	Usa	1950	20,221	208	27	22	1,077	ex Oceanic Independence-82, Independence-74
Norwegian Crown	(2)	Bhs	1988	34,242	188	28	22	1,240	ex Crown Odyssey-03, Norwegian Crown-00, Crown Odyssey-96
Norwegian Dawn	(me2)	Bhs	2002	92,250	292	32	25	2,500	I/dn SuperStar Sagittarius
Norwegian Dream	(2)	Bhs	1992	50,764	230	29	18	2,100	ex Dreamward-98 (len-98)
Norwegian Majesty	(2)	Bhs	1992	40,876	207	28	19	2,324	ex Royal Majesty-97 (len-99)
Norwegian Jewel	(me2)	Bhs	2005	91,740	294	32	24	2,400	
Norwegian Spirit	(me2)	Bhs	1998	75,338	269	32	24	(1,966)	ex SuperStar Leo-04
Norwegian Star	(me2)	Bhs	2001	91,740	294	32	24	2,500	I/dn SuperStar Libra
Norwegian Sun	(me2)	Bhs	2001	78,309	258	32	20	2,359	
Norwegian Wind	(2)	Bhs	1993	50,760	230	29	18	2,100	ex Windward-98 (len-98)
Pride of Aloha	(me2)	Usa	1999	77,104	260	32	20	2,450	ex Norwegian Sky-04, I/a Costa Olympia
Pride of America	(me2)	Usa	2005	80,439	276	32	22	2,146	
Pride of Hawaii	(me2)	Usa	2006	92,250	294	32	24	2,400	
United States *	(st4)	Usa	1952	38,216	302	31	30	1,930	

newbuildings

Name	Eng	Flag	Year	GRT	Loa	Bm	Kts	Pass	Former names
Norweigan Pearl	(me2)	Bhs	2007	93,000	294	32	24	2,400	
Norwegian Gem	(me2)	Bhs	2007	93,000	294	32	24	2,384	

* laid up pending rebuilding or ** pending probable demolition.

Saga Holidays. SAGA ROSE. *Phil Kempsey*

Silversea Cruises. SILVER WIND. *Hans Kraijenbosch*

Name	Eng	Flag	Year	GRT	Loa	Bm	Kts	Pass	Former names
Orient Lines/UK									

Orient Lines/UK

Funnel: *White with broad blue band above narrow white and red bands, black top.*
Hull: *Black with red boot-topping.*

Name	Eng	Flag	Year	GRT	Loa	Bm	Kts	Pass	Former names
Marco Polo	(2)	Bhs	1965	22,080	176	24	20	850	ex Aleksandr Pushkin-91

Transocean Tours   Germany

Funnel: *White with blue 't' symbol inside blue ring (*interupting pale blue over blue narrow bands).*
Hull: *White with pale blue over blue bands, red boot-topping.*

Name	Eng	Flag	Year	GRT	Loa	Bm	Kts	Pass	Former names
Arille †	(2)	Cyp	1971	23,149	194	24	21	1,194	ex Aquamarine-06, Carousel-05, Nordic Prince-95
Astor *	(2)	Bhs	1987	20,606	176	23	18	650	ex Fedor Dostoevskiy-95, Astor-88
Astoria **	(2)	Bhs	1981	18,591	164	23	18	540	ex Arkona-02, Astor-85

managed by Passat Shipmanagement Ltd., Cyprus
* chartered from Sovcomflot AKP, Russia to 2007, ** from Seetours International, Germany (Carnival Corp-Princess Cruises) to 2010 and † from Louis Cruise Lines Ltd, Cyprus.

TUI Group   Germany

Hapag-Lloyd Cruises/Germany

Funnel: *Orange with blue 'HL'*
Hull: *White with orange/blue band, red boot-topping*

Name	Eng	Flag	Year	GRT	Loa	Bm	Kts	Pass	Former names
Bremen †	(2)	Bhs	1990	6,752	112	17	16	184	ex Frontier Spirit-93
C. Columbus **	(2)	Bhs	1997	15,067	145	22	18	423	
Europa	(me2)	Bhs	1999	28,437	199	24	21	408	
Hanseatic *	(2)	Bhs	1991	8,378	123	18	14	188	ex Society Adventurer-92
Sea Cloud ‡	(as2)	Mlt	1931	2,532	110	15	-	68	ex Sea Cloud of Grand Cayman-87, Sea Cloud-80, Antarna-79, Patria-64, Angelita-61, Sea Cloud-52, Hussar-35
Sea Cloud II ‡	(as2)	Mlt	2000	3,849	117	16	14	96	

* chartered from Hanseatic Cruises GmbH until 2008 and ** chartered from NSB Niederelbe Schiffahrts. GmbH & Co. KG.
‡ operated for Sea Cloud Cruises (managed by Hansa Shipmanagement GmbH or † operated by Radisson Seven Seas Cruises q.v.

Thomson Cruises/UK

Funnel: *Pale blue with red 'tui' logo.*
Hull: *White with blue over yellow over red bands, blue or red boot-topping.*

Name	Eng	Flag	Year	GRT	Loa	Bm	Kts	Pass	Former names
The Emerald	(st2)	Grc	1958	23,428	178	26	20	960	ex Regent Rainbow-96, Diamond Island-92, Santa Rosa-90
Thomson Celebration **	(2)	Nld	1984	33,933	215	27	21	1,340	ex Noordam-05
Thomson Destiny	(2)	Cyp	1982	37,773	215	28	20	1,595	ex Sunbird-05, Song of America-99
Thomson Spirit *	(2)	Bhs	1983	33,930	215	27	21	1,374	ex Spirit-03, Nieuw Amsterdam-02, Patriot-02, Nieuw Amsterdam-00

Chartered from Louis Cruise Lines or * on sub-charter or ** directly from Holland America Line (see under Carnival Corp.)

Other Passenger Cruise Ships

Abercrombie & Kent Inc, USA

Name	Eng	Flag	Year	GRT	Loa	Bm	Kts	Pass	Former names
Explorer		Lbr	1969	2,398	73	14	14	102	ex Society Explorer-92, Lindblad Explorer-85
Explorer II *	(2)	Bhs	1996	12,331	133	20	16	428	ex Alexander von Humboldt-05, Explorer II-05, Saga Pearl-05, Minerva-03, I/a Okean

Owned by Explorer Shipping Corp., US and managed by V. Ships Leisure SAM, Monaco.
Seasonally chartered to Noble Caledonia or * to Phoenix Reisen, Germany q.v.

Caspi Shipping, Israel

Name	Eng	Flag	Year	GRT	Loa	Bm	Kts	Pass	Former names
Dream Princess	(2)	Bhs	1970	22,945	194	24	20	1,196	ex Sundream-04, Song of Norway-97

Managed for Lance Shipping, Cyprus.

Clipper Cruise Line, USA

Name	Eng	Flag	Year	GRT	Loa	Bm	Kts	Pass	Former names
Clipper Adventurer *	(2)	Bhs	1975	4,376	100	16	17	116	ex Alla Tarasova-97
Clipper Odyssey	(2)	Bhs	1989	5,218	103	15	18	128	ex Oceanic Odyssey-98, Oceanic Grace-97
Yorktown Clipper *	(2)	Usa	1988	2,354	78	13	-	149	

* owned by New World Shipmanagement, USA.

Star Cruise. MEGASTAR TAURUS. *Hans Kraijenbosch*

Star Cruise (Norwegian Cruise). NORWEGIAN JEWEL. *Hans Kraijenbosch*

Star Cruise (Norwegian Cruise). NORWEGIAN WIND. *Hans Kraijenbosch*

Name	Eng	Flag	Year	GRT	Loa	Bm	Kts	Pass	Former names
Clipper Group, Denmark									
Corinthian II *	(2)	Mlt	1991	4,200	91	15	15	114	ex Island Sun-05, Sun-04, Renai I-03, Renaissance Seven-01, Regina Renaissance-98, Renaissance Seven-92
Island Sky	(2)	Bhs	1992	4,200	90	15	15	114	ex Sky-04, Renai II-03, Renaissance Eight-01

*Managed by International Shipping Partners and chartered out to Noble Caledonia or * Travel Dynamics*

Name	Eng	Flag	Year	GRT	Loa	Bm	Kts	Pass	Former names
Club Cruise, Netherlands									
Van Gogh	(2)	Vct	1975	15,402	156	22	22	640	ex Club 1-99, Club Cruise I-99, Odessa Sky-98, Gruziya-95

On charter to Travelscope. Also see Phoenix Seereisen, Germany.

Name	Eng	Flag	Year	GRT	Loa	Bm	Kts	Pass	Former names
Compagnie des Isles du Ponant, France									
Le Diamant *	(2)	Wlf	1974	8,282	124	16	16	265	ex Song of Flower-04, Explorer Starship-89, Begonia-87, Fernhill-74
Le Levant	(2)	Wlf	1990	3,504	100	14	16	95	

* co-owned by Tapis Rouge Cruises, Spain. Also operates sail-cruise vessels La France and Le Ponant.

Name	Eng	Flag	Year	GRT	Loa	Bm	Kts	Pass	Former names
Croatia Cruise Lines, Croatia									
Dalmacija	(2)	Hrv	1964	5,619	117	17	17	312	

Name	Eng	Flag	Year	GRT	Loa	Bm	Kts	Pass	Former names
Cruise West, USA									
Spirit of Oceanus	(2)	Bhs	1991	4,200	90	15	16	114	ex MegaStar Sagittarius-01, Sun Viva-00, Renaissance Five-97, Hanseatic Renaissance-92, Renaissance Five-91

Name	Eng	Flag	Year	GRT	Loa	Bm	Kts	Pass	Former names
Delphin Seereisen GmbH, Germany									
Delphin	(2)	Mlt	1975	16,214	156	22	21	554	ex Kazakhstan II-96, Byelorussiya-93

Name	Eng	Flag	Year	GRT	Loa	Bm	Kts	Pass	Former names
D&P Cruises, Italy									
Paloma I	(2)	Vct	1980	12,586	134	21	20	376	ex Dmitriy Shostakovich-00

on charter to Hansa Touristik, Germany.

Name	Eng	Flag	Year	GRT	Loa	Bm	Kts	Pass	Former names
Discoverer Reederei GmbH, Germany									
World Discoverer	(2)	Gbr	1969	6,072	108	16	15	299	ex Dream 21-01, Delfin Star-97, Baltic Clipper-92, Sally Clipper-92, Delfin Clipper-90

Owned by World Adventurer Pte Ltd., Singapore and managed by V. Ships Leisure SAM, Monaco.

Name	Eng	Flag	Year	GRT	Loa	Bm	Kts	Pass	Former names
EasyCruise Ltd, UK									
EasyCruiseOne	(2)	Cyp	1990	4,077	88	16	15	170	ex The Neptune 2-05, The Neptune-04, Renaissance Two-98

newbuilding : Company report order of 7,500 grt cruise ship (100 x 18m) with 504 berths, but no indication as to builder or dates.
Managed by V. Ships Leisure SAM, Monaco.

Name	Eng	Flag	Year	GRT	Loa	Bm	Kts	Pass	Former names
Elegant Cruises & Tours Inc, USA									
Andrea		Lbr	1960	2,549	87	13	16	169	ex Harald Jarl-02

Currently operated seasonally by Noble Caledonia or Scantours Inc, USA

Name	Eng	Flag	Year	GRT	Loa	Bm	Kts	Pass	Former names
Elysian Cruises Line, USA									
Grand Victoria	(2)	Grc	1966	11,429	150	21	18	536	ex World Renaisance-05, Awani Dream-98, World Renaisance-95, Homeric Renaissance-78, Renaissance-77
New Flamenco *	(2)	Bhs	1972	17,042	163	25	25	700	ex Elysian Flamenco-04, Flamenco-04, Southern Cross-97, Starship Majestic-95, Sun Princess-89, Spirit of London-74

* chartered to Spanish Travelplan.

Name	Eng	Flag	Year	GRT	Loa	Bm	Kts	Pass	Former names
Enchanted Islands Corp, Ecuador									
Galapagos Explorer II	(2)	Ecu	1990	4,077	88	16	15	100	ex Renaissance Three-97

Operated by Canodros SA, Ecuador

Name	Eng	Flag	Year	GRT	Loa	Bm	Kts	Pass	Former names
Enterprises Shipping & Trading, Greece									
Cruise One	(2)	Jpn	1990	21,884	174	24	21	626	ex Orient Venus-05

TUI Group (Thomson Cruises). THOMSON CELEBRATION. *G. J. de Boer*

Club Cruise. VAN GOGH. *Hans Kraijenbosch*

Name	Eng	Flag	Year	GRT	Loa	Bm	Kts	Pass	Former names

Eurasia International, Hong Kong (China)

| Golden Princess | (2) | Bhs | 1967 | 12,704 | 158 | 20 | 22 | 725 | ex Joy Wave-00, Oriental Pearl-99, Costa Playa-98, Pearl-95, Ocean Pearl-93, Pearl of Scandinavia-88, Innstar-82, Finnstar-81, Finlandia-78 |

Gute Bucher Fur Alle EV ('Good Books for All'), Germany

Doulos		Mlt	1914	6,804	130	17	13	-	ex Franca C-78, Roma-52, Medina-49
Logos II *	(2)	Mlt	1968	4,804	110	16	10	129	ex Argo-88, Antonio Lazaro-88
Logos Hope	(2)	Fro	1973	12,252	129	21	22	-	ex Norrona I-04, Norrona-03, Gustav Vasa-83

* owned by Educational Book Exhibits Ltd., Germany.

Hebridean Island Cruises Ltd, UK

| Hebridean Princess | (2) | Gbr | 1964 | 2,112 | 72 | 14 | 14 | 49 | ex Columba-89 |
| Hebridean Spirit | (2) | Gbr | 1991 | 4,200 | 91 | 15 | 15 | 79 | ex Capri-01, MegaStar Capricorn-01, Sun Viva 2-00, Renaissance Six-98 |

Helios Shipping, Greece

| Constellation | | Vct | 2002 | 2,842 | 89 | 14 | 13 | 96 | ex Corinthian-04, Sun Bay II-03 |

Chartered to Travel Dynamics.

Holiday Kreuzfahrten, Germany

| Lili Marleen * | (2) | Grc | 1976 | 16,795 | 164 | 23 | 18 | 950 | ex Ocean Countess-05, Olympia Countess-04, Olympic Countess-01, Awani Dream 2-98, Cunard Countess-96 |
| Mona Lisa | (2) | Bhs | 1966 | 28,891 | 210 | 27 | 21 | 720 | ex Victoria-03, Sea Princess-95, Kungsholm-79 |

Chartered from Technical Marine, Greece or * from Majestic International Cruises, Greece.

Hoteles Playaventura SL, Canary Islands

| Vistamar | (2) | Esp | 1989 | 7,478 | 121 | 17 | 17 | 350 | |

operated by Plantours & Partner GmbH, Germany.

Imperial Majesty Cruise Line, USA

| Regal Empress | (2) | Bhs | 1953 | 21,909 | 186 | 24 | 18 | 1,160 | ex Caribe 1-93, Caribe-82, Olympia-82 |

International Shipping Partners Inc., USA

| Enchanted Capri | (2) | Bhs | 1975 | 15,410 | 156 | 22 | 21 | 650 | ex Island Holiday-98, Arkadiya-97, Azerbaydzhan-96 |

Japan Cruise Line, Japan

| Pacific Venus | (2) | Jpn | 1998 | 26,518 | 183 | 25 | 20 | 720 | |

Kristina Cruises Ltd., Finland

| Kristina Regina | | Fin | 1960 | 4,295 | 100 | 15 | - | 353 | ex Borea-87, Bore-77 |

Lindblad Expeditions, USA

| National Geographic Endeavour | | Bhs | 1966 | 3,132 | 89 | 14 | 15 | 110 | ex Endeavour-05, Caledonian Star-01, North Star-89, Lindmar-83, Marburg-82 |
| Polaris | (2) | Ecu | 1960 | 2,138 | 72 | 13 | 14 | 82 | ex Lindblad Polaris-87,Oresund-81 |

Lindos Maritime, Greece

| Clelia II | (2) | Bhs | 1990 | 4,077 | 88 | 15 | 15 | 84 | ex Renaissance Four-96 |

Chartered by Classical Cruises.

Marina Cruises, Monaco

| Adriana | (2) | Vct | 1972 | 4,490 | 104 | 14 | 16 | 312 | ex Aquarius-87 |

Managed by V. Ships Leisure SAM, Monaco.

Mercy Ships International, USA

Africa Mercy	(2)	Mlt	1960	16,071	152	23	17	-	ex Ingrid-00, Dronning Ingrid-99
Anastasis	(2)	Mlt	1953	11,701	159	21	13	-	ex Victoria-78
Caribbean Mercy		Pan	1952	2,125	80	12	13	172	ex Polarlys-94

Operating world-wide as hospital ships.

EasyCruise. EASYCRUISE ONE. *M. D. J. Lennon*

Gute Bucher fur Alle. DOULOS. *Phil Kempsey*

Name	Eng	Flag	Year	GRT	Loa	Bm	Kts	Pass	Former names

Norwegian Coastal Voyages / Expedition Cruises, Norway

Name	Eng	Flag	Year	GRT	Loa	Bm	Kts	Pass	Former names
Lofoten		Nor	1964	2,621	87	13	16	223	
Midnatsol	(2)	Nor	2003	16,151	135	22	18	828	
Nordkapp	(2)	Nor	1996	11,386	123	20	15	490	
Nordnorge	(2)	Nor	1997	11,384	123	20	18	464	
Nordstjernen		Nor	1956	2,191	81	13	15	179	
Polar Star *	(me3)	Brb	1969	3,963	87	21	18	105	

Current and former 'Hurtigruten' vessels operating seasonal voyages to Alaska, Antarctica and Central America.
* owned by Karlson Shipping, Norway and seasonally chartered to Noble Caledonia.

New Century Cruise Lines, Singapore

Name	Eng	Flag	Year	GRT	Loa	Bm	Kts	Pass	Former names
Leisure World	(2)	Bhs	1969	15,653	160	23	-	920	ex Continental World-93, Fantasy World-93, Asian World-92, Shangri La World-92, Skyward-91

Odessa Shipping Co Ltd, Ukraine

Name	Eng	Flag	Year	GRT	Loa	Bm	Kts	Pass	Former names
Odessa	(2)	Vct	1974	11,889	136	22	16	482	ex Odessa I-01, Odessa-99, Copenhagen-75

Currently laid-up.

Osterreichischer Lloyd, Cyprus

Name	Eng	Flag	Year	GRT	Loa	Bm	Kts	Pass	Former names
Orient Queen	(2)	Pan	1968	15,781	160	23	20	928	ex Bolero-04, Starward-95

Page & Moy Holidays, UK

Name	Eng	Flag	Year	GRT	Loa	Bm	Kts	Pass	Former names
Ocean Majesty	(2)	Prt	1966	10,417	131	19	20	613	ex Homeric-95, Ocean Majesty-95, Olympic-95, Ocean Majesty-94, Kypros Star-89, Sol Christiana-86, Juan March-85
Ocean Monarch	(2)	Prt	1955	15,833	162	21	17	500	ex Ocean Odyssey-02, Switzerland-02, Daphne-96, Akrotiri Express-74, Port Sydney-72

Chartered from Majestic International Cruises, Greece

The Peace Boat, Japan

Name	Eng	Flag	Year	GRT	Loa	Bm	Kts	Pass	Former names
The Topaz	(st2)	Pan	1956	32,327	195	26	20	1,050	ex Olympic-98, FiestaMarina-94, Carnivale-93, Queen Anna Maria-75, Empress of Britain-64

Managed by Technical Marine, Greece and operating world cruises on charter to non-governmental organisation as 'The Peace Boat'.

Quark Expeditions Inc, USA

Name	Eng	Flag	Year	GRT	Loa	Bm	Kts	Pass	Former names
Lyubov Orlova	(2)	Mlt	1976	4,251	100	16	17	206	

Chartered from Lubov Orlova Shipping, Switzerland and also operates Russian research ships and ice-breakers on Antarctic cruises.

ResidenSea Ltd., Norway

Name	Eng	Flag	Year	GRT	Loa	Bm	Kts	Pass	Former names
The World	(2)	Bhs	2002	43,188	196	29	18	656	

operated by Silversea Cruises Ltd and with accommodation comprising110 privately owned apartments and 88 guest suites

Salamis Lines (Hellas) Ltd., Cyprus

Name	Eng	Flag	Year	GRT	Loa	Bm	Kts	Pass	Former names
Salamis Glory	(2)	Cyp	1962	10,392	150	20	17	480	ex Regent Spirit-96, Morning Star-92, Constellation-92, Danaos-78, Anna Nery-78

SeaDream Yacht Club, Norway

Name	Eng	Flag	Year	GRT	Loa	Bm	Kts	Pass	Former names
SeaDream I	(2)	Bhs	1984	4,333	105	15	17	116	ex Seabourn Goddess I-01, Sea Goddess I-00
SeaDream II	(2)	Bhs	1985	4,333	105	15	17	116	ex Seabourn Goddess II-01, Sea Goddess II-00

Seawise Foundation, USA

Name	Eng	Flag	Year	GRT	Loa	Bm	Kts	Pass	Former names
Explorer	(2)	Bhs	2001	24,318	178	26	27	836	ex Olympia Explorer-04, I/a Olympic Explorer

Chartered from Stella Maritime, Bahamas for use as a floating University

Sete Yacht Management, Greece

Name	Eng	Flag	Year	GRT	Loa	Bm	Kts	Pass	Former names
Columbus Caravelle	(2)	Bhs	1990	7,560	116	17	17	330	ex Sally Caravelle-91, Delfin Caravelle-91

Shatiek Shipping SA

Name	Eng	Flag	Year	GRT	Loa	Bm	Kts	Pass	Former names
Madagascar	(2)	Ukr	1960	3,008	88	14	18	180	ex Bordeaux-05, Viking Bordeaux-04, Stella Maris II-98, Bremerhaven-65

Managed by Dmiks, Ukraine

Japan Cruise Line. PACIFIC VENUS. *Hans Kraijenbosch*

Lindos Maritime. CLELIA II. *M. D. J. Lennon*

Name	Eng	Flag	Year	GRT	Loa	Bm	Kts	Pass	Former names

Societe Services et Transports, Monaco

Club Med 2	(as/me2)	Fra	1992	14,983	187	20	15	441	

Operated by Club Mediterranee and managed by V. Ships Leisure; see also Radisson Seven Seas Cruises.

StarLine Cruises Ltd., Kenya

Royal Star	(2)	Bhs	1956	5,067	112	16	15	276	ex Ocean Islander-90, City of Andros-84, San Giorgio-76

operated by Africa Safari Club

Viajes Iberojet Cruceros, Spain

Grand Mistral	(me2)	Mhl	1999	47,276	216	29	19	1,667	ex Mistral-05
Grand Voyager	(2)	Grc	2000	24,391	180	26	28	836	ex Voyager-06, Olympia Voyager-04, Olympic Voyager-01

Managed by V. Ships Leisure SAM, Monaco.

Voyages of Discovery, UK

Discovery	(2)	Bmu	1972	20,216	169	25	18	689	ex Platinium-02, Hyundai Pungak-01, Island Princess-99, Island Venture-72

Managed by V. Ships Leisure SAM, Monaco.

Voyages of Discovery. DISCOVERY. *Phil Kempsey*

Right: **BP Shipping's** BRITISH MERLIN and two **OMI** tankers at Europoort. *Hans Kraijenbosch*

PART TWO
Cargo Vessels
and Tankers

Name	Eng	Flag	Year	GRT	DWT	Loa	Bm	Kts	Type	Former names

Abu Dhabi National Tanker Co

United Arab Emirates

Funnel: Black with yellow 'eagle' symbol on white square, narrow blue over white over red bands beneath narrow black top.
Hull: Black with grey boot-topping

Name	Eng	Flag	Year	GRT	DWT	Loa	Bm	Kts	Type	Former names
Al Dhabiyyah	Are	1983	19,245	32,055	178	28	15	T	
Al Dhibyaniyyah	Are	1984	34,240	57,211	232	32	14	T	
Arzanah	Are	1983	19,245	32,027	178	28	15	T	
Baynunah	Are	1983	34,240	57,211	232	32	14	T	
Diyyinah	Are	1983	24,699	38,602	193	30	16	T	

Owned by Abu Dhabi National Oil Co., which also controls National Gas Shipping Co. with 8 large LNG tankers

Christian F Ahrenkiel GmbH & Co

Germany

Funnel: Buff or buff with houseflag on blue band, or charterers colours.
Hull: Black, dark blue, green or grey with red boot-topping.

Name	Eng	Flag	Year	GRT	DWT	Loa	Bm	Kts	Type	Former names
Amalia del Bene *	Pan	1989	34,838	64,221	225	32	14	B	
Anglia	Lbr	1999	26,047	31,000	196	30	21	CC	ex Columbus Australia-05, Cherokee-03, Panthermax-02, CanMar Supreme-02, Panther Max-01
Aquitania	Lbr	2000	26,044	31,000	196	30	21	CC	ex Maersk Aquitania-03, Corrado-03, Lion Max-02
Bahamian Express	Mhl	2000	17,167	21,150	169	27	20	CC	
Batu	Lbr	1997	24,987	42,648	183	31	14	B	
Calapadria	Deu	2000	19,131	25,360	189	27	20	CC	ex Samaria-04, P&O Nedlloyd Samaria-03, Samaria-00
Cimbria	Lbr	2002	27,779	39,358	222	30	22	CC	
CMA CGM Greece	Lbr	2003	27,779	39,421	222	30	22	CC	ex Carpathia-04
CMA CGM Puma	Lbr	2000	19,131	24,973	189	27	22	CC	ex Scandia-03, P&O Nedlloyd Scandia-02, Scandia-02
CMA CGM Ukraine	Lbr	2003	27,779	39,418	222	30	22	CC	ex Cardonia-03
Cordelia	Lbr	2003	27,779	40,878	222	30	22	CC	
CSAV Rio Rapel	Lbr	2000	26,047	28,337	195	30	21	CC	ex Asturia-04, Comanche-03, Ocelot Max-02
Danubia	Lbr	2004	38,975	68,524	229	32	15	T	ex Ocean Principal-05, Tavropos-04
Franconia	Lbr	1979	16,198	18,821	177	27	18	CC	ex Eagle Integrity-95, Sea Breeze-92, CMB Motion-91, European Senator-90, Franklin 1-87, TFL Franklin 86, Seatrain Bennington-80
Kersaint	Lux	2001	23,232	37,263	183	27	14	T	
Magpie	Lbr	1999	23,843	35,930	183	27	14	T	
Melide	Lbr	1999	23,843	35,841	183	27	14	T	
Montreux	Lbr	1999	23,843	35,953	183	27	14	T	
Norasia Rigel	Lbr	2003	27,779	40,878	222	30	22	CC	ex Carinthia-04
Nordscot	Lbr	2001	23,740	35,770	183	27	14	T	
Robin	Lbr	1999	23,843	35,966	183	27	14	T	
Safmarine Illovo	Lbr	2000	26,047	30,850	196	30	20	CC	ex Alicantia-05, Commander-03, Jaguar Max-02
Safmarine Mono	Lbr	2001	26,047	30,703	196	30	20	CC	ex Andalusia-04, Centurion-03, Puma Max-02
Saxonia	Lbr	1999	19,131	25,414	189	27	20	CC	ex P&O Nedlloyd San Francisco-05, Saxonia-99
Silvia	Lbr	2000	23,842	35,000	183	27	14	T	
St. Katharinen	Lbr	1999	25,202	43,760	182	30	14	T	
Tasman Trader	Tuv	1990	17,331	22,568	177	27	18	Co	ex El Dorado-01
Turin Express	Lbr	2000	19,131	25,414	189	27	20	CC	ex Scotia -06, P&O Nedlloyd Scotia-02, Scotia-01
YM Izmir	Lbr	1995	17,285	22,148	175	29	20	CC	ex Masovia-05
YM Jakarta	Lbr	1997	17,287	22,148	175	29	20	CC	ex Montania-04

newbuildings - four 27,779 grt container ships and seven 47,600 grt 73,400 dwt tankers for 2006-7 delivery.
*Managed by Ahrenkiel Shipmanagement GmbH & Co KG including * for Del Bene SA, Argentina*

Allocean Ltd

UK

Funnel: Charterers colours.
Hull: Black with red boot-topping.

Name	Eng	Flag	Year	GRT	DWT	Loa	Bm	Kts	Type	Former names
Algerian Express	Hkg	1995	15,095	18,294	169	27	17	CC	ex Young Liberty-05, Choyang Leader-01, Kuo Fah-95
Andalusian Express	Hkg	1995	15,095	18,585	169	27	17	CC	ex Young Chance-03, Choyang Challenger-01
CP Master	Gbr	1999	24,836	11,000	217	27	25	CC	ex Lykes Master-05, Perth-04, ADCL Sultana-00, Norasia Sultana-00
CSCL America *	Cyp	2004	90,645	101,612	334	43	25	CC	
CSCL Europe *	Cyp	2004	90,645	101,612	334	43	25	CC	
Hertford	Gbr	1999	24,836	14,169	217	27	25	CC	ex Lykes Competitor-05, Hertford-04, ADCL Selina-01, Norasia Selina-00

Name	Eng	Flag	Year	GRT	DWT	Loa	Bm	Kts	Type	Former names
Kota Merdesa *		Sgp	2002	13,764	16,794	154	25	19	CC	ex Pac Aries-04
Kota Mesra *		Sgp	2002	13,764	16,742	154	25	19	CC	ex Pac Aquarius-02
Maersk Derby *		Cyp	2004	39,941	50,814	260	32	23	CC	ex P&O Nedlloyd Caracas-05
Maersk Deva *		Cyp	2004	39,941	50,828	260	32	23	CC	ex P&O Nedlloyd Caribbean-06
MSC Amsterdam		Hkg	1995	28,892	41,624	203	31	20	CC	ex Trade Selene-03, MSC Amsterdam-02, Trade Selene-01
MSC Belem		Hkg	1995	29,195	35,534	196	32	20	CC	ex Trade Harvest-02
MSC Greece		Hkg	1995	29,195	35,534	196	32	20	CC	ex Trade Maple-02, MSC Hamburg-02, Trade Maple-01
MSC Zurich		Hkg	1995	28,892	41,553	203	31	20	CC	ex Trade Eternity-04, MSC London-02, Trade Eternity-01
Ocean Preface		Hkg	1993	37,550	70,255	225	32	13	B	ex Geeta-04, De Poterne-95
Ocean Prelate		Gbr	2002	30,011	52,433	190	32	15	B	ex John Oldendorff-05
Ocean Prelude		Gbr	1995	36,097	68,541	225	32	14	B	ex Magnus Stove-03
Ocean Premier		Hkg	1996	18,070	27,348	175	26	14	B	ex Asteriks-04, Spring Venture-97
Ocean President		Hkg	2001	28,647	50,913	190	32	-	B	ex Sea Angel-04
Ocean Pride		Ita	1997	9,914	14,015	143	22	14	T	ex Sapphire-04
Pac Antlia *		Sgp	2001	13,764	16,794	154	25	19	CC	ex H.H. Ruth-01
Pac Aquila *		Sgp	2002	13,764	16,400	154	25	19	CC	
Priya		Gbr	1996	25,202	44,128	182	30	14	T	ex Jag Priya-03, Olympic Venture-01

* owned or managed by Allocean Maritime Ltd., UK.

Alpha Ship GmbH   Germany

Funnel: *Green with wide light green and narrow light blue 'darts' on broad cream band or charterers colours*
Hull: *Green or brown with red boot-topping.*

Name	Eng	Flag	Year	GRT	DWT	Loa	Bm	Kts	Type	Former names
Astor		Deu	1995	14,241	18,395	159	24	18	CC	ex APL Caracus-01, Astor-00, Infanta-97, I/a Astor
Cap Matatula		Ant	1997	14,241	18,445	159	24	19	CC	ex Castor-05, TMM Guadalajara-99, Castor-97
Cap Van Diemen		Ant	1999	23,722	29,240	194	28	21	CC	ex Uranus-06
Cap Vincent		Deu	1998	23,722	29,240	194	28	21	CC	ex Neptun-02, Kota Perdana-00, Neptun-99
Columbus Waikato		Ant	1998	23,722	29,240	194	28	21	CC	ex Taurus-02, Kota Perabu-01, Taurus-99
Condor		Ant	1995	14,241	18,395	159	24	18	CC	ex TMM Chiapas-01, Condor-99, Recife-97, Condor-95
Maersk Hong Kong		Ant	1997	21,199	25,039	178	28	21	CC	ex Nadir-98
Maersk Itajai		Ant	2000	23,722	29,240	194	28	21	CC	ex Aries-01
Maersk Valparaiso		Ant	2000	23,722	29,240	194	28	21	CC	ex Maersk Wellington-01, Maersk Itajai-01, Vega-00
Mars		Ant	1996	14,241	18,449	159	24	19	CC	ex Sea Viking-99, CMBT Mars-97, CGM La Bourdonnais-97, Mars-96
Merkur		Ant	1996	14,241	18,447	159	24	19	CC	ex Sea Valiant-99, Merkur-97, CMBT Endeavour-97, Merkur-96
Orion		Ant	1997	21,199	25,107	178	28	21	CC	ex Maersk Lima-99, Orion-98, TNX Mercury-98, I/a Orion
Pegasus		Ant	1997	23,722	29,229	194	28	21	CC	
Pluto		Ant	1999	23,722	29,210	194	28	21	CC	
Pollux		Ant	1997	14,241	18,400	159	24	18	CC	
Safmarine Amazon		Ant	1998	21,199	24,049	178	28	21	CC	ex Maersk Wellington-01, Zenit-98
Safmarine Memling		Ant	1999	23,722	29,240	194	28	21	CC	ex SCL Memling-02, Poseidon-99
Saturn		Ant	1996	14,241	18,400	159	24	18	CC	ex TMM Leon-01, CMB Endurance-97, Saturn-96
Sirius		Ant	1998	21,199	25,107	183	28	21	CC	
Venus		Ant	1996	14,241	18,400	159	24	19	CC	ex CMBT Encounter-97, Venus-96

Angelicoussis Group   Greece

Anangel Shipping Enterprises SA/Greece

Funnel: *White with green 'trefilli' between two narrow red bands beneath black top.*
Hull: *Light grey, dark grey or blue with red boot-topping.*

Name	Eng	Flag	Year	GRT	DWT	Loa	Bm	Kts	Type	Former names
Anangel Ambition *		Grc	1994	81,120	161,587	280	44	13	B	
Anangel Argonaut *		Grc	1981	36,782	65,668	223	32	14	B	ex Thorsdrake-82
Anangel Dawn		Grc	1994	75,871	149,321	270	43	14	B	ex Stellar Era-01
Anangel Destiny *		Grc	1999	87,523	171,997	289	45	15	B	
Anangel Dynasty		Grc	1999	86,600	171,101	289	45	14	B	ex Yangtze Ore-02
Anangel Eagle		Grc	1983	20,432	34,070	178	27	14	B	ex Libexport-86
Anangel Enosis *		Grc	1995	38,859	75,464	225	32	14	B	
Anangel Eternity		Grc	1999	86,600	171,176	289	45	14	B	ex Virginie Venture-02

Name	Eng	Flag	Year	GRT	DWT	Loa	Bm	Kts	Type	Former names
Anangel Express		Grc	1982	34,407	61,537	223	32	14	B	ex Oak Sun-87
Anangel Fortune		Grc	2005	88,844	175,000	289	45	14	B	
Anangel Galini *		Grc	2002	39,941	74,374	225	32	15	B	
Anangel Innovation		Grc	2004	87,050	171,681	289	45	15	B	
Anangel Legend *		Grc	1996	81,151	161,059	280	45	14	B	ex Bavang-03
Anangel Loyalty *		Grc	1995	38,131	71,550	224	32	14	B	ex Panagiotis A-02
Anangel Omonia *		Grc	1996	38,859	73,519	225	32	14	B	
Anangel Power *		Grc	1982	20,432	34,170	178	27	14	B	ex Libexpress-86
Anangel Pride *		Grc	1993	81,569	161,643	280	45	13	B	
Anangel Progress *		Grc	1989	36,781	69,406	225	32	13	B	ex Channel Express-89
Anangel Solidarity *		Grc	1993	81,569	161,545	280	44	13	B	
Anangel Splendour *		Grc	1993	81,120	161,643	280	45	13	B	
Anangel Venture *		Grc	1989	36,781	69,406	225	32	13	B	ex Channel Enterprise-89
Anna L **		Grc	1984	22,215	38,213	188	28	14	B	ex Frangiscos C.K.-03
Antonis I. Angelicoussis *		Grc	1989	36,986	69,346	225	32	13	B	ex Channel Endeavour-89
Pioneer		Grc	2004	87,050	171,681	289	45	15	B	
Sky L **		Grc	1979	10,274	17,199	146	21	14	C	ex Anangel Sky-02, Suncaribe-82, Anangel Sky-79

newbuildings - eight 171-175,000 dwt bulk carrier due for 2006-7 delivery.
* managed by Anangel Maritime Services Inc. or ** by Lomar Shipping & Management Inc., both Greece.

Kristen Navigation Inc/Greece
Funnel: *Dark blue with dark blue disc on broad light blue band.*
Hull: *Black with red boot-topping.*

Name	Flag	Year	GRT	DWT	Loa	Bm	Kts	Type	Former names
Andromeda Voyager *	Bhs	2005	160,808	320,472	332	58	-	T	
Antonis I. Angelicoussis *	Bhs	2000	156,758	306,085	332	58	15	T	
Aries Voyager *	Bhs	2006	160,808	320,870	332	58	16	T	
Astro Altair	Grc	1997	53,074	98,805	248	43	15	T	
Astro Antares	Grc	1996	53,074	98,876	248	43	15	T	
Astro Arcturus	Grc	1997	53,074	98,805	248	43	15	T	
Astro Callisto	Grc	1999	157,833	299,167	332	58	15	T	ex Picardie-03
Astro Canopus	Grc	1998	79,714	159,899	274	48	15	T	
Astro Capella	Grc	1998	79,714	147,998	275	48	15	T	
Astro Carina	Grc	2003	153,911	306,314	332	58	15	T	
Astro Cassiopeia	Grc	2003	83,000	159,000	274	48	15	T	
Astro Castor	Grc	2001	153,911	306,344	332	58	16	T	
Astro Centaurus	Grc	1995	156,565	300,294	332	58	15	T	ex Mindoro-00
Astro Challenge	Pan	2002	157,878	299,222	332	58	15	T	ex Maia-04, I/a Uvas
Astro Chorus	Grc	2001	159,016	305,704	332	58	16	T	ex Zeeland-03
Astro Corona	Grc	2003	153,911	305,870	332	58	16	T	
Astro Cygnus	Grc	2001	153,911	306,317	332	58	16	T	
Astro Leon	Grc	1992	153,427	285,771	328	57	15	T	ex Ambon-00
Astro Libra	Grc	1992	153,437	286,006	328	57	15	T	ex Irian-00
Astro Luna	Grc	1995	147,007	264,340	322	58	15	T	ex Tango-02, Diamond Iris-01
Astro Lupus	Grc	1989	137,893	257,589	321	57	15	T	ex Navix Seibu-00
Astro Lyra	Grc	1995	153,429	284,410	328	57	15	T	ex Flores-00
Astro Perseus	Grc	2004	80,620	158,982	274	48	15	T	
Astro Phoenix	Grc	2004	85,000	159,000	274	48	15	T	
Astro Polaris	Grc	2004	85,000	159,460	274	48	15	T	
Astro Saturn	Grc	2003	57,022	105,167	248	43	-	T	
Astro Sculptor	Grc	2003	57,022	105,108	248	43	-	T	
Astro Sirius	Grc	1996	53,074	98,805	248	43	15	T	
Elizabeth I. Angelicoussis	Grc	2004	83,000	159,000	274	48	15	T	
Gemini Voyager *	Bhs	1999	160,036	310,138	330	58	16	T	ex Richard H. Matzke-03
Regulus Voyager *	Bhs	2000	160,036	310,138	331	58	16	T	ex Chang-Lin Tien-03

newbuildings - one 306,000 dwt and four 95,000 grt Lng tankers on order for 2005-6 delivery.
* managed by ChevronTexaco Shipping Co. LLC q.v.

Alpha Tankers & Freighters International Ltd/Greece
Funnel: *White with black 'A' between narrow red bands below black top.*
Hull: *Blue with red boot-topping.*

Name	Flag	Year	GRT	DWT	Loa	Bm	Kts	Type	Former names
Alpha Action	Grc	1994	77,211	150,790	274	45	14	B	ex Action-02, World Action-02
Alpha Afovos	Grc	2001	39,941	74,428	225	32	15	B	ex Anangel Afovos-01
Alpha Century	Grc	2000	87,407	170,415	289	45	14	B	ex Anangel Century-02
Alpha Cosmos	Grc	2001	87,378	169,770	289	45	15	B	ex Mineral York-02, Mineral Trader-01
Alpha Effort	Grc	1999	38,564	72,844	225	32	15	B	
Alpha Era	Grc	2000	87,407	170,387	289	45	14	B	ex Mineral Sakura-02
Alpha Flame	Grc	1999	38,852	74,545	225	32	14	B	ex United Support-04

Alpha Ship GmbH. ORION. *Hans Kraijenbosch*

Angelicoussis Group (Kristen Navigation). ASTRO CHORUS. *Hans Kraijenbosch*

Angelicoussis Group (Alpha Tankers). ALPHA FRIENDSHIP. *F. de Vries*

Name	Eng	Flag	Year	GRT	DWT	Loa	Bm	Kts	Type	Former names
Alpha Friendship		Grc	1996	81,140	161,524	280	45	14	B	ex Anangel Friendship-02
Alpha Future		Grc	1999	38,564	72,893	225	32	15	B	
Alpha Gemini		Grc	1985	34,541	65,298	222	32	14	B	ex Ios-97
Alpha Happiness		Grc	1999	38,564	72,800	225	32	15	B	
Alpha Harmony		Grc	2001	39,941	74,492	225	32	14	B	ex Alpha Harmony I-02, Alpha Harmony-01
Alpha Melody		Grc	2002	39,941	74,374	225	32	15	B	I/a Anangel Melody
Alpha Millennium		Grc	2000	87,407	170,415	280	45	15	B	ex Anangel Millennium-02
Annoula		Grc	1997	36,559	70,281	225	32	14	B	
Maria A. Angelicoussi		Grc	2001	86,201	169,163	289	45	15	B	I/a Fabulous
Marvellous		Grc	2000	86,201	169,150	289	45	15	B	ex Mineral Marvel-04, Marvel-04

related family company.

Atlanship SA　　　　　　　　　　　　　　　　　　Switzerland

Funnel: *White with narrow red diagonal line aft of blue triangle.*
Hull: *Stone or white with red boot-topping.*

Orange Blossom		Lbr	1985	9,984	15,108	145	22	-	Tfj	
Orange Sky		Lbr	2000	22,063	26,863	172	27	14	Tfj	I/a May Oldendorff (conv B-02)
Orange Star		Lbr	1975	9,981	12,320	156	21	24	Tfj	ex Fife-86, Andalucia Star-84
Orange Wave		Lbr	1993	13,444	16,700	157	26	18	Tfj	

newbuilding: one 33,000 grt 42,500 dwt fruit juice carrier on order for 2006 delivery.

Seereederei Baco-Liner GmbH　　　　　　　　　　Germany

Funnel: *Black with yellow/black 'bl' symbol on broad white band.*
Hull: *Blue with white 'BACO-LINER', red boot-topping.*

Baco-Liner 1		Lbr	1979	22,345	21,801	204	29	15	LC	
Baco-Liner 2		Lbr	1980	22,345	21,801	201	29	14	LC	
Baco-Liner 3		Lbr	1984	22,528	21,771	204	29	14	LC	

BBG-Bremer Bereederungs GmbH & Co KG　　　Germany

Funnel: *White with blue 'BBG' on white diamond on blue band or charterers colours.*
Hull: *Blue or black with red boot-topping.*

Atalanta		Lbr	1999	28,148	44,593	185	32	15	Co	ex CCNI Arauco-04
Cape Darnley		Mhl	2003	23,132	30,346	193	28	19	Co	
Cape Delfaro		Mhl	2004	23,132	30,000	193	28	19	Co/hl	
Cape Delgardo		Mhl	2003	23,132	30,000	193	28	19	Co/hl	
Cape Donington		Mhl	2003	23,132	30,343	193	28	19	Co/hl	ex Golden Isle-04, Cape Donington-03
CCNI Antartico		Mhl	2002	23,132	30,490	193	28	15	Co/hl	ex CSAV Genova-04, Cape Dorchester-03
CCNI Magallanes		Mhl	2002	23,132	30,586	193	28	15	Co/hl	ex Cape Dyer-03
Conti Singa *		Deu	1996	42,336	41,460	242	32	22	CC	ex MSC Switzerland-05, Norasia Singa-02
Conti Shanghai *		Deu	1996	42,323	41,510	242	32	22	CC	ex Norasia Shanghai-02
Maersk Itaqui *		Lbr	1994	42,323	41,570	242	32	22	CC	ex P&O Nedlloyd Dammam-05, MSC Italy-05, Norasia Sharjah-02
Maersk Itea *		Lbr	1994	42,323	41,570	242	32	22	CC	ex P&O Nedlloyd Shanghai-05, MSC Munich-04, Norasia Hong Kong-02, MSC Houston-99, Norasia Hong Kong-98
MSC Boston		Mlt	1993	42,323	41,570	242	32	22	CC	ex Norasia Fribourg-97
MSC New York		Lbr	1994	42,323	41,570	242	32	22	CC	ex Norasia Kiel-97
Zim Houston III		Atg	1993	10,742	14,111	163	22	17	CC	ex Lukas-99, Kaedi-99, Kano-98, Lukas-98

* managed for Conti Rederei, Germany

Belships ASA　　　　　　　　　　　　　　　　　　Norway

Funnel: *Blue with blue 'S' inside 'C' above blue anchor within narrow blue ring on white disc.*
Hull: *Blue or dark grey with red boot-topping.*

Belnor		Nis	1996	26,449	47,369	190	31	14	B	
Ondina		Pan	1996	26,449	47,639	190	31	14	B	ex Western Ondina-04
Stove Campbell		Nis	1999	26,966	46,223	186	31	14	Co	ex Western Onyx-01
Stove Trader		Nis	1999	26,966	46,223	186	31	14	Co	ex Western Obelisk-01
Stove Tradition		Nis	1998	26,966	46,223	186	31	14	Co	ex Western Opal-01
Stove Transport		Nis	1998	26,966	46,223	186	31	16	Co	ex Western Olivin-01
Super Adventure *		Pan	1996	17,977	28,630	172	27	14	B	ex IVS Super Adventure-03, Super Adventure-01

Name	Eng	Flag	Year	GRT	DWT	Loa	Bm	Kts	Type	Former names
Super Challenge		Pan	1996	17,977	28,581	172	27	14	B	ex IVS Super Challenge-03, Super Challenge-02

*Managed by Belships Management Singapore Pte. Ltd., Singapore or * managed for Dowa Line Co. Ltd., Japan*
Also see Belchem Singapore Pte. Ltd. (formed jointly with Chemikalien Seetransport GmbH q.v.)

Beluga Shipping GmbH   Germany

Funnel: *Buff with dark green 'G'.*
Hull: *Dark green with white 'GREENFLEET', red boot-topping.*

Name	Eng	Flag	Year	GRT	DWT	Loa	Bm	Kts	Type	Former names
BBC India		Gib	1998	11,894	17,539	143	22	16	Co	ex Maria Green-04
Marion Green		Gib	1999	11,894	17,539	143	22	16	Co	
Margaretha Green		Gib	1999	11,894	17,539	143	22	16	Co	ex Newpac Cumulus-05, Margaretha Green-04, Nirint Voyager-02, Coral Green-01, Margaretha Green-00

newbuildings: two 14,000 grt container ships for 2007 delivery from Chinese builder.
Also owns several 8-9,600 grt vessels, some with heavy lift cranes.

Bergesen Worldwide Ltd   Norway

Funnel: *Blue with white 'B' above 'W' or plain blue with narrow black top.*
Hull: *Black with red or grey boot topping.*

Name	Eng	Flag	Year	GRT	DWT	Loa	Bm	Kts	Type	Former names
Nile		Pan	1991	153,407	285,739	328	57	15	T	ex Argo Pallas-00
Norna **		Pan	1974	20,812	37,797	186	26	15	T	ex Akti A-01, Seafriend-97, Alice G-91, Faith I-91, Faith-97, Varanger-84
Norsea **		Mlt	1977	19,351	33,401	171	26	13	T	ex Sea Elevi-01, Vincenzina-00, Silina-95, Petrobulk Sterling-93, Capri Alfa-90, Fort Kingston-90, Capri Alfa-89, Panama-88
Noto		Pan	1992	153,437	286,006	328	57	14	T	ex Argo Thetis-00
Nuri		Sgp	1992	153,427	285,933	328	58	15	T	ex Argo Daphne-00
Nysa		Sgp	2000	157,814	299,543	332	58	15	T	ex Argo Artemis-00
Sala		Pan	1993	153,506	293,376	328	58	15	T	
Sebu		Pan	1993	153,506	293,238	332	57	15	T	ex Seki-94
Soro		Pan	1993	156,539	299,718	332	58	15	T	
Suva		Pan	1993	153,332	293,371	328	57	15	T	ex Argo Medea-00, Suva-98
Sylt		Pan	1993	153,332	293,297	328	57	15	T	
Taos		Pan	1990	144,567	275,993	326	57	14	T	ex General Monarch-96, Sea Duke-91
Ubud		Pan	1999	149,383	299,990	330	60	16	T	
Ulan		Pan	2000	157,814	277,370	332	58	15	T	
Ural		Pan	2000	149,383	299,990	330	60	16	T	
Utah *		Hkg	2001	157,814	299,498	332	58	15	T	
Utik		Hkg	2001	157,814	299,150	332	58	15	T	
World Lake		Hkg	2004	156,500	298,500	332	58	15	T	
World Lion		Hkg	2004	156,500	298,500	332	58	15	T	
World Luck		Pan	2003	158,993	298,555	332	58	15	T	
World Luna		Pan	2003	158,993	298,555	332	58	15	T	

newbuildings - two 306,000 dwt tankers, one 23,000 grt, two 47,000 grt Lpg tankers and three 95,000 grt Lng tankers for 2007-8 delivery.
Controlled by Sohmen family, Hong Kong (China) and managed by BW Shipping Managers Pte. Ltd., Singapore.
*Owned by subsidiaries * The Green Tankers AS, France or ** Norchart AS, Norway*

Bergesen Worldwide Gas ASA/Norway

Funnel: *White with deep black top containing white houseflag with black anchor and diagonal light green stripe.*
Hull: *Light green with blue boot-topping or red with light green diagonal stripe and red or grey boot-topping*

Name	Eng	Flag	Year	GRT	DWT	Loa	Bm	Kts	Type	Former names
Berge Arctic		Pan	2001	91,563	174,285	292	48	-	B	
Berge Arrow		Nis	1978	44,502	48,821	229	32	15	Lpg	ex Northern Arrow-84
Berge Atlantic		Nis	1998	91,962	172,704	292	48	16	B	
Berge Boston	(st)	Nis	2003	93,844	77,410	277	43	19	Lng	
Berge Captain		Nis	1991	45,032	56,945	224	36	16	Lpg	
Berge Challenger		Nis	1992	45,032	56,885	224	36	16	Lpg	
Berge Clipper		Nis	1992	45,032	56,864	224	36	16	Lpg	
Berge Commander		Nis	1991	45,032	56,875	224	36	16	Lpg	
Berge Danuta		Nis	2000	49,288	50,260	226	36	18	Lpg	
Berge Denise *		Atf	2001	49,292	56,745	226	36	18	Lpg	
Berge Eagle		Nis	1978	44,502	48,986	229	32	17	Lpg	ex Northern Eagle I-84
Berge Everett	(st)	Nis	2003	93,844	77,410	277	43	19	Lng	
Berge Fjord ***		Pan	1986	159,534	310,698	332	57	13	O	ex Docefjord-00
Berge Frost		Nis	1983	50,699	56,174	250	36	17	Lpg	ex Floreal-91
Berge Hugin		Nis	2002	22,902	26,616	174	28	16	Lpg	ex Lancashire-05
Berge Munin		Nis	1989	19,719	29,171	166	27	16	Lpg	ex Cheshire-05

Name	Eng	Flag	Year	GRT	DWT	Loa	Bm	Kts	Type	Former names
Berge Nantes ***		Atf	2003	35,190	44,773	216	32	17	Lpg	
Berge Nice ***		Atf	2003	35,346	44,639	216	32	17	Lpg	
Berge Nord		Nis	1997	107,512	218,283	305	53	15	B	
Berge Odin		Nis	2005	25,994	29,000	180	29	-	Lpg	
Berge Pacific	(2)	Nis	1986	118,491	231,850	315	56	13	B	ex Iron Pacific-98
Berge Phoenix		Pan	1986	154,098	290,793	334	62	14	Obo	ex Grand Phoenix-00
Berge Rachel		Nis	1984	49,130	63,296	228	36	14	Lpg	
Berge Racine		Nis	1985	49,130	63,254	228	36	14	Lpg	
Berge Ragnhild		Nis	1985	49,130	63,258	228	36	14	Lpg	
Berge Saga		Nis	1979	44,151	55,303	225	34	16	Lpg	
Berge Shan		Nis	1986	100,070	200,692	300	50	13	B	ex Chiribetsu-00, Chiribetsu Maru-95
Berge Sisu		Nis	1978	44,076	55,172	225	34	16	Lpg	
Berge Spirit		Nis	1980	44,076	55,173	225	34	16	Lpg	ex Golar Frost-89
Berge Stadt *		Atf	1994	160,467	306,951	332	58	16	T	
Berge Stahl		Nis	1986	175,720	364,767	343	64	13	O	
Berge Strand		Nis	1982	43,849	55,361	225	34	16	Lpg	
Berge Sund		Nis	1981	43,849	55,303	225	34	16	Lpg	
Berge Sword		Nis	1979	44,502	48,996	229	32	17	Lpg	ex Excaliber-88, Hoegh Sword-86
Berge Vik		Pan	1987	159,534	310,686	332	57	13	O	ex Tijuca-02
Bergeland		Nis	1992	154,030	322,941	339	55	14	O	
Century		Nis	1974	26,097	22,036	182	29	-	Lgc	ex Lucian-80
Harriette N		Sgp	2003	34,582	47,232	216	32	17	Lpg	ex Cantarell-00, l/a Petrogas II
Havdrott		Nis	1978	34,577	43,386	220	29	16	Lpg	ex Galpara-87
Havfrost		Nis	1991	34,946	49,513	205	32	15	Lpg	
Havfru		Nis	1973	26,097	22,041	182	29	20	Lgc	ex Vanda-87, Venator-86
Havglimt		Nis	1978	30,950	38,534	206	31	16	Lpg	ex Centum-87
Havis		Nis	1993	34,951	49,513	205	32	15	Lpg	
Havkong		Nis	1978	34,577	43,386	220	29	17	Lpg	ex Galconda-87
Havrim		Nis	1980	26,207	27,480	197	29	-	Lpg	ex Smolnyy-94
Hebris		Nis	1983	15,397	20,566	158	24	17	Lpg	
Hedda		Nis	1993	22,521	30,815	170	27	18	Lpg	
Hekabe		Nis	1977	34,572	43,386	220	29	16	Lpg	ex Garinda-86
Helga		Nis	1994	22,521	30,800	170	27	16	Lpg	
Helice		Nis	1991	34,974	49,513	205	32	16	Lpg	
Helios		Nis	1992	34,974	49,513	205	32	15	Lpg	
Hemina		Nis	1979	34,577	43,386	220	29	16	Lpg	ex Garala-87
Herakles		Nis	1982	20,531	31,485	158	28	15	Lpg	ex Berge Fister-88
Hugo N		Nis	1980	34,582	46,486	216	32	-	Lpg	ex Ahkatun-99
LNG Benue		Bmu	2005	97,561	83,000	285	43	-	Lng	
LNG Enugu		Bmu	2005	97,561	83,068	285	43	-	Lng	
LNG River Orashi		St	2004	97,561	83,068	285	43	-	Lng	
LNG Oyo		Bmu	2005	97,561	83,068	285	43	-	Lng	
SG Enterprise †		Bhs	1997	108,083	211,485	312	51	14	B	ex Jedforest-00, SG Enterprise-98
SG Prosperity †		Bhs	1996	108,083	211,201	312	51	14	B	ex Lauderdale-00, SG Prosperity-98
Steven N **		Pan	1979	33,807	40,605	217	32	17	Lpg	ex Monterrey-99

newbuildings: eight tankers between 29,000 - 78,000 dwt on order for 2006-8 delivery.
*Wholly controlled by Sohmen family's World Nordic ApS and * managed by The Green Tankers AS, France, ** by Anglo-Eastern Shipmanagement Ltd., Singapore or *** by International Tanker Management Ltd., UAE † on charter to Chinese steelmaker until 2012*

Neu Seeschiffahrt GmbH/Germany

Funnel: Blue with 'NEU' on blue/white/blue horizontally striped flag on white rectanglr.
Hull: Black, dark grey or brown with red boot-topping.

Name	Eng	Flag	Year	GRT	DWT	Loa	Bm	Kts	Type	Former names
Alfred N		Pan	1991	131,479	260,826	325	54	13	B	ex Lyra-02
Alster N		Pan	1988	171,924	305,893	340	57	13	Obo	ex Alster Ore-03
Amy N		Pan	1997	155,051	322,457	332	58	13	B	ex Neckar Ore-01
Arthur N		Pan	1991	131,479	260,823	325	54	13	B	ex Athesis Ore-02
Constance N		Pan	1983	113,272	224,666	315	50	-	B	ex Gargantua-05, Global Spirit-98, Chishirokawa Maru-93
Edward N	(2)	Pan	1979	112,947	225,162	313	50	17	Obo	ex Berge Athene-04, Pankar Theodoros-88, Konkar Theodoros-87
Faith N		Pan	1990	131,479	260,783	325	54	13	B	ex Auriga-02
Grace N		Lbr	1983	113,342	224,222	312	50	13	B	ex Elbe Ore-05, Frontier Maru-96
Julian N		Lbr	1993	77,090	149,394	270	43	13	B	ex Anja-05, Chou Shan-03

Atlanship SA. ORANGE SKY. *N. Kemps*

Bergesen Worldwide. BERGE ARCTIC. *Hans Kraijenbosch*

Bergesen Worldwide. BERGE NANTES. *J. M. Kakebeeke*

Name	Eng	Flag	Year	GRT	DWT	Loa	Bm	Kts	Type	Former names
Mosel N		Lbr	1995	63,152	122,311	266	41	14	B	ex Mosel Ore-03
Ruhr N		Lbr	1987	171,924	305,863	340	57	13	Obo	ex Ruhr Ore-03
Saar N		Lbr	1995	63,152	122,331	266	41	14	B	ex Saar Ore-03
Waterman N		Pan	1985	129,325	259,296	329	54	12	B	ex Hyundai Giant-03

51% interest controlled by Bergesen Worldwide Gas ASA.

Bergshav Shipholding AS Norway

Funnel: *Red with white 'B' and narrow white band beneath black top.*
Hull: *Brown with red or grey boot-topping.*

Name	Eng	Flag	Year	GRT	DWT	Loa	Bm	Kts	Type	Former names
Berana		Pan	1985	43,733	83,890	229	32	14	T	ex Danita-00
Bergitta		Nis	1999	56,207	105,641	239	42	14	T	
Bertora		Bhs	2001	55,796	100,257	238	42	14	T	
Bregen	(2)	Nis	1994	10,012	13,941	150	21	13	T	
Cypress Pass **		Lbr	1988	42,447	12,763	184	31	18	V	
Hyundai No. 203 **		Pan	1988	41,353	12,762	184	31	18	V	ex Atlantic Beauty-92, Hyundai No.203-90
Vibeke *	(2)	Bhs	1996	16,940	23,025	169	24	17	Ro	ex Sochi-05
Vinni *	(2)	Mlt	1994	16,940	13,480	169	24	17	Ro	ex Novorossiysk-04

Newbuildings: 57,000 grt 105,000 dwt tanker for 2007 delivery from Japanese builder.
*Company over 60% owned by Frontline q.v. * on charter to Wallenius-Wilhelmsen or ** to Eukor Car Carriers Inc. q.v.*

Bibby Line Ltd UK

Funnel: *Pink with black top or 'Stolt' colours.*
Hull: *Black or red with red or green boot-topping.*

Name	Eng	Flag	Year	GRT	DWT	Loa	Bm	Kts	Type	Former names
Stolt Dorset		Pan	1997	12,140	19,299	148	23	14	T	ex Botany Triumph-02
Stolt Kent		Iom	1998	12,141	19,125	148	23	15	T	

Blystad Shipmanagement Ltd UK

Funnel: *Yellow with red 'B' on broad white band edged with narrow blue bands, narrow black top.*
Hull: *Black or red wih red boot-toping.*

Name	Eng	Flag	Year	GRT	DWT	Loa	Bm	Kts	Type	Former names
Anabel		Mhl	1980	23,847	42,662	176	32	15	T	ex Tanja Jacob-04
Songa Ancora		Mhl	1989	77,931	142,031	269	45	14	T	ex Ancora-05, Leon Spirit-04, Boria Tapias-04, Jahre Trader-98
Songa Anette		Lbr	1989	38,878	62,326	225	32	14	T	ex Anette-05, Annette-00, Nichian-00, World S-95, World Shanghai-95, I/a Cabo de Homos
Songa Eva		Mhl	1989	10,948	17,485	151	22	14	T	ex Lake Eva-06, Jakov Sverdlov-03
Songa Maya		Mhl	1988	10,948	17,485	151	22	14	T	ex Lake Maya-06, Kapitan Rudnev-03
Team Actinia *		Cyp	1993	22,633	40,296	176	32	14	T	ex Actinia-00
Team Anemonia *		Cyp	1995	22,633	40,296	176	32	14	T	ex Anemonia-00
Team Anatas		Mhl	1986	22,620	40,158	174	32	-	T	ex Anatas-05, Maribel-04, Ferncourt-93, Antonio Dovali J-89, I/a Ferncourt
Team Aniara		Lbr	1985	25,362	40,738	178	32	14	T	ex Aniara-03, Levant-89, Avanti-88
Team Anja		Mhl	1997	28,027	44,640	183	32	14	T	ex Simunye-05, Engen Simunye-00
Team Jupiter **		Nis	2000	27,185	48,338	182	32	14	T	
Team Leopard		Mhl	1985	26,113	46,100	172	32	14	T	ex Leopard-04, Petrobulk Leopard-96, Naess Leopard-86
Team Mars		Mhl	1982	21,057	42,010	184	30	14	T	ex Team Troma-98, Troma-82
Team Merkur		Mhl	1981	24,330	41,985	184	30	14	T	ex Team Frosta-98, Frosta-82
Team Neptun **		Nis	2000	27,185	48,309	182	32	14	T	
Team Panther		Mhl	1985	26,113	46,100	172	32	14	T	ex Panther-04, Petrobulk Panther-96, Naess Panther-86
Team Saturn		Mhl	1987	24,653	45,831	186	30	14	T	ex Team Hada-98
Team Tiger		Mhl	1985	26,113	44,987	172	32	14	T	ex Tiger-04, Petrobulk Tiger-96, Jahre Tiger-86

newbuildings: Six 26,900 grt 40,000 dwt tankers on order for 2007-9 delivery from Croatian builder.
*Norwegian subsidiary Team Tankers AS operating pool including vessels owned * by Consultores de Navegacion SA, Spain or ** by Chemikalien Seetransport GmbH, Germany q.v.*

Name	Eng	Flag	Year	GRT	DWT	Loa	Bm	Kts	Type	Former names

Aug Bolten Wm Miller's Nachfolger (GmbH & Co) KG   Germany

Funnel: *Black with black 'B' over red diagonal crosses on white houseflag or (*) black 'L' on blue-edged white disc at centre of blue diagonal crossed and edged houseflag on broad white band.*
Hull: *Black with red boot-topping.*

Name	Eng	Flag	Year	GRT	DWT	Loa	Bm	Kts	Type	Former names
Andros		Cyp	1996	14,599	24,279	157	26	-	B	ex Sea Wisdom-03
Delos		Cyp	1997	15,888	24,000	160	26	16	B	ex Sea Master-01
Dorothea		Cyp	1984	13,021	22,025	155	23	14	B	ex Garnet Star-94
Elisabeth Bolten		Lbr	2001	10,132	13,275	127	21	14	Co	
Marielle Bolten		Lbr	1997	19,354	29,538	181	26	14	Co	
Milos *		Cyp	1997	14,397	24,045	154	26	13	B	ex Pacific Trader-03
Natalie Bolten		Lbr	2001	10,132	13,275	127	21	14	Co	
Naxos		Mhl	1995	15,164	23,825	153	26	14	B	ex Hirosaki Cherry-04, Hirosaki Rainbow-01
Nord Spirit		Mhl	1997	25,967	47,260	186	31	14	B	ex Sea Orion-03
Paros *		Cyp	1997	14,397	23,984	154	26	14	B	ex Pacific Bridge-03
Santorin II *		Cyp	1984	14,147	23,899	160	24	14	B	ex Cynthia No. 5-93, Jovian Lark-90, Sanko Melody-85
Sigrun Bolten		Lbr	1997	19,354	29,538	181	26	14	Co	ex Cielo di Savona-01. Sigrun Bolten-97
Skyros *		Cyp	1998	14,781	24,128	154	26	14	B	ex Diamond Star-03
Tinos		Cyp	1995	14,431	23,725	151	26	13	B	ex Bright Nextage-03
William		Cyp	1995	15,164	23,829	153	26	14	B	ex Pacific Rainbow II-01

* owned by subsidiary Lydia Shipping Co. SA, Greece.

A/S Borgestad ASA   Norway

Funnel: *Dark blue with dark blue 'B' on white shield overlapping white band or * white with red 'W' symbol.*
Hull: *Grey, orange or * green with red boot-topping.*

Name	Eng	Flag	Year	GRT	DWT	Loa	Bm	Kts	Type	Former names
Westwood Anette		Bhs	1987	28,805	45,252	200	31	15	BC	
Westwood Columbia *		Bhs	2002	32,551	45,000	200	31	17	BC	
Westwood Marianne		Bhs	1986	28,805	45,252	200	31	15	BC	
Westwood Olympia *		Bhs	2004	32,500	45,000	200	31	17	BC	
Westwood Rainier *		Bhs	2002	32,551	45,000	200	31	17	BC	
Westwood Victoria *		Bhs	2003	31,772	45,851	200	31	17	BC	

newbuildings: three further 45,000 dwt (Westwood Fraser, Westwood Cascade and Westwood Robson) due for 2007-8 delivery
* managed for Westwood Shipping Lines Inc.(Weyerhaeuser Co.), USA. Also see Gearbulk Ltd (Kristian Gerhard Jebsen Skips)

BP Plc   UK

BP Shipping Ltd/UK

Funnel: *Red with green band on broad white band beneath black top.*
Hull: *Black with red boot-topping.*

Name	Eng	Flag	Year	GRT	DWT	Loa	Bm	Kts	Type	Former names
Alaskan Explorer †		Usa	2005	95,000	185,000	287	50	15	T	
Alaskan Frontier †		Usa	2004	95,000	185,000	287	50	15	T	
Alaskan Legend †		Usa	2006	95,000	185,000	287	50	15	T	
Alaskan Navigator †		Usa	2005	95,000	185,000	287	50	15	T	I/dn Alaskan Adventurer
British Beech *		Iom	2003	58,200	106,138	241	42	15	T	
British Chivalry		Iom	2005	29,335	46,803	183	32	15	T	
British Cormorant		Iom	2005	63,661	114,809	250	44	-	T	
British Courtesy		Iom	2005	28,000	46,080	183	32	14	T	
British Curlew		Iom	2004	63,562	114,809	250	44	15	T	
British Cygnet		Iom	2005	63,462	113,782	250	44	15	T	
British Eagle		Iom	2006	64,500	113,120	250	44	15	T	
British Endeavour **		Gbr	2002	23,235	37,224	183	27	15	T	
British Endurance **		Gbr	2002	23,235	37,296	183	27	14	T	
British Energy		Gbr	2001	23,682	35,970	183	27	14	T	
British Engineer		Iom	2003	23,240	37,343	183	27	14	T	ex Baltic Commodore-05
British Enterprise		Gbr	2001	23,682	35,858	183	27	14	T	
British Environment		Iom	2003	23,240	37,330	183	27	14	T	ex Baltic Crusader-05
British Esteem		Gbr	2003	23,235	37,220	183	27	15	T	
British Excellence		Iom	2003	23,240	37,330	183	27	14	T	ex Baltic Challenger-05
British Experience		Iom	2003	23,240	37,333	183	27	14	T	ex Baltic Champion-05
British Explorer		Gbr	2003	23,235	37,321	183	27	15	T	
British Falcon		Iom	2006	64,500	113,120	250	44	15	T	
British Fidelity		Iom	2004	29,335	46,803	183	32	14	T	
British Gannet		Iom	2005	63,661	114,809	250	44	15	T	
British Harmony		Iom	2005	29,335	46,803	183	32	14	T	

Bergesen Worldwide. HEDDA. *Vandriessche Guido*

Bergshav Shipholding. BERGITTA. *Hans Kraijenbosch*

Blystad Shipmanagement. TEAM ANATAS. *Hans Kraijenbosch*

Aug Bolten Wm Miller's Nachfolger. ELISABETH BOLTEN. *N. Kemps*

BP Shipping. BRITISH ENDURANCE. *C. Lous*

Brostrom AB. BRO EDWARD. *N. Kemps*

Name	Eng	Flag	Year	GRT	DWT	Loa	Bm	Kts	Type	Former names
British Hawthorn **		Iom	2003	57,567	81,697	241	42	15	T	
British Hazel *		Iom	2004	58,070	106,085	241	42	15	T	
British Holly *		Iom	2004	58,070	106,085	241	42	15	T	
British Innovator	(st)	Iom	2002	92,900	67,850	279	43	19	Lng	
British Integrity		Iom	2004	29,335	46,803	183	32	15	T	
British Kestrel		Iom	2006	64,500	113,120	250	44	15	T	
British Laurel **		Iom	2002	57,567	106,500	241	42	15	T	
British Liberty		Iom	2004	29,335	46,803	183	32	14	T	
British Loyalty		Iom	2004	29,335	46,803	183	32	14	T	
British Mallard		Iom	2005	63,661	114,809	250	44	15	T	
British Merchant	(st)	Iom	2003	93,498	67,850	279	43	19	Lng	
British Merlin		Iom	2003	63,661	114,761	250	44	15	T	
British Oak **		Iom	2003	57,567	106,500	241	42	15	T	
British Osprey		Iom	2003	63,661	101,760	250	44	15	T	
British Pioneer		Iom	1999	160,216	306,397	334	58	15	T	
British Pride		Iom	2000	160,216	305,994	334	58	15	T	
British Progress		Iom	2000	160,216	306,497	334	58	15	T	
British Purpose		Iom	2000	160,216	306,307	334	58	15	T	
British Robin		Iom	2005	63,462	113,782	250	44	15	T	
British Security		Iom	2004	28,000	46,080	183	32	14	T	
British Serenity		Iom	2005	28,000	46,080	183	32	14	T	
British Swift		Iom	2003	63,661	114,809	250	44	15	T	
British Tenacity		Iom	2004	28,000	46,080	183	32	14	T	
British Trader	(st)	Iom	2003	93,498	75,109	279	43	19	Lng	
British Tranquility		Iom	2005	28,000	46,080	183	32	14	T	
British Unity		Iom	2004	28,000	46,080	183	32	14	T	
British Vine *		Iom	2004	58,200	106,000	241	42	15	T	
British Willow		Iom	2003	57,500	106,000	241	42	15	T	

newbuildings - five 155,000 cm Lng and four 48,000 grt Lpg tankers (British Commerce, Confidence, Courage and Counsellor) .
* managed by Executive Ship Management Pte. Ltd., Singapore or ** managed for Seaworld Management & Trading Inc., Greece.
† owned by BP Oil Shipping Co, subsidiary of BP Amoco Corporation, USA.
Also see Alaska Tanker Co. (formed jointly with Keystone Shipping Co. and Overseas Shipholding Group Inc, both USA) under OSG.

Brostrom AB Sweden

Brostrom Tankers SA/France

Funnel: *Blue with houseflag (blue 'AB' on white disc over red/blue horizontal bands) overlapping green rectangle on white band.*
Hull: *Blue or grey with red boot-topping.*

Name	Eng	Flag	Year	GRT	DWT	Loa	Bm	Kts	Type	Former names
Bro Albert		Atf	1995	28,226	46,768	183	32	14	T	ex Port Albert-00
Bro Alexandre		Atf	1995	28,226	46,738	183	32	14	T	ex Port Alexandre-00
Bro Anton *		Swe	1999	11,375	16,376	144	23	15	T	ex United Anton-00
Bro Arthur		Atf	1995	28,226	46,802	183	32	14	T	ex Port Arthur-00
Bro Atland *		Swe	1999	11,377	16,326	144	23	15	T	ex United Atland-00, United Albert-99
Bro Axel *		Swe	1998	11,324	16,389	144	23	13	T	ex United Axel-00
Bro Caroline		Atf	1995	29,083	45,014	183	32	14	T	ex Port Caroline-00
Bro Catherine		Atf	1997	29,083	44,922	180	32	14	T	ex Port Catherine-00
Bro Cecile		Atf	1997	29,083	44,936	180	32	14	T	ex Port Cecile-00
Bro Charlotte		Atf	1997	29,083	44,970	181	32	14	T	ex Port Charlotte-00
Bro Deliverer	(2)	Swe	2006	10,660	14,500	147	22	13	T	
Bro Designer	(2)	Swe	2006	10,660	14,500	147	22	13	T	
Bro Edward		Atf	2005	26,659	37,300	184	30	14	T	
Bro Elizabeth		Atf	2001	24,099	37,026	184	30	15	T	
Bro Elliot		Atf	2005	26,659	37,300	184	30	14	T	
Bro Ellen		Atf	2002	24,100	37,000	184	30	15	T	
Bro Etienne		Atf	2004	26,659	37,300	184	30	14	T	
Bro Premium		Nld	1999	29,289	45,790	183	32	15	T	ex Iver Exact-06
Bro Priority		Swe	2001	21,517	31,265	177	28	14	T	ex Iver Progress-05
Bro Promotion		Nld	1999	29,289	45,790	183	32	15	T	ex Iver Example-06
Bro Provider		Swe	2001	21,517	31,265	177	28	14	T	ex Iver Prosperity-06
Bro Sincero ‡		Swe	2002	11,855	16,008	146	22	14	T	
Bro Stella *		Swe	1995	40,958	70,260	213	36	14	T	ex United Stella-01
Cilaos †		Atf	1996	29,083	44,885	180	32	14	T	ex Port Christine-98
Evinco ‡		Swe	2005	13,769	19,500	156	24	-	T	

newbuildings: two further 10,660 grt and one 25,000 grt tanker due for 2007 delivery.
* owned by Brostrom Tankers AB (managed by Brostrom Ship Management AB).
† jointly owned with Societe d'Armement et de Transport (SOCATRA), France or ‡ with Rederi Donsotank A/B, Sweden.

Name	Eng	Flag	Year	GRT	DWT	Loa	Bm	Kts	Type	Former names

Hermann Buss GmbH & Cie

Germany

Funnel: White with houseflag or charterers colours.
Hull: Green with red boot-topping or charterers colours..

Name	Eng	Flag	Year	GRT	DWT	Loa	Bm	Kts	Type	Former names
Atlantic Trader	Atg	1996	16,165	22,250	168	27	19	CC	ex Calaparati-05, Atlantic Trader-04, CSAV Rauten-98, Sea Vista-97, Atlantic Trader-96
Baltrum Trader	Atg	1999	25,361	34,017	207	30	21	CC	ex P&O Nedlloyd Fremantle-01, Baltrum Trader-99
Cala Palmira	Atg	1995	11,987	14,717	157	24	22	CC	ex Melfi Canada-04, Maersk La Guaira-03, Weser Trader-97, CTE Algeciras-96, Weser Trader-95
CMA CGM Kiwi	Deu	1998	16,803	22,900	185	25	19	CC	ex Maruba Trader-04, I/a Szczecin Trader
CMA CGM Springbok	Atg	1996	16,165	22,250	168	27	21	CC	ex Warnow Trader-03, Libra Valencia-99, Warnow Trader-96
CMA CGM Tucano	Deu	1998	23,792	30,340	188	30	20	CC	ex Arkona Trader-03, Cielo d'Italia-02, Arkona Trader-99
CP Canada	Atg	1998	25,361	34,041	207	30	20	CC	ex Cielo del Canada-05, Juist Trader-99
CSAV Hamburgo	Atg	1998	25,361	33,976	207	30	21	CC	ex Brasil Star-99, Borkum Trader-98
CSAV New York	Atg	1998	25,361	33,919	207	30	21	CC	ex Lykes Osprey-03, ECL Rotterdam-02, Maersk Sao Paulo-99, Helgoland Trader-99
DAL Reunion	Atg	1994	15,895	22,525	168	27	21	CC	ex Elbe Trader-04, Zim Argentina III-04, CSAV Rauli-98, Elbe Trader-95
Ems Trader	Atg	2000	25,535	33,917	200	30	21	CC	ex Alemania Express-05, Sea Cheetah-02, I/a Ems Trader
Jade Trader	Atg	1995	11,987	14,700	157	24	20	CC	ex OOCL Accord-98, Jade Trader-96
Leda Trader	Atg	2000	25,535	33,934	200	30	22	CC	ex Cap Castillo-05, I/a Leda Trader
Maersk Fuji	Atg	2005	9,981	11,798	139	23	19	CC	
Maersk Fukuoka	Atg	2005	9,981	11,798	139	23	19	CC	
Maruba Cathay	Deu	1998	23,783	30,360	188	30	21	CC	ex Oder Trader-05, Zim Lisbon I-03, Oder Trader-03, Cielo d'America 02, Maersk Rio Grande-99, Oder Trader-98
Maruba Trader	Atg	1997	16,165	22,250	168	27	21	CC	ex Cap Serrat-05, Dollart Trader-04, Libra Genova-00, Repubblica de la Boca-99, Dollart Trader-97
Monteverde	Atg	1998	25,355	33,987	207	30	21	CC	I/a Jumme Trader
Ocean Trader	Atg	1996	16,165	22,250	168	27	19	CC	ex Calapadria-03, Zim Brasil I-01, Atlantico-98, Ocean Trader-96
Pacific Trader	Atg	1996	16,165	22,525	168	27	19	CC	ex CSAV Recife-98, Maersk Sao Paulo-97, Pacific Trader-96
Trave Trader	Atg	1994	15,922	22,525	168	27	21	CC	ex CSAV Yokohama-04, Trave Trader-03, Zim Montevideo-98, Trave Trader-96

newbuildings - five further 10,000 grt 12,000 dwt container ships due for 2006 delivery from Chinese builder.

Carl Buttner-Bremen GmbH & Co KG Tankreederei

Germany

Funnel: Yellow with white 'CB' and four corner stars on red houseflag, narrow black top.
Hull: Black with red boot-topping.

Name	Eng	Flag	Year	GRT	DWT	Loa	Bm	Kts	Type	Former names
Admiral	Gib	2002	16,914	23,998	168	26	15	T	
Apollo	Gib	2003	16,914	24,028	169	26	15	T	
Apatura	Gib	2004	16,901	24,064	168	26	15	T	
Aurelia	Gib	2006	16,900	23,400	168	26	15	T	
Aurora	Gib	2004	16,901	24,086	168	26	15	T	
Avalon	Gib	2006	16,900	23,000	168	26	15	T	
Songa Arctic *	Deu	1991	14,332	23,470	170	25	14	T	ex Dorsch-06

* formerly owned, now time chartered until 2010 from Blystad q.v..

Cardiff Marine Inc

Greece

Funnel: Black with broad blue band edged with narrow yellow bands or blue with black top.
Hull: Black or grey with red boot-topping

Name	Eng	Flag	Year	GRT	DWT	Loa	Bm	Kts	Type	Former names
Agrari	Mlt	1984	38,627	63,953	229	32	11	T	ex Andromeda-01
Alameda	Mlt	2001	86,743	170,662	290	45	14	B	ex Cape Araxos-05
Alona *	Mlt	2002	29,054	48,640	191	32	15	B	ex Georgia T-05, I/a Transworld 3
Belmonte	Mlt	2004	40,160	73,601	225	33	14	B	
Bonita	Mlt	2006	57,711	106,144	247	42	-	T	
Catalina	Mlt	2005	40,485	74,432	225	32	14	B	
Conquistador	Mlt	1991	53,724	95,773	232	42	14	T	ex Minerva Grace-04, Green Century-00
Conrad Oldendorff	Pan	2002	39,727	76,623	225	32	14	B	

Name	Eng	Flag	Year	GRT	DWT	Loa	Bm	Kts	Type	Former names
Corcovado		Mlt	2005	58,418	104,635	244	42	-	T	
Coronado		Mlt	2000	38,818	75,706	225	32	14	B	ex Seafarer II-05, Seafarer-04
Daytona *		Mlt	1989	36,269	69,703	225	32	14	B	ex Macanudo-05, Chiyoshima Maru-99
Flecha *		Mlt	1982	37,661	65,081	228	32	15	B	ex Clipper Star-00, Microba-89, Hutland Venture-83
Iguana		Mlt	1996	36,559	70,349	225	32	14	B	ex Pacific Carrier-04, Pacific Fortune-01
Ipanema		Mlt	1992	39,175	70,914	225	32	14	T	ex Seamusic III-02, Pacific 3-93
Kamari		Mlt	1997	53,829	96,315	243	42	14	T	ex Spyros-04
La Jolla		Mlt	1997	37,707	72,126	224	32	14	B	ex Konkar Maroula-05, World Refresh-03, I/a Valiant
Lacerta *		Mlt	1994	37,629	71,862	225	32	14	B	ex Kiyoh-00
Lanikai *		Mlt	1988	36,120	68,676	224	32	14	B	ex Magic Wand-05, Penelope V-04, Lolcos Sapphire-03, Sapphire-98
Linda Oldendorff		Lbr	1995	39,279	75,275	225	32	14	B	
Lovina		Mlt	2005	58,418	104,493	244	42	-	T	
Manasota		Mlt	2004	88,129	171,061	289	45	14	B	ex Katerina V-05
Matira		Mlt	1994	25,943	45,863	190	31	14	B	ex Minoan Pride-05, New Generation-04
Montego		Pan	2006	62,400	105,000	244	42	-	T	
Mostoles *		Mlt	1981	44,985	75,395	243	32	14	Obo	ex Maersk Mostoles-91, Mostoles-89, Viator-84 (conv Obo-96, conv T-98)
Netadola		Mlt	1993	77,372	149,475	270	43	14	B	ex Meridian Polaris-05, Saikyo-00
Ocean Crystal		Mlt	1999	38,372	73,688	225	32	14	B	ex Samsara-05, Ocean Crystal-05
Olinda		Mlt	1996	79,643	149,258	276	45	14	T	ex Tribute-04
Panormos *		Mlt	1995	37,821	71,747	224	32	14	B	ex Royal Taian-03, Maersk Taian-00
Paragon		Mlt	1995	38,205	71,259	225	32	13	B	ex Oceanic Enterprise-05
Pink Sands		Mlt	1993	55,048	93,891	242	42	14	T	ex Angelo D'Amato-01, Sanko Protector-99
Primo Stealth		Mlt	2005	58,418	104,479	235	42	-	T	
Saetta		Mlt	1984	37,949	60,882	228	32	14	T	ex Bright Eagle-01
Sarasota		Mlt	1992	56,855	96,828	242	42	14	T	ex Tsunami-05, Minerva Concert-03, Stena Concert-99
Shibumi		Mlt	1984	92,568	166,058	290	47	12	B	ex Huang Shan-00, Atara-89, I/a Patria
Sonoma *		Mlt	2001	40,437	74,786	225	32	14	B	ex Yong Kang-05
Striggla *		Mlt	1982	37,519	64,747	228	32	14	B	ex Madonna Lily-97, Magnolia I-86, Santa Amelia Maru-86
Tamara		Mlt	1990	52,511	97,151	247	42	14	T	ex CSK Valiant-02
Tigani		Mlt	1991	52,603	97,114	247	42	14	T	ex Seafalcon-05
Tonga *		Mlt	1984	36,303	66,798	230	32	16	B	ex Stefanos-05, Ming Mercy-03
Toro		Mlt	1995	38,567	73,034	225	32	14	B	ex Stalo-04
Vadella		Mlt	2005	58,446	104,635	244	42	-	T	
Voutakos		Pan	1987	95,748	188,334	291	48	-	B	ex K. Jasmine-06, Jasmine-98
Waikiki		Mlt	1995	39,385	75,473	225	32	14	B	ex Giuseppe D'Amato-05
Xanadu		Mlt	1999	37,722	72,270	225	32	14	B	ex CMB Daisy-05, Sea Daisy-04

newbuildings: eight 177,000 dwt and two 75,000 dwt bulk carriers, one 163,000 dwt and five 105,000 dwt tankers due for 2006-9 delivery.
Management subsidiary of Liberian-owned, Greek-based DryShips Inc., 57% owned by Economou family.
* operating in Baumarine Pool

Carisbrooke Shipping PLC UK

Funnel: *Buff with buff 'CS' on blue rectangle.*
Hull: *Light grey with green waterline over red boot-topping*

Name	Eng	Flag	Year	GRT	DWT	Loa	Bm	Kts	Type	Former names
Greta-C		Gbr	2002	14,159	19,150	156	24	14	Co	I/a Dina-C
Mark-C		Iom	2003	14,357	19,460	160	24	14	Co	ex Innogy Sprite-05, Dina-C-03

Ceres Hellenic Shipping Enterprises Ltd Greece

Funnel: *Blue with three white bands, middle band interupted by white diamond.*
Hull: *Black with red boot-topping.*

Name	Eng	Flag	Year	GRT	DWT	Loa	Bm	Kts	Type	Former names
Captain Vangelis L		Lbr	1992	78,504	145,856	278	43	14	B	ex Captain Vangelis-03, Bulktirreno-03, Maria Rebecca-96
Kyla		Lbr	1982	70,517	134,806	270	42	16	B	ex Bulktiger-03, Gallant Teger-96, Juanita II-88, Onstad Trader-85
Santa Esmeralda		Lbr	1990	36,725	69,458	225	32	14	B	ex Oceanic Ensign-05, Oceanic Esprit-04, Merchant Pride-98
Santa Markela		Lbr	1990	38,022	71,749	224	32	14	B	ex Anemi Breeze-05, Universal Harmony-04, C.Filyos-03, Maritime Nancy-97
Santa Victoria		Lbr	2002	40,030	75,966	225	32	14	B	ex Santa Vitoria-05

Name	Eng	Flag	Year	GRT	DWT	Loa	Bm	Kts	Type	Former names
Thetis		Lbr	1993	38,891	73,653	225	32	14	B	

newbuildings: five 81,500 grt 157,700 dwt tankers and two 88,000 grt bulk carriers due for 2006-7 delivery.
Also see vessels operating in 'Seachem Pool' under Odfjell ASA.

Coeclerici Armatori SpA/Italy

Funnel: *Blue with black top.*
Hull: *Black with red boot-topping.*

Name	Eng	Flag	Year	GRT	DWT	Loa	Bm	Kts	Type	Former names
Bulk Africa		Lbr	2002	87,590	170,578	289	45	14	B	
Bulk Atlanta		Lbr	1990	77,096	149,495	270	43	13	B	ex Cape Asia-00
Bulk Australia		Lbr	2002	87,590	170,578	289	45	14	B	
Bulk Cedar *		Lbr	1998	38,995	73,322	225	32	14	B	ex Red Cedar-06
Bulk Fern *		Lbr	1998	38,995	73,326	225	32	14	B	ex Red Fern-06, I/a Halla Pride
Bulk Leher		Lbr	1992	77,273	149,532	270	43	13	B	ex Bulk Ispat Leher-05, Aberous-99
Bulkazores		Pan	1977	34,705	61,131	225	32	15	B	ex NL Trader-94, Bergitta-91, Continental Trader-89
Capo Noli		Mlt	1981	14,454	23,683	160	25	17	Bu	ex Timpe-95, Cynthia No.4-88, Great Tempo-86, World Tempo-85
Porto Cervo		Mlt	1983	46,518	87,659	259	32	15	B	ex Cetra Lyra-95, Hunga-87, Louis L.D.-84, I/a Richfield
Prosperous		Pan	1990	77,273	149,498	270	43	13	B	ex Bulkprosperous-03, Prosperous-97

newbuildings - 14 large bulk carriers on order for 2006-8 delivery from various owners to be time-chartered for 7-10 years.
Owns controlling interest (65%) in jointly owned Coeclerici Ceres Bulk Carriers NV.
* formerly owned, now time-chartered to Coeclerici Ceres from DryLog Bulk Carriers (Peter Livanos) until 2012.

Chandris (Hellas) Inc
Greece

Funnel: *Dark blue with large white 'X'.*
Hull: *Dark blue with red boot-topping.*

Name	Eng	Flag	Year	GRT	DWT	Loa	Bm	Kts	Type	Former names
Aktea		Grc	2005	60,007	107,091	248	43	-	T	
Al Nabila 4		Egy	1982	16,595	27,841	171	25	15	T	ex Gate-00, Sandgate-00, Ras al Barshah-87
Alexia		Egy	1982	54,537	91,740	245	40	15	T	ex Enalios Zephyros-02, Mexico-98, Esso Mexico-94
Althea		Grc	1999	56,841	84,992	248	43	15	T	
Amira		Egy	2001	39,818	74,401	225	32	14	B	
Astrea		Grc	1999	56,841	84,999	248	43	15	T	
Athinea		Grc	2006	62,300	115,000				T	
Australis		Grc	2003	156,914	299,095	330	60	16	T	ex Saga-04, I/a Front Saga
Britanis		Grc	2002	157,581	304,732	332	58	16	T	
Maribella		Grc	2004	39,736	76,629	225	32	15	B	
Marichristina		Grc	2001	40,121	74,410	225	32	15	R	ex SA Warrior-03
Marietta		Grc	2004	40,135	73,880	225	32	15	B	ex World Prosperity-04
Marijeannie		Grc	2001	40,121	74,410	225	32	15	B	ex SA Gladiator-03
Marinicki		Grc	2005	39,738	76,629	225	32	15	B	
Marivic		Pan	1981	50,169	81,283	232	44	15	T	ex Ocean Victor-94, Kenyo Maru-88
Myrto		Grc	2001	39,831	74,470	225	32	14	B	
Patris		Grc	2000	157,496	298,543	332	58	15	T	
Sharifa 3		Egy	1984	38,529	66,800	231	32	15	T	ex Elbe-04, Mantinia-89, Urania Coulouthros-89
Zeinat 2		Egy	1986	46,632	82,424	211	48	14	T	ex Ist-05

newbuildings: one further 62,300 grt 115,000 dwt tanker due for 2006 delivery.

Chemikalien Seetransport GmbH
Germany

Funnel: *Blue with white 'ST' inside large white outlined 'C' on blue square on broad white band.*
Hull: *Black or red with blue or red boot-topping.*

Name	Eng	Flag	Year	GRT	DWT	Loa	Bm	Kts	Type	Former names
African Future		Lbr	2005	25,400	40,263	176	31	15	T	
Athens Star		Deu	2005	41,966	73,400	229	32	-	T	
Belgreeting *		Lbr	1987	25,865	43,549	197	30	14	Obo	ex Western Greeting-96, I/a Pacific Greeting
Chemtrans Lyra		Lbr	1993	53,829	97,097	243	42	15	T	ex Eagle Lyra-03, Neptune Lyra-94, Athina II-94, Dalby-93, I/a Consensus Dalby
Chemtrans Moon		Lbr	2004	40,763	72,296	229	32	-	T	I/a Silver Dolphin
Chemtrans Ray		Lbr	2000	40,516	71,637	227	32	15	T	ex Emerald Ray-03
Chemtrans Sea		Lbr	2004	40,764	72,365	229	32	-	T	
Chemtrans Sky		Lbr	2000	37,033	63,381	229	32	14	T	ex Asopos-04
Chemtrans Star		Lbr	2000	37,033	63,331	229	32	15	T	ex Aliakmon-03
Chemtrans Sun		Lbr	1999	40,516	71,675	227	32	15	T	ex Emerald Sun-03
Cinderella	(st)	Vct	1965	22,062	14,066	201	25	17	Lng	ex Jules Range-89, Jules Verne-88
Green Point		Lbr	2003	29,982	49,511	183	32	14	T	

Name	Eng	Flag	Year	GRT	DWT	Loa	Bm	Kts	Type	Former names
Hamburg Star		Deu	2005	40,000	73,400	229	32	-	T	
Hans Scholl *		Lbr	2004	25,399	40,250	176	31	15	T	
London Star		Deu	2006	40,000	73,400	229	32	-	T	
Maersk Rhine		Lbr	1999	22,181	35,000	171	31	14	T	ex Ras Maersk-00
Maersk Riga		Lbr	2001	22,184	34,999	171	27	14	T	ex Roy Maersk-03
Maersk Rouen		Lbr	2000	22,181	35,000	171	27	15	T	ex Maersk Rye-03
Maersk Rugen		Lbr	2001	22,181	35,000	171	27	14	T	ex Maersk Ramsey-03
MS Simon		Lbr	2004	25,399	37,247	176	31	15	T	
MS Sophie		Lbr	2004	25,399	37,247	176	31	15	T	I/a Chemtrans Sophie
St. Jacobi *		Lbr	1999	25,202	43,760	182	30	14	T	
St. Petri *		Lbr	2000	28,534	47,228	183	32	14	T	
Tapatio †		Lbr	2003	26,914	46,764	183	32	14	T	
Trans Atlantic		Lbr	2001	40,437	74,823	225	32	14	B	ex Yong Ler-05, Yong Le-01
Trans Ocean *		Lbr	1983	44,910	75,568	244	32	15	Obo	ex Chemtrans Belocean-03, Belocean-94
Trans Pacific *		Lbr	2004	40,485	74,403	225	32	14	B	ex CMB Eline-05

newbuildings: one further 40,000 grt (New York Star) and two further 25,400 grt tankers for 2007 delivery.
* owned by subsidiary Chemtrans Overseas (Cyprus) Ltd, Cyprus and managed by Belchem Singapore Pte. Ltd. (formed jointly with Belships). Partner in Star Tankers Pool with Heidmat Inc and in Baumarine Pool. † managed for Laurin Tankers America Inc.
Also see Team Tankers Pool under Blystad Shipmanagement Ltd.

Chevron Corporation USA

ChevronTexaco Shipping Co LLC/USA

Funnel: *White with three narrow blue bands, narrow black top.*
Hull: *Black with red boot-topping.*

Name	Eng	Flag	Year	GRT	DWT	Loa	Bm	Kts	Type	Former names
Aberdeen		Bhs	1996	47,274	87,055	222	37	14	T	
Antares Voyager *		Bhs	1998	160,036	309,995	333	58	16	T	ex Frank A. Shrontz-03
Arizona Voyager	(gt)	Usa	1977	22,664	39,836	199	29	16	T	ex Chevron Arizona-02
Colorado Voyager	(gt)	Usa	1976	22,735	39,842	199	29	15	T	ex Chevron Colorado-03
Dynamic Energy		Bhs	2002	46,506	53,556	227	36	17	Lpg	
Dynamic Vision		Bhs	2001	46,506	53,503	227	36	17	Lpg	
Kometik ‡	(2)	Can	1997	76,216	126,646	272	46	14	T	
Maria A. Angelicoussis		Bhs	2000	156,505	300,000	332	58	15	T	
Neptune Voyager		Bhs	2003	58,156	104,875	244	42	-	T	
Northwest Swan	(st)	Bmu	2004	96,165	73,676	280	43	19	Lng	
Orion Voyager		Bhs	1994	88,919	156,447	275	50	15	T	ex Chevron Employee Pride-02, Chevron Africa-94
Phoenix Voyager *		Bhs	1999	160,036	310,137	331	58	16	T	ex J. Bennet Johnston-03
Star Ohio †		Bhs	1992	80,569	143,750	274	49	14	T	ex Citadelle-92
Stellar Voyager		Bhs	2003	58,088	104,801	244	42	-	T	
Vega Voyager		Bhs	2003	58,088	104,864	244	42	-	T	
Washington Voyager	(gt)	Usa	1976	22,761	39,795	199	29	15	T	ex Chevron Washington-03

newbuildings: two 63,500 grt tankers and three 95,000 grt Lng tankers from Samsung for 2006-9 delivery.
* managed for Cambridge Petroleum Transport Corp.
† owned by Texaco Panama Inc (Texaco Marine Services Inc) managed by Northern Marine Management, UK
‡ jointly owned with Mobil Oil Corp (Exxon Mobil) and Murphy Oil Corp.managed by Canship Ugland Ltd.
See also Frontline Ltd

China Ocean Shipping (Group) Co (COSCO) China

Cosco Container Lines Co Ltd/China

Funnel: *Blue with white vertical line through white ring above white 'COSCO', broad yellow base and narrow black top.*
Hull: *Grey or black with blue 'COSCO', green or red boot-topping.*

Name	Eng	Flag	Year	GRT	DWT	Loa	Bm	Kts	Type	Former names
An Ting		Chn	1970	9,992	14,517	152	21	18	C	ex Kunlunshan-71
Beauty River		Pan	1990	22,712	33,667	188	28	18	BC	ex Belstar-90
Bing He		Chn	1985	23,542	33,389	201	28	15	CC	
Buyihe *		Pan	1997	36,772	44,911	243	32	21	CC	
Chao He		Chn	1985	19,835	25,955	170	28	17	CC	
Chuanhe		Chn	1997	65,140	69,285	280	40	24	CC	
Chun He		Chn	1984	19,835	25,955	170	28	17	CC	
Cosco Antwerp		Hkg	2001	65,531	68,910	280	40	25	CC	
Cosco Dalian		Pan	2005	66,380	67,209	279	40	25	CC	
Cosco Felixstowe		Bhs	2002	65,532	69,107	280	40	24	CC	
Cosco Hamburg		Hkg	2001	65,531	69,193	280	40	24	CC	
Cosco Hong Kong		Bhs	2002	65,531	68,895	280	40	24	CC	
Cosco Qingdao		Pan	1997	65,140	69,285	280	40	24	CC	ex Yun He-01

Name	Eng	Flag	Year	GRT	DWT	Loa	Bm	Kts	Type	Former names
Cosco Rotterdam		Bhs	2002	65,531	69,224	280	40	25	CC	
Cosco Shanghai		Hkg	2001	65,531	69,192	280	40	25	CC	
Cosco Singapore		Hkg	2001	65,531	69,196	280	40	25	CC	
Cosco Tianjin		Pan	2005	66,380	67,209	279	40	24	CC	
Cosco Xiamen		Pan	2005	66,380	67,209	279	40	24	CC	
Da He		Chn	1994	49,375	51,950	275	32	25	CC	
Dainty River		Pan	1993	22,746	33,650	188	28	18	CC	
Dong He		Chn	1990	37,143	47,625	236	32	19	CC	
Empress Dragon		Pan	1994	46,734	46,103	276	32	24	CC	
Empress Heaven		Pan	1993	46,734	46,099	276	32	24	CC	ex Ming Heaven-01, Empress Heaven-98
Empress Phoenix		Pan	1994	46,734	46,125	276	32	24	CC	
Empress Sea		Pan	1994	46,734	46,074	276	32	24	CC	
Fei He		Chn	1994	48,311	51,280	275	32	24	CC	
Fei Yun He		Chn	2000	20,569	25,723	180	28	20	CC	
Fengyunhe		Pan	1998	16,737	24,251	183	28	19	CC	
Gao He		Chn	1990	37,143	47,625	236	32	19	CC	
Hanihe *		Pan	1997	36,772	44,911	243	32	21	CC	
Hong Yun He		Chn	1999	20,624	26,027	180	28	20	CC	
Honor River		Pan	1990	22,712	33,661	188	28	16	CC	ex Canstar-90, Belhaven-90
Hua Yun He **		Chn	2000	20,624	25,850	180	28	20	CC	
Jin He		Pan	1997	65,140	69,285	280	40	24	CC	
Jin Yun He		Pan	2000	16,737	23,850	183	28	19	CC	
Jing Po He *		Pan	1997	36,772	44,911	243	32	21	CC	
Liao He		Chn	1983	19,915	26,025	170	28	17	CC	
Ling Yun He		Chn	2000	20,569	25,723	180	28	20	CC	
Lu He *		Pan	1997	65,140	69,285	280	40	24	CC	
Luan He		Chn	1978	18,503	25,550	169	26	15	Co	ex Victoria Bay-83, Columbia 81, Arabian Strength-79, I/a Columbia
Luo Ba He		Pan	1998	36,772	44,700	243	32	21	CC	
Luo He		Chn	1983	19,915	26,025	170	28	17	CC	
Mi Yun He		Pan	2001	16,738	23,850	183	28	19	CC	
Min He		Chn	1989	37,143	47,625	236	32	19	CC	
Naxihe		Pan	1997	36,772	44,911	243	32	21	CC	
Pretty River		Pan	1993	22,746	33,650	188	28	18	CC	
Pu He		Chn	1990	35,963	46,136	236	32	19	CC	
Qing Yun He		Chn	2000	20,624	21,200	180	28	20	CC	
Qiu He		Chn	1984	19,732	25,808	171	29	15	CC	
River Elegance		Pan	1994	48,161	49,945	277	32	24	CC	
River Wisdom		Pan	1994	48,161	49,955	277	32	24	CC	
Sha He		Chn	1983	19,915	26,025	171	28	17	CC	
Shan He		Chn	1994	49,375	51,985	275	32	24	CC	
Song He		Chn	1986	24,438	33,265	199	29	16	CC	
Song Yun He		Pan	1998	16,737	23,831	183	28	19	CC	
Tai He		Chn	1989	35,963	45,987	236	32	19	CC	
Teng He		Chn	1994	48,311	51,280	275	32	24	CC	
Teng Yun He		Chn	2000	20,569	25,723	180	28	20	CC	
Wanhe *		Pan	1997	65,140	69,285	280	40	24	CC	
Xiang He		Chn	1985	24,043	30,939	200	28	17	CC	
Xibohe		Pan	1997	36,772	44,911	243	32	21	CC	
Xing He		Chn	1985	19,237	25,925	170	28	15	CC	
Yin He		Chn	1984	19,237	25,925	172	29	17	CC	
Yu He		Chn	1986	24,043	30,940	200	29	17	CC	
Yuan He		Chn	1994	48,311	51,280	275	32	24	CC	
Yue He *		Pan	1997	65,140	69,285	280	40	24	CC	
Yuguhe		Pan	1997	65,140	69,285	280	40	24	CC	
Zhen He		Chn	1993	49,375	51,985	275	32	24	CC	
Zhong He		Chn	1993	48,311	51,280	264	32	23	CC	
Zhuang He		Chn	1985	24,438	33,240	199	29	17	CC	

newbuildings - numerous including eight 98,100 grt 120,000 dwt and five 53,500 grt container ships for 2006-8 delivery.
* operated by Cosco (Cayman) Fortune Holdings Ltd., Singapore ** managed by Eurasia International (China) Ltd (see Schulte Group)

Cosco (HK) Shipping Co Ltd/Hong Kong (China)

Funnel: *Blue with white 'CHS' and black top or * yellow with red band beneath black top.*
Hull: *Grey with green boot-topping.*

Name	Eng	Flag	Year	GRT	DWT	Loa	Bm	Kts	Type	Former names
Aleslevada		Pan	1990	36,544	70,231	225	32	13	B	ex Channel Victory-90
Beatanavis		Hkg	1985	24,950	39,924	184	31	14	B	
Bright City		Hkg	1988	36,120	68,200	224	32	14	B	ex Bright Field-98, Oceanus-90
Bright Days		Hkg	1989	36,120	68,676	224	32	14	B	ex Garnet-91

China Ocean Shipping. COSCO HAMBURG. *G. J. de Boer*

China Ocean Shipping. YUGUHE. *Hans Kraijenbosch*

Cosco (HK) Shipping. COS LUCKY. *J. M. Kakebeeke*

China Shipping. XIN YAN TIAN. *Hans Kraijenbosch*

Chiquita Brands Inc. CHIQUITA BELGIE. *J. M. Kakebeeke*

Name	Eng	Flag	Year	GRT	DWT	Loa	Bm	Kts	Type	Former names
Bright State		Hkg	1989	36,120	68,676	224	32	14	B	ex Belore-90
CHS Moon		Pan	1990	75,054	151,040	270	43	14	B	ex Bartolomeu Dias-05
CHS Star		Pan	1991	75,675	150,149	269	43	13	B	ex Mercurian Virgo-05, Nord-Energy-01
Cos Angel *		Sgp	1983	32,649	65,029	228	32	14	B	ex Sunny Glorious-96, Sunrise Glory-85, Ocean Prosper-84
Cos Bonny *		Sgp	1996	26,759	46,840	187	32	14	B	
Cos Cherry *		Sgp	1996	26,759	46,840	187	32	14	B	
Cos Fair *		Pan	1999	26,829	46,689	187	32	14	B	
Cos Glory *		Pan	1999	26,829	46,680	187	32	14	B	
Cos Hero *		Pan	1998	25,982	45,574	186	30	14	B	
Cos Intrepid *		Hkg	2001	39,795	74,119	225	32	14	B	
Cos Joy *		Hkg	2001	39,795	74,119	225	32	14	B	
Cos Knight *		Pan	2002	30,053	52,323	190	32	-	B	
Cos Lucky *		Pan	2003	30,053	52,395	190	32	-	B	
Festivity		Pan	1982	27,423	45,548	193	32	14	B	
Full Beauty		Hkg	1994	36,586	70,198	225	32	14	B	
Full City		Pan	1995	15,873	26,758	167	26	14	B	
Full Comfort		Hkg	1994	36,586	70,181	225	32	14	B	
Full Sources		Hkg	1994	36,639	69,573	225	32	14	B	
Full Spring		Hkg	1994	36,639	69,587	225	32	14	B	
Full Strong		Hkg	1994	36,586	70,171	225	32	14	B	
Full Wealth		Hkg	1995	24,055	43,217	185	31	14	B	
Grand View		Hkg	1994	26,818	43,980	190	31	14	B	
Grand Way		Hkg	1994	26,818	44,006	190	31	14	B	
Joviality		Hkg	1982	28,224	45,564	193	32	14	B	
Joyous Age		Hkg	1994	35,879	69,271	225	32	14	B	
Joyous Land		Hkg	1994	35,879	69,283	225	32	15	B	
Joyous Society		Hkg	1994	35,879	69,274	225	32	15	B	
Joyous World		Hkg	1995	35,879	69,286	225	32	15	B	
Jurong Sea *		Sgp	1983	38,107	69,203	235	32	13	B	ex Eaton Breeze-95, Donpafu-93
Mass Enterprise		Pan	1993	36,560	69,555	225	32	13	B	
Mass Glory		Pan	1993	36,560	69,555	225	32	13	B	
Mass Prosperity		Pan	1993	36,560	69,555	225	32	13	B	
Salusnavis		Hkg	1985	24,950	39,940	185	31	14	B	
Sea Crane *		Sgp	1985	26,951	46,040	190	32	13	B	ex New League-94
Sea Gloria ‡		Pan	1994	80,203	157,600	280	43	14	B	ex Sea Glory I-94
Sea Grace ‡		Pan	1994	80,203	157,600	280	43	14	B	
Searadiance		Hkg	1977	38,412	71,733	228	32	15	B	ex Orient City-78
Tian Fu Hai †		Chn	1998	79,480	149,135	270	44	14	B	
Tian Li Hai †		Chn	1999	79,480	150,000	270	44	14	B	
Tian Yang Hai		Pan	1997	85,676	169,999	289	45	17	B	
Weddell Sea		Pan	1978	19,911	33,789	182	27	16	B	
Xinfa Hai †		Chn	2004	88,856	174,766	289	45	15	B	
Xinwang Hai †		Chn	2003	88,856	174,732	289	45	15	B	

* owned by Cosco (Singapore) Pte. Ltd., Singapore, † by Cosco Bulk Carrier Co. Ltd. or ‡ by Cosco Qingdao Ocean Shipping Co.
COSCO is the world's largest shipping group with numerous subsidiaries owning about 650 vessels, the above being a cross section from over 215 bulk carriers between 22,000 dwt and 175,000 dwt operated by the main subsidiaries.
Also see Chinese-Polish Joint Stock Co. (Chinsko-Polskie Towarzystwo Okretowe SA) under Polish Ocean Line.

China Shipping (Group) Co China

China Shipping Container Lines Co Ltd

Funnel: Blue with blue 'CIS' on broad white/yellow band.
Hull: Green with white 'China Shipping Line', red boot-topping

Name	Eng	Flag	Year	GRT	DWT	Loa	Bm	Kts	Type	Former names
CSCL Africa *		Hkg	2005	90,645	101,612	334	43	25	CC	
CSCL Asia		Hkg	2004	90,645	101,612	334	43	25	CC	
CSCL Chiwan *		Hkg	2001	39,941	50,488	260	32	24	CC	
CSCL Dalian *		Hkg	2002	39,941	50,871	260	32	24	CC	
CSCL Felixstowe *		Hkg	2002	39,941	50,789	260	32	24	CC	
CSCL Hamburg *		Hkg	2001	39,941	50,500	260	32	24	CC	
CSCL New York *		Hkg	2005	39,941	50,500	263	32	24	CC	
CSCL Ningbo *		Hkg	2002	39,941	50,789	260	32	24	CC	
CSCL Oceania *		Cyp	2004	90,645	101,810	334	43	25	CC	
Xin Bei Lun		Chn	2005	41,482	52,000	263	32	24	CC	
Xin Chang Sha		Chn	2005	41,482	52,000	263	32	24	CC	
Xin Chang Shu		Chn	2005	66,452	69,303	280	40	25	CC	

Name	Eng	Flag	Year	GRT	DWT	Loa	Bm	Kts	Type	Former names
Xin Chi Wan		Chn	2004	66,452	69,271	280	40	25	CC	
Xin Chong Qing		Chn	2003	50,188	50,500	263	32	24	CC	
Xin Da Lian		Chn	2003	66,433	68,000	280	40	26	CC	
Xin Dan Dong		Chn	2006	41,482	52,000	263	32	24	CC	
Xin Fang Cheng		Chn	2005	41,482	52,000	263	32	24	CC	
Xin Fu Zhou		Chn	2004	66,452	69,303	280	40	26	CC	
Xin Hai Kou		Chn	2005	41,482	52,000	263	32	24	CC	
Xin Huang Pu		Chn	2005	41,482	50,500	263	32	24	CC	
Xin Jin Zhou		Chn	1982	33,267	34,477	216	32	18	CC	ex Maple River-02, Tor Bay-93
Xin Lian Yun Gang		Chn	2003	66,433	69,023	280	40	26	CC	
Xin Nan Sha		Chn	2005	41,482	52,000	263	32	24	CC	
Xin Nan Tong		Chn	2003	41,482	50,151	263	32	24	CC	
Xin Ning Bo		Chn	2003	66,433	69,303	280	40	26	CC	
Xin Nanjing		Chn	2004	46,000	52,000	263	32	24	CC	
Xin Pu Dong		Chn	2003	66,433	68,000	280	40	26	CC	
Xin Qin Huang Dao		Chn	2004	66,452	69,303	280	40	26	CC	
Xin Qing Dao		Chn	2003	66,433	69,423	280	40	26	CC	
Xin Quan Zhou		Chn	2005	41,482	50,500	263	32	24	CC	
Xin Ri Zhou		Chn	2005	41,482	52,000	263	32	24	CC	
Xin Shan Tou		Chn	2005	41,482	52,000	263	32	24	CC	
Xin She Kou		Chn	1983	33,267	34,477	216	32	18	CC	ex River Crystal-02, Providence Bay-93
Xin Su Zhou		Chn	2004	41,482	50,137	263	32	24	CC	
Xin Tian Jin		Chn	2003	66,433	68,000	280	40	26	CC	
Xin Wei Hai		Chn	2006	41,482	52,000	263	32	24	CC	
Xin Xia Men		Chn	2004	66,433	69,259	280	40	25	CC	
Xin Yan Tia		Chn	2005	66,452	69,303	280	40	26	CC	
Xin Yan Tian		Chn	2004	66,433	68,023	280	40	26	CC	
Xin Yang Shan		Chn	2005	41,482	52,000	263	32	24	CC	
Xin Yang Zhou		Chn	2004	41,482	50,137	263	32	24	CC	
Xin Ying Kou		Chn	2004	41,482	52,000	263	32	24	CC	

newbuildings: Over 30 container ships on order between 41,000-107,200 dwt for 2006-8 delivery.
* chartered from Seaspan Container Lines Ltd., Cyprus (Washington Corp, USA)
In addition to the above, the company owns many smaller container ships, while other subsidiaries of China Shipping operate about 250 bulk carriers and tankers between 10,000-158,000 grt. See other chartered vessels with 'CSCL' prefix in index.

Chiquita Brands Inc   USA

Great White Fleet Ltd/Belgium

Funnel: Buff with white diamond on red band beneath black top.
Hull: White with white 'Chiquita' on blue oval, red boot-topping.

Name	Eng	Flag	Year	GRT	DWT	Loa	Bm	Kts	Type	Former names
Chiquita Belgie *		Bhs	1992	13,049	13,930	158	24	22	R	
Chiquita Bremen		Bmu	1992	10,842	12,890	157	23	21	R	
Chiquita Deutschland *		Bhs	1991	13,049	13,930	158	24	22	R	
Chiquita Italia *		Bhs	1992	13,049	13,930	158	24	22	R	
Chiquita Nederland *		Bhs	1991	13,049	13,930	158	24	21	R	
Chiquita Rostock		Bmu	1993	10,842	12,850	157	24	21	R	
Chiquita Scandinavia *		Bhs	1992	13,049	13,930	159	24	21	R	
Chiquita Schweiz *		Bhs	1992	13,049	13,930	158	24	22	R	
Courtney L		Bmu	1992	19,595	15,672	203	27	21	CC	ex Martha L-92
Edyth L		Bhs	1990	19,595	15,672	203	27	21	CC	
Frances L		Bhs	1991	19,595	15,646	203	27	21	CC	
Puritan		Bmu	1983	13,998	9,649	148	26	17	CC	ex Eagle Prestige-96, Puritan-93

* owned by K/S Difko companies, Denmark.

Cido Shipping HK Ltd   Hong Kong (China)

Funnel: Charterers colours
Hull: Black or long-term charterers colours with red boot-topping.

Name	Eng	Flag	Year	GRT	DWT	Loa	Bm	Kts	Type	Former names
Belo Horizonte		Hkg	2004	40,014	76,801	225	32	14	B	
Caribbean Emerald		Pan	1985	24,929	9,234	151	27	17	V	ex Bellflower-92
Danann Island		Pan	2006	38,900	76,000	225	32	14	B	
Dream Angel		Pan	2006	40,500	13,500	117	28	-	V	
Dream Beauty		Pan	2006	40,500	13,500	117	28	-	V	
European Emerald ‡		Pan	1984	37,996	13,208	175	29	18	V	ex Nissan Maru-92
Fortune Ocean		Hkg	2006	40,040	76,600	225	32	14	B	
Grand Choice ‡		Pan	1999	50,309	16,669	179	32	19	V	

Name	Eng	Flag	Year	GRT	DWT	Loa	Bm	Kts	Type	Former names
Grand Cosmo		Pan	2006	59,217	17,750	200	32	20	V	
Grand Duke		Pan	2005	59,217	18,315	200	32	20	V	
Grand Mark ‡		Pan	2000	50,310	16,681	179	32	19	V	
Grand Mercury		Pan	2002	58,947	19,121	200	32	20	V	
Grand Neptune		Pan	2006	59,217	13,500	200	32	20	V	
Grand Orion		Pan	2006	59,217	13,500	200	32	20	V	
Grand Pace ‡		Pan	1999	50,309	16,714	179	32	19	V	
Grand Pavo **		Pan	2005	59,217	18,376	200	32	20	V	
Grand Phoenix **		Pan	2005	59,217	18,383	200	32	20	V	
Grand Pioneer		Pan	2002	58,947	19,120	200	32	20	V	
Grand Quest ‡		Pan	2000	50,309	16,702	179	32	19	V	
Grand Race ‡		Pan	2000	50,309	16,689	179	32	19	V	
Grand Venus		Pan	2006	59,217	13,500	200	32	20	V	
Great Dream		Hkg	2004	19,829	33,745	169	28	14	B	
Great Leader		Hkg	2004	19,829	33,745	169	28	14	B	
Great River		Hkg	2004	19,829	33,700	175	28	14	B	
Great Summit		Hkg	2005	19,829	33,745	169	28	14	B	
Hoegh Oceania †		Pan	2003	58,947	19,121	200	32	19	V	ex Hual Oceania-05
Hual Dubai †		Pan	2004	58,947	19,121	200	32	19	V	
Magic Sky		Pan	1982	21,574	10,642	166	22	17	V	ex Morning Sky-01, Magic Sky-00, Maersk Sky-97, Rich Seven-89
Magic Wave ‡		Pan	1980	23,304	7,300	153	26	21	V	ex Maersk Wave-96
Magic Wind ‡		Pan	1981	23,304	7,300	153	26	21	V	ex Maersk Wind-96
Marine Reliance ‡		Mhl	1987	35,750	11,676	174	30	17	V	
Modern Chance ‡		Lbr	1999	33,863	10,834	164	28	18	V	
Modern Express ‡		Pan	2001	33,831	10,817	164	28	21	V	
Modern Link ‡		Pan	2000	33,831	10,419	164	28	18	V	
Modern Peak ‡		Pan	1999	33,831	10,817	164	28	18	V	
Morning Ace		Pan	1976	23,679	8,773	175	25	18	V	ex Canadian Ace II-03, Lotus Ace-86, Laurel-83
Morning Breeze ‡		Pan	1977	24,278	8,545	169	26	16	V	ex Morning Grace-99, Puebla-95, Amoroso-93, North Blaze-90, Polar Ace-87
Morning Charm ‡		Pan	1978	21,757	8,045	153	25	18	V	ex Arabian Star-95, Young Soldier-91
Morning Ivy		Pan	1981	47,847	17,637	190	32	18	V	ex Princess Arrow-04, European Venture-90, I/a Automobile Venture
Morning Light ‡		Pan	1978	30,070	10,601	180	28	17	V	ex Californian Star-95, Donaire-92, Young Splendour-90
Morning Power		Pan	1981	42,657	16,984	199	30	18	V	ex Vermilion Highway-02
Morning Prince ‡		Pan	1979	45,423	13,910	190	32	19	V	ex Prince-95, Prince No.10-94, Prince Maru No.10-86
Morning Queen ‡		Pan	1978	38,974	18,426	199	30	18	V	ex Hamburg Star-95, Golden Ace-91
Morning Rise		Pan	1977	17,720	18,624	154	24	15	V	ex Kashima-00, Kashima Maru-87 (conv C-98)
Morning Saga ‡		Lbr	1981	41,868	13,834	186	32	18	V	ex Viking Star-96, Viking Ace-92, Paramount Ace-90
Morning Sun		Pan	1982	14,663	5,775	156	19	15	V	ex Koushun-99, Orange Coral-89
Pacific Honor		Pan	2003	28,144	45,800	180	32	14	T	
Pacific Oasis		Pan	2004	28,799	47,999	180	32	14	T	
Pacific Polaris		Pan	2004	28,799	47,999	180	32	14	T	
Pos Courage		Hkg	2004	40,014	76,810	225	32	14	B	
Pos Dignity		Hkg	2004	40,014	76,810	225	32	14	B	
Pos Eternity		Hkg	2004	39,964	76,295	225	32	14	B	
Pos Freedom		Hkg	2005	30,743	55,695	190	32	14	B	
Pos Glory		Hkg	2004	39,964	76,508	225	32	14	B	
Pos Harmony		Hkg	2005	30,743	55,700	190	32	14	B	
Pos Island		Hkg	2006	31,000	55,000	190	32	14	B	
Saracen Star ‡		Pan	1984	26,758	11,554	158	28	17	V	ex Oscar Ace-92
Topaz Ace *		Pan	1995	48,210	14,696	180	32	18	V	
Trigger		Lbr	1976	25,909	9,993	188	23	18	V	ex Barcelona-92, Trigger-91, Nosac Trigger-88, Trigger-85, Hoegh Trigger-84

newbuildings: 12 bulk carriers, 12 container ships, 21 tankers and 14 vehicle carriers for 2006-10 delivery.
* on charter to Mitsui OSK, ** to Kawasaki, † to Leif Hoegh & Co or ‡ belived to be on charter to Eukor Car Carriers Inc. (see under Wallenius-Wilhelmsen) but not confirmed by company.

Clipper Group (Management) Ltd

Bahamas

Clipper Denmark APS/Denmark

Funnel: *Black with white 'C' symbol.*
Hull: *Black with white 'CLIPPER', red boot-topping.*

Clipper Group (Dockendale Shipping). CLIPPER MERCURY. *N. Kemps*

Clipper Group (Dockendale Shipping). CLIPPER VALOUR. *Hans Kraijenbosch*

CMA CGM Holding. CMA CGM PUCCINI. *J. M. Kakebeeke*

Name	Eng	Flag	Year	GRT	DWT	Loa	Bm	Kts	Type	Former names
Changsha **		Bhs	1999	14,118	20,730	158	23	15	Co	ex Clipper Sterling-05, VOC Sterling-04, Clipper Sterling-00
Clipper Eagle †		Bhs	1994	11,542	16,906	149	23	14	B	
Clipper Falcon †		Bhs	1995	11,542	16,900	149	23	14	B	
Clipper Flamingo		Bhs	1997	19,354	29,516	181	26	14	Co	ex VOC Flamingo-04, Cielo di Calgary-01, Clipper Flamingo-00, Chuqui-00, Clipper Flamingo-97
Clipper Frontier		Bhs	1997	19,354	28,106	181	26	14	Co	ex VOC Frontier-04, Clipper Frontier-00, Pudahuel-99, Clipper Frontier-97
Clipper Melody		Bhs	1997	16,405	25,069	172	25	14	B	ex Jan Zizka-99
Clipper Ranger		Bhs	2002	12,578	20,200	155	24	16	B	l/a Clipper Reunion
Clipper Regal		Bhs	2002	12,578	20,035	155	24	16	B	ex VOC Regal-03
Clipper Reunion		Bhs	2002	12,578	20,001	155	24	16	B	ex VOC Reunion-03
Magdalena Green *		Nld	2001	11,894	17,520	141	22	15	Co	
Makiri Green *		Nld	1999	11,894	17,539	143	22	16	Co	
Marinus Green *		Nld	2000	11,894	16,000	143	22	16	Co	
Marissa Green *		Nld	2000	11,894	16,000	143	22	16	Co	
Marlene Green *		Nld	2001	11,894	17,500	143	22	16	Co	
Pacific Fantasy		Bhs	1996	19,354	29,538	181	26	14	Co	ex DS Fantasy-04, Cielo di Spagna-01, Clipper Fantasy-00, Paipote-98, Clipper Fantasy-97, Paipote-97, Clipper Fantasy-96
Pacific Future		Bhs	1998	18,597	29,538	181	26	14	Co	ex Barachois-05
VOC Progress †		Bhs	1989	26,128	40,908	196	28	13	B	ex Papendrecht-04, Kosice-97
VOC Pioneer †		Bhs	1989	26,128	40,908	196	28	13	B	ex Pendrecht-04, Vitkovice-97

newbuildings:
* management by CEC Shipmanagement NL BV, Netherlands or ** owned by Van Ommeren Clipper Shipping BV, Netherlands.
† owned by Lomar Shipping, Greece.

Clipper Bulk (Portland) Inc/USA

Name	Eng	Flag	Year	GRT	DWT	Loa	Bm	Kts	Type	Former names
Clipper Harvest		Bhs	2004	19,730	32,040	168	29	14	B	
Clipper Horizon		Bhs	2004	19,900	32,040	168	29	14	B	
Clipper Labrador *		Bhs	1998	17,784	28,215	169	27	14	B	ex Pactimber-04
Clipper Lagoon		Bhs	2004	16,954	28,200	169	27	14	B	
Clipper Lake		Hkg	2001	16,953	28,492	169	27	14	B	ex Pacforest-04
Clipper Lancaster *		Bhs	1996	17,209	28,249	170	27	14	B	ex Paclogger-04, Sea Dream-99
Clipper Lancelot *		Lbr	1997	16,794	28,426	169	27	14	B	ex Pactrader-04, Sea Winner-99
Clipper Lasco		Bhs	2004	16,954	28,200	169	27	14	B	
Clipper Lis *		Bhs	1996	16,041	27,609	169	26	14	B	ex Pacrose-04
Pacstar		Lbr	1986	17,275	26,863	174	28	12	B	ex Sun Light-89
Pacsun		Lbr	1986	17,142	26,943	174	28	12	B	ex Port Star-89, Pacific Stream-87, Hope River-87, River Star-86
VOC Orchid *		Bhs	1996	27,610	45,513	190	31	14	B	ex Grand Orchid-04

* managed by associated Dockendale Shipping Co. Ltd.

Dockendale Shipping Co Ltd/Bahamas

Funnel: White with red 'D' and 'S' above points of black anchor.
Hull: Black with white 'DOCKENDALE' or 'DOCKSHIP' red boot-topping.

Name	Eng	Flag	Year	GRT	DWT	Loa	Bm	Kts	Type	Former names
African Eagle		Bhs	2003	17,944	27,102	178	26	14	B	ex DS Mascot-03
African Falcon		Bhs	2003	17,944	27,101	178	26	14	B	ex Clipper Majestic-03
African Hawk		Bhs	2004	17,944	27,101	178	26	14	B	
African Sanderling		Bhs	1984	13,911	20,412	154	23	15	Co	ex DS Attica-04, Albert Oldendorff-01, Attica-99, Vaimama-96, Attica-96, Ushuaia-95, Mostween 8-92, Silver Gulf-89
Austyn Oldendorff		Bhs	2002	22,072	34,655	179	28	14	B	ex IVS Valiant-03
Clipper Faith		Bhs	1998	19,354	28,106	181	26	14	Co	ex Cielo di Victoria-01, Clipper Faith-00
Clipper Mercury		Bhs	2004	17,944	27,082	178	26	14	B	
Clipper Mermaid		Bhs	2001	17,944	27,105	178	26	14	B	
Clipper Morning		Bhs	2002	17,944	27,141	178	26	14	B	
Clipper Valour		Bhs	2003	22,072	34,790	179	28	14	B	
DS Fiesta		Bhs	1997	19,354	29,516	181	26	14	Co	ex Clipper Fiesta-01
DS Freeway		Bhs	1998	18,597	29,227	181	26	14	Co	ex Mirande-04
DS Manatee		Bhs	2002	17,944	27,128	178	26	14	B	
DS Mirage		Bhs	1997	16,405	25,096	172	25	14	B	ex Clipper Mirage-03, Prokop Holy-99
DS Montrose		Bhs	2001	17,944	27,028	178	26	14	B	
DS Regent		Bhs	2003	12,578	20,001	155	24	16	B	
DS Splendour		Bhs	1999	14,118	20,742	158	23	15	Co	ex Splendour-02
DS Vanguard		Bhs	2004	22,072	34,300	179	28	14	B	

Name	Eng	Flag	Year	GRT	DWT	Loa	Bm	Kts	Type	Former names
Kuiseb		Bhs	2002	17,944	30,850	179	28	14	B	ex Claire-05, Enterprise-04, Millenium Africa-02, Fortuna Africa-01, Griffin Elara-99, Adriatic Bulker-98, Tiger Island-97, Fayrouz I-94
Leopold Oldendorff		Bhs	2002	22,072	34,656	179	28	14	B	ex IVS Victory-03

Associated company.

CMA CGM Holding SA France

Funnel: *White with red 'CMA' and blue 'CGM' inside blue oval, narrow blue top.*
Hull: *Blue with white 'CMA CGM', red boot-topping.*

Name	Eng	Flag	Year	GRT	DWT	Loa	Bm	Kts	Type	Former names
ANL Explorer		Bhs	1985	35,739	34,194	218	30	20	CC	ex CMA CGM Enterprise-02, Australian Enterprise-01, Asia Venus-97, California Venus-95, Med Kobe-95, California Venus-94
CMA CGM Arno	(2)	Pan	1979	32,428	30,998	210	32	22	CC	ex Fort Royal-03
CMA CGM Bellini *		Bhs	2004	69,022	72,500	277	40	24	CC	
CMA CGM Berlioz		Atf	2001	73,157	80,250	300	40	25	CC	
CMA CGM Bizet		Atf	2001	73,157	77,200	300	40	25	CC	
CMA CGM Chopin		Bhs	2004	69,022	72,500	277	40	24	CC	
CMA CGM Debussy		Atf	2001	73,157	80,251	300	40	26	CC	
CMA CGM Eiffel *		Bhs	2002	49,855	58,344	282	32	26	CC	
CMA CGM Fidelio		Bhs	2006	99,500	100,000	334	43	24	CC	l/a CMA CGM Othello
CMA CGM Fort St. Georges		Fra	2003	26,047	30,450	198	30	21	CC	
CMA CGM Fort St. Louis		Fra	2003	26,210	30,804	198	30	21	CC	
CMA CGM Fort St. Pierre		Atf	2003	26,047	30,450	198	30	21	CC	
CMA CGM Fort Ste. Marie		Fra	2003	26,210	30,450	198	30	21	CC	
CMA CGM Hudson	(2)	Pan	1980	32,428	30,998	210	32	22	CC	ex Fort Fleur d'Epee-03
CMA CGM Junior S		Mlt	1994	9,600	12,582	150	22	18	CC	ex Active F-04, Perak-04, Sea Scandia-97, Maersk Miami-96, Finna I-94
CMA CGM La Tour *		Bhs	2001	26,050	30,500	196	30	22	CC	
CMA CGM Manet *		Bhs	2001	26,050	30,442	196	30	21	CC	
CMA CGM Makassar ‡		Grc	1990	37,193	44,044	243	32	21	CC	ex Hanjin Felixstowe-03
CMA CGM Matisse		Atf	1999	25,777	32,274	196	30	21	CC	
CMA CGM Medea		Fra	2006	99,600	100,000	334	43	24	CC	
CMA CGM Mozart		Bhs	2004	69,022	72,500	277	40	24	CC	
CMA CGM Nabucco		Bhs	2006	99,600	100,000	334	43	24	CC	
CMA CGM Norma		Bhs	2006	99,600	100,000	334	43	24	CC	
CMA CGM North Africa 1		Mlt	1985	9,764	12,710	149	22	17	CC	ex Wilma-04, Coral Wilma-01, Wilma-00, Weserland-95, Sea Lake-93, Antartico-92, Red Sea Endeavour-89, Sudan Crown-87, Royal Eagle-85, Weserland-85
CMA CGM North Africa 2		Mlt	1984	9,764	12,816	149	22	17	CC	ex P&O Nedlloyd Christine-04, Christine Eberhardt-03, MSC Christine-01, Coral Christine-01, Christine Eberhardt-00, Horizon-00, Christine Eberhardt-99, Melbridge Christine-99, CGM de Lesseps-98, Christine Eberhardt-97, Maersk la Plata-97, Hannoverland-94, Sea Beach-93, Hannoverland-91, Columbus Oregon-91, ACT 9-90, Hannoverland-86, Lloyd Londres-86, Hannoverland-85
CMA CGM Otello		Bhs	2005	90,100	100,000	334	43	24	CC	l/a CMA CGM Fidelio
CMA CGM Potomac		Pan	1980	31,154	28,955	215	31	21	CC	ex Douce France-03, Fort Saint Charles-95
CMA CGM Puccini		Bhs	2004	69,022	72,500	277	40	24	CC	
CMA CGM Puget *		Bhs	2002	50,561	58,548	282	32	24	CC	
CMA CGM Ravel		Atf	2001	73,059	79,465	300	40	25	CC	
CMA CGM Rigoletto		Bhs	2006	99,600	100,000	334	43	24	CC	
CMA CGM Rossini		Bhs	2004	73,059	72,500	277	40	24	CC	
CMA CGM Seine ‡		Grc	1990	37,193	43,940	243	32	21	CC	ex Hanjin Hamburg-03, l/a Hanjin Vancouver
CMA CGM Simba		Atg	1994	11,062	15,166	158	23	18	CC	ex TMM Durango-05, MSC Nigeria-04, P&O Nedlloyd San Pedro-01, Kent Merchant-99, Maersk Libreville-98, Antje-97, Lanka Amila-97, Antje-94
CMA CGM Straus *		Bhs	2004	69,022	72,500	277	40	24	CC	
CMA CGM Tage		Pan	1980	31,154	28,955	215	31	21	CC	ex Fort Desaix-03
CMA CGM Tosca		Bhs	2006	99,600	100,000	334	43	24	CC	
CMA CGM Traviata		Fra	2006	99,600	100,000	334	43	24	CC	
CMA CGM Utrillo		Atf	1999	25,777	32,274	196	30	21	CC	

Name	Eng	Flag	Year	GRT	DWT	Loa	Bm	Kts	Type	Former names
CMA CGM Verdi *		Bhs	2004	69,022	72,500	277	40	24	CC	
CMA CGM Vivaldi *		Pan	2004	90,745	101,661	334	43	24	CC	
CMA CGM Wagner *		Bhs	2004	69,022	72,500	277	40	24	CC	
Ville d'Aquarius		Deu	1996	40,465	49,229	259	32	24	CC	ex Lykes Tiger-03, Ville d'Aquarius-02
Ville de Mars		Pan	1990	37,235	43,714	242	32	22	CC	ex Australian Endurance-00, Lykes Challenger-99, CGM Pasteur-98, Nedlloyd Pasteur-98, CGM Pasteur-95, Ville de Virgo-91, CGM Pasteur-90

newbuildings: four more 99,600 grt, twelve 53,453 grt, two 50,500 grt, two 41,480 grt and a 17,000 grt container ship for 2007-9 delivery.
* owned by CMA CGM (UK) Shipping Ltd., UK. ‡ on charter from Magnus Carriers Corp, Greece.
See other vessels with 'CMA CGM' or 'ANL' prefixes in index

Delmas Armement/France

Funnel: Blue with white ships wheel.
Hull: Black with white 'DELMAS', red boot-topping.

Name	Eng	Flag	Year	GRT	DWT	Loa	Bm	Kts	Type	Former names
Adeline Delmas		Atf	1985	23,275	33,520	176	30	14	BC	
Blandine Delmas		Atf	1986	23,275	33,611	176	30	14	BC	
Caroline Delmas		Atf	1986	23,275	33,611	176	30	14	BC	
Delmas Surcouf †		Bhs	1983	17,280	22,312	170	27	17	Co	ex DSR Qingdao-95, Delmas Surcouf-94, C.R.Libreville-91
Delmas Sycamore †		Cyp	1977	17,146	21,081	165	26	18	Co	ex Expert-01, Woermann Expert-00, CMB Esprit-92, Apapa Palm-88, Menestheus-96, Lloyd Parana-85, Menestheus-84, Barber Menestheus-84, Menestheus-80
Delphine Delmas		Atf	1986	23,275	33,520	176	30	14	BC	
Elisa Delmas		Hkg	2002	16,916	20,979	169	27	20	CC	
Flora Delmas ***		Hkg	2002	16,916	21,420	169	27	20	CC	
Gaby Delmas ***		Hkg	2002	16,916	20,944	169	27	20	CC	
Julie Delmas		Bhs	2002	26,047	30,453	196	30	21	CC	
Kamina *		Bhs	1982	20,829	26,288	177	28	18	CC	ex Renee Delmas-00, CGM Mascareignes-96, Renee Delmas-95, Nedlloyd Bordeaux-92, Ville de Rouen-91, Ibn Zaidoun-91, Ville de Rouen-90, Renee Delmas-87
Kumasi		Bhs	2001	26,061	30,450	196	30	21	CC	ex WAL Ubangi-04, Catherine Delmas-03
Laura Delmas		Hkg	1979	35,748	22,564	197	32	20	Ro	ex Kintampo-02, Towada-98, Kintampo-97, Nedlloyd Rochester-96, Rochester-88, Nedlloyd Rochester-86
Lucie Delmas *		Hkg	1979	35,748	22,564	197	32	19	Ro	ex Kagoro-03, Nedlloyd Rotterdam-96, Rotterdam-88, Nedlloyd Rotterdam-86
Marie Delmas		Bhs	2001	26,061	30,450	196	30	21	CC	
MOL Horizon *		Bhs	1982	20,829	26,287	177	28	17	CC	ex Suzanne Delmas-03, Suzanne-99, Marfret Caraibes-98, Suzanne Delmas-97, Ville de Marseille-89, Suzanne Delmas-87
MOL Rainbow		Bhs	2003	26,047	30,450	196	30	21	CC	ex Louis Delmas-03
Nicolas Delmas		Bhs	2002	26,061	30,450	196	30	21	Co	
Patricia Delmas *		Bhs	1982	20,424	26,287	177	28	18	CC	ex Patricia D-98, Patricia-98, Patricia Delmas-97
Rokia Delmas **		Lbr	1985	32,924	27,601	185	32	16	Ro	ex Rosa Blanca-98
Roland Delmas		Bhs	1980	30,774	24,223	187	32	17	Ro	ex Grand Bereby-94, Saint Roparzh-92, Hoegh Banniere-91, Woermann Banniere-90, Hoegh Banniere-89
Rosa Delmas **		Lbr	1985	32,951	27,577	185	32	16	Ro	ex Rosa Tucano-98, Calapoggio-95, Rosa Tucano-93
Saint Roch		Bhs	1980	16,744	24,260	187	32	18	Ro	ex Hoegh Belle-81
Ursula Delmas		Bhs	1984	30,750	32,709	189	32	18	CC	ex MSC Ipanema-04, Ursula Delmas-03, Sherbro-94, Nedlloyd Zaandam-91, Ursula Delmas-90, Etienne Denis-89
Veronique Delmas		Bhs	1984	30,750	31,983	189	32	18	CC	

* owned by Otal Investments Ltd. (OT Africa Line) and managed by V. Ships UK.
** managed by Dohle IOM Ltd or *** Midocean Management, Isle of Man. † chartered from Primera Maritime (Hellas) Ltd., Greece.

NV CMB SA   Belgium

Bocimar International NV/Belgium

Funnel: Blue with blue 'B' on broad cream band
Hull: Black or orange with blue or red boot-topping.

Name	Eng	Flag	Year	GRT	DWT	Loa	Bm	Kts	Type	Former names
CMB Florentina		Bel	2005	40,060	76,838	225	32	-	B	
CMB Talent		Hkg	2001	30,053	46,719	190	32	14	B	ex United Talent-04

CMA CGM Holding (Delmas Armement). JULIE DELMAS. *J. M. Kakebeeke*

CMA CGM Holding (Delmas Armement). LAURA DELMAS. *N. Kemps*

CMB SA (Bocimar International). MINERAL OAK. *N. Kemps*

Name	Eng	Flag	Year	GRT	DWT	Loa	Bm	Kts	Type	Former names
Mineral Antwerpen ‡		Pan	2003	87,495	172,150	289	45	15	B	
Mineral Azalea †		Hkg	1999	85,386	171,199	281	45	14	B	ex Sea Azalea-03
Mineral Beijing		Bel	2004	88,930	173,880	289	45	15	B	
Mineral Belgium		Bel	2005	88,930	173,806	289	45	-	B	
Mineral China		Bel	2003	88,292	171,448	289	45	14	B	l/a CIC Oslo
Mineral Noble		Lbr	2004	88,179	170,649	289	45	15	B	ex Mineral Kiwi-04
Mineral Oak ‡		Pan	1996	85,721	165,693	288	44	13	B	
Mineral Poterne		Bel	1997	87,368	172,091	289	45	14	B	ex Channel Poterne-04
Mineral Shanghai		Bel	2004	88,930	173,880	289	45	15	B	
Mineral Sines ‡		Pan	2002	87,495	172,319	289	45	15	B	
Mineral Tianjin		Bel	2004	88,930	173,691	289	45	15	B	
Mineral Viking		Bel	2001	87,363	172,964	289	45	15	B	ex Bagru-04

newbuildings: six 74-76,000 dwt and two 177,000 dwt bulk carriers due 2006-8 from South Korean and Chinese builders.
Partner in Cape International Pool formed jointly with Ofer (Zodiac), Belships, Moller, Torvald Klaveness and Overseas Shipholding Corp.
Managed by subsidiary Tecto NV, † by 28% owned Wah Kwong Ship Management, Hong Kong or ‡ by Oak Maritime (Canada) Ltd., Canada.

Euronav Luxembourg SA/Luxembourg

Funnel: *Black, white flag with narrow red horizontal cross on broad white cross on blue disc or * ** blue with gold overlapping 'GO'.*
Hull: *Black with red boot-topping.*

Name	Eng	Flag	Year	GRT	DWT	Loa	Bm	Kts	Type	Former names
Algarve		Atf	1999	157,833	298,969	332	58	15	T	
Artois		Atf	2001	159,456	298,330	334	60	16	T	
Bourgogne		Bel	1996	161,287	296,230	333	58	13	T	
Cap Diamant *		Grc	2001	94,729	160,044	277	53	14	T	
Cap Georges *		Grc	1998	81,148	147,443	274	48	14	T	
Cap Jean *		Grc	1998	81,148	146,439	274	48	14	T	
Cap Laurent *		Grc	1998	81,148	147,436	274	48	14	T	
Cap Leon *		Grc	2003	81,328	159,048	274	48	-	T	
Cap Pierre *		Grc	2004	81,328	159,048	274	48	-	T	
Cap Romuald *		Grc	1998	81,148	146,639	274	48	14	T	
Famenne		Atf	2001	159,456	298,412	333	60	15	T	
Fantasy *		Grc	2002	57,683	106,560	241	42	-	T	
Fidelity *		Grc	2002	57,683	106,548	241	42	-	T	
Filikon *		Grc	2002	78,845	150,709	274	48	15	T	ex Paros-04
Finesse *		Grc	2003	78,845	150,709	274	48	15	T	ex Anafi-04
Flandre		Lux	2004	159,016	305,704	332	58	15	T	
Golden Stream **		Pan	1995	144,149	275,616	326	57	14	T	
Luxembourg		Atf	1999	157,833	298,997	332	58	15	T	
Namur		Bel	2000	159,397	298,628	333	60	15	T	ex Ichiban-03, Berge Ichiban-02
Pacific Lagoon **		Bel	1999	163,346	305,839	333	58	15	T	
Provence		Atf	1994	153,778	284,912	327	57	15	T	ex Provence I-94
Savoie		Bel	1993	160,214	304,430	331	58	14	T	ex Berge Sigval-04
TI Asia		Mhl	2001	234,006	441,893	380	68	16	T	ex Hellespont Alhanbra-04
TI Creation		Bel	1998	156,505	298,324	332	58	15	T	ex Crude Creation-05, World Creation-04
TI Europe		Mhl	2002	234,006	442,000	380	68	16	T	ex Hellespont Tara-04
TI Guardian		Bel	1993	162,361	290,927	333	58	15	T	ex Crude Guardian-05, Ocean Guardian-04
TI Hellas		Bel	2005	161,127	319,254	333	60	16	T	ex Chrysanthemium-05
TI Topaz		Bel	2002	161,135	318,934	333	60	16	T	ex Crude Topaz-05, Oriental Topaz-05

*Formerly wholly controlled by CMB SA and now demerged with vessels managed by France Shipmanagement SA or * by Euronav Ship Management Hellas Ltd.,*
Greece and operating mainly in Tankers International Pool (48 ULCC and VLCC tankers) formed jointly with Klaius Oldendorff, Sanko, Overseas Shipholding
Group, Shinyo, Petronas, Oak Maritime, Wah Kwong and Essar Shipping.
*** managed for Golden Ocean Services (UK) Ltd, UK in which Frontline (Hemen Holdings) have largest shareholding*

Exmar NV/Belgium

Funnel: *Blue with red 'E' on broad white band.*
Hull: *Red with dark red boot-topping.*

Name	Eng	Flag	Year	GRT	DWT	Loa	Bm	Kts	Type	Former names
Brugge Venture ‡		Hkg	1997	22,352	26,777	170	27	17	Lpg	
Brussels		Bel	1997	22,323	26,943	170	27	16	Lpg	ex Oxfordshire-05
Carli Bay		Bel	1998	17,527	20,613	155	26	17	Lpg	
Chaconia		Bel	1990	19,643	29,271	166	27	16	Lpg	
Courcheville		Bel	1989	19,719	29,171	166	27	16	Lpg	ex Nyhall-96
Donau		Bel	1985	23,508	32,339	183	30	15	Lpg	ex Gaz Nordsee-96, Donau-91
Eeklo		Bel	1995	23,519	28,993	179	27	16	Lpg	
Excalibur	(st)	Lux	2002	93,786	77,822	268	43	19	Lng	
Excel (st)		Bel	2003	93,786	77,774	277	43	-	Lng	l/a Peace River
Excelerate	(st)	Bel	2006	93,786	77,822	277	43	-	Lng	
Excellence	(st)	Bel	2005	93,719	77,348	277	43	-	Lng	
Flanders Harmony		Bel	1992	47,597	64,220	228	36	-	Lpg	

Name	Eng	Flag	Year	GRT	DWT	Loa	Bm	Kts	Type	Former names
Flanders Tenacity ‡‡		Bel	1996	47,027	54,155	230	36	19	Lpg	
Gent		Bel	1985	18,155	26,820	155	27	16	Lpg	
Kemira Gas		Bel	1995	10,018	13,289	143	21	16	Lpg	
Methania	(st)	Bel	1978	81,792	67,879	280	42	19	Lng	
Reggane *		Lbr	1999	47,174	54,592	230	36	16	Lpg	
Touraine ‡		Hkg	1996	25,337	30,309	196	29	19	Lpg	ex Antwerpen Venture-97

newbuildings: five 38000 cubic metre Lpg tankers for 2006 delivery to Exmar Pool (Bergesen (2), Moller (2) and Exmar (1)) + lng + 48000grt lpg
Partly demerged from CMB Group, also operates LNG tankers in joint venture with Golar and Lpg tankers in Pool with Moller and Bergesen.
*Managed by subsidiary Tecto Belgium NV, * for Sonatrach Gas Carrier, Belgium*
‡ jointly owned with or ‡‡ time chartered from Wah Kwong Shipping Agency Co. Ltd., Hong Kong (China)

Cobelfret NV   Belgium

Funnel: *Yellow with red 'C' on white diamond on blue band.*
Hull: *Black or grey with green boot-topping.*

Name		Flag	Year	GRT	DWT	Loa	Bm	Kts	Type	Former names
CSK Beilun *		Sgp	1999	87,522	172,561	289	45	14	B	ex Pierre LD-04
Lowlands Beilun		Bel	1999	85,906	170,162	289	45	14	B	
Lowlands Brilliance		Bel	2002	85,906	169,631	289	45	-	B	
Lowlands Comfort *		Pan	2000	39,126	75,961	225	32	14	B	
Lowlands Ghent *		Hkg	2004	40,014	76,801	225	32	14	B	
Lowlands Grace *		Hkg	1991	77,273	149,518	270	43	12	B	ex CSK Everest-93
Lowlands Longevity		Bel	2001	86,848	173,000	289	45	15	B	
Lowlands Maine *		Pan	2005	40,039	76,600	225	32	-	B	
Lowlands Mimosa *		Pan	2002	29,885	52,479	190	32	14	B	
Lowlands Nello *		Sgp	2004	40,040	76,830	225	32	-	B	
Lowlands Orchid *		Pan	2005	88,594	176,193	289	45	-	B	
Lowlands Patrasche *		Hkg	2002	28,553	51,104	189	32	14	B	
Lowlands Phoenix *		Pan	2004	89,543	177,036	289	45	14	B	
Lowlands Prosperity		Bel	2001	86,201	169,229	289	45	14	B	ex Lowlands Prosperous-04
Lowlands Saguenay		Pan	1985	37,721	66,995	228	32	16	B	ex Northern Enterprise-01
Lowlands Sumida *		Pan	1998	37,689	72,493	225	32	-	B	ex Federal Sumida-06
Lowlands Sunrise *		Pan	2003	88,594	176,298	289	45	15	B	
Lowlands Trader *		Phl	2001	87,390	172,517	289	45	15	B	

Operated by Cobelfret SA, Luxembourg or Cobelfret Bulk Carriers NV, Belgium and managed by Anglo-Eastern (Antwerp) NV.
* on long term time-charter from various Philippine, Singapore and Japanese owners.

Compania SudAmericana de Vapores SA   Chile

Funnel: *Red with deep black top.*
Hull: *Grey or white with red or green boot-topping.*

Name		Flag	Year	GRT	DWT	Loa	Bm	Kts	Type	Former names
Braztrans I *		Bra	1980	22,011	38,186	194	28	15	B	ex Docemarte-99
Mapocho		Chl	1999	16,986	21,182	168	27	20	CC	ex Kribi-02, ANL Okapl-02, Fesco Endeavor-01, Kribi-00
Pacific Explorer		Mhl	1978	38,970	18,069	199	30	20	V	ex Asian Highway-93
Pacific Runner		Mhl	1977	38,754	18,099	199	30	20	V	ex Grand Lebanon-04, Pacific Runner-03, American Highway-92
Pacific Winner		Mhl	1987	48,688	18,845	213	30	18	Ro	ex Republica di Pisa-03
Rio Blanco **		Chl	1981	41,208	18,142	199	30	17	V	ex Fuji Ace-98
Rio Bueno		Pan	1980	25,984	11,076	161	27	16	V	ex Pacific Winner-94, Subaru Maru-92
Rio Enco		Chl	1978	19,867	7,426	139	26	18	V	ex Bright Ace-94, Singa Satu-83

newbuildings: three 65,600 grt (Chacabuco, Choapa, Cholguan) and three 42,382 grt (Laja, Limari, Longavi) container ships for 2006 delivery.
*Managed by Southern Shipmanagement (Chile) Ltd. Owned * by subsidiary Cia. Libra de Navegacao or ** jointly with Mitsui OSK Lines.*
Wholly owns Norasia Services SA, Switzerlandand has minority 27% interest in Navieros Group controlled Compania Chilena de Navegacion Interoceanica SA, Chile (CCNI) - see chartered vessels with 'CSAC', 'Norasia' and 'CCNI' prefixes in index
See other jointly owned vessels under Kristian Gerhard Jebsen and Odfjell ASA.

ConocoPhillips Inc   USA

Conoco Shipping Co/Usa
Funnel: *Red with white 'globe' device*
Hull: *Black with red boot-topping.*

Name		Flag	Year	GRT	DWT	Loa	Bm	Kts	Type	Former names
Constitution		Mhl	1999	58,242	104,700	244	42	15	T	
Continental *		Lbr	1993	53,848	96,683	243	42	14	T	
Guardian		Lbr	1992	53,772	96,920	243	42	14	T	
Patriot		Lbr	1992	53,772	96,920	248	42	14	T	
Pioneer *		Lbr	1993	53,858	96,724	248	42	14	T	

Name	Eng	Flag	Year	GRT	DWT	Loa	Bm	Kts	Type	Former names
Polar Adventure **	(2)	Usa	2004	85,387	141,739	273	46	16	T	
Polar Alaska **	(st)	Usa	1979	83,675	127,000	290	51	15	T	ex Arco Alaska-00
Polar California **	(st)	Usa	1980	83,675	127,003	290	51	15	T	ex Arco California-00
Polar Discovery **	(2)	Usa	2003	85,387	140,320	273	46	16	T	
Polar Endeavour **	(2)	Usa	2001	85,387	141,740	273	46	16	T	l/a Arco Endeavour
Polar Enterprise **	(2)	Usa	2005	85,387	141,739	273	46	16	T	
Polar Resolution **	(2)	Usa	2002	85,387	141,737	273	46	16	T	
Randgrid	(me2)	Nor	1995	75,273	122,535	266	46	15	T	ex Heidrun-96
Sentinel		Pan	1999	58,242	104,700	244	42	15	T	

*owned by ConocoPhillips Marine or ** by Polar Tankers Inc., both USA*

Costamare Shipping Co SA   Greece

Funnel: *Blue with black top or charterers colours*
Hull: *Grey or black with red boot-topping.*

Name	Eng	Flag	Year	GRT	DWT	Loa	Bm	Kts	Type	Former names
Britain Star *		Lbr	1978	14,050	15,270	157	25	18	CC	ex Zim Britain-04, MSC Chiwan-99, Ratana Pailin-97, ACX Jasmin-94, TSK Melody-91, Korean Senator-89, Democracy-88, Durga Felixstowe-87, TFL Democracy-86
China Sea		Grc	2002	53,453	62,740	294	32	24	CC	ex Zim New York-04
City of Glasgow **		Grc	1978	14,050	15,270	157	25	18	CC	ex Express-98, Choyang Express-98, Express-93, MSC Laura-90, Zim Guam-90, Express-88, Durga Osaka-87, Express-87, Nedlloyd Express-86, TFL Express-86, Alltrans Express-80
Cosco Guangzhou		Crc	2006	88,600	109,000	360	43	-	CC	
Cosco Ningbo		Crc	2006	88,600	109,000	360	43	-	CC	
Horizon *		Lbr	1991	15,783	14,764	167	27	18	CC	ex S. Caboto-05
Hyundai Challenger		Grc	1986	39,678	37,915	233	32	21	CC	ex Navarino-04, Zim Shenzhen-02, California Zeus-98, Hidaka Maru-88
Kuala Lumpur Express		Grc	2000	54,437	66,781	294	32	24	CC	
Liguria		Grc	1978	14,050	15,451	157	25	18	CC	ex MSC Liguria-03, MSC Romania-02, MSC Busan-99, Captain George-97, Eagle Nova-96, ACX Orchid-95, Ratana Thevi-91, Pylos-91, Leon-91, Freedom-91, Zim Venezia-91, JSS Los Angeles-88, British Senator-88, Freedom-87, TFL Freedom-86
Maersk Kalamata		Grc	2003	74,656	81,094	304	40	25	CC	
Maersk Kolkata		Grc	2003	74,656	81,577	304	40	25	CC	
Maersk Mandraki		Grc	1988	52,191	60,639	294	32	23	CC	ex Marit Maersk-04
Maersk Mykonos		Grc	1988	52,191	60,639	294	32	23	CC	ex Marchen Maersk-05
Maersk Toba		Grc	1982	43,325	53,690	270	32	24	CC	ex Leda Maersk-98
Maersk Tokyo		Grc	1981	43,325	53,540	270	32	23	CC	ex Lexa Maersk-97
Maersk Toyama		Grc	1984	40,238	48,600	256	32	24	CC	ex MSC Attica-04, Safmarine Victory-02, Maersk Toyama-01, Laust Maersk-98
MSC Alabama *		Grc	1996	37,518	42,966	243	32	23	CC	ex APL Italy-01, Chetumal-00, TMM Chetumal-97
MSC Antwerp		Grc	1976	34,382	37,852	223	31	21	CC	ex Maersk Bilbao-05, MSC Antwerp-03, Vancouver-98, Maersk Vancouver-98, Alva Maersk-95
MSC Austria *		Lbr	1977	38,991	40,624	241	32	21	CC	ex Houston Express-03, Rotterdam Express-00, Duesseldorf Express-97
MSC Germany *		Lbr	1978	38,991	40,849	240	32	21	CC	ex Genua Express-03, Nurnberg Express-00, Nurnberg Atlantic-93, Nurnberg Express-87
MSC Japan *		Grc	1996	37,518	42,938	243	32	23	CC	ex APL Panama-01, Manzanillo-00, TMM Manzanillo-97, Manzanillo-96, Carmen-96
MSC Korea		Grc	1996	37,518	42,938	243	32	23	CC	ex APL Spain-01, Sinaloa-00, TMM Sinaloa-97, Sinaloa-96
MSC Mexico *		Lbr	1978	38,991	40,849	241	32	22	CC	ex Koeln Express-03, Koln Atlantic-93, Koln Express-87
MSC Namibia		Grc	1977	27,754	27,893	204	31	20	CC	ex Namibia-04, MSC Namibia-03, Cap Vilano-00, Laser Stream-96, Advisor-93, CGM Provence-90, Advisor-85, Asia Winds-84, Advisor-83
MSC Romania II *		Lbr	1979	16,471	19,261	179	25	18	CC	ex MSC Genova-02, Shanghai-98, MSC Shanghai-98, Heung-A Strait-97, Zim Genova-95, Zim Koper-91, Enterprise-88, TFL Enterprise-86, Eagle Faith-85, TFL Enterprise-85, Alltrans Enterprise-82, Incotrans Enterprise-82,

NV CMB (Euronav). TI HELLAS. *Hans Kraijenbosch*

CMB SA (Exmar NV). KEMIRA GAS. *Vandriessche Guido*

Costamare Shipping Co SA. MSC VENICE (on charter to Mediterranean Shipping). *G. J. de Boer*

Name	Eng	Flag	Year	GRT	DWT	Loa	Bm	Kts	Type	Former names
										TFL Enterprise-81, Alltrans Enterprise-79
MSC Serena *		Pan	1977	38,991	40,624	241	32	21	CC	ex Zim Eilat I-02, New York Express-98, Maersk Algeciras-96, Stuttgart Express-92 (len-85)
MSC Sicily		Grc	1978	20,676	24,382	186	28	20	CC	ex Carmen-01, MSC China-00, Prestige-98, California Express-93, Carmen-92, Asian Pearl-91
MSC Sudan		Grc	1976	27,971	27,795	204	31	21	CC	ex Caribia Express-03, Woermann Ulanga-91, ScanDutch Ledra-90, Caribia Express-87
MSC Tuscany		Grc	1978	20,676	24,383	186	24	14	CC	ex Mumbai-01, Indamex Mumbai-01, MSC Singapore-00, Nedlloyd Java-98, Asian Jade-91
MSC Venice *		Lbr	1978	16,471	19,261	179	25	18	CC	ex MSC Osaka-98, Osaka-97, Zim Osaka-96, Liberty-88, TFL Liberty-86
MSC Washington		Grc	1984	43,332	53,325	270	32	22	CC	ex Maersk Trondheim-05, Lars Maersk-99
MSC Yokohama		Grc	1979	30,249	27,738	203	31	21	CC	ex Romanos-97, Hyundai Vancouver-97, Gulf Speed-94, OOCL Brilliance-93, Gulf Speed-91, Incotrans Speed-86, China Winds-84, Incotrans Speed-83
New York Express		Grc	2000	54,437	66,818	294	32	24	CC	
Reunion *		Lbr	1983	20,345	28,422	174	28	18	CC	ex DAL Reunion-02, Delmas Mascareignes-02, SEAL Ubena-00, Sea Merchant-97, Hongkong Senator-88, Ubena-87
River Mas *		Bhs	1987	18,353	19,710	172	25	17	CC	ex Budi Waja-06, MSC Indonesia-02, Admiralty-01, Mecklenburg I-98, Mecklenburg-96, Ernst Thalmann-90
Safmarine Antwerp		Grc	2003	74,661	81,183	304	40	25	CC	ex Maersk Kobe-03
Safmarine Himalaya		Grc	2000	74,661	81,584	304	40	25	CC	ex Sealand Virginia-03
Safmarine Igoli		Grc	1987	42,304	39,579	250	32	22	CC	ex APL Costa Rica-03, APL Pacific-01, MSC Pacific-01, Houston Express-99, Saturn-98, California Saturn-97
Sealand Illinois		Grc	2000	74,661	81,584	304	40	25	CC	
Sealand Michigan		Grc	2000	74,661	81,584	304	40	25	CC	
Sealand New York		Grc	2000	74,661	81,584	304	40	25	CC	
Sealand Washington		Grc	2000	74,661	81,584	304	40	25	CC	
Sierra Express		Grc	1977	27,970	23,020	204	31	20	CC	ex Cordillera Epress-83
Singapore Express		Grc	2000	54,415	66,793	294	32	24	CC	
Sophia Britannia		Grc	1993	50,501	59,567	292	32	23	CC	ex Kirishima-99
Strait Mas *		Bhs	1987	18,353	19,710	172	25	17	CC	ex Montreal Senator-06, Brandenburg-98, Wilhelm Pieck-90
Westmed II *		Lbr	1978	16,471	19,621	179	25	17	CC	ex City of Dublin-98, Zim Yokohama-96, Independence-88, TFL Independence-86
Windward *		Lbr	1974	14,400	21,885	171	23	16	CC	ex Pelayo-05, Windward-03, Werra-84, Werra Express-84, Freudenfels-80, Aristotelis-76 (conv C/len-79)
Yangtze Star		Grc	2004	53,453	62,740	294	32	24	CC	ex Zim Piraeus-05
Zim Shanghai		Mlt	2002	53,453	66,597	294	32	24	CC	

newbuildings - five 99,500 grt (9200 teu) container ships due 2006 from South Korean builder for charter to COSCO.
* owned or managed by associated Ciel Shipmanagement SA, Greece, or ** Shanghai Costamare Ship Management, China.

Reederei Frank Dahl   Germany

Funnel: *Blue with yellow 'mibau+stema', red boot-topping.*
Hull: *White with yellow 'H' over yellow wave on blue square, narrow black top.*

Name	Eng	Flag	Year	GRT	DWT	Loa	Bm	Kts	Type	Former names
Nordnes *		Atg	2001	17,765	28,100	166	25	14	Bu	ex Rocknes-05, Kvitnes-03
Sandnes *		Atg	2005	17,357	28,000	167	25	15	Bu	
Splittnes	(2)	Pan	1994	9,855	16,073	148	21	14	B	ex Kari Arnhild-02
Stones *		Atg	2001	17,357	28,115	166	25	14	Bu	

* managed for H.J.Hartmann and operated by Mibau & Stema.

D'Amico Societa di Navigazione SpA   Italy

Funnel: *Yellow with blue 8-pointed star.*
Hull: *Grey or black with white or yellow 'd'AMICO', red boot-topping.*

Name	Eng	Flag	Year	GRT	DWT	Loa	Bm	Kts	Type	Former names
Cielo d'America †		Ita	2002	25,580	34,019	202	30	21	CC	
Cielo d'Europa †		Ita	2002	25,580	34,038	202	30	21	CC	
Cielo del Baltico		Lbr	1986	16,282	27,350	170	23	15	T	ex Maersk Baltic-01, Magdelena-97, Rita Maersk-96
Cielo di Baffin †		Iom	1986	16,282	27,350	170	23	15	T	ex Maersk Baffin-01, Rasmine Maersk-96
Cielo di Barents †		Nis	1986	16,282	27,350	170	23	15	T	ex Maersk Barents-02, Edzard-97,

Name	Eng	Flag	Year	GRT	DWT	Loa	Bm	Kts	Type	Former names
										Maersk Barents-97, Robert Maersk-97
Cielo di Biscaglia		Lbr	1986	16,282	27,350	170	23	15	T	ex Maersk Biscay-01, Ras Maersk-97
Cielo di Bothnia		Lbr	1986	16,282	27,350	170	23	15	T	ex Maersk Bothnia-01, Rebecca-97,
										Maersk Bothnia-97, Romo Maersk-97
Cielo di Guangzhou †		Lbr	2006	25,507	38,875	168	29	-	T	
Cielo di Londra		Lbr	2001	23,680	36,032	183	27	-	T	
Cielo di Milano *		Ita	2003	25,400	40,081	176	31	15	T	
Cielo di Monfalcone		Ita	2002	27,839	37,420	186	29	14	Co	
Cielo di Napoli		Ita	2003	25,400	40,081	176	31	15	T	
Cielo di Parigi		Lbr	2001	23,680	36,032	183	27	-	T	
Cielo di Roma *		Ita	2003	25,382	40,096	176	31	15	T	
Cielo di Salerno **		Lbr	2002	23,680	36,023	183	27	15	T	
Cielo di Vaiano †		Lbr	1998	19,712	31,962	172	27	16	B	ex Asteri J-05, Astro Ace-04
Cielo di Vancouver		Ita	2002	27,828	37,420	186	29	14	Co	
High Challenge		Lbr	1999	28,238	46,473	183	32	14	T	
High Courage		Lbr	2005	30,048	46,991	183	32	14	T	
High Endeavour		Lbr	2004	30,028	46,991	183	32	14	T	
High Endurance		Lbr	2004	30,028	46,991	183	32	14	T	
High Energy ‡		Pan	2004	28,245	46,874	180	32	15	T	
High Harmony ‡		Pan	2005	28,059	45,913	180	32	15	T	
High Light		Pan	2005	28,245	46,843	180	32	15	T	
High Performance **		Lbr	2005	30,100	51,303	183	32	15	T	
High Power ‡		Pan	2004	28,245	46,866	180	32	15	T	
High Presence ‡		Sgp	2005	28,245	48,400	180	32	15	T	
High Priority ‡		Sgp	2005	28,245	46,847	180	32	15	T	
High Progress		Lbr	2005	30,081	51,302	183	32	15	T	
High Spirit		Lbr	1999	28,238	46,473	183	32	14	T	
High Valor		Lbr	2005	30,048	46,991	183	32	-	T	
High Wind		Lbr	1999	28,238	46,473	183	32	14	T	
Medi Dubai		Ita	2001	29,367	52,523	190	32	14	B	ex Medi Monaco
Medi Tokyo		Ita	1999	38,835	74,356	225	32	14	B	
Rita D'Amato		Ita	2004	25,400	40,081	176	31	15	T	

* managed for Perseveranza SpA di Nav, Italy or ** for CoGeMa, Monaco. † owned by D'Amico Dry Ltd and managed by Ishima Pte Ltd , both Singapore.
‡ chartered from Japanese finance houses. Smaller tankers operating on 'Handytankers' Pool.
Also 18 other bulk carriers (52-76,000 dwt) with 'Medi' prefix and 11 newbuildings being chartered from various owners.

Danaos Shipping Co Ltd

Greece

Funnel: Blue or charterers colours.
Hull: Black with red boot-topping.

Name	Eng	Flag	Year	GRT	DWT	Loa	Bm	Kts	Type	Former names
Achilleas		Pan	1994	35,879	69,180	225	32	14	B	ex Milky Ace-02, Milky Star-02
Alexandra I		Pan	1994	35,886	69,090	225	32	14	B	ex Ocean Cherry-02
APL Belgium		Sgp	2002	65,792	67,500	277	40	24	CC	
APL England		Sgp	2001	65,792	67,967	277	40	24	CC	
APL Holland		Sgp	2001	65,792	67,500	277	40	24	CC	
APL Scotland		Sgp	2001	65,792	67,500	277	40	24	CC	
CMA CGM Elbe		Grc	1991	37,134	44,008	243	32	22	CC	ex Hanjin Bremen-03
CMA CGM Kalamata		Grc	1991	37,134	43,967	243	32	22	CC	ex Hanjin Singapore-03
CMA CGM Komodo		Grc	1991	37,134	43,966	243	32	22	CC	ex Hanjin Elizabeth-03
Dimitris C		Pan	1994	26,824	43,815	190	31	14	B	ex Aditya Gopal-02, Skausund-94
Eagle Express		Bhs	1978	28,078	23,047	204	31	21	CC	ex MSC Izmir-01, Eagle Quest-97, OOCL
										Beacon-95, Eagle Express-93,
										America Express-83
Fivos		Pan	1994	36,561	69,659	225	32	14	B	ex Global Ace-02, Global Star-02
Henry		Pan	1986	41,280	38,717	245	32	22	CC	ex APL Guatemala-05, Henry-04, APL
										Guatemala-04, Zim Xingang-01, Cape Henry-99
Hyundai Commodore		Grc	1992	51,836	61,152	275	37	25	CC	
Hyundai Duke		Grc	1992	51,836	61,152	275	37	26	CC	
Independence		Pan	1986	41,413	38,624	248	32	22	CC	ex MOL Independence-03, Alligator
										Independence-01
Maersk Constantia *	(2)	Bel	1979	52,615	50,027	258	32	22	CC	ex S.A. Waterberg-01
Maria C		Pan	1994	26,093	45,205	188	31	14	B	ex May Star-02
Norasia Hamburg		Cyp	1989	46,697	44,851	275	32	22	CC	ex APL Arabia-04, ANL Hamburg-04,
										Norasia Hamburg-03, Cosco Bremerhaven-01,
										Honour-00, OOCL Honour-00, APL Arabia-97,
										OOCL Honour-96
Roberto C		Pan	1994	26,057	45,210	188	31	14	B	ex Azusa-02

Name	Eng	Flag	Year	GRT	DWT	Loa	Bm	Kts	Type	Former names
S.A. Helderberg *	(2)	Bel	1977	52,615	49,579	258	32	21	CC	
S.A. Sederberg *	(2)	Bhs	1978	52,615	48,878	258	32	21	CC	
S.A. Winterberg *	(2)	Bhs	1978	52,615	50,017	258	32	22	CC	ex Transvaal-95, S.A. Winterberg-92
Sofia III		Cyp	1998	37,978	69,146	225	32	14	B	ex Aifos-03, Ever Victory-02
Victory I		Pan	1988	42,809	40,638	253	32	22	CC	ex MOL Victory-03, Alligator Victory-01
YM Milano		Grc	1988	41,786	45,036	248	32	21	CC	ex MSC Pegasus-03, Pegasus-02, Maersk Livorno-99, Pegasus-98, California Pegasus-98, Yamaaki Maru-92
Zim Mumbai		Cyp	1984	30,500	35,472	240	30	20	CC	ex Pacific Bridge-06, MSC Fremantle-02, Pacific Bridge-98, Zim Mumbai-98, Hyundai Seattle-96, Pacific Bridge-94, Makalu-89, Pacific Bridge-86 (len-89)
YM Yantian		Cyp	1989	46,697	45,570	276	32	22	CC	ex Hope-03, OOCL Hope-00

newbuildings: two 107,200 grt container ships for 2008 delivery.
* managed by Safmarine Ship Management, South Africa

Herm Dauelsberg GmbH & Co   Germany

Funnel: White with black 'D' on cream band between narrow blue bands, or charterers colours.
Hull: Black or grey with red boot-topping.

Name		Flag	Year	GRT	DWT	Loa	Bm	Kts	Type	Former names
Bellavia		Mhl	2005	53,807	66,501	294	32	25	CC	
Cala Pintada		Lbr	2001	23,652	30,375	188	30	21	CC	ex Lobivia-04
Cala Providencia		Lbr	1995	14,968	20,176	167	25	19	CC	ex Novia-04, P&O Nedlloyd Slauerhoff-03, P&O Nedlloyd Mumbai-02, Novia-01, Sea Novia-97, Novia-95
Cap Sunion		Lbr	1995	23,691	30,743	188	30	21	CC	ex Bonavia-04, Safmarine Maluti-04, Maersk Algerciras-01, Contship Auckland-97, Bonavia-95
Cherokee Bridge		Mhl	2005	40,952	55,490	261	32	24	CC	l/a Clivia
Chesapeake Bay Bridge		Mhl	2005	40,952	55,497	261	32	24	CC	l/a Silvia
Lindavia		Lbr	1996	23,825	30,615	188	30	21	CC	ex Maersk Sydney-00, Lindavia-98, Sea Lindavia-98, Lindavia-96
Magnavia		Lbr	1996	23,825	30,743	188	30	21	CC	ex MOL Waratah-02, Alligator Unity-01, Maersk Oceania-00, Magnavia-97
Marivia		Lbr	2001	23,652	30,375	188	30	21	CC	
Octavia		Mhl	2005	53,807	66,501	294	32	25	CC	
Olivia			1995	14,968	20,176	167	25	19	CC	ex P&O Nedlloyd Mahe-02, Olivia-01
Safmarine Tugela		Lbr	1995	23,691	30,743	188	30	21	CC	ex Altavia-03, Safmarine Tugela-03, Maersk Nagoya-01, Maersk Santos-99, Choyang Fortune-97, Altavia-95

Del Monte Fresh Fruit International Inc   Bermuda

Funnel: Dark green with white 'Del Monte' on yellow edged red fruit symbol.
Hull: White with green boot-topping.

Name		Flag	Year	GRT	DWT	Loa	Bm	Kts	Type	Former names
Alcazar Carrier *		Bhs	1979	15,834	15,200	169	26	22	R	ex Winter Moon-99, Zenit Moon-87, Winter Moon-85
Algeciras Carrier		Bhs	1979	15,834	15,200	169	26	22	R	ex Winter Sun-00, Zenit Sun-87, Winter Sun-84
Alicante Carrier *		Bhs	1979	15,834	15,200	169	26	22	R	ex Winter Star-99, Zenit Star-87, Winter Star-85
Cadiz Carrier *		Bhs	1979	15,833	15,100	169	26	22	R	ex Winter Water-99, Zenit Water-87, Winter Water-85
Malaga Carrier *		Bhs	1979	15,834	15,100	169	26	22	R	ex Winter Wave-99, Zenit Wave-87, Winter Wave-85
Segovia Carrier *		Bhs	1980	15,834	15,200	169	26	22	R	ex Winter Sea-99, Zenit Sea-87, Winter Sea-85
Valencia Carrier		Bhs	1984	12,340	10,126	148	24	19	R	ex Spring Bride-02

Owned by subsidiary Network Shipping Ltd., USA and managed by Norbulk Shipping UK Ltd. or * by DFM Ltd., Poland.

Horn-Linie (GmbH & Co)/Germany

Funnel: Grey with white 'H' on blue above red bands
Hull: White with red boot-topping.

Name		Flag	Year	GRT	DWT	Loa	Bm	Kts	Type	Former names
Hornbay		Lbr	1990	12,887	9,069	154	23	20	Rr	
Horncap		Lbr	1991	12,887	9,069	154	23	20	Rr	
Horncliff		Lbr	1992	12,877	9,184	154	23	20	Rr	

Del Monte Fresh Fruit International. SEGOVIA CARRIER. *Hans Kraijenbosch*

Del Monte (Horn-Linie). HORNCLIFF. *Hans Kraijenbosch*

Name	Eng	Flag	Year	GRT	DWT	Loa	Bm	Kts	Type	Former names

Dockwise NV   Netherlands

Funnel: *Dark blue with black 'D' on white disc on light blue square on white band.*
Hull: *Black, orange or green with 'DOCKWISE', red boot-topping.*

Name	Eng	Flag	Year	GRT	DWT	Loa	Bm	Kts	Type	Former names
Black Marlin *		Ant	2000	37,938	57,021	218	42	14	HLS	
Blue Marlin *		Ant	2000	51,821	76,051	218	63	14	HLS	(wid-03)
Dock Express 10	(2)	Nld	1979	13,110	12,928	154	27	15	HLS	ex Dock Express France-94, Dock Express 10-87
Dock Express 12	(2)	Nld	1979	13,110	12,928	159	27	15	HLS	
Enterprise	(2)	Ant	1984	17,395	8,727	158	29	12	LC	ex Smit Enterprise-03, Danube Express-98, Nikolay Markin-92
Explorer	(2)	Ant	1984	19,453	8,638	159	31	13	LC	ex Smit Explorer-03, Pavel Antokolskiy-99
Mighty Servant 1	(me2)	Nld	1983	19,954	23,473	160	40	14	HLS	(len/wid-98)
Mighty Servant 3	(me2)	Nld	1984	22,391	27,720	181	40	14	HLS	
Super Servant 3	(2)	Ant	1982	10,224	14,138	140	32	13	HLS	
Super Servant 4	(2)	Ant	1982	12,642	17,600	140	32	13	HLS	
Swan		Ant	1981	22,788	30,060	181	32	16	HLS	ex Sea Swan-96, Swan H.L.-89, Dyvi Swan-88
Swift		Ant	1983	22,835	32,187	183	32	15	HLS	ex Sea Swift-96, Swift H.L.-89, Dyvi Swift-88
Teal		Ant	1984	22,835	32,101	181	32	15	HLS	ex Sea Teal-96, Teal H.L.-89, Dyvi Teal-88
Tern		Ant	1982	22,788	30,060	181	32	16	HLS	ex Sea Tern-96, Tern H.L.-89, Dyvi Tern-88
Transshelf	(2)	Ant	1987	26,547	34,030	173	40	15	HLS	

newbuildings: 16,250 grt and 37,500 grt yacht carriers on order for 2006-7 delivery.
Company owned by Heerema BV, Netherlands (70%) and Van Ommeren (30%) with vessels managed by Anglo-Eastern (UK) Ltd., UK
* operated for Offshore Heavy Transport ASA, Norway (35% owned by Wilh. Wilhelmsen and 13% by Dyvi)

Peter Döhle Schiffahrts-KG   Germany

Funnel: *Black, black 'PD' on white diamond on broad red band bordered by narrow white bands, black with yellow 'ICL' above yellow wave inside yellow rectangular outline (Independent) or charterers colours.*
Hull: *Dark grey or black with red boot-topping.*

Name	Eng	Flag	Year	GRT	DWT	Loa	Bm	Kts	Type	Former names
Adonia		Lbr	2006	51,350	58,341	286	32	-	CC	
Aglaia		Mhl	2001	14,278	15,315	159	26	22	CC	I/a Sandy Rickmers
Ajama *		Cyp	1994	30,526	34,079	205	32	19	CC	ex CP Pathfinder-06, Lykes Pathfinder-05, DAL East London-04, Ajama-02, Sea Star-99, Choyang Grace-97, Delaware Bay-95, Sea Musketeer-94, Ajama-94, I/a Charles de Foucauld
Alabama		Lbr	1998	38,440	74,002	225	32	14	B	ex Belgrano-03, Golden Disa-99
Alana		Gbr	2004	9,981	11,390	134	23	-	CC	I/d Adelina
Alda		Lbr	2006	74,000	85,500	-	-	-	CC	
Alianca Hong Kong ‡		Deu	1998	25,608	34,015	208	30	21	CC	ex Columbus Chile-04, Alianca Rotterdam-02, Lykes Traveler-01, CMA CGM Gauguin-01, CGM Gaugin-00, Charlotta-98
Alicia		Lbr	2005	40,494	73,901	225	32	14	B	
Amalthea		Mhl	2001	14,290	14,901	159	26	22	CC	
Angela		Atg	2005	9,962	11,403	134	23	-	CC	
APL Jakarta ‡		Lbr	2003	35,645	41,850	220	32	22	CC	ex Julia-03, Alessa-03, I/a Carmen
APL Shanghai		Lbr	2003	35,645	42,062	220	32	22	CC	ex Azalea-03, I/a Clarissa
Atlantica ‡		Mhl	1995	39,017	72,506	219	32	14	B	ex Atlantic Crown-00, Atlantic Rose-95
Attila *		Iom	1997	38,520	73,049	225	32	14	B	ex Aspen-02, NOL Pollux-00
Baltic Swan		Gbr	2004	9,981	11,360	134	23	-	CC	
Cap Norte ‡		Deu	1997	25,608	34,015	208	30	21	CC	ex Santos Express-03, Sea Ocelot-02, Transroll Argentina-99, Cap Norte-99, Impala-98, Brasil Star-98, Impala-97
CCNI Antillanca		Lbr	2005	35,645	41,850	220	32	22	CC	ex Demeter-06
CCNI Atacama †		Deu	1998	28,148	46,376	185	32	15	Co	I/a Valbella
CCNI Punta Arenas		Lbr	2005	30,047	35,741	208	32	-	CC	
Chacabuco **		Lbr	2006	65,600	67,970	276	40	-	CC	
Chaiten		Lbr	2006	64,600	67,970	276	40	-	CC	I/d Anguila
Chillan		Lbr	2006	66,280	67,970	276	40	-	CC	I/d Arizona
Choapa **		Lbr	2005	66,280	67,970	276	40	-	CC	
Cholguan **		Lbr	2006	65,600	67,970	276	40	-	CC	
Clan Gladiator		Cyp	1992	21,053	30,007	182	29	18	CC	ex Alberta-05, Fesco Enterprise-00, Nedlloyd Singapore-99, Santa Victoria-96, MSC Victoria-95, Muscat Bay-94, Santa Victoria-92
Copiapo		Lbr	2004	66,280	68,228	276	40	-	CC	ex Amazonia-04
CSAV Chicago ‡		Cyp	1997	25,608	34,015	208	30	21	CC	ex Maersk Freeport-99, Liberta-99, Montebello-99, I/a Liberta
CSAV Rio Trancura		Lbr	2005	35,881	41,802	220	32	22	CC	ex Coletta-05

Name	Eng	Flag	Year	GRT	DWT	Loa	Bm	Kts	Type	Former names
Daniel		Lbr	2006	9,990	11,360	134	23	-	CC	
Glen Helen **		Lbr	1998	25,537	46,570	183	31	14	B	ex Alicahue-04
Glen Maye **		Lbr	1998	25,537	46,570	183	31	14	B	ex Allipen-05
Glen Mooar **		Lbr	1998	25,537	46,570	183	31	14	B	ex Antuco-05
Glen Vine		Mhl	1981	29,496	51,267	194	32	14	Ce	ex Big One-05, Cielo di Parma-04, Nebraska-97, Onda Chiara-94, Serafino Ferruzzi-90 (conv B-87, conv T-05)
MSC Bilboa ‡		Lbr	2006	88,600	97,400	334	43	25	CC	l/d Bremen
MSC Paris ‡		Lbr	2006	88,600	97,430	334	43	25	CC	l/d Hamburg
MSC Valencia ‡		Lbr	2006	88,600	97,400	334	43	25	CC	l/d Jork
Hispania ‡		Lbr	1995	25,503	43,222	185	30	14	B	ex Pacific Governor-03
Holland Maas Caraibes		Atg	2005	9,962	11,200	134	23	-	CC	
Husum		Lbr	2006	26,626	34,465	210	30	21	CC	
Independent Action		Lbr	1992	14,867	20,140	167	25	17	CC	ex Cielo di Colombia-99, Annabella D-98, CSAV Rupanco-97, Augusta-97, Brasil Express-94, Annabella D-92, l/a Auriga
Independent Endeavor		Lbr	1995	14,923	20,406	167	25	19	CC	ex Astoria D-00, Libra New York-99, Libra Valencia-97, l/a Astoria
Independent Pursuit		Lbr	2005	17,000	19,500	168	25	-	CC	
Independent Spirit		Cyp	1991	12,997	17,610	152	25	17	CC	ex Erika E-97, Nuova Asia-97, Alabama-96, Atlantic Express-93, Donata Schulte-91
Independent Trader		Cyp	1991	12,997	17,610	150	25	17	CC	ex Carola E-97, Caroline-96, America-96, Carolina-91
Independent Venture		Lbr	1993	14,849	20,540	167	25	19	CC	ex Sea Voyager-99, Nautique-98
Libra Ipanema		Lbr	2005	26,626	34,500	210	30	21	CC	ex Emden-06
Libra Rio ‡		Atg	2003	35,645	41,850	221	32	22	CC	l/a Katharina, l/d Albona
Libra Santos		Lbr	2003	35,881	41,850	220	32	22	CC	ex Patricia-04, Amasia-03, l/a Cyrill
Limari **		Lbr	2005	42,382	51,870	268	32		CC	
Lircay		Lbr	2006	42,300	51,870	268	32		CC	l/d Ariba
Loa		Lbr	2005	42,382	51,870	268	32	-	CC	l/a Adda
Longavi **		Lbr	2006	42,300	51,870	268	32		CC	
Lontue		Lbr	2006	42,300	51,870	268	32		CC	
Maersk Vera Cruz *		Iom	2004	17,188	22,513	179	28	21	CC	l/a Pyxis
Maersk Victoria *		Iom	2004	17,188	22,506	179	28	21	CC	l/a Palomar
Minna		Lbr	2005	35,881	41,800	220	32	-	CC	ex Zeus-05
MOL Americas		Atg	2000	16,803	22,967	184	25	19	CC	ex Amanda-04, Libra Livorno-03, l/a Amanda
MSC Yorkshire		Gbr	2005	9,962	11,150	134	23	-	CC	
Norasia Atlas ‡		Lbr	2005	35,881	42,157	220	32	22	CC	
Norasia Alya		Lbr	2004	35,881	41,748	220	32	22	CC	ex Renata-04
Norasia Balkans		Atg	2001	35,645	42,300	220	32	22	CC	ex Norasia Taurus-05, APL Mexico-04, l/a Katjana, l/d Celine
Norasia Enterprise		Deu	2003	51,350	58,341	286	32	-	CC	ex Amaranta-03
Norasia Makalu		Atg	2002	35,645	42,200	220	32	22	CC	ex APL Portugal-05, l/a Antonia, l/d Chloe
OOCL Narva ‡		Deu	2004	9,981	11,360	134	23	18	CC	l/a Finnlandia
Paine **		Lbr	2006	74,000	85,500	-	-	-	CC	
Safmarine Mbashe		Lbr	2006	17,189	22,300	179	28	21	CC	ex Viona-06
Safmarine Mgeni		Deu	2000	16,803	22,968	184	25	20	CC	ex Altonia-04, Safmarine Buffalo-03, Maersk Felixstowe-01, CSAV Marsella-00
TS Keelung		Lbr	2006	17,100	22,300	179	28	21	CC	
Valdivia		Lbr	2006	17,189	22,308	179	28	21	CC	
Vasco da Gama		Lbr	2006	32,300	39,600	212	32	21	CC	

newbuildings: four further 85,500 dwt (Abba/Anita/Palena/Puelo), one more 43,100 dwt (William Shakespeare), five 41,800 dwt (Daphne/Leto/Hebe/Hera/Maia), two 39,200 dwt (Amerigo Vespucci/Marco Polo) and eight 33,800 dwt container ships due for 2006-8 delivery
Owns minority 13% interest in Navieros Group controlled Compania Chilena de Navegacion Interoceanica SA, Chile (CCNI)
* managed by Dohle IOM Ltd, UK, ** by Southern Shipmanagement (Chile) Ltd, Chile, † by Uniteam Marine Shipping or ‡ by Hammonia Reederei GmbH & Co. KG, both Germany (joint venture with HCI Hanseatische Capital GmbH)

Dole Food Company   Costa Rica

Funnel: Dark blue with with red 'Dole' symbol on white band or charterers colours.
Hull: White or cream with red 'Dole' symbol above blue line, blue boot-topping.

Name	Eng	Flag	Year	GRT	DWT	Loa	Bm	Kts	Type	Former names
Dole Africa		Bhs	1994	10,584	10,288	150	23	21	R	
Dole America		Bhs	1994	10,584	10,288	150	23	21	R	
Dole Asia		Bhs	1994	10,584	10,288	150	23	21	R	
Dole California		Ita	1989	16,488	11,800	179	27	20	CC	
Dole Chile		Bhs	1999	31,779	30,145	205	32	21	CC	
Dole Colombia		Bhs	1999	31,779	30,145	205	32	21	CC	

Dockwise NV. BLUE MARLIN. *Hans Kraijenbosch*

Dockwise NV. SUPER SERVANT 3. *Hans Kraijenbosch*

Peter Dohle Schiffahrts. CCNI ATACAMA (on charter to CCNI). *G. J. de Boer*

Dole Food Company. DOLE AFRICA. *Hans Kraijenbosch*

Eletson Corp. SKOPELOS. *Hans Kraijenbosch*

Ethiopian Shipping Lines. NETSANET. *Hans Kraijenbosch*

Name	Eng	Flag	Year	GRT	DWT	Loa	Bm	Kts	Type	Former names
Dole Costarica		Ita	1991	16,488	11,800	179	27	20	CC	
Dole Ecuador		Ita	1989	16,488	11,800	179	27	20	CC	
Dole Europa		Bhs	1994	10,584	10,288	150	23	21	R	
Dole Honduras		Ita	1991	16,488	11,800	179	27	20	CC	
Tropical Mist		Lbr	1986	9,749	11,998	149	22	20	R	
Tropical Morn		Lbr	1986	9,749	11,998	149	22	20	R	
Tropical Sky		Lbr	1986	9,749	11,998	149	22	20	R	
Tropical Star		Lbr	1986	9,749	11,998	149	22	20	R	

Managed by subsidiary Reefership Marine Services Ltd.

DT-Bereederungs GmbH & Co KG   Germany

Funnel: *Charterers colours*
Hull: *Black or red with red boot-topping.*

Name	Eng	Flag	Year	GRT	DWT	Loa	Bm	Kts	Type	Former names
Gloria		Atg	2001	16,803	22,967	185	25	20	CC	ex P&O Nedlloyd Pessoa-04, P&O Nedlloyd Lagos-02, I/a Gloria
Montemar Europa		Atg	2003	16,803	22,900	185	25	20	CC	
Olympia		Atg	1986	10,287	12,500	148	23	18	CC	ex P&O Nedlloyd Cesme-05, Olympia-03, ACX Swallow-00, QC Mallard-00, Hansa Coral-99, Sea Eagle-92, Contship Australia-90, Ocean Australia-89, Fine Eagle-88
Xanadu		Atg	1984	24,844	40,891	183	31	14	B	ex Maria-02, Cedrela-89, Western Jade-88, Dimitros Criticos-88, Kepbrave-86

formerly Danz und Tietjens Schiffahrts KG with vessels managed by BBC-Burger Bereederungs Contor GmbH.

Dyvi AS   Norway

Funnel: *Black with blue 'D' between two narrow blue bands on broad white band.*
Hull: *Grey with blue boot-topping or ** dark blue with light blue diagonal stripes.*

Name	Eng	Flag	Year	GRT	DWT	Loa	Bm	Kts	Type	Former names
Dyvi Adriatic		Hkg	1988	39,187	9,772	183	30	18	V	ex Wolfsburg-03
Dyvi Baltic		Hkg	1989	39,043	9,772	183	30	17	V	ex Hannover-02
Dyvi Kattegat		Nis	1973	25,615	9,652	188	23	18	V	ex Dyvi Antwerpen-04, Dyvi Kattegat-03
Dyvi Pamplona		Nis	1999	37,237	12,778	180	31	19	V	
Dyvi Puebla		Nis	1999	37,237	12,780	180	31	19	V	
Kassel		Pan	1999	51,204	17,297	180	32	19	V	

Eletson Corp   Greece

Funnel: *Black with red boot-topping.*
Hull: *Buff base with blue five-pointed star on broad white band, edged with narrow blue bands beneath black top.*

Name	Eng	Flag	Year	GRT	DWT	Loa	Bm	Kts	Type	Former names
Agathonissos		Grc	2002	57,062	106,149	244	42	15	T	
Alkyonis		Grc	1992	39,265	66,895	228	32	14	T	
Alonissos		Grc	2004	57,062	106,290	244	42	15	T	
Angistri		Grc	2000	39,283	76,019	213	37	15	T	
Argironissos		Grc	1992	29,506	45,425	183	32	14	T	
Erikoussa		Grc	2003	41,679	70,142	228	32	15	T	
Folegandros		Grc	1992	29,506	45,425	183	32	14	T	
Halki		Grc	1989	27,793	46,538	183	32	14	T	
Kandilousa		Grc	1995	28,507	46,700	183	32	14	T	
Kastelorizo		Grc	1991	29,506	45,425	183	32	14	T	
Makronissos		Grc	2002	57,062	106,149	244	42	15	T	
Megalonissos		Grc	2004	57,062	106,290	244	42	15	T	
Parapola		Grc	1994	38,792	68,232	243	32	14	T	
Pelagos		Grc	1999	39,283	76,020	213	37	15	T	
Psara		Grc	1989	27,793	46,538	183	32	14	T	
Salamina		Grc	1991	29,506	45,425	183	32	14	T	
Samothraki		Grc	1989	27,793	46,538	183	32	14	T	
Serifopoulo		Grc	1995	28,507	46,700	183	32	14	T	
Serifos		Grc	1995	28,507	46,700	183	32	14	T	
Shinoussa		Grc	1990	27,793	46,538	183	32	14	T	
Skiropoula		Grc	1995	38,792	68,232	242	32	14	T	
Skopelos		Grc	2003	41,679	70,142	228	32	15	T	
Sporades		Grc	1993	39,265	66,895	228	32	14	T	
Stavronisi		Grc	1996	38,667	68,232	243	32	14	T	
Velopoula		Grc	1993	39,265	66,895	228	32	14	T	

Name	Eng	Flag	Year	GRT	DWT	Loa	Bm	Kts	Type	Former names

John T Essberger GmbH & Co
Germany

DAL Deutsche Afrika-Linien GmbH & Co

Funnel: *Buff, narrow red band on black-edged broad white band and black top or buff with broad green band.*
Hull: *Light grey or black with red boot-topping*

Name	Eng	Flag	Year	GRT	DWT	Loa	Bm	Kts	Type	Former names
DAL Kalahari		Lbr	2005	50,567	62,994	266	37	24	CC	
Helvetia		Pan	1980	16,235	24,000	185	23	15	Ce	
Invicta		Pan	1983	9,948	16,730	145	22	15	Ce	
Karonga		Lbr	1991	14,793	17,238	159	24	16	C	ex Nordana Advisor-99, Karonga-98, Prosperity-96
Sanaga		Lbr	1998	17,784	28,215	169	27	14	B	ex Paclogger-98
Selinda		Lbr	2001	17,784	28,107	169	27	14	B	
Swakop		Lbr	2001	17,784	28,083	169	27	14	B	

newbuildings - four 62,300 grt 115,000 dwt tankers from South Korean builder for 2006-7 delivery.
managed by associated Transocean Shipmanagement GmbH, Germany.

The Ethiopian Shipping Lines
Ethiopia

Funnel: *Green with yellow lion on brown eight-spoke wheel, deep red top.*
Hull: *Grey with red boot-topping.*

Name	Eng	Flag	Year	GRT	DWT	Loa	Bm	Kts	Type	Former names
Abbay Wonz		Eth	1984	11,292	15,107	137	23	16	C	ex Mengistu H.M.-84
Abyot		Eth	1985	11,292	15,107	137	23	16	C	
Admas		Eth	1986	11,573	13,593	150	22	16	C	ex Spica-95, Warszawa II-93
Andinet		Eth	1985	11,731	14,897	137	23	15	C	
Netsanet		Eth	1985	11,731	14,894	137	23	15	C	
Tekeze		Eth	1990	13,651	18,145	166	23	15	Co	ex Lim-99, Norviken-97, Moraca-95

Evergreen Marine Corp (Taiwan) Ltd
Taiwan

Funnel: *Black with green eight-pointed star above 'EVERGREEN' within brown globe outline on broad white band.*
Hull: *Black or dark green with red or green boot-topping.*

Name	Eng	Flag	Year	GRT	DWT	Loa	Bm	Kts	Type	Former names
Ever Able		Pan	1996	14,807	15,605	165	27	18	CC	
Ever Ally		Pan	1996	14,807	15,605	165	27	18	CC	
Ever Apex		Pan	1997	14,807	15,605	165	27	18	CC	
Ever Dainty		Pan	1997	52,700	55,604	294	32	25	CC	
Ever Decent		Pan	1997	52,090	55,604	294	32	25	CC	
Ever Delight		Pan	1998	52,090	55,515	294	32	25	CC	
Ever Deluxe		Pan	1998	52,090	54,300	294	32	25	CC	
Ever Develop		Pan	1998	52,090	55,515	294	32	25	CC	
Ever Devote		Pan	1998	52,090	55,604	294	32	25	CC	
Ever Diadem		Pan	1998	52,090	55,604	294	32	25	CC	
Ever Diamond		Pan	1998	52,090	55,515	294	32	25	CC	
Ever Divine		Pan	1998	52,090	55,604	294	32	25	CC	
Ever Dynamic		Pan	1998	52,090	55,515	294	32	25	CC	
Ever Gaining		Pan	1987	46,410	53,240	270	32	20	CC	
Ever Garden		Twn	1984	37,023	43,401	231	32	20	CC	
Ever Gather		Pan	1984	37,023	43,401	231	32	20	CC	ex LT Gather-04, Ever Gather-02, Cosco Durban-01, Ever Gather-00
Ever General		Pan	1987	46,410	53,240	270	32	20	CC	
Ever Genius		Twn	1984	37,023	43,401	231	32	20	CC	
Ever Gentle		Twn	1984	37,023	43,401	231	32	20	CC	
Ever Gentry		Twn	1984	37,023	43,401	231	32	20	CC	
Ever Giant		Pan	2004	37,023	43,198	231	32	20	CC	ex LT Giant-06, Ever Giant-99
Ever Gifted		Twn	1984	37,023	43,401	231	32	20	CC	
Ever Given		Pan	1986	46,410	53,240	270	32	20	CC	
Ever Gleamy		Pan	1985	37,023	43,401	231	32	20	CC	ex LT Gleamy-04, Ever Gleamy-02, LT Gleamy-00, Ever Gleamy-00
Ever Golden		Twn	1985	37,023	43,401	231	32	20	CC	
Ever Goods		Pan	1985	46,410	53,240	270	32	20	CC	
Ever Govern		Twn	1985	37,023	43,401	231	32	20	CC	
Ever Grade		Pan	1984	37,042	43,198	231	32	20	CC	
Ever Growth		Twn	1984	37,023	43,401	231	32	20	CC	
Ever Guard		Pan	1983	37,042	43,198	231	32	20	CC	ex LT Guard-05, Ever Guard-02, Cosco Santos-01, Ever Guard-00
Ever Guest		Pan	1986	46,410	53,240	270	32	21	CC	
Ever Guide		Pan	1983	37,042	43,198	231	32	20	CC	ex Cosco New York-02, Ever Guide-00

Name	Eng	Flag	Year	GRT	DWT	Loa	Bm	Kts	Type	Former names
Ever Peace		Pan	2002	17,887	19,309	182	28	18	CC	ex LT Peace-04, I/a Ever Peace
Ever Pearl		Pan	2002	17,887	19,309	182	28	18	CC	ex LT Pearl-04
Ever Power		Pan	2002	17,887	19,309	182	25	18	CC	ex LT Power-05, Ever Power-02
Ever Racer		Pan	1994	53,359	57,904	294	32	23	CC	
Ever Reach		Pan	1994	53,359	57,904	294	32	23	CC	
Ever Refine		Pan	1995	53,103	58,912	266	32	23	CC	
Ever Renown		Pan	1994	53,101	58,912	294	32	23	CC	
Ever Repute		Pan	1995	53,103	58,912	294	32	23	CC	
Ever Result		Pan	1994	53,103	58,912	294	32	23	CC	
Ever Reward		Pan	1994	53,103	58,912	294	32	23	CC	
Ever Safety		Pan	2006	75,200	78,700	300	43	-	CC	
Ever Salute		Pan	2006	75,200	78,700	300	43	-	CC	
Ever Steady		Pan	2006	75,200	78,700	300	43	-	CC	
Ever Strong		Pan	2006	75,200	78,700	300	43	-	CC	
Ever Summit		Pan	2006	75,200	78,700	300	43	-	CC	
Ever Uberty		Pan	1999	69,246	63,216	285	40	25	CC	
Ever Ultra		Pan	1996	69,218	63,388	285	40	24	CC	
Ever Unific		Pan	1999	69,246	63,216	285	40	25	CC	
Ever Union		Pan	1997	69,218	63,388	285	40	24	CC	
Ever Unique		Pan	1997	69,218	63,388	285	40	24	CC	
Ever Unison		Pan	1996	69,218	63,388	285	40	24	CC	
Ever United		Pan	1996	69,218	62,386	285	40	24	CC	ex LT United-03, Ever United-00
Ever Unity		Pan	1999	69,246	62,700	285	40	25	CC	ex LT Unity-04, Ever Unity-00
Ever Uranus		Pan	1999	69,246	63,216	285	40	24	CC	
Ever Urban		Pan	2000	69,200	63,216	285	40	24	CC	
Ever Ursula		Pan	1999	69,200	62,700	285	40	25	CC	ex LT Ursula-04, Ever Ursula-00
Ever Useful		Pan	1999	69,200	62,700	285	40	24	CC	
Ever Utile		Pan	2000	69,246	63,216	285	40	25	CC	ex LT Utile-05, Ever Utile-00
Green Modest		Pan	1976	12,406	16,858	163	23	15	CC	ex Uni-Modest-02, Access-84, Galleon Topaz-82, Ever Modest-80
Green Moral		Pan	1976	12,406	16,858	163	23	15	CC	ex Uni-Moral-02, Achieve-84, Galleon Opal-84, Galleon Onyx-81, Ever Moral-80
Hatsu Eagle *		Gbr	2001	76,022	75,898	300	43	25	CC	I/a Ever Eagle
Hatsu Elite *		Gbr	2002	76,022	75,898	300	43	25	CC	
Hatsu Envoy *		Gbr	2002	76,067	75,898	300	43	25	CC	I/a Ever Envoy
Hatsu Ethic *		Gbr	2002	76,067	75,898	300	43	24	CC	
Hatsu Excel *		Gbr	2002	76,022	75,898	300	43	25	CC	
Hatsu Pride *		Gbr	2003	17,887	19,309	182	28	19	CC	
Hatsu Prima *		Gbr	2003	17,887	19,309	182	28	18	CC	
Hatsu Shine *		Gbr	2005	75,246	78,693	300	43	-	CC	
Hatsu Sigma *		Gbr	2005	75,246	78,693	300	43	-	CC	
Hatsu Smart *		Gbr	2006	75,246	78,693	300	43	-	CC	
Hatsu Smile *		Gbr	2006	75,246	78,693	300	43	-	CC	
LT Ulysses		Pan	2000	69,200	62,700	285	40	25	CC	ex Ever Ulysses-00
LT Unicorn		Pan	2000	69,200	62,700	285	40	25	CC	I/a Ever Unicorn
Uni-Accord		Hkg	1997	14,796	15,300	165	27	18	CC	ex Cosco Redsea-02, Uni-Accord-01
Uni-Active		Twn	1998	14,796	15,300	165	27	18	CC	
Uni-Adroit		Twn	1998	14,807	15,511	165	27	18	CC	
Uni-Ahead		Pan	1997	14,796	15,477	165	27	18	CC	
Uni-Ample		Pan	1997	14,796	15,300	165	27	18	CC	
Uni-Angel		Pan	1997	14,796	15,300	165	27	18	CC	
Uni-Ardent		Pan	1998	14,807	15,511	165	27	18	CC	
Uni-Arise		Pan	1997	14,796	15,300	165	27	18	CC	
Uni-Aspire		Pan	1998	14,807	15,511	165	27	18	CC	
Uni-Assent		Pan	1999	14,807	15,511	165	27	18	CC	
Uni-Assure		Pan	1999	14,807	15,511	165	27	18	CC	
Uni-Chart		Pan	1992	12,405	17,446	152	26	17	CC	
Uni-Concert		Pan	1993	12,405	17,446	152	26	17	CC	
Uni-Concord		Pan	1992	12,405	17,445	153	26	17	CC	
Uni-Corona		Pan	1992	12,405	17,445	152	26	17	CC	
Uni-Crown		Pan	1992	12,404	17,446	152	26	17	CC	
Uni-Forever		Pan	1979	13,995	18,813	162	23	15	CC	ex Ever Forever-84, Green Forever-83
Uni-Order		Pan	1982	18,337	26,671	180	23	15	CC	ex Ever Order-94
Uni-Pacific		Pan	1999	17,887	19,309	182	28	18	CC	
Uni-Patriot		Pan	1999	17,887	19,309	182	28	18	CC	

Name	Eng	Flag	Year	GRT	DWT	Loa	Bm	Kts	Type	Former names
Uni-Perfect		Pan	2000	17,887	19,100	182	28	18	CC	
Uni-Phoenix		Pan	2000	18,300	19,100	182	28	18	CC	
Uni-Popular		Pan	2000	17,887	15,418	182	28	18	CC	
Uni-Premier		Pan	2001	17,887	19,309	182	28	18	CC	
Uni-Probity		Pan	2001	17,887	19,309	182	28	18	CC	
Uni-Promote		Pan	2001	17,887	19,308	182	28	18	CC	
Uni-Prosper		Pan	2001	17,887	19,309	182	28	18	CC	I/a Uni-Pioneer
Uni-Prudent		Pan	2000	17,887	19,309	182	28	18	CC	

newbuildings: eight 95,000 grt 98,500 dwt, one 53,000 grt and one 35,000 grt container ships for 2006-7 delivery
* owned by subsidiary Hatsu Marine Ltd., UK

Italiana Marittima SpA/Italy

Funnel: *Cream with blue 'LT' below narrow blue band, blue top.*
Hull: *Black with white 'L TRIESTINO' and green boot-topping.*

Name	Eng	Flag	Year	GRT	DWT	Loa	Bm	Kts	Type	Former names
Ital Garland		Ita	1988	46,445	44,424	270	32	20	CC	ex LT Garland-06, Ever Garland-99
Ital Universo		Ita	2001	68,888	63,216	285	40	25	CC	ex LT Universo-06
LT Genova *		Ita	1993	38,395	41,500	234	32	21	CC	ex Nuova Genova-01
LT Glamour		Ita	1987	46,445	53,240	270	32	20	CC	ex Ever Glamour-99
LI Going		Ita	1983	37,042	43,198	231	32	20	CC	ex Ever Going-99
LT Grace		Ita	1984	37,023	43,198	231	32	20	CC	ex Fver Grace-99
LT Greet		Ita	1984	37,042	43,293	231	32	20	CC	ex Ever Greet-99
LT Lloydiana *		Ita	1989	35,629	40,196	231	32	20	CC	ex Nuova Lloydiana-00, LT Lloydiana-00, Nuova Lloydiana-99
LT Trieste *		Ita	1993	38,395	41,700	234	32	21	CC	ex Nuova Trieste-00
LT Unica		Ita	2001	68,888	63,216	285	40	25	CC	
LT Usodimare		Ita	2000	69,200	63,216	285	40	25	CC	

* formerly owned now on charter from Technomar Shipping Inc, Greece.
other vessels believed to be renamed with 'Ital' prefix during 2006

Exxon Mobil Corp   USA

SeaRiver Maritime Inc/USA

Funnel: *Blue with narrow white band separated from upper broad red band by further narrow white band, narrow black top.*
Hull: *Black with red or blue boot-topping.*

Name	Eng	Flag	Year	GRT	DWT	Loa	Bm	Kts	Type	Former names
S/R American Progress		Usa	1997	26,092	45,435	183	32	14	T	ex American Progress-00
S/R Baytown		Usa	1984	32,136	59,625	238	32	15	T	ex Exxon Baytown-93
S/R Columbia Bay	(st)	Usa	1978	94,547	188,099	290	51	14	T	ex B.T. Alaska-03
S/R Hinchinbrook		Usa	1977	44,869	92,017	273	32	16	T	ex Overseas Ohio-00
S/R Long Beach		Usa	1987	94,999	214,853	301	51	16	T	ex Exxon Long Beach 93
S/R Wilmington		Usa	1984	27,508	48,779	194	32	16	T	ex Exxon Wilmington-93

International Marine Transportation Ltd/UK

Funnel: *Black with white 'IMT' on blue rectangle on large white disc.*
Hull: *Black or dark grey with red boot-topping.*

Name	Eng	Flag	Year	GRT	DWT	Loa	Bm	Kts	Type	Former names
Alrehab		Mhl	1999	160,279	301,620	335	58	15	T	
Eagle		Mhl	1993	160,347	284,493	332	58	16	T	
Hawk		Mhl	2000	159,414	306,320	335	58	16	T	
Kestrel		Mhl	2000	159,414	306,278	335	58	16	T	
Mediterranean		Mhl	1986	94,999	214,853	301	51	16	T	ex S/R Mediterranean-05, Exxon Mediterranean-93, Exxon Valdez-90
Osprey		Mhl	1999	160,279	284,893	335	58	16	T	
Ras Laffan		Mhl	1999	57,066	105,424	244	42	14	T	
Raven		Mhl	1996	160,348	301,653	332	58	15	T	
Valiant		Mhl	1999	57,066	105,476	244	42	14	T	

Fednav Ltd   Canada

Funnel: *White, red design incorporating part of maple leaf with interlinked 'F' and 'C', broad black top.*
Hull: *Red with dark red boot-topping.*

Name	Eng	Flag	Year	GRT	DWT	Loa	Bm	Kts	Type	Former names
Arctic		Can	1978	20,236	28,418	221	23	15	Obo	
Federal Agno		Phl	1985	17,821	29,643	183	23	14	BC	ex Federal Asahi-89
Federal Asahi ‡		Hkg	1999	20,659	36,500	200	24	14	B	
Federal Danube ‡		Cyp	2004	23,100	35,000	200	24	14	B	
Federal Elbe ‡		Cyp	2003	22,600	37,000	200	24	14	B	
Federal Ems ‡		Cyp	2002	22,654	37,058	200	24	14	B	

Name	Eng	Flag	Year	GRT	DWT	Loa	Bm	Kts	Type	Former names
Federal Hudson		Hkg	2000	20,659	36,563	200	24	14	B	
Federal Hunter		Hkg	2001	20,659	36,563	200	24	14	B	
Federal Kivalina		Hkg	2000	20,659	36,563	200	24	14	B	
Federal Kumano ‡		Hkg	2003	20,661	36,489	200	24	14	B	
Federal Kushiro ‡		Pan	2004	19,200	32,762	190	24	14	B	
Federal Leda ‡		Cyp	2003	22,600	37,000	200	24	14	B	
Federal Maas		Brb	1997	20,837	34,372	200	24	14	B	
Federal Manitou †		Atg	2004	18,825	27,783	185	24	-	B	
Federal Matane †		Atg	2004	18,825	27,780	185	24	-	B	
Federal Mattawa †		Lbr	2005	18,825	27,000	185	24	-	B	
Federal Miramichi †		Lbr	2006	18,825	27,000	185	24	-	B	
Federal Nakagawa ‡		Hkg	2005	20,661	36,489	200	24	14	B	
Federal Oshima		Hkg	1999	20,500	36,563	200	24	14	B	
Federal Progress		Hkg	1989	21,469	36,445	177	30	14	B	
Federal Rhine		Brb	1997	20,837	34,372	200	23	14	B	
Federal Rideau		Hkg	2000	20,500	36,563	200	24	14	B	
Federal Saguenay		Brb	1996	20,837	34,372	200	23	14	B	
Federal Schelde		Brb	1997	20,837	34,372	200	23	14	B	
Federal Shimanto ‡		Pan	2001	19,125	32,787	190	24	14	B	
Federal St. Laurent		Brb	1996	20,837	34,372	200	23	14	B	
Federal Venture		Hkg	1989	21,469	36,445	177	30	14	B	ex Northern Venture-02
Federal Welland		Hkg	2000	20,659	35,750	200	24	14	B	
Federal Weser ‡		Cyp	2002	21,300	35,000	200	24	14	B	
Federal Yoshino ‡		Pan	2001	19,125	32,845	190	24	14	B	
Federal Yukon		Hkg	2000	20,659	36,563	200	24	14	B	
Lake Erie		Mhl	1980	22,734	38,294	223	23	14	B	ex Federal Ottawa-95
Lake Michigan		Mhl	1981	22,734	38,294	222	23	14	B	ex Federal Maas-95
Lake Ontario		Mhl	1980	22,734	38,294	222	23	14	B	ex Federal Danube-95
Lake Superior		Mhl	1981	22,734	38,294	222	23	14	B	ex Federal Thames-95
Orsula ‡		Hrv	1996	20,837	34,198	200	24	14	B	ex Federal Calumet-97

newbuildings: one 19,000 grt 31,500 dwt and seven chartered 52-56,000 dwt bulk carriers for 2006-8 delivery.
managed by Anglo-Eastern Ship Management Ltd. Hong Kong. Also has 50% interest in The CSL Group Inc (Canada Steamship Lines)
† chartered from Sunship Schiffahrts subsidiary of Reederei M Lauterjung KG, Germany or ‡ from various other owners. Nearly 40 other vessels chartered from
Onassis, Rendsburg (Karl Schluter), Spar Shipping or Viken Ship Management (Ludwig Mowinckels Rederi) .

Frontline Ltd Bermuda

Funnel: White with light blue 'f' symbol on dark blue vertical rectangle above 'FRONTLINE'.
Hull: Black, brown or light blue with red or dark blue boot-topping.

Name	Eng	Flag	Year	GRT	DWT	Loa	Bm	Kts	Type	Former names
Altair Voyager †		Bhs	1993	80,914	135,829	259	48	15	T	ex Condoleezza Rice-01
Ariake		Bhs	2001	159,397	298,530	333	60	15	T	ex Berge Ariake-01
Cygnus Voyager †		Bhs	1993	88,919	156,835	275	50	15	T	ex Samuel Ginn-03
Edinburgh		Lbr	1993	156,408	302,493	332	58	15	T	ex Golar Edinburgh-01
Front Ace		Lbr	1993	144,652	275,546	325	57	15	T	ex General Ace-00, Sea Princess-93
Front Ardenne		Nis	1998	79,633	152,550	258	46	15	T	ex Ardenne-00
Front Birch		Nis	1991	78,443	151,680	267	46	14	T	ex Birch-99
Front Brabant		Nis	1998	79,633	152,550	269	46	15	T	ex Brabant-00
Front Breaker		Nis	1991	89,004	169,146	285	45	14	Obo	
Front Climber		Sgp	1991	89,004	169,146	285	45	14	Obo	
Front Comanche		Atf	1999	159,423	300,133	333	60	15	T	ex Stena Comanche-01
Front Comor		Nis	1993	77,931	142,031	269	45	14	T	ex Comor-99
Front Driver		Nis	1991	89,004	169,146	285	45	14	Obo	
Front Duchess		Sgp	1993	149,997	284,480	322	56	14	T	ex Sea Duchess-96
Front Duke		Sgp	1992	149,945	284,420	322	56	14	T	ex Sea Duke-96
Front Energy		Cyp	2004	164,300	305,213	330	60	-	T	ex Sea Energy-05, I/a Mt. Pertamina 2
Front Falcon		Bhs	2002	160,904	308,875	333	58	-	T	I/a Mosfalcon
Front Force **		Cyp	2004	156,873	305,442	330	60	-	T	ex Sea Force-05, I/a Mt. Pertamina 1
Front Glory		Nis	1995	79,979	149,834	269	46	15	T	ex London Glory-97
Front Granite		Nis	1991	77,931	142,031	269	45	14	T	ex Granite-01
Front Guider		Sgp	1991	89,004	169,146	285	45	14	Obo	
Front Highness		Sgp	1991	149,945	284,317	322	56	14	T	ex Sea Highness-96
Front Horizon		Mhl	1988	80,274	134,832	279	46	-	T	ex New Horizon-04
Front Lady		Sgp	1991	149,945	284,497	322	56	14	T	ex Sea Lady-96
Front Leader		Sgp	1991	89,004	169,146	285	45	14	Obo	
Front Lord		Sgp	1991	149,945	282,057	322	56	14	T	ex Sea Lord-96
Front Maple		Nis	1991	78,443	151,680	267	46	14	T	ex Maple-99

Name	Eng	Flag	Year	GRT	DWT	Loa	Bm	Kts	Type	Former names
Front Page		Lbr	2002	156,916	299,164	330	60	-	T	I/a Front Saga
Front Pride		Nis	1993	79,978	149,686	269	46	15	T	ex London Pride-98
Front Rider		Sgp	1992	89,004	169,146	285	45	14	Obo	
Front Sabang		Sgp	1990	153,644	285,715	328	57	14	T	ex Sabang-00, Damar-94, Argo Dione-91
Front Scilla		Iom	2000	160,805	302,561	333	60	16	T	ex Oscilla-05
Front Serenade		Lbr	2002	157,000	298,300	333	60	16	T	
Front Splendour		Nis	1995	79,979	148,835	269	46	15	T	ex London Splendour-97
Front Stratus		Lbr	2002	156,916	299,157	330	60	-	T	
Front Striver		Sgp	1992	89,004	169,204	285	45	14	Obo	
Front Sunda		Nis	1992	77,931	142,031	269	45	14	T	ex Sunda-99
Front Target **		Nis	1990	77,931	142,031	269	45	14	T	ex Genmar Centaur-04, Crude Target-03, Nord-Jahre Target-00, Jahre Target-93
Front Tobago ‡		Lbr	1993	147,580	260,619	333	56	15	T	ex Toba-00
Front Transporter **		Nis	1989	77,870	142,053	269	45	14	T	ex Genmar Transporter-04, Crude Transporter-03, Nord-Jahre Transporter-00, Jahre Transporter-93
Front Traveller §		Nis	1990	77,931	142,031	269	45	14	T	ex GenmarTraveller-04, Crude Traveller-03, Nord-Jahre Traveller-00, Jahre Traveller-93
Front Vanadis		Sgp	1990	153,413	285,872	327	57	14	T	ex Vanadis-00
Front Vanguard		Mhl	1998	159,423	300,058	333	60	14	T	ex New Vanguard-04
Front Viewer		Sgp	1992	89,004	169,146	285	45	14	Obo	
Front Vista		Mhl	1998	159,423	300,149	333	60	14	T	ex New Vista-04
Marble **		Bhs	1992	77,931	152,000	269	45	14	T	
Mindanao		Sgp	1998	81,265	147,447	274	48	15	T	
Navix Astral		Pan	1996	144,127	275,644	324	56	15	T	
Ocana ††		Iom	1999	159,423	300,144	333	60	16	T	ex Front Commerce-04, Stena Commerce-01
Omala ††		Pan	1999	163,346	306,009	333	58	15	T	ex New Circassia-04, I/a Golden Circassia
Opalia ††		Iom	1999	159,756	302,193	333	60	15	T	
Otina ††		Iom	2002	159,383	298,465	333	60	15	T	ex Hakata-04
Sirius Voyager			Bhs	1994	88,919	156,382	275	50	15	T	ex Chevron Mariner-02
Virgo Voyager †		Bhs	1992	88,946	155,127	275	50	15	T	ex William E. Crain-02

Controlled by John Fredriksen owned Hemen Holdings, which has 64% control of * Seatankers Management Co. Ltd, Cyprus and 11% interest in General Maritime Corporation q.v.
Managed by V Ships (UK) Ltd, V Ships Norway AS, International Tanker Management Holding Ltd, UAE or Thome Ship Management.
** managed by Frontline Management AS, Norway and ‡ jointly owned by Overseas Shipholding (30%) and CMB-Euronav (30%) q.v.
† chartered to ChevronTexaco Shipping LLC or †† to Royal Dutch-Shell Group.
§ owned by The OSM Group, Norway and managed by Wallem Shipmanagement Inc, USA
Also see Euronav SA (under CMB) and other chartered ships with 'Front' prefix in index.

Golar LNG Ltd/Bermuda

Name	Eng	Flag	Year	GRT	DWT	Loa	Bm	Kts	Type	Former names
Gimi	(st)	Gbr	1976	96,235	72,703	294	42	19	Lgc	
Golar Freeze	(st)	Gbr	1977	95,879	66,200	288	43	20	Lng	
Golar Frost	(st)	Lbr	2004	115,156	67,100	288	68	119	Lng	
Golar Mazo	(st)	Lbr	2000	111,835	76,210	290	47	19	Lng	
Golar Spirit	(st)	Gbr	1981	106,577	80,239	289	45	19	Lng	
Golar Viking	(st)	Mhl	2005	93,750	79,950	280	43	19	Lng	
Golar Winter	(st)	Gbr	2004	93,899	80,810	277	43	19	Lng	
Hilli	(st)	Gbr	1975	96,235	72,703	293	42	19	Lgc	ex Golar Glacier-75
Khannur	(st)	Gbr	1977	96,235	73,074	293	42	19	Lgc	
Methane Princess	(st)	Gbr	2003	93,899	77,707	277	43	-	Lng	

newbuildings: three 95,800 grt 145,700 cm Lng tankers on order.
Also operates LNG vessels in joint venture with Exmar q.v.

General Maritime Corporation LLC   USA

Funnel: Black with yellow 'G' on yellow edged green diamond on yellow edged broad blue band.
Hull: Black with red boot-topping.

Name	Eng	Flag	Year	GRT	DWT	Loa	Bm	Kts	Type	Former names
Genmar Agamemnon		Lbr	1995	53,829	96,213	243	42	14	T	ex Emilie-98
Genmar Ajax		Lbr	1996	53,829	96,183	243	42	14	T	ex Julie-98
Genmar Alexandra		Mhl	1992	56,012	102,262	241	42	14	T	ex Nordpacific-00, Skaunord-00
Genmar Argus		Mhl	2000	81,151	159,901	274	48	15	T	ex Crude Tria-03
Genmar Constantine		Lbr	1992	56,021	102,262	241	42	14	T	ex Artois-98, Seahope D.Y.-96
Genmar Defiance *		Lbr	2002	56,225	105,538	239	42	15	T	ex Peneda-04
Genmar Gabriel		Mhl	1990	52,512	94,993	247	42	14	T	ex Silver Venus-99, Pacific Saturn-97
Genmar Gulf		Mhl	1991	81,135	141,844	274	48	14	T	ex Crudegulf-03, landsort-97
Genmar Harriet G		Lbr	2006	79,325	150,205	274	48	14	T	
Genmar Hope		Sgp	1999	81,526	159,539	274	48	15	T	ex Crude Hope-03, Nord Hope-00

Fednav. FEDERAL HUNTER. *Hans Kraijenbosch*

Frontline (Golar LNG). GOLAR SPIRIT. *Hans Kraijenbosch*

The Great Eastern Shipping Co. JAG PRADIP. *Hans Kraijenbosch*

Grimaldi Group. GRANDE AMBURGO. *Hans Kraijenbosch*

Grimaldi Group. GRANDE SCANDINAVIA. *Phil Kempsey*

Hapag-Lloyd. SAVANNAH EXPRESS. *Hans Kraijenbosch*

Name	Eng	Flag	Year	GRT	DWT	Loa	Bm	Kts	Type	Former names
Genmar Horn		Mhl	1999	81,526	159,474	274	48	15	T	ex Crude Horn-03, Nord Horn-00
Genmar Kara G		Lbr	2006	79,300	150,200	274	48	14	T	
Genmar Minotaur		Lbr	1995	53,829	96,213	243	42	14	T	ex Stephanie-98
Genmar Orion		Mhl	2002	81,381	159,992	274	48	-	T	ex Crude Okto-03, Antares-02
Genmar Phoenix		Mhl	1999	80,058	153,015	269	46	15	T	ex Crude Ena—03
Genmar Princess		Lbr	1991	52,164	96,765	228	42	14	T	ex Crude Princess-04, Genmar Princess-03, Crude Princess-03, Nord-Jahre Princess-00, Jahre Princess-93
Genmar Progress		Lbr	1991	52,164	96,765	228	42	14	T	ex Crude Progress-04, Genmar Progress-03, Crude Progress-03, Nord-Jahre Progress-00, Jahre Progress-93
Genmar Revenge *		Lbr	1994	53,773	96,755	244	42	14	T	ex Sintra-04, Astro Perseus-00, Yuhsei Maru-99
Genmar Spyridon		Mhl	2000	81,151	159,959	274	48	15	T	ex Crude Dio-03
Genmar Strength *		Lbr	2003	56,225	105,674	239	42	15	T	ex Portel-04
Genmar Sun *		Mhl	1985	50,272	89,636	244	40	15	T	ex Stavanger Sun-00, Glefi III-90, Atlantic Amity-90

* owned by subsidiary General Maritime Management (Portugal) Lda (formerly Soponata SA)

The Great Eastern Shipping Co. Ltd.   India

Funnel: Yellow with 'AHB' on white diamond on red and green diagonally divided houseflag, narrow black top.
Hull: Grey or black with 'Great Eastern', red boot-topping.

Name	Eng	Flag	Year	GRT	DWT	Loa	Bm	Kts	Type	Former names
Ardeshir H Bhiwandiwalla		Ind	1992	146,541	264,301	322	58	15	T	ex Seaking-04, Izusan Maru-00
Jag Anjali		Ind	1986	36,512	66,203	230	32	14	T	ex Suzanne-03
Jag Arnav *		Ind	1995	38,265	71,122	225	32	14	B	ex Floral Deigo-01
Jag Arpan		Ind	1986	36,512	66,183	230	32	14	T	
Jag Laadki		Ind	1992	78,710	145,242	270	44	14	T	ex Knock Adoon-93
Jag Labh		Ind	1988	52,247	96,551	232	42	15	T	ex Sealoyalty-05, Tromaas-01
Jag Lakshya		Lbr	1989	79,552	139,753	267	46	14	T	ex Geres Knock-04, Sheen-99
Jag Lalit		Ind	2005	81,396	158,344	274	48	-	T	
Jag Lamha		Ind	1987	52,764	98,214	247	42	14	T	ex Sudong Spirit-03, Full Moon River-95
Jag Lata		Ind	2003	57,508	105,709	244	43	14	T	
Jag Lavanya		Ind	2004	58,400	105,000	244	43	14	T	
Jag Laxmi		Ind	1999	58,374	105,051	243	42	14	T	
Jag Leela		Ind	1999	58,374	105,148	243	42	14	T	
Jag Leena		Ind	1985	55,903	95,007	246	44	14	T	ex Magellan Spirit-03, Nikko Maru-95
Jag Leher		Ind	1986	58,853	107,544	246	43	14	T	ex Genmar Pacific-03, North Pacific-03, Nord Pacific-93
Jag Lok		Ind	2005	81,396	158,280	274	48	-	T	
Jag Padma *		Ind	1982	27,771	47,803	183	32	15	T	ex Paula Maersk-92
Jag Pahel		Ind	2004	27,627	46,321	183	32	14	T	
Jag Palak *		Ind	1985	18,542	27,402	170	26	15	T	
Jag Pankhi		Ind	2003	27,627	46,272	183	32	14	T	
Jag Pari *		Ind	1982	20,302	28,679	171	27	14	T	
Jag Pavitra		Ind	1985	28,010	50,600	183	32	15	T	ex Olivia Maersk-97, Evelyn Maersk-93
Jag Prachi		Ind	1996	25,202	44,124	182	30	14	T	ex Torm Lily-01
Jag Pradip		Ind	1996	27,627	45,683	183	32	14	T	
Jag Pragati		Ind	1985	18,542	27,402	170	26	15	T	
Jag Praja		Ind	1982	17,199	29,990	171	26	15	T	ex Rossi-95, Novorossiysk-91, World Product-82
Jag Pranam		Ind	1984	28,010	50,600	183	32	15	T	ex A.P. Moller-96
Jag Pratap		Ind	1995	27,627	45,692	183	32	14	T	
Jag Prayog		Ind	1982	17,199	29,990	171	26	15	T	ex Stavropol-95
Jag Preeti *		Ind	1981	20,302	29,138	171	27	14	T	
Jag Rahul *		Ind	2003	30,011	52,239	190	32	-	B	ex Philipp Oldendorff-05
Jag Rani *		Ind	1984	24,643	41,545	183	31	14	B	ex Malaya-99, Spring Stork-96, Sanko Stork-86
Jag Ratna *		Ind	1977	21,396	35,100	185	27	14	B	ex Captain John D.Pateras-89, Pantanassa-79
Jag Ravi		Ind	1997	26,322	45,342	190	32	-	B	ex Sea Satin-05, Oriental Express-02
Jag Reena *		Ind	1999	26,010	45,659	186	30	-	B	ex Cora Oldendorff-05
Jag Rishi *		Ind	1984	24,111	41,093	185	30	14	B	ex Spring Peacock-96, Sanko Peacock-86
Jag Vayu		Ind	1978	21,308	28,400	192	26	19	Lpg	ex Herdis-97, Helios-91, Lord Kelvin-87
Jag Vidya *		Ind	1977	16,926	27,490	170	26	15	B	ex Amita-88, Syra-87
Jag Vikas *		Ind	1977	16,393	26,781	177	23	16	B	ex Polychronis-89
Jag Vikram *		Ind	1980	16,910	27,463	170	26	15	B	ex Jag Kranti-89, Radhika-87, Mia-86
Jag Viraj		Ind	1991	17,778	17,577	160	26	15	Lpg	ex Gaz Diamond-04, Spic Diamond-00

Name	Eng	Flag	Year	GRT	DWT	Loa	Bm	Kts	Type	Former names
Nisha †		Vct	1977	16,931	27,481	170	26	15	B	ex Jag Vishnu-98, Gayatri-88, Petropolis-87, Triton-82

newbuildings - three 23,200 grt 37,000 dwt and three 30,028 grt 47,400 dwt taners for 2007 delivery.
* managed by Five Stars Shipping Co. Pte. Ltd., or † by The Great Eastern Shipping Co. London Ltd., UK

Grimaldi Group   Italy

Funnel: *Yellow with red 'Gt' symbol or blue with either white 'I' or 'A' symbol or white 'S' within white ring.*
Hull: *Yellow with black 'GRIMALDI LINES' on white upperworks, red boot-topping.*

Name	Eng	Flag	Year	GRT	DWT	Loa	Bm	Kts	Type
Gran Bretagna *		Ita	1999	51,714	18,461	181	32	18	Ro
Grand Benelux *		Ita	2001	37,712	12,594	176	31	20	Ro
Grande Africa		Ita	1998	56,642	26,195	214	32	18	Ro
Grande Amburgo §		Ita	2003	56,642	26,170	214	32	18	Ro
Grande America		Mlt	1997	56,642	26,169	214	32	18	Ro
Grande Anversa		Ita	2004	38,651	12,353	177	31	20	Ro
Grande Atlantico		Ita	1999	56,640	26,170	214	32	18	Ro
Grande Buenos Aires		Swe	2004	56,642	26,169	214	32	18	Ro
Grande Detriot		Ita	2005	38,651	12,353	176	31	20	Ro
Grande Ellade *		Ita	2001	52,000	18,440	181	32	18	Ro
Grande Europa *		Ita	1998	51,714	18,461	181	32	18	Ro
Grande Francia §		Ita	2002	56,642	26,170	214	32	18	Ro
Grande Italia *		Ita	2001	37,712	12,594	176	31	20	Ro
Grande Lagos *		Ita	2004	44,408	13,740	196	31	19	Ro
Grande Mediterraneo *		Ita	1998	51,714	18,427	181	32	18	Ro
Grande Napoli		Ita	2003	42,600	14,900	201	31	20	Ro
Grande Nigeria §		Ita	2002	56,642	26,170	214	32	18	Ro
Grande Portogallo *		Ita	2002	37,712	12,594	176	31	20	Ro
Grande Roma		Ita	2003	42,600	14,900	201	31	20	Ro
Grande San Paolo		Ita	2003	56,642	26,170	214	32	18	Ro
Grande Scandinavia *		Ita	2001	52,000	18,440	181	32	18	Ro
Grande Sicilia *		Ita	2006	41,900	14,900	179	31	20	Ro
Grande Spagna *		Ita	2002	37,712	12,594	176	31	20	Ro
Repubblica Argentina †		Ita	1998	51,925	23,882	206	30	20	Ro
Repubblica del Brasile †		Ita	1998	51,925	23,800	206	30	20	Ro
Repubblica di Amalfi		Ita	1989	42,574	25,450	216	30	18	Ro
Repubblica di Genova *		Ita	1988	42,567	25,450	216	30	18	Ro
Repubblica di Roma §		Ita	1992	42,001	19,287	184	30	19	Ro
Repubblica di Venezia †		Ita	1987	48,622	18,730	213	30	18	Ro

newbuildings: three 55,000 grt and three 41,900 grt ro-ro vessels for 2006-7 delivery
Ships owned by related Italian companies * Atlantica SpA di Navigazione, † by Grandi Traghetti SpA di Navigazione or § by Industria Armamento Meridionale SpA, who also operate other ferries and ro-ro vessels in the Mediterranean.

ACL Shipmanagement AB/Sweden

Funnel: *White with blue 'ACL' over wavy line, black top.*
Hull: *Black with white 'ACL' symbol.*

Name	Eng	Flag	Year	GRT	DWT	Loa	Bm	Kts	Type	Former names
Atlantic Cartier		Swe	1985	58,358	51,648	292	32	17	Ro	
Atlantic Companion		Swe	1984	57,255	51,648	292	32	17	Ro	ex Companion Express-94, Atlantic Companion-87
Atlantic Compass		Swe	1984	57,255	51,648	292	32	17	Ro	
Atlantic Concert		Swe	1984	57,255	51,648	292	32	17	Ro	ex Concert Express-94, Atlantic Concert-87
Atlantic Conveyor		Swe	1985	58,438	51,648	292	32	17	Ro	
Grande Argentina		Swe	2001	56,642	26,170	214	32	18	Ro	
Grande Brasile		Ita	2000	56,642	26,170	214	32	18	Ro	

Hanjin Shipping Co Ltd   South Korea

Funnel: *Orange with white 'H' inside white ring.*
Hull: *Black with white 'HANJIN', red boot-topping.*

Name	Eng	Flag	Year	GRT	DWT	Loa	Bm	Kts	Type
Alexander Carl		Pan	1993	110,627	208,189	312	50	13	B
Empress **		Pan	1992	76,925	151,662	274	45	13	B
Frontier **		Pan	1992	76,925	151,492	274	45	13	B
Goodwill **		Pan	1992	75,277	149,401	269	43	14	B
Hanjin Antwerp *		Kor	1996	16,252	27,367	167	26	14	B
Hanjin Beijing *		Kor	1996	65,893	67,115	279	40	25	CC
Hanjin Berlin *		Kor	1997	66,403	67,236	279	40	25	CC
Hanjin Bombay *		Kor	1994	16,252	27,029	167	26	14	B

Name	Eng	Flag	Year	GRT	DWT	Loa	Bm	Kts	Type	Former names
Hanjin Brisbane *		Kor	1997	16,252	27,327	167	26	14	B	
Hanjin Busan †		Cyp	1979	17,682	18,782	201	24	18	CC	
Hanjin Calcutta *		Kor	1997	16,270	27,365	167	26	14	B	
Hanjin Capetown		Pan	1993	76,954	147,631	274	45	13	B	
Hanjin Dampier		Kor	1989	110,541	207,346	309	50	13	B	
Hanjin Gladstone		Lbr	1990	110,541	207,391	309	50	13	B	
Hanjin Haypoint		Kor	1990	77,650	151,431	274	45	13	B	
Hanjin Houston *		Kor	1995	16,232	27,209	167	26	14	B	
Hanjin Istanbul *		Kor	1997	16,270	27,369	167	26	14	B	
Hanjin Kaohsiung ‡		Cyp	1990	37,134	43,925	243	32	22	CC	
Hanjin Kwangyang †		Cyp	1978	14,953	20,195	187	25	17	CC	ex Ever Victory-83
Hanjin London *		Kor	1996	66,687	67,298	279	40	26	CC	
Hanjin Los Angeles		Pan	1997	51,754	62,700	290	32	24	CC	
Hanjin Madras		Kor	1990	77,650	150,431	274	45	13	B	
Hanjin Malta		Kor	1993	51,299	62,649	290	32	24	CC	
Hanjin Marseilles		Pan	1993	51,299	62,681	290	32	24	CC	
Hanjin Melbourne		Kor	1987	93,643	186,260	292	48	13	B	ex Westin Seven-89
Hanjin Muscat	(st)	Pan	1999	93,765	75,463	280	43	20	Lng	
Hanjin Nagoya		Pan	1998	51,754	62,500	290	32	24	CC	
Hanjin New Orleans		Kor	1994	37,550	70,337	225	32	13	B	
Hanjin Oslo		Pan	1998	65,469	68,993	279	40	25	CC	
Hanjin Paris		Pan	1997	66,687	68,500	279	40	25	CC	
Hanjin Penang *		Kor	1997	16,270	27,369	167	26	14	B	
Hanjin Pittsburg		Kor	1990	25,461	38,393	186	28	15	B	ex Pittsburg-93
Hanjin Pohang †		Cyp	1979	17,933	18,798	201	24	17	CC	
Hanjin Port Kembla		Pan	1993	68,243	126,267	264	41	13	B	
Hanjin Portland		Kor	1993	50,792	62,716	290	32	24	CC	
Hanjin Pyeong Taek	(st)	Pan	1995	90,004	71,041	269	43	19	Lng	
Hanjin Ras Laffan	(st)	Pan	2000	93,769	75,079	280	43	20	Lng	
Hanjin Richards Bay		Pan	1997	75,752	149,322	269	43	14	B	
Hanjin Roberts Bank		Pan	1994	73,706	135,069	268	43	14	B	
Hanjin Rome		Pan	1998	65,469	68,955	280	40	25	CC	
Hanjin San Francisco *		Kor	1996	50,792	62,681	290	32	24	CC	
Hanjin Seoul †		Cyp	1979	17,675	18,835	201	24	17	CC	
Hanjin Shanghai		Pan	1995	50,792	62,799	290	32	24	CC	
Hanjin Sur	(st)	Pan	2000	93,769	75,193	280	43	20	Lng	
Hanjin Sydney		Kor	1987	95,513	188,117	291	48	13	B	ex Westin Nine-89
Hanjin Tacoma		Pan	1994	37,550	70,347	225	32	13	B	
Hanjin Tampa *		Kor	1995	16,252	27,209	167	26	14	B	
Hanjin Valencia		Pan	1998	51,754	62,799	290	32	24	CC	
Hanjin Vancouver ‡		Cyp	1990	35,745	44,764	241	32	20	CC	ex Hanjin Hamburg-90
Hanjin Washington		Pan	1997	65,643	67,272	279	40	25	CC	
Hanjin Wilmington		Pan	1997	50,792	62,799	290	32	24	CC	
Keoyang Majesty **		Pan	1997	43,181	48,618	221	32	15	Bw	
Keoyang Noble **		Pan	1997	43,181	51,662	221	32	15	Bw	
Keoyang Orient **		Pan	1997	75,752	149,322	269	43	14	B	
Pos Bravery **		Kor	1992	110,593	207,096	309	50	13	B	
Pos Challenger **		Pan	1992	75,277	140,302	269	43	13	B	
Pos Dedicator **		Kor	1993	110,627	208,393	312	50	13	B	
Pos Harvester **		Pan	1992	75,277	140,302	269	43	13	B	

newbuildings: eight 74,000 grt container ships for 2006-8 delivery.
* owned by Korea French Banking Corp. (formed jointly with Societe Generale SA) and by subsidary ** Keoyang Shipping Co. Ltd.
Formerly owned now chartered from † Varship Shipping Co. Ltd., or ‡ from Samartzis Maritime Enterprises Co. SA, both Greece

Senator Lines GmbH/Germany
80% owned affiliate company only operating chartered vessels.
See chartered vessels with 'Senator' suffix under Reederei F. Laeisz GmbH and NSB Niederelbe Schiffahrts. GmbH & Co. KG and in index.

Hansa Mare Reederei GmbH & Co KG   Germany

Funnel: *Black with red dot over blue wave on broad white band or charterers colours.*
Hull: *Blue or grey with red boot-topping.*

Name	Eng	Flag	Year	GRT	DWT	Loa	Bm	Kts	Type	Former names
APL Argentina		Atg	2000	40,306	52,250	261	32	22	CC	ex YM Savannah-04, Trade Hallie-03, Mare Caribicum-01
APL Chile		Atg	2000	40,306	52,250	261	32	22	CC	ex Mare Arcticum-04, YM New York-04, Trade Tesia-03, Mare Arcticum-01

Name	Eng	Flag	Year	GRT	DWT	Loa	Bm	Kts	Type	Former names
APL Panama		Atg	2000	40,306	52,250	261	32	22	CC	ex Mare Arcticum-04, YM Wilmington-04, Trade Freda-03, I/a Mare Britannicum
APL Peru *		Atg	2002	41,834	53,554	266	32	-	CC	ex Delaware Bridge-05, HLL Atlantic-03
CMA CGM Rodin **		Atg	2001	27,093	33,220	210	30	22	CC	I/a Ansgaritor
Dalian Express		Atg	1998	40,306	52,329	261	32	24	CC	ex Maersk Tirana-06, P&O Nedlloyd Cartagena-05, Elbe Bridge-04, Mare Superum-98
HHL Biscay *		Atg	2006	14,000	19,980	164	23	15	T	
Ibuki †		Atg	1994	16,266	22,494	168	25	19	CC	ex Mare Ibericum-04, Indamex Impala-03, ANL Impala-01, Mare Ibericum-01, Carina Challenger-01, Mare Ibericum-97, CSAV Ranco-97, Mare Ibericum-94
Kota Ekspres		Atg	1997	29,383	34,670	196	32	22	CC	ex Mare Africum-02
Maersk Dammam *		Atg	2003	41,834	53,511	266	32	-	CC	I/a HLL Pacific
Maersk Dublin *		Atg	1995	50,698	62,441	292	32	24	CC	ex Dragor Maersk-02
Maersk Petersburg		Atg	1997	29,383	34,705	196	32	22	CC	ex Mare Thracium-04, MSC Oregon-01, Mare Thracium-00
Maersk Peterhead		Atg	1997	29,750	34,800	196	32	21	CC	ex OOCL Harmony-04, Mare Ionium-00
Maersk Pittsburg		Atg	1997	29,383	34,705	196	32	22	CC	ex Mare Internum-04
Maersk Portland		Atg	1995	29,383	34,625	196	32	21	CC	ex Mare Caspium-04, ANL China-02, NYK Minerva-01, Mare Caspium-00
Maersk Tangier		Atg	1998	40,306	52,357	261	32	25	CC	ex P&O Nedlloyd Tiger-05, Weser Bridge-04, I/a Mare Siculum
Mare Adriaticum		Atg	1993	9,581	12,721	150	23	17	CC	ex Mekong Stream-03, Mare Adriaticum-03, ACX Wagle-02, Mare Adriaticum-00, Rotterdam Stad-98, Mare Adriaticum-97, Sea Nordic-95, Independent Trader-94, Mare Adriaticum-94
Mare Balticum		Atg	1993	9,584	12,712	150	23	17	CC	ex X-Press Konkan-02, Mare Balticum-01, Saudi Dammam-99, Mare Balticum-99, Maersk Euro Octavo-94, Mare Balticum-93
Mare Doricum		Atg	1995	9,590	12,705	150	22	17	CC	ex ACX Falcon-02, Mare Doricum-00, Dreda Stad 98, Mare Doricum-97, Sea Nordic-95, Mare Doricum-95
Mare Gallicum		Deu	1996	29,383	34,671	196	32	22	CC	ex Ipex Emperor-02, OOCL Haven-01, Mare Gallicum-00, Acapulco-98, TMM Acapulco-97, Mare Gallicum-96
Mare Hibernum		Atg	1995	9,600	12,571	150	22	17	CC	ex ACX Seagull-02, Saudi Buraydah-00, Mare Hibernum-98
Mare Phoenicium		Atg	1999	40,306	52,330	261	32	24	CC	ex Ems Bridge 01, I/a Mare Phoenicium
MCT Alioth *		Lbr	1999	12,358	17,563	149	24	15	T	ex Alioth-04
MCT Almak *		Lbr	1999	12,358	17,561	149	24	15	T	ex Almak-03
MCT Altair *		Lbr	1999	12,358	17,553	149	24	15	T	ex Altair-03
MCT Arcturus *		Lbr	1999	12,358	17,563	149	24	15	T	ex Arcturus-03
MCT Matterhorn *		Atg	2006	14,000	19,980	164	23	15	T	I/a HLL Arctic
Mekong Spirit		Atg	1996	9,616	12,705	150	22	17	CC	ex MSC Biscay-05, Mare Tuscum-01, Ankara-01, DNOL Ankara-99, Mare Tuscum-98, CGM Jean Laborde-98, Mare Tuscum-97
MSC Scandinavia		Atg	2000	40,306	52,250	261	32	24	CC	ex Donau Bridge-04, Mare Atlanticum-01
Mumbai Express		Atg	1999	40,306	47,660	261	32	24	CC	ex Mare Lycium-06, P&O Nedlloyd Cobra-05, Mare Lycium-03, Mosel Bridge-02, I/a Mare Lycium

newbuildings - four 41,800 grt container ships and six further 14,000 grt 18,500 dwt tankers for 2007-8 delivery.
*Company jointly owned by * Hanseatic Lloyd Reederei and ** Schlussel Reederei KG, both Germany.*
† managed by Uniteam Marine Shipping, Germany.

Hapag-Lloyd AG   Germany

Funnel: *Orange with blue 'HL' symbol.*
Hull: *Black with white 'Hapag-Lloyd' and red boot-topping.*

Name	Eng	Flag	Year	GRT	DWT	Loa	Bm	Kts	Type	Former names
Antwerpen Express		Deu	2000	54,437	67,145	294	32	24	CC	ex Tokyo Express-99
Berlin Express		Deu	2002	88,493	100,019	320	43	26	CC	
Bonn Express		Deu	1989	35,919	45,977	236	32	20	CC	
Brasil Express †		Pan	1997	13,448	15,421	160	25	18	CC	ex Sanuki-05
Bremen Express		Deu	2000	54,465	66,971	294	32	24	CC	

Name	Eng	Flag	Year	GRT	DWT	Loa	Bm	Kts	Type	Former names
Caribia Express **		Bhs	1992	21,053	30,078	182	28	19	CC	ex Cap Vilano-04, Libra Brasil-03, P&O Nedlloyd Pinta-02, P&O Nedlloyd Tema-00, Santa Rosa-99, Panatlantic-97, Santa Rosa-97, Nedlloyd van Rees-96, Santa Rosa 95
Colombo Express		Deu	2005	93,750	103,800	335	43	25	CC	
Dresden Express		Deu	1991	53,883	67,680	294	32	23	CC	
Dusseldorf Express		Deu	1998	53,523	66,525	294	32	23	CC	
Essen Express		Deu	1993	53,815	67,680	294	32	23	CC	
Frankfurt Express	(2)	Sgp	1981	57,540	51,540	288	32	23	CC	
Hamburg Express		Deu	2001	88,493	100,003	320	43	26	CC	
Hannover Express		Deu	1991	53,783	67,680	294	32	23	CC	
Heidelburg Express		Deu	1989	35,919	45,977	236	32	20	CC	ex Ville De Verseau-91, Heidelberg Express-91
Hoechst Express		Deu	1991	53,833	67,680	294	32	23	CC	
Hong Kong Express		Deu	2002	88,493	100,016	320	43	26	CC	ex Berlin Express-02
Humboldt Express *		Sgp	1984	32,444	34,037	200	32	16	CC	
Kobe Express		Deu	1998	53,523	67,537	294	32	23	CC	ex Shanghai Express-02
Kyoto Express		Deu	2005	93,750	103,890	335	43	25	CC	
Leverkusen Express		Deu	1991	53,783	67,680	294	32	23	CC	
London Express		Deu	1998	53,523	66,577	294	32	23	CC	
Ludwigshafen Express		Deu	1992	53,833	67,680	294	32	23	CC	
Norfolk Express		Deu	1995	36,606	45,362	245	32	24	CC	ex OOCL Atlantic-03, Norfolk Express-02, Hong Kong Express-02, Northern Majesty-96
Paris Express		Deu	1994	53,815	67,613	294	32	23	CC	ex Hamburg Express-01
Rotterdam Express		Deu	2000	54,400	66,975	294	32	24	CC	
Santiago Express		Sgp	1984	32,444	33,997	206	32	18	CC	ex Isla de la Plata-96, Cordillera Express-84
Shanghai Express		Deu	2002	88,493	100,006	320	43	26	CC	l/a Berlin Express
Stuttgart Express		Deu	1993	53,815	67,640	294	32	23	CC	
Tokyo Express		Deu	2000	54,437	54,766	294	32	24	CC	

newbuildings - five 100,000 grt (335 x 43m) container ships on order for 2007-8 delivery.
Subsidiary of TUI Group.
* owned by subsidiary Hapag-Lloyd (Eastwind) Pte. Ltd., Singapore and ** managed by V. Ships Norway.
† chartered from Eagle Maritime. See other chartered ships under Costamare, Norddeutsche and Schepers.

CP Ships Inc/Canada

Funnel: *Dark blue with red and white chequered houseflag.*
Hull: *Red with red boot-topping.*

Name	Eng	Flag	Year	GRT	DWT	Loa	Bm	Kts	Type	Former names
Barcelona Express		Bmu	1987	40,439	40,744	270	32	20	CC	ex CP Sinaloa-06, TMM Sinaloa-05, Ming Promotion-01
Canberra Express		Gbr	2000	23,652	29,841	188	30	20	CC	ex CP Eagle-6, Lykes Eagle-05, Clivia-00
Copenhagen Express **		Bmu	1987	39,132	44,966	259	32	21	CC	ex CP Explorer-06, Lykes Explorer-05, Genevieve Lykes-98, President Arthur-96, l/a Doctor Lykes
CP Ambassador		Gbr	1987	40,436	40,845	270	32	20	CC	ex Lykes Ambassador-05, Ming Plenty-01
CP Bravery **		Bmu	1978	26,383	33,869	219	31	23	CC	ex CanMar Bravery-05, Cast Privilege-01, CanMar Bravery-99, OOCL Bravery-98, Canadian Explorer-90, Dart Canada-81
CP Challenger		Bmu	1986	40,464	40,744	270	32	20	CC	ex Lykes Challenger-05, Ming Peace-01
CP Discoverer		Usa	1987	39,132	44,966	259	32	21	CC	ex Lykes Discoverer-05, Margaret Lykes-97, President Harding-96, l/a James Lykes
CP Endurance *		Bmu	1983	32,152	32,424	222	32	22	CC	ex CanMar Endurance-05, Cast Performance-03, Contship Endeavour-99, CanMar Endeavour-98, Alligator Joy-95, Tokyo Maru-90
CP Everglades		Gbr	2002	40,146	36,644	243	32	20	CC	ex Lykes Ranger-05
CP Glory **		Bmu	1979	16,145	18,964	177	27	22	CC	ex CanMar Glory-05, Sea Falcon-94, CMB Monarch-91, CMB Mover-90, Asian Senator-90, Jefferson-88, TFL Jefferson-86, Seatrain Saratoga-80
CP Hero		Bmu	1986	41,023	40,009	243	32	22	CC	ex Lykes Hero-05, Cast Progress-03, Alligator Reliance-01, Astro Prosperity-96
CP Honour *		Bmu	1998	39,174	40,120	245	32	21	CC	ex CanMar Honour-05
CP Liberator		Usa	1987	39,132	44,966	259	32	21	CC	ex Lykes Liberator-05, Stella Lykes-97, President Garfield-96, Tillie Lykes-87

Name	Eng	Flag	Year	GRT	DWT	Loa	Bm	Kts	Type	Former names
CP Los Angeles *		Bmu	1996	33,663	33,659	216	32	20	CC	ex Cielo di Los Angeles-05, Cast Premier-05, OOCL Canada-03
CP Margosa ‡		Cyp	2006	39,941	50,000	260	32	24	CC	
CP Navigator		Usa	1987	39,132	44,966	259	32	21	CC	ex Lykes Navigator-05, Almeria Lykes-98, President Buchanan-96, I/a Almeria Lykes
CP Power *		Bmu	1982	31,570	32,207	223	32	22	CC	ex Montreal Senator-05, Cast Power-03, Contship Success-99, CanMar Success-98, Alligator Excellence-95, America Maru-90
CP Pride *		Bmu	1998	39,174	40,881	245	32	21	CC	ex CanMar Pride-05
CP Rotoiti	(me2)	Bmu	1977	22,228	20,270	203	26	-	Ro	ex Rotoiti-05, Union Rotoiti-99
CP Shenandoah **		Gbr	2002	40,146	40,478	243	32	21	CC	ex TMM Colima-05, Contship Tenacity-02
CP Spirit *		Gbr	2003	55,994	62,300	294	32	-	CC	ex CanMar Spirit-05
CP Triumph **		Bmu	1978	16,289	18,606	177	27	19	CC	ex CanMar Triumph-05, CMB Marque-90, American Senator-89, Dart Americana-87, Seapac Independence-81, Seatrain Independence-81
CP Valour		Bmu	1979	15,145	18,800	177	27	18	CC	ex CanMar Valour-05, OOCL Assurance-97, Taiwan Senator-90, Dart Britain-87, Seapac Oriskany-81, Seatrain Oriskany-81
CP Venture *		Gbr	2003	55,994	62,300	294	32	-	CC	ex CanMar Venture-05
CP Victor ‡		Cyp	2006	39,941	50,000	260	32	24	CC	I/d Lykes Victor
CP Victory **		Bmu	1979	16,289	18,381	177	27	18	CC	ex CanMar Victory-05, American Senator-90, Singapore Senator-89, Dart Atlantica-87, Seapac Chesapeake-81, Seatrain Chesapeake-81
CP Yellowstone **		Gbr	2002	40,146	35,200	244	32	22	CC	ex TMM Guanajuato-05
Dubai Express ‡		Cyp	2006	39,941	50,500	260	32	24	CC	ex CP Corbett-06, I/a CP Guerrero, I/d TMM Guerrero
Fremantle Express		Gbr	1995	23,540	30,645	187	30	19	CC	ex CP Voyager-06, Lykes Voyager-05, P&O Nedlloyd Bandar Abbas-01, P&O Nedlloyd Yafo-99, Pax-98, CMBT Melbourne-97, Contship Melbourne-97, I/a Pax
Jakarta Express ‡		Cyp	2006	39,600	50,500	260	32	24	CC	ex CP Dartmoor-06, CP Banyan-06, I/d Contship Banyan
Lahore Express ‡		Cyp	2006	39,941	50,000	260	32	24	CC	ex CP Morelos-06
Lisbon Express *		Bmu	1996	33,735	34,330	216	32	20	CC	ex CP Prospect-06, Cast Prospect-05, CanMar Fortune-03
Livano Express		Usa	1991	37,474	43,084	242	32	21	CC	ex Lykes Motivator-06, Jupiter-01, Ville de Jupiter-01, CGM Pascal-00, Nedlloyd Pascal-98, CGM Pascal-95
Lykes Osprey ¶		Cyp	1984	16,517	22,233	166	27	18	CC	ex MSC Patagonia-04, Heicon-99, Sea Victory-97, Heicon-97, CSAV Rauten-96, Heicon-95, CSAV Rubens-95, Heicon-94, CGM Iguacu-94, Calapadria-93, Red Sea Energy-91, Belgian Senator-90, Euro Texas-89, Heicon-88
Maersk Dayton *		Gbr	2003	46,009	54,220	281	32	25	CC	ex CP Borealis-06, Contship Borealis-05
Maersk Dale		Gbr	2002	46,009	54,157	281	32	25	CC	ex CP Australis-06, Contship Australis-05
Maersk Dexter		Gbr	2002	46,009	54,156	281	32	25	CC	ex CP Aurora-06, Contship Aurora-05
New Delhi Express ‡		Cyp	2005	39,941	50,500	260	32	24	CC	ex CP Kanha-06, I/a CP Charger, I/d Lykes Charger
New Orleans Express		Gbr	1989	35,958	42,976	240	32	21	CC	ex CP Campeche-06, TMM Campeche-05, Choyang Park-01
Philadelphia Express **		Usa	2003	40,146	40,478	243	32	22	CC	ex CP Yosemite-06, TMM Yucatan-05
Saigon Express ‡		Cyp	2006	39,600	50,500	260	32	24	CC	ex CP Jasper-06, CP Trader-06, I/d Lykes Trader
Sydney Express *		Gbr	1994	23,540	30,621	187	30	19	CC	ex CP Dynasty-06, CanMar Dynasty-05, TMM Guadalajara-03, P&O Nedlloyd Melbourne-01, Coral Seatel-89, Contship Sydney-98, Coral Seatel-94
Valencia Express *		Bmu	1996	33,735	34,330	216	32	20	CC	ex CP Performer-06, Lykes Performance-05, Cast Prominence-05, CanMar Courage-03
Washington Express **		Gbr	2003	40,146	40,478	243	32	22	CC	ex CP Denali-06, Lykes Flyer-05
Wellington Express		Gbr	2001	23,652	29,894	188	30	21	CC	ex CP Tabasco-06, TMM Tabasco-05, Silvia-01

newbuildings: five further 39,900 grt 50,500 dwt container ships for 2006-7 delivery from South Korean builder.
* managed by Anglo-Eastern Ship Management Ltd., Hong Kong (China) or ** by Split Ship Management, Croatia.
† chartered from Oceanbulk Maritime SA, Greece, ¶ from Wilco Maritime Ltd, UK (managed by Fleet Management Ltd, Hong Kong) or ‡ on 10-year charter from Seaspan Container Lines Ltd., Cyprus (Washington Corp, USA). Also see other vessels in index with 'CP' or 'Lykes' prefix.

Hanjin Shipping Co. HANJIN BERLIN. *Vandriessche Guido*

Hanjin Shipping Co. HANJIN PYEONG TAEK. *Hans Kraijenbosch*

Emil Hartmann. SEALING. *C. Lous*

Hartmann Schiffahrts. CSAV RIO LONTUE. *Hans Kraijenbosch*

Leif Hoegh & Co ASA. HUAL DURBAN. *N. Kemps*

Hyundai Merchant Marine. HYUNDAI BANNER. *Hans Kraijenbosch*

Name	Eng	Flag	Year	GRT	DWT	Loa	Bm	Kts	Type	Former names

Harren & Partners Schiffahrts GmbH — Germany

Funnel: *Cream with two dark sails above three waves.*
Hull: *Light grey with red boot-topping.*

Name	Eng	Flag	Year	GRT	DWT	Loa	Bm	Kts	Type	Former names
Maersk Naantali	Cyp	2005	11,935	16,400	144	23	14	T	ex Patricia-05
Maersk Nairn	Cyp	2006	11,935	16,400	144	23	14	T	l/a Patagona
Maersk Newport	Cyp	2005	11,935	16,664	144	23	14	T	ex Patalya-05
Maersk Nordenham	Cyp	2005	11,935	16,716	144	23	14	T	ex Patrona-05
Paiute	Atg	1995	36,615	70,273	225	32	14	B	
Peoria	Atg	1996	36,615	70,231	225	32	14	B	
Pochard	Atg	2003	22,655	37,384	199	24	14	B	l/a Panarea
Puffin	Atg	2003	22,654	37,641	199	24	14	B	
Sibulk Premier	Atg	2003	29,985	53,609	190	32	14	B	ex Sibulk Pioneer-03
VOC Gallant *	Bhs	2002	30,928	51,215	190	32	14	B	ex DS Gallant-04
VOC Galaxy *	Bhs	2002	30,928	51,201	190	32	14	B	ex Clipper Galaxy-03
VOC Gemini *	Atg	2003	30,928	51,187	192	32	14	B	ex Clipper Gemini-03

newbuildings: two further 11,000 grt 16,400 dwt tankers on order from Chinese builder for 2007 delivery.
* on charter to Van Ommeren Clipper Holdings (Clipper Group)

Emil Hartmann — Germany

Funnel: *Yellow with red 'GT' on white segments of white/blue diagonally quartered flag, narrow black top.*
Hull: *Black with red boot-topping.*

Name	Eng	Flag	Year	GRT	DWT	Loa	Bm	Kts	Type	Former names
Seabass	Deu	2001	21,353	32,480	178	28	14	T	
Seaconger	Deu	2005	21,329	32,200	178	28	16	T	
Seadevil	Deu	1996	21,367	32,250	178	28	14	T	
Seahake	Deu	2003	21,329	32,480	178	28	16	T	
Sealing	Deu	2003	21,356	32,480	178	28	16	T	
Seamullet	Deu	2001	21,353	32,230	178	28	15	T	
Searay	Deu	2004	21,353	32,310	178	28	16	T	
Seashark	Deu	2004	21,329	32,310	178	28	16	T	
Seaturbot	Deu	2000	21,353	32,230	178	28	14	T	

newbuildings - three 21,300 grt tankers for 2006 delivery
Managed by German Tanker Shipping GmbH & Co KG.

Hartmann Schiffahrts GmbH & Co KG — Germany

Funnel: *White with blue 'h' symbol.*
Hull: *Blue with red boot-topping.*

Name	Eng	Flag	Year	GRT	DWT	Loa	Bm	Kts	Type	Former names
Barranquilla	Cyp	1995	13,695	22,051	158	25	14	B	ex UBC Barranquilla-04, Bernes-01
BBC Korea *	Cyp	2003	12,993	17,477	143	23	15	Co	ex Atlantic Pendant-05
BBC Russia *	Cyp	2003	12,993	17,471	143	23	15	Co	ex Atlantic Progress-03
Beaumont	Cyp	1995	13,695	22,056	158	25	14	B	ex UBC Beaumont-04, Brunes-01
Cabo Prior	Lbr	2004	25,406	33,829	207	30	-	CC	l/a Frisia Lissabon
Cap Doukato	Lbr	2004	25,406	33,847	207	30	-	CC	l/a Frisia Kiel
Cap Saray	Deu	2004	25,406	33,784	207	30	-	CC	l/a Frisia Rotterdam
Cosco Karachi	Deu	2005	27,915	37,900	215	30	-	CC	ex Frisia Kopenhagen-05
Cosco Sydney	Lbr	2004	27,915	37,978	215	30	-	CC	l/a Frisia Leipzig
CSAV Rio Lontue	Lbr	2004	25,406	27,400	207	30	-	CC	l/a Frisia Wismar
CSAV Santos	Lbr	2004	25,406	33,900	207	30	-	CC	l/a Frisia Rostock
DAL Madagascar	Lbr	2001	16,803	23,051	184	25	19	CC	ex Sagittarius-04
Frisia Loga	Lbr	2006	25,360	33,900	207	30	-	CC	
Johann Oldendorff	Lbr	1995	26,890	46,601	188	32	14	B	ex San Paolo-04
Libra Santa Catarina	Lbr	2004	25,406	33,781	207	30	22	CC	ex Frisia Lubeck-04
Lyra Pioneer **	Pan	2003	28,059	45,985	180	32	14	T	
Mount Adamello **	Cyp	2004	22,521	40,002	182	27	14	T	
Mount Fuji **	Cyp	2003	22,515	40,055	182	27	14	T	
Mount McKinney **	Cyp	2004	22,518	39,997	182	27	14	T	
Mount Olympus **	Cyp	2003	22,515	40,011	182	27	14	T	
Mount Rainier **	Cyp	2004	22,518	40,012	182	27	14	T	
Mount Robson **	Cyp	2004	22,518	40,014	182	27	14	T	
Nord Sound **	Pan	2003	28,059	45,975	180	32	14	T	
Santos Star	Lbr	2005	25,406	27,400	207	30	-	CC	l/a Frisia Helsinki
UBC Stavanger *	Cyp	2004	19,748	31,751	172	27	14	B	
UBC Tampico *	Cyp	2004	24,140	37,821	182	29	14	B	

newbuildings: four 65,000 grt, three 27,779 grt, two 25,360 grt and four 10,000 grt container ships for 2006-8 delivery.
Owned by subsidiaries * Intership Navigation Co. Ltd or ** Donnelly Tanker Management Ltd., both Cyprus

Name	Eng	Flag	Year	GRT	DWT	Loa	Bm	Kts	Type	Former names

Leif Hoegh & Co ASA Norway

Funnel: *White with blue top and houseflag interrupting white band.*
Hull: *Dark grey with dark blue 'HOEGH AUTOLINERS' on white superstructure or blue 'HOEGH LINES', red boot-topping.*

Name	Eng	Flag	Year	GRT	DWT	Loa	Bm	Kts	Type	Former names
Alliance New York **		Usa	2005	57,280	15,990	200	32	-	V	ex Hoegh New York-05, Hual New York-05
Arctic Lady ‡		Nis	2006	123,000	74,400	288	49	-	Lng	
Arctic Princess ‡		Nis	2006	123,000	74,400	288	49	-	Lng	
Hoegh Berlin		Nis	2005	57,280	16,006	200	32	-	V	
Hoegh Galleon	(st)	Nis	1974	71,822	50,746	250	40	19	Lng	ex Mystic Lady-00, Asake Maru-98, Mystic Lady-98, Asake Maru-98, Pollenger-87, LNG Challenger-79
Hoegh Gandria ‡	(st)	Nis	1977	96,011	71,630	288	44	20	Lng	
Hoegh Tracer		Nis	1981	33,236	12,961	180	29	18	V	ex Hual Tracer-06, Tracer-95, Hual Tracer-94
Hoegh Transit		Nis	1981	45,573	17,650	190	32	19	V	ex Hual Transit-05, Hual Transita-00, Kyushu-96, Kyushu Maru-88
Hoegh Traveller		Nis	1983	35,022	15,370	180	29	18	V	ex Hual Traveller-05
Hoegh Trinity		Nis	1981	45,365	17,938	190	32	19	V	ex Hual Trinity-05, Hual Trinita-00, Yokohama-95, Yokohama Maru-88
Hoegh Trooper		Bhs	1995	56,164	21,414	200	32	20	V	ex Hual Trooper-05
Hoegh Tropicana *		Nis	1980	33,359	12,003	180	32	17	V	ex Hual Tropicana-05, Hual Lisita-00, Lisita-82
Hoegh Trotter		Nis	1983	35,022	15,370	180	29	18	V	ex Hual Trotter-05
Hoegh Trove *		Bhs	2000	57,200	21,200	200	32	19	V	ex Hual Trove-05, Hual Maritita-00
Hoegh Trubadour		Nis	1980	33,369	12,165	180	29	17	V	ex Hual Trubadour-05, Hual Ingrita-00, Ingrita-82
Hual Asia		Bhs	2000	57,200	21,200	200	32	19	V	
Hual Durban		Pan	2004	58,947	19,121	200	32	20	V	
Hual Paris		Nis	2005	57,280	21,081	200	32	20	V	
Hual Seoul		Nis	2004	57,280	21,500	200	32	20	V	
Hual Tokyo		Nis	2004	57,280	21,500	200	32	20	V	
Hual Trader		Bhs	1998	56,816	16,393	200	32	20	V	
Hual Tramper		Bhs	1980	33,369	12,169	180	29	17	V	Hual Rolita-00, ex Rolita-82
Hual Transporter		Bhs	1999	57,757	21,300	200	32	20	V	
Hual Trapeze		Nis	1983	41,871	15,500	180	31	17	V	ex Hual Carmencita-00
Hual Trapper		Nis	1981	33,236	12,961	180	29	18	V	
Hual Treasure *		Bhs	1999	58,684	21,199	200	32	19	V	ex Hual Carolita-00
Hual Trekker		Nis	1981	33,374	11,977	180	29	17	V	ex Hual Angelita-00, Angelita-82
Hual Trident		Bhs	1995	56,164	21,423	200	32	20	V	
Hual Triumph		Nis	1988	53,578	20,885	200	32	18	V	ex Hual Margarita-00
Kiwi Auckland		Nis	1985	37,841	13,295	175	29	18	V	ex Cosmo Spirit-05, Excelsior-99, Young Skipper-91
Morning Mercator		Bhs	1988	52,422	23,096	200	32	18	V	ex Hual Tricorn-04, Hual Champ-00, Auto Champ-00
Morning Meridian		Bhs	1988	52,422	23,052	200	32	18	V	ex Hual Triton-04, Auto Diana-00, l/a Auto Daewoo
Morning Rose		Nis	1980	45,007	15,603	194	32	18	V	ex Hual Trailer-04, Hual Karinita-00, Karinita-82
Norman Lady ‡	(st)	Nis	1973	71,469	50,922	250	40	18	Lgc	

newbuildings: four 48,000 grt and four 57,000 grt vehicle carriers for 2006-8 delivery.
*Managed by Hoegh Fleet Services AS, * by IUM Shipmanagement AS, both Norway or ** by Liberty Maritime Corp, USA.*
‡ jointly owned with Mitsui OSK Lines Ltd., Japan q.v.

Hyundai Corporation South Korea

Hyundai Merchant Marine Co Ltd/South Korea

Funnel: *White with yellow edged green triangle.*
Hull: *Blue with white 'HYUNDAI', red boot-topping.*

Name	Eng	Flag	Year	GRT	DWT	Loa	Bm	Kts	Type	Former names
Asian Jade		Pan	2005	57,164	106,062	244	42	-	T	ex KWK Jade-05
Forest Pioneer		Pan	1998	39,548	51,300	218	32	15	Bw	
Global Victory *		Pan	1996	76,068	149,155	270	43	14	B	
Global Winner *		Pan	1997	81,152	161,121	280	45	14	B	
Hyundai Advance		Pan	1997	21,611	24,777	182	30	22	CC	ex Wan Hai 251-00, Hyundai Advance-98
Hyundai Aquapia	(st)	Pan	2000	113,998	77,564	289	48	20	Lng	
Hyundai Atlas		Pan	1995	76,068	149,310	270	43	13	B	
Hyundai Banner		Kor	1996	151,977	281,074	330	58	15	T	
Hyundai Bridge		Pan	1998	21,611	24,766	182	30	21	CC	
Hyundai Confidence		Pan	2003	64,845	68,114	275	40	25	CC	
Hyundai Continental		Kor	1988	101,466	200,269	309	50	13	B	
Hyundai Cosmpia	(st)	Pan	2000	113,998	77,591	289	48	20	Lng	
Hyundai Cosmos		Kor	1986	85,678	163,256	290	45	13	B	

Name	Eng	Flag	Year	GRT	DWT	Loa	Bm	Kts	Type	Former names
Hyundai Fortune		Pan	1996	64,054	68,539	275	40	25	CC	
Hyundai Freedom		Pan	1996	64,054	68,363	275	40	25	CC	
Hyundai Future		Pan	1997	21,611	24,600	182	30	21	CC	
Hyundai General		Kor	1996	64,054	68,378	275	40	25	CC	
Hyundai Glory		Pan	2004	53,352	63,404	294	32	25	CC	
Hyundai Greenpia	(st)	Pan	1996	103,764	71,684	274	47	18	Lng	
Hyundai Highness		Kor	1996	64,054	68,379	275	40	25	CC	
Hyundai Highway		Pan	1998	21,611	24,799	182	30	21	CC	
Hyundai Island		Kor	1986	67,897	127,852	274	43	12	B	
Hyundai Oceania		Kor	1983	74,052	139,887	267	43	15	B	
Hyundai Oceanpia	(st)	Pan	2000	113,998	77,000	288	48	20	Lng	
Hyundai Olympia		Kor	1987	93,005	186,330	292	46	13	B	
Hyundai Power		Pan	1998	76,068	135,000	269	43	14	B	
Hyundai Progress		Pan	1997	21,611	24,766	182	30	22	CC	ex Wan Hai 252-00, Hyundai Progress-98
Hyundai Prosperity		Kor	1990	77,650	151,257	274	45	13	B	
Hyundai Spirit		Pan	1993	68,093	126,051	263	41	18	B	
Hyundai Sprinter		Pan	1997	21,611	24,600	182	30	21	CC	
Hyundai Star		Pan	1995	151,592	281,199	330	58	15	T	
Hyundai Stride		Pan	1997	21,611	24,777	182	30	21	CC	
Hyundai Sun		Pan	1998	156,692	301,178	330	58	15	T	
Hyundai Technopia	(st)	Pan	1999	113,998	77,584	289	48	20	Lng	
Hyundai Universal		Kor	1990	101,604	200,052	309	50	13	B	
Hyundai Utopia	(st)	Pan	1994	103,764	71,909	274	47	18	Lng	
Hyundai Vladivostok		Cyp	1997	21,611	24,766	182	30	21	CC	ex CMA Oakland-01, Hyundai Vladivostok-99
Kiani Satu		Pan	1997	16,660	16,717	165	26	14	C	
Oriental Green		Pan	1996	25,503	43,229	185	31	14	B	
Pacific Champ *		Pan	1996	25,503	43,229	185	31	14	B	
Pacific Courage		Pan	1992	145,403	258,096	338	58	15	T	ex Stena Comfort-00, Wisteria-97
Pacific Royal *		Pan	1997	25,503	43,210	185	31	14	B	
Pacific Success		Kor	1989	24,790	38,412	186	28	14	B	
Pacific Superior		Pan	1994	146,849	269,605	338	58	15	T	ex Apollo Akama-04
Universal Brave		Pan	1997	156,692	278,900	331	58	15	T	
Universal Crown		Pan	2005	163,465	309,316	333	60	-	T	
Universal Hope †		Pan	1993	158,475	299,700	344	56	14	T	ex Eugen Maersk-04, British Vigilance-02, Emma Maersk-97
Universal Peace †		Pan	1995	158,475	299,700	344	56	14	T	ex Emma Maersk-04, Ellen Maersk-97
Universal Prime		Pan	1997	156,692	278,900	331	58	15	T	
Universal Queen		Pan	2005	163,465	309,373	333	60	-	T	
VL Malibu		Pan	1989	137,024	248,976	324	58	15	T	ex Nichioh-03

newbuildings: two 300,000 dwt tankers, eight 55,000 grt, three 74,400 grt and four 88,600 grt container ships for 2006-8 delivery.
* owned by subsidiary Haeyoung Maritime Services Co. Ltd., South Korea and † managed by Wallem Ship Management.
See also Eukor Car Carriers Inc (under Wallenius Wilhelmsen)

International Shipholding Corporation   USA

Central Gulf Lines Inc/USA

Funnel: *White with blue symbol within blue ring, narrow black top or buff with 8-pointed white star on white edged broad red band or green with two broad white bands.*
Hull: *Black with red boot-topping.*

Name	Eng	Flag	Year	GRT	DWT	Loa	Bm	Kts	Type	Former names
Asian Emperor		Pan	1999	55,729	21,479	228	32	20	V	(len. 06)
Asian King ‡		Pan	1998	55,729	21,511	200	32	19	V	
Atlantic Forest **	(2)	Usa	1984	37,460	40,881	263	32	20	LC	ex Aleksey Kosygin-96
Bali Sea	(2)	Sgp	1982	29,594	22,220	175	36	13	HL	ex Super Servant 5-95, Dan Lifter-85
Banda Sea	(2)	Sgp	1982	29,594	22,239	175	36	13	HL	ex Super Servant 6-95, Dan Mover-85
Green Cove		Usa	1994	50,308	16,178	179	32	19	V	ex Shohjin-00
Green Dale *		Usa	1999	50,087	15,894	179	32	19	V	ex Altair Leader-99
Green Lake		Usa	1998	57,623	22,799	200	32	19	V	ex Cygnus Leader-01
Green Point		Usa	1994	51,819	14,930	180	32	19	V	ex Triton Diamond-98
Green Ridge		Pan	1998	57,449	21,523	200	32	19	V	ex Hercules Leader-05
Hickory †	(2)	Pan	1989	38,282	40,796	263	32	18	LC	ex Gaysin-97, Ernesto Che Guevara-96
P&O Nedlloyd Buenos Aires *		Usa	1984	23,790	29,730	183	31	17	CC	ex Nedlloyd van Noort-98
P&O Nedlloyd Veracruz *		Usa	1984	23,790	29,730	183	31	18	CC	ex Nedlloyd van Diemen-98

Hyundai Merchant Marine. HYUNDAI CONFIDENCE. *Hans Kraijenbosch*

International Shipholding Corp. ATLANTIC FOREST. *Hans Kraijenbosch*

Interorient Navigation Co. AZTECA (in charterers colours). *J. M. Kakebeeke*

Name	Eng	Flag	Year	GRT	DWT	Loa	Bm	Kts	Type	Former names
Rhine Forest **	Mhl	1972	35,826	44,799	261	32	18	LC		ex Bilderdyk-86

*managed by LMS Shipmanagement Inc. including for * for Waterman Steamship Corp. and ** for Forest Lines subsidiaries.*
† managed by Dobson Fleet Management Ltd, Cyprus and ‡ possibly chartered to Eukor Car Carriers Inc. (see under Wallenius-Wilhelmsen)

Interorient Navigation Co. Ltd. Cyprus

Funnel: Buff with blue 'IN' inside blue ring.
Hull: Black with red boot-topping.

Name	Eng	Flag	Year	GRT	DWT	Loa	Bm	Kts	Type	Former names
Arctic Point *		Cyp	2003	23,235	37,389	183	27	14	T	I/a Baltic Adonia
Azteca		Cyp	1993	13,237	17,546	155	23	16	Co	ex ANL Progress-03, Melanesian Chief-02, Barnes Bridge-01, Island Chief-00, Chengtu-99, Barnes Bridge-98, SEAL Mauritius-97, Santander-94, Kapitan E. Freyman-93
Baltic Action		Cyp	2005	23,240	37,340	183	27	14	T	
Baltic Advance		Mhl	2006	23,240	37,340	183	27	14	T	
Baltic Ambassador		Cyp	2005	23,240	37,340	183	27	14	T	
Baltic Ambition		Cyp	2005	23,240	37,340	183	27	14	T	
Baltic Captain I		Cyp	2000	23,235	37,389	183	27	14	T	ex Baltic Captain-02, I/a Androcles
Baltic Chief I		Cyp	2000	23,235	37,389	183	27	14	T	ex Baltic Chief-01, Baltic Carrier-01, I/a Armodius
Baltic Commander I		Cyp	2000	23,235	37,418	183	27	14	T	ex Baltic Commander-02, I/a Antifon
Baltic Sun II *		Mlt	2005	23,235	37,305	183	27	15	T	ex Baltic Sun-05
Baltic Wave *		Mlt	2003	23,235	37,300	183	27	15	T	ex Prostar-05, Ice Point-03
Baltic Wind *		Mlt	2003	23,235	37,296	183	27	15	T	ex Prosky-05
CMA CGM Dardanelles *		Mhl	1997	31,206	38,502	210	32	22	CC	ex Indamex Delaware-04, Champion-03, Contship Champion-02, I/a Telendos
Conti Harmony		Deu	1997	31,207	38,400	210	32	22	CC	ex Contship Innovator-02, Contship Harmony-99, Conti Harmony-97, I/a Timarchos
Flores *		Mlt	2001	23,235	37,272	183	27	14	T	ex Flores I-01
Giannutri *		Mlt	2004	23,235	37,272	183	27	14	T	
Glacier Point *		Cyp	2003	23,235	37,389	183	27	15	T	ex Baltic Sea-03
Indamex Delaware		Deu	1997	31,207	38,400	210	32	22	CC	ex Champion-03, Contship Champion-02, I/a Telendos
Jolly		Cyp	1992	27,103	25,904	178	32	18	CC	ex Kota Setia-02, Jolly-01, Jolly Topazio-00, Jolly Oro-99, Croatia Express-98
Kerel *		Mlt	2002	23,235	37,272	183	27	14	T	
Norasia Tegesos *		Deu	1996	31,207	38,400	210	32	22	CC	ex Tegesos-04, Contship Action-03, Tegesus-97
Norasia Telamon		Cyp	1996	31,207	38,400	210	32	22	CC	ex Telamon-04, Contship Ambition-03, Telamon-96
Nordamerika *		Mhl	2000	23,740	35,775	183	27	14	T	
Sea Navigator *		Gib	1995	14,961	20,406	167	25	19	CC	ex Indamex Mississippi-01, Sea Navigator-00, Nauplius-99, TNX Sprint-98, Zim Brasil-98, Energy-97, Nauplius-95
Sicilia *		Mlt	2001	23,235	37,272	183	27	14	T	
Sinotrans Tokyo		Cyp	2005	9,966	13,950	148	23	-	CC	ex Olympian Racer-05
Tolteca		Cyp	1992	13,231	17,300	155	23	16	Co	ex NDS Kuito-03, Tower Bridge-02, Lykes Leader-01, Tower Bridge-00, Nordana Challenger-99, Tower Bridge-98, Maersk Abidjan-98, Kapitan Moshchinskiy-97, Isla Pinzon-96, Kapitan Moshchinskiy-96, Nedlloyd Cristobal-95, Kapitan Moshchinskiy-94, Zim Jamaica-94, Kapitan Moshchinskiy-92
Tula		Cyp	1994	13,258	17,493	155	23	16	Co	ex Kew Bridge-03, Jolly Ambra-03, Kew Bridge-02, Seaboard Houston-02, Lykes Striker-01, Kew Bridge-00, Zim Houston 1-99, Kew Bridge-98, SEAL Reunion-97, Kapitan N. Petrosyan-94
Zapoteca		Bhs	1992	13,237	17,491	155	24	16	Co	ex NDS Bengela-03, Waterloo Bridge-03, Nordana Defender-99, Waterloo Bridge-98, Zim Mexico-97, Zim Santos-96, Kapitan N. Kladko-92

newbuildings: two 108,170 dwt, 11 further 37,340 dwt, five 36,000 dwt tankers and a 10,000 grt container ship for 2006-8 delivery.
* *owned or managed by subsidiary INC Interorient Navigation Hamburg GmbH & Co KG, Germany.*

Islamic Republic of Iran Shipping Lines Iran

Funnel: Red base with broad white band below green top.
Hull: Light grey with black 'IRISL' and red or green boot-topping, or black with red boot-topping

Name	Eng	Flag	Year	GRT	DWT	Loa	Bm	Kts	Type	Former names
Iran Abozar		Irn	1986	25,770	43,365	190	30	14	B	
Iran Adi		Irn	1983	22,027	37,537	186	28	15	B	ex World Fraternity-84

Name	Eng	Flag	Year	GRT	DWT	Loa	Bm	Kts	Type	Former names
Iran Afzal		Irn	1983	22,027	37,588	186	28	15	B	ex Manila Faith-84, Primelock-83
Iran Akhavan		Irn	1984	20,576	34,859	198	24	15	B	ex Philippine Success-84
Iran Amanat		Irn	1983	20,576	34,859	198	24	15	B	ex Manila Pride-84
Iran Ardebil		Irn	2004	25,369	37,875	207	30	22	CC	
Iran Ashrafi		Irn	1985	25,768	43,342	190	30	14	B	
Iran Azadi		Irn	1979	20,672	35,839	180	28	15	B	ex Oinoussian Friendship-81
Iran Azarbayjan		Irn	2000	39,424	72,642	225	32	14	B	
Iran Baabael		Irn	1998	15,670	22,882	168	26	16	Co	
Iran Baakeri		Irn	1998	15,670	22,882	168	26	16	Co	
Iran Baghaei		Irn	1979	12,775	17,970	170	23	18	C	ex Ydra-93, Almas-92, Tannenbels-86, Stratherrol-82
Iran Bahonar		Irn	1983	21,959	40,325	176	32	14	T	ex Cleon-83
Iran Baluchestan		Irn	2000	16,694	22,600	174	26	16	Co	
Iran Bayan		Irn	1974	9,891	16,265	150	21	16	C	ex Arya Sepand-80, Aristonimos-75
Iran Beheshti		Irn	1979	22,048	39,026	205	26	15	T	ex Selma-82
Iran Borhan		Irn	1975	10,205	16,265	150	21	16	C	ex Arya Gohar-80
Iran Broojerdi		Irn	1978	13,917	17,970	170	23	18	C	ex Arastou-93, Merbabu-86, Rheinbels-83, Strathelgin-82
Iran Chamran		Irn	1985	25,768	43,309	190	30	14	B	
Iran Dastghayb		Irn	1984	25,768	43,369	190	30	14	B	
Iran Deyanat		Irn	1983	25,168	44,169	200	20	15	B	ex Odinlook-81
Iran Eghbal		Irn	1986	25,768	40,345	191	30	14	B	
Iran Ehsan		Irn	1975	9,891	16,265	150	21	16	C	ex Arya Akhtar-80, Aristaios-75
Iran Entekhab		Irn	1978	20,811	35,896	180	28	15	B	ex Oinoussian Prestige-81
Iran Eshraghi		Irn	1985	25,768	43,369	190	30	14	B	
Iran Esteghlal		Irn	1978	20,811	35,839	180	28	15	B	ex Oinoussian Virtue-81
Iran Ghafari		Irn	1985	25,768	43,369	190	30	14	B	
Iran Ghazi		Irn	1985	25,768	43,442	190	30	14	B	
Iran Gheyamat		Irn	1978	14,433	19,212	167	25	18	C	ex Arya Shams-80
Iran Ghodousi		Irn	1986	25,770	43,480	190	30	14	B	
Iran Gilan		Irn	2000	39,424	63,400	225	32	14	B	
Iran Golestan		Irn	2001	39,517	72,162	225	32	14	B	
Iran Hamedan		Irn	2001	39,517	72,162	225	32	14	B	
Iran Hamzeh		Irn	1986	25,770	43,288	190	30	14	B	
Iran Hesabi		Irn	1998	15,670	22,882	168	26	16	Co	
Iran Hormozgan		Irn	2000	36,014	41,962	240	32	22	CC	
Iran Ilam		Irn	2004	25,369	37,600	207	30	22	CC	
Iran Isfahan		Irn	2000	36,014	41,971	240	32	22	CC	
Iran Jamal		Irn	1985	25,768	40,422	190	30	14	B	
Iran Jomhuri		Irn	1978	20,811	35,830	180	28	15	B	ex Oinoussian Leadership-81
Iran Kashani		Irn	1984	25,768	43,309	190	30	14	B	
Iran Kerman		Irn	2000	36,014	41,970	240	32	22	CC	
Iran Kermanshah		Cyp	2001	40,609	75,249	225	32	14	B	ex Cape Tenaron-03
Iran Khorasan		Irn	2000	39,424	72,622	225	32	14	B	
Iran Khuzestan		Irn	1999	16,694	23,116	174	26	16	Co	
Iran Kordestan		Irn	1999	16,694	23,116	174	26	16	Co	
Iran Lorestan		Irn	1999	16,694	23,176	174	26	16	Co	
Iran Madani		Irn	1985	25,768	43,345	190	30	14	B	
Iran Mahallati		Irn	1978	13,914	16,905	170	23	18	C	ex Lindenbels-88, Strathewe-82
Iran Makin		Irn	1997	16,621	24,065	174	26	17	Co	
Iran Matin		Irn	1996	16,621	22,948	174	26	16	Co	
Iran Mazandaran		Irn	2000	39,424	72,642	225	32	14	B	
Iran Meezan		Irn	1975	9,888	16,265	150	21	16	C	ex Arya Sooroosh-80
Iran Mobin		Irn	1996	16,621	22,982	174	26	16	Co	
Iran Modares		Irn	1977	20,049	33,667	182	27	15	B	ex Gentle River-83, Treana-78
Iran Mufateh		Irn	1985	25,768	43,262	190	30	14	B	
Iran Nabuvat		Irn	1977	14,856	19,212	167	25	18	C	ex Arya Shahab-60
Iran Navab		Irn	1986	25,768	43,342	190	30	14	B	
Iran Piroozi		Irn	2003	25,369	33,853	207	30	22	CC	
Iran Rajai		Irn	1983	22,097	40,367	176	32	14	T	ex Ferncraig-83
Iran Sadoughi		Irn	1985	25,768	43,369	190	30	14	B	
Iran Sadr		Irn	1985	25,768	43,265	190	30	14	B	
Iran Saeidi		Irn	1986	25,768	43,369	190	30	14	B	
Iran Salam		Irn	1975	8,364	12,140	153	18	18	C	ex Arya Zar-80
Iran Sarbaz		Irn	1984	20,576	34,859	198	24	15	B	
Iran Sattari		Irn	1998	15,670	22,882	168	26	16	Co	
Iran Seestan		Irn	1999	16,694	23,176	174	26	16	Co	
Iran Sepah		Irn	1976	19,701	33,856	186	26	14	B	ex Ocean Cosmos-84

Interorient Navigation Co. BALTIC CAPTAIN I. *Hans Kraijenbosch*

Iran Shipping Lines. IRAN KORDESTAN. *J. M. Kakebeeke*

Iran Shipping Lines. IRAN SHARIATI. *N. Kemps*

Iran Shipping Lines. IRAN ZANJAN. *Hans Kraijenbosch*

Ernst Jacob. FOUR SCHOONER. *Hans Kraijenbosch*

Kristian Gerhard Jebsen. PINE ARROW (in Gearbulk colours). *Vandriessche Guido*

Name	Eng	Flag	Year	GRT	DWT	Loa	Bm	Kts	Type	Former names
Iran Shahryar		Irn	1999	15,670	22,882	168	26	16	Co	
Iran Shariat		Irn	1983	25,168	44,468	200	29	15	B	ex Thorlock-84
Iran Shariati		Irn	1985	25,768	40,422	190	30	14	B	
Iran Sokan		Irn	1975	9,888	16,265	150	21	16	C	ex Arya Navid-80
Iran Tabatabaei		Irn	1998	15,670	22,621	168	26	16	Co	
Iran Takhti		Irn	1978	16,173	23,720	159	25	16	Co	ex Sargodha-84
Iran Taleghani		Irn	1985	25,768	43,309	190	30	14	B	
Iran Tehran		Irn	2000	36,014	41,937	240	32	22	CC	
Iran Teyfouri		Irn	1979	16,173	23,720	159	25	16	Co	ex Simba-84
Iran Vahdat		Irn	1977	14,856	19,212	167	25	18	C	ex Arya Keyhan-80
Iran Vojdan		Irn	1975	9,891	16,265	150	21	16	C	ex Arya Kay-80, Aristonidas-75
Iran Yamin		Irn	1996	16,621	22,967	174	26	17	Co	
Iran Yasooj		Irn	2004	25,369	33,850	207	30	20	CC	
Iran Yazd		Cyp	2001	40,609	72,642	225	32	14	B	ex Cape Race-03
Iran Zanjan		Irn	2003	25,391	33,757	207	30	-	CC	

newbuildings - over 40 container ships and bulk carriers on order for 2006-8 delivery.

Irano-Hind Shipping Co Ltd/Iran

Funnel: Black with green/brown diagonally quartered flag with white 'I' and 'H' in upper and lower quarters respectively or * blue.
Hull: Black with red boot-topping.

Name	Eng	Flag	Year	GRT	DWT	Loa	Bm	Kts	Type	Former names
Attar		Mlt	1994	25,885	43,706	186	30	14	B	ex Parisian Trader-00
ISI Olive *		Mlt	1992	81,135	141,861	274	48	14	T	ex Mastera-02
Sattar		Mlt	1992	24,155	43,419	185	31	14	B	ex Belstar-01
Teen		Mlt	1995	26,828	43,671	190	31	14	B	ex Oriental Dream-03, Eun Ji-97

*Formed jointly with The Shipping Corporation of India Ltd (49%) and * managed by International tanker Management Ltd., UAE.*

Ernst Jacob GmbH & Co KG   Germany

Funnel: Black, white diagonal cross on broad blue band with blue 'J' on white centre diamond
Hull: Grey or red with red boot-topping or white with blue boot-topping.

Name	Eng	Flag	Year	GRT	DWT	Loa	Bm	Kts	Type	Former names
Chaleur Bay *		Mlt	2000	40,705	71,345	229	32	15	T	
Four Ketch		Cym	2003	40,037	69,995	229	32	15	T	
Four Schooner †		Cym	2000	40,037	73,083	229	32	15	T	
Four Smile †		Cym	2001	81,236	160,573	274	48	14	T	
Four Sun †		Cym	2003	81,236	160,292	274	48	14	T	
Jill Jacob		Cym	2003	40,037	72,909	229	32	15	T	ex Four Clipper-04
Johann Jacob		Cym	2000	40,037	73,001	229	32	15	T	ex Four Brig-04
Kim Jacob		Lbr	1998	81,265	159,211	274	48	15	T	ex Celebes-98
Los Roques		Cym	2000	40,705	61,130	229	32	15	T	
Mara *		Mhl	1989	39,836	64,850	225	32	15	Obo	ex Mara Lolli-Ghetti-90
Margara *		Cym	1999	40,705	60,913	229	32	14	T	
Max Jacob		Lbr	2000	81,565	157,449	274	48	14	T	ex Soyang-01
Noemi *		Ant	2004	41,690	72,700	225	32	14	T	ex Colin Jacob
Oliver Jacob		Lbr	1999	81,565	157,326	274	48	14	T	ex Columbia-02
Santa Ana **		Cym	2002	24,252	39,768	190	28	14	T	ex Greenock-02, I/a Diamant
Senatore *		Mhl	2004	41,526	72,700	225	32	14	T	ex Ariadne Jacob-05
Venice *		Mlt	2001	43,822	81,408	240	36	14	T	
3 Maj *		Mhl	1988	39,836	64,850	225	32	13	Obo	

** managed by Scorpio Ship Management SAM or ** by IndoChina Ship Management (UK) Ltd.*
† deployed in Jacob Scorpio tanker pool.

Jahre Dahl Bergesen AS   Norway

Funnel: Various operating company or charterers colours.
Hull: Various including black with red boot-topping.

Name	Eng	Flag	Year	GRT	DWT	Loa	Bm	Kts	Type	Former names
Esperanza		Lbr	1993	62,390	106,684	246	42	15	T	ex Grab Esperanza-03
Eurydice		Cyp	1986	52,862	94,941	244	42	14	T	ex Jahre Prince-00, Friendship Venture-87
Hyundai Explorer		Bhs	1986	39,892	43,567	244	32	21	CC	ex P&O Nedlloyd Pusan-03, Hyundai Explorer-02
Hyundai Frontier		Bhs	1986	39,892	43,567	244	32	21	CC	ex MSC Pretoria-04, Hyundai Frontier-02, Lalandia-92, Hyundai Frontier-88
Hyundai Innovator		Pan	1986	39,892	43,567	244	32	21	CC	
Maersk Tampa		Bhs	1984	43,332	53,325	270	32	24	CC	ex Louis Maersk-99
MSC Parana		Nis	1987	23,761	34,380	202	28	17	CC	ex Cielo di Valencia-02, Lynx-00, Cast Lynx-99, Norasia Mubarak-94
MSC Peru		Nis	1987	23,761	34,380	202	28	17	CC	ex P&O Nedlloyd Falcon-03, Cielo di Livorno-01, Bear-00, Cast Bear-99, Norasia Al-Muntazah-94
Skauboard		Nis	1997	34,885	49,370	196	32	15	B	

Name	Eng	Flag	Year	GRT	DWT	Loa	Bm	Kts	Type	Former names
Skaubryn		Nis	1982	43,312	41,666	183	32	14	Ro	ex Skeena-91
Skaugran		Nis	1979	41,905	42,424	183	32	14	Ro	
Thorsriver *		Bhs	1989	23,761	34,380	202	28	17	CC	ex HSH Ubin-05, Kota Sahabat-02, HSH Ubin-00, Cast Elk-99, Norasia Sun-94
Thorstream		Bhs	1989	23,761	34,380	202	28	17	CC	ex HSH Kusu-05, Cast Wolf-99, Norasia Singa-94

*Ship management company owned by AS Thor Dahl Shipping (52.5%), Bulls Tankrederi A/S-Jorgen Jahre (22.5%), Gluteus Medius AS (Tom Bergesen). Vessels managed by Jahre-Wallem AS (JDB 50%, Wallem 40% and B. Skaugen 10%) or * by OW Shipmanagement, Singapore.*
See also Eukor Car Carriers Inc. (under Wallenius Willhelmsen)

Kristian Gerhard Jebsen Skipsrederi AS   Norway

Funnel: *Black with white pennant flag on broad blue band or * pale green with white 'SKS' on broad red band.*
Hull: *Black or * red with red or green boot-topping.*

Name	Eng	Flag	Year	GRT	DWT	Loa	Bm	Kts	Type	Former names
Apalis Arrow		Bhs	1983	30,767	42,149	208	32	14	BC	ex Emerald Coast-98, Star Everwin-87, Everwin-00
Avocet Arrow		Bhs	1985	27,470	39,239	199	30	15	BC	ex City of Alberni-98, Belwood-93
Barbet Arrow		Bhs	1985	27,470	39,260	199	30	15	BC	ex City of New Westminster-98, Belforest-93
Canelo Arrow		Bhs	1997	32,520	48,077	187	31	14	B	
CHL Innovator †		Sgp	1976	19,426	26,931	175	26	15	B	ex Rodney-86, Cape Rodney-85
CHL Progressor †		Sgp	1985	32,333	48,251	189	32	-	B	ex Therassia-89
Gannet Arrow		Bhs	1985	27,470	39,260	199	30	15	BC	ex City of Nanaimo-98, Beltimber-93
Jaeger Arrow		Bhs	2001	29,103	24,101	171	25	18	Cp	
Kestrel Arrow		Bhs	1983	30,767	42,149	208	32	15	BC	ex Jade Forest-98, Star Everace-87, Everace-83
Pinc Arrow		Bhs	1996	32,520	48,041	190	31	14	BC	
SKS Mersey		Nis	2003	70,933	120,499	250	44	15	Obo	
SKS Mosel		Nis	2003	70,933	121,000	250	44	15	Obo	
SKS Tagus *		Nis	1997	63,515	109,933	244	42	15	Obo	
SKS Tana *		Nis	1996	63,515	109,906	244	42	14	Obo	
SKS Tanaro *		Nis	1999	63,515	109,787	244	42	14	Obo	
SKS Tiete *		Nis	1999	63,515	109,773	244	42	14	Obo	
SKS Torrens *		Nis	1999	63,515	109,846	244	42	14	Obo	
SKS Trent *		Nis	1997	63,515	109,832	244	42	15	Obo	
SKS Trinity *		Nis	1999	63,515	109,798	244	42	14	Obo	
SKS Tugela *		Nis	1997	63,515	109,913	244	42	15	Obo	
SKS Tweed *		Nis	1999	63,515	109,832	244	42	15	Obo	
SKS Tyne *		Nis	1996	63,515	109,891	244	42	14	Obo	

newbuildings: four 82,000 grt 159,000 dwt tankers and one 13,100 grt bitumen tanker (Sunbird Arrow) on order for 2006-7 delivery.
* owned by SKS OBO Ltd formed jointly with Nordship and managed by V.Ships Norway A/S
† managed for CHL Shipping BV, Netherlands (subsidiary of TNT Shipping & Development Ltd., Australia)

Gearbulk Shipowning Ltd/Bermuda

Funnel: *Black with large white 'G'.*
Hull: *Black with white 'GEARBULK', red boot-topping.*

Name	Eng	Flag	Year	GRT	DWT	Loa	Bm	Kts	Type	Former names
Alouette Arrow		Bhs	1980	12,688	14,602	159	21	16	Cp	ex Chimo-94, Finnarctis-91
Auk Arrow		Bhs	1984	27,962	43,952	188	29	13	BC	ex Heina-91
Borg Arrow		Nis	1992	29,369	46,998	199	31	15	BC	ex Westwood Borg-04, Spero-98, Saga Ocean-95
Breeze Arrow		Nis	1992	29,369	46,908	199	31	15	BC	ex Westwood Breeze-03, Saga Breeze-98
Bridge Arrow *		Nis	1992	29,369	46,956	199	31	15	BC	ex Westwood Bridge-05, Saga River-03, Sea River-92
Bergen Arrow *		Bhs	1984	25,063	38,800	182	29	14	BC	ex Bergen Thistle-86
Cedar Arrow		Bhs	2001	32,458	47,818	190	31	14	BC	
Condor Arrow		Bhs	1979	25,846	38,618	182	29	15	BC	ex Molda-81
Cormorant Arrow		Bhs	1986	28,005	43,074	188	29	13	BC	
Crane Arrow		Bhs	1984	27,818	42,913	188	29	14	BC	ex Chelsfield-89
Dunlin Arrow		Bhs	1986	27,012	38,760	183	29	13	BC	ex Aris-04, Rio Acre-93
Eagle Arrow **		Bhs	1977	30,719	45,063	201	31	15	BC	ex Norsul Bahia-04, Cielo d'Europa-01, Star Europa-96, Cielo d'Europa-91, Star Mallard-89, Hoegh Mallard-87
Emu Arrow		Bhs	1997	36,008	51,419	200	32	14	B	
Falcon Arrow		Bhs	1986	28,805	45,295	200	31	15	BC	ex Norsul Europa-04, Westwood Belinda-03
Finch Arrow		Bhs	1984	26,130	39,273	183	29	13	BC	ex Francois LD-90
Grebe Arrow		Bhs	1997	35,998	51,633	200	32	16	B	
Grouse Arrow		Bhs	1991	44,398	42,276	185	30	15	B	
Gull Arrow		Bhs	1982	25,846	38,787	182	29	16	BC	ex Horda-91
Harefield		Bhs	1985	27,818	41,651	188	29	13	BC	
Hawk Arrow		Bhs	1985	28,092	40,269	188	29	14	BC	
Hornbill Arrow		Bhs	1980	21,139	31,247	180	28	15	BC	ex Star Bettina-05, Alberni Dawn-03

Name	Eng	Flag	Year	GRT	DWT	Loa	Bm	Kts	Type	Former names
Ibis Arrow		Bhs	1986	28,239	42,497	188	29	14	BC	
Kite Arrow		Bhs	1997	36,008	51,800	200	32	16	B	
Kiwi Arrow		Bhs	1981	27,069	38,695	182	29	14	BC	
Mandarin Arrow		Bhs	1996	35,998	51,733	200	32	16	B	
Merlin Arrow		Bhs	1999	36,008	51,459	200	32	15	BC	ex Tolten-04
Mozu Arrow		Bhs	1992	44,398	42,276	185	30	15	B	
Nandu Arrow		Bhs	1978	25,063	38,618	182	29	14	BC	
Osprey Arrow		Bhs	1985	27,938	42,596	188	29	13	BC	
Pelican Arrow		Bhs	1982	25,846	38,787	182	29	16	BC	ex Folga-91
Penguin Arrow		Bhs	1997	36,008	51,738	200	32	16	B	
Petersfield		Bhs	1985	27,818	41,646	188	29	13	BC	
Petrel Arrow		Bhs	1985	27,824	42,964	188	29	14	BC	ex Alain LD-90
Plover Arrow		Bhs	1997	36,008	51,880	200	32	14	B	
Poplar Arrow		Bhs	2005	35,250	47,818	190	31	14	BC	
Puffin Arrow		Bhs	1981	27,069	38,695	183	29	13	BC	ex Brierfield-89, La Sierra-83
Raven Arrow		Bhs	1981	24,855	38,771	182	29	14	BC	
Rhein		Bhs	1979	26,948	38,596	183	29	14	BC	ex Maya-89, Sun Maya-86, Charles LD-83
Rhone		Bhs	1978	26,204	38,542	182	29	16	BC	ex Rokko-89, Sun Rokko-86, La Cordillera-83
Siskin Arrow		Bhs	1985	26,130	39,151	183	29	14	BC	ex Monique LD-90
Spruce Arrow		Bhs	2002	32,458	47,818	190	31	14	BC	
Sun Suma		Bhs	1978	26,204	38,542	182	29	16	BC	ex La Costa-84
Swan Arrow		Bhs	1987	28,805	45,295	200	31	15	BC	ex Norsul America-04, Westwood Jago-03
Swift Arrow		Bhs	1992	44,398	42,276	185	30	15	B	
Teal Arrow		Bhs	1984	27,962	43,002	188	29	13	BC	ex Lista-91
Tern Arrow		Bhs	1986	28,239	42,570	188	29	14	BC	
Tiwai Maru		Pan	1984	11,867	18,703	151	22	13	B	ex Southland Maru-84
Toki Arrow **		Bhs	1980	21,139	31,247	180	28	17	BC	ex Harmac Dawn-04
Toucan Arrow		Bhs	1996	35,998	51,880	200	32	16	B	
Tsuru Arrow		Bhs	1987	28,805	45,295	200	31	15	BC	ex Norsul Vancouver-04, Westwood Cleo-02
Weaver Arrow		Bhs	1997	36,008	51,364	200	32	14	B	
Westfield		Bhs	1985	27,818	41,619	188	29	13	BC	
Windfield		Bhs	1980	26,942	38,715	183	29	14	BC	ex Pierre LD-86
Wren Arrow		Bhs	1985	27,824	41,637	188	29	13	BC	ex Charles LD-90

*Minority of 40% in Gearbulk owned by Mitsui OSK, Japan q.v. * managed by Borgestad ASA, Norway or ** SMT Shipmanagement, Cyprus.*

Jungerhans Maritime Services GmbH & Co KG   Germany

Funnel: *White with pale blue 'J' inside pale blue diamond outline between two narrow pale blue bands or charterers colours*
Hull: *Black or grey with red boot-topping.*

Name	Eng	Flag	Year	GRT	DWT	Loa	Bm	Kts	Type	Former names
ACX Plumeria *		Deu	1997	18,233	26,260	177	28	20	CC	ex City of Stuttgart-05, Klaus J-02, Irma Delmas-02, Maersk San Antonio-99, TNX Express-98, Aldebaren-97, I/a Klaus J
Ara J *		Atg	1998	11,153	16,833	148	25	18	CC	ex Safmarine Italia-02, SCL Italia-00, Schwerin-98, Ara J-98
Clan Praetorian *		Atg	1997	18,233	26,260	178	28	20	CC	ex Helene J-05, ANL Oryx-03, Helene J-02, Fesco Express-00, Maersk Manzanillo-99, TNX Sprint-98, Antares-97, Helene J-97
Libra J		Atg	1998	12,004	14,174	149	23	19	CC	ex Tausala Samoa-05, I/a Libra J
Maersk Ravenna		Gib	2001	14,000	18,400	156	25	18	CC	I/a Auriga J
Maersk Rio Grande		Gib	2002	16,129	16,794	161	25	19	CC	ex Corona J-02
Maersk Rosario		Gib	2003	16,129	16,824	161	25	19	CC	ex Crux J-03
Maersk Rostock		Atg	2002	14,062	18,832	156	25	19	CC	ex Taurus J-03
Maersk Rotterdam		Gib	2002	14,062	18,400	156	25	18	CC	I/a Antares J

* owned by subsidiary Astor Shiffahrts GmbH.

Kahn Scheepvaart BV   Netherlands

Funnel: *White with red elephant and red/blue eight-pointed star between narrow green bands.*
Hull: *Dark blue with white 'WWW.JUMBOSHIP.NL', red boot-topping.*

Name	Eng	Flag	Year	GRT	DWT	Loa	Bm	Kts	Type	Former names
Fairpartner		Ant	2004	15,071	11,350	143	27	17	Co/hl	
Jumbo Javelin		Ant	2004	15,022	12,870	143	27	17	Co/hl	

Also owns several smaller heavy lift vessels.

Kristian Gerhard Jebsen (Gearbulk). SWIFT ARROW. *Hans Kraijenbosch*

Kahn Scheepvaart (Jumboship). FAIRPARTNER. *Hans Kraijenbosch*

Name	Eng	Flag	Year	GRT	DWT	Loa	Bm	Kts	Type	Former names

Kawasaki Kisen KK   Japan

Funnel: *Bright red with white 'K', above grey base.*
Hull: *Grey with red boot-topping.*

Name	Eng	Flag	Year	GRT	DWT	Loa	Bm	Kts	Type	Former names
Akashi Bridge		Pan	1993	48,237	47,425	277	32	24	CC	
Akinada Bridge		Pan	2001	68,687	71,366	285	40	25	CC	
American Highway		Pan	2000	49,212	16,750	179	32	20	V	
Arcadia Highway		Pan	1994	49,012	15,507	180	32	20	V	
Atlantic Highway		Pan	2002	55,493	17,232	200	32	20	V	
Atlas Highway		Lbr	1987	45,742	14,487	180	32	20	V	
Baltic Highway		Pan	2001	42,238	17,828	179	32	20	V	
Bauhinia Bridge		Hkg	1993	48,342	47,425	277	32	24	CC	ex Seto Bridge-04
Bay Bridge		Lbr	1985	34,467	35,396	227	32	20	CC	
Bosphoros Bridge		Pan	1993	48,220	47,359	277	32	25	CC	
Californian Highway		Pan	1983	43,407	16,519	183	32	18	V	
Cape Acacia		Pan	2005	104,732	206,237	300	50	-	B	
Cape Apricot		Pan	2004	90,091	180,310	289	45	14	B	
Cape Awoba		Pan	1996	87,803	171,978	289	45	14	B	ex Cape Acacia-05
Cape Azalea		Pan	1996	87,799	171,846	289	45	14	B	
Cape Camellia		Pan	2000	87,322	172,502	289	45	14	B	ex Cape Daisy-04
Cape Enterprise		Pan	2003	92,993	185,909	290	47	14	B	
Cape Flora		Pan	2000	83,056	164,361	280	47	14	B	
Cape Future		Pan	2002	92,993	185,820	290	47	14	B	
Cape Glory		Pan	2003	89,529	177,173	289	45	14	B	
Cape Jacaranda		Pan	1995	93,698	183,863	290	46	14	B	
Cape Liberty		Pan	2005	92,993	185,897	290	47	14	B	
Cape Lotus		Pan	2000	83,849	170,780	289	45	16	B	
Cape Maple		Pan	2005	104,932	206,204	300	50	-	B	
Cape Olive		Pan	1996	85,663	169,963	290	46	14	B	
Cape Orchid		Pan	2001	87,322	172,569	289	45	14	B	
Cape Rosa		Pan	2005	101,911	203,163	300	50	-	B	
Cape Salvia		Pan	2002	87,341	172,559	289	45	14	B	
Cape Sentosa		Sgp	2003	89,545	177,346	289	45	14	B	
Cape Sophia		Pan	2005	55,285	99,047	250	43	-	B	
Cape Triumph		Pan	2004	88,594	176,343	289	45	15	B	
Cape Victory		Pan	2003	89,492	177,359	289	45	14	B	
Cape Wakaba		Pan	1996	87,803	171,978	289	45	14	B	ex Cape Maple-05
Cape Wisteria		Pan	1997	87,322	172,846	289	45	14	B	ex Cape Rosa-04
Caribbean Highway		Pan	2002	42,238	17,866	179	32	20	V	
Century Highway No. 1		Pan	1984	43,198	15,363	186	32	18	V	
Century Highway No. 2		Pan	1985	44,616	15,509	186	32	18	V	
Century Highway No. 3		Pan	1986	46,186	14,304	186	32	18	V	
Century Highway No. 5		Pan	1986	44,969	15,380	190	32	18	V	
Chang Jiang Bridge		Pan	1992	48,237	47,425	277	32	24	CC	ex Brooklyn Bridge-01
Chiswick Bridge		Pan	2001	68,687	68,280	285	40	25	CC	
Colorado Highway		Pan	2005	44,382	12,806	183	30	-	V	
Concord Bridge		Pan	1998	47,541	51,805	275	32	23	CC	
Continental Highway		Pan	2001	55,493	17,201	200	32	20	V	
Coral Highway		Pan	1987	49,439	14,597	180	32	20	V	ex Michigan Highway-95
Emden		Pan	1987	38,062	13,898	178	29	17	V	
European Highway		Pan	1999	48,039	15,057	180	32	20	V	
Genoa Bridge		Pan	2002	66,292	67,197	279	40	25	CC	
George Washington Bridge		Pan	2006	68,687	71,000	285	40	25	CC	
Glen Canyon Bridge		Pan	2006	68,687	71,000	285	40	25	CC	
Global Highway		Pan	1982	51,087	15,148	200	32	18	V	
Golden Gate Bridge		Pan	2001	68,687	71,376	285	40	25	CC	
Greenwich Bridge		Pan	2006	68,687	71,000	285	40	25	CC	
Guang Dong Bridge		Pan	2006	68,687	71,000	285	40	25	CC	
Henry Hudson Bridge		Jpn	1987	42,407	40,934	241	32	22	CC	
Hercules Highway		Jpn	1987	46,875	14,977	180	32	18	V	
Humber Bridge		Jpn	1988	48,305	47,539	277	32	24	CC	
Hume Highway		Pan	1985	51,235	16,169	200	32	18	V	
Indiana Highway		Jpn	2003	55,457	17,442	200	32	20	V	
James River Bridge		Pan	2001	68,687	71,336	285	40	25	CC	
Kentucky Highway		Jpn	1987	50,320	15,587	180	32	19	V	
Lions Gate Bridge		Pan	2001	68,687	71,395	285	40	25	CC	
Long Beach Bridge		Pan	2001	66,332	68,280	279	40	25	CC	
Mackinac Bridge		Jpn	1986	42,414	40,982	241	32	22	CC	

Name	Eng	Flag	Year	GRT	DWT	Loa	Bm	Kts	Type	Former names
Manhattan Bridge		Pan	1987	42,394	40,934	241	32	22	CC	
Marble Highway		Pan	1984	33,131	11,907	173	28	18	V	
Mediterranean Highway		Pan	2002	55,493	17,228	200	32	20	V	
Melbourne Highway		Pan	1983	43,259	16,483	183	32	18	V	
Mineral Kyoto		Pan	2004	90,398	177,462	289	45	14	B	
Morning Noble		Pan	1984	45,699	13,687	180	32	18	V	ex Tokyo Highway-05
Morning Sapphire		Jpn	1985	45,706	13,684	180	32	18	V	ex New York Highway-05
Newport Bridge		Pan	1993	48,220	47,384	277	32	25	CC	
Nippon Highway		Pan	1999	49,212	16,827	179	32	20	V	
Normandie Bridge		Lbr	1989	48,235	47,351	277	32	23	CC	ex YM Tacoma-05, Normandie Bridge-02
Ocean Highway		Pan	2000	49,212	16,733	179	32	20	V	
Olympian Highway		Pan	1995	47,077	14,226	180	32	20	V	
Oriental Highway		Lbr	1980	28,997	12,434	175	27	17	V	
Orion Highway		Lbr	1984	44,576	14,384	179	32	19	V	
Pacific Highway		Pan	2000	48,039	15,127	180	32	20	V	
Pegasus Highway		Pan	1994	49,012	15,553	180	32	18	V	
Princes Highway		Pan	1986	51,233	16,191	200	32	18	V	
Rhein Bridge		Pan	1989	48,235	46,200	277	32	24	CC	
Sapphire Highway		Pan	1986	49,098	14,683	179	32	19	V	ex London Highway-94
Scandinavian Highway		Pan	1986	48,014	14,569	190	32	18	V	ex European Highway-96
Seven Seas Highway		Pan	2001	55,493	17,232	200	32	20	V	
Shanghai Bridge		Pan	2001	68,687	68,280	285	40	25	CC	
Shanghai Highway		Pan	2005	48,927	15,413	180	32	-	V	
Shenandoah Highway		Pan	1992	47,368	12,308	180	32	18	V	
Shing Star		Pan	2004	88,490	177,662	289	45	14	B	
Sinfonia		Pan	1991	93,788	184,403	290	46	13	B	ex Mikasa-98
Sirius Highway		Pan	1984	44,576	14,301	179	32	18	V	
Suez Canal Bridge		Pan	2002	68,687	71,359	285	40	25	CC	
Texas Highway		Jpn	2003	55,458	17,200	200	32	20	V	
Tianjing Highway		Pan	2005	48,927	15,410	180	32	-	V	
Tower Bridge		Sgp	1985	34,487	34,775	227	32	20	CC	
Triton Highway		Jpn	1987	45,783	14,484	180	32	18	V	
Tsing Ma Bridge		Pan	2002	68,687	68,280	285	40	25	CC	
Valencia Bridge		Pan	2004	54,519	65,006	294	32	23	CC	
Vancouver Bridge		Pan	2005	54,519	65,002	294	32	23	CC	
Vecchio Bridge		Pan	2005	54,519	64,983	294	32	23	CC	
Venice Bridge		Pan	2005	54,519	64,989	294	32	23	CC	
Verrazano Bridge		Pan	2004	54,519	65,038	294	32	23	CC	
Victoria Bridge		Pan	2005	54,519	64,906	294	32	23	CC	
Vincent Thomas Bridge		Pan	2005	54,519	65,023	294	32	23	CC	
Virginia Bridge		Pan	2004	54,519	64,990	294	32	23	CC	
Washington Highway		Jpn	1986	50,334	14,081	190	32	19	V	
West Gate Bridge		Jpn	1986	42,000	40,928	241	32	22	CC	ex George Washington Bridge-05
Williamsburg Bridge		Pan	1998	47,541	51,759	275	32	23	CC	ex Victoria Bridge-05
Yamato		Pan	1991	93,699	184,349	290	46	13	B	
YM Bremen		Pan	2001	66,332	67,170	279	40	25	CC	ex Bremen Bridge-04
YM Chicago		Pan	2001	66,332	67,170	279	40	25	CC	ex Chicago Bridge-04
YM Rotterdam		Pan	2001	66,332	68,280	285	40	25	CC	ex Rotterdam Bridge-04

newbuilldings: about 60 on order including five 89,000 grt container ships, two 315,000 dwt tankers, and vehicle, Lpg and bulk carriers.
The company and its many subsidiaries own or manage over 210 vessels, only the larger container ships, car and bulk carriers being listed. The owned, managed and chartered fleet also includes 24 other 'capesize' bulk carriers (143-173,000 dwt), about 65 'panamax' or 'handy' bulk carriers, 13 woodchip carriers, 4 VLCC tankers, 10 'Aframax', product and Lpg tankers, 29 Lng tankers (18 on order) and 27 vehicle carriers.
Also see Cido Shipping and various other chartered container ships with 'Bridge' suffix in index.

Klaveness Maritime Logistics AS

Norway

Funnel: *Yellow with blue 'K' on white disc and blue edged narrow white band.*
Hull: *Grey or orange with red boot-topping.*

Name	Eng	Flag	Year	GRT	DWT	Loa	Bm	Kts	Type	Former names
Al Mansour		Mhl	2002	38,889	72,562	225	32	-	Bcs	
Bakra		Mhl	1993	37,550	70,456	225	32	13	Bu	ex Bakar-99, Beskydy-98
Balder		Mhl	2002	30,739	48,184	190	32	-	B	
Ballangen		Mhl	1987	24,621	41,734	184	31	14	Bu	ex Yamburg-92, Oinoussian Fighter-89
Balsfjord		Mhl	1996	37,550	70,120	225	32	13	Bu	ex Sumava-98
Banasol		Mhl	2001	38,889	72,562	225	32	14	Bcs	
Banastar		Mhl	2001	38,889	72,700	225	32	16	Bcs	
Bandar		Lbr	1982	46,996	81,659	259	32	15	B	ex Bulkgulf-03
Baniyas		Nis	2001	38,889	72,562	225	32	-	Bcs	

Name	Eng	Flag	Year	GRT	DWT	Loa	Bm	Kts	Type	Former names
Bantry		Mhl	2005	38,883	72,562	225	32	-	Bcs	
Barkald		Mhl	2002	28,912	49,900	190	32	-	B	
Bauta		Mhl	1987	24,621	41,756	184	31	14	Bu	ex Yasnaya Polyana-92, Oinoussian Prudence-89
Clipper Gem *		Bhs	1990	36,433	64,619	225	32	14	B	ex China Pride-05, Alaska-02, China Pride-02
Clipper Glory *		Bhs	1990	36,433	65,652	226	32	14	B	ex China Glory-04
Clipper Jade *		Bhs	1994	38,679	70,046	225	32	14	B	ex China Spirit-04
Clipper Jasmine *		Bhs	1994	38,657	70,109	225	32	14	B	ex China Hope-04
Clipper Joy *		Bhs	1994	38,679	70,044	225	32	14	B	ex China Joy-04
KCL Bardu		Lbr	1979	21,630	33,684	177	27	15	B	ex Bardu-05, Swan Cliff-99, Bardu-95
KCL Barracuda		Pan	1984	10,880	17,722	147	23	13	B	ex Thai Ho-04, Kiwi Star-93

newbuildings - 38,900 grt 72,450 dwt bulk carrier for 2007 delivery from Japanese builder.
* owned by subsidiary American Bulker KS and managed by Dockendale Shipping Co. Ltd or Clipper Bulk (Portland) Inc (Clipper Group).
Also operates time-chartered vessels in Bulkhandling and Baumarine Pools

Knohr & Burchard Germany

Funnel: White with blue houseflag or charterers colours.
Hull: Dark blue with black or red boot-topping.

Name	Eng	Flag	Year	GRT	DWT	Loa	Bm	Kts	Type	Former names
Barmbeck		Deu	2005	16,324	15,955	169	27	21	CC	
Cast Prestige		Deu	2005	16,324	15,952	169	27	21	CC	ex Reinbek-05
Cast Prosperity		Deu	2005	16,324	15,952	169	27	21	CC	ex Eibeck-05
Flottbek		Deu	2005	16,324	15,952	169	27	21	CC	

Knutsen OAS Shipping AS Norway

Funnel: Black with two red bands.
Hull: Orange (larger vessels with white 'KNUTSEN OAS'), red boot-topping.

Name	Eng	Flag	Year	GRT	DWT	Loa	Bm	Kts	Type	Former names
Anna Knutsen	(2)	Nor	1987	69,313	129,154	257	46	14	T	
Anneleen Knutsen		Nis	2002	24,242	35,140	183	27	15	T	
Betty Knutsen		Nis	1999	24,185	35,807	183	27	14	T	
Bilbao Knutsen	(st)	Cni	2004	90,920	68,530	284	43	-	Lng	
Cadiz Knutsen	(st)	Cni	2003	90,835	68,411	284	43	-	Lng	
Catherine Knutsen		Nis	1992	77,352	141,200	277	43	14	T	ex Tanana-99, Wilomi Tanana-98, Tanana-98, Wilomi Tanana-97
Elisabeth Knutsen *	(me2)	Nor	1997	71,880	124,788	265	43	14	T	
Ellen Knutsen †		Nis	1991	11,433	17,071	142	23	13	T	
Gerd Knutsen *		Iom	1996	79,244	134,510	277	44	14	T	ex Knock An-03
Hanne Knutsen	(2)	Gbr	2000	72,245	123,851	265	43	15	T	
Heather Knutsen		Can	2005	80,918	148,644	277	46	-	T	l/a Rose Knutsen
Helene Knutsen ‡		Nis	1992	11,737	14,848	142	23	13	T	
Hilda Knutsen		Nis	1989	11,425	14,910	142	23	13	T	
Isabel Knutsen		Gbr	2001	13,753	22,377	160	23	15	T	ex Chembulk Savannah-00
Jasmine Knutsen		Nis	2005	80,918	148,706	277	46	-	T	
Jorunn Knutsen	(2)	Nis	2000	72,651	125,772	265	43	15	Ts	ex Asgard C-05, Jorunn Knutsen-00
Karen Knutsen *	(2)	Lbr	1999	87,827	154,390	276	50	14	T	ex Knock Whillan-03
Kitty Knutsen		Gbr	1980	63,101	127,747	264	41	16	T	ex Norrisia-03, Gerina-87
Kristin Knutsen †		Nis	1998	12,184	19,152	148	23	15	T	
Maria Knutsen		Gbr	2001	13,753	22,377	160	23	15	T	l/a Chembulk Barcelona
Navion Europa *	(me2)	Nor	1995	73,637	130,596	265	43	15	T	ex Jorunn Knutsen-98
Navion Norvegia *		Nor	1995	73,637	130,865	265	43	15	T	ex Hanne Knutsen-98
Pascale Knutsen		Gbr	1993	11,688	14,848	142	23	13	T	
Ragnhild Knutsen		Gbr	1987	69,321	128,772	260	46	14	T	
Rita Knutsen **	(2)	Nor	1986	70,434	124,472	252	46	14	T	ex Nordic Sarita-05, Sarita-98
Sallie Knutsen *	(2)	Iom	1999	87,827	154,390	276	50	14	T	ex Knock Sallie-03
Sidsel Knutsen		Nis	1993	15,806	22,625	163	23	13	T	
Siri Knutsen		Gbr	2004	24,242	35,309	187	27	15	T	
Synnove Knutsen †		Nis	1992	11,433	17,071	142	23	13	T	
Tordis Knutsen *		Nor	1993	66,671	123,848	265	43	14	T	
Torill Knutsen		Nis	1990	11,425	14,910	142	23	13	T	ex Vinga Knutsen-90
Tove Knutsen *		Nor	1989	60,719	112,508	243	43	14	T	
Turid Knutsen		Nis	1993	15,689	22,617	142	23	13	T	
Vigdis Knutsen *		Nor	1993	66,671	123,423	265	43	14	T	

newbuildings: 24,240 grt tanker, also 90,900 grt and 95,800 grt Lng tanker for 2006-7 delivery
* operated by Navion ASA (see under Teekay Shipping Corp.) or † by JO Tankers (J. O. Odfjell A/S), Norway q.v.
‡ managed by AS Norske Shell. ** operated for Petroleum Geo-Services (PGS) prior to conversion to floating production unit (FSPO).

Knutsen OAS Shipping. BETTY KNUTSEN. *Hans Kraijenbosch*

Knutsen OAS Shipping. HILDA KNUTSEN. *N. Kemps*

Name	Eng	Flag	Year	GRT	DWT	Loa	Bm	Kts	Type	Former names

Reederei Ernst Komrowski   Germany

Funnel: *White with white diamond at centre of blue/red diagonally quartered flag or charterers colours*
Hull: *Black or grey with red boot-topping.*

Name	Eng	Flag	Year	GRT	DWT	Loa	Bm	Kts	Type	Former names
Bonanza		Ant	2004	40,160	73,513	225	32	14	B	
Dorian		Lbr	1994	16,191	22,426	179	25	19	CC	ex DAL Karoo-02, Dorian-01, Karawa-00, Dorian-99, Sea Bold-98, Dorian-98, Sea Bold-97, Maersk Charleston-97, TSL Bold-96, Dorian-94
Fujian		Ant	1996	39,385	75,264	225	32	14	B	ex Umberto D'Amato-03
Hainan		Ant	1996	39,385	75,230	225	32	14	B	ex Luigi D'Amato-03
TMM Hidalgo		Lbr	1997	16,793	22,994	185	25	19	CC	ex Delmas Tourville-03, Adrian-03, Ivory Star-02, TMM Manzanillo-01, Adrian-01, CSAV Barcelona-01, Adrian-99, Santa Paula-98, Adrian-97, Jan Ritscher-97
Vulkan		Lux	1996	16,800	22,982	185	25	19	CC	ex Marfret Caraibes-05, CMA CGM Karukera-04, Vulkan-01, CMA CGM Karukera-01, Vulkan-01, Cap York-00, Vulkan-99, CSAV Rengo-99, Vulkan-06

newbuildings: three 10,000 grt container ships and two further 39,900 grt bulk carriers for 2006-7 delivery

Kuwait Oil Tanker Co (SAK)   Kuwait

Funnel: *Red with gold Arabic characters on green oval disc on broad white band beneath black top.*
Hull: *Black with red or grey boot-topping.*

Name	Eng	Flag	Year	GRT	DWT	Loa	Bm	Kts	Type	Former names
Al Awdah		Kwt	1991	149,647	284,533	322	56	14	T	
Al Badiyah		Kwt	1989	26,356	35,643	183	32	13	T	
Al Deerah		Kwt	1989	26,356	35,643	183	32	13	T	
Al Funtas		Kwt	1983	160,010	294,739	336	60	14	T	ex Middletown-89, Al Funtas-87
Al Kuwaitiah		Kwt	1988	26,351	35,643	183	32	13	T	
Al Maqwa		Kwt	1983	43,970	66,652	241	32	15	T	ex West Kirby-88, Umm Al Jathathel-87
Al Sabiyah		Kwt	1988	26,356	35,644	183	32	13	T	
Al Salheia		Kwt	1998	158,503	310,453	334	58	15	T	
Al Samidoon		Kwt	1992	149,719	284,889	322	57	14	T	
Al Shegaya		Kwt	1998	158,503	310,433	334	58	15	T	
Al Shuhadaa		Kwt	1992	149,719	285,116	322	57	14	T	
Al Tahreer		Kwt	1991	149,719	284,532	322	56	14	T	
Arabiyah		Kwt	1988	75,029	121,109	250	43	13	T	
Gas Al Ahmadi		Kwt	1979	42,904	47,471	230	35	16	Lpg	ex Gas Princess-89, Gas Al Ahmadi-87
Gas Al Burgan		Kwt	1979	42,904	47,471	230	35	21	Lpg	ex Gas King-89, Gas Al Burgan-87
Gas Al-Gurain		Kwt	1993	44,868	49,874	230	37	16	Lpg	
Gas Al Minagish		Kwt	1980	42,904	47,471	231	35	16	Lpg	ex Gas Prince-89, Gas Al Minagish-87
Gas Al Mutlaa		Kwt	1993	44,868	49,874	230	37	16	Lpg	
Hadiyah		Kwt	1988	75,029	121,109	250	43	13	T	
Kazimah		Kwt	1982	160,010	294,739	336	60	14	T	ex Townsend-88, Kazimah-87
Keefan		Kwt	1982	43,970	66,652	241	32	15	T	ex Hoylake-88, Umm Al Roos-87
Warbah		Kwt	1982	43,970	66,652	241	32	15	T	ex Helsby-88, Umm Ruwaisat-87

newbuildings: two 161,000 grt, two 38,900 grt and one 61,000 grt tankers and two 47,000 grt Lpg tankers for 2006-8 delivery.
Subsidiary of Kuwait Petroleum Corporation

F Laeisz Schiffahrts GmbH & Co   Germany

Funnel: *Yellow or charterers colours.*
Hull: *Black with red boot-topping or white with blue boot-topping.*

Name	Eng	Flag	Year	GRT	DWT	Loa	Bm	Kts	Type	Former names
Bussewitz		Lbr	1983	14,377	13,935	152	23	12	Lpg	
Chrismir ‡		Lbr	1997	81,329	159,829	280	45	-	B	
Hanjin Colombo		Pan	1994	50,792	62,850	290	32	24	CC	
Hanjin Osaka		Pan	1992	51,754	62,681	290	32	24	CC	ex Ville de Shanghai-99, Hanjin Osaka-98
Hanjin Philadephia		Lbr	2002	50,242	58,810	282	32	24	CC	
Hanjin Phoenix		Lbr	2002	50,242	58,423	282	32	24	CC	
Hanjin Praha *		Lbr	2001	50,242	58,423	280	32	24	CC	I/a Praha
Hanjin Pretoria *		Lbr	2002	50,242	58,768	282	32	24	CC	
Kota Pahlawan		Lbr	1997	25,499	33,950	200	30	21	CC	ex CMA CGM Emerald-04, Pembroke Senator-03, P&O Nedlloyd Fos-01, ECL Europa-99, Pembroke Senator-99
Kota Pelangi		Lbr	1996	31,131	38,650	210	32	22	CC	ex Potsdam-02, Ipex Emperor-99, Sea Elegance-97, Potsdam-96
Kota Pusaka		Lbr	1996	31,131	38,650	210	32	22	CC	ex Pommern-02, P&O Nedlloyd Unity-01, Pommern-97, Sea Excellence-97, Pommern-96

Name	Eng	Flag	Year	GRT	DWT	Loa	Bm	Kts	Type	Former names
Luise Oldendorff		Lbr	1994	38,513	72,873	225	32	14	B	
Matilde ‡		Mhl	1997	81,329	160,013	280	45	-	B	
MSC Basel		Lbr	1992	34,231	45,696	216	32	19	CC	ex Shanghai Senator-04, DSR-Atlantic-97
MSC Chile		Lbr	1997	28,701	32,500	202	31	20	CC	ex Priwall-02, Sea Panther-01, Priwall-97
MSC Palermo		Lbr	1992	34,231	45,696	216	32	19	CC	ex Palermo Senator-03, DSR-Baltic-96
Pacific Senator		Lbr	1992	34,231	45,696	216	32	19	CC	ex DSR-Pacific-97
Pacific Viking		Lbr	2005	35,853	42,937	205	32	19	Lpg	
Panama		Lbr	1989	18,000	26,288	177	28	18	CC	ex MSC Amazonia-02, MSC Andes-01, Panama-98, Panama Senator-97, Contship Noumea-96, Panama Senator-96
Paradise N		Lbr	1997	155,051	322,398	332	58	13	B	ex Peene Ore-02
Paris		Lbr	1990	18,000	26,288	177	28	17	CC	ex Sunrise-97, Choyang Pride-96, Paris-93, Paris Senator-93
Patmos Senator		Lbr	1992	34,231	45,696	216	32	19	CC	ex DSR-Europe-97
Peking Senator **		Deu	1997	53,324	63,527	294	32	23	CC	ex Cho Yang Ark-00
Penang Senator **		Deu	1997	53,324	63,533	294	32	23	CC	ex Cho Yang Atlas-01
Pequot		Lbr	1996	36,615	70,165	225	32	15	B	
Pilgrim †		Lbr	1994	7,743	7,721	131	20	19	R	ex Crystal Pilgrim-96
Pilsum		Lbr	1997	38,364	73,762	225	32	14	B	ex Andhika Loreto-03, Corona Challenge-02
Pittsburg †		Lbr	1994	7,743	7,721	131	20	19	R	ex Pioneer-96, Crystal Pioneer-96
Pohang Senator		Deu	1998	53,324	63,537	294	32	23	CC	
Polar Viking		Lbr	2004	35,853	42,854	205	32	16	Lpg	
Pontremoli		Lbr	2006	27,800	33,000	213	32	22	CC	
Port Said		Lbr	1994	19,819	22,300	174	27	19	CC	ex Port Said Senator-05, DSR-Port Said-00, Northern Pleasure-94
Portland Senator **		Deu	1997	53,324	63,645	294	32	23	CC	ex Cho Yang Alpha-01
Portugal Senator		Deu	1998	53,324	63,645	294	32	23	CC	
Powhatan		Lbr	1995	36,615	69,045	225	32	15	B	
Pride *		Lbr	1992	7,743	7,726	131	20	19	R	ex Crystal Pride-03
Privilege *		Lbr	1992	7,743	7,726	131	20	19	R	ex Crystal Privilege-03
Pudong Senator		Deu	1997	53,324	62,057	294	32	23	CC	
Pugwash Senator		Deu	1997	53,324	62,200	294	32	23	CC	
Punjab Senator		Deu	1997	53,324	63,645	294	32	23	CC	
Puritan		Lbr	1983	13,998	9,649	148	26	17	CC	ex Eagle Prestige-96, Puritan-93
Pusan Senator		Deu	1997	53,324	63,584	294	32	23	CC	
William Oldendorff		Lbr	1997	38,215	73,726	225	32	15	B	ex Wiltrader-03, Win Trader-02

newbuildings: one further 27,800 grt (Pontresina) and two 28,400 grt container ships for 2007 delivery.
*Owned or managed by Reederei F. Laeisz GmbH including * managed for Dr. Peters KG fund and ** for Norddeutsche Vermogensanlage GmbH & Co., both Germany. † chartered to Seatrade Groningen BV and ‡ to Overseas Shipholding Group (until 2010) q.v.*
Also see managed vessels under NSB Niederelbe Schiffahrts. GmbH.

Latvian Shipping Company Latvia

Funnel: Dark brown with dark brown 'Lat' on broad white band or blue with white 'L+C' overlapping broad red band.
Hull: Black or red with red boot-topping.

Name	Eng	Flag	Year	GRT	DWT	Loa	Bm	Kts	Type	Former names
Abava		Mlt	1992	7,057	6,366	140	19	16	R	ex Chiquita Abava-93
Akademikis Vavilovs		Mlt	1985	9,552	7,673	138	23	20	R	ex Akademik N. Vavilov-91
Akademikis Zavarickis		Mlt	1986	9,552	7,673	138	23	20	R	ex Akademik Zavaritskiy-91
Amata		Mlt	1991	7,392	6,231	140	19	16	R	ex Chiquita Amata-93, Amata-91, Mazoiusze-91
Antonio Gramsi		Lbr	1978	25,726	39,870	195	28	16	T	ex Antonio Gramsci-91
Aries **		Mhl	1993	18,094	29,790	175	26	14	T	ex Parnar-00
Asari		Cyp	1984	18,526	28,750	179	25	15	T	ex Georgiy Kholostyakov-92
Atair Star *		Mhl	1984	10,937	17,550	151	22	-	T	ex Makatsarija-00
Bulduri		Cyp	1983	18,625	28,750	179	25	15	T	ex Dmitriy Medvedyev-91
Davids Sikeiross		Lbr	1976	25,679	40,030	195	28	16	T	ex David Siqueiros-91
Dubulti		Mlt	1982	17,532	29,610	179	25	14	T	ex General Pliyev-91
Dzintari		Lbr	1985	10,944	16,341	152	22	15	T	ex Moris Bishop-91
Dzons Rids		Lbr	1978	25,726	39,870	195	28	16	T	ex John Reed-91
Estere		Cyp	1989	18,625	28,610	178	25	14	T	ex Esther-94
Hose Marti		Lbr	1978	25,726	39,870	195	28	16	T	ex Jose Marti-91
Indra		Lbr	1994	21,183	28,840	179	25	14	T	ex Puikovo-94
Inga		Lbr	1990	18,625	28,610	179	25	14	T	
Kaltene		Mhl	2003	23,217	37,000	183	27	14	T	ex Pink Star-04
Kemeri		Lbr	1985	10,944	17,610	152	22	15	T	ex Yuliy Danishevshiy-91
Klements Gotvalds		Lbr	1978	25,726	39,870	195	28	16	T	ex Klement Gottwald-91
Kolka		Mhl	2003	23,217	37,000	183	27	14	T	ex Purple Star-04
Kuldiga		Mhl	2003	23,217	37,237	183	27	14	T	ex Coral Star-04

Name	Eng	Flag	Year	GRT	DWT	Loa	Bm	Kts	Type	Former names
Kurzeme		Lbr	1997	18,503	23,100	160	26	15	Lpg	
Latgale		Mlt	2001	39,085	68,467	229	32	14	T	ex Inca-01
Lielupe		Lbr	1979	25,726	39,870	195	28	16	T	ex Sukhe Bator-92
Majori		Lva	1980	17,521	27,235	179	25	14	T	ex Grigoriy Nikolayev-91
Mar		Lbr	1990	18,625	28,610	178	25	14	T	
Mercure *		Mhl	1992	18,094	29,751	175	26	14	T	ex Danila-00
Ojars Vacietis		Cyp	1985	10,944	16,341	152	22	15	T	ex Oyar Vatsietis-91
Pablo Neruda		Lbr	1978	25,726	39,870	195	28	16	T	ex Pols Robsons-04, Paul Robeson-91
Pumpuri		Cyp	1987	18,526	28,750	179	25	14	T	ex Mikhail Gromov-92
Riga		Mlt	2001	39,085	68,467	229	32	14	T	ex Aztec-01
Ropazi		Cyp	1985	10,944	16,341	152	22	15	T	ex Ropazhi-93, Panteleymon Ponomarenko-91
Rundale		Cyp	1977	13,704	17,025	160	23	15	T	ex Leninsk Kuznetskiy-91
Samburga		Cyp	1976	13,704	17,200	160	23	15	T	ex Samburg-92
Skulptors Tomskis		Mlt	1986	9,552	7,673	138	23	20	R	ex Skulptor Tomskiy-91
Vidzeme		Lbr	1997	18,503	23,100	160	26	15	Lpg	
Zanis Griva		Lbr	1985	10,944	16,341	152	22	15	T	ex Zhan Griva-91
Zemgale		Mlt	2001	39,085	68,467	229	32	14	T	ex Maya-01
Zoja I		Cyp	1988	18,625	28,610	179	25	14	T	ex Don-89
Zoja II		Lva	1989	18,625	28,610	178	25	14	T	ex Kmir-90

Newbuildings: ten 30,060 grt and four 23,240 grt tankers for 2006-7 delivery.
*managed by LSC Shipmanagement Sia, Latvia except * by Columbia Shipmanagement Ltd., Cyprus,*

J. Lauritzen Holding A/S Denmark

NYKLauritzenCool AB/Sweden

Funnel: *Deep red base and broad blue top withblue and red arcs on broad white central band.*
Hull: *Red, cream or white with red/blue 'NYKLauritzenCool', red or blue boot-topping.*

Name		Flag	Year	GRT	DWT	Loa	Bm	Kts	Type	Former names
Amer Annapurna §		Lbr	1987	10,298	11,022	146	23	18	R	ex Arctic Spirit-99, Arctic Universal-97
Amer Choapa		Cyp	1987	13,312	12,848	152	24	18	R	ex Choapa-96
Amer Everest §		Cyp	1989	9,072	11,622	149	21	19	R	ex Hokkaido Rex-95
Amer Fuji §		Cyp	1990	9,070	11,540	149	21	17	R	
Amer Himalaya §		Cyp	1990	9,070	11,595	149	21	17	R	
Amer Whitney §		Cyp	1990	9,070	11,633	149	21	20	R	ex Californian Reefer-98, Humboldt Rex-94
Atlantic Reefer		Pan	1998	10,991	12,633	145	23	21	R	
Atlantik Frigo		Hrv	1989	10,366	11,000	143	23	19	R	
Belgian Reefer		Bhs	1983	12,383	14,786	145	24	18	R	ex Anne B-92
Brazilian Reefer		Bhs	1984	12,383	14,786	145	24	16	R	ex Betty B-92
Chaiten **		Lbr	1988	13,312	12,838	152	24	18	R	
Chilean Reefer		Dis	1992	7,944	11,095	141	20	22	R	ex Carelian Reefer-97
Crown Emerald *		Pan	1996	10,519	10,351	152	23	18	R	
Crown Garnet *		Pan	1996	10,519	10,322	152	23	21	R	
Crown Jade *		Pan	1997	10,519	10,332	152	23	21	R	
Crown Opal *		Pan	1997	10,519	10,332	152	23	21	R	
Crown Ruby *		Pan	1997	10,519	10,338	152	23	21	R	
Crown Sapphire *		Pan	1997	10,519	10,334	152	23	21	R	
Crown Topaz *		Pan	1999	10,527	10,318	152	23	21	R	
Cygnus Reefer *		Lbr	1990	8,818	9,679	144	22	20	R	
Ditlev Lauritzen **		Dis	1990	14,406	16,950	164	24	20	R	
Dominica †		Bhs	1993	13,077	13,981	158	24	22	R	ex Geest Dominica-97
Galaxy Harvest *		Pan	1988	8,519	8,800	142	21	19	R	ex Gallant Harvest-93
Global Harvest *		Pan	1993	8,520	8,752	144	21	19	R	
Glorious Harvest *		Pan	1989	8,519	8,830	142	21	19	R	ex Glorious Express-93
Ivar Lauritzen **		Dis	1990	14,406	16,950	165	24	19	R	
Ivory Ace		Vut	1990	10,394	10,713	150	23	20	R	
Ivory Dawn		Bhs	1991	10,412	10,600	150	23	20	R	
Ivory Girl		Vut	1996	11,438	10,432	154	24	21	R	
Ivory Tirupati §		Lbr	1989	11,438	10,432	150	23	20	R	ex Ivory Bay-89
Jorgen Lauritzen **		Dis	1991	14,406	16,950	164	24	19	R	
Knud Lauritzen **		Dis	1991	14,406	16,950	164	24	19	R	
Lady Korcula		Mhl	2000	11,443	12,913	155	23	20	R	
Lady Racisce		Hrv	2000	11,443	12,913	155	23	20	R	
Mexican Reefer		Pan	1994	10,203	11,575	145	22	20	R	
Orion Reefer *		Pan	1989	8,818	9,643	144	22	20	R	
Pacific Reefer		Pan	1998	10,991	12,633	145	23	21	R	
Peruvian Reefer		Dis	1992	7,944	11,092	141	20	22	R	ex Savonian Reefer-97
Rauma Reefer ‡		Cym	1985	12,411	14,499	145	24	18	R	ex Australian Reefer-00
Scandinavian Reefer		Dis	1992	7,944	11,054	141	20	22	R	

J Lauritzen (NYKLauritzenCool). ATLANTIC REEFER. *Hans Kraijenbosch*

J Lauritzen (NYKLauritzenCool). DOMINICA. *Hans Kraijenbosch*

J Lauritzen (NYKLauritzenCool). SUMMER MEADOW. *Hans Kraijenbosch*

Name	Eng	Flag	Year	GRT	DWT	Loa	Bm	Kts	Type	Former names
Skier Star **		Bhs	1981	12,061	12,475	156	23	22	R	ex Skier-02, Tundra Skier-91, Hilco Skier-88
Southern Harvest *		Sgp	1990	8,483	8,946	141	23	19	R	ex Serene Harvest-00
Splendid Harvest *		Lbr	1988	8,483	8,955	141	21	19	R	
St. Lucia †		Bhs	1993	13,077	13,981	158	24	22	R	ex Geest St. Lucia-97
Summer Bay **		Bhs	1985	12,660	13,613	169	24	24	R	ex Summer Breeze-00, Chiquita Baracoa-96, Ellen D-90
Summer Flower **		Bhs	1984	12,659	13,556	169	24	22	R	ex Chiquita Baru-96, Vivian M-90
Summer Meadow **		Bhs	1985	12,659	13,584	169	24	20	R	ex Chiquita Bocas-96, Irma M-90
Summer Wind **		Bhs	1985	12,660	13,636	169	24	24	R	ex Chiquita Burica-96, Edyth L-90
Supreme Harvest *		Vut	1988	8,483	8,937	141	21	19	R	
Triton Reefer *		Lbr	1990	8,818	9,683	144	22	18	R	
Wild Cosmos *		Pan	1998	9,859	10,097	150	22	20	R	
Wild Heather *		Pan	1998	9,859	10,114	150	22	20	R	
Wild Jasmine *		Pan	1998	9,859	10,110	150	22	20	R	
Wild Lotus *		Pan	1998	9,859	10,139	150	22	20	R	
Wild Peony *		Pan	1998	9,859	10,110	150	22	20	R	

*Joint venture with * NYK, also operating refrigerated ships chartered from various owners including ** Chartworld Shipping Corp., Greece, † Geest PLC (FII Fyffes Ltd), ‡ DFM, Poland and § Amer Shipping Ltd. See also vessels chartered from Leonhardt & Blumberg Reederei.*
Company also involved in 'handy-size' bulker pool operated with South African based Island View Shipping (Grindrod Group)

C M Lemos & Co Ltd   UK
Nereus Shipping SA/Greece
Funnel: Yellow with blue 'L' on white houseflag, black top.
Hull: Black or grey with red boot-topping.

Name	Eng	Flag	Year	GRT	DWT	Loa	Bm	Kts	Type	Former names
Authentic		Grc	2004	78,922	150,249	274	48	15	T	
Cosmic		Grc	2000	78,918	150,284	274	48	15	T	
Emerald		Grc	1986	27,535	46,793	189	32	14	B	
Majestic		Grc	2000	78,918	150,284	274	48	15	T	
North Star		Grc	1996	79,832	148,561	269	46	15	T	
Poetic		Grc	2003	78,922	150,103	274	48	15	T	
Romantic		Grc	2004	78,922	150,247	274	48	15	T	
Symphonic		Grc	2006	157,200	300,000	-	-	-	T	
Topaz		Grc	1985	27,535	46,874	189	32	14	B	

newbuildings: one further 157,200 grt tanker on order for 2006 delivery.

Leonhardt & Blumberg Schiffahrts GmbH & Co KG   Germany
Funnel: Black with red 'x' and black '+' combined on broad white band, * black with blue single wave on white rectangle with white Maltese Cross on dark blue square in top corner or charterers colours.
Hull: Dark grey, blue or black with red boot-topping or white with blue boot-topping.

Name	Eng	Flag	Year	GRT	DWT	Loa	Bm	Kts	Type	Former names
Al Shamiah		Deu	1998	15,988	20,840	170	25	20	CC	ex Hansa Trondheim-04, MSC Thailand-04, Hansa Trondheim-02, Direct Hawk-01, Hansa Trondheim-01, Direct Jabiru-00, Maersk Reunion-99, Hansa Trondheim-98
Al Yamamah		Lbr	2001	20,461	20,700	170	25	16	CC	ex Hansa Aalesund-04, MSC New Plymouth-04, Hansa Aalesund-02
APL Australia *		Lbr	2002	50,243	58,486	282	32	24	CC	ex MSC Lausanne-04, HS Explorer-02, I/a Hansa Explorer
APL Italy *		Lbr	2002	50,243	58,213	282	32	24	CC	ex MSC Arizona-05, HS Voyager-03, I/a Hansa Voyager
Cap Azul		Lbr	2002	18,334	23,493	175	27	19	CC	ex P&O Nedlloyd Nelson-04, Hansa Nordburg-02
Cap Lobos		Lbr	1997	16,915	21,519	168	27	19	CC	ex Hansa Catalina-03, CMA Xiamen-00, P&O Nedlloyd Abidjan-99, Hansa Catalina-97
CMA CGM Mercure *		Lbr	2002	50,242	58,512	280	32	24	CC	ex HS Caribe-02, I/a Hansa Caribe
CP Condor		Lbr	2000	18,335	23,579	175	27	18	CC	ex Direct Condor-05, Hansa Flensburg-00
CP Jabiru		Lbr	2000	18,335	23,600	175	27	18	CC	ex Direct Jabiru-05, Hansa Rendsburg-01
CP Kestrel		Lbr	2000	18,037	23,579	175	27	18	CC	ex Direct Kestrel-05, Hansa Sonderburg-01
CSCL Seattle *		Lbr	2001	65,131	68,100	275	40	26	CC	I/a HS Columbia, I/dn Hansa Columbia
CSCL Xiamen *		Lbr	2000	25,369	33,899	207	30	21	CC	ex Hansa Victory-00
CSCL Yantian *		Lbr	2000	25,369	33,912	207	30	21	CC	ex Hansa Liberty-00
Damaskus		Deu	1998	16,915	21,480	168	27	19	CC	ex CMA Mersin-00, Hansa Castella-99
Delmas Kerguelen		Lbr	2002	18,334	23,493	175	27	19	CC	ex Hansa Oldenburg-03
EWL Antilles		Lbr	1993	9,606	12,575	150	22	18	CC	ex Nedlloyd Curacao-97, Sea-Land Panama-95, Maya Star-94, Hansa Wismar-93
H. Kirkenes		Lbr	2002	15,988	20,463	175	27	18	CC	I/a Hansa Kirkenes

Name	Eng	Flag	Year	GRT	DWT	Loa	Bm	Kts	Type	Former names
Hansa Africa		Lbr	1997	37,398	43,378	243	32	22	CC	ex ANL Excellence-03, Ville de Venus-02, Ibn Zaidoun-00, Hansa Africa-97
Hansa Arendal		Lbr	2001	15,988	20,700	170	25	16	CC	ex TMM Chiapas-05, Hansa Arendal-02
Hansa Bergen		Lbr	1997	15,988	20,887	170	25	20	CC	ex Columbus Bondi—01, Hansa Bergen-00, Maersk Windhoek-99, Maersk Gothenburg-98, Hansa Bergen-98
Hansa Berlin		Lbr	1993	9,609	12,582	150	22	17	CC	ex P&O Nedlloyd Orinoco-05, APL Manaus-05, MB Caribe-04, Melbridge Berlin-03, EWL Venezuela-99, Hansa Berlin-98, Eagle Wisdom-95, Hansa Berlin-93
Hansa Bremen ‡		Lbr	1989	10,842	12,942	157	23	21	R	
Hansa Centaur		Lbr	1998	16,927	20,860	168	27	19	CC	ex Pacific Merchant-01, CMA Qingdao-00, P&O Nedlloyd Luanda-99, I/a Hansa Centaur
Hansa Century		Lbr	1997	31,730	34,954	193	32	22	CC	ex Kota Perdana-04, Zim Pusan I-02, Hansa Century-98, Ibn Duraid-98, Hansa Century-97
Hansa Commodore		Lbr	1997	16,915	21,470	168	27	19	CC	
Hansa Greifswald		Mlt	1996	9,605	12,559	150	22	17	CC	ex EWL West Indies-04, Hansa Greifswald-96
Hansa Kristiansand		Lbr	2001	15,988	20,700	170	25	16	CC	ex Kota Machan-03, Hansa Kristiansand-02
Hansa London		Lbr	1992	9,608	12,575	150	22	17	CC	ex Marfret Normandie-99, Maersk Zambezi-98, Gouritz-97, Hansa London-96, Maersk Santiago-96, Hansa London-92
Hansa Lubeck ‡		Lbr	1990	10,842	12,942	157	23	21	R	
Hansa Narvik		Lbr	1998	15,988	20,630	170	25	20	CC	ex Kota Serikat-03, Hansa Narvik-02, Direct Eagle-00, Hansa Narvik-99
Hansa Rostock		Lbr	1994	9,606	12,575	150	23	18	CC	
Hansa Stavanger		Deu	1997	15,988	20,526	170	25	18	CC	ex Lykes Trader-05, Cap Pasado-04, Hansa Stavanger-03, Direct Condor-00, Maersk Gauteng-99, Maersk Izmir-98, Hansa Stavanger-98
Hansa Stockholm ‡		Lbr	1991	10,842	12,942	157	23	21	R	
Hansa Stralsund		Lbr	1993	9,603	12,577	150	22	17	CC	ex Chile Star-98, Hansa Stralsund-97, Eagle Wave-96, Hansa Stralsund-93
Hansa Visby ‡		Lbr	1989	10,842	12,942	157	23	21	R	
HS Challenger ††		Lbr	2004	30,123	35,600	207	32	22	CC	ex Hansa Challenger-04
HS Discoverer ††		Lbr	2003	30,123	35,600	207	32	22	CC	ex Hansa Discovery-04
HS Norma *		Lbr	2004	62,796	115,633	250	44	15	T	
HS Tosca *		Lbr	2004	62,796	115,630	250	44	15	T	
Maersk Athens		Lbr	1998	16,915	21,473	168	27	19	CC	ex Hansa Centurion-00, CMA Kobe-00, Hansa Centurion-99
Maersk Auckland		Lbr	2003	18,334	23,493	175	27	19	CC	ex Hansa Brandenburg-03
Maersk Dampier *		Lbr	2002	50,242	57,600	280	32	24	CC	ex CMA CGM Neptune-06, I/a HS Colon-02, I/dn Hansa Colon
Maersk Danbury ††		Lbr	2005	54,271	66,762	294	32	-	CC	ex Ernest Hemingway-05
Maersk Darmstadt *		Mlt	2004	54,271	68,187	294	32	23	CC	ex HS Livingstone-04, I/d Maersk Dunkirk
Maersk Davenport ††		Lbr	2005	54,271	66,762	294	32	-	CC	
Maersk Dortmund *		Mlt	2004	54,271	66,672	294	32	23	CC	ex HS Humboldt-04
Maersk Dresden		Deu	1996	50,644	62,399	292	32	24	CC	ex Dagmar Maersk-04, Hansa Atlantic-96
Maersk Duisburg		Deu	1996	50,644	62,400	277	32	24	CC	ex Dorthe Maersk-04, Hansa Pacific-96
Maersk Malaga		Deu	1998	16,927	21,563	168	27	19	CC	ex Hansa Caledonia-03, CSAV Suape-98, Hansa Caledonia-98
Maersk Marseille		Lbr	1994	16,927	21,480	168	27	19	CC	ex CMA Inchon-00, P&O Nedlloyd Accra-99, Nedlloyd River Plate-97, Hansa Riga-94
Maersk Pireaus		Lbr	1998	16,915	21,480	168	27	19	CC	ex Hansa Calypso-00, Maersk Pireaus-00, Hansa Calypso-00, CMA Hakata-00, Hansa Calypso-99
Maersk Vaasa		Lbr	2003	16,145	20,367	170	25	19	CC	I/a H. Fyn
Maersk Ventspils		Lbr	2004	15,000	17,600	175	27	19	CC	I/a H. Ronneburg
Maersk Vilnius		Lbr	2003	18,335	23,606	175	27	18	CC	ex Hansa Augustenburg-03
Maersk Volos		Lbr	2003	18,334	17,600	175	27	19	CC	I/a H.Freyburg, I/dn Hansa Freyburg
Maersk Voshod		Deu	2003	18,334	23,600	175	27	18	CC	ex Cap Aguilar-05, Hansa Augustenburg-03
MOL Accord †		Lbr	2003	16,145	20,700	170	25	19	CC	ex H. Langeland-06, CSAV Ilha Bela-05, Cap Pilar-04, H. Langeland-03
MSC Donata		Lbr	2002	40,108	52,806	258	32	24	CC	
MSC Sarah *		Lbr	1999	53,208	67,795	294	32	24	CC	ex Saudi Yanbu-02
Norasia Alps *		Deu	1997	31,730	34,954	193	32	22	CC	ex Hansa Constitution-05, MSC Florida-03, Hansa Constitution-98, Ibn Al Akfani-98, Hansa Constitution-97

Name	Eng	Flag	Year	GRT	DWT	Loa	Bm	Kts	Type	Former names
NYK Prestige		Deu	1994	37,563	43,600	243	32	22	CC	ex Hansa India-04, P&O Nedlloyd Yantian-02, Largs Bay-99

newbuildings: six 16,000 grt container ships, three 18,334 grt, four 53,500 grt (HS Livingstone, HS Humboldt, HS Columbus and HS Barents), (*) four 36,000 grt and (††) four 27,000 grt container ships on order for 2006-7 delivery.
* owned or managed by Hansa Shipping GmbH & Co. KG, or † by Hansa Hamburg Shipping or †† Hansa Treuhand, all Germany. ‡ chartered out to NYKLauritzenCool AB q.v.

Livanos Group Greece

Sun Enterprises Ltd

Funnel: *Black with red 'L' between 'greek key' borders on broad white band.*
Hull: *Grey with red boot-topping.*

Name	Eng	Flag	Year	GRT	DWT	Loa	Bm	Kts	Type	Former names
Achilleus		Grc	1983	22,587	39,731	174	32	15	T	ex Sylvan Arrow-02, Mobil Challenge-92
Alfios		Grc	1983	21,963	38,452	171	30	15	T	ex Saucon-02, Mobil Enterprise-91
Amazon Beauty		Grc	2003	43,075	72,909	228	40	15	T	
Amazon Brilliance		Grc	2005	43,075	72,910	228	40	15	T	
Amazon Explorer		Grc	2002	43,075	72,826	228	40	15	T	
Amazon Gladiator		Grc	2001	43,075	72,910	228	40	15	T	
Amazon Guardian		Grc	1999	43,075	72,910	228	40	15	T	
Artemis		Grc	1983	22,587	39,776	174	32	15	T	ex Royal Arrow-01, Mobil Courage-91
Athina Zafirakis		Grc	2002	38,727	74,204	225	32	14	B	ex Jin Tai-04, Jin Hui-02
Atlantic Hawk		Bhs	2002	38,727	74,204	225	32	14	B	ex Jin Kang-04
Chios		Grc	1993	157,213	301,824	327	58	14	T	
Christina		Grc	1999	158,110	309,344	335	58	16	T	
Evros		Grc	2005	30,020	47,120	183	32	14	T	
Ioannis Zafirakis		Grc	2004	38,700	74,000	225	32	14	B	
Lita		Grc	2002	56,573	104,459	241	42	14	T	
Meandros		Grc	1988	52,159	91,680	244	42	14	T	ex Wenatchi-02, American Pegasus-99, Neptune Pegasus-94, Caribbean First-92
Pacific Fighter *		Bhs	1998	18,597	29,538	181	26	14	Co	ex Clipper Fighter-04, Dolisle-04
Strymon		Grc	2005	30,020	47,120	183	32	14	T	

newbuildings: two 30,100 grt 45,800 dwt tankers for 2006 delivery.
* managed by Clipper Denmark ApS

Louis Dreyfus Armateurs SAS France

Funnel: *Black with blue 'LD & C' on white band between two narrow red bands.*
Hull: *Black*

Name	Eng	Flag	Year	GRT	DWT	Loa	Bm	Kts	Type	Former names
Edouard LD	(st)	Fra	1977	79,252	67,460	281	42	20	Lng	
Jean LD		Atf	2005	89,076	171,908	289	45	-	B	
Pierre LD		Atf	2006	89,100	172,000	289	45	-	B	

Operated by subsidiary Louis Dreyfus Armateurs SNC, the main partner in G.I.E. CETRAGPA group.

Joint Stock Co LUKoil Russia

Funnel: *Black with logo on white square over white above pale blue above red bands.*
Hull: *Black with red boot-topping.*

Name	Eng	Flag	Year	GRT	DWT	Loa	Bm	Kts	Type	Former names
Astrakhan		Rus	2000	13,767	19,995	156	25	15	T	
Kaliningrad		Rus	2001	13,767	19,996	156	25	15	T	
Magas		Rus	2000	13,817	19,996	156	25	15	T	
Maikop		Rus	1999	10,321	15,441	145	23	14	T	
Murmansk		Rus	1999	10,321	15,441	145	23	14	T	
Perm		Rus	1997	10,298	15,855	145	23	14	T	
Saint Petersburg		Rus	1999	10,321	15,541	145	23	14	T	ex Sankt-Peterburg-99
Saratov		Rus	2002	13,767	19,995	154	25	15	T	
Usinsk		Rus	2002	13,815	19,800	154	25	15	T	
Volgograd		Rus	1998	10,298	15,855	145	23	14	T	

Owned by LUKoil Arctic Tanker Joint Stock Co and managed by Riverlake Shipping SA or Unicom Management Services (Cyprus) Ltd.

Murmansk Shipping Co/Russia

Funnel: *Blue with white polar bear, (or white with polar bear on broad blue band) and black top.*
Hull: *Grey, black or red with red boot-topping.*

Name	Eng	Flag	Year	GRT	DWT	Loa	Bm	Kts	Type	Former names
Admiral Ushakov		Rus	1979	14,141	19,885	162	23	14	BC	
Aleksandr Nevskiy		Rus	1978	14,141	19,885	162	23	14	BC	
Aleksandr Sledzyuk		Rus	1975	13,153	17,200	160	23	16	T	ex Urengoy-02
Aleksandr Suvorov		Rus	1979	14,141	19,885	162	23	14	BC	

Livanos Group (Sun Enterprises). AMAZON EXPLORER. *Hans Kraijenbosch*

LUKoil. MAIKOP. *Hans Kraijenbosch*

LUKoil (Murmansk Shipping). ALEKSANDR SUVOROV. *M. D. J. Lennon*

Name	Eng	Flag	Year	GRT	DWT	Loa	Bm	Kts	Type	Former names
Anatoliy Lyapidevskiy *		Cyp	1984	14,141	19,252	162	23	15	BC	
Arctic Trader *		Mlt	1994	28,420	48,170	192	32	15	B	ex Goldstar-94
Arctic Voyager *		Mlt	1994	28,420	48,131	192	32	15	B	ex Silverstar-94
Arkhangelsk *		Cyp	1983	18,627	19,943	174	25	17	Ro	
Dmitriy Donskoy		Rus	1977	14,141	19,885	162	23	14	BC	
Dmitriy Pozharskiy		Rus	1978	14,141	19,885	162	23	14	BC	
Georgiy Kononovich		Rus	1976	13,204	17,200	160	23	15	T	ex Nizhnevartovsk-03
Indiga		Rus	1976	11,290	16,420	164	22	14	T	ex Lunni-03
Ivan Bogun		Rus	1981	14,141	19,885	162	23	14	BC	
Ivan Papanin		Rus	1990	14,400	10,105	166	23	17	Ro	
Ivan Susanin		Rus	1981	14,141	19,885	162	23	14	BC	
Kandalaksha		Rus	1984	18,627	19,943	177	25	17	ROl	
Kapitan Bochek *		Cyp	1982	14,141	19,252	162	23	14	BC	
Kapitan Chukhchin		Rus	1981	14,141	19,240	162	23	14	BC	
Kapitan Danilkin		Rus	1987	18,574	19,763	174	25	17	Ro	
Kapitan Kudlay *		Cyp	1983	14,009	19,252	162	23	15	BC	
Kapitan Nazarev *		Cyp	1984	14,141	19,252	162	23	15	BC	
Kapitan Sviridov		Rus	1982	14,141	19,240	162	23	14	BC	
Kapitan Vakula *		Cyp	1983	14,141	19,252	162	23	15	BC	
Kapitan Vodenko *		Cyp	1982	14,141	19,240	162	23	15	BC	
Khatanga		Rus	1987	14,937	23,050	158	26	15	T	ex Bauska-04, Nord Skagerrak-87
Kola		Rus	1983	18,627	19,943	177	25	17	ROl	
Kolguyev		Rus	1987	16,344	28,358	180	23	13	B	ex Kolguev-04, Great Laker-03, ex Green Laker-94
Kuzma Minin		Rus	1980	14,141	19,885	162	23	14	BC	
Mikhail Kutuzov		Rus	1979	14,141	19,885	162	23	14	BC	
Mikhail Strekalovskiy		Rus	1981	14,141	19,250	162	23	14	BC	
Monchegorsk *		Cyp	1983	18,672	19,943	177	25	17	ROl	
Norilsk *		Cyp	1982	18,627	19,942	174	25	17	ROl	
Pavel Vavilov		Rus	1981	14,141	19,240	162	23	15	BC	
Pyotr (Petr) Velikiy		Rus	1978	14,141	19,885	162	23	14	BC	
Tim Buck *		Cyp	1983	14,141	19,240	162	23	14	BC	
Varzuga		Rus	1977	11,290	16,420	164	22	14	T	ex Uikku-03
Viktor Tkachyov		Rus	1981	14,141	19,240	162	23	15	BC	
Yemelyan Pugachev		Rus	1980	13,572	19,885	162	22	15	BC	
Yuriy Arshenevskiy		Rus	1986	18,574	19,724	177	25	17	ROl	
Yuriy Dolorukiy		Rus	1980	14,141	19,885	162	22	15	BC	

* owned by NB Shipping subsidiaries (managed by NB Maritime Management (Cyprus) Ltd.).

Lundqvist Rederierna   Finland

Funnel: White with yellow diamond interrupting thin blue band on blue edged broader yellow band.
Hull: Brown or black with red boot-topping.

Name		Flag	Year	GRT	DWT	Loa	Bm	Kts	Type	Former names
Alfa Britannia		Bhs	1998	56,115	99,280	248	43	14	T	
Alfa Germania		Bhs	1998	56,115	99,193	248	43	14	T	
Alfa Italia		Bhs	2002	59,719	105,588	249	43	15	T	
Hildegaard		Bhs	1999	56,115	99,122	248	43	14	T	
Katja		Bhs	1995	52,067	97,220	232	42	15	T	
Penelop		Bhs	2006	62,300	100,000	-	-	-	T	
Sarpen		Bhs	2002	59,719	105,655	248	43	15	T	
Thornbury		Bhs	2001	56,115	99,220	248	43	15	T	

MACS - Maritime Carrier AG   Switzerland

Funnel: Blue with white 'macs'.
Hull: Black with white rhinoceros symbol and 'macs', some with white band above red boot-topping.

Name		Flag	Year	GRT	DWT	Loa	Bm	Kts	Type	Former names
Algoa Bay		Mhl	1978	18,600	26,901	173	24	16	BC	ex St. Blaize-93, Rosebank-91, Virgo-89, Victory-86
Amber Lagoon		Mhl	1997	23,401	31,916	187	27	17	Co	
Blue Master *		Sgp	1971	20,578	28,876	179	26	16	Co	ex Nahoda Biru-86, Blue Master-84
Diamond Land		Mhl	1981	21,826	28,042	177	27	18	Ro	ex Columbine-94, Conti Bavaria-89, Genova-86, Conti Bavaria-85, Costa Ligure-84
Green Cape		Mhl	1981	21,826	28,052	177	27	18	Ro	ex Natal-94, Bandama-92, Conti Hammonia-91, Als Dedication-89, Conti Hammonia-87, Manhattan-86, Conti Hammonia-85, Costa Arabica-84
Grey Fox		Lbr	1998	23,401	33,684	192	27	16	Co	

Name	Eng	Flag	Year	GRT	DWT	Loa	Bm	Kts	Type	Former names
Purple Beach		Lbr	1998	23,401	31,916	187	27	17	Co	
Silverfjord *		Sgp	1972	20,584	28,876	179	26	15	Co	ex Chung Shing-87, Silverfjord-83
Stellenbosch		Vct	1978	18,600	26,847	173	24	15	BC	ex Vidal-93, Rowanbank-91, Vento-89, Venture-86
Viborg *		Sgp	1971	20,578	28,876	179	26	15	Co	ex Golden Isle-98, Tropical Isle-87, Arica-85, Taurus-81, Norbeth-78

Operated by MACS - Maritime Carrier Shipping GmbH & Co, Germany
* owned by Choosan Shipping Pte. Ltd subsidiary of Singa Ship Management Pte. Ltd., Singapore.

Malaysian International Shipping Corp Berhad   Malaysia

Funnel: Blue, broad red band divided by white band with yellow star.
Hull: Black or red with white 'MISC' or 'MISC Malaysia', red or grey boot-topping.

Name	Eng	Flag	Year	GRT	DWT	Loa	Bm	Kts	Type	Former names
Armata		Cym	1980	50,244	89,920	246	40	14	T	ex Handy Sonata-96, Kikuwa-90, Kikuwa Maru No.2-90
Bertina		Mys	1982	39,673	65,975	235	32	14	T	ex Petrobulk Saturn-89, Kohyoh Maru-88
Bunga Anggerik		Mys	1989	18,453	29,995	172	26	15	T	
Bunga Bidara		Mys	1990	17,215	23,518	177	27	18	CC	
Bunga Cenderawasih		Mys	1989	18,453	29,928	172	26	15	T	
Bunga Delima		Mys	1990	17,215	23,518	177	27	18	CC	
Bunga Kantan Dua		Sgp	2005	11,590	19,766	144	24	-	T	
Bunga Kantan Satu		Sgp	2005	11,590	19,774	144	24	-	T	
Bunga Kantan Tiga		Sgp	2005	11,590	19,734	144	24	-	T	
Bunga Kasturi ‡		Mys	2003	156,967	299,999	330	60	-	T	
Bunga Kasturi Dua †		Mys	2005	157,008	300,542	330	60	-	T	
Bunga Kekaras ‡		Mys	1995	20,378	29,990	178	30	14	T	
Bunga Kelana 3		Mys	1998	57,017	105,784	244	42	14	T	
Bunga Kelana Dua **		Mys	1997	57,017	105,575	244	42	14	T	
Bunga Kelana Empat		Mys	1999	57,017	105,815	244	42	14	T	
Bunga Kelana Enam		Mys	1999	57,017	105,811	244	42	14	T	
Bunga Kelana Lima		Mys	1999	57,017	105,400	244	42	14	T	
Bunga Kelana Satu †		Mys	1997	57,017	105,575	244	42	14	T	
Bunga Kelana Tudjuh		Mys	2004	57,500	105,000	244	42	14	T	
Bunga Kenanga ‡		Mys	2000	40,037	73,083	229	32	15	T	ex Four Cutter-00
Bunga Kenari		Mys	1991	17,215	23,574	177	27	18	CC	
Bunga Kerayong ‡		Mys	1994	12,994	18,130	160	26	13	T	
Bunga Mawar		Mys	1990	18,453	29,974	172	26	15	T	
Bunga Melati Dua		Mys	1997	22,254	32,169	177	30	14	T	
Bunga Melati Empat		Mys	1999	22,116	31,967	177	30	14	T	
Bunga Melati Enam		Mys	2000	22,116	30,000	177	30	15	T	
Bunga Melati Lima		Mys	1999	22,116	30,000	177	30	15	T	
Bunga Melati Satu		Mys	1997	22,254	32,127	177	30	14	T	
Bunga Melati Tiga		Mys	1999	22,116	31,986	177	30	15	T	
Bunga Melati Tudjuh		Mys	2000	23,000	30,000	177	30	15	T	
Bunga Pelangi		Mys	1992	53,521	61,428	275	37	24	CC	
Bunga Pelangi Dua		Mys	1995	53,521	61,777	275	37	24	CC	
Bunga Raya Dua		Mys	1998	39,582	48,244	258	32	24	CC	
Bunga Raya Satu		Mys	1998	39,582	48,304	258	32	24	CC	
Bunga Saga 9		Mys	1999	38,972	73,127	225	32	-	B	
Bunga Semarak		Mys	1990	9,951	16,924	143	22	13	T	
Bunga Seroja Satu		Mys	2006	88,600	97,000	-	-	-	CC	
Bunga Siantan		Mys	1991	9,951	16,924	143	22	13	T	
Bunga Tanjung		Mys	1991	18,453	29,980	172	26	14	T	
Bunga Terasek		Mys	1991	17,215	20,000	177	27	19	CC	
Bunga Teratai		Mys	1998	21,339	24,612	184	27	19	CC	ex Bunga Teratai Satu-01
Bunga Teratai Dua		Mys	1998	21,339	24,554	184	27	19	CC	
Bunga Teratai 4		Mys	1998	21,339	24,561	184	27	19	CC	ex Bunga Teratai Empat-05
Bunga Teratai Tiga		Mys	1998	21,339	24,554	184	27	19	CC	
Pernas Amang		Mys	1987	36,369	64,944	225	32	14	B	
Quasar **		Mys	1989	52,500	97,197	247	42	14	T	ex Freja Svea-97, Paola-89

newbuildings: four 157,000 grt tankers for 2006-8 delivery and one 88,600 grt container ship for 2007 delivery.
Controlled (62.4%) by national oil company Petronas Group (Petroleum Nasional Berhad), also own or manage 10 Lng tankers,
* on charter to Fednav Ltd. q.v. and ** managed by Anglo-Eastern Ship Management (Singapore) Pte. Ltd, † by Eagle Management or ‡ by Espl Fleet Management Sdn Berhad, Malaysia.

Name	Eng	Flag	Year	GRT	DWT	Loa	Bm	Kts	Type	Former names

American Eagle Tankers Inc Ltd/Bermuda

Funnel: *White with dark blue 'AET' symbol incorporating ships bow and six small red dashes, narrow black top.*
Hull: *Orange with red boot-topping.*

Name	Eng	Flag	Year	GRT	DWT	Loa	Bm	Kts	Type	Former names
C.S. Stealth		Mhl	2006	58,418	104,500	244	42	-	T	
C.V. Stealth		Mhl	2005	58,418	104,499	244	42	-	T	
Eagle Albany		Sgp	1998	57,929	107,160	247	42	14	T	
Eagle Anaheim		Sgp	1999	57,929	107,160	247	42	14	T	
Eagle Atlanta		Sgp	1999	57,929	107,160	247	42	14	T	
Eagle Augusta		Sgp	1999	58,156	105,345	244	42	14	T	
Eagle Auriga		Sgp	1993	55,962	102,352	241	42	14	T	ex Neptune Auriga-94
Eagle Austin		Sgp	1998	58,156	105,000	244	42	14	T	
Eagle Baltimore		Sgp	1996	57,456	99,405	253	44	14	T	
Eagle Beaumont		Sgp	1996	57,456	99,448	253	44	14	T	
Eagle Birmingham		Sgp	1997	57,456	99,343	253	44	14	T	
Eagle Boston		Sgp	1996	57,456	99,328	253	44	14	T	
Eagle Carina		Sgp	1993	52,504	95,639	247	42	14	T	ex Neptune Carina-94
Eagle Centaurus		Sgp	1992	52,504	95,644	247	42	14	T	ex Neptune Centaurus-94
Eagle Charlotte		Sgp	1997	57,949	107,169	247	42	14	T	
Eagle Columbus		Sgp	1997	57,949	107,166	247	42	14	T	
Eagle Corona		Sgp	1993	52,504	79,993	235	42	14	T	ex Neptune Corona-94
Eagle Memphis		Sgp	1987	53,483	104,499	236	43	13	T	ex Neptune Pisces-95
Eagle Milwaukee		Sgp	1987	53,483	104,385	236	43	13	T	ex Neptune Phoenix-95
Eagle Otome		Sgp	1994	52,504	95,663	247	42	14	T	ex Neptune Otome-00
Eagle Phoenix		Sgp	1998	56,346	105,500	241	42	14	T	ex Paola I-01
Eagle Subaru		Sgp	1994	52,504	95,675	247	42	14	T	ex Neptune Subaru-99
Eagle Tacoma		Sgp	2002	57,950	107,123	247	42	14	T	
Eagle Tampa		Sgp	2003	58,166	107,123	247	42	14	T	
Eagle Toledo		Sgp	2002	58,166	107,092	247	42	14	T	
Eagle Trenton		Sgp	2003	58,166	107,123	247	42	14	T	
Eagle Tucson		Sgp	2003	58,166	107,123	247	42	14	T	
Eagle Valencia		Sgp	2005	160,046	306,999	333	58	-	T	
Eagle Venice		Mys	2005	160,046	309,164	333	58	-	T	
Eagle Vermont		Sgp	2002	161,233	318,338	333	60	16	T	
Eagle Vienna		Sgp	2004	161,233	306,999	333	60	-	T	
Eagle Virginia		Sgp	2002	161,233	318,338	333	60	16	T	

newbuildings: two 57,900 dwt tankers for 2007 delivery.
Managed by Eagle Shipmanagement, Singapore.

PNSL Holdings Berhad

Subsidiary, associated with Tong Joo Shipping Pte. Ltd., owning 6 vessels and controlling Anglo-Eastern Ship Management Ltd., Hong Kong (formed by amalgamation with Denholm Ship Management Ltd) and Pacific Basin Bulk Shipping, Hong Kong (33 bulk carriers and 1 newbuilding) operating mainly in Far Eastern waters.

Marconsult Schiffahrt (GmbH & Co) KG   Germany

Funnel: *Charterers colours.*
Hull: *Black or grey with red boot-topping.*

Name	Eng	Flag	Year	GRT	DWT	Loa	Bm	Kts	Type	Former names
Lydia Oldendorff		Lbr	1998	13,066	20,526	153	24	17	Co	
MSC Java		Lbr	2000	13,066	20,567	153	24	17	Co	ex Julia Oldendorff-04
MSC Maracaibo		Lbr	1999	13,066	20,567	153	24	17	Co	ex Georg Oldendorff-03, Libra Ecuador-02, CSAV Estambul-00, Georg Oldendorff-00
MSC Toulouse		Lbr	2000	13,066	20,500	153	24	17	Co	ex Trina Oldendorff-04, Cielo del Caribe-03, Trina Oldendorff-01
Shanghai Star I		Deu	1994	16,269	23,465	165	28	19	CC	ex Buxsund-04, Maersk Shimizu-02, Contship Europe-98
Tasman Challenger		Lbr	1992	17,726	24,190	177	27	18	CC	ex Margret Oldendorff-04, NDS Proteus-03, MSC Damas-03, Margret Oldendorff-02, CCNI Austral-99

Compagnie Maritime Marfret   France

Funnel: *Blue with red 'MF', black top.*
Hull: *Black or light grey with red or pink boot-topping.*

Name	Eng	Flag	Year	GRT	DWT	Loa	Bm	Kts	Type	Former names
Delmas Forbin		Lbr	2003	18,334	23,579	175	27	18	CC	ex Durande-03, I/a Hansa Sonderburg
Marfret Douce France		Fra	2004	14,067	17,145	155	25	18	CC	ex Sima Prime-04
Providence		Fra	1995	16,252	23,334	179	25	19	CC	ex Nordcloud-96

Malaysian International Shipping. BUNGA KELANA 3. *Hans Kraijenbosch*

Malaysian International Shipping. BUNGA PELANGI DUA. *N. Kemps*

Name	Eng	Flag	Year	GRT	DWT	Loa	Bm	Kts	Type	Former names

Martime-Gesellschaft fur Maritime Diens GmbH   Germany

Funnel: *Large blue 'M' or charterers colours.*
Hull: *Grey with red boot-topping.*

Name	Eng	Flag	Year	GRT	DWT	Loa	Bm	Kts	Type	Former names
Alianca Bahia		Lbr	2002	25,587	33,940	201	30	21	CC	ex Kassandra-02
Alianca Shanghai		Lbr	1998	25,499	34,116	200	30	21	CC	ex P&O Nedlloyd Eagle-03, Columbus Texas-01, Gallia-98
Barbarossa		Atg	1980	16,868	21,569	164	29	18	CC	ex Nuova Australia-98, Zura Bhum-96, Barbarossa-94, Alum Bay-94, Sea Progress-92, Hoechst Express-91, JSS Britannia-88, JSS Los Angeles I-86, JSS Los Angeles-86, Barbarossa-86, Ibn Al-Akfani-83, I/a Barbarossa
Cap Bonavista		Lbr	1999	25,535	33,917	200	30	21	CC	ex P&O Nedlloyd La Spezia-02, I/a Cap Bonavista
Cap Cortes		Lbr	1997	16,211	20,983	168	27	21	CC	ex Fresena-03, Cabo Creus-03, Monte Rosa-01, Azteca-00, Columbus la Plata-99, Fresena-98
Cap Delgado		Lbr	2000	25,535	34,026	200	30	21	CC	ex P&O Nedlloyd Salerno-02, Cap Delgado-00
Cap Ortegal		Lbr	1998	25,500	34,362	199	30	21	CC	ex CMA CGM Delacroix-02, Cap Ortegal-00, Gemini-98
Cap Reinga		Deu	1998	16,211	20,976	168	28	21	CC	ex Columbus Coromandel-04, I/a Hispania
Clan Tribune		Lbr	1993	21,034	29,931	182	28	19	CC	ex Eyrene-05, CSAV Seoul-03, Norasia Seoul-01, CSAV Seattle-00, P&O Nedlloyd San Jose-00, Nedlloyd San Jose-98, Eyrene-93
Columbus Florida		Lbr	1997	16,211	21,008	168	27	21	CC	ex Fiducia-97
Cosco Brisbane		Lbr	2005	27,915	38,121	215	30	-	CC	
Cosco Panama		Lbr	2005	27,915	37,900	215	30	-	CC	
CSCL Lianyungang		Lbr	2001	25,535	35,976	200	30	21	CC	ex Katharina-01
CSCL Longkou		Lbr	2001	25,535	33,917	200	30	21	CC	ex Juturna-01
CSCL Yantai		Lbr	2001	25,535	33,894	200	30	21	CC	I/a Jasmin
Dolores		Lbr	1987	20,344	29,358	181	29	20	CC	ex CSAV Rio Amazonas-04, Dolores-03, P&O Nedlloyd Nina-02, Dolores-01, Kota Sempena-01, Zim Chicago-00, Dolores-99, City of Haifa-99, Dolores-98, Nelson Bay-98, Dolores-94, OOCL Breeze-93, Dolores-91, ScanDutch Gallia-90, Dolores-87
Igloo Moon *		Lbr	1987	10,195	13,125	142	22	16	Lpg	ex Gaschem Moon-87
Igloo Star *		Lbr	1986	10,195	13,125	142	22	16	Lpg	ex Gaschem Star-86
Medusa		Lbr	2006	27,915	37,900	215	30	-	CC	
Nona		Lbr	2006	27,915	37,900	215	30	-	CC	
Sea Bright		Lbr	1994	22,738	33,250	188	28	19	CC	ex Med Kaohsiung-95, Ming Bright-95
TS Shanghai		Lbr	1996	15,859	20,084	167	27	19	CC	ex Helvetia-05, Columbus Pacific-03, Sea Amazon-97, Helvetia-96, Columbus Olinda-96, Helvetia-96
X-Press Resolute		Lbr	1994	21,034	29,931	182	28	19	CC	ex CCNI Valparaiso-05, Kota Permasan-04, Elisabeth-99, Cielo di Los Angeles-99, Elisabeth-94

newbuildings: one further 27,900 grt container ship for 2007 delivery.
* managed for Tankreederei Ahrenkiel GmbH & Co. (Christian F. Ahrenkiel) q.v.

Mediterranean Shipping Co SA   Switzerland

Funnel: *Cream with cream 'MSC' on black disc, narrow black band below black top.*
Hull: *Black with red boot-topping.*

Name	Eng	Flag	Year	GRT	DWT	Loa	Bm	Kts	Type	Former names
Hyundai Pioneer *		Pan	1986	39,892	43,567	244	32	21	CC	ex MSC Pioneer-04, Hyundai Pioneer-04, P&O Nedlloyd Miami-03, Hyundai Pioneer-02
MSC Adele		Pan	1986	21,633	31,205	187	28	17	CC	ex Norasia Sharjah-94
MSC Adriana		Pan	1998	25,219	18,779	216	27	25	CC	ex MSC Malaysia-04, Warwick-03, ADCL Sheba-02, Norasia Sheba-00
MSC Agata *		Pan	1982	20,345	28,422	174	28	18	CC	ex DAL Madagascar-03, SEAL Usaramo-00, Sea Trade-97, Usaramo-87
MSC Alexa		Pan	1996	42,307	51,111	244	32	22	CC	
MSC Alexandra		Pan	1987	31,340	41,771	199	32	18	BC	ex MSC Orinoco-99, Toluca-99, MSC Nicole-99, Toluca-98
MSC Alice		Pan	1976	35,535	38,984	252	31	23	CC	ex OOCL Explorer-95, Oriental Explorer-91, Seapac Princeton-83, Oriental Statesman-81 (len-82)

Name	Eng	Flag	Year	GRT	DWT	Loa	Bm	Kts	Type	Former names
MSC Alpana *		Pan	1978	28,060	28,153	204	31	20	CC	ex Indfex SCI-02, Angela-01, Zim Beijing-01, Angela-99, Oregon Star-98, Angela-97, Uruguay Express-96, Alemania Express-92
MSC Alyssa		Pan	2001	43,575	61,487	274	32	23	CC	
MSC America *		Pan	1993	34,231	45,696	216	32	19	CC	ex American Senator-04, DSR-America-00
MSC Amy *		Pan	1992	11,872	14,342	157	23	17	CC	ex Pellini-04, Esteclipper-04, MSC Ukraine-03, Esteclipper-01, Melbridge Pride-99, Cielo del Venezuela-98, Esteclipper-97, Nedlloyd Catarina-97, Aurora-95, Esteclipper-92, l/a Kalamazoo
MSC Anahita *		Pan	1985	34,285	36,377	224	32	20	CC	ex CMC Pearl-04, Harbour Bridge-02
MSC Anastasia		Pan	1970	16,670	21,307	181	28	20	CC	ex POL Baltic-95, Leverkusen Express-90, CGM Lorraine-86, Leverkusen Express-85, pt.ex Leverkusen-78 (len/wid-78)
MSC Angela *		Pan	1975	12,364	17,110	159	23	18	Co	ex Mananjary-93, Mungo-90, Calvados-83
MSC Aniello		Pan	2000	40,631	56,916	260	32	23	CC	
MSC Annamaria		Pan	1987	21,633	31,205	187	28	17	CC	ex Norasia Al-Mansoorah-94
MSC Annick *		Pan	1988	13,315	16,768	159	23	15	CC	ex Promotor N-04, Contship Asia-03, NDS Benguela-02, Contship Asia-02, Tiger Wave-98, Jurong Express-96, Columbus Ohio-96
MSC Ans		Pan	2004	53,500	67,800	294	32	24	CC	
MSC Antonia		Pan	1985	22,667	33,864	188	28	18	CC	ex Mixteco-94, Birthe Oldendorff-93, Ville de Castor-92, DSR Oakland-92, London Senator-91, ScanDutch Hispania-89, Commander-87, Astoria-86, World Champion-85
MSC Ariane *		Pan	1970	10,837	14,714	153	23	20	Co	ex Ninghai-91, Tausala Samoa-90, Santa Clara-84, Torm America-83, Goldenfels-81, Atlantica Montreal-76, Goldenfels-72
MSC Asli **		Pan	2000	24,836	14,150	217	27	25	CC	ex Lincoln-04, ADCL Salwa-02, Norasia Salwa-00
MSC Atlantic ‡		Pan	1991	37,071	46,975	237	32	21	CC	ex Rostock Senator-02, DSR-Rostock-00
MSC Augusta		Pan	1986	21,648	31,205	187	28	17	CC	ex Norasia Pearl-94
MSC Aurora *		Pan	1971	13,276	18,534	175	23	19	CC	ex Aurora-94, Acadia-86, Atlantica Genova-76, Gruenfels-71 (len-73)
MSC Ayala *		Pan	1985	36,124	35,382	215	32	20	CC	ex Alen-04, Oasis Altair-03, Ligwa-03, Great Rizal-96, Oasis Altair-90
MSC Barbara		Pan	2002	73,819	85,250	304	40	25	CC	
MSC Benedetta		Sgp	2006	55,150	67,600				CC	
MSC Brianna		Pan	1986	40,177	43,288	244	32	19	CC	ex Neptune Jade-97
MSC Caitlin		Pan	1998	25,219	18,779	216	27	25	CC	ex Oxford-05, ADCL Shamsaa-01, Norasia Shamsaa-00, Norasia Salome-99
MSC Camille *	(2)	Pan	1970	15,769	16,070	174	26	21	Co	ex MSC Diego-98, Diego-94, San Francisco-86
MSC Canberra		Pan	1995	29,181	41,583	203	31	19	CC	ex Joseph-01, TMM Puebla-01, Joseph-00, Zim Venezia I-98, Med Fos-97, Joseph Lykes-96
MSC Carina *		Pan	1986	42,260	45,725	241	32	22	CC	ex MSC Europe-03, Rainbow Bridge-02
MSC Carla *		Pan	1986	35,953	43,300	241	32	20	CC	ex Hanjin Longbeach-01
MSC Carmen *		Pan	1979	20,391	21,457	186	27	21	CC	ex Nuova Rosandra-93, Pancaldo-89 (conv Ro-89)
MSC Carole *		Pan	1980	16,600	21,936	179	23	15	Co	ex Vega-03, Seaboard Santiago-02, Vega-02, Pamina-83, CP Hunter-81, Pamina-80
MSC Carolina		Pan	2005	65,483	72,000	275	40		- CC	
MSC Chelsea *		Pan	1983	17,468	25,412	166	29	18	CC	ex Concordia-04, Hyundai Inchon-95, Concordia-95, Nedlloyd Seoul-95, Red Sea Eureka-93, Concordia-92, Incotrans Pacific-90, Concordia-87, JSS Los Angeles-86, Concordia-86, ScanDutch Concordia-85, Concordia-83
MSC Chiara		Pan	1988	31,430	41,828	199	32	18	BC	ex TMM Morelos-01, Morelos-00
MSC Chitra		Pan	1980	33,113	38,485	231	32	23	CC	ex Crystal I-04, APL Crystal-02, NOL Crystal-00, Neptune Crystal-96
MSC Claudia	(2)	Pan	1971	50,303	35,737	261	32	24	CC	ex Oceanus Osaka-95, Kamakura Maru-88
MSC Clorinda		Pan	1981	32,238	30,714	222	32	23	CC	ex Ace Concord-94, Neptune Accord-86, Kawana-84, Ace Concord-82
MSC Corinna		Pan	1984	32,703	38,466	207	32	20	CC	ex Med Singapore-97, Ville de Sirius-94, Rhein Express-91, Verhaeren-84
MSC Corsica ††		Mhl	1980	27,994	27,631	204	31	20	CC	ex Safmarine Infant-02, SCL Infanta-00, Author-99, Benarmin-82, Author-81
MSC Cristiana *		Pan	1984	17,700	20,221	184	25	18	Co	ex Absalon-03, Kota Maha-01, Absalon-00, Kenya Star I-00, Absalon-99, Presidente Sarmiento-98, Lanka Abhaya-87, Andalusia-85, Euro Star-84

Name	Eng	Flag	Year	GRT	DWT	Loa	Bm	Kts	Type	Former names
MSC Daniela *		Pan	1972	11,506	15,967	155	23	16	Co	ex MSC Aniello-99, Aniello-94, Jogoo-80, Turmalin-78
MSC Deborah		Pan	2006	55,150	-	-	-	-	CC	
MSC Deila *		Pan	1979	20,391	21,457	186	27	21	Ro	ex Nuova Piave-93, Da Mosto-89 (conv Ro-89)
MSC Denisse *		Pan	1977	28,176	23,058	204	31	21	CC	ex CanMar Force-01, Caraibe-00
MSC Didem *		Pan	1987	35,598	43,108	241	32	21	CC	ex Savannah-05, SCI Asha-03, Savannah-02, Hanjin Savannah-01
MSC Diego		Pan	1999	40,631	56,889	260	32	23	CC	
MSC Don Giovanni		Pan	1996	29,181	41,583	203	31	19	CC	ex Jean-96, I/a Jean Lykes
MSC Dymphna		Pan	1988	36,420	43,224	241	32	22	CC	ex Hanjin Rotterdam-98
MSC Edith		Pan	1998	25,219	18,779	216	27	25	CC	ex Lykes Crusader-05, Ayrshire-04, Safmarine Prime-04, Ayrshire-03, ADCL Samantha-01, Norasia Samantha-00
MSC Edna		Pan	1977	35,599	38,686	252	31	23	CC	ex OOCL Educator-96, Oriental Educator-88, Seapac Lexington-83, Oriental Researcher-81, I/a Oriental Chevalier
MSC Ela		Pan	2004	54,304	67,800	294	32	24	CC	
MSC Elena *		Pan	1994	30,971	36,887	202	32	21	CC	ex TMM Sonora-04, Houston Express-00, Sonora -99
MSC Eleni **		Pan	2004	54,881	67,800	294	32	24	CC	
MSC Eleonora *		Pan	1994	28,892	41,667	203	31	20	CC	ex MSC Beijing-03, Trade Cosmos-02, Sea Excellence-96, Trade Cosmos-95
MSC Eliana		Pan	1970	13,875	14,258	187	23	18	CC	ex Ming Hope-90, Ho Ming-77, Hai Mou-73 (len-79)
MSC Emilia S *		Pan	1970	10,932	14,336	153	23	20	Co	ex Emilia S-94, Sternenfels-80
MSC Emma		Pan	2003	53,500	67,800	294	32	24	CC	
MSC Erminia *		Pan	1979	17,304	14,520	170	25	19	CC	ex MSC Provence-04, City of Liverpool-03, Zim Liverpool I-00, Mor Canada-99, Nikolay Golovanov-94
MSC Esthi		Lbr	2006	95,000	107,850	337	46	-	CC	
MSC Eyra *		Pan	1982	21,586	21,370	203	25	20	CC	ex Pelineo-04, Miden Agan-02, Maersk Toronto-00, Miden Agan-97, CMA Le Cap-95, Kapitan Kozlovskiy-95 (len-89)
MSC Fabienne		Pan	2004	54,774	66,825	294	32	24	CC	
MSC Federica *	(2)	Cyp	1974	21,296	21,101	209	27	18	CC	ex MSC Gina-99, Gina-94, Water Gina-91, Gina S-90, Australia-86, Malmros Monsoon-84
MSC Fiorenza		Lbr	2006	95,000	107,850	337	46	-	CC	
MSC Florentina		Pan	2003	75,590	85,000	304	40	25	CC	
MSC Floriana		Pan	1986	21,648	31,205	187	28	17	CC	ex Princess-95, Norasia Princess-94
MSC Francesca *		Pan	1971	10,837	14,819	153	23	20	Co	ex Francesca-94, Stockenfels-80
MSC Gabriella *		Pan	1983	13,038	17,330	158	23	15	Co	ex Pearl Merchant-01, New Hailong-95, Ciudad de Buenaventura-93, Webber's Post-88, Nedlloyd Cristobal-86, Giahara-86, Woermann Wangoni-85, Family Irini-84
MSC Gianna *		Pan	1983	27,758	42,077	209	30	15	BC	ex Hellen C-03, Jolly Ebano-01, Hellen C-00, Ellen Hudig-97
MSC Gina		Pan	1999	40,631	56,889	260	32	23	CC	
MSC Giorgia		Pan	1985	22,667	33,823	188	28	18	CC	ex Maya-94, DSR Yokohama-93, Tokyo Senator-91, ScanDutch Massilia-88, Azuma-87, Pacific Pride-86
MSC Giovanna		Pan	1987	27,103	25,904	178	32	18	CC	ex MSC Provence-99, Dubrovnik Express-99, Koper Express-96
MSC Giulia		Pan	1970	16,670	21,185	181	28	21	CC	ex POL Gulf-93, Ludwigshafen-90, Ludwigshafen Express-90, pt ex Ludwigshafen-79 (len/wid-79)
MSC Grace *		Pan	1991	13,861	17,298	155	23	16	Co	ex Putney Bridge-02, Melanesian Chief-00, Putney Bridge-99, Mikhail Tsarev-97, Zim Rio-96, Mikhail Tsarev-94, Contship Columbus-93, Mikhail Tsarev-93
MSC Hailey *		Pan	1994	38,395	46,967	236	32	21	CC	ex Alva Star-05, Norasia Malta-01, MSC Jasmine-98, Norasia Malta-96
MSC Heidi		Pan	2006	95,000	107,850	332	43	25	CC	
MSC Hina		Pan	1984	21,585	21,370	203	25	20	CC	ex Leixoes-03, MSC Melbourne-01, Leixoes-98, Tikhon Kiselyev-95
MSC Ilaria *		Pan	1977	20,408	16,167	181	27	18	CC	ex Antigoni-00, Norasia Toronto-00, Antigoni-99, MSC Granada-99, Antigoni-98, UB Tiger-98, Malacca Glory-98, Alkistis-96, Eastern Trader-95, Golfo de Chiriqui-95, Ciudad de Quito-84

Mediterranean Shipping Co. MSC DANIELA. *Hans Kraijenbosch*

Mediterranean Shipping Co. MSC EYRA. *J. M. Kakebeeke*

Mediterranean Shipping Co. MSC FLORENTINA. *Vandriessche Guido*

Name	Eng	Flag	Year	GRT	DWT	Loa	Bm	Kts	Type	Former names
MSC Imma *		Pan	1983	27,758	42,077	209	30	17	BC	ex Princess Stefanie-04, Jolly Avorio-01, Princess Stefanie-00, Prince Nicolas-00, Cornelis Verolme-97
MSC Immacolata *		Pan	1979	17,304	14,719	170	25	20	CC	ex Immacolata-04, Sumatra-04, MSC Sumatra-03, Essex-02, Mor UK-00, Nadezhda Obukhova-94
MSC India *		Pan	1991	13,258	17,298	155	23	16	Co	ex Albert Bridge-02, Kiribati Chief-01, Niugini Chief-01, Chekiang-99, Albert Bridge-98, Nedlloyd Everest-97, Aleksandr Marinesko-95, Orient Shreyas-95, Aleksandr Marinesko-93
MSC Ines		Lbr	2006	88,600	-	-	-	-	CC	
MSC Ingrid *		Pan	1999	53,208	67,678	294	32	25	CC	ex Saudi Jeddah-02
MSC Insa *	(3)	Pan	1972	51,608	40,227	269	32	27	CC	ex Maersk Tacoma-96, North Sea-94, Elbe Maru-89
MSC Iris *		Pan	1982	21,586	21,370	203	25	20	CC	ex Pelat-04, MSC Eyra-04, Pelat-04, Lisboa-02, P&O Nedlloyd Ottawa-00, Sea-Land Canada-99, Lisboa-97, Kapitan Gavrilov-95 (len-89)
MSC Jade *		Pan	1986	36,514	43,293	241	32	20	CC	ex Hanjin Yokohama-01
MSC Jasmine		Pan	1988	31,430	41,828	199	32	18	BC	ex TMM Oaxaca-00, Contship Houston-97, Oaxaca-96
MSC Jeanne *		Pan	1979	33,113	38,492	233	32	23	CC	ex CMC Diamond-04, APL Diamond-02, NOL Diamond-98, Neptune Diamond-96
MSC Jemima ‡‡		Pan	1994	30,971	36,887	202	32	20	CC	ex Nuevo Leon-05, TMM Nuevo Leon-03, Nuevo Leon-00
MSC Jenny *		Pan	1988	39,990	43,537	245	32	21	CC	ex Hyundai Commander-04, NYK Pride-04, Hyundai Commander-00
MSC Jessica *		Pan	1980	23,291	23,930	202	30	19	CC	ex Columbus Olivos-01, Alianca Hamburgo-98, Columbus Olivos-97, Monte Pascoal-96, Columbus Olivos-95, Monte Pascoal-90, Dunedin-86
MSC Jilhan *		Pan	1986	14,068	19,560	162	25	18	CC	ex Kapitan Kurov-04, Contship Italy-93, Red Sea Europa-91, CGM Roussillon-90, Sandra K-88, Sea Merchant-88, JSS Scandinavia-88, I/a Sandra K
MSC Joanna		Lbr	2006	95,000	107,850	337	46	25	CC	
MSC Jordan ‡		Lbr	1993	37,071	47,120	237	32	21	CC	ex Sovcomflot Senator-03
MSC Judith		Pan	2006	90,300	101,000	325	43	25	CC	
MSC Katherine Ann *		Pan	1985	17,700	20,169	184	25	18	CC	ex Alter Ego-04, Kota Mutiara-01, Alter Ego-00, Dr. Juan B. Alberdi-98, Lanka Amitha-87, Aquitania-85, I/a Eurosun
MSC Katie		Pan	1977	35,599	38,908	252	31	23	CC	ex OOCL Executive-95, Oriental Executive-89 (len-81)
MSC Katrina		Pan	1979	30,249	27,738	203	31	21	CC	ex Gulf Spirit-97, Eagle Pride-95, Gulf Spirit-94, OOCL Blossom-93, Gulf Spirit-91, Incotrans Spirit-86
MSC Kerry		Pan	1995	37,323	45,530	240	32	22	CC	ex Ville de Norma-98
MSC Lara *		Pan	1994	28,892	38,270	203	31	20	CC	ex MSC Bruxelles-04, Trade Apollo-02, Jadroplov Trader-95, Chesapeake Bay-95, Sea Excellence-94, Trade Sol-94
MSC Laura		Pan	2002	75,590	85,928	300	40	24	CC	
MSC Lauren		Pan	1982	32,238	30,790	222	32	25	CC	ex OOCL Charisma-93, Oriental Patriot-91
MSC Laurence		Pan	1977	32,341	30,937	222	32	23	CC	ex Dragon Komodo-97, NOL Coral-96, Neptune Coral-96
MSC Lea **		Pan	2000	24,836	14,150	217	27	25	CC	ex Shropshire-04, ADCL Sabrina-01, I/a Norasia Sabrina
MSC Leanne *		Pan	1983	17,702	20,128	184	25	18	Co	ex Honour-03, MSC Leanne-03, Honour-03, Kota Molek-01, Delmas Surville-00, Honour-99, Ocean Sirius-95, Lanka Asitha-89, Laredo-84
MSC Leila *		Pan	1987	13,315	16,804	159	23	16	CC	ex Tiger Cloud-05, Heluan-03, Dubai Confidence-98, Heluan-96, Columbus Olinda-96
MSC Levina		Pan	1989	36,420	43,140	241	32	21	CC	ex Hanjin Le Havre-98
MSC Lieselotte *		Pan	1983	21,586	21,370	203	25	20	CC	ex Aveiro-03, Tiger Sea-02, Aveiro-02, Nikolay Tikhonov-95 (len-89)
MSC Linzie		Pan	2003	54,881	68,209	294	32	23	CC	
MSC Lisa		Pan	2004	54,304	68,577	294	32	24	CC	
MSC Lorena		Pan	2006	50,000	54,450	261	32	24	CC	
MSC Loretta		Pan	2002	73,819	85,801	304	40	25	CC	
MSC Lucia *		Pan	1978	14,953	20,239	187	25	17	CC	ex Tiger Star-04, Hanjin Cheju-00, Ever Voyager-83

Name	Eng	Flag	Year	GRT	DWT	Loa	Bm	Kts	Type	Former names
MSC Lucy		Pan	2005	89,954	101,661	325	43	25	CC	
MSC Ludovica		Pan	2003	75,590	85,882	304	40	25	CC	
MSC Luisa		Pan	2002	75,590	84,920	304	40	25	CC	
MSC Madeleine		Lbr	2006	88,600	-	-	-	-	CC	
MSC Maeva		Pan	2005	89,954	101,661	325	43	25	CC	
MSC Magali *		Pan	1980	33,113	38,485	231	32	23	CC	ex Amber I-03, APL Amber-01, NOL Amber-00, Neptune Amber-96
MSC Malin *		Pan	1982	21,586	21,370	203	25	20	CC	ex Pelado-04, Tavira-03, Maersk Montreal-00, Tavira-97, Kapitan Kanlevskiy-95 (len-89)
MSC Mandy ‡		Pan	1993	37,071	47,120	237	32	21	CC	ex SCI Vaibhav-04, Bremen Senator-03
MSC Manu ‡	(2)	Pan	1978	52,682	49,217	259	32	22	CC	ex Kalahari-05, DAL Kalahari-05, Maersk Hamburg-95, Aberdeen Bay-93, Ortelius-92, London Express-92, Ortelius-91, London Express-90, Nuptse-88, Ortelius 86
MSC Mara		Pan	2006	55,150	-	-	-	-	CC	
MSC Maria *		Pan	1985	21,586	21,370	203	26	20	CC	ex Delphic Spirit-03, Zim Seoul-99, Delphic Spirit-99, MSC Uruguay-98, Miden River-98, Spevde Vradcos-97, Algoa Bay-95, Professor Tovstykh-95
MSC Maria Laura		Pan	1988	36,343	42,513	229	32	20	CC	ex Sea Cheetah-00, Cap Verde-00, CGM La Perouse-98, Ville de la Fontaine-93, La Fontaine-92, CGM La Perouse-91
MSC Maria Pia		Pan	1997	29,115	40,117	196	32	22	CC	ex MSC Bremen-04, Lykes Innovator-03, Safmarine Erebus-02, CMBT Erebus-01, Northern Vision-97
MSC Marianna		Pan	2002	73,819	85,250	304	40	25	CC	ex MSC Loraine-02
MSC Marina		Pan	2003	73,819	85,806	304	40	25	CC	
MSC Marta		Pan	2005	65,483	72,000	275	40	-	CC	
MSC Martina		Pan	1993	37,398	43,378	243	32	22	CC	ex Maersk Hong Kong-97, Hansa America-93
MSC Marylena		Pan	1998	25,219	18,779	216	27	25	CC	ex Cheshire-05, ADCL Savannah-01, Norasia Savannah-00
MSC Matilde *		Pan	1999	53,208	67,615	294	32	25	CC	ex Saudi Jubail-02
MSC Maureen		Pan	2003	75,590	85,832	304	40	25	CC	
MSC Maya		Pan	1988	35,598	43,184	242	32	21	CC	ex Maersk Levant-04, MSC Jamie-02, Hanjin Seattle-98
MSC Mediterranean		Pan	1995	29,181	41,583	203	31	19	CC	ex Nautic II-04, CMA CGM Monet-02, James-00, James Lykes-96
MSC Mee May		Pan	1970	16,670	21,185	181	29	21	CC	ex Mee May-94, Erlangen Express-86, Incotrans Progress-82, Erlangen Express-81, Erlangen-79 (len/wid-79)
MSC Melissa		Pan	2002	73,819	85,250	304	40	25	CC	
MSC Mia Summer		Pan	1999	25,219	18,779	216	27	25	CC	ex Buckinghamshire-05, ADCL Scarlet-01, Norasia Scarlet-00
MSC Michaela		Pan	2002	73,819	85,797	304	40	25	CC	
MSC Michele		Pan	1971	16,670	21,185	181	29	21	CC	ex Michele-94, Incotrans Pacific-86, Hoechst Express-84, Incotrans Promise-83, Hoechst Express-81, Hoechst-79 (len/wid-79)
MSC Mirella *		Pan	1989	27,103	25,904	178	32	18	CC	ex Zagreb Express-99,
MSC Monica		Pan	1993	37,398	43,378	243	32	22	CC	ex Ville d'Aquila-97, Hansa Asia-93
MSC Natalia *		Pan	1986	40,177	43,403	244	32	21	CC	ex MSC California-01, Vision-99, Choyang Vision-98, Neptune Garnet-96
MSC Nederland ‡		Pan	1992	37,071	47,120	237	32	21	CC	ex Vladivostok Mariner-03, Vladivostok Senator-02
MSC Nerissa		Pan	2004	54,881	67,800	294	32	24	CC	
MSC Nicole		Pan	1989	31,430	41,828	199	32	18	BC	ex Contship America-00, Monterrey-00, MSC Lima-98, Nedlloyd Montevideo-98, Monterrey-97
MSC Nilgun		Pan	1994	30,971	36,887	202	32	20	CC	ex P&O Nedlloyd Pinta-05, Contship Inspiration-02, TMM Yucatan-01, Yucatan-00
MSC Noa *		Pan	1986	35,953	43,270	241	32	20	CC	ex Hanjin Newyork-02
MSC Normandie ‡‡		Pan	1983	20,345	28,422	174	28	18	CC	ex New Challenge-02, DAL Reunion-02, Catherine Delmas-00, Sea Commerce-97, Usambara-87, Victoria Bay-86, Usambara-84
MSC Nuria	(2)	Pan	1977	44,154	39,454	249	32	19	CC	ex Australian Venture-96
MSC Olga		Sgp	2006	55,150	-	-	-	-	CC	
MSC Ornella		Pan	2004	54,304	67,800	294	32	24	CC	
MSC Pamela		Pan	2005	107,849	110,592	337	46	-	CC	
MSC Paola *		Pan	1978	20,295	19,974	202	26	22	CC	ex Safmarine Nomzi-01, Nomzi-00, Boringia-95

Name	Eng	Flag	Year	GRT	DWT	Loa	Bm	Kts	Type	Former names
MSC Patricia *		Pan	1990	13,651	18,150	166	24	14	Co	ex Torm America-02, Tisno-98, Torm America-97, Vardar Delmas-92, Vardar-91
MSC Peggy		Pan	1984	32,696	38,981	207	32	20	CC	ex Atlantic Bridge-98, CMBT Maeterlinck-97, Med Barcelona-96, Ville de Canopus-94, ScanDutch Helvetia-91, Maeterlinck-89
MSC Perle *		Pan	1983	17,414	25,329	166	29	18	CC	ex Corona-03, Nautic I-02, City of Dublin-00, City of Antwerp-98, City of London-97, Pacific Span-93, Incotrans Pacific-90, ScanDutch Arcadia-90, Korean Senator-88, Corona-87, Atlantic Corona-85, Corona-84, ScanDutch Corona-84, Corona-83
MSC Pilar *		Pan	1984	30,751	30,458	189	32	17	CC	ex Rigena-04, MSC Pilar-04, Rigena-04, Argolikos-03, Morgane Delmas-03, MSC Bogota-01, Argolikos-98, Nedlloyd Pernambuco-97, Deppe Texas-95, Yolande Delmas-95
MSC Poh Lin		Pan	2004	54,774	66,786	294	32	24	CC	
MSC Rachele		Pan	2005	91,038	101,898	335	43	-	CC	
MSC Rafaela		Pan	1996	42,307	51,210	243	32	22	CC	
MSC Rania		Pan	2006	94,489	107,500	332	43	-	CC	
MSC Regina		Pan	1999	40,631	56,890	260	32	23	CC	
MSC Rita		Pan	2005	89,954	101,661	325	43	-	CC	
MSC Roberta *		Pan	1986	39,892	43,567	244	32	21	CC	ex Hyundai Challenger-05, P&O Nedlloyd Panama-04, Hyundai Challenger-03
MSC Rosa M *		Cyp	1978	20,418	20,185	186	27	23	CC	ex Rosa M-94, D'Albertis-87 (con Ro-97)
MSC Rosalba		Pan	2006	95,000	107,500	332	43	-	CC	
MSC Rossella **		Pan	1993	37,396	43,878	243	32	22	CC	ex Ville de Carina-97, Hansa Europe-93
MSC Sabrina		Pan	1989	35,598	43,078	243	32	21	CC	ex Hanjin Oakland-98
MSC Samantha *		Pan	1982	30,955	34,098	210	32	18	CC	ex Pacific Sky-04, Safmarine Vaal-02, S.A. Vaal-00, Vaal-96, S.A. Vaal-87
MSC Samia	(2)	Pan	1973	40,944	35,480	265	32	26	CC	ex Maersk Kobe-94, Verrazano Bridge-93
MSC Sandra		Pan	2001	43,575	61,468	274	32	23	CC	
MSC Santhya ‡		Pan	1991	37,071	46,600	237	32	21	CC	ex Baykal Senator-04, DSR Senator-00, Vladivostok-91
MSC Sariska *		Pan	1971	13,276	18,836	175	23	18	CC	ex MSC Alexa-96, Alexa-94, Carmen Mare-87, Ville de Zenith-86, Carmen Mare-86, Passero-85, Ruhr Express-85, Geyerfels-80, Seatrain Bremen-80, Geyerfels-79, Seatrain Valley Forge-78, Atlantic Livorno-77, I/a Geyerfels (len-74)
MSC Selin *		Pan	1981	22,131	17,993	173	32	17	Ro	ex Puerto Cortes-04, Kota Eagle-89, Contender Argent-87, Cavara-86, Contender Argent-84
MSC Selma *		Mar	1985	13,769	18,155	166	23	16	CC	ex Mina—04, Kuang Ming Taichung-02, Sinar Nusa-00, Tiger Cape-96, Impala-94, Ruhland-91
MSC Shannon ‡		Pan	1991	37,071	47,120	237	32	21	CC	ex Berlin Senator-04
MSC Shaula *		Pan	1977	20,295	19,974	202	26	21	CC	ex MSC Mbashi-00, Mbashi-99, CMBT America-96, Fionia-95
MSC Sheila ‡		Pan	1999	12,396	16,211	150	23	14	CC	ex Atlantik Trader-05
MSC Silvana		Pan	2006	94,489	107,500	332	43	-	CC	
MSC Sonia	(2)	Pan	1972	50,646	40,929	261	32	24	CC	ex Sea Dominance-96, Double Haven-95, Rhine Maru-95
MSC Sophie		Pan	1993	37,398	43,294	243	32	22	CC	ex Maersk Colombo-97, Hansa Australia-93
MSC Stefania		Pan	1969	23,881	24,245	213	30	23	CC	ex Stefania-94, Shireen-88, Crescent-88, Hakozaki Maru-81
MSC Stella		Pan	2004	73,819	85,680	304	40	-	CC	
MSC Suez ‡		Pan	1993	37,071	47,120	237	32	21	CC	ex Hamburg Senator-02
MSC Sukaiyna *		Pan	1987	22,746	24,362	198	28	18	CC	ex La Boheme-04, Antares-98, Isla Gran Malvina-98
MSC Susanna		Pan	2005	107,849	109,600	337	46	-	CC	
MSC Tasmania *		Pan	1993	34,231	45,696	216	32	19	CC	ex Japan Senator-04, Choyang Elite-98, DSR-Asia-96
MSC Teresa *	(2)	Pan	1974	22,042	20,770	209	27	22	CC	ex MSC Rafaela-96, Rafaela S-94, Seagull-88, Tavara-86, Tamara-84
MSC Tina *		Pan	1986	42,259	45,721	249	32	22	CC	ex Ambassador Bridge-04
MSC Tomoko		Pan	2006	95,000	107,500	332	43	-	CC	
MSC Trinidad †		Pan	1984	31,248	37,933	203	32	18	CC	ex Jaguar-03, Maipo-02
MSC Valeria *		Pan	1970	10,837	14,666	153	23	15	C	ex Tamaitai Samoa-91, Santa Monica-84, Torm Africa-83, Deneb-81, Gutenfels-80, Atlantica New York-73, Gutenfels-72

Mediterranean Shipping Co. MSC MARIANNA. *J. M. Kakebeeke*

Mediterranean Shipping Co. MSC ORNELLA. *J. M. Kakebeeke*

Mediterranean Shipping Co. MSC PATRICIA. *J. M. Kakebeeke*

Name	Eng	Flag	Year	GRT	DWT	Loa	Bm	Kts	Type	Former names
MSC Vanessa		Pan	2003	75,590	85,844	300	40	25	CC	
MSC Veronique		Pan	1976	32,341	30,934	222	32	23	CC	ex NOL Pearl-97, Neptune Pearl-96
MSC Vittoria		Pan	2006	90,300	100,000	-	-	-	CC	
MSC Viviana		Pan	2003	73,819	85,250	304	40	25	CC	
MSC Zrin §		Mlt	1994	29,912	35,100	201	32	18	CC	ex CSAV Peru-01, Zrin-98, Columbus Bahia-98, Alemania Express-97, MSC Zrin-96, Zrin-94, Antoine de Padoue-94

newbuildings: three 107,200 grt (MSC Asya, MSC Candice, MSC Pina, MSC Sylvana), two 95,000 grt (MSC Roma, MSC Lisbon), two 51,700 grt (MSC Leigh, MSC Rosaria)

World's second largest container carrier (by vessels and capacity) - see other chartered ships in index with 'MSC' prefix
* managed by MSC Ship Management (Hong Kong) Ltd., Hong Kong or ** owned by Mediterranean Shipping Co. SrL, Italy.
‡ managed by Dobson Fleet Management Ltd., Cyprus or ‡‡ by DFM Ltd, Poland
† chartered from Technomar Shipping Inc, †† fromTarget Marine SA or § from Jadroplov International.

Minerva Marine Inc   Greece

Funnel: *Black with light blue 'MINERVA' or red with red boot-topping.*
Hull: *Dark blue with light blue over dark blue trianges on broad white band.*

Name	Eng	Flag	Year	GRT	DWT	Loa	Bm	Kts	Type	Former names
Atalandi		Grc	2004	59,781	105,306	244	42	14	T	ex Valpiave-04
Minerva Alexandra		Grc	2000	58,125	104,643	244	42	14	T	
Minerva Alice		Grc	1999	28,246	46,408	182	32	14	T	
Minerva Anna		Mlt	2005	30,050	50,922	183	32	15	T	ex Pine Venture-02
Minerva Astra		Grc	2001	59,693	105,830	248	43	15	T	l/a Stromness
Minerva Concert		Grc	2003	56,477	105,817	241	42	15	T	
Minerva Eleonora		Grc	2004	58,156	104,875	244	42	14	T	
Minerva Ellie		Grc	2005	58,156	103,194	244	42	14	T	
Minerva Emma		Grc	1999	58,125	105,000	244	42	14	T	
Minerva Grace		Mlt	2005	30,053	50,922	183	32	14	T	
Minerva Helen		Grc	2004	58,156	104,875	244	42	14	T	
Minerva Iris		Grc	2004	58,156	103,124	244	42	14	T	
Minerva Joanna		Grc	2000	28,246	46,541	183	32	14	T	
Minerva Julie		Grc	2000	28,246	46,270	183	32	14	T	
Minerva Libra		Grc	1999	58,156	105,344	244	42	15	T	l/a Al Bizzia
Minerva Lisa		Grc	2004	58,156	103,622	244	42	14	T	
Minerva Maya		Grc	2002	57,508	105,709	244	42	14	T	
Minerva Nike		Grc	2004	57,301	105,330	244	42	14	T	
Minerva Nounou		Grc	2000	80,870	147,450	274	48	14	T	
Minerva Rita		Mlt	2005	30,050	50,922	183	32	14	T	
Minerva Roxanne		Grc	2004	58,156	103,622	244	42	14	T	
Minerva Zen		Grc	1999	28,246	46,344	183	32	14	T	
Minerva Zenia		Grc	2002	59,693	105,946	248	43	15	T	ex Torness-02, l/a Wrabness
Minerva Zoe		Grc	2004	57,000	105,000	244	42	14	T	
Sanko Brave		Pan	2003	56,500	105,400	239	42	14	T	
Sanko Bright		Pan	2003	56,172	104,075	239	42	15	T	
Stemnitsa		Grc	2000	80,870	147,092	274	48	14	T	
Surfer Rosa		Mlt	2004	29,327	46,719	183	32	14	T	ex Kazbek-04

newbuildings: one 58,400 grt 105,000 dwt and three 28,238 grt 50,930 dwt tankers for 2006 delivery from Far Eastern builders.
Associated with Thenamaris (Ships Management) Inc.

Mitsui OSK Lines Ltd   Japan

Funnel: *Bright red.*
Hull: *Light blue or grey with green waterline and red boot-topping.*

Name	Eng	Flag	Year	GRT	DWT	Loa	Bm	Kts	Type	Former names
Ambassador Norris		Pan	2001	27,955	45,290	180	32	15	T	
Amity Ace		Pan	1981	41,705	18,169	199	30	18	V	ex Meiyo Maru-99
APL Chiwan *		Pan	1995	59,622	63,440	299	37	24	CC	ex MOL Tyne-02, Tyne-01
APL Dubai *		Pan	1995	60,133	62,905	300	37	24	CC	ex MOL Rhine-02, Rhine-01
APL Ningpo *		Pan	1995	58,531	61,470	300	37	24	CC	ex MOL Loire-02, La Loire-01
APL Qingdao		Pan	1995	58,923	61,489	300	37	23	CC	ex MOL Mosel-02, Mosel-00
Aquarius Ace *		Pan	1998	36,615	14,353	175	29	15	V	
Asian Spirit *		Lbr	1988	53,578	21,835	200	32	18	V	ex Hual Tribute-04
Astral Ace		Pan	2000	36,615	14,280	175	29	18	V	
Atlixco		Pan	1982	41,697	18,217	199	30	18	V	ex Clover Ace-99
Azalea Ace		Pan	1979	27,874	12,672	175	27	18	V	ex Sevenseas-92, Sevenseas Highway-88
Bravery Ace *		Pan	2000	52,276	17,686	189	32	20	V	
Brilliant Ace		Pan	1987	47,505	14,189	180	32	17	V	
Camellia Ace *		Pan	1994	55,336	18,938	200	32	18	V	

Name	Eng	Flag	Year	GRT	DWT	Loa	Bm	Kts	Type	Former names
Cattleya Ace *		Vut	1988	56,823	18,762	199	32	21	V	
Celestial Wing *		Pan	2005	44,146	15,438	180	30	-	V	
Comet Ace		Pan	2000	36,615	14,283	175	29	18	V	
Cosmos Ace *		Pan	1998	46,346	15,439	182	31	19	V	
Cosmos Venture *		Lbr	1986	46,051	17,750	188	31	18	V	
Courageous Ace *		Pan	2003	56,439	19,927	198	32	-	V	
Crystal Ace		Pan	1983	27,566	10,538	161	27	16	V	
Dynamic Express ***		Pan	1993	25,644	42,253	180	31	14	T	
Eminent Ace *		Pan	2005	58,616	18,947	200	32	-	V	
Esteem Splendour		Pan	2005	56,163	106,493	243	42	14	T	
Eternal Ace *		Pan	1988	55,380	18,701	200	32	19	V	
Euro Spirit *		Lbr	1998	46,346	15,483	188	31	19	V	
Favorite Ace		Pan	2006	59,800	17,100	200	32	20	V	
Felicity Ace		Pan	2006	59,800	17,100	200	32	20	V	
Firmament Ace		Pan	2006	59,800	17,100	200	32	20	V	
Freedom Ace *		Pan	2005	60,175	19,093	200	32	-	V	
Frontier Ace *		Pan	2000	52,276	17,693	189	32	20	V	
Frontier Express ***		Pan	1993	40,721	00,520	220	32	11	T	
Glorious Ace *		Pan	1981	46,047	17,743	190	32	18	V	
Harmony Ace *		Pan	1992	47,819	14,256	180	32	19	V	
Heroic Ace *		Pan	2002	56,439	19,879	198	32	20	V	
Iris Ace *		Pan	1983	33,521	16,461	190	32	19	V	ex Rainbow Ace-93
Liberty Ace *		Pan	2004	60,175	19,106	200	32	20	V	
Maple Ace II *		Lbr	1992	38,349	15,361	188	28	18	V	
Martorell		Pan	2003	57,789	19,531	200	32	-	V	
Marvelous Ace		Pan	2006	59,422	18,900	200	32	-	V	
Mercury Ace		Jpn	1985	44,979	16,603	176	29	17	V	
MOL Advantage		Pan	2001	66,332	66,532	279	40	25	CC	
MOL Callao †		Iom	1997	23,734	30,461	188	30	21	CC	ex City of London-04, CGM Caravelle-01, City of London-98
MOL Bravery		Pan	1995	41,114	39,788	245	32	23	CC	ex Alligator Bravery-01
MOL Columbus		Pan	1991	41,144	40,331	245	32	21	CC	ex Alligator Columbus-00
MOL Confidence **		Pan	1994	51,841	61,152	275	37	24	CC	ex Federal-04, Hyundai Federal-03
MOL Discovery		Pan	1991	42,812	40,499	253	32	22	CC	ex Alligator Discovery-01, OOCL Shanghai-98, Alligator Discovery-96
MOL Elbe		Jpn	1990	50,352	58,112	292	32	23	CC	ex Elbe-01
MOL Efficiency		Pan	2002	53,822	63,160	294	32	24	CC	
MOL Encore		Pan	2003	53,096	61,441	294	32	24	CC	
MOL Endeavor		Pan	2003	53,096	61,441	294	32	24	CC	
MOL Endurance		Pan	2003	53,096	61,441	294	32	24	CC	
MOL Enterprise		Pan	2004	53,600	49,600	294	32	24	CC	
MOL Eternity		Jpn	1985	35,234	33,687	205	32	19	CC	ex Southern Cross Maru-01
MOL Excellence		Pan	2003	53,822	50,800	294	32	24	CC	
MOL Expeditor		Pan	2003	53,822	62,800	294	32	24	CC	
MOL Express *		Pan	2003	53,400	62,800	294	32	24	CC	
MOL Fortune		Lbr	1986	40,354	41,513	226	32	20	CC	ex Alligator Fortune-01
MOL Glory		Lbr	1986	39,283	40,817	226	32	20	CC	ex Aligator Glory-01
MOL Golden Wattle		Lbr	1986	40,354	41,474	226	32	19	CC	ex Alligator Hope-01
MOL Integrity		Pan	2001	66,332	66,800	279	40	25	CC	
MOL Ingenuity *		Pan	1992	50,204	58,986	292	32	24	CC	ex MOL Danube-02, Danube-01
MOL Initiative *		Pan	1988	50,030	59,488	290	32	23	CC	ex La Seine-02
MOL Liberty *		Pan	1986	42,117	38,512	246	32	22	CC	ex Alligator Liberty-02
MOL Maas *		Lbr	1995	60,133	62,905	300	37	23	CC	ex Maas-01
MOL Miracle		Pan	1991	41,495	40,330	245	32	21	CC	ex Alligator Miracle-02, Alligator America-99
MOL Paramount		Pan	2005	72,000	72,968	293	40	-	CC	
MOL Performance *		Pan	2001	74,071	74,453	294	40	27	CC	
MOL Precision		Pan	2002	71,902	72,300	293	40	25	CC	
MOL Pride *		Lbr	1988	41,126	40,192	245	32	21	CC	ex Alligator Pride-01
MOL Priority *		Pan	2002	74,071	74,453	294	40	26	CC	
MOL Progress *		Pan	2002	71,902	72,300	293	40	25	CC	
MOL Promise		Pan	2002	71,902	72,300	293	40	25	CC	
MOL Solution		Pan	2001	71,902	72,300	293	40	25	CC	
MOL Thames *		Pan	1990	50,628	59,056	290	32	23	CC	ex Thames-00
MOL Triumph		Lbr	1988	43,082	40,540	253	32	22	CC	ex Alligator Triumph-01
MOL Wellington		Pan	1979	32,163	29,888	216	32	22	CC	ex Wellington Maru-01, Canberra Maru-87
MOL Wisdom		Pan	1995	41,114	59,814	245	32	23	CC	ex Alligator Wisdom-01
Mona Century *		Pan	2000	87,523	172,036	289	45	15	B	
Mona Liberty		Sgp	1992	77,195	151,533	273	43	14	B	ex Kohju-01

Name	Eng	Flag	Year	GRT	DWT	Loa	Bm	Kts	Type	Former names
Mona Linden *		Pan	2000	84,507	170,473	289	45	14	B	
Neptune Ace *		Pan	1985	44,979	16,560	176	29	17	V	
Nord Sun		Sgp	2004	40,300	76,830	225	32	14	B	
Nordholt		Hkg	2005	30,688	55,697	190	32	-	B	
Ocean Ace		Pan	1983	43,684	16,149	184	32	18	V	ex Meiho Maru-88
Ocean Spirit *		Lbr	1985	47,561	16,770	191	32	19	V	ex San Laurel-97, Nissan Laurel-95
Olive Ace		Lbr	1977	38,772	13,873	176	32	19	V	
Oriental Phoenix *		Lbr	1985	27,658	11,824	159	28	17	V	
Pacific Spirit *		Nis	1987	53,578	20,885	200	32	18	V	ex Hual Trophy-05, Hual Favorita-01
Paradise Ace		Pan	2004	60,175	19,080	200	32	20	V	
Pearl Ace *		Pan	1994	45,796	15,194	188	31	18	V	
Pegasus Ace *		Pan	1998	36,615	14,348	175	29	19	V	
Planet Ace *		Pan	1992	38,349	15,327	188	28	18	V	
Polaris Ace *		Pan	1997	46,346	15,522	182	31	19	V	
Progress Ace		Pan	2003	57,789	19,512	200	32	20	V	
Prominent Ace		Pan	2004	57,789	19,550	200	32	20	V	
Rainbow Wing *		Pan	1986	41,643	15,199	190	32	19	V	ex Salvia Ace-00, Continental Wing-97
Ruby Express ***		Pan	2004	57,468	106,516	241	42	14	T	
Sapphire Ace		Pan	1993	45,796	15,204	188	31	18	V	
Solar Wing *		Lbr	1988	41,604	13,224	187	32	19	V	
Splendid Ace *		Pan	2003	56,439	19,893	198	32	-	V	
Sun Ace *		Pan	1981	29,973	13,051	179	27	17	V	
Triumph Ace *		Pan	2000	55,880	20,131	194	32	20	V	
Universal Spirit *		Lbr	1985	39,948	13,025	173	30	19	V	ex Sanwa-98, Sanwa Maru-91
Victory Ace		Pan	1985	36,026	16,068	200	28	18	V	(len-87)
World Spirit		Lbr	1998	37,949	14,101	175	29	19	V	

newbuildings: Over 110 on order including container ships (16), vehicle carriers (16), tankers (23), Lng carriers (6), bulk and ore carriers (32).
* owned or managed by MO Ship Management Co. Ltd., Japan, ** by Jahre-Wallem AS, Norway or *** by Thome Ship Management, Singapore. † chartered from Andrew Weir Shipping Ltd., UK

MOL Tankship Management Ltd/UK

Name	Eng	Flag	Year	GRT	DWT	Loa	Bm	Kts	Type	Former names
African Ruby		Pan	1994	81,803	147,638	278	45	15	T	
Asian Progress II **		Sgp	2000	160,079	314,026	333	60	15	T	
Asian Progress III **		Sgp	2004	159,875	306,352	333	60	14	T	
Atlantic Hero		Pan	1992	51,984	96,687	232	42	13	T	ex Stena Concertina-99
Atlantic Liberty		Pan	1995	164,373	311,625	330	58	15	T	
Atlantic Prosperity		Pan	1996	164,373	310,000	330	58	15	T	
Bandaisan *		Pan	2000	149,282	281,037	330	60	15	T	
Chinook Maiden		Pan	1996	27,915	45,217	180	32	14	T	
Diamond Hope **		Pan	1995	146,865	259,999	322	58	15	T	
Diamond Jasmine *		Pan	1999	152,041	281,050	330	60	16	T	
Glen Maye		Pan	1992	79,595	140,991	272	46	14	T	
Glen Roy		Pan	1992	79,479	144,100	273	43	14	T	
Grand Mountain		Hkg	1993	149,323	269,141	330	59	15	T	ex Mitsumine-04
Ibukisan *		Pan	2000	160,079	299,999	330	60	15	T	
Ikomasan *		Pan	2000	160,079	299,986	333	60	15	T	
Iwatesan *		Pan	2003	159,912	300,667	333	60	16	T	
Kaimon **		Pan	1991	142,463	258,076	324	56	15	T	
Kaimon II *		Pan	2002	160,079	314,014	333	60	15	T	
Kaminesan *		Pan	2003	159,813	303,896	333	60	16	T	
Katori *		Pan	1995	146,510	259,999	324	56	15	T	
Maracas Bay		Bhs	1998	20,573	30,977	175	28	15	T	
Midnight Sun		Pan	1997	27,915	45,219	180	32	14	T	
Millennium Explorer		Pan	2000	56,695	100,063	241	42	15	T	
Naparima		Pan	1996	20,573	30,947	175	28	15	T	
Nariva		Bhs	1998	20,573	30,977	175	28	15	T	
Navix Azalea		Pan	1995	146,745	269,141	333	58	15	T	
Nichihiko		Jpn	1999	154,159	281,705	333	60	15	T	
Nichinori		Pan	2002	159,477	298,414	333	60	16	T	
Nichioh		Pan	2004	159,872	303,994	330	60	14	T	
Nichiryu		Pan	1991	137,025	249,037	324	58	15	T	
Nichiwa		Pan	1992	137,651	249,107	324	58	15	T	ex Nissho-97
Ohminesan *		Pan	1996	151,039	259,984	333	60	15	T	
Oriental Jade		Pan	2004	159,875	306,352	333	60	14	T	
Oriental Venture		Pan	1992	154,071	281,018	330	59	14	T	
Orion Trader *		Pan	1998	151,039	267,736	333	60	15	T	
Pacific Partner		Pan	2004	57,226	105,946	244	42	14	T	
Perseus Trader *		Pan	2003	160,066	299,992	333	60	16	T	

Mediterranean Shipping Co. MSC RACHELE. *Vandriessche Guido*

Minerva Marine. MINERVA ANNA. *F. de Vries*

A. P. Moller-Maersk. GUNVOR MAERSK. *Hans Kraijenbosch*

Name	Eng	Flag	Year	GRT	DWT	Loa	Bm	Kts	Type	Former names
Rokkosan *		Pan	2003	160,066	300,257	333	60	16	T	
Ruby III		Pan	1990	140,850	243,850	325	58	16	T	ex Dynamic City-06, Diamond City-00
Ryuohsan *		Pan	2000	149,282	281,050	330	60	16	T	
Selene Trader *		Pan	2003	159,912	299,991	333	60	-	T	
Takase		Pan	1999	160,220	259,993	333	60	15	T	
Vega Trader *		Pan	2003	159,813	299,985	333	60	-	T	
Washusan *		Pan	2000	152,041	281,050	330	60	16	T	
Welsh Venture		Pan	1991	151,127	280,491	330	56	14	T	
Yohteisan *		Pan	2000	149,282	281,050	330	60	16	T	

* owned or managed by subsidiary International Energy Transport Co. Ltd. or ** MOL Shipmanagement Asia, Singapore.
MOL is one of the world's largest shipping groups with many subsidiaries owning or managing over 500 vessels with many more charter. Only the largest container ships, tankers and vehicle carriers are listed, in addition to which there are numerous bulk carriers, wood-chip carriers, product tankers and Lng carriers.

A P Moller-Maersk   Denmark

Funnel: *Black with white seven-pointed star on broad light blue band.*
Hull: *Light blue with black 'Maersk Line' or 'MAERSK SEALAND', red boot-topping.*

Name	Eng	Flag	Year	GRT	DWT	Loa	Bm	Kts	Type	Former names
Donax *		Sgp	2001	61,764	79,000	245	42	15	T	ex Maersk Prosper-01
Dromus *		Sgp	1999	61,764	110,000	245	42	15	T	ex Maersk Prime-04
Eli Maersk		Dis	2000	159,187	259,999	333	58	16	T	
Ellen Maersk		Dis	2000	159,187	308,491	333	58	16	T	
Else Maersk		Dis	2000	159,187	308,491	333	58	16	T	
Hans Maersk		Dis	1993	18,360	23,257	160	26	16	Lpg	
Helene Maersk		Dis	1993	18,360	23,270	160	26	16	Lpg	
Henning Maersk		Dis	1994	18,360	23,267	160	26	16	Lpg	
Henriette Maersk		Dis	1994	18,360	23,267	160	26	16	Lpg	
Jakob Maersk		Dis	1991	23,878	36,160	185	27	16	Lpg	
Jesper Maersk		Dis	1991	23,878	36,160	185	27	16	Lpg	
Jessie Maersk		Dis	1991	23,878	36,160	185	27	16	Lpg	
Maersk Curlew		Gbr	1983	52,175	99,800	236	40	15	T	ex Maersk Dorset-97, Bin He-95, Dorthe Maersk-92
Maersk Greenock		Dis	2006	50,698	50,425	292	32	24	CC	
Maersk Holyhead		Ven	2000	17,980	20,815	159	26	18	Lpg	
Maersk Pelepas ‡		Lbr	2000	32,322	39,300	211	32	22	CC	
Maersk Perth ‡		Lbr	2001	32,322	39,300	211	32	22	CC	l/a Meta
Maersk Plymouth ‡		Lbr	2000	32,322	39,300	211	32	22	CC	ex Alexandra-00
Maersk Princess		Dis	2005	61,000	109,637	245	42	14	T	
Maersk Ras Laffan	(st)	Dis	2004	93,226	73,705	279	43	20	Lng	
Maersk Scotland		Ven	1991	11,822	16,263	158	21	15	Lpg	ex Risanger-98, Saulkrasti-91
Niels Maersk		Nis	1991	11,822	16,259	158	21	15	Lpg	ex Ravnanger-98, Salacgriva-91
Nora Maersk		Dis	2000	27,733	30,194	199	30	21	CC	
Nysted Maersk		Dis	2001	27,733	30,194	197	30	21	CC	
Paula Maersk		Dis	2000	61,764	109,354	245	42	15	T	
Peter Maersk		Dis	1999	61,764	109,693	244	32	15	T	
Ras Maersk		Dis	2003	22,181	34,999	171	27	14	T	
Ribe Maersk		Dis	2004	22,181	35,000	171	27	14	T	
Richard Maersk		Dis	2001	22,184	34,909	171	27	14	T	
Rita Maersk		Dis	2004	22,184	35,199	171	27	14	T	
Robert Maersk		Dis	2003	22,181	34,801	171	27	14	T	
Romoe Maersk		Dis	2003	22,161	34,808	171	27	14	T	
Rosa Maersk		Dis	2005	22,184	35,192	171	27	14	T	
Roy Maersk		Dis	2005	22,184	35,190	171	27	14	T	
Sea-Land Defender **		Usa	1980	32,629	30,379	257	31	20	CC	
Sea-Land Endurance **		Usa	1980	32,629	30,224	257	31	20	CC	

newbuildings - about 106 large deep-sea vessels on order including nine 300,000 dwt, four 110,000 dwt, eight 29,000 dwt and six 16,400 dwt tankers, four 47,000 grt Lpg tankers, 70 container ships between 25-106,700 grt, five 138-153,000cm LNG carriers for 2006-10 delivery.
Worlds largest container carrier (by vessels and capacity) - see other chartered ships with 'Maersk' prefix or suffix in index.
* chartered to Shell International Trading & Shipping Co Ltd, UK and ** managed by U.S. Ship Management Inc.
‡ on charter from Reederei Stefan Patjens, Germany,

Maersk Line/Denmark

Funnel: *As above, dark blue with orange band or * red with blue 5-pointed star on white disc below narrow white band and black top.*
Hull: *Black, blue or grey with red or blue boot-topping.*

Name	Eng	Flag	Year	GRT	DWT	Loa	Bm	Kts	Type	Former names
A. P. Moller		Dis	2000	91,560	104,750	347	43	25	CC	
Adrian Maersk		Dis	2004	93,496	109,000	353	43	25	CC	
Agnete Maersk		Dis	1998	14,120	17,375	155	25	18	CC	
Albert Maersk		Dis	2004	93,496	105,750	352	43	25	CC	

Name	Eng	Flag	Year	GRT	DWT	Loa	Bm	Kts	Type	Former names
Alexander Maersk		Dis	1998	14,120	17,375	155	25	18	CC	ex Adrian Maersk-04
Anna Maersk		Dis	2003	93,496	109,000	352	43	25	CC	
Arafura		Gbr	1991	37,902	44,541	241	32	18	CC	
Argonaut †	(st)	Usa	1979	17,902	16,401	186	24	20	CC	
Arnold Maersk		Dis	2003	93,496	109,000	352	43	25	CC	
Arthur Maersk		Dis	2003	93,496	105,750	352	43	25	CC	
Axel Maersk		Dis	2003	93,496	109,000	352	43	25	CC	
Caroline Maersk		Dis	2000	91,560	104,700	347	43	25	CC	
Carsten Maersk		Dis	2000	91,560	104,750	347	43	25	CC	
Cecilie Maersk		Dis	1994	20,842	28,550	190	28	18	CC	
Charlotte Maersk		Dis	2002	91,750	104,000	347	43	25	CC	
Chastine Maersk		Dis	2001	91,560	104,750	347	43	25	CC	
Christian Maersk		Dis	1992	18,979	25,375	176	28	18	CC	
Claes Maersk		Dis	1994	20,842	28,550	190	28	18	CC	
Clara Maersk		Dis	1992	18,979	25,275	176	28	18	CC	
Clementine Maersk		Dis	2002	91,921	104,750	347	43	25	CC	
Clifford Maersk		Dis	1999	91,560	104,700	348	43	25	CC	
Columbine Maersk		Dis	2002	91,921	110,000	347	43	25	CC	
Cornelia Maersk		Dis	2002	91,921	104,750	347	43	25	CC	
Cornelius Maersk		Dis	2000	91,560	104,700	347	43	25	CC	
Dirch Maersk		Dis	1996	50,698	62,418	292	32	24	CC	
Endeavor †		Usa	1991	23,953	31,829	181	31	18	CC	ex Ibn Khaldoun-97, China Sea-94, CMB Drive-91
Endurance †		Usa	1991	23,953	31,829	181	31	18	CC	ex Ibn Jubayr-97, I/a CMB Dolphin
Enterprise †		Usa	1992	23,953	31,829	181	31	18	CC	ex Ibn Zuhr-97, CMB Dawn-92
Gerd Maersk		Dis	2006	97,900	115,700	367	43	25	CC	
Gjertrud Maersk		Dis	2005	97,933	115,700	367	43	25	CC	
Glasgow Maersk		Gbr	1999	50,698	62,400	292	32	24	CC	
Gosport Maersk		Gbr	2000	50,698	51,100	292	32	24	CC	
Grasmere Maersk		Gbr	2000	50,698	62,007	292	32	24	CC	
Greenwich Maersk		Gbr	2000	50,698	62,228	292	32	24	CC	
Grete Maersk		Dis	2005	97,933	115,700	367	43	25	CC	
Gudrun Maersk		Dis	2005	97,933	115,700	367	43	25	CC	
Gunvor Maersk		Dis	2005	97,900	115,700	367	43	25	CC	
Jens Maersk		Dis	2001	30,166	27,300	216	32	23	CC	
Jepperson Maersk		Dis	2001	30,166	35,097	216	32	22	CC	
Johannes Maersk		Dis	2001	30,166	27,300	216	32	23	CC	
Jervis Bay *		Gbr	1992	50,235	59,093	292	32	22	CC	
Josephine Maersk		Dis	2002	30,166	27,300	216	32	23	CC	
Karen Maersk		Dis	1996	81,488	82,135	318	43	25	CC	
Kate Maersk		Dis	1996	81,488	84,900	318	43	25	CC	
Katrine Maersk		Dis	1997	81,488	84,900	318	43	25	CC	
Kirsten Maersk		Dis	1997	81,488	90,456	318	43	25	CC	
Knud Maersk		Dis	1996	81,488	84,900	318	43	25	CC	
Lars Maersk		Dis	2004	50,657	62,994	267	37	24	CC	
Laura Maersk		Dis	2001	50,721	63,200	266	37	24	CC	
Laust Maersk		Dis	2001	50,721	63,000	266	37	24	CC	
Leda Maersk		Dis	2001	50,721	63,200	266	37	24	CC	
Lexa Maersk		Dis	2001	50,721	63,400	266	37	24	CC	
Lica Maersk		Dis	2001	50,721	63,400	266	37	24	CC	
Luna Maersk		Dis	2002	50,721	63,400	266	37	25	CC	
Madison Maersk		Dis	1991	52,181	60,350	294	32	23	CC	
Maersk Aberdeen		Sgp	1999	14,130	17,720	155	25	18	CC	
Maersk Ahram ††		Egy	1998	14,063	17,728	155	25	18	CC	
Maersk Alabama		Usa	1998	14,120	17,375	155	25	18	CC	ex Alva Maersk-04
Maersk Antwerp		Sgp	1999	14,063	17,720	155	25	18	CC	
Maersk Arkansas		Usa	1998	14,120	17,375	155	25	18	CC	ex Angelica Maersk-04, Albert Maersk-04
Maersk Arun		Gbr	1999	14,063	14,175	155	25	18	CC	
Maersk Atlantic		Sgp	1999	14,063	17,720	155	25	18	CC	ex Swan River Bridge-00, Maersk Atlantic-99
Maersk Avon		Gbr	1999	14,063	17,728	155	25	18	CC	
Maersk Carolina		Usa	1998	50,698	62,229	292	32	24	CC	ex Grete Maersk-02
Maersk Dalton *		Gbr	1992	50,350	59,093	292	32	22	CC	ex Repulse Bay-06
Maersk Darlington *		Gbr	1993	50,350	59,093	292	32	22	CC	ex Newport Bay-06
Maersk Dartford *		Gbr	1993	50,350	59,093	292	32	23	CC	ex Singapore Bay-06
Maersk Dauphin *		Gbr	1994	50,350	59,093	292	32	22	CC	ex Providence Bay-06, Shenzen Bay-94
Maersk Delano *		Gbr	1994	50,350	59,093	292	32	22	CC	ex Shenzen Bay-06
Maersk Delmont *		Gbr	1995	50,350	59,093	292	32	22	CC	ex Colombo Bay-06
Maersk Gairloch		Gbr	2002	50,698	62,242	292	32	24	CC	
Maersk Garonne		Fra	2003	50,698	62,007	282	32	24	CC	

Name	Eng	Flag	Year	GRT	DWT	Loa	Bm	Kts	Type	Former names
Maersk Gateshead		Iom	2002	50,686	62,242	292	32	24	CC	
Maersk Gironde		Atf	2002	50,698	62,007	292	32	24	CC	
Maersk Kampala		Nld	2001	80,654	88,967	300	43	24	CC	ex P&O Nedlloyd Houtman-06
Maersk Kalmar		Nld	1998	80,942	82,700	300	43	24	CC	ex P&O Nedlloyd Rotterdam-06
Maersk Karachi		Gbr	1998	80,600	82,700	300	43	24	CC	ex P&O Nedlloyd Kobe-06
Maersk Kiel		Gbr	1998	80,942	82,702	300	43	24	CC	ex P&O Nedlloyd Southampton-06
Maersk Kimi		Nld	1998	80,600	82,700	300	43	24	CC	ex P&O Nedlloyd Kowloon-06
Maersk Kingston		Nld	2001	80,654	87,343	300	43	24	CC	ex P&O Nedlloyd Stuyvesant-06
Maersk Kithira		Gbr	2001	80,654	83,370	300	43	24	CC	ex P&O Nedlloyd Cook-06
Maersk Kyrenia		Gbr	2001	80,654	87,343	300	43	24	CC	ex P&O Nedlloyd Shackleton-06
Maersk Malacca		Sgp	1990	49,779	56,049	294	32	24	CC	ex Munkebo Maersk-03, Alsia-93
Maersk Merlion		Sgp	1990	49,874	55,971	294	32	24	CC	ex Marstal Maersk-03, Arosia-93
Maersk Miami *		Nld	1994	56,248	55,238	279	38	23	CC	ex Nedlloyd Hongkong-06
Maersk Missouri		Usa	1998	50,698	62,226	292	32	24	CC	ex Gerd Maersk-02
Maersk Nara		Nld	1985	37,814	53,726	243	32	20	CC	ex P&O Nedlloyd Brisbane-06, Nedlloyd Tokyo-97, Raleigh Bay-96, Sea Cavalier-94, Nedlloyd Tokyo-94, Maersk Tokyo-90, C.R.Tokyo-87
Maersk Nolanville *		Lbr	2004	26,833	34,287	210	30	21	CC	ex P&O Nedlloyd Susana-05, I/a Rio Taku
Maersk Nottingham *		Lbr	2004	26,833	34,000	210	32	21	CC	ex P&O Nedlloyd Regina-06, I/dn Regina Star
Maersk Palermo		Nld	1999	31,207	38,400	210	32	22	CC	ex P&O Nedlloyd Auckland-06
Maersk Patras		Gbr	1998	31,333	37,845	210	32	19	CC	ex P&O Nedlloyd Marseille-06
Maersk Pembroke		Nld	1998	31,333	38,400	210	32	22	CC	ex P&O Nedlloyd Sydney-06
Maersk Penang		Nld	1998	31,333	38,170	210	32	22	CC	ex P&O Nedlloyd Jakarta-06
Maersk Phuket		Mhl	1998	31,333	37,845	210	32	22	CC	ex P&O Nedlloyd Genoa-06
Maersk Sana *		Lbr	2004	94,724	94,724	335	43	24	CC	ex P&O Nedlloyd Mondriaan-06, Mondriaan Star-04
Maersk Santana *		Lbr	2005	94,724	94,724	335	43	24	CC	ex P&O Nedlloyd Manet-06, Manet Star-05
Maersk Sarnia *		Lbr	2005	94,724	94,724	335	43	24	CC	ex P&O Nedlloyd Michelangelo-06, Michelangelo Star-05
Maersk Seville *		Deu	2006	94,724	94,700	335	43	24	CC	ex P&O Nedlloyd Mahler-06
Maersk Sheerness *		Lbr	2006	94,724	94,700	335	43	24	CC	ex P&O Nedlloyd Mendelssohn-06
Maersk Sidney *		Lbr	2005	94,724	94,724	335	43	24	CC	ex P&O Nedlloyd Miro-06, Miro Star-05
Maersk Taranaki		Gbr	1981	30,080	27,930	200	32	20	Ro	ex P&O Nedlloyd Adelaide-06, Australia Star-99, Pyrmont Bridge-96, Heinrich Oldendorff-93, Kazimierz Pulaski-92
Maersk Virginia		Usa	2002	50,686	62,009	292	32	24	CC	ex Maersk Geelong-03
Maersk Vungtau		Nld	1980	30,175	23,678	206	31	21	CC	ex P&O Nedlloyd Los Angeles-05, Nedlloyd Zeelandia-98, Zeelandia-86, Java Winds-84, Nedlloyd Zeelandia-83, Benattow-82, Zeelandia-80
Magleby Maersk		Dis	1990	52,181	60,350	294	32	23	CC	
Majestic Maersk		Dis	1990	52,181	60,639	294	32	23	CC	
Maren Maersk		Dis	1989	52,191	60,639	294	32	23	CC	
Margrethe Maersk		Dis	1989	52,191	60,639	294	32	23	CC	
Marie Maersk		Dis	1990	52,181	60,350	294	32	23	CC	
Mathilde Maersk		Dis	1989	52,191	60,640	294	32	23	CC	
Mayview Maersk		Dis	1991	52,181	60,350	294	32	23	CC	
Mc-Kinney Maersk		Dis	1991	52,181	60,350	294	32	23	CC	
Mette Maersk		Dis	1989	52,191	60,639	294	32	23	CC	
Nedlloyd Adelaide	(2)	Bhs	1977	52,007	49,262	259	32	23	CC	ex P&O Nedlloyd Adelaide-06, Aramac-00, Nedlloyd Houtman-98, Largs Bay-90, Nedlloyd Houtman-86, Largs Bay-82, Nedlloyd Houtman-80
Nedlloyd Adriana *		Lbr	2003	26,833	34,567	210	30	21	CC	ex P&O Nedlloyd Adriana-06, Adriana Star-03
Nedlloyd Africa *		Nld	1992	48,508	50,792	266	32	21	CC	
Nedlloyd America *		Nld	1992	48,508	50,620	266	32	21	CC	
Nedlloyd Asia *		Nld	1991	48,508	50,620	266	32	21	CC	
Nedlloyd Barentsz		Nld	2000	66,526	67,785	278	40	25	CC	ex P&O Nedlloyd Barentsz-05
Nedlloyd Clarence		Nld	1983	33,405	38,351	210	32	18	CC	ex Ibn Bajjah-97, Nedlloyd Clarence-95, Algeciras Bay-94, Ibn Bajjah-94, Nedlloyd Clarence-91, Clarence-88, Nedlloyd Clarence-86
Nedlloyd Clement		Nld	1983	33,405	37,581	210	32	19	CC	ex Clement-88, Nedlloyd Clement-86
Nedlloyd Colombo		Nld	1982	32,114	32,841	211	32	19	CC	ex P&O Nedlloyd Colombo-06, Genua Express-04, Nedlloyd Colombo-03
Nedlloyd de Liefde		Lbr	1995	10,917	13,700	151	24	18	CC	ex P&O Nedlloyd de Liefde-06, Milena-05, Sigrid Wehr-04, Washington Express-01, Sigrid Wehr-00, Independent Venture-98, Sigrid Wehr-96, Cape Scott-95

A. P. Moller-Maersk. JOHANNES MAERSK. *Hans Kraijenbosch*

A. P. Moller-Maersk. ROSA MAERSK. *N. Kemps*

A. P. Moller-Maersk. NEDLLOYD HONSHU. *N. Kemps*

Name	Eng	Flag	Year	GRT	DWT	Loa	Bm	Kts	Type	Former names
Nedlloyd Drake		Gbr	2000	66,590	67,500	278	40	25	CC	ex P&O Nedlloyd Drake-06
Nedlloyd Dubai	(2)	Nld	1978	51,982	49,730	259	32	23	CC	ex P&O Nedlloyd Dubai-06, Heemskerck-05, Transvaal-87
Nedlloyd Europa *		Nld	1991	48,508	50,792	266	32	21	CC	
Nedlloyd Evita *		Lbr	2004	26,833	34,567	210	30	22	CC	ex P&O Nedlloyd Evita-06
Nedlloyd Honshu *		Nld	1995	56,248	55,238	279	38	24	CC	
Nedlloyd Houston		Nld	1983	23,930	30,040	183	31	17	CC	ex P&O Nedlloyd Houston-06, Nedlloyd van Neck-98
Nedlloyd Hudson		Nld	2000	66,526	67,900	278	40	24	CC	ex P&O Nedlloyd Houston-06
Nedlloyd Juliana *		Lbr	2003	26,833	34,315	210	30	22	CC	ex P&O Nedlloyd Juliana-06, Juliana Star-03
Nedlloyd Marita *		Lbr	2003	26,833	34,296	210	30	21	CC	ex P&O Nedlloyd Marita-05, Marita Star-04
Nedlloyd Maxima *		Lbr	2004	26,833	34,567	210	30	22	CC	ex P&O Nedlloyd Maxima-05
Nedlloyd Mercator		Nld	2000	66,526	67,785	278	40	25	CC	ex P&O Nedlloyd Mercator-06
Nedlloyd Muscat	(2)	Gbr	1977	52,055	47,196	259	32	23	CC	ex P&O Nedlloyd Ningbo-05, City of Cape Town-05, Table Bay-96, Tolaga Bay-91, Table Bay-82, Barcelona-81, Table Bay-79
Nedlloyd Nina		Gbr	1981	31,207	30,684	200	32	22	CC	ex P&O Nedlloyd Nina-06, P&O Nedlloyd Malacca-02, P&O Nedlloyd Khaleej-00, P&O Nedlloyd Piraeus-00, Asia Star-99, Maersk Hakata-99, Choyang Sydney-98, Singapore Express-96, Neptune Lazuli-94, Gebe Oldendorff-93, Tadeusz Kosciuszko-92
Nedlloyd Oceania *		Nld	1992	48,508	50,620	266	32	21	CC	
Nedlloyd Tasman		Gbr	1999	66,526	67,900	278	40	24	CC	ex P&O Nedlloyd Tasman-06
Nedlloyd Teslin *		Lbr	2004	26,833	34,567	210	30	22	CC	ex P&O Nedlloyd Teslin-05, I/dn Rio Teslin
Nedlloyd Valentina *		Lbr	2004	26,833	32,000	210	32	19	CC	ex P&O Nedlloyd Valentina-06, I/dn Valentina Star
Nele Maersk		Dis	2000	27,733	30,194	199	30	21	CC	
Nexø Maersk		Dis	2001	27,733	30,420	199	30	21	CC	
Nicolai Maersk		Dis	2000	27,733	30,420	199	30	21	CC	
Nicoline Maersk		Dis	2000	27,733	30,191	199	30	21	CC	
Olga Maersk		Dis	2003	34,202	41,028	237	32	24	CC	
Olivia Maersk		Dis	2003	34,202	41,097	237	32	24	CC	
Oluf Maersk		Dis	2003	34,202	41,028	237	32	24	CC	
Oriental Bay §		Gbr	1989	50,538	59,285	291	32	23	CC	
Peninsular Bay		Gbr	1989	50,538	59,285	290	32	23	CC	
Regina Maersk		Dis	1996	81,488	82,135	318	43	25	CC	
Sally Maersk		Dis	1998	91,560	104,696	348	43	25	CC	
Sea-Land Champion		Gbr	1995	49,985	59,840	292	32	24	CC	
Sea-Land Eagle		Gbr	1997	49,985	59,961	292	32	24	CC	
Sea-Land Freedom		Mhl	1980	32,629	30,416	257	31	20	CC	
Sea-Land Intrepid		Usa	1997	49,985	59,000	292	32	24	CC	
Sea-Land Lightning		Usa	1996	49,985	59,938	292	32	24	CC	
Sea-Land Mariner		Mhl	1980	32,629	30,489	257	31	20	CC	
Sea-Land Mercury		Gbr	1995	49,985	59,840	292	32	24	CC	
Sea-Land Meteor		Usa	1996	49,985	59,938	292	32	24	CC	
Sea-Land Pride		Usa	1985	47,667	47,171	261	32	21	CC	ex Galveston Bay-94, Mary Anne-88, American Kentucky-87
Sea-Land Value		Sgp	1984	47,667	44,751	261	32	21	CC	ex Kim D-88, American Utah-87
Sea-Land Racer		Gbr	1997	49,985	59,964	292	32	24	CC	
Sine Maersk		Dis	1998	91,560	104,696	348	43	25	CC	
Skagen Maersk		Dis	1999	91,500	104,700	348	43	25	CC	
Sofie Maersk		Dis	1999	91,500	104,696	348	43	25	CC	
Sorø Maersk		Dis	1999	91,500	104,696	348	43	25	CC	
Sovereign Maersk		Dis	1997	91,560	104,886	348	43	25	CC	
Susan Maersk		Dis	1997	91,560	104,886	348	43	25	CC	
Svend Maersk		Dis	1999	91,500	104,896	348	43	25	CC	
Svendborg Maersk		Dis	1998	91,560	104,696	348	43	25	CC	
Tåsinge Maersk		Dis	1994	20,842	28,550	190	28	18	CC	ex Maersk California-02, Caroline Maersk-97
Thies Maersk		Dis	1992	16,982	21,825	162	28	18	CC	ex Cornelia Maersk-01
Thomas Maersk		Dis	1994	18,859	25,368	176	28	18	CC	ex Maersk Tennesse-02, Thomas Maersk-97
Thurø Maersk		Dis	1991	16,982	21,825	162	28	18	CC	ex Chastine Maersk-01
Tinglev Maersk		Dis	1994	18,859	25,431	176	28	18	CC	ex Maersk Texas-02, Tinglev Maersk-97
Tobias Maersk		Gbr	1990	17,700	21,229	161	28	18	CC	ex TRSL Antares-96, Tobias Maersk-95
Torben Maersk		Gbr	1990	17,700	21,238	161	28	18	CC	
Tove Maersk		Dis	1992	16,982	21,825	162	28	18	CC	ex Charlotte Maersk-01
Trein Maersk		Gbr	1990	17,700	21,229	161	28	18	CC	ex TRSL Arcturus-97, Trein Maersk-95

Name	Eng	Flag	Year	GRT	DWT	Loa	Bm	Kts	Type	Former names
Troense Maersk	Dis		1992	16,982	21,825	162	28	18	CC	ex Maersk Colorado-03, Clifford Maersk-97

newbuildings - five 94,724 grt and four 26,700 grt container ships for 2006-7 delivery to Reederei Blue Star GmbH.
Company formed to integrate former 'P&O Nedlloyd' fleet with existing 'Sea-Land' vessels. Recent and imminent renamings are included, but further renamings and reorganisation is expected later in 2006.
Vessels are owned by subsidiaries Blue Star Ship Management BV, Netherlands, * by Reederei Blue Star GmbH, Germany, † Farrell Mediterranean Express, USA or †† owned by subsidiary Maersk Egypt SAE, Egypt.. § managed for Zodiac Maritime Agencies Ltd., UK (see Ofer Bros.)
Also see other chartered ships with 'Nedlloyd' or 'Maersk' prefixes in index.

A P Moller Singapore Pte Ltd/Singapore

Name	Eng	Flag	Year	GRT	DWT	Loa	Bm	Kts	Type	Former names
Effie Maersk		Sgp	2000	159,187	307,190	333	58	16	T	
Elisabeth Maersk		Sgp	1999	159,187	307,190	333	58	-	T	
Emilie Maersk		Sgp	1999	159,187	307,190	333	58	-	T	
Maersk Cloud *		Sgp	1983	30,588	11,164	167	28	17	V	ex Rich Victoria-89
Maersk Crest *		Sgp	1983	30,572	11,430	167	28	17	V	ex Rich Queen-89
Maersk Jewel		Sgp	2006	23,000	29,000	180	29	-	Lpg	
Maersk Phoenix		Sgp	2005	61,724	109,571	245	42	15	T	
Maersk Pointer		Sgp	2001	61,764	110,000	245	42	15	T	
Maersk Pristine		Sgp	2004	61,764	109,637	245	42	15	T	
Maersk Radiant		Sgp	2004	22,184	34,806	171	27	14	T	
Maersk Sea *		Sgp	1987	27,887	7,902	158	27	19	V	
Maersk Sun *		Sgp	1987	27,887	7,894	158	27	19	V	
Maersk Taiki *		Sgp	1998	44,219	12,490	179	32	19	V	
Maersk Taiyo *		Sgp	1996	44,219	13,778	179	32	19	V	
Maersk Teal *		Sgp	1998	44,219	12,490	179	32	19	V	
Maersk Tide *		Sgp	1997	44,219	12,490	179	32	19	V	
Maersk Wave *		Sgp	2000	51,770	12,473	180	32	20	V	
Maersk Welkin		Sgp	2006	52,691	21,500	199	32	20	V	
Maersk Willow		Sgp	2005	52,691	21,500	199	32	20	V	
Maersk Wind *		Sgp	2000	51,720	12,473	180	32	20	V	

newbuildings: two 110,000 dwt tankers, three 57,000 grt vehicle carriers and two 23,000 grt Lpg tankers for 2006-7 delivery.
* on charter to Wallenius-Wilhelmsen q.v.

The Maersk Co Ltd/UK

Name	Eng	Flag	Year	GRT	DWT	Loa	Bm	Kts	Type	Former names
CMA CGM Hispaniola		Gbr	1990	17,700	21,238	161	28	18	CC	ex Marienborg-04, Thorkil Maersk-01
Loch Rannoch ‡	(2)	Gbr	1998	75,526	130,031	270	46	14	T	
Maersk Barry		Gbr	2006	21,000	29,000	176	29	14	T	
Maersk Humber		Iom	1998	17,980	20,815	159	26	18	Lpg	ex Burgos-05, Maersk Humber-00
Maersk Ramsey		Gbr	2004	22,184	34,656	171	27	14	T	
Maersk Rapier		Iom	2000	22,181	35,000	171	27	15	T	ex Robert Maersk-00
Maersk Regent		Gbr	2003	22,181	35,000	171	27	14	T	
Maersk Richmond		Gbr	2003	22,181	35,000	171	27	14	T	
Maersk Rosyth		Gbr	2003	22,184	34,811	171	27	14	T	
Maersk Rye		Gbr	2004	22,184	34,656	171	27	14	T	
North Sea Producer *		Iom	1983	52,434	99,800	236	40	15	T	ex Dagmar Maersk-96
Sea-Land Developer		Usa	1980	32,629	30,296	257	31	20	CC	
Sea-Land Independence		Usa	1980	32,629	30,374	257	31	20	CC	
Sea-Land Innovator		Usa	1980	32,629	30,341	257	31	20	CC	

* owned by Maersk Contractors Ltd, UK and ‡ managed by BP Shipping Ltd., UK

Maersk Line Ltd/USA

Name	Eng	Flag	Year	GRT	DWT	Loa	Bm	Kts	Type	Former names
Maersk Alaska		Usa	1975	40,594	30,866	239	31	21	CC	ex SP5 Eric G. Gibson-99, pt. Adrian Maersk-94, pt. Axel Maersk-84 (len-78, len-84)
Maersk Arizona		Usa	1975	40,594	30,866	239	31	21	CC	ex LTC Calvin P. Titus-99, pt. Albert Maersk-95, pt. Adrian Maersk-84 (len-78, len-84)
Maersk Constellation		Usa	1980	20,529	21,213	182	27	18	Ro	ex Elisabeth Maersk-88, C.R. Marseille-88, Elisabeth Maersk-87
Maersk Georgia		Usa	1998	50,698	62,400	292	32	24	CC	ex Gudrun Maersk-02
Maersk Rhode Island		Usa	2002	22,161	34,801	171	27	14	T	l/a Maersk Ramsey
Sea-Land Achiever		Usa	1984	57,075	59,869	290	32	18	CC	ex Galveston Bay-02, Sea-Land Achiever-94, Leyla A-88, American Alabama-87
Sea-Land Atlantic		Usa	1985	57,075	58,943	290	32	19	CC	ex Karen H-88, American Oklahoma-87
Sea-Land Charger		Usa	1997	49,985	59,961	292	32	24	CC	
Sea-Land Comet		Usa	1995	49,985	59,840	292	32	24	CC	
Sea-Land Commitment		Usa	1985	57,075	58,869	290	32	19	Cc	ex OOCL Inspiration-00, CGM Ile de France-93, Sea-Land Commitment-91, Marguerite-88, American California-87
Sea-Land Explorer		Usa	1980	32,629	30,298	257	31	20	CC	
Sea-Land Express		Usa	1980	32,629	30,422	257	31	20	CC	

Name	Eng	Flag	Year	GRT	DWT	Loa	Bm	Kts	Type	Former names
Sea-Land Integrity		Usa	1984	57,075	58,869	290	32	19	CC	ex Virginia-88, Jacqueline-88, American Virginia-87
Sea-Land Liberator		Usa	1980	32,629	30,250	227	31	20	CC	
Sea-Land Motivator		Usa	1984	47,667	46,987	261	32	21	CC	ex Raleigh Bay-94, Elizabeth L-88, American New Jersey-87
Sea-Land Patriot		Usa	1980	32,629	30,225	257	31	20	CC	
Sea-Land Performance		Usa	1985	57,075	58,869	290	32	19	CC	ex Ruth W-88, American Washington-87
Sea-Land Quality		Usa	1985	57,075	58,869	290	32	19	CC	ex Patricia M-88, American Illinois-87
Sea-Land Voyager		Usa	1980	32,629	30,390	257	31	20	CC	
Sea-Land Florida		Usa	1984	57,075	58,943	290	32	19	CC	ex Nedlloyd Holland-00, Catherine K-88, American New York-87

Also owns seven other vessels long-term chartered to US military fleet

Safmarine Container Lines/Belgium

Funnel: *Blue with 'Safmarine' houseflag on large white disc.*
Hull: *White with blue 'Safmarine', red or green boot-topping.*

Name	Eng	Flag	Year	GRT	DWT	Loa	Bm	Kts	Type	Former names
Safmarine Asia	Iom	1985		21,887	31,290	189	28	17	CC	ex CMBT Asia-00, Norasia Samantha-84 (len-89)
Safmarine Basilea *	Che	2005		9,990	12,680	140	22	17	Co	ex SCL Basilea-05
Safmarine Cameroun	Bel	2004		24,488	28,936	196	32	20	CC	
Safmarine Concord	Bel	1988		18,037	26,152	177	28	17	CC	ex Zoe Delmas-00, Concord-99, CMBT Concord-97, Hansa Concord-95, POL East-93, Ville de Mars-92
Safmarine Cotonou	Bel	1986		21,054	29,800	182	29	18	CC	ex Maersk Cotonou-00, Nomaza-98, Mediterraneo-98, Zim Australia-96, Nedlloyd van Linschoten-94, ScanDutch Edo-89, Santa Catarina-86
Safmarine Europe	Iom	1985		21,887	31,290	189	28	17	CC	ex CMBT Europe-00, Norasia Susan-94 (len-89)
Safmarine Ibhayi ‡	Lbr	2000		32,322	39,300	211	32	22	CC	ex Maersk Pelepas-03, Heike-01
Safmarine Ikapa ‡	Lbr	2001		32,322	39,300	211	32	22	CC	ex MSC Canada-03, Liwia-02
Safmarine Kuramo	Bel	2004		24,488	28,844	196	32	20	CC	
Safmarine Leman *	Che	2005		9,990	12,680	140	22	17	Co	ex SCL Leman-05
Safmarine Nimba	Bel	2004		24,488	28,900	196	32	20	CC	
Safmarine Nokwanda	Gbr	2005		50,657	62,994	266	37	24	CC	
Safmarine Nolizwe †	Mhl	1981		20,799	25,070	186	28	20	CC	ex Nolizwe-01, CMB Plantin-94, Plantin-89
Safmarine Nomazwe	Gbr	2004		50,657	62,994	266	37	25	CC	
Safmarine Oranje	Zaf	1991		27,103	29,651	178	32	18	CC	ex Oranje-05, Safmarine Oranje-04, S.A. Oranje-00, Oranje-96

newbuildings: four 50,700 grt container ships for 2006-7 delivery.
Managed by Safmarine Technical Organisation, South Africa.
* on charter from Enzian Shipping AG, Switzerland, † from Transman Shipmanagers SA, Greece or ‡ from Reederei Stefan Patjens, Germany.
Also see other vessels in index with 'Safmarine' prefix.

A/S J Ludwig Mowinckels Rederi   Norway

Vista Ship Management AS/Norway
Funnel: *Yellow with narrow blue band on white band on broad red band beneath black top*
Hull: *Black, grey or brown with red boot-topping.*

Name	Eng	Flag	Year	GRT	DWT	Loa	Bm	Kts	Type	Former names
Borga		Nis	1992	66,671	123,665	265	43	14	T	ex Marie Knutsen-94
Fosna		Nis	1992	52,157	96,314	232	42	14	T	
Grena		Bhs	2003	80,691	148,553	278	46	14	T	
Lista	(2)	Nor	1995	17,751	27,892	170	24	14	T	
Molda		Nis	1994	52,157	96,347	238	42	14	T	

Viken Ship Management AS/Norway
Funnel: *Cream with narrow blue band on white band on broad red band beneath black top*
Hull: *Black, grey or brown, or dark green with red boot-topping.*

Name	Eng	Flag	Year	GRT	DWT	Loa	Bm	Kts	Type	Former names
Daviken *		Bhs	1987	23,306	34,752	222	23	14	B	ex Malinska-97
Erviken		Nis	2004	87,400	152,146	275	48	14	T	
Federal Fuji *		Bhs	1986	17,814	29,536	183	23	14	B	
Federal Polaris *		Bhs	1985	17,815	29,536	183	23	14	B	
Goviken *		Bhs	1987	23,306	34,752	222	23	14	B	ex Omisalj-97
Inviken *		Bhs	1986	17,313	30,070	189	23	15	B	ex Bar-97
Sandviken		Bhs	1986	23,271	34,750	222	23	-	B	ex Petka-00
Storviken		Nis	2005	82,647	151,000	-	-	-	T	
Tanea **		Iom	2005	62,806	115,340	250	44	-	T	
Torinia **		Iom	2005	62,806	115,340	250	44	-	T	
Trochus **		Iom	2006	62,806	115,345	250	44	-	T	

Name	Eng	Flag	Year	GRT	DWT	Loa	Bm	Kts	Type	Former names
Utviken *		Bhs	1987	17,191	30,052	189	23	16	B	ex C. Bianco-95, Bijelo Polje-92

*On charter to * Fednav Ltd., Canada or long-term bareboat charter to ** Royal Dutch-Shell Group q.v.*

MPC Munchmeyer Petersen Steamship GmbH   Germany

Funnel: *Charterers colours.*
Hull: *Grey with red boot-topping.*

Name	Eng	Flag	Year	GRT	DWT	Loa	Bm	Kts	Type	Former names
Cabo Creus	Deu		2003	25,703	33,795	208	30	-	CC	ex Rio Valiente-03
CSCL Hong Kong	Lbr		2001	65,059	68,122	275	40	-	CC	
CSCL Shanghai	Lbr		2000	65,059	68,122	275	40	-	CC	
Hugo Oldendorff	Mlt		1998	25,791	44,144	199	30	14	B	
Maersk Naples	Lbr		2004	27,059	34,415	212	30	22	CC	
Maersk Narbonne *	Lbr		2005	27,059	34,426	212	30	22	CC	ex Coral Bay, l/d Caroline E
Maersk Narvik	Lbr		2005	27,059	34,444	212	30	22	CC	l/a Rio Eider
Maersk Nashville *	Lbr		2005	27,059	34,200	212	30	22	CC	l/d Andres E
Rio Adour	Lbr		2006	27,322	34,200	212	30	22	CC	
Rio Ardeche	Lbr		2006	27,322	34,200	212	30	22	CC	
Rio Branco	Lbr		1998	13,066	20,501	153	24	17	Co	ex Julius Oldendorff-03, P&O Nedlloyd Djibouti-00, l/a Julius Oldendorff
Rio Grande	Lbr		1998	13,066	20,567	153	24	17	Co	ex Friedrich Oldendorff-03, Cielo del Peru-01, Friedrich Oldendorff-01
Rio Lawrence	Lbr		2005	9,978	12,545	149	23	-	CC	
Rio Negro	Lbr		1999	13,066	20,567	153	24	17	Co	ex Hermann Oldendorff-03
Rio Rubio	Lbr		1999	13,066	20,567	153	24	17	Co	ex Johann Oldendorff-02
Rio Stora	Lbr		2006	28,000	28,325	189	29	-	CC	
Rio Susa	Lbr		2006	28,000	28,325	189	29	-	CC	
Yangtze River	Lbr		1998	25,791	44,114	199	30	15	B	ex Gerdt Oldendorff-05
Zella Oldendorff	Lbr		2001	39,893	73,931	225	32	14	B	ex Trave River-01

newbuildings - one 28,000 grt and five 25,000 grt container ships for 2006-8 delivery,
* managed by NSC Schiffahrts GmbH

The National Shipping Company of Saudi Arabia   Saudi Arabia

Funnel: *White with yellow palm tree and crossed swords between two narrow green bands, narrow black top.*
Hull: *Green or red with yellow 'NSCSA', red or blue boot-topping.*

Name	Eng	Flag	Year	GRT	DWT	Loa	Bm	Kts	Type	Former names
Abqaiq	Bhs		2002	159,990	302,986	333	58	16	T	
Al Farabi †	Sau		1986	26,464	41,158	178	32	14	T	
Ghawar	Bhs		1996	163,882	300,361	340	56	15	T	
Harad	Bhs		2001	159,990	303,115	333	58	17	T	l/a Hellespont Burnside
Hawtah	Bhs		1996	163,882	300,361	340	56	15	T	
Matjam	Bhs		2002	159,990	303,115	333	58	17	T	
NCC Arar *	Nis		1982	14,627	23,016	159	23	14	T	ex Austanger-90
NCC Asir *	Nis		1982	14,627	23,016	159	23	16	T	ex Bow Explorer-90, Grenanger-90
NCC Baha *	Nis		1985	15,817	24,728	172	28	14	T	ex Bow Falcon-90, Fjellanger-90, Northern Falcon-89, Portela-88
NCC Hijaz	Pan		2005	29,575	46,000	183	32	-	T	
NCC Jizan **	Nis		1976	17,561	28,025	171	25	17	T	ex Bow Saint-90, Torvanger-90
NCC Jubail **	Nis		1996	23,197	37,449	183	32	16	T	
NCC Madinah **	Nis		1976	17,561	28,060	171	25	17	T	ex Bow Selene-90, Nordanger-90
NCC Mekka **	Nis		1995	23,197	37,272	183	32	16	T	
NCC Najd	Pan		2005	29,575	45,998	183	32	-	T	
NCC Riyad **	Nis		1994	23,197	37,252	183	32	16	T	
NCC Tihama	Pan		2006	29,575	46,200	183	32	-	T	
NCC Yamamah **	Nis		1977	17,561	28,053	171	25	17	T	ex Bow Stellar-90, Spinanger-90
Ramlah	Bhs		1996	163,882	300,361	340	56	15	T	
Safaniyah	Bhs		1997	163,882	300,361	340	56	15	T	
Safwa	Bhs		2002	159,990	302,977	333	58	16	T	
Saudi Abha	Sau		1983	44,171	42,600	249	32	18	Ro	
Saudi Diriyah	Sau		1983	44,171	42,600	249	32	18	Ro	
Saudi Hofuf	Sau		1983	44,171	42,600	249	32	18	Ro	
Saudi Tabuk	Sau		1983	44,171	42,600	249	32	18	Ro	
Uqba Ibn Nafi	Sau		1985	28,195	42,825	180	32	14	T	
Watban	Bhs		1996	163,882	300,361	340	56	15	T	

** owned by subsidiary National Chemical Carriers Ltd., and managed by Mideast Ship Management Ltd or ** by Odfjell ASA , Norway q.v.*
† owned by Arabian Chemical Carriers (formed jointly with United Arab Shipping Co.) and managed by Mideast Ship Management Ltd, UAE.

Name	Eng	Flag	Year	GRT	DWT	Loa	Bm	Kts	Type	Former names

Navalmar (UK) Ltd

UK

Funnel: Black
Hull: Black or grey with red boot-topping.

Name	Eng	Flag	Year	GRT	DWT	Loa	Bm	Kts	Type	Former names
Bio Bio		Cym	1979	26,078	38,542	182	29	14	BC	ex Bio Bio I-95, Bio Bio-93, Grebe Arrow-92, Mannar-90, Sun Maiko-86, La Primavera-85
Dover Castle		Cym	1982	28,964	41,800	187	30	15	Co	ex Waardrecht-01, Westwood Fuji-98, Waardrecht-94, Med Sky-94, Puebla-93, Med Sky-92, Waardrecht-89, Westwood Magellan-86, Waardrecht-85, Willine Tokyo-85, Waardrecht-84, Ibn al Kadi-83, l/a Waardrecht
Fjordstone		Vct	1978	21,193	31,945	162	27	15	BC	ex Dryso-98
Houston		Cym	1979	23,239	31,507	183	27	18	Co	ex Rickmers Houston-03, Hoegh Clipper-97
Humboldt Current		Vct	1981	16,992	24,432	193	23	16	Co	ex Torm S.P.-93, Simo Matavulj-91, Konkar Thetis-87
Leeds Castle		Cym	1982	26,964	41,880	187	30	16	BC	ex CSAV Barcelona-01, Leeds Castle-01, Wieldrecht-01, Westwood Halla-99, Star Livorno-95, Yucatan-93, Star Livorno-92, Wieldrecht-90
Luni Castle *		Mlt	1982	20,919	31,960	183	28	15	B	ex Lokris-04, Bunga Kenanga-99
Med Carrara		Cym	1981	26,847	43,300	177	33	14	B	ex ICL Jayam Kondan-00, Howard Smith-92
Med Lerici		Cym	1979	15,959	22,857	177	23	15	Co	ex Med Neapolis-98, Ionian Star-96, Meissen-92
Med Riva		Mlt	1978	16,161	23,340	177	23	15	Co	ex Med Sorrento-98, Sky I-96, Ionian Sky-96, Jena-92
Med Salvador		Irl	1982	30,013	49,228	190	32	14	B	ex Iman-03, Neslihan-92, Baiona-90, Suo Maru-88
Olinda Castle *		Irl	1981	21,284	32,680	183	28	-	BC	ex Timberland-03, Ljubljana-02, Cielo di Firenze-98, Ljubljana-93, Ioannis Zafirakis-88, Brazil Venture-86
Patara *		Vct	1979	16,281	24,274	177	23	15	Co	ex Rio Express-03, Med Pisa-98, Rover-95, Star Rover-88, Searover-88, Feng Shiang-87, Fengtien-86
Portinari		Mlt	1978	21,669	28,800	201	25	16	CC	ex Vermeer-02, Lontue-99, Ville de Bordeaux-91, Red Sea Entente-90, Ville de Bordeaux-89, Hapag Lloyd Kiel-82, Ville de Bordeaux-81, Seatrain West Point-79, Ville de Bordeaux-78 (len/conv C-82)
Rembrandt **		Vct	1975	16,166	26,680	171	25	14	B	ex Finiki-98, Pacduchess-93
Rossel Current		Vct	1981	16,992	24,491	193	23	16	Co	ex Juraj Dalmatinac-93, Konkar Doris-87
Rubens		Mlt	1977	21,449	29,240	198	25	20	CC	ex Limari-99, Ville d'Anvers-91, Apapa-91, Red Sea Envoy-89, Antsiranana-87, Ville d'Anvers-87 (len/conv C-80)
Taurus		Cym	1981	16,992	37,425	182	30	13	Co	ex Great Trans-01, Leopold Oldendorff-01, Great Trans-99, Infanta-94, Taurus-88
Valpolicella		Vct	1983	20,627	32,243	183	28	15	B	ex Swordfish-04, Packing-03
Van Dyck *		Vct	1976	16,166	26,681	171	25	14	B	ex Eliki-98, Pacbaron-93
Verona Castle		Pan	1981	29,709	49,000	190	32	14	B	ex Fanfare-05, Fanoula-03, Mosdeep-98, Casuarina-89, Yamaoki Maru-88
Windsor Castle		Cym	1982	26,964	41,820	187	30	16	BC	ex Wennsdrecht-01, Nedlloyd Abidjan-97, Star Lorraine-95, Altamira-93, Star Lorraine-92, Woensdrecht-90
York Castle		Cym	1985	29,660	46,650	196	32	17	BC	ex Maria-03, Mitla-99

*Managed by B Navi SpA, Italy and * owned by subsidiaries Navalmar Transportes Maritimos Ltda, Madeira or ** Navalmar Lanka (Pvt) Ltd., Sri Lanka.*

MC Shipping Inc/Bermuda

Funnel: White with red 'MC', narrow black top or charterers colours.
Hull: Grey with red boot-topping.

Name	Eng	Flag	Year	GRT	DWT	Loa	Bm	Kts	Type	Former names
Ankara		Bhs	1975	33,401	37,129	239	31	24	CC	ex Maersk Bahrain-04, Anna Maersk-98, pt ex Anders Maersk-84 (len-78/84)
Galileo		Iom	1982	39,932	47,594	210	31	17	Lpg	ex Isomeria-05
La Forge		Bhs	1981	42,501	45,587	225	32	15	Lpg	ex Benny Queen-96
Maersk Barcelona *		Bhs	1975	33,400	37,115	239	31	24	CC	ex Axel Maersk-98, pt ex Anna Maersk-84 (len- 78/84)
Maersk Belawan		Bhs	1976	33,401	37,212	239	31	24	CC	ex Arthur Maersk-98 (len-78/83)
Maersk Brisbane		Bhs	1976	33,401	37,129	239	31	24	CC	ex Anders Maersk-98, pt ex Arthur Maersk-83 (len-78/83)

* managed by Munia Mobilien GmbH & Co. KG.

Name	Eng	Flag	Year	GRT	DWT	Loa	Bm	Kts	Type	Former names

Navigation Maritime Bulgare

Bulgaria

Funnel: *Yellow with broad red band.*
Hull: *Black with red boot-topping.*

Name	Eng	Flag	Year	GRT	DWT	Loa	Bm	Kts	Type	Former names
Adalbert Antonov		Bgr	1979	23,363	38,510	202	28	14	B	
Aleko Konstantinov		Bgr	1985	12,554	15,442	159	23	17	CC	
Alexander Dimitrov		Mlt	1985	23,609	38,524	199	28	15	B	
Balgarka		Mlt	2004	25,065	41,425	186	30	14	B	ex Dolly-03
Balkan		Bgr	1975	15,865	24,386	185	23	14	B	
Belmeken		Bgr	1973	16,151	23,738	185	23	15	B	
Bogdan		Bgr	1997	10,220	14,011	142	22	13	B	
Bulgaria		Bgr	1978	30,596	52,975	215	32	14	B	
Dimitrovsky Komsomol		Mlt	1985	23,444	38,545	201	28	15	B	
General Vladimir Zaimov		Bgr	1973	16,150	23,661	185	23	15	B	
Geo Milev		Bgr	1985	12,174	14,814	159	23	18	C	
Georgi Grigorov		Mlt	1986	23,540	38,518	199	28	15	B	
Kamenitza		Bgr	1980	16,188	24,150	185	20	11	B	
Kapitan Georgi Georgiev		Bgr	1980	16,188	24,150	185	23	14	B	
Kom		Mlt	1997	10,220	13,971	142	22	13	B	
Koznitsa		Bgr	1984	16,502	24,100	185	23	14	B	
Liliana Dimitrova		Bgr	1982	23,779	38,135	202	28	16	B	
Malyovitza		Bgr	1983	16,188	24,456	184	23	14	B	
Midjur		Mlt	1992	13,834	21,537	168	25	13	B	
Milin Kamak		Bgr	1979	16,166	24,596	185	23	14	B	
Okoitchitza		Bgr	1982	16,188	24,148	184	23	14	B	
Perelik		Mlt	1998	10,220	13,900	142	22	13	B	
Persenk		Mlt	1998	10,228	13,887	142	22	13	B	
Petimata OT RMS		Bgr	1978	23,363	38,400	202	28	14	B	
Peyo Yavorov		Bgr	1984	12,554	15,104	159	23	18	C	
Plana		Mlt	1991	13,834	19,985	169	25	13	B	
Plovdiv		Mlt	1989	11,982	14,101	157	23	16	CC	ex Nedlloyd Marne-97, Armada Sprinter-97, Nedlloyd Marne-96, Waterdrager-91
Rila		Bgr	1977	16,166	24,354	185	23	14	B	
Rodina		Bgr	1978	30,596	52,975	215	32	14	B	
Rodopi		Bgr	1978	16,166	24,708	185	23	14	B	
Rojen		Bgr	1978	16,166	24,500	185	23	14	B	ex Sakar-78
Rousse		Mlt	1989	11,982	14,101	157	23	16	CC	ex Nedlloyd Musi-97, Wateraids-91, Kariba-91, Wateralds-91, CMB Effort-90, Wateraids 89
Sakar		Mlt	1995	13,957	21,591	168	25	13	B	
Shipka		Bgr	1979	16,166	24,285	185	23	14	B	
Slavianka		Bgr	1978	16,166	24,685	185	23	14	B	
Sofia		Mlt	1988	11,977	13,800	157	23	16	CC	ex Nedlloyd Maas-96, Waterkoning-91, Contship Singapore-90, Waterkoning-89, AEL America-89, Waterkoning-88
Svilen Russev		Bgr	1982	23,779	38,142	202	28	14	B	
Trapezitsa		Bgr	2003	13,967	21,250	169	25	-	B	
Tzarevetz		Mlt	1998	13,965	21,470	169	25	-	B	
Vitosha		Bgr	1977	16,166	25,864	185	23	14	B	
Vola 1		Mlt	1992	13,834	20,620	168	25	13	B	ex Vola-03
Yordan Lutibrodski		Vct	1986	23,589	38,519	198	28	15	B	
Yordanka Nikolova		Bgr	1979	23,363	38,400	202	28	14	B	

newbuildings: three 24,700 dwt bulk carriers for 2006-7 delivery.
Part owned (43.7%) by British Orient Holdings.

Neptune Orient Lines Ltd

Singapore

Funnel: *Blue with horizontal blue and diagonal green triple wave design on broad white band, narrow black top or dark blue with white eagle and stars on red band (APL vessels)*
Hull: *Light grey with blue 'NOL' or black with white 'APL' with red or dark grey boot-topping*

Name	Eng	Flag	Year	GRT	DWT	Loa	Bm	Kts	Type	Former names
Alba †		Iom	1997	38,520	73,049	225	32	14	B	ex Hawthorn-01, NOL Sirius-00
APL Agate		Sgp	1997	65,475	63,693	272	40	24	CC	ex NOL Agate-00
APL Alexandrite		Sgp	1992	49,716	59,603	288	32	25	CC	ex MOL Ideal-02, APL Alexandrite-02, Neptune Alexandrite-01
APL Almandine		Sgp	1993	49,716	59,560	288	32	23	CC	ex Tokyo Bay-98, Neptune Almandine-96
APL Amazonite		Sgp	1993	49,716	59,603	288	32	24	CC	ex APL Sweden-01, NOL Amazonite-00, Osaka Bay-97, NOL Amazonite-96, Neptune Amazonite-95

National Shipping Co. Of Saudi Arabia. NCC JUBAIL. *C. Lous*

Navigation Maritime Bulgare. PEYO YAVOROV. *Hans Kraijenbosch*

Neptune Orient Lines. APL SPAIN. *G. J. de Boer*

Nippon Yusen Kaisha. CAPE CHARLES. *C. J. Dornom*

Nippon Yusen Kaisha. LYRA LEADER. *Phil Kempsey*

Name	Eng	Flag	Year	GRT	DWT	Loa	Bm	Kts	Type	Former names
APL Cairo		Sgp	2001	25,305	34,133	207	30	21	CC	
APL China *		Usa	1995	64,502	67,432	276	40	24	CC	
APL Coral		Sgp	1998	65,475	64,145	275	40	24	CC	ex NOL Coral-01
APL Cyprine		Sgp	1997	65,475	64,156	272	40	24	CC	ex NOL Cyprine-00
APL Dalian		Sgp	2002	25,305	34,133	207	30	21	CC	ex Indamex Dalian-04, APL Dalian-03
APL Germany §		Lbr	2003	66,462	67,109	281	40	-	CC	
APL Hong Kong §		Lbr	2002	66,573	67,009	280	40	-	CC	
APL Iolite		Sgp	1997	63,900	62,693	272	40	26	CC	ex MSC Hudson-04, APL Iolite-03, NOL Iolite-00
APL Ireland §		Lbr	2002	66,462	67,009	280	40	-	CC	
APL Iris		Sgp	1998	63,900	62,693	272	40	24	CC	ex NOL Iris-01
APL Jade		Sgp	1995	53,519	66,647	294	32	24	CC	ex Hyundai Grace-05, APL Jade-04, NOL Sheratan-98, I/a Neptune Sheratan
APL Japan		Sgp	1995	64,502	66,520	276	40	24	CC	
APL Jeddah		Sgp	2001	25,305	34,122	207	30	21	CC	ex Indamex Malabar-04, APL Jeddah-03
APL Kennedy		Sgp	1988	61,296	54,665	275	39	24	CC	ex President Kennedy-03
APL Korea *		Usa	1995	64,502	66,370	276	40	24	CC	
APL Orchid		Sgp	1984	13,488	18,437	161	25	17	CC	ex Eagle Orion-99, Dragon Nias-97, Neptune Jasper-96, Anro Adelaide-93, Neptune Jasper-89
APL Pearl		Sgp	1998	65,475	64,050	275	40	24	CC	ex NOL Pearl-99
APL Pusan		Sgp	2002	25,305	34,122	207	30	21	CC	ex Indamex Chesapeake-04, APL Pusan-02
APL Philippines		Usa	1996	64,502	66,370	276	40	24	CC	
APL Singapore *		Usa	1995	64,502	66,370	276	40	24	CC	
APL Spain §		Lbr	2004	66,300	66,100	281	40	-	CC	
APL Thailand *		Usa	1995	64,502	66,370	276	40	24	CC	
APL Topaz		Sgp	1989	47,893	51,534	276	32	24	CC	ex MOL Commitment-05, APL Topaz-04, America-01, President Hoover-99, NOL Topaz-98, Neptune Topaz-96
APL Tulip		Sgp	1984	13,488	18,437	161	25	17	CC	ex NOL Beryl-99, Neptune Beryl-97, Anro Fremantle-93, Neptune Beryl-89
APL Turquoise		Sgp	1996	52,086	60,323	294	32	24	CC	ex NOL Turquoise-98
MOL Innovation		Sgp	1995	52,086	60,323	294	32	24	CC	ex APL Tourmaline-04, MOL Innovation-04, MOL Tourmaline-03, APL Tourmaline-02, NOL Tourmaline-98
MOL Velocity		Sgp	1996	53,519	66,511	294	32	24	CC	ex APL Spinel-05, MOL Velocity-04, APL Spinel-03, MOL Velocity-03, APL Spinel-02, NOL Spinel-98
Hyundai Garnet		Sgp	1995	53,519	66,565	294	32	24	CC	ex APL Garnet-05, MOL Vigor-05, MSC Louisiana-03, APL Garnet-02, NOL Seginus-98, Neptune Seginus-95
MOL Vision		Sgp	1995	53,519	65,598	294	32	24	CC	ex MSC Maryland-03, APL Sardonyx-02, NOL Sardonyx-98, Neptune Sardonyx-96
New Dynamic		Sgp	2001	13,764	16,400	154	25	19	CC	
Pole ‡		Iom	1997	38,520	73,049	225	32	14	B	ex Polaris-02, NOL Castor-00
President Adams *		Usa	1988	61,296	53,613	275	39	24	CC	
President Grant *		Usa	1988	47,893	51,437	276	32	24	CC	ex NOL Ruby-98, Neptune Ruby-96
President Jackson *		Usa	1988	61,296	53,613	275	39	24	CC	
President Polk *		Usa	1988	61,296	53,613	275	39	24	CC	
President Truman *		Usa	1988	61,296	53,613	275	39	24	CC	
President Wilson *		Usa	1989	47,893	51,534	276	32	24	CC	ex NOL Zircon-98, Neptune Zircon-96

*managed by Neptune Shipmanagement Services (Pte.) Ltd., Singapore, except * by subsidiary American Ship Management LLC, USA.*
† managed by Dohle IOM Ltd, Isle of Man or ‡ by Augustea Ship Management S.r.l., Italy. § chartered from Japanese owners or banks.

Neste Oil Corporation Finland

Funnel: *Black with diamond divided green over blue.*
Hull: *Black or dark blue, some with pale green or white 'NESTESHIP', red or pink boot-topping.*

Name	Eng	Flag	Year	GRT	DWT	Loa	Bm	Kts	Type
Futura		Fin	2004	15,980	25,084	170	24	14	T
Jurmo		Fin	2004	15,980	25,049	169	24	14	T
Mastera	(me2)	Fin	2003	64,259	106,208	252	44	14	T
Natura		Fin	1993	51,161	91,263	242	40	14	T
Neste		Fin	2004	15,980	25,117	170	24	14	T
Palva		Fin	1986	28,292	48,376	200	30	14	T
Purha		Fin	2003	15,980	25,000	170	24	14	T
Sotka		Fin	1976	11,290	16,420	164	22	14	T
Tempera	(me2)	Fin	2002	64,259	106,034	252	44	14	T
Tervi		Fin	1986	28,292	48,375	202	30	14	T

Name	Eng	Flag	Year	GRT	DWT	Loa	Bm	Kts	Type	Former names

Nippon Yusen Kaisha

Japan

Funnel: Black with two narrow red bands on broad white band.
Hull: Black with red boot-topping.

Name	Eng	Flag	Year	GRT	DWT	Loa	Bm	Kts	Type	Former names
Aegean Leader		Pan	1993	47,171	13,157	180	32	18	V	ex Ocean Beluga-99, Mercury Diamond-96
Alioth Leader		Pan	1998	51,790	14,909	180	32	19	V	
Andromeda Leader		Pan	2004	62,195	21,443	200	32	-	V	
Anna **		Nis	1978	39,710	17,224	196	30	19	V	ex Hojin Maru-89
Aquarius Leader		Pan	1998	57,623	22,815	200	32	19	V	
Baltic Leader		Pan	1982	27,424	10,449	161	27	16	V	ex Brava-99, Jinyo Maru-87
Bellona		Pan	1985	45,495	15,160	184	32	18	V	ex Centry Leader No. 2-94
Bijin		Pan	1988	47,521	14,126	180	32	17	V	
Blue Hawk		Lbr	1978	40,711	14,407	186	32	18	V	
Bujin		Pan	1993	41,931	17,189	196	29	18	V	
California Jupiter *		Lbr	1986	41,668	38,438	248	32	22	CC	
California Mercury		Jpn	1987	41,442	38,538	248	32	22	CC	
Cape Charles		Pan	1986	41,843	38,449	249	32	22	CC	
Cape May		Jpn	1986	42,145	38,217	248	32	22	CC	ex Yamataka Maru-91
Capricornus Leader		Pan	2004	61,854	20,120	200	32	-	V	
Cassiopeia Leader		Pan	1999	57,455	21,547	200	32	19	V	
Centaurus Leader		Pan	2004	62,195	21,471	200	32	-	V	
Century Leader No.1		Pan	1984	45,422	11,772	180	32	18	V	
Century Leader No.3		Jpn	1986	44,830	14,154	179	32	18	V	
Century Leader No.5		Jpn	1986	50,867	15,293	200	32	18	V	
Champion Peace		Pan	1999	56,249	106,042	241	42	15	T	
Champion Pride		Pan	1998	58,141	99,997	244	42	13	T	
Columbia Leader		Pan	1987	38,659	13,491	182	30	18	V	ex Green Bay-01
Delphinus Leader		Pan	1998	57,391	21,514	200	32	19	V	
Dresden		Pan	2000	37,237	12,743	177	32	19	V	
Eijin		Pan	1982	41,195	14,361	180	32	18	V	ex Eijin Maru-85
Equuleus Leader		Pam	2005	61,804	20,141	200	32	20	V	
Eufonia **		Pan	1981	27,163	10,480	165	28	18	V	ex Yujin-92, Yujin Maru-85
Fanta **		Pan	1983	36,437	13,732	190	29	16	V	ex Evviva-98, Madonna-93, Aso Maru-90
Festa **		Pan	1983	36,439	13,656	190	29	16	V	ex Amagi Maru-90
Fontana		Pan	1977	52,214	16,602	196	30	19	V	ex Ryujin Maru-88
Fuji		Lbr	1984	47,751	16,204	190	32	18	V	ex Fuji Maru-90
Ganta		Pan	1978	25,431	11,311	165	27	17	V	ex Beach-90, Pioneer Racer-90
Gas Aries *		Lbr	1991	44,493	50,357	230	37	16	Lpg	
Gas Capricorn *		Lbr	2003	46,021	49,999	230	37	16	Lpg	
Hakone		Pan	1983	35,309	29,733	212	32	21	CC	ex Hakone Maru-99
Heijin *		Pan	1989	47,521	14,366	180	32	18	V	
Hojin *		Vut	1990	55,470	18,273	200	32	19	V	
Hudson Leader		Pan	1987	47,707	14,104	180	32	18	V	ex Green Lake-01
Jingu Maru *		Jpn	1992	42,164	17,216	196	32	18	V	
Jinsei Maru		Jpn	1990	55,489	17,914	199	32	19	V	
Jupiter Diamond		Sgp	1978	45,998	14,687	214	29	18	V	
Kaga		Jpn	1988	51,047	59,188	289	32	23	CC	
Kaijin *		Pan	1994	41,931	17,183	196	29	18	V	
Kamakura *		Pan	1988	50,462	59,441	290	32	23	CC	
Katsuragi *		Pan	1990	50,437	59,418	292	32	23	CC	ex Kowloon Bay-98, Katsuragi-96
Kitano		Jpn	1990	50,618	59,804	288	32	23	CC	
Koh Jin		Vut	1981	49,844	19,712	199	32	18	V	
Leo Leader		Pan	1999	57,566	22,733	200	32	19	V	
Linden Pride *		Pan	2001	46,021	49,999	230	37	16	Lpg	
Lyra Leader		Pan	2005	32,510	21,453	200	32	20	V	
Morning Melody		Pan	1988	47,068	13,162	180	32	18	V	ex Phoenix Diamond-04
Nada V *		Pan	1984	43,101	14,820	186	32	18	V	
New Nada *		Pan	1992	47,519	14,180	180	32	19	V	
Nippon *		Pan	2002	159,613	298,399	333	60	15	T	
NYK Andromeda *		Pan	1998	75,637	81,819	300	40	23	CC	
NYK Antares *		Pan	1997	75,637	81,819	300	40	23	CC	
NYK Aphrodite *		Pan	2003	75,484	81,171	300	40	25	CC	
NYK Apollo *		Pan	2002	75,484	81,171	300	40	25	CC	
NYK Aquarius		Pan	2003	75,484	81,171	300	40	25	CC	
NYK Argus		Pan	2004	75,484	81,000	300	40	25	CC	
NYK Artemis		Pan	2003	75,484	81,171	300	40	25	CC	
NYK Athena		Pan	2003	75,484	81,171	300	40	25	CC	
NYK Atlas		Pan	2004	75,519	81,171	300	40	25	CC	

Name	Eng	Flag	Year	GRT	DWT	Loa	Bm	Kts	Type	Former names
NYK Canopus		Pan	1998	76,847	82,275	300	40	23	CC	
NYK Castor *		Pan	1998	76,847	82,275	300	40	23	CC	
NYK Kai *		Pan	1993	50,606	59,658	288	32	24	CC	ex Kai-95
NYK Leo *		Pan	2002	75,201	77,900	300	40	27	CC	
NYK Libra		Pan	2002	75,201	77,900	300	40	26	CC	
NYK Loadstar *		Pan	2001	75,201	77,900	300	40	27	CC	
NYK Lynx		Pan	2002	75,201	77,950	300	40	26	CC	
NYK Lyra *		Pan	2002	75,201	78,000	300	40	26	CC	
NYK Pegasus *		Pan	2003	76,199	80,270	300	40	25	CC	
NYK Phoenix *		Pan	2003	76,199	80,270	300	40	25	CC	
NYK Procyon *		Pan	1995	60,117	63,179	300	37	22	CC	
NYK Sirius		Pan	1998	76,847	82,271	300	40	23	CC	
NYK Springtide *		Pan	1992	43,213	39,394	253	32	23	CC	
NYK Starlight *		Pan	1991	43,327	39,015	251	32	23	CC	
Ocean Ceres		Sgp	1999	88,385	171,850	289	45	14	B	ex Charles LD-04
Orion Diamond		Vut	1982	53,251	15,396	214	32	18	V	
Orion Leader		Pan	1999	57,513	21,526	200	32	19	V	
Pacific Leader		Pan	1983	47,129	16,138	184	32	17	V	ex Prospero-99, Jinkai Maru-90
Pegasus Diamond		Jpn	1986	47,164	13,068	180	32	18	V	
Pegasus Leader		Pan	1999	57,566	22,747	200	32	19	V	
Perseus Leader		Pan	1999	57,449	21,503	200	32	19	V	
Phoenix Leader		Pan	2004	61,804	20,146	200	32	20	V	
Pioneer Leader **		Pan	1980	41,116	17,859	200	32	17	V	
Procyon Leader		Pan	2000	51,259	17,361	180	32	19	V	
Provider *		Lbr	1978	30,575	31,227	215	31	24	CC	ex NYK Provider-00, P&O Nedlloyd Otago-00, Provider-99, NYK Providence-98, Neptune Rhodonite-96, Hira II-91, Hira Maru-87
Pyxis Leader		Pan	2004	62,195	21,466	200	32	20	V	
Ryujin		Pan	1993	47,737	14,080	180	32	19	V	
Sagittarius Leader		Pan	2005	61,804	20,098	200	32	20	V	
Satsuma		Bhs	1993	150,167	258,019	332	58	15	T	
Seijin		Pan	1984	42,177	15,397	200	32	17	V	ex Seijin Maru-88
Sirius Leader		Pan	2000	51,496	16,451	180	32	19	V	
Taizan		Pan	2002	160,084	300,405	333	60	15	T	
Tajima		Pan	1996	148,330	258,096	333	60	16	T	
Takachiho II		Pan	1998	149,376	280,889	330	60	16	T	
Takasago Maru *		Jpn	1999	149,376	281,050	330	60	16	T	
Takasuzu *		Pan	2000	152,139	279,989	330	60	16	T	
Tateyama		Pan	2002	160,072	300,373	333	60	15	T	
Tenryu		Lbr	1999	152,139	281,050	330	60	16	T	
Tohdoh		Pan	1991	149,356	258,096	330	59	15	T	
Tokachi *		Pan	1999	149,376	280,973	330	60	16	T	
Tsurusaki *		Pan	2002	154,338	300,838	333	60	16	T	
Vega Leader		Pan	2000	51,496	16,396	180	32	19	V	
Virgo Leader		Pan	2004	61,854	20,111	200	32	20	V	

newbuildings - over 100 vessels on order including 8 bulk carriers over 170,000 dwt, 10 container ships over 71,000 dwt and 13 vehicle carriers.
* managed by NYK Ship Management Co. Ltd., Singapore or ** NYK Ship Management, Hong Kong.
The company and its subsidiaries own or manage over 310 vessels with several hundred others on charter. In addition to the container ships, vehicle carriers and tankers listed, the company also owns, manages or operates 26 large Lng tankers, 20 wood-chip carriers, many bulk carriers, tankers and smaller vehicle carriers. See also NYKLauritzenCool AB (under Lauritzen), Ray Shipping, Stolt-Nielsen, Torm and Vroon.

Nordcapital GmbH Germany

ER Schiffahrt GmbH & Cie KG

Funnel: *Charterers colours.*
Hull: *Blue with pink boot-topping or charterers colours.*

Name	Eng	Flag	Year	GRT	DWT	Loa	Bm	Kts	Type	Former names
APL Canada		Lbr	2001	65,792	68,025	277	40	26	CC	ex E.R. Canada-01
APL Denmark		Sgp	2002	65,792	67,935	277	40	26	CC	ex E.R. Denmark-02
APL India		Sgp	2002	65,792	68,025	277	40	26	CC	ex E.R. India-02
APL Sweden		Sgp	2002	65,792	68,025	277	40	26	CC	ex E.R. Sweden-02
China Star		Lbr	1996	30,280	35,962	202	32	22	CC	ex E.R. Darwin-02, Ganges-02, Hanjin Genoa-00
CMA CGM Aegean		Lbr	1996	30,280	35,966	202	32	22	CC	ex E.R. Brisbane-03, Pan Crystal-02
CMA CGM Camellia		Lbr	2006	27,779	39,200	222	30	23	CC	
CMA CGM Egypt		Lbr	1996	30,280	35,966	202	32	22	CC	ex E.R. Albany-04, Rhein-02, Zim Sydney-00
CMA CGM Jaguar		Lbr	2004	26,836	34,289	210	30	-	CC	ex E.R. Caen-04
CMA CGM Kingston		Lbr	2003	39,941	50,900	264	32	24	CC	ex E.R. Kingston-04, CMA CGM Kingston-03, I/a E.R. Kingston

Name	Eng	Flag	Year	GRT	DWT	Loa	Bm	Kts	Type	Former names
CMA CGM La Boussole		Lbr	2005	26,836	34,263	210	30	-	CC	ex E.R. Cannes-05
CMA CGM L'Astrolabe		Lbr	2005	26,718	34,567	210	30	-	CC	
CMA CGM L'Etoile		Lbr	2005	26,626	34,500	210	30	-	CC	ex E.R. Camargue-05
CMA CGM Marmara		Lbr	1998	30,280	35,798	202	32	22	CC	ex CSCL Nile-03, Nile-02, Hyundai Nobility-01
CMA CGM Nilgai		Lbr	2003	39,941	50,900	264	32	24	CC	ex ANL Pacific-05, CMA CGM New York-03, I/a E.R. New York
CMA CGM Parsifal		Lbr	2006	95,000	100,800	335	43	25	CC	I/a E.R. Toulon
CMA CGM Power		Lbr	1996	30,280	35,962	202	32	22	CC	ex CMA CGM Virginia-05, Indamex Mumbai-04, E.R. Canberra-03, Donau-02, Hanjin Dalian-00
CMA CGM Rose		Lbr	2005	27,779	39,200	222	30	23	CC	ex E.R. Marseille-05
CMA CGM Turkey		Lbr	1998	30,280	35,848	202	32	22	CC	ex CSCL Indus-03, Indus-02, Hyundai Infinity-01
CMA CGM Violet		Lbr	2006	27,779	39,200	222	30	23	CC	
CMA CGM Yantian		Lbr	2003	39,941	53,000	264	32	24	CC	I/a E.R. Yantian
Cosco China		Lbr	2005	91,649	100,800	335	43	25	CC	I/a E.R. Tianan
Cosco Long Beach		Lbr	2004	83,133	93,572	300	43	25	CC	
Cosco Seattle		Pan	2004	83,133	93,728	300	43	25	CC	
Cosco Shenzen		Pan	2004	83,133	93,643	300	43	25	CC	I/dn E.R. Shenzen
Cosco Vancouver		Pan	2004	83,133	93,638	300	43	25	CC	
Cosco Yokohama		Pan	2004	83,133	93,659	300	43	25	CC	
CSAV Ningbo		Lbr	1998	26,125	30,720	196	30	19	CC	ex Copiapo-04, I/a E.R. Santiago
CSAV Shanghai		Lbr	1998	26,125	30,721	196	30	19	CC	ex Aconcagua-99 I/a E.R. Hamburg
CSCL Fuzhou		Lbr	2000	25,500	33,855	207	30	21	CC	ex E.R. Lubeck-01, E.R. Fuzhou-01
CSCL Kobe		Lbr	2001	66,289	68,196	277	40	26	CC	I/a E.R. Kobe
CSCL Los Angeles		Lbr	2001	66,289	68,131	277	40	26	CC	I/a E.R. Los Angeles
E.R. Amsterdam		Deu	2000	66,289	67,557	277	40	26	CC	ex P&O Nedlloyd Magellan-05, I/a E.R. Amsterdam
E.R. Cape Town		Lbr	1995	16,175	22,900	185	26	19	CC	ex Panatlantic-04, Quadrant Express-99
E.R. Felixstowe		Lbr	2000	66,289	67,500	277	40	26	CC	ex P&O Nedlloyd Torres-06, I/a E.R. Felixstowe
E.R. London		Deu	2000	66,289	67,566	277	40	26	CC	ex P&O Nedlloyd Vespucci-05, I/a E.R. London
E.R. Sydney		Deu	1998	36,603	45,400	232	32	23	CC	ex YM Napoli-04, Amazonas-02, Choyang Zenith-01, I/a Zenith Globe
Indamex Cauvery		Lbr	1998	36,603	45,383	232	32	23	CC	ex CMA CGM Constellation-04, Safmarine Vinson-03, E.R. Melbourne-02, Congo-02, Choyang Honour-01
Kota Pekarang		Lbr	2005	28,927	39,275	222	30	-	CC	ex E.R. Manchester-05
Kota Pemimpin		Lbr	2005	27,779	39,200	222	30	23	CC	ex E.R. Malta-05
Kota Permai		Lbr	2005	27,779	39,200	222	30	23	CC	ex E.R. Malma-05
Maersk Dallas		Lbr	2004	54,592	67,170	294	32	25	CC	ex E.R. Dallas-04
Maersk Denver		Lbr	2004	54,592	67,170	294	32	25	CC	ex E.R. Denver-04
Maersk Napier		Lbr	1999	25,630	33,855	207	30	21	CC	ex E.R. Stralsund-05, Indamex Tuticorin-04, E.R. Stralsund-03, Maersk Mendoza-02, I/a E.R. Stralsund
Maersk New Orleans		Lbr	2002	27,322	33,800	212	30	22	CC	ex E.R. Wilhelmshaven-02
Maersk Newark		Lbr	2002	26,200	33,800	212	30	22	CC	ex E.R. Cuxhaven-02
Maersk Newcastle		Lbr	2003	26,200	33,800	212	30	22	CC	ex E.R. Elsfleth-03
Maersk Norfolk		Lbr	2003	27,322	33,800	212	30	22	CC	ex E.R. Bremen-03
Maersk Valencia		Lbr	1999	25,630	33,855	207	30	21	CC	ex E.R. Copenhagen-99
Maersk Verona		Lbr	1999	16,803	23,075	185	26	19	CC	ex E.R. Durban-04, Direct Falcon-03, Griffin Clio-99
MSC Hobart		Lbr	1994	22,736	33,523	188	28	18	CC	ex E.R. Hobart-04, Mosel-02, Zim Koper-98, Hyundai Longview-96
Norasia Atria		Lbr	2004	41,855	53,611	264	32	24	CC	ex E.R. Wellinghton-04, I/a E.R. Auckland
Norasia Integra		Lbr	2004	41,855	53,610	264	32	24	CC	ex E.R. Auckland-04, I/a E.R. Wellington
OOCL France		Lbr	2001	66,289	67,591	277	40	26	CC	ex E.R. Paris-01
OOCL Germany		Lbr	2000	66,289	67,660	277	40	26	CC	ex E.R. Berlin-01
OOCL Los Angeles		Lbr	2000	66,289	67,737	277	40	26	CC	I/a E.R. Pusan
OOCL Malaysia		Lbr	2000	66,289	66,298	277	40	26	CC	ex E.R. Seoul-00
OOCL New York		Lbr	1999	66,289	67,660	277	40	26	CC	I/a E.R. Hong Kong
OOCL Shanghai		Lbr	1999	66,289	67,473	277	40	26	CC	I/a E.R. Shanghai
Safmarine Cunene		Lbr	2002	27,332	33,800	212	30	22	CC	ex E.R. Bremerhaven-02
Safmarine Zambezi		Lbr	2002	27,322	34,608	212	30	22	CC	ex E.R. Helgoland-02
YM Chiwan		Lbr	2006	40,300	38,200	-	-	-	CC	
YM Tianjin		Lbr	2006	40,300	38,200	-	-	-	CC	
Zim Beijing		Lbr	2005	54,626	66,939	294	32	25	CC	

Name	Eng	Flag	Year	GRT	DWT	Loa	Bm	Kts	Type	Former names
Zim Savannah		Lbr	2004	54,626	67,170	294	32	25	CC	ex E.R. Savannah-04

newbuildings: seven 95,000 grt (ER T's), eight 27,779 grt and six 40,300 grt (ER M's) container ships for 2006 delivery.
Shipping subsidiary of Erck Rickmers' investment group Nordcapital Ges. Fur Unternehmensbeteiligungen mbH & Cie.

Norddeutsche Reederei Germany

Funnel: *Charterers colours*
Hull: *Black or red with red boot-topping.*

Name	Eng	Flag	Year	GRT	DWT	Loa	Bm	Kts	Type	Former names
Alianca Singapore		Lbr	2001	25,713	33,900	208	30	21	CC	ex Cap Matapan-04, Northern Endurance-03, Andhika Fatima-01
APL Arabia		Lbr	2000	54,415	66,895	294	32	24	CC	ex MOL Vigilance-03, Vantage-03, MOL Vantage-02, APL Arabia-02, l/a Northern Grace
APL Egypt		Lbr	2000	54,415	66,922	294	32	24	CC	ex MOL Virtue-03, APL Egypt-02
APL Malaysia		Lbr	2000	54,415	66,910	294	32	24	CC	ex MOL Value-03, APL Malaysia-02, l/a Northern Glance
Bangkok Express		Deu	2003	75,590	85,400	300	40	25	CC	ex Northern Magnitude-04
Barcelona Bridge		Lbr	2003	41,078	48,874	260	32	-	CC	ex Northern Delicacy-03
Busan Express		Deu	2004	75,590	85,400	300	40	25	CC	
Cap Frio		Lbr	2001	25,713	33,900	208	30	21	CC	ex Northern Endeavour-03, Andhika Loreto-01
Cap Salinas		Lbr	2001	25,713	33,836	208	30	21	CC	ex NYK Freesia-05, Cap Salinas-04, Northern Enterprise-03, Andhika Lourdes-02
Conti Arabian		Lbr	1990	18,000	26,288	177	28	18	CC	ex Delmas Mascareignes-03, Kaedi-02, Conti Arabian-00, Maruba Challenger-00, Conti Arabian-97, Arabian Senator-97
Duburg		Lbr	1990	18,000	26,288	177	28	18	CC	ex Kota Perkasa-02, Japan Senator-98
Houston Express		Deu	2005	94,483	101,500	332	43	-	CC	l/d Northern Jade
Indamex Godavari		Lbr	1997	36,606	45,131	245	32	23	CC	ex MSC Bursa-04, P&O Nedlloyd Barcelona-02, Northern Diversity-98
Los Angeles Express		Lbr	2003	75,590	85,400	300	40	25	CC	l/a Northern Magnum
Luetjenburg		Deu	1995	37,323	45,530	239	32	23	CC	ex Garden Bridge-03, Heaven River-00, Lutjenburg-98
Maersk Stralsund		Lbr	2005	95,000	101,500	332	43	-	CC	ex P&O Nedlloyd Marilyn-05
MSC Delhi		Lbr	2004	35,954	42,186	231	32	22	CC	ex Northern Distinction-04
MSC Queensland		Lbr	2004	35,697	42,186	231	32	22	CC	l/a Northern Devotion
Northern Divinity		Lbr	1997	36,606	44,117	245	32	23	CC	ex P&O Nedlloyd Damietta-05, OOCL Europe-02, P&O Nedlloyd Damietta-01, Northern Divinity-97
Potomac Bridge		Lbr	2003	41,078	48,923	260	32	23	CC	l/a Northern Decency
San Francisco Express		Deu	2004	75,590	85,400	300	40	25	CC	
Savannah Express		Deu	2005	94,483	101,500	332	43	-	CC	l/d Northern Julie
Sinotrans Dalian		Lbr	2005	27,437	37,800	222	30	-	CC	
Sinotrans Qingdao		Lbr	2005	27,437	37,800	222	30	-	CC	
Sinotrans Shanghai		Lbr	2005	27,437	37,800	222	30	-	CC	l/a Northern Valence
Sinotrans Tianjin		Lbr	2005	27,437	37,800	222	30	-	CC	l/a Northern Vivacity
Tiger Sky		Lbr	1991	16,236	23,596	163	28	17	CC	ex Mildburg-02, Direct Condor-99, Mildburg-96, Contship Australia-95
Troyburg		Lbr	1988	18,037	26,070	177	28	17	CC	ex MSC Callao-02, Troyburg-98, NOL Koi-98, Deppe Florida-96, Troyburg-94, Ville de Venus-93
Yokohama Senator		Lbr	1998	53,324	63,615	294	32	23	CC	ex Cho Yang Ace-01

newbuildings: five 40,300 grt container ships for 2008-9 delivery.
Also see vessels managed by F. Laeisz Schiffahrts GmbH

Dampskibsselskabet 'Norden' A/S Denmark

Funnel: *Black with narrow red band on broard white band.*
Hull: *Black or dark blue with red boot-topping.*

Name	Eng	Flag	Year	GRT	DWT	Loa	Bm	Kts	Type	Former names
Nord Stealth		Dis	2001	56,346	105,300	239	42	14	T	
Nord Stream		Pan	2003	28,059	45,974	180	32	15	T	
Nordasia		Dis	1998	57,009	105,994	244	42	13	T	
Nordatlantic		Dis	2001	56,346	105,322	239	42	15	T	
Nordbright *		Pan	2001	29,999	52,827	190	32	14	B	
Nordeuropa		Dis	2000	23,740	35,752	183	27	14	T	
Nordglimt		Pan	2000	27,986	50,236	190	32	14	B	

Name	Eng	Flag	Year	GRT	DWT	Loa	Bm	Kts	Type	Former names
Nordpacific		Dis	2003	56,346	105,344	239	42	14	T	
Nordstjernen *		Dmk	2001	29,963	53,553	190	32	15	B	
Nordsund *		Pan	2001	27,980	50,296	190	32	14	B	
Spirit		Pan	2000	26,091	45,526	186	30	14	B	ex Nordholm-06

newbuildings: two 38,500 dwt tankers and a 53,000 dwt bulk carrier for 2006-7 delivery
In addition to the vessels listed, the company operates or charters between 115-130 bulk carriers and tankers.
* owned by Eagle Bulk Shipping, USA and time chartered back until 2007
32% owned by A/S Dampskibsselskabet Torm, Denmark q.v.

Novorossiysk Shipping Co   Russia

Funnel: Blue with red and black intertwined ropes between narrow diagonal blue bands on broad diagonal white band.
Hull: Black, brown or red with red boot-topping.

Name	Eng	Flag	Year	GRT	DWT	Loa	Bm	Kts	Type	Former names
Adygeya	I hr		2005	57,177	105,926	244	42	-	T	ex Four Stream-05
Akademik Vereshchagin		Mlt	1989	18,625	28,610	179	25	14	T	
Aleksandr Pokryshkin *		Lbr	1987	37,884	67,980	243	32	15	T	
Boris Livanov		Rus	1986	16,502	23,920	185	23	15	B	
Elbrus *		Mlt	2004	28,000	46,080	183	32	14	T	
General Zamora		Ven	1993	39,036	68,198	224	32	15	T	ex Amity-01
Grigoriy Nesterenko *		Mlt	1986	18,625	28,610	179	25	14	T	
Ilya Erenburg		Rus	1987	10,949	15,970	152	22	15	T	
Kaluga *		Lbr	2003	62,395	114,800	250	44	-	T	
Kazan *		Lbr	2003	62,395	115,727	250	44	-	T	
Khirurg Vishnevskiy		Rus	1988	10,949	15,970	152	22	15	T	
Khudozhnik Moor		Rus	1983	16,502	24,110	185	23	14	B	
Krasnodar *		Lbr	2003	62,395	115,605	250	44	-	T	
Krymsk *		Lbr	2003	62,395	115,605	250	44	-	T	
Kuban *		Lbr	2000	56,076	106,562	243	42	14	T	I/a Moscow Glory
Leonid Sobolyev		Rus	1985	16,502	23,940	184	23	14	B	
Leonid Utesov		Rus	1989	10,949	15,970	152	22	15	T	
Marshal Bagramyan *		Lbr	1984	37,884	67,980	243	32	15	T	
Marshal Chu(y)kov *		Lbr	1984	37,916	67,980	243	32	15	T	
Marshal Vasilyevskiy		Rus	1982	37,916	67,980	243	32	15	T	
Moscow *		Lbr	1998	56,076	99,600	243	42	15	T	
Moscow Kremlin *		Lbr	1998	56,076	106,521	243	42	15	T	
Moscow River *		Lbr	1999	56,075	106,552	243	42	15	T	
Moscow Stars *		Lbr	1999	56,076	106,450	243	42	14	T	
Moscow University *		Lbr	1999	56,076	106,521	243	42	15	T	
Pamir *		Mlt	2004	28,000	46,000	183	32	14	T	
Pob(y)eda		Rus	1981	37,916	67,980	243	32	15	T	
Pyotr (Petr) Shmidt *		Mlt	1987	18,526	28,610	179	25	14	T	
Sergey Lemesh(y)ev		Rus	1983	16,502	24,110	185	23	14	B	
Sorokaletiye Pobedy *		Lbr	1985	38,916	67,980	243	32	15	T	
Stena Concord		Lbr	2004	27,500	47,400	183	32	-	T	
Stena Consul		Lbr	2004	27,500	47,400	183	32	-	T	
Taganrog *		Lbr	1996	26,218	40,713	181	32	14	T	
Taman *		Lbr	1996	26,218	40,818	181	32	15	T	
Tambov *		Lbr	1996	26,218	40,727	181	32	14	T	
Temryuk *		Lbr	1996	26,218	40,584	181	32	14	T	
Tikhoretsk *		Lbr	1996	26,218	40,791	181	32	14	T	
Tikhvin *		Lbr	1996	26,218	40,727	181	32	15	T	
Timashevsk *		Lbr	1996	26,218	40,584	181	32	15	T	
Tomsk *		Lbr	1997	26,218	40,703	181	32	15	T	
Trogir *		Mlt	1995	26,218	40,727	181	32	14	T	
Troitsk *		Lbr	1996	26,218	40,816	181	32	15	T	
Tula *		Lbr	1997	26,218	40,584	181	32	14	T	
Tver *		Lbr	1996	26,218	40,743	181	32	15	T	
Valeriy Chkalov *		Mlt	1988	18,625	28,610	179	25	14	T	
Vera Mar(y)etskaya		Rus	1983	16,508	24,110	185	23	14	B	
Vladimir Kokkinaki *		Mlt	1986	18,526	28,750	179	25	15	T	
Vladimir Vysotskiy		Rus	1988	10,949	15,970	152	22	15	T	
Yevgeniy Titov *		Mlt	1986	18,625	28,640	179	25	14	T	

newbuildings: 19 tankers between 40,000-114,000 grt for 2006-8 delivery.
Owned by Government of The Republic of Russia and * managed by subsidiary Novoship (UK) Ltd., UK.

NSB Niederelbe Schiffahrtsges mbH & Co KG   Germany

Funnel: *Blue with blue 'NSB' on white diamond or blue 'N' on square on broad white band or charterers colours.*
Hull: *Black, blue or dark grey with red boot-topping.*

Name	Eng	Flag	Year	GRT	DWT	Loa	Bm	Kts	Type	Former names
Aka Bhum	Deu		1990	16,236	23,596	163	28	17	CC	ex Conti La Spezia-04, MSC Amazonia-01, Buxlady-99, Contship La Spezia-95
ANL Esprit	Deu		1998	25,713	33,995	206	30	21	CC	ex CMA CGM Falcon-04, CSCL Nantong-03, Sea Leopard-01, Buxhansa-98
ANL Georgia	Deu		1997	40,465	49,238	259	32	23	CC	ex Ville de Mimosa-04
APL Melbourne	Deu		1997	24,053	27,100	205	27	20	CC	ex Vancouver-04, Ivory Star 1-03, Conti Seattle-02, CCNI Antartico-02, Sea Lynx-00, Conti Seattle-97
Buxcrown	Deu		1989	18,000	26,288	177	28	17	CC	ex Kota Pertama-01, Buxcrown-98, Singapore Senator 95
Buxfavourite	Deu		1997	25,713	34,083	206	30	21	CC	ex CSCL Yingkou-03, Sea Puma-01, Buxfavourite-98
Buxhill	Deu		1995	16,259	23,465	163	30	18	CC	ex CSAV Santos-04, Buxhill-03, Indamex Malabar-03, Buxhill-02, Contship Ticino-98
Buxlagoon	Deu		1994	16,270	23,130	163	28	17	CC	ex YM Surabaya-04, Indamex New Delhi-03, Kota Perwira-00, Contship Italy-98
Buxlink	Deu		2002	25,375	33,817	207	30	23	CC	ex P&O Nedlloyd Hunter Valley-05
Buxmaster	Deu		1986	16,250	23,465	163	28	18	CC	ex Delmas Ango-05, WAL Ulangi-04, Buxmaster-04, Cotonou Star-02, Buxmaster-01, WEC Rotterdam-01, Buxmaster-98, CMB Melody-96, Red Sea Endurance-92, Ville de Pluton-91
California Senator	Deu		1994	34,617	45,025	216	32	21	CC	ex Sea Initiative-95, Chesapeake Bay-94, Californian Senator-94
Canada Senator	Lbr		1992	30,567	31,160	203	31	19	CC	ex Northern Joy-01, CMA Xingang-01, Contship Mexico-99, Northern Joy-98, Sea Vigor-97, Hyundai Tacoma-96, Sea Hawk-94, Northern Joy-93
Cap Ferrato	Deu		2002	25,375	33,864	207	30	21	CC	
Cap Pilar	Deu		1997	25,713	34,083	205	27	20	CC	ex Conti Cartagena-05, CMA CGM Eagle-04, Conti Cartagena-03, MSC Provence-01, Sea-Land Argentina -00, I/a Conti Cartagena
CMA CGM Alabama *	Deu		1997	31,730	34,731	193	32	22	CC	ex Indamex Alabama-04, Conti Wellington-03, Contship Vision-03, I/a Conti Wellington
CMA CGM Balzac	Deu		2001	73,172	77,941	300	40	26	CC	ex Conti Paris-01
CMA CGM Baudelaire	Deu		2001	73,172	77,946	300	40	26	CC	ex Conti Lyon-01
CMA CGM Capella	Deu		1995	35,595	42,673	240	32	22	CC	ex Ville de Capella-02, Northern Honour-95
CMA CGM Hugo	Pan		2004	90,745	101,662	334	43	25	CC	
CMA CGM Verlaine	Deu		2001	72,760	77,900	300	40	26	CC	I/a Buxcliff
CMA CGM Vernet	Deu		1994	35,595	42,673	240	32	22	CC	ex Northern Pioneer-02, Ville de Sagitta-01, I/a Northern Pioneer
CMA CGM Voltaire	Lbr		2001	72,760	77,900	300	40	26	CC	I/a Buxcoast
Conti Albany	Deu		1997	31,730	34,790	193	32	22	CC	ex ANL Albany-03, Conti Albany-03, Contship Optimism-02, I/a Conti Albany
Conti Asia	Deu		1993	16,282	23,596	163	28	18	CC	ex Contship Asia-98
Conti Barcelona	Deu		1991	16,236	23,596	164	28	17	CC	ex Tiger Speed-01, Conti Barcelona-01, Maersk Barcelona-01, Conti Barcelona-99, New York Express-98, Conti Barcelona-97, Contship Barcelona-96
Conti Esperance	Deu		1996	31,730	34,800	193	32	22	CC	ex Contship Romance-03, I/a Conti Esperance
Conti Germany	Deu		1992	16,236	23,596	164	28	17	CC	ex MSC Victoria-01, Contship Germany-98
Conti Jork	Deu		1990	16,236	23,596	163	28	17	CC	ex Kota Permas-00, Conti Jork-99, Contship Jork-97
Conti Malaga *	Deu		1998	25,713	24,083	205	27	20	CC	ex MSC Chile-02, Sea-Land Uruguay-01, Conti Malaga-98

Nippon Yusen Kaisha. NYK LYRA. *N. Kemps*

NSB Niederelbe Schiffs. CONTI MALAGA. *Hans Kraijenbosch*

Name	Eng	Flag	Year	GRT	DWT	Loa	Bm	Kts	Type	Former names
Conti Sydney *		Deu	1990	16,236	23,596	163	28	17	CC	ex MSC Sydney-04, Conti Sydney-03, MSC Senegal-01, Conti Sydney-99, Direct Currawong-98, Contship Ipswich-95, I/a Contship Sydney
Conti Valencia		Deu	1998	25,713	34,051	206	30	21	CC	ex MSC Spain-05, Conti Valencia-03, Lykes Hunter-01, Ivaran Hunter-99, Sea Tiger-98, Conti Valencia-98
Doria		Deu	1987	10,811	13,464	147	23	15	CC	ex ANL Pioneer-04, MSC Kiwi-02, Everett Express-01, Doria-00, OOCL Admiral-98, Doria-97, Sea-Land Mexico-94, Doria-94, Contship Asia-91, Ocean Asia-88, Doria-88
Ever Champion *		Mhl	2005	90,449	100,949	334	43	25	CC	
Ever Charming *		Mhl	2005	90,465	98,700	334	43	25	CC	
Ever Chilvary *		Mhl	2006	90,465	98,700	334	43	25	CC	
Ever Conquest *		Mhl	2006	90,465	98,700	334	43	25	CC	
Hanjin Amsterdam *		Deu	1999	66,278	67,900	279	40	26	CC	I/a Conti Canberra
Hanjin Athens *		Deu	2000	66,278	67,900	279	40	26	CC	ex YM Athens-05, Hanjin Athens-03, Conti Melbourne-00
Hanjin Baltimore		Mhl	2005	83,133	92,964	300	43	-	CC	
Hanjin Basel *		Mhl	2003	65,918	68,200	279	40	26	CC	ex Hanjin Lisbon-03
Hanjin Boston *		Pan	2005	83,133	92,964	300	43	-	CC	
Hanjin Brussels *		Deu	2000	66,278	67,900	279	40	26	CC	ex Conti Brussel
Hanjin Cairo *		Deu	2001	65,131	68,045	275	40	25	CC	
Hanjin Chicago *		Lbr	2003	65,918	68,037	278	40	26	CC	
Hanjin Copenhagen *		Deu	1999	66,278	68,996	279	40	26	CC	ex Conti Darwin-99
Hanjin Dallas *		Pan	2005	83,133	92,964	300	43	-	CC	
Hanjin Geneva *		Deu	2000	65,918	68,263	279	40	26	CC	ex Cosco Tianjin-05, Hanjin Geneva-03, Conti Porto-00
Hanjin Gothenburg *		Deu	2002	65,131	68,045	275	40	25	CC	I/a Conti Goteborg
Hanjin Helsinki *		Deu	2002	65,131	68,045	275	40	25	CC	
Hanjin Lisbon *		Lbr	2003	65,918	67,979	279	40	26	CC	
Hanjin Madrid *		Mhl	2003	65,918	67,979	279	40	26	CC	
Hanjin Miami *		Pan	2005	83,133	92,964	300	43	-	CC	
Hanjin Ottawa *		Deu	2000	66,278	68,834	278	40	26	CC	ex Conti Melbourne-00
Hanjin Taipei *		Deu	2001	65,131	68,086	275	40	25	CC	
Hanjin Vienna *		Deu	2000	65,918	68,263	279	40	26	CC	ex Conti Lissabon-00
Hanjin Yantian *		Pan	2005	83,133	92,964	300	43	-	CC	
Hatsu Courage *		Mhl	2005	90,465	98,700	334	43	25	CC	
Hatsu Crystal *		Mhl	2006	90,465	98,700	334	43	25	CC	
Hongkong Senator		Deu	1995	34,617	45,470	216	32	21	CC	
Ibn Sina		Deu	1993	34,454	45,470	216	32	24	CC	ex Tokyo Senator-97, Sea Progress-96, Tokyo Senator-94
Ital Contessa *		Mhl	2006	90,465	100,800	334	43	25	CC	ex LT Contessa-06
Kota Pertama		Deu	1997	25,713	34,083	206	30	22	CC	ex CMA CGM Albatross-04, Conti Bilbao-03, Brasilia-02, Sea-Land Brasil-99, I/a Conti Bilbao
London Senator		Deu	1994	34,454	45,696	216	32	24	CC	ex Sea Endeavour-95, Delaware Bay-94, London Senator-94
LT Cortesia *		Mhl	2005	90,449	100,863	334	43	25	CC	
Marfret Caraibes		Deu	1993	16,282	23,465	163	28	19	CC	ex Buxsailor-05, City of York-03, Buxsailor-01, CSAV Salerno-00, Libra Houston-00, CMBT Amboseli-98, Contship Atlantic-97
Melbourne Star I		Deu	1995	16,270	23,130	163	28	18	CC	ex YM Kwang Yang-04, Buxmoon-03, Maersk Osaka-02, Contship Lavagna-98
MOL Wish		Deu	1996	37,549	44,731	241	32	24	CC	ex Caribbean Sea-06, MSC Madrid-03, Sea-Land Endeavour-01, Sea Endeavour-96, Caribbean Sea-96
MSC Alessia *		Deu	2001	75,590	84,920	304	40	25	CC	
MSC Flaminia *		Deu	2001	75,590	84,920	304	40	24	CC	I/a Buxclipper
MSC Geneva		Deu	2006	51,700					CC	I/a Buxsong
MSC Ilona *		Deu	2001	75,590	84,920	304	40	25	CC	I/a Buxcomet
MSC Lausanne		Deu	2005	50,963	54,450	275	32	-	CC	
MSC Texas		Mhl	2004	90,745	101,898	334	43	25	CC	
Northern Delight		Deu	1994	19,819	22,246	174	27	19	CC	ex P&O Nedlloyd Rumba-05, Kairo-05, P&O Nedlloyd Dubai-03, Kairo-03, Northern Delight-03, Zim Chicago II-01, Kota Sejati-00, Northern Delight-99, P&O Nedlloyd Dubai-99, Dubai Bay-98, Nedlloyd Sao Paulo-96, Northern Delight-94

Name	Eng	Flag	Year	GRT	DWT	Loa	Bm	Kts	Type	Former names
Northern Faith		Deu	1994	35,595	42,673	240	32	22	CC	ex Indamex Mumbai-05, Contship Innovator-04, Northern Faith-02, Ville de Libra-02
Northern Felicity		Deu	1994	19,819	22,246	174	27	19	CC	ex P&O Nedlloyd Beirut-05, Northern Felicity-03, CMA Los Angeles-00, Northern Felicity-99, P&O Nedlloyd Dammam-99, Dammam Bay-98, Nedlloyd Salvador-96, Northern Felicity-94
Northern Happiness		Deu	1994	19,819	22,273	174	27	19	CC	ex Cap Velas-04, Northern Happiness-03, Kairo-00, DNOL Kairo-99, Kairo-98, Northern Happiness-94
Northern Reliance		Deu	1994	35,595	42,085	240	32	22	CC	ex Indamex New York-05, Contship Champion-04, Northern Reliance-02, Ville de Vela-02
Pacific Link		Deu	2004	90,745	101,661	334	43	25	CC	
Rialto Bridge *		Deu	1996	37,549	44,647	241	32	24	CC	ex Safmarine Kimley-03, Sea-Land Mistral-02, l/a White Sea
San Pedro Bridge		Deu	1996	37,549	44,690	241	32	24	CC	ex Sea-Land Initiative-00, Sea Initiative-96, Sargasso Sea-96
Ville d'Orion '		Deu	1997	40,465	49,208	259	32	23	CC	ex ANL California-03, Ville d'Orion-03
Ville de Taurus		Deu	1997	40,400	49,238	259	32	23	CC	
Washington Senator		Deu	1994	34,454	45,455	216	32	20	CC	ex Maersk Antwerp-95, Tor Bay-94, Washington Senator-94
Yellow Sea *		Deu	1996	37,549	44,765	241	32	24	CC	ex City of Edinburgh-03, Humen Bridge-02, Sea-Land Victory-00, Yellow Sea-96
YM Ibiza *		Deu	1997	31,730	34,894	193	32	22	CC	ex P&O Nedlloyd Newark-05, Contship Nobility-03, Conti Brisbane-97
YM Pearl River I		Mhl	1989	18,000	26,288	177	28	19	CC	ex Conti Hong Kong-03, MSC Guayaquil-01, Conti Hong Kong-99, MSC Guayaquil-98, Nedlloyd Zaandam-97, Buxmerchant-95, Choyang Star-94, Hongkong Senator-91
YM Xingang I *		Deu	1993	16,236	23,596	163	28	18	CC	ex MSC France-04, Conti France-03, Maersk Jakarta-99, Conti France-98, Contship France-98

newbuildings - ten 85,000 grt, two 55,000 grt and eight 95,000 grt container ships for Conti, five 27,400 dwt (190 x 28m) for 2007/8 delivery.
Company associated with W. Harms GmbH & Co. KG. and * managed for associated Conti Reederei, Germany.

Odfjell ASA   Norway

Funnel: *White with blue diagonal chain link symbol, black top*
Hull: *Orange with blue 'ODFJELL SEACHEM', red or black boot topping*

Name	Eng	Flag	Year	GRT	DWT	Loa	Bm	Kts	Type	Former names
Bow Americas ‡‡		Pan	2004	11,924	19,707	146	24	-	T	
Bow Andes †		Chl	1977	17,561	28,021	171	25	17	T	ex Bow Sun-98
Bow Architect ‡‡		Pan	2005	18,405	30,058	170	26	-	T	
Bow Cardinal		Nis	1997	23,196	37,479	183	32	16	T	
Bow Cecil		Nis	1998	23,206	37,545	183	32	16	T	
Bow Cedar		Nis	1996	23,196	37,455	183	32	16	T	
Bow Century		Nis	2000	23,206	37,438	183	32	16	T	
Bow Chain		Nis	2002	23,190	37,518	183	32	16	T	
Bow Cheetah		Sgp	1988	22,637	40,257	171	32	14	T	ex Santa Anna-00, Falkanger-91, Fort Cheetah-89, Northern Cheetah-88
Bow Clipper		Nis	1995	23,197	37,221	183	32	16	T	
Bow Condor †		Mhl	1978	17,561	28,084	171	25	17	T	ex Bow Sea-05
Bow Eagle		Nis	1985	15,829	24,728	172	28	14	T	ex Northern Eagle-89, Mangueira-88
Bow Europe ‡‡		Pan	2005	11,690	19,728	144	24	-	T	ex North Contender-05
Bow Fagus		Nis	1995	23,197	37,221	183	32	16	T	
Bow Faith		Nis	1997	23,196	37,479	183	32	16	T	
Bow Favour		Nis	2001	23,190	37,467	183	32	16	T	
Bow Fertility *		Sgp	1987	27,963	39,611	177	32	14	T	ex Fertility L-04
Bow Fighter		Nis	1982	20,478	35,100	174	32	15	T	
Bow Firda		Nis	2003	23,190	37,000	183	32	16	T	
Bow Flora		Nis	1998	23,206	37,369	183	32	16	T	
Bow Flower		Nis	1994	23,197	37,221	183	32	16	T	
Bow Fortune		Nis	1999	23,206	37,395	183	32	16	T	
Bow Fraternity		Sgp	1987	27,262	45,593	177	32	14	T	ex Fraternity L-04
Bow Heron		Nis	1979	20,362	35,210	174	32	15	T	ex Iver Heron-91
Bow Hunter		Sgp	1983	14,627	23,002	158	23	15	T	
Bow Lady **		Nis	1978	18,438	32,227	171	26	17	T	ex Golar Petrosun-89
Bow Lancer		Nis	1980	20,478	35,050	174	32	15	T	ex Berganger-90
Bow Leopard		Sgp	1988	22,637	40,257	171	32	14	T	ex Fort Leopard-89, Northern Leopard-88

149

Name	Eng	Flag	Year	GRT	DWT	Loa	Bm	Kts	Type	Former names
Bow Lion		Sgp	1987	22,637	40,272	171	32	14	T	ex Fort Lion-89, Northern Lion-88
Bow Maasslot ***		Sgp	1982	24,794	38,039	172	32	15	T	ex Maasslot L-04, Maasslot-93
Bow Maasstad ***		Sgp	1983	24,794	38,039	172	32	15	T	ex Maasstad L-04, Maasstad-94
Bow Maasstroom ***		Sgp	1983	24,794	38,039	172	32	15	T	ex Maasstroom L-04, Maasstroom-93
Bow Merkur ‡		Nis	1975	17,561	27,954	171	25	17	T	ex Bow Fortune-98
Bow Neptun ‡		Nis	1976	17,561	28,160	171	25	17	T	ex Bow Spring-04
Bow Orion ‡		Nis	1977	17,561	28,085	171	25	17	T	ex Bow Sky-04
Bow Pacifico †		Chl	1982	12,198	15,200	161	23	15	T	ex Bow Saphir-01
Bow Panther		Sgp	1986	22,714	40,263	171	32	14	T	ex Northern Panther-89
Bow Peace *		Sgp	1987	28,001	45,655	177	32	14	T	ex Peaceventure L-00
Bow Petros **		Nis	1984	22,589	37,250	174	32	14	T	ex Petros-92, Owl Petros-84, Atlas Petros-94
Bow Pioneer		Sgp	1982	14,627	23,016	158	23	15	T	
Bow Power		Sgp	1987	28,001	39,571	177	32	14	T	ex Powerventure L-00
Bow Pride *		Sgp	1987	28,001	39,586	177	32	14	T	ex Pridevenure L-00
Bow Prima *		Sgp	1987	28,001	45,655	177	32	14	T	ex Primaventure L-00
Bow Prosper *		Sgp	1987	28,008	39,574	177	32	14	T	ex Prosperventure L-00
Bow Puma		Sgp	1986	22,714	40,091	171	32	14	T	ex Santa Maria-91, Finnanger-91, Fort Puma-89, Northern Puma-86
Bow Santos ‡		Pan	2004	11,986	19,997	148	24	-	T	
Bow Saturn ‡		Nis	1976	17,561	28,085	171	25	17	T	ex Bow Star-98
Bow Sky		Sgp	2005	29,965	39,942	183	32	15	T	
Bow Spring		Nis	2004	29,965	39,942	183	32	15	T	
Bow Star		Nis	2004	29,971	39,832	183	32	15	T	
Bow Summer		Sgp	2005	29,965	39,942	183	32	15	T	
Bow Sun		Sgp	2003	29,965	39,942	183	32	15	T	I/a Multicarrier
Bow Viking		Sgp	1981	19,639	33,695	183	30	16	T	ex Mauranger-90, Kaupanger-81

newbuildings - one 28,000 grt 45,000 dwt tanker for 2007 delivery.
Majority managed by Odfjell Ship Management Asia or Odfjell Singapore Pte. Ltd, both Singapore or * by Ceres Hellenic Shipping Enterprises Ltd, Greece q.v. (partners in Seachem Pool), ** by Hanseatic Shipping Co. Ltd., Cyprus (The Schulte Group) or *** by OSM Ship Management AS, Norway. † jointly owned by Odfjell y Vapores SA, Chile and CSAV, managed by Southern Shipmanagement (Chile) Ltd. q.v. ‡ owned by Salhus Shipping AS, Norway or ‡‡ chartered from other owners.
See also time-chartered vessels under The National Shipping Company of Saudi Arabia, Saudi Arabia.

J O Odfjell A/S   Norway
JO Tankers AS

Funnel: Blue with white interlinked 'JO' symbol.
Hull: Orange with blue 'JO TANKERS', red boot-topping

Name	Eng	Flag	Year	GRT	DWT	Loa	Bm	Kts	Type	Former names
Bryggen		Nis	1981	15,393	26,328	173	23	14	T	ex Jo Elm-03, Lake Anne-91
Jo Acer *		Nis	2004	18,703	29,709	170	26	14	T	
Jo Ask		Nis	1997	12,317	19,087	148	23	16	T	
Jo Betula *		Nis	2003	15,992	25,032	159	25	15	T	
Jo Birk		Nis	1982	22,772	39,293	175	32	16	T	
Jo Brevik		Nis	1986	19,685	33,490	183	30	15	T	
Jo Cedar		Nld	1994	22,415	36,733	182	32	15	T	
Jo Clipper **		Nis	1981	19,889	33,695	183	30	15	T	ex Polux-81
Jo Eik		Nis	1998	12,249	19,234	148	23	16	T	
Jo Gran **	(2)	Nis	1980	23,194	37,532	175	32	16	T	ex Johnson Chemstar-88
Jo Kashi †		Pan	2003	15,895	25,148	159	26	14	T	
Jo Kiri		Pan	2003	11,769	19,508	145	24	14	T	
Jo Lind **	(2)	Nis	1982	19,809	33,532	183	30	15	T	ex Johnson Chemspan-88
Jo Lonn		Nis	1982	22,772	39,273	175	32	16	T	
Jo Oak		Nis	1983	22,772	39,270	175	32	16	T	
Jo Rogn **	(2)	Nis	1980	23,189	37,572	175	32	14	T	ex Johnson Chemsun-88
Jo Selje		Nld	1993	22,380	36,800	182	32	15	T	
Jo Sequoia *		Nis	2003	23,129	37,622	183	32	15	T	
Jo Spruce		Nld	1993	22,415	36,778	182	32	15	T	
Jo Sycamore *		Nis	2000	23,200	37,500	183	32	15	T	
Jo Sypress		Nld	1998	22,415	36,752	182	32	15	T	

Managed by JO Tankers AS; also see A/S Borgestad ASA and Knutsen O.A.S. Shipping A/S, both Norway.
* managed by JO Tankers UK Ltd or ** by Executive Ship Management, Singapore.
† chartered from Japanese owner (managed by Fleet Management, Hong Kong).

Odfjell ASA. BOW MAASSTROOM. *Hans Kraijenbosch*

J O Odfjell A/S (JO Tankers). JO ACER. *Hans Kraijenbosch*

Rudolf A. Oetker (HSDG). MONTE SARMIENTO. *Hans Kraijenbosch*

Name	Eng	Flag	Year	GRT	DWT	Loa	Bm	Kts	Type	Former names

Rudolf A Oetker — Germany

Hamburg-Sudamerikanische Dampfschiffahrts-ges (HSDG)

Funnel: *White with red top.*
Hull: *Red or white with red boot-topping.*

Name	Eng	Flag	Year	GRT	DWT	Loa	Bm	Kts	Type	Former names
Alianca Maua	Deu		2005	69,132	64,730	272	40	-	CC	ex Monte Verde-05
Alianca Urca	Bra		1981	24,270	23,520	185	28	17	CC	ex Columbus Canterbury-02, Monte Rosa-96
Cap Carmel	Lbr		2003	25,705	33,600	207	30	22	CC	
Cap Finisterre	Deu		1991	29,841	32,675	200	32	18	CC	
Cap Melville	Lbr		2003	25,705	33,836	207	30	22	CC	
Cap Nelson	Deu		2004	25,709	33,925	207	30	22	CC	ex Santos Express-05, Cap Nelson-04
Cap Palmas	Lbr		2003	25,709	33,795	208	30	21	CC	ex NYK Fantasia-05, Cap Palmas-03
Cap Polonia	Deu		1990	29,739	33,221	200	32	18	CC	
Cap Roca	Deu		1990	35,303	42,221	234	32	21	CC	ex New York Express-96, Berlin Express-93, POL Jos-92, Berlin Express-91
Cap San Antonio	Lbr		2001	40,085	51,060	257	32	23	CC	
Cap San Augustin	Lbr		2001	40,085	51,087	257	32	23	CC	
Cap San Lorenzo	Lbr		2001	40,085	51,045	257	32	23	CC	
Cap San Marco	Lbr		2001	40,085	51,087	257	32	23	CC	
Cap San Nicolas	Lbr		2001	40,085	51,101	257	32	22	CC	
Cap San Raphael	Lbr		2002	40,085	51,059	257	32	22	CC	
Cap Trafalgar	Lbr		1990	29,739	33,222	200	32	19	CC	ex CMA CGM Pasteur-06, CGM Pasteur-01, Cap Trafalgar-99
Cap Verde	Deu		2003	25,703	33,741	208	29	-	CC	ex Alianca Sao Paulo-05, Rio Verde-03
Carmel Bio-Top	Lbr		2004	17,500	15,052	186	25	-	CC	
Carmel Eco-Fresh	Lbr		2003	18,931	15,052	186	25	-	CC	I/a Rio Alexandre
Monte Cervantes	Deu		2004	69,132	64,730	272	40	23	CC	ex P&O Nedlloyd Salsa-06, Monte Cervantes-05
Monte Olivia	Deu		2004	69,132	64,730	272	40	23	CC	
Monte Pascoal	Deu		2004	69,132	65,066	272	40	23	CC	ex P&O Nedlloyd Lambada-06, Monte Pascoal-05
Monte Rosa	Deu		2004	69,132	64,888	272	40	23	CC	
Monte Sarmiento	Deu		2004	69,132	65,028	272	40	23	CC	

newbuildings: ten 69,000 grt container ships for 2008 delivery.
All managed by Columbus Shipmanagement GmbH.

Alianca Navegacao e Logistica Ltd/Brazil

Funnel: *Yellow with broad white over red bands beneath black top, black triangular 'A' on white band or HSDG colours.*
Hull: *Blue with white 'ALIANCA', red boot-topping.*

Name	Eng	Flag	Year	GRT	DWT	Loa	Bm	Kts	Type	Former names
Alianca Brasil	Bra		1994	28,397	32,984	200	32	18	CC	
Alianca Europa	Bra		1994	28,397	32,984	200	32	18	CC	
Copacabana	Bra		1984	20,995	26,848	179	31	18	CC	
Flamengo	Bra		1985	20,994	26,868	179	31	18	CC	
Leblon	Bra		1982	24,270	23,560	185	28	16	CC	ex Columbus California-00, Monte Cervantes-93
Lily	Bra		1984	28,347	47,043	201	27	15	B	ex Arpoador-85

Maritime Services Aleuropa GmbH/Germany

Funnel: *White with red half-circle on broad blue top above broad green band.*
Hull: *White.*

Name	Eng	Flag	Year	GRT	DWT	Loa	Bm	Kts	Type	Former names
Carlos Fischer	Lbr		2002	33,005	43,067	204	32	20	Tfj	
Ouro do Brasil	Lbr		1993	15,218	19,519	173	26	20	Tfj	
Premium do Brasil	Lbr		2003	33,005	43,002	205	32	20	Tfj	
Sol do Brasil	Lbr		1994	15,218	19,563	173	26	20	Tfj	

Managed for Group Fischer, Brazil.

Ofer Brothers (Holdings) Ltd — Israel

Funnel: *Blue or charterers colours.*
Hull: *Various.*

Name	Eng	Flag	Year	GRT	DWT	Loa	Bm	Kts	Type	Former names
Atlantic Fortune	Mlt		1994	26,136	44,820	187	30	14	B	ex Aqua Crest-01, Halla Neptune-98
Bengal Sea *	Lbr		1992	37,071	47,120	237	32	21	CC	ex SCI Gaurav-04, German Senator-02, Choyang Volga-98
Black Sea *	Mlt		1990	36,584	44,014	240	32	22	CC	ex Zim Ravenna I-05, Choyang Glory-98
Cap Blanco	Mlt		1984	32,150	37,042	203	32	15	CC	ex CGM Magellan-97, Andes-94
Cap Brett *	Cyp		1979	24,080	23,628	184	28	18	CC	ex Columbus Canada-04, CMB Memling-94, Monte Sarmiento-86, Columbus Canterbury-83
Cap Domingo	Mlt		1984	31,446	34,680	201	32	19	CC	ex Alianca Mexico-99, Cap Corrientes-98, Laser Pacific-96, Bo Johnson-93

Name	Eng	Flag	Year	GRT	DWT	Loa	Bm	Kts	Type	Former names
Cap York *		Mlt	1979	24,270	24,320	184	28	19	CC	ex City of Istanbul-04, Columbus Queensland-03
Cape Carmel		Bmu	1996	92,194	179,869	290	46	14	B	ex Pytchley-05, SGC Capital-98
Cape Lowlands		Lbr	1999	92,194	172,515	289	45	15	B	ex La Selva-04
Car Bridge I		Lbr	1981	41,368	17,344	199	30	17	V	ex Zimcar 1-01, Delborg-00, Primavera-96, Jinto Maru-89
Car Star 1 *		Cyp	1981	41,363	17,427	199	30	17	V	ex Thonborg-99, Margherita-96, Jinmu Maru-90
Caribbean Sea		Lbr	1992	37,071	46,975	237	32	21	CC	ex Zim Florida-05, St. Petersburg Mariner-03, St. Petersburg Senator-02
Columbus Victoria *		Cyp	1979	24,081	23,165	168	28	19	CC	ex Oregon Star-94, Columbus Louisiana-91
CSCL Qingdao		Mlt	2001	39,941	50,953	260	32	24	CC	
CSCL Rotterdam		Mlt	2002	39,500	50,863	260	32	24	CC	
CSCL Tianjin		Mlt	2001	39,941	50,953	260	32	24	CC	
Dafnls		Mlt	1981	13,586	16,728	160	24	15	Co	ex Bonny-98, Zagreb-95
Durban Star III		Mlt	1982	15,611	22,918	166	27	16	Co	ex Hillary-99, Earnest Venture-96
India Lotus		Mlt	1981	36,263	39,967	239	32	22	CC	ex Zim Haifa I-02, Zim Savannah-98, M.Savannah-90, Zim Savannah-90
Kestrel I		Mlt	1988	30,824	25,684	202	31	17	CC	ex Pelican I-03, Zim Antwerp I-02, Asia Opal-02, LT Mediterranea-99, Nuova Mediterranea-99, Genova-96, Erna Oldendorff-81, H. Cegielski-91
Lina		Lbr	1994	16,282	23,276	163	28	18	CC	ex Rejane Delmas-04, Contship New Zealand-97
Marmara Sea *		Cyp	1990	36,584	44,025	241	32	23	CC	ex Zim Dalian-05, Choyang Victory-98
Mombasa Star		Pan	1979	15,879	22,954	166	27	15	C	ex Valerie I-00, Concord Asia-96, Grand Wing-86
MSC Andalucia II		Mlt	1978	20,408	21,857	181	27	17	CC	ex Lora-02, MSC Andalucia-02, Lora-00, Norasia Alexandria-00, Lora-99, Diana-96, Asean Unity-94, Ciudad de Pasto-93 (con C-95)
North Sea *		Lbr	1992	37,071	47,120	237	32	21	CC	ex Zim Singapore-04, Korea Star-03, Moscow Mariner-02, Moscow Senator-02, Choyang Moscow-98
Ori A		Pan	1978	14,741	21,513	163	24	14	T	ex Marina-94, Terutoku Maru-93
Philippine Star		Mlt	1986	22,667	33,852	188	28	19	CC	ex Zim Mumbai 1-02, MSC Cameroon-01, Zim Shanghai-01, Vesta-95, Ville de Vesta-94, Japan Sea-93, Ville de Vesta-89, Pacific Prosperity-88
Qingdao Star		Mlt	1985	22,667	32,934	188	28	18	CC	ex CSCL Huangpu-02, Zim India-00, Zim Singapore-98, Vega-95, Ville de Vega-94, Pacific Progress-88
SCI Mahima		Mlt	1985	37,814	53,726	243	32	19	CC	ex Zim Chicago-04, Zim Venezia II-02, Alma A-01, Houston-00, Houston Express-97, Sea Premier-94, CGM Paris-94, Maersk Tacoma-88, C.R. Paris-87
White Swan *		Cyp	1989	30,824	26,132	202	31	17	CC	ex Zim Hamburg I-02, Asia Jade-02, LT Nipponica-99, Nuova Nipponica-99, Trieste-96, T. Wenda-91
Zim Keelung		Mlt	1981	36,263	39,967	239	32	22	CC	ex M.Keelung-91, Zim Keelung-91
Zim Marseille		Mlt	1981	31,694	28,615	222	31	21	CC	ex Azov Sea-01, Asia Crown-01, APL Monterrey-01, Asia Crown-00, Zim Osaka-98, Asia Crown-96, California Ceres-96, Shin-Kashu Maru-81
Zim Novorossiysk		Mlt	1977	15,560	18,834	187	25	21	CC	ex Gulf Glory-02, Penang Glory-01, Hanjin Kunsan-98, Ever Valiant-85

Owned by Ofer (Ships Holding) Ltd except * by subsidiary Kotani Shipmanagement Ltd, Cyprus formed jointly with Zodiac Maritime Agencies Ltd., UK.

Zodiac Maritime Agencies Ltd/UK

Funnel: Blue with blue 'Z' on globe outline on white disc.
Hull: Black, grey/red or white with red boot-topping.

Name	Eng	Flag	Year	GRT	DWT	Loa	Bm	Kts	Type	Former names
Alanya		Gbr	1986	27,012	38,792	183	29	13	B	ex Rio Purus-93
Amber *		Pan	1986	93,509	181,884	290	46	13	B	ex Concorde Spirit-99, Concorde Maru-91
Andes Mountains		Lbr	1983	7,988	8,410	142	20	18	R	ex Greenland Rex-95
Asian Beauty **		Gbr	1994	44,481	13,308	185	31	18	V	
Asian Glory **		Gbr	1994	44,818	13,363	184	31	18	V	
Asian Trader		Lbr	1991	16,731	22,735	175	28	19	CC	ex Asian Pollux-03
Atlas Mountains		Lbr	1982	8,041	8,778	140	21	18	R	ex Winfast Reefer-96, Frontier Reefer-94, Kijima-89
Belsize Park		Gbr	2003	11,590	19,937	146	24	15	T	
Brazil Star		Lbr	1983	100,912	201,227	299	50	12	B	ex Tsukuba Maru-94
Broadgate		Lbr	1984	20,986	35,287	176	28	14	B	ex Marine Royal-95, Unyo Maru-88
Brother Glory		Gbr	1998	27,105	46,211	190	31	13	B	
Buccleuch		Bmu	1993	90,820	182,675	284	47	13	B	
Cape Eagle		Gbr	1993	81,589	161,475	280	45	14	B	

Name	Eng	Flag	Year	GRT	DWT	Loa	Bm	Kts	Type	Former names
Cape Falcon		Gbr	1993	81,589	149,480	280	45	14	B	
Cape Flamingo		Gbr	2005	90,092	180,201	290	45	-	B	
Cape Hawk		Gbr	1995	81,589	161,425	280	45	14	B	
Cape Kestrel		Gbr	1993	81,589	161,475	280	45	14	B	
Cape Merlin		Gbr	1994	77,503	150,966	273	43	-	B	ex Universal Spirit-02
Cape Osprey		Gbr	1996	81,589	161,448	280	45	14	B	ex Sanko Oriole-03
Cape Pelican		Gbr	2005	90,091	180,235	289	45	-	B	
Cape Stork		Gbr	1996	83,658	171,039	278	45	14	B	ex Lowlands Rose-04
Captain Aysuna		Lbr	1986	16,080	26,914	168	27	13	B	ex New Venus-97, Helm Star-92, Liberty Star-88
CMA CGM Carolina *		Lbr	1980	40,077	47,841	260	32	23	CC	ex APL Emerald-05, President Eisenhower-98, Neptune Jade-84
CMA CGM Sapphire		Lbr	1991	36,627	44,013	240	32	22	CC	ex Grand Vision-03, Choyang Giant-01
CMA CGM Virginia *		Lbr	1980	40,077	47,841	260	32	23	CC	ex APL Ivory-05, President F.D. Roosevelt-98, Neptune Garnet-84 (len-81)
Cotswold		Bmu	1986	80,578	151,016	289	45	14	B	
CP Deliverer		Gbr	2003	39,800	50,500	260	32	24	CC	ex Lykes Deliverer-05
CP Indigo		Gbr	2003	39,941	50,900	260	32	24	CC	ex Contship Indigo-05, APL Panama-04
CP Monterrey		Gbr	2003	39,941	50,813	260	32	24	CC	ex TMM Monterrey-05
Cumbria		Lbr	1990	13,455	13,453	146	23	14	Lpg	ex Victoire-04, Kelvin-96
Duhallow		Bmu	1993	63,240	122,774	266	41	14	B	
Eastgate		Lbr	1990	17,066	27,877	177	26	14	B	ex Japan Rainbow II-01
Eridge		Bmu	1993	63,153	122,792	266	41	14	B	
Fernie		Bmu	1996	63,153	122,292	266	41	14	B	
Grafton		Bmu	1996	63,153	122,301	266	41	14	B	
Grand View		Lbr	1991	36,627	44,006	242	32	22	CC	ex P&O Nedlloyd Xiamen-04, Choyang World-01
Green Mountain		Pan	1983	7,777	8,488	142	20	17	R	ex Manila Tiger-95, Reefer Tiger-89
Green Park		Gbr	2003	11,590	19,940	146	24	15	T	
Hammonia Express		Gbr	2003	39,941	50,800	260	32	24	CC	ex CP Aguascalientes-06, TMM Aguascalientes-05
Heythrop		Bmu	1996	85,364	165,729	288	44	13	B	
Highgate		Gbr	1985	29,660	46,650	196	32	17	BC	ex Colima-96
Holsatia Express		Gbr	2003	39,941	50,500	260	32	24	CC	ex CP Provider-06, Lykes Provider-05
Hyde Park *		Lbr	1982	22,103	38,892	174	32	14	T	ex Stolt Reliant-96, Stolt Luisa Pando-90, M. Luisa de Pando-83
Hyundai Admiral		Gbr	1992	51,836	61,152	275	37	24	CC	
Hyundai Baron		Gbr	1992	51,836	61,152	275	37	24	CC	
Hyundai Discovery		Gbr	1996	64,054	51,120	275	40	25	CC	
Hyundai Dominion		Gbr	2001	74,373	60,494	304	40	26	CC	
Hyundai Emperor		Gbr	1992	51,836	61,152	275	37	26	CC	
Hyundai Independence		Gbr	1996	64,054	68,537	275	40	25	CC	
Hyundai Kingdom		Gbr	2001	74,373	80,551	304	40	26	CC	
Hyundai Liberty		Gbr	1996	64,054	68,539	275	40	25	CC	
Hyundai National		Gbr	2001	74,373	60,494	304	40	26	CC	
Hyundai Patriot		Gbr	2001	74,373	60,494	304	40	26	CC	
Hyundai Republic		Gbr	2001	74,373	80,000	304	40	26	CC	
Hyundai No. 106 **		Lbr	1987	42,469	12,939	184	31	18	V	
Hyundai No. 107 **		Lbr	1987	42,469	12,989	184	31	18	V	
Hyundai No. 108 **		Lbr	1987	30,024	9,783	174	28	18	V	
Hyundai No. 109 **		Lbr	1987	31,367	9,694	174	28	19	V	ex Toronto-99, Hyundai No.109-97
Irfon		Bmu	1996	84,921	165,628	288	44	13	B	
Irongate *		Lbr	1982	92,614	179,618	299	48	13	B	ex Kinokawa-96, Kinokawa Maru-93
Kenwood Park *		Lbr	1982	22,103	39,015	174	32	14	T	ex Stolt Resolute-96, Stolt Maria Pando-90, A. Maria de Pando-83
Kildare		Bmu	1996	108,083	211,320	312	50	14	B	ex SGC Express-98
Kyushu Star *		Lbr	1982	73,657	142,936	270	43	14	B	ex Kitaura Maru-95
Lake Phoenix		Gbr	1992	7,303	8,075	134	21	19	R	ex Amber Rose-96
London Tower		Lbr	1994	17,651	23,884	183	28	19	CC	ex Nantai Queen-99
Lucky Transporter		Lbr	1984	15,763	26,650	167	26	14	B	ex Prime Unity-96, Maersk Pine-92, Mercury Island-90
Maersk Darwin		Gbr	1996	51,938	60,348	294	32	23	CC	ex ANL Indonesia-03, Indonesia-02, APL Indonesia-01
Maersk Doha		Gbr	1996	51,938	60,348	294	32	23	CC	ex P&O Nedlloyd Caribbean-03, Germany-02, APL Germany-02, OOCL Germany-98
Maersk Dundee		Gbr	1996	51,931	60,348	294	32	23	CC	ex France-03, APL France-01, OOCL France-98
Marine Phoenix		Gbr	1994	7,313	7,957	134	21	19	R	ex Amber Lily-97
Meynell		Bmu	1997	93,629	185,767	292	48	15	B	ex SG Universe-98
Moorgate		Lbr	1990	25,965	45,875	190	31	13	B	ex Federal Kumano-97
Morning Cloud		Lbr	1983	36,304	66,755	230	32	15	B	ex Morning Camellia-90, Panamax Neptune-86

Ofer Brothers (Zodiac Marine Agencies). RICHMOND PARK. *C. Lous*

Ofer Brothers (Zodiac Marine Agencies). SURREY. *J. M. Kakebeeke*

Name	Eng	Flag	Year	GRT	DWT	Loa	Bm	Kts	Type	Former names
MSC Krittika		Gbr	1994	30,971	36,999	202	32	21	CC	ex Lykes Commander-05, TMM Mexico-01, Sea Guardian-96, Mexico-94
MSC Napoli		Gbr	1991	53,409	60,173	276	37	24	CC	ex CMA CGM Normandie-04, Nedlloyd Normandie-01, CGM Normandie-95
Mulungisi *		Lbr	1984	9,057	9,340	149	21	19	R	ex Koala-95
Newforest		Bmu	1996	93,629	185,688	292	48	15	B	ex SGC Foundation-98
Noa		Lbr	1985	26,014	43,590	186	30	14	B	ex Soarer Adonis-97
Norasia Bellatrix		Lbr	2002	50,000	58,000	282	32	24	CC	ex Hanjin Pennsylvania-04
Northgate *		Lbr	1984	93,049	179,422	299	48	13	B	ex Kii Maru-97
Northumberland		Gbr	1990	11,822	16,137	158	21	15	Lpg	ex Nelly Maersk-03, Reinanger-98, Anne-Laure-97, Sloka-93
Ormond		Bmu	1986	96,794	187,025	300	47	13	B	
Pacific Quest *		Lbr	1983	31,403	32,631	218	32	21	CC	ex Richmond Bridge-98, Hyundai Portland-97, Maersk Rotterdam-94, Richmond Bridge-93
Peggy Dow		Ant	1985	11,335	10,570	155	23	23	R	
Quorn		Bmu	1996	92,194	179,869	290	46	14	B	ex SG China-98
Regents Park		Gbr	1984	15,163	23,169	171	24	15	T	ex Lacerta-96, R.F. Potomac-94, Mercantil Parati-91, Jacuhy-88
Richmond Park		Lbr	1984	15,163	23,814	171	24	15	T	ex Tamara I-96, R.F. Carioca-93, Mercantil Cabo Frio-92, Jutahy-88
River Phoenix *		Gbr	1993	7,313	8,044	134	21	19	R	ex Clover Moon-99, Dover Phoenix-97
Rutland		Bmu	1997	85,848	170,013	292	46	14	B	ex SG Fortune-98
Sandra Azul		Gbr	1994	60,117	63,163	300	37	23	CC	ex NYK Altair-01
Sandra Blanca *		Gbr	1995	60,117	63,014	300	37	23	CC	ex NYK Vega-01
Santa Barbara		Lbr	1992	43,213	39,402	253	32	23	CC	ex NYK Surfwind-99
Santa Cruz		Gbr	1991	43,209	38,970	252	32	23	CC	ex NYK Sunrise-99
Santa Monica		Lbr	1991	43,213	39,376	253	32	23	CC	ex NYK Seabreeze-99
Sea Phoenix *		Pan	1992	7,303	8,056	134	21	19	R	ex Amber Cherry-96
Seagate		Gbr	1989	17,590	28,836	170	27	14	C	ex Alabama Rainbow-01
Shetland		Iom	1981	14,102	18,270	153	25	17	Lpg	ex Maersk Shetland-01, Svendborg Maersk-94
Silvergate		Lbr	1987	37,025	68,158	225	32	14	B	ex Glory Hope-97
Sinar Toba		Gbr	1990	16,731	22,734	185	28	19	CC	ex Kota Perabu-05, Millenia Tower-03, ACX Rose-00
Snowdon		Bmu	1998	85,848	170,013	292	46	14	B	l/a SG Creation
Somerset		Gbr	1981	14,046	18,270	153	25	17	Lpg	ex Maersk Somerset-01, Sally Maersk-93
Southgate		Gbr	1982	15,274	25,417	161	25	14	B	ex Menina Elisa-93, Oriental Swan-89
Springwood		Lbr	1984	22,009	37,694	188	28	14	B	ex Spring Hawk-93, Sanko Hawk-86
Stafford		Gbr	1984	14,102	18,270	153	25	17	Lpg	ex Maersk Stafford-01, Sine Maersk-93, Olga Maersk-92
Stonegate *		Lbr	1984	107,083	187,011	305	51	13	B	ex Sunny Ocean-98, River Star-97
Suffolk		Gbr	1984	14,102	18,270	153	25	17	Lpg	ex Maersk Suffolk-01, Sofie Maersk-93, Oluf Maersk-92
Summer Phoenix		Gbr	1993	7,326	8,041	134	21	19	R	ex Spring Phoenix-01, Windward Phoenix-99
Surrey		Gbr	1982	14,102	18,270	153	25	17	Lpg	ex Maersk Surrey-01, Svend Maersk-93
Sussex		Gbr	1981	14,102	18,270	153	25	17	Lpg	ex Maersk Sussex-01, Susan Maersk-92
Taunton		Bmu	1986	95,835	186,324	300	47	13	B	ex Marine Crusader-89
Thuringia Express		Gbr	2003	39,941	50,500	260	32	24	CC	ex CP Tamarind-06, Contship Tamarind-05, APL Honduras-04
Tineke		Ant	1984	11,335	10,510	155	23	23	R	
Ullswater		Bmu	1990	63,106	114,741	266	42	14	B	
Ural Mountains *		Lbr	1984	8,063	8,238	142	20	18	R	ex Mistrau-95
Vine		Bmu	1990	63,106	114,975	266	42	14	B	
Waterford		Bmu	1990	77,113	149,513	270	43	12	B	
YM Hamburg		Gbr	1997	40,268	49,238	259	32	23	CC	ex Ville de Virgo-04
YM Hongkong II		Lbr	1991	17,156	22,219	186	28	18	CC	ex Tiger Shark-04, Recife-01, Pacific Vista-98, Tokyo Bridge-98,
YM Kaohsiung		Gbr	1998	40,068	49,238	259	32	23	CC	ex Ville de Tanya-05
YM Moji		Lbr	1994	16,708	24,444	183	28	19	CC	ex Tiger Bridge-04, Libra Australia II-02, Libra Australia-00
YM Shanghai		Gbr	1997	40,268	49,000	259	32	23	CC	ex Ville d'Antares-04
York		Bmu	1990	77,113	149,513	270	43	13	B	
Zetland		Bmu	1985	74,003	145,905	267	43	13	B	ex Mosbulk-90
Zim Panama		Gbr	2002	53,453	55,000	294	32	24	CC	
Zim Pusan		Gbr	2004	53,453	62,740	294	32	24	CC	
Zim Shenzhen		Gbr	2004	53,453	62,740	294	32	24	CC	

newbuildings: five 74,400 grt and five 75,300 grt container ships for 2006 and 2009 delivery respectively.
* owned by SAMAMA (Societe Anon. Monegasque d'Admin. Maritime et Aerienne)
** believed to be chartered to Eukor Car Carriers Inc. (see under Wallenius-Wilhelmsen)

Name	Eng	Flag	Year	GRT	DWT	Loa	Bm	Kts	Type	Former names

Tanker Pacific Management Singapore (Pte) Ltd/Singapopre

Name	Eng	Flag	Year	GRT	DWT	Loa	Bm	Kts	Type	Former names
Gateway	Nis	1988	79,544	152,385	267	46	14	T	ex Kronviken-04, Eurus-97, Golar Jane-91
Genmar Challenger	Lbr	1991	57,082	95,002	243	38	14	Obo	ex SCF Challenger-01, SKS Challenger-95
Genmar Champ	Lbr	1992	57,082	96,027	243	38	14	Obo	ex Genmar Champion-03, SCF Champion-01, SKS Champion-95
Genmar Endurance	Lbr	1991	57,082	96,027	243	38	14	Obo	ex SCF Endurance-01, SKS Endurance-95
Genmar Hector	Lbr	1992	57,082	96,027	243	38	14	Obo	ex SC Horizon-00, SKS Horizon-95, Scanobo Horizon-92
Genmar Pericles	Lbr	1992	57,082	96,027	243	38	14	Obo	ex SC Breeze-00, SKS Breeze-95, Scanobo Breeze-92
Genmar Spirit	Lbr	1992	57,082	96,027	243	38	14	Obo	ex SCF Spirit-01, SKS Spirit-95, Scanobo Spirit-92
Genmar Star	Lbr	1992	57,082	96,027	243	38	14	Obo	ex SCF Star-01, SKS Star-95
Genmar Trader	Lbr	1991	57,082	96,043	243	38	14	Obo	ex SCF Trader-01, SKS Trader-95
Genmar Trust	Lbr	1992	57,082	96,027	243	38	14	Obo	ex SCF Trust-01, SKS Trust-95, Scanobo Trust-92
Hadra	Iom	1994	28,277	40,549	183	32	14	T	
Halia	Iom	1993	28,277	40,549	183	32	14	T	
Headway	Nis	1989	79,544	152,385	267	40	14	T	ex Solviken-04, Corus-97, Golar Colleen-91
Kingsway	Lbr	1992	84,488	140,059	271	49	14	T	ex Genmar Honour-05, Erati-04
Nara	Sgp	1996	28,433	47,172	183	32	15	T	ex Eagle Vela-04, NOL Vela-00
Queensway	Lbr	1993	84,488	159,878	271	49	14	T	ex Genmar Conqueror-05, Inago-04
Savannah	Sgp	1996	28,433	47,172	183	32	15	T	ex Eagle Sagitta-04, NOL Sagitta-00
Starway	Mhl	1991	88,946	155,103	275	48	15	T	ex Genmar Zoe-06, J. Dennis Bonney-00

A cross-section of the 56 vessels currently owned or managed by the company.

Zim Integrated Shipping Services/Israel

Funnel: *White with blue 'ZIM' below seven gold stars (four above three).*
Hull: *White or grey with green boot-topping, or black with white 'ZIM' and red boot-topping.*

Name	Eng	Flag	Year	GRT	DWT	Loa	Bm	Kts	Type	Former names
Blue Sky	Lbr	1983	93,052	166,013	290	47	15	D	ex Hadora-03
Zim Adriatic	Mlt	1982	36,263	39,967	239	32	22	CC	ex Adriatic-97, Zim Iberia-97
Zim America	Isr	1990	37,209	47,230	236	32	21	CC	
Zim Asia	Isr	1996	41,507	45,850	254	32	21	CC	
Zim Atlantic	Isr	1996	41,507	45,850	254	32	21	CC	
Zim Barcelona	Mlt	2004	53,450	54,740	294	32	24	CC	
Zim California	Isr	2002	53,453	62,740	294	32	24	CC	
Zim Canada	Isr	1990	37,209	47,230	236	32	21	CC	
Zim China	Isr	1997	41,507	45,850	254	32	21	CC	
Zim Europa	Isr	1997	41,507	45,850	254	32	21	CC	
Zim Haifa	Isr	2004	54,626	66,938	254	32	24	CC	
Zim Hong Kong	Isr	1992	37,209	47,230	230	32	21	CC	
Zim Iberia	Isr	1998	41,507	46,350	254	32	21	CC	
Zim Israel	Isr	1992	37,209	47,230	236	32	22	CC	
Zim Italia	Isr	1991	37,209	47,230	236	32	21	CC	
Zim Jamaica	Isr	1997	41,507	45,850	254	32	21	CC	
Zim Japan	Isr	1991	37,209	47,230	236	32	21	CC	
Zim Korea	Isr	1991	37,209	47,230	236	32	21	CC	
Zim Mediterranean	Isr	2002	53,453	62,686	294	32	24	CC	
Zim Pacific	Isr	1996	41,507	45,850	254	32	21	CC	
Zim U.S.A.	Isr	1997	41,200	46,250	254	32	21	CC	
Zim Virginia	Isr	2002	53,453	62,740	294	32	24	CC	

Controlled by Israel Corporation, which is 57.3% owned by Ofer Bros. See other chartered ships with 'Zim' prefix in index.

Reederei Claus-Peter Offen GmbH & Co   Germany

Funnel: *Black with white Maltese Cross on broad blue band edged with narrow white bands, or charterers colours.*
Hull: *Black, light grey or red with red boot-topping.*

Name	Eng	Flag	Year	GRT	DWT	Loa	Bm	Kts	Type	Former names
Cala Palamos	Deu	1997	21,531	30,173	182	30	20	CC	ex P&O Nedlloyd Salsa-05, Santa Giannina-02, P&O Nedlloyd Kingston-02, l/a Santa Giannina
Canmar Promise	Deu	1997	21,531	30,202	182	30	20	CC	ex Santa Giorgina-03, P&O Nedlloyd Rio Grande-03, Santa Giorgina-97
CCNI Tokyo	Lbr	1991	21,049	30,007	182	28	19	CC	ex Santa Barbara I-04, Indfex SCI-02, Santa Barbara I-01, P&O Nedlloyd Bahrain-01, Santa Barbara I-98, Santa Barbara-97, Sea Jade-97, Khaleej Bay-96, Maersk Kanagawa-95, Santa Barbara-94, Puebla-94, Santa Barbara-93

Name	Eng	Flag	Year	GRT	DWT	Loa	Bm	Kts	Type	Former names
Clan Legionary		Deu	1994	21,054	29,744	182	29	20	CC	ex Santa Margherita-05, P&O Nedlloyd Caribbean-02, P&O Nedlloyd Douala-01, Cielo di Livorno-99, Santa Margherita-94
Clan Tangun		Lbr	1996	21,531	30,201	182	30	19	CC	ex Santa Giuliana-05, P&O Nedlloyd Orinoco-01, Nedlloyd Orinoco-99, Santa Giuliana-96
Maersk Damascus		Lbr	2002	45,803	53,081	281	32	25	CC	ex P&O Nedlloyd Palliser-06, I/a Santa Romana
Maersk Decartur		Lbr	2002	45,803	53,410	281	32	25	CC	ex P&O Nedlloyd Encounter-06, I/a Santa Rebecca
Maersk Denia		Lbr	2002	45,803	53,328	281	32	25	CC	ex P&O Nedlloyd Remuera-06, I/a Santa Rafaela
Maersk Denton		Lbr	2002	45,803	53,115	281	32	25	CC	ex P&O Nedlloyd Mairangi-06, Santa Rufina-02
Maersk Detroit		Deu	2005	54,771	66,821	294	32	-	CC	ex Santa Palagia-05
Maersk Dieppe		Lbr	2005	54,809	67,310	294	32	-	CC	ex P&O Nedlloyd Doha-05, Santa Placida-04
Maersk Dolores		Deu	2005	54,809	67,255	294	32	-	CC	ex P&O Nedlloyd Delft-05, I/d Santa Patricia
Maersk Dominica		Deu	2002	45,803	53,462	281	32	25	CC	ex Sydney Express-06, P&O Nedlloyd Pegasus-03, I/a Santa Roberta
Maersk Donegal		Deu	2005	54,771	62,400	295	32	-	CC	ex P&O Nedlloyd Dublin-05, I/d Santa Paula
Maersk Douglas		Deu	2005	54,771	66,800	294	32	-	CC	wx Santa Petrissa-05
Maersk Driscoll		Deu	2005	54,809	67,310	294	32	-	CC	ex P&O Nedlloyd Dalian-05
Maersk Duffield		Lbr	2002	45,803	52,800	281	32	25	CC	ex Columbus New Zealand-06, P&O Nedlloyd Resolution-02, Santa Rosanna-02
Maersk Dunafare		Deu	2002	45,803	53,452	281	32	25	CC	ex P&O Nedlloyd Botany-05, I/a Santa Ricarda
Maersk Dunedin		Deu	2005	54,809	67,247	295	32	-	CC	ex P&O Nedlloyd Detroit-05, I/a Santa Pamina
Maersk Durham		Deu	2005	54,809	67,310	294	32	-	CC	ex P&O Nedlloyd Dover-05
Maersk Ipanema		Deu	1995	36,028	45,170	246	32	24	CC	ex P&O Nedlloyd Seattle-05, Chesapeake Bay-98, Santa Ana-95
Mercosul Palometa		Lbr	1993	15,778	20,278	167	28	19	CC	ex P&O Nedlloyd Zanzibar-01, San Vicente-99, CGM Santos Dumont-98, San Vicente-97
MOL Caledon		Deu	2005	58,289	64,519	294	32	-	CC	ex P&O Nedlloyd Livingstone-06
MOL Cullinan		Deu	2005	58,289	64,519	294	32	-	CC	ex P&O Nedlloyd Heemskerck-06
MSC Beijing		Lbr	2005	89,954	100,870	325	43	25	CC	
MSC Bruxelles		Lbr	2005	107,849	110,000	337	46	25	CC	
MSC Busan		Lbr	2005	89,954	100,000	325	43	25	CC	
MSC Charleston		Pan	2006	90,300	100,000	325	43	25	CC	
MSC Chicago		Lbr	2005	107,849	109,600	337	46	25	CC	
MSC Johannesburg		Deu	1995	36,028	45,170	246	32	24	CC	ex Santa Elena-04, Maersk Rotterdam-01, New York Senator-98, Santa Elena-95
MSC Shanghai		Lbr	2005	65,483	72,000	275	40	-	CC	I/a Santa Viola
MSC Tokyo		Lbr	2005	65,483	71,949	275	40	-	CC	I/a Santa Vanessa
MSC Toronto		Pan	2006	90,300	100,000	325	43	25	CC	
OOCL Korea		Lbr	2001	66,500	67,796	277	40	24	CC	I/a Santa Victoria
OOCL Thailand		Lbr	2002	65,289	67,644	277	40	24	CC	I/a Santa Virginia
San Clemente		Lbr	1994	15,778	20,219	167	28	19	CC	ex Cielo del Chile-03, San Clemente-01, Columbus Bahia-01, San Clemente-99
San Cristobal		Lbr	1995	15,859	20,156	167	28	19	CC	ex Maersk Abidjan-04, San Cristobal-01, Lykes Hawk-00, San Cristobal-99, CGM Saint Exupery-98, Equinox-97, San Cristobal-95
San Felipe		Lbr	1996	15,859	20,058	167	28	19	CC	ex Puerto Limon-04, San Felipe-02, Columbus Mexico-01, Lykes Eagle-00, Ivaran Eagle-99, San Felipe-98
San Fernando		Lbr	1996	15,859	20,219	167	28	19	CC	ex P&O Nedlloyd Tema-04, San Fernando-02, Lykes Condor-01, Ivaran Condor-99, San Fernando-98
San Francisco		Lbr	1996	15,859	20,200	167	28	19	CC	ex Lykes Pilot-06, Maersk Apapa-04, San Francisco-01, Lykes Raven-00, Ivaran Raven-99, San Francisco-98, Contship Brasil-97, Francisco-96, San Francisco-96
San Lorenzo		Lbr	1993	15,778	20,278	167	28	19	CC	ex Columbus Ohio-02, Altamira-00, San Lorenzo 1-98, San Lorenzo-97
Santa Adriana		Deu	2000	25,294	32,323	207	30	22	CC	ex P&O Nedlloyd Algoa-05, MOL Parana-02, P&O Nedlloyd Algoa-01, I/a Santa Adriana
Santa Alexandra		Deu	2000	25,294	32,391	207	30	22	CC	ex P&O Nedlloyd Abidjan-05, MOL San Paulo-02, P&O Nedlloyd Abidjan-01, Santa Alexandra-00

Reederei Claus-Peter Offen. MERCOSUL PALOMETA. *Hans Kraijenbosch*

Reederei Claus-Peter Offen. MSC TOKYO. *Vandriessche Guido*

Name	Eng	Flag	Year	GRT	DWT	Loa	Bm	Kts	Type	Former names
Santa Alina		Deu	2001	25,294	32,299	207	30	22	CC	ex P&O Nedlloyd Apapa-05, MOL Santos-02, P&O Nedlloyd Apapa-01, I/a Santa Alina
Santa Annabella		Lbr	2000	25,294	32,308	207	30	22	CC	ex P&O Nedlloyd Agulhas-05, MOL Paraguay-02, P&O Nedlloyd Agulhas-01, Santa Annabella-00
Santa Arabella		Deu	2000	25,294	32,321	207	30	22	CC	ex P&O Nedlloyd Accra-06, MOL Salvador-02, P&O Nedlloyd Accra-01, Santa Arabella-00
Santa Carlotta		Lbr	2000	37,113	40,018	243	32	23	CC	ex P&O Nedlloyd Olinda-05, I/a Santa Carlotta
Santa Carolina		Lbr	2000	37,113	40,125	243	32	22	CC	ex P&O Nedlloyd Surat-05, Santa Carolina-01
Santa Catalina		Lbr	2001	37,113	40,102	243	32	23	CC	ex P&O Nedlloyd Dejima-05, I/a Santa Catalina
Santa Celina		Deu	2001	37,113	40,018	243	32	23	CC	ex P&O Nedlloyd Chusan-05, Santa Celina-01
Santa Cristina		Lbr	2001	37,113	39,300	243	32	23	CC	ex P&O Nedlloyd Bantam-05, I/a Santa Cristina
Santa Fabiola		Lbr	1999	21,583	30,135	183	30	20	CC	ex P&O Nedlloyd Singapore-05, I/dn Santa Fabiola
Santa Federica		Deu	1998	21,583	29,700	182	30	20	CC	ex P&O Nedlloyd Santiago-02, I/a Santa Fredericia
Santa Felicita		Deu	1999	21,583	30,135	183	30	20	CC	ex P&O Nedlloyd Seoul-02, I/dn Santa Felicita
Santa Fiorenzo		Lbr	1998	21,583	30,007	183	30	20	CC	ex P&O Nedlloyd Arica-02, I/a Santa Fiorenzo
Santa Francesca		Deu	1998	21,583	30,029	183	30	20	CC	ex P&O Nedlloyd Sao Paulo-02, I/a Santa Francesca
Santa Giovanna		Deu	1996	21,531	30,201	182	30	20	CC	ex P&O Nedlloyd Amazonas-01, Santa Giovanna-01, P&O Nedlloyd Amazonas-01, Nedlloyd Amazonas-99, Santa Giovanna-96
Santa Giulietta		Deu	1997	21,531	30,252	182	30	20	CC	ex P&O Nedlloyd Parana-02, I/a Santa Giulietta
Santa Maddalena		Deu	1994	21,054	29,610	182	29	20	CC	ex Delmas Bourgainville-04, P&O Nedlloyd Hawkes Bay-03, P&O Nedlloyd Durban-02, Nedlloyd van Nassau-99, Santa Maddalena-95
Santa Monica		Lbr	1991	21,049	30,007	182	28	18	CC	ex P&O Nedlloyd Samba-05, Santa Monica I-03, P&O Nedlloyd Dubai-00, P&O Nedlloyd van Nes-99, Nedlloyd van Nes-98, Genoa Senator-95, Santa Monica-94
Tiger Island		Lbr	1986	21,049	30,007	182	29	18	CC	ex Sitc Manila-06, Santa Isabella-04, P&O Nedlloyd Dammam-01, Santa Isabella-99, P&O Nedlloyd Salvador-98, Santa Isabella-97, Nedlloyd van Cloon-97, ScanDutch Helvetia-89, I/a Holsten Sea
YM Fukuoka		Lbr	1993	15,778	20,326	166	28	19	CC	ex Maersk Accra-05, YM Fukuoka-05, San Isidro-01, P&O Nedlloyd Lome-00 San Isidro-98

newbuildings: nine 110,000 dwt, eleven 60,000 grt and various smaller containers ships due 2006-7.

Egon Oldendorff OHG
Germany

Funnel: Grey with white 'EO' on broad blue band, or charterers colours.
Hull: Grey, black or red with red boot-topping

Name	Eng	Flag	Year	GRT	DWT	Loa	Bm	Kts	Type	Former names
Albert Oldendorff *		Lbr	2004	19,883	31,647	172	27	-	BC	
Alfred Oldendorff		Lbr	1996	25,074	46,489	190	31	-	B	ex Diamond Halo-04
Alice Oldendorff *		Lbr	2000	28,747	48,000	190	32	14	Bu	
Alwine Oldendorff §		Lbr	1990	35,350	66,088	225	32	13	B	ex Tatry-98
Auguste Oldendorff		Lbr	2001	11,194	18,320	148	23	13	B	
Beatriz		Lbr	1993	13,696	22,145	158	25	14	B	ex Dorothea Oldendorff-04
Bernhard Oldendorff †		Lbr	1991	43,332	77,548	245	32	14	Bu	ex Yeoman Burn-94
Carl Oldendorff *		Lbr	2002	19,822	31,350	172	27	14	B	
Cathrin Oldendorff *		Lbr	2003	19,883	31,643	172	27	14	B	
Christoffer Oldendorff †		Lbr	1981	37,959	62,732	228	32	14	Bu	ex CSL Innovator-93, Atlantic Huron-88, Pacific Peace-86
Dorthe Oldendorff **		Lbr	1994	13,712	22,059	158	25	14	B	
Eduard Oldendorff *		Lbr	2001	19,882	31,640	172	27	14	B	
Edwine Oldendorff		Lbr	2000	11,194	18,315	148	23	13	B	
Eibe Oldendorff		Lbr	1983	18,220	29,364	162	26	13	BC	ex Georgia Gal-05, Eibe Oldendorff-04, Global America-00, Eibe Oldendorff-99, Captain Bougainville-91, Hyundai No.23-89
Elisabeth Oldendorff **		Lbr	1992	13,696	22,154	158	25	14	B	

Name	Eng	Flag	Year	GRT	DWT	Loa	Bm	Kts	Type	Former names
Elise Oldendorff		Lbr	1997	13,781	20,427	149	23	14	BC	
Elsa Oldendorff *		Pan	1998	14,397	24,021	154	26	13	B	ex Stellar Kohinoor-02
Ernst Oldendorff		Lbr	1997	16,405	26,045	172	25	14	B	ex Jan Hus-98
Frederike Oldendorff		Lbr	1997	26,586	48,224	189	31	14	B	ex Mercury Trader-03
Gebe Oldendorff *		Pan	1998	14,762	23,510	155	26	14	B	ex J. Captain Trader-02
Gertrude Oldendorff *		Lbr	2001	19,882	31,635	172	27	14	B	
Gisela Oldendorff		Lbr	1997	13,781	20,100	149	23	14	B	
Gitta Oldendorff §		Pan	2005	19,883	32,833	172	27	-	B	
Gretke Oldendorff **		Lbr	1994	13,690	22,050	158	25	14	B	
Harmen Oldendorff		Lbr	2005	39,568	69,700	225	32	14	B	
Hedwig Oldendorff *		Lbr	1984	90,747	149,863	281	54	13	Obo	ex Behemoth-05, Grouper-04, Algarrobo-02, Nord Atlantic-93, Cast Orca-84
Helena Oldendorff *		Lbr	1984	18,469	28,354	196	23	14	B	ex Noble River-86
Henry Oldendorff		Lbr	1998	16,405	26,031	172	25	14	B	ex Jan Zelivsky-98
Hille Oldendorff		Lbr	2005	30,988	55,566	190	32	14	B	ex Josco Tongzhou-05
Imme Oldendorff		Lbr	1999	28,078	48,913	190	32	14	B	ex Royal Chance-03
Jobst Oldendorff *		Lbr	1995	14,743	23,569	155	26	13	B	ex Tinker Bell-03
Kent Pioneer		Lbr	1999	13,781	20,427	149	23	14	BC	ex Mathilde Oldendorff-05
Kent Timber		Lbr	1999	13,781	20,427	149	23	14	BC	ex Antonie Oldendorff-05
Lily Oldendorff		Lbr	2003	19,883	31,350	172	27	14	B	
Lucas Oldendorff *		Lbr	2002	19,882	31,643	172	27	14	B	
Lucy Oldendorff **		Lbr	1992	13,696	22,160	157	25	14	B	
Ludolf Oldendorff §		Phl	2000	26,010	45,578	186	30	15	B	
Magdalena Oldendorff		Lbr	1998	14,762	23,515	154	26	14	B	ex Ocean Breeze-04
Max Oldebdorff		Lbr	1997	26,586	48,225	189	31	14	B	ex Million Trader-03
May Oldendorff		Lbr	1997	26,040	45,205	188	31	14	B	ex Houyu-03
Mina Oldendorff §		Phl	1999	26,010	45,630	186	30	14	B	
Pacific Faithful		Lbr	1996	19,354	29,516	181	26	14	Co	ex Christiane Oldendorff-04, Tamaya-99, Christiane Oldendorff-96
Pacific Freedom		Lbr	1996	19,354	29,512	181	26	14	Co	ex Ilsabe Oldendorff-05, CSAV Livorno-02, Ilsabe Oldendorff-01, Cielo di Monfalcone-99, Andacollo-98, Ilsabe Oldendorff-97
Paul Oldendorff		Lbr	2003	21,185	35,117	178	28	14	B	
Regina Oldendorff *		Lbr	2006	24,140	-	-	-	-	B	
Rosario		Lbr	1976	32,173	22,691	206	31	21	Ro	ex Rosanne-04, Daisy-00, Euroshipping 2-97, Magnitogorsk-96
Roxanne		Lbr	1976	32,173	21,002	206	31	21	Ro	ex Nicole-00, Kotlini-97, Komsomolsk-95
Sophie Oldendorff †		Lbr	2000	41,428	70,034	225	32	14	Bu	
Tasman Adventurer		Atg	1992	15,901	21,679	165	26	16	Co	ex Helga Oldendorff-99, FMG Mexico-99, Helga Oldendorff-96, POL Europe-95
Tasman Discoverer *		Atg	1992	15,900	21,763	165	26	16	Co	ex Henrietta Oldendorff-99, FMG Santiago-99, Henrietta Oldendorff-96, POL Asia-95
Texas Gal		Lbr	1983	18,220	29,338	162	26	13	BC	ex Eckert Oldendorff-05, Texas Gal-04, Eckert Oldendorff-03, Global Asia-00, Eckert Oldendorff-99, Captain Padon-91, Hyundai No.22-89
Theodor Oldendorff		Lbr	1999	12,192	17,786	141	23	13	B	
Yeoman Brook ‡		Lbr	1991	43,332	77,548	245	32	14	Bu	

newbuildings - four 22,800 grt bulk carriers for 2006-7 delivery.
* managed by subsidiary Oldendorff Carriers GmbH & Co. KG and ** owned by Investeringsgruppen Danmark A/S, Denamrk
† operated in joint Pool with CSL Group Inc., Canada or ‡ on time charter to Foster Yeoman Ltd until 2011.
§ on time-charter from various owners (currently about 80 such vessels) or ¶ on bareboat charter with purchase option from MPC q.v.

Reederei 'NORD' Klaus E Oldendorff Ltd　　　Cyprus

Funnel: *Grey with white 'N' inside white ring on broad blue band or charterers colours.*
Hull: *Light grey with red or black boot-topping.*

Name	Eng	Flag	Year	GRT	DWT	Loa	Bm	Kts	Type	Former names
Cala Puebla		Deu	1997	16,264	22,350	179	25	19	CC	ex Nordcoast-05, Safmarine Nahoon-02, DAL East London-02, Nordcoast-01, Alianca Parana-00, Nordcoast-00, CSAV Buenos Aires-99, Nordcoast-97
Cala Pilar		Cyp	1997	16,252	22,420	179	25	19	CC	ex City of Stuttgart-02, Safmarine Inyathi-01, Nordriver-01, Pacific Eagle-01, Nordriver-00, Bogata-99, Nordriver-98
Cala Pinar del Rio		Cyp	1994	14,619	20,275	167	25	17	CC	ex Nordpol-05, Indamex Taj-02, Abidjan Star II-00, Nordpol-99, TNX Mercury-98, Nordpol-98, San Marino-97, Nordpol-94

Name	Eng	Flag	Year	GRT	DWT	Loa	Bm	Kts	Type	Former names
CMA CGM Carioca		Cyp	1997	24,053	27,100	206	27	20	CC	ex Nordfalcon-04, CSAV Taipei-01, Panamerican-99, Nordfalcon-97
CMA CGM Colombie		Cyp	1997	24,053	27,100	206	27	20	CC	ex CSAV Livorno-03, Nordhawk-02, Libra Buenos Aires-01, Zim Sao Paulo-99, Panbrasil-98, I/a Nordhawk
CMA CGM Condor		Cyp	1994	14,619	20,255	165	25	19	CC	ex Cala Palamos-04, Nordpartner-01, Cielo del Cile-01, Nordpartner-99, San Miguel-96
CMA CGM Intensity		Iom	2003	25,407	33,900	207	30	22	CC	ex Nordmed-04
CMA CGM Romania		Iom	2003	25,407	33,900	207	30	22	CC	ex Nordbaltic-03
Delmas Kenya		Cyp	1991	11,998	14,190	157	23	17	CC	ex Nordcliff-02, New Achiever-01, Nordcliff-00, Tui Pacific-00, Nordcliff-97, Lanka Asitha-97, Nordcliff-91
Libra Corcovado		Cyp	2003	25,407	33,701	207	30	22	CC	ex Lykes Envoy-05, Nordpacific-03
Libra Niteroi		Cyp	2003	25,407	33,853	207	30	22	CC	ex Nordatlantic-05, Cala Palos-04, Nordatlantic-03
Libra Patagonia		Cyp	1997	16,252	22,330	179	25	19	CC	ex Nordcloud-03, Niver Austral-99, Nordcloud-98
Nordbeach		Cyp	1991	11,998	14,100	157	23	17	CC	ex Abidjan Star-99, Nordbeach-98, X-Press Mumbai-97, Lanka Aruna-96, Nordbeach-92
Nordeagle		Cyp	1997	24,053	27,100	206	27	20	CC	ex Libra Houston-01, CSAV Seoul-00, Panatlantic-99, Nordeagle-97
Nordelbe		Cyp	2001	40,605	75,259	225	32	14	B	
Nordems		Cyp	2001	40,605	75,253	225	32	14	B	
Nordenergy		Cyp	2003	161,306	319,174	333	60	16	T	
Nordmark		Cyp	1998	57,148	89,999	244	42	15	T	
Nordmars		Cyp	2004	40,000	74,999	225	32	14	T	
Nordmerkur		Cyp	2004	40,000	74,999	225	32	14	T	
Nordmillennium		Cyp	2000	156,417	302,000	331	58	15	T	
Nordmoritz		Cyp	1995	39,027	72,610	225	32	14	B	
Nordmosel		Cyp	2001	40,605	75,080	225	32	14	B	
Nordneptune		Cyp	2004	40,000	74,999	225	32	14	T	
Nordpower		Cyp	2003	161,308	319,012	333	60	16	T	
Nordrhine		Cyp	2001	40,605	75,080	225	32	14	B	
Nordseas		Cyp	1996	16,264	22,386	178	25	19	CC	ex MOL Sprinter-04, Malacca Star-03, Nordsea-01, Nordseas-01, Pacific Voyager-01, Nordsea-00, Panaustral-98, Nordsea-97
Nordsky		Cyp	1990	11,998	14,140	157	23	17	CC	ex Peru Star-00, Nordsky-97, Alaska-96, Nordsky-92, Karawa-92, Nordsky-92
Nordstar		Cyp	1998	16,803	23,007	185	25	19	CC	ex P&O Nedlloyd Pampas-02, Nordstar-01, Niver Austral-00, Nordstar-99, CSAV Rio Uruguay-99
Nordstrand		Cyp	1993	30,526	34,079	205	32	19	CC	ex Nautic-00, Nordstrand-99, Byron Bay-98, Nordstrand-97, Med Marseilles-96, Saint Corentin-94
Nordstrength		Cyp	1998	57,148	89,999	244	42	15	T	
Nordsun		Cyp	1991	11,998	14,140	157	23	17	CC	ex Chile Star II-99, Kent Scout-98, CGM La Bourdonnaise-97, Nordsun-97, Lanka Abhaya-97, Nordsun-92
Nordtrave		Cyp	2001	40,605	75,080	225	32	14	B	
Nordvenus		Lbr	2004	40,000	74,999	225	32	14	T	
Nordwelle		Cyp	2005	27,093	34,600	210	30	-	CC	
Nordweser		Cyp	2001	40,605	75,321	225	32	14	B	
YM Okinawa		Cyp	1994	16,202	22,450	179	25	19	CC	ex Nordlake-05, CSAV Lonquimay-98, Nordlake-96

Newbuildings: one 27,000 grt and four 36,000 grt container ships for 2006-8 delivery.

Fred Olsen & Co   Norway

Funnel: *Black with red band.*
Hull: *Dark grey or red with red or pink boot-topping.*

Name	Eng	Flag	Year	GRT	DWT	Loa	Bm	Kts	Type	Former names
Knock Adoon		Sgp	1985	133,940	244,942	318	54	14	T	ex El Greco-05, Tagawa Maru-01
Knock Allan		Sgp	1992	78,710	145,242	274	44	14	T	
Knock Stocks		Sgp	1993	78,710	145,242	274	44	14	T	

Owned by subsidiary Red Band AS, Norway (operated by First Olsen Tankers Ltd., Liberia) and managed by V.Ships Norway AS.

Reederei 'NORD' Klaus E. Oldendorff. CALA PILAR. *M. D. J. Lennon*

Reederei 'NORD' Klaus E. Oldendorff. NORDMERKUR. *F. de Vries*

Name	Eng	Flag	Year	GRT	DWT	Loa	Bm	Kts	Type	Former names

Schiffahrts Oltmann Verwaltung GmbH

Germany

Funnel: *Mainly in charterers colours.*
Hull: *Dark grey with red boot-topping.*

Name	Eng	Flag	Year	GRT	DWT	Loa	Bm	Kts	Type	Former names
APL Beijing *	Lbr	2004	54,605	67,022	294	32	-	CC	
APL Brazil *	Bhs	2004	40,952	55,461	261	32	-	CC	
APL Vietnam *	Lbr	2005	54,605	67,025	294	32	-	CC	
CMA CGM Vega *	Bhs	2001	39,812	51,020	258	32	24	CC	
CP Rangitoto	Deu	1998	25,359	33,964	207	30	20	CC	ex Contship Rangitoto-05, Cielo di San Francisco-05, Ute Oltmann-99
CSAV Yokohama	Deu	2005	25,630	33,742	207	30	22	CC	ex JPO Gemini-05
Libra Buenos Aires	Atg	2000	25,381	33,937	207	30	22	CC	CMA CGM Chili-02, JPO Aquarius-01
Maersk Dabou	Lbr	2005	41,359	52,450	264	32	-	CC	ex P&O Nedlloyd Cardenas-05, JPO Cancer-05
Maersk Danville	Lbr	2005	41,359	52,786	264	32	-	CC	ex P&O Nedlloyd Cardigan-05, JPO Capricornus-05
MOL Renaissance	Lbr	2005	35,881	41,743	220	32	-	CC	ex JPO Leo-05
Montebello	Deu	1998	25,361	33,919	207	30	21	CC	ex Anika Oltmann-99, Montebello-99, Anika Oltmann-98
MSC Christina **	Cyp	1998	37,579	56,902	243	32	23	CC	ex P&O Nedlloyd Chicago-04
MSC Ulsan *	Bhs	2002	40,108	51,020	258	32	24	CC	
P&O Nedlloyd Carolinas	Lbr	2005	41,359	52,786	264	32	-	CC	ex JPO Libra-05
P&O Nedlloyd Carthago	Lbr	2005	41,359	52,786	264	32	-	CC	ex JPO Pisces-05
Trade Rainbow	Atg	2001	25,361	33,900	207	30	22	CC	ex TCL Challenger-02, JPO Aries-01

newbuildings: two 34,600 grt container ships (JPO Sagittarius/JPO Scorpius) on order for 2006-7 delivery.
* owned by D Oltmann or ** by Reimarus Schiffahrts, both Germany.

OMI Marine Services LLC

USA

Funnel: *Black with large white 'O' on broad red band edged with narrow white bands.*
Hull: *Brown or blue with red boot-topping*

Name	Eng	Flag	Year	GRT	DWT	Loa	Bm	Kts	Type	Former names
Adair	Mhl	2003	81,074	159,199	274	48	T		
Amazon	Mhl	2002	28,539	47,275	183	32	14	T	
Angelica	Mhl	2004	81,074	159,106	274	48	-	T	
Arlene	Mhl	2003	84,789	165,000	274	50	15	T	
Ashley	Mhl	2001	23,217	37,270	183	27	14	T	
Brazos	Mhl	2005	29,242	46,889	183	32	14	T	
Charente	Mhl	2001	23,740	35,751	183	27	14	T	
Dakota	Mhl	2002	81,270	159,435	274	48	-	T	
Delaware	Mhl	2002	85,000	159,169	274	48	-	T	
Fox	Mhl	2004	23,200	37,000	183	27	14	T	
Ganges	Mhl	2004	23,246	37,106	183	28	14	T	
Garonne	Mhl	2004	23,346	37,178	183	27	14	T	
Guadalupe	Mhl	2000	28,539	47,037	183	32	14	T	ex Alam Bakti-00
Horizon	Mhl	2004	29,242	46,955	183	32	14	T	
Hudson	Mhl	2000	81,093	152,592	274	48	-	T	ex Front Sun-03
Ingeborg	Mhl	2003	84,789	165,010	274	50	15	T	
Isere	Mhl	1999	22,848	35,406	185	27	15	T	
Janet	Mhl	2004	81,074	159,100	274	48	-	T	ex Athenian Olympics-04
Jeanette	Mhl	2004	29,242	46,921	183	32	14	T	
Kansas	Mhl	2006	29,242	46,922	184	32	14	T	
Lauren	Mhl	2005	29,242	46,911	183	32	14	T	
Loire	Mhl	2004	23,200	37,106	183	27	14	T	
Madison	Lbr	2000	23,842	35,833	183	27	14	T	ex Nina-01
Marne	Mhl	2001	23,217	37,230	183	27	14	T	l/a Ruby Star
Moselle	Mhl	2003	28,567	47,038	183	32	14	T	
Neches	Mhl	2000	28,539	47,052	183	32	14	T	ex Alam Bayu-00
Ohio	Mhl	2001	23,235	37,278	183	27	14	T	l/a Borak
Orontes	Mhl	2002	23,235	37,382	183	27	14	T	
Ottawa	Mhl	2003	42,771	70,296	228	32	-	T	
Potomac	Mhl	2000	81,093	152,592	274	48	-	T	ex Front Sky-03
Rhine	Mhl	2006	23,200	37,000	183	27	14	T	
Rhone	Mhl	2000	23,740	35,769	183	27	-	T	ex Prospero-01
Rosetta	Mhl	2003	28,567	47,037	183	32	14	T	
Ruby	Mhl	2004	23,240	37,384	183	27	14	T	ex Baltic Admiral-04
Sacramento	Mhl	1998	81,565	157,411	274	48	14	T	
San Jacinto	Mhl	2002	28,539	47,038	183	32	15	T	
Saone	Mhl	2004	23,246	36,986	183	27	14	T	

Name	Eng	Flag	Year	GRT	DWT	Loa	Bm	Kts	Type	Former names
Seine		Mhl	1999	22,848	35,407	185	27	15	T	
Somjin		Mhl	2001	83,723	160,183	274	48	14	T	
Tamar		Mhl	2003	43,000	70,100	228	32	-	T	
Tevere		Mhl	2005	23,246	36,990	183	28	14	T	
Thames		Mhl	2005	29,214	47,036	184	32	14	T	
Trinity		Lbr	2000	23,842	35,833	183	27	14	T	ex Snipe-01
Wabash		Mhl	2006	29,000	47,000	184	32	14	T	

newbuildings: two 29,000 grt tankers for 2006 delivery.

Onassis Group   Monaco
Olympic Shipping and Management SA

Funnel: *Orange, large white disc with blue/yellow pennant and five interlocking coloured rings above and below*
Hull: *Black with red boot-topping*

Name	Flag	Year	GRT	DWT	Loa	Bm	Kts	Type	Former names
Calliroe Patronicola	Grc	1985	17,879	29,608	183	23	15	B	
Olympic Faith	Grc	1991	81,192	147,457	274	45	14	T	
Olympic Flag	Grc	2004	80,591	155,099	274	47	16	T	
Olympic Flair	Grc	1991	81,192	147,396	274	45	14	T	
Olympic Future	Grc	2004	80,591	155,039	274	47	16	T	
Olympic Galaxy	Pan	1982	35,417	64,931	225	32	14	B	ex Ikan Bawal-86
Olympic Legacy	Grc	1996	160,129	302,789	332	58	14	T	
Olympic Legend	Grc	2003	160,083	308,500	333	60	15	T	
Olympic Liberty	Grc	2003	160,083	304,992	333	60	15	T	
Olympic Loyalty	Grc	1993	160,129	303,184	332	58	15	T	
Olympic Melody	Grc	1984	17,879	29,640	182	23	14	B	
Olympic Mentor	Grc	1984	17,879	29,693	182	23	14	B	ex Patricia R-88, Calliroe Patronicola-84
Olympic Merit	Grc	1985	17,879	29,611	182	23	14	B	
Olympic Miracle	Pan	1984	17,879	29,670	182	23	14	B	
Olympic Serenity	Grc	1991	52,127	96,733	232	42	13	I	
Olympic Spirit II	Grc	1997	52,197	96,773	232	42	13	T	
Olympic Sponsor	Grc	1994	52,196	96,547	232	42	13	T	
Olympic Symphony	Grc	1990	52,086	96,547	232	42	13	T	

Orient Overseas (International) Ltd   Hong Kong (China)
Orient Overseas Container Line Ltd

Funnel: *Yellow with red and gold flower.*
Hull: *Light grey with red 'OOCL', orange with white 'OOCL' or black with red boot-topping.*

Name	Flag	Year	GRT	DWT	Loa	Bm	Kts	Type	Former names
China Act *	Sgp	1995	77,135	151,688	270	43	15	B	
China Fortune *	Sgp	1992	77,096	149,402	270	43	15	B	
China Peace *	Hkg	2005	88,930	174,413	289	45	14	B	
China Progress *	Hkg	2006	88,900	174,400	289	45	14	B	
China Prosperity *	Sgp	1986	83,474	151,013	288	45	14	B	
OOCL Ability †	Pan	1997	16,750	24,346	183	28	19	CC	
OOCL Acclaim †	Pan	1997	16,750	23,850	183	28	18	CC	
OOCL Ambition †	Pan	1997	16,750	23,850	183	28	18	CC	
OOCL America	Hkg	1995	66,047	67,741	276	40	24	CC	
OOCL Atlanta	Hkg	2005	89,097	99,620	323	43	25	CC	
OOCL Authority †	Pan	1997	16,750	23,850	183	28	18	CC	
OOCL Belgium	Hkg	1998	39,174	40,972	245	32	21	CC	
OOCL Britain	Hkg	1996	66,046	67,958	276	40	24	CC	
OOCL California	Hkg	1995	66,046	67,765	276	40	24	CC	
OOCL Chicago	Hkg	2000	66,677	67,278	277	40	25	CC	
OOCL China	Hkg	1996	66,046	67,625	276	41	24	CC	
OOCL Envoy	Hkg	1979	37,238	39,766	251	32	25	CC	ex China Container-91 (len-82)
OOCL Exporter	Hkg	1976	41,266	41,587	275	31	22	CC	ex Oriental Chief-89 (len-82)
OOCL Fair	Hkg	1987	40,980	44,448	241	32	21	CC	ex Oriental Fair-89
OOCL Faith	Hkg	1985	40,980	44,448	241	32	21	CC	ex Veracruz-98, TMM Veracruz-97, Vera Cruz-96, OOCL Faith-96, Oriental Faith-89
OOCL Fidelity	Hkg	1987	40,980	44,477	241	32	21	CC	ex Brooklyn Bridge-91
OOCL Fortune	Hkg	1985	40,978	44,433	241	32	21	CC	ex Oriental Fortune-89
OOCL Freedom	Hkg	1985	40,978	44,452	241	32	21	CC	ex Eagle Malaysia-98, OOCL Freedom-96, Oriental Freedom-89
OOCL Friendship	Hkg	1987	41,664	45,863	241	32	22	CC	ex Anahuac-98, Eagle Anahuac-97, OOCL Friendship-96, Oriental Friendship-89

OMI Marine Services. GANGES. *Vandriessche Guido*

OMI Marine Services. SOMJIN. *Hans Kraijenbosch*

166

Orient Overseas Container Line. OOCL AMBITION. *Hans Kraijenbosch*

Overseas Shipholding Group. DELPHINA. *F. de Vries*

Name	Eng	Flag	Year	GRT	DWT	Loa	Bm	Kts	Type	Former names
OOCL Hamburg		Hkg	2004	89,097	99,618	323	43	25	CC	
OOCL Hong Kong		Hkg	1996	66,046	67,637	276	40	24	CC	
OOCL Japan		Hkg	1995	66,046	67,752	276	40	24	CC	
OOCL Long Beach		Hkg	2003	89,097	99,508	323	43	25	CC	
OOCL Melbourne †		Hkg	2003	34,610	43,093	235	32	22	CC	
OOCL Montreal		Hkg	2003	55,994	47,840	294	32	24	CC	
OOCL Netherlands		Hkg	1997	66,016	67,700	276	40	24	CC	
OOCL Ningbo		Hkg	2004	89,000	99,500	323	43	25	CC	
OOCL Osaka †		Pan	2003	34,610	43,093	235	32	22	CC	
OOCL Qingdao		Hkg	2004	89,097	99,600	323	43	25	CC	
OOCL Rotterdam		Hkg	2004	89,097	99,500	323	43	25	CC	
OOCL San Francisco		Hkg	2000	66,677	67,286	277	40	25	CC	
OOCL Shenzhen		Hkg	2003	89,097	99,518	323	43	25	CC	
OOCL Singapore		Hkg	1997	66,086	67,480	276	40	24	CC	
OOCL Sydney †		Sgp	2003	34,610	43,093	235	32	22	CC	
OOCL Tianjin		Hkg	2005	89,097	99,500	323	43	25	CC	
OOCL Xiamen †		Pan	2003	34,610	43,093	235	32	22	CC	

newbuildings: four 89,000 grt 99,500 dwt, six 40,500 grt and two 41,400 grt container ships for 2006-8 delivery.
* owned by subsidiary Chinese Maritime Transport Ltd., Taiwan or † on charter from various Japanese owners or finance houses.

Associated Maritime Co (Hong Kong) Ltd

Name	Eng	Flag	Year	GRT	DWT	Loa	Bm	Kts	Type	Former names
New Ace		Lbr	1987	52,967	88,878	244	40	14	T	ex Atlantic Ace-92
New Alliance		Lbr	1998	56,311	106,118	241	42	14	T	
New Amber		Lbr	1987	50,272	89,601	244	40	15	T	ex Sidelia-99
New Ambition		Lbr	1987	52,967	88,761	244	40	14	T	ex Ambition-91
New Amity		Lbr	1998	56,311	106,120	241	42	14	T	
New Argosy		Lbr	1987	52,967	88,782	244	40	14	T	ex Atlantic Argosy-92
New Assurance		Lbr	1986	50,272	81,274	244	40	15	T	ex Atlantic Assurance-92
New Century		Lbr	2004	156,973	299,031	330	60	14	T	
New Fortuner		Lbr	1992	78,958	146,041	277	44	14	T	
New Spirit		Lbr	2005	156,973	298,972	330	60	14	T	
New Valor		Lbr	1992	156,317	281,598	328	57	13	T	
New Venture		Lbr	1992	156,307	291,640	328	57	13	T	
New Victory		Lbr	1993	156,307	291,613	328	57	14	T	
New Vitality		Lbr	1993	153,808	290,691	330	56	15	T	
Pacific Enterprise		Hkg	1996	79,542	149,363	270	44	14	B	
Pacific Navigator		Hkg	1997	85,711	165,779	288	44	14	B	
Pacific Vitality		Hkg	1996	85,711	165,794	288	45	14	B	

newbuildings: two 157,000 grt tankers for 2009 delivery.
Subsidiary formed jointly with Ming Wah Shipping Co. Ltd, Hong Kong (China)

Overseas Shipholding Group   USA

Funnel: Blue with white 'OSG' ('S' having waves in lower part), black top.
Hull: Black with red boot-topping.

Name	Eng	Flag	Year	GRT	DWT	Loa	Bm	Kts	Type	Former names
Alcesmar		Cyp	2004	30,058	45,965	183	32	14	T	
Alcmar		Cyp	2004	30,058	45,965	183	32	14	T	
Alvheim **	(me)	Nor	2001	65,676	91,676	265	43	15	T	ex Odin-05, Navion Odin-03
Andromar		Cyp	2004	30,058	45,965	183	32	14	T	
Ania *		Mhl	1994	53,341	94,847	245	42	14	T	
Antigmar		Cyp	2004	30,100	45,800	183	32	14	T	
Ariadmar		Cyp	2004	30,058	45,800	183	32	14	T	
Beryl *		Mhl	1994	53,341	93,302	245	42	14	T	
Cabo Hellas *		Mhl	2003	38,900	69,250	228	32	14	T	
Cabo Sounion *		Mhl	2004	40,038	69,636	228	32	14	T	
Compass 1 *		Pan	1992	52,552	97,078	247	42	14	T	ex Stena Compass-00, Hawaiian Prince-96, Seto
Crown Unity *		Mhl	1996	156,852	300,482	330	58	14	T	
Delphina		Mhl	1989	22,972	39,673	186	27	14	T	
Denali †		Usa	1978	94,647	188,099	290	51	14	T	ex B.T. San Diego-94
Eliane *		Mhl	1994	53,341	94,813	245	42	14	T	
Equatorial Lion *		Mhl	1997	156,880	273,539	330	58	15	T	
Jacamar		Pan	1999	60,804	104,901	247	42	15	T	
Kenai †	(st)	Usa	1979	64,329	123,114	265	42	17	T	
Kodiak †	(st)	Usa	1978	64,329	122,805	265	42	17	T	ex Tonsina-05
Majestic Unity *		Pan	1996	156,852	300,549	330	58	14	T	
Neptune		Mhl	1989	22,946	40,085	186	27	14	T	

Name	Eng	Flag	Year	GRT	DWT	Loa	Bm	Kts	Type	Former names
Overseas Allenmar		Pan	1988	25,740	41,750	182	30	14	T	ex Allenmar-05, Petrobulk Challenger-01, Osprey Challenger-96, Pacific Challenger-94
Overseas Almar		Pan	1996	28,357	46,162	183	32	14	T	ex Almar-05, Osprey Altair-01
Overseas Ambermar		Cyp	2002	23,843	35,700	183	27	14	T	ex Ambermar-05
Overseas Ann *		Mhl	2001	157,883	309,327	335	58	15	T	
Overseas Aquamar		Cyp	1998	28,400	47,236	183	32	15	T	ex Aquamar-05, Alam Berkat-02
Overseas Atalmar		Cyp	2004	30,058	45,800	183	32	15	T	ex Atalmar-05
Overseas Athens		Mhl	1987	24,584	39,729	193	32	14	T	ex City University-05, Ocean Challenger-93
Overseas Camar		Pan	1988	26,113	45,372	172	32	14	T	ex Camar-05, Petrobulk Cougar-01
Overseas Capemar		Pan	1988	23,127	37,615	175	30	15	T	ex Capemar-05, Petrobulk Cape-01, Osprey Cape-96, Telaga Ayu-93, Creation-91, l/a Atlantic Chivalry Bride-93, Seto Bridge-92
Overseas Cathy *		Mhl	2004	62,371	112,700	250	44	14	T	
Overseas Chicago †	(st)	Usa	1977	44,869	90,638	273	32	16	T	
Overseas Chris *		Mhl	2001	157,883	308,700	335	58	15	T	
Overseas Cleliamar *		Mhl	1993	38,653	68,600	226	32	13	T	ex Cleliamar-05, Double Pride-98, l/a Chemoil Pride
Overseas Colmar		Cyp	1987	24,584	39,729	193	32	14	T	ex Colmar-05, Ocean Conqueror-93
Overseas Donna *		Mhl	2000	157,883	309,498	335	58	15	T	
Overseas Ermar		Pan	1989	22,838	34,999	186	27	14	T	ex Ermar-05, Petrobulk Power-01, Torm Helene-90
Overseas Fran *		Mhl	2001	62,385	112,700	250	44	14	T	
Overseas Fulmar		Cyp	1989	25,368	39,521	182	31	15	T	ex Fulmar-05, Kobe Spirit-93
Overseas Harriette		Usa	1977	15,531	25,515	173	23	15	B	
Overseas Goldmar *		Mhl	2002	40,343	69,684	228	32	14	T	ex Goldmar-05, l/a LMZ Mandi
Overseas Jademar *		Mhl	2002	38,900	69,250	228	32	14	T	ex Jademar 05
Overseas Jamar		Lbr	1988	26,113	46,100	172	32	14	T	ex Jamar-05, Petrobulk Jaguar-01
Overseas Josefa Camejo *		Mhl	2001	62,385	112,200	250	44	14	T	
Overseas Joyce		Usa	1987	48,017	16,141	269	42	16	V	
Overseas Keymar *		Cyp	1993	54,953	95,822	242	42	14	T	ex Keymar-05, Takamane Maru-98
Overseas Limar		Pan	1996	28,357	46,170	183	32	14	T	ex Limar-05, Osprey Lyra-01
Overseas Luxmar		Usa	1997	28,357	46,162	183	32	14	T	ex Luxmar-05, Petrobulk Pollux-01
Overseas Maremar		Cyp	1998	28,400	47,225	183	32	15	T	ex Maremar-05, Alam Belia-02
Overseas Marilyn		Usa	1978	15,531	25,515	173	23	15	B	
Overseas Mulan *		Mhl	2002	161,233	319,029	333	60	16	T	
Overseas Nedimar		Cyp	1996	28,326	43,999	183	32	14	T	ex Nedimar-05
Overseas New Orleans		Usa	1983	24,016	43,644	201	27	15	T	ex Exxon Yorktown-89, Hunter Armistead-84
Overseas New York †	(st)	Usa	1977	44,869	91,843	273	32	16	T	
Overseas Pearlmar *		Mhl	2002	38,900	69,250	228	32	14	T	ex Pearlmar-05
Overseas Petromar		Pan	2001	23,740	35,000	183	27	14	T	ex Petromar-05, l/a Nordatrika
Overseas Philadelphia		Usa	1982	21,446	43,648	201	27	14	T	ex Exxon Princeton-89, Eileen Ingram-84
Overseas Polys *		Cyp	1993	38,653	68,623	226	32	14	T	ex Polys-05, Double Glory-97
Overseas Portland *		Mhl	2001	62,385	112,700	250	44	14	T	
Overseas Primar		Cyp	1988	25,368	39,538	182	31	14	T	ex Primar-05, BP Advocate-93, l/a Onomichi Spirit
Overseas Reginamar		Lbr	2004	38,900	69,250	228	32	14	T	ex Reginamar-05
Overseas Reinemar		Lbr	2004	38,900	69,250	228	32	14	T	ex Reinemar-05
Overseas Reymar *		Lbr	2004	38,900	69,250	228	32	14	T	ex Reymar-05
Overseas Rimar		Pan	1998	28,357	46,162	183	32	14	T	ex Rimar-05, Petrobulk Sirius-01
Overseas Rosalyn *		Mhl	2003	161,233	291,850	333	60	15	T	
Overseas Rosemar *		Mhl	2002	40,343	69,697	228	32	14	T	ex Rosemar-05
Overseas Rubymar *		Mhl	2002	40,343	69,697	228	32	14	T	ex Rubymar-05
Overseas Shirley *		Mhl	2001	62,385	112,056	250	44	14	T	
Overseas Silvermar *		Mhl	2002	40,343	69,609	228	32	14	T	ex Overseas-05, l/a LMZ Zacvi
Overseas Sophie *		Mhl	2003	62,371	112,700	250	44	14	T	
Overseas Washington †	(st)	Usa	1978	44,906	91,967	273	32	16	T	
Pacific Ruby *		Mhl	1994	53,830	84,999	247	42	15	T	ex Burwain Electra-95
Pacific Sapphire *		Mhl	1994	53,830	96,173	247	42	15	T	ex Burwain Helena-95
Prince William Sound †	(st)	Usa	1975	64,340	123,936	268	41	17	T	
Puget Sound		Usa	1983	24,668	50,860	201	32	14	T	ex S/R Puget Sound-04, Potomac Trader-00
Raphael *		Mhl	2000	157,883	308,700	335	58	15	T	
Rebecca *		Mhl	1994	53,341	94,872	245	42	14	T	
Regal Unity *		Mhl	1997	164,371	309,966	330	58	16	T	
Sovereign Unity *		Mhl	1996	164,371	309,892	330	58	16	T	
TI Africa		Grc	2002	234,006	441,893	380	68	16	T	ex Hellespont Metropolis-04
TI Oceania		Grc	2002	234,006	442,470	380	68	16	T	ex Hellespont Fairfax-04

Name	Eng	Flag	Year	GRT	DWT	Loa	Bm	Kts	Type	Former names
Takamar		Pan	1998	60,504	103,244	247	42	15	T	ex P. Alliance-01
Tanabe *		Mhl	2002	159,383	298,561	333	60	16	T	
Uranus		Mhl	1988	22,046	39,451	186	27	14	T	
Vega		Mhl	1989	22,972	39,710	186	27	14	T	

newbuildings: six 120,000 grt Lng tankers for 2007-8 delivery.
*owned by OSG Ship Management Greece Ltd or * by OSG Ship Management (UK) Ltd or Tanker Management UK Ltd, UK or ** managed by OSG Ship Management, Norway. † managed by subsidiary Alaska Tanker Co. LLC (formed jointly with Keystone Shipping Co., USA and BP Shipping Ltd, UK) or ‡ by OSG Ship Management Greece Ltd., Greece. †† owned by Shoei Kisen Kaisha Ltd., Japan.*
See also Navion ASA (under Teekay) and Tanker International Pool under CMB (Euronav Luxembourg SA).

Pacific International Lines (Pte) Ltd Singapore

Funnel: *Red with black 'PIL' on broad white band.*
Hull *Black or grey with red boot-topping.*

Name		Flag	Year	GRT	DWT	Loa	Bm	Kts	Type	
Kota Ganteng		Hkg	2002	28,676	37,087	227	32	22	CC	
Kota Gemar		Hkg	2002	28,676	37,115	227	32	22	CC	
Kota Gembira		Hkg	2002	28,676	37,114	227	32	22	CC	
Kota Gunawan		Hkg	2003	28,676	37,100	227	32	22	CC	
Kota Kado		Sgp	2005	31,070	39,916	233	32	-	CC	
Kota Kamil		Sgp	2006	31,700	39,400	233	32	-	CC	
Kota Kaya		Sgp	2006	31,700	39,400	233	32	-	CC	

newbuildings: one 21,000 grt and eight 41,482 grt container ships for 2006-8 delivery.
Operates from Far East to Europe in joint service with Wan Hai Lines q.v. also fleet of 55 other smaller container ships in Far East.
Also see chartered ships with 'Kota' prefix in index.

Papachristidis Ltd UK

Funnel: *Blue with broad above narrow blue bands, interupted by blue 'ºµ¶' within blue ring on white disc.*
Hull *White with red boot-topping.*

Name		Flag	Year	GRT	DWT	Loa	Bm	Kts	Type	Former names
Hellespont Pride		Mhl	2006	42,100	73,630	229	32	14	T	
Hellespont Progress		Mhl	2006	42,100	73,630	229	32	14	T	
Hellespont Promise		Mhl	2006	42,100	73,630	229	32	14	T	
Hellespont Prosperity		Mhl	2006	42,100	73,630	229	32	14	T	
Hellespont Protector		Mhl	2006	42,100	73,630	229	32	14	T	
Hellespont Providence		Mhl	2006	42,100	73,630	229	32	14	T	
Hellespont Tatina		Mhl	1999	56,324	105,535	239	42	14	T	ex Minerva Anna-04, Pine Venture-02
Hellespont Trader *		Mhl	1996	79,832	148,435	269	46	-	T	ex Sea Star-05
Hellespont Trinity *		Mhl	1996	80,637	148,017	274	48	14	T	ex Marina M-05
Hellespont Trooper *		Mhl	1996	80,637	147,916	274	48	14	T	ex Spetses-05

*Operated by Greek subsidiary Hellespont Steamship Corp and * managed by Hellespont Hammonia.*

Dr Peters KG Fund Germany

Funnel: *Charterers colours.*
Hull *Various.*

Name		Flag	Year	GRT	DWT	Loa	Bm	Kts	Type	Former names
Ashna		Mhl	1999	156,417	301,438	330	58	15	T	ex Nordbay-04
Bahamas Spirit ††		Bhs	1996	57,947	107,261	247	42	17	T	ex Sanko Trader-01
Cape Hatteras ‡		Cyp	1992	10,396	12,854	147	24	17	CC	ex P&O Nedlloyd Inca-05, Cape Hatteras-03, Cala Panama-03, Cape Hatteras-02, Maersk Cebu-00, Cape Hatteras-98, Eagle Dawn-98, Cape Hatteras-95, ACX Iris-95, Cape Hatteras-93
Cape Henry ‡		Lbr	1992	10,376	12,835	147	24	17	CC	ex Safmarine Athi-02, Cape Henry-02, Avon-98, Halla Liberty-98, Kinabalu-97, Tiger Ocean-96, ACX Aster-95, Ratana Manee-94, TSL Bravo-93, Cape Henry-92
Cape Race ‡		Lbr	1993	29,912	35,071	201	32	20	CC	ex MSC Perth-05, Cape Race-03, MSC Argentina-02, Cape Race-01, CSAV Callao-99, Copiapo-98, Jean Bosco-95, Yucatan-94, Jean Bosco-93
Cape Spear ‡		Lbr	1998	10,917	13,623	151	24	18	CC	ex MSC Coimbra-03, Cape Spear-01
Deja Bhum ‡		Gib	1996	10,917	13,700	151	24	18	CC	ex Cape Sable-06
DS-Performer *		Lbr	2000	61,764	84,999	245	42	15	T	ex Paula Maersk-05
DS-Power *		Lbr	1999	61,764	110,000	245	42	15	T	ex Peter Maersk-05
Eagle Excellence ‡		Lbr	1995	17,285	22,148	175	27	20	CC	ex Cape Natal-96
Ernst Salamon ‡		Lbr	1999	38,888	74,002	225	32	14	B	ex Far Eastern Queen-01
Elversele §		Lux	1996	23,519	28,993	179	27	18	Lpg	
Eupen §		Lux	1999	23,952	29,121	180	27	16	Lpg	
Front Century †		Bhs	1998	157,976	311,189	334	58	15	T	

Pacific International Lines. KOTA GEMAR. *Hans Kraijenbosch*

Polish Ocean (Chinese-Polish Joint Stock Shg). CHIPOLBROK SUN. *J. M. Kakebeeke*

Polish Steamship Co. IRMA. *Hans Kraijenbosch*

Name	Eng	Flag	Year	GRT	DWT	Loa	Bm	Kts	Type	Former names
Front Champion †		Bhs	1998	157,976	311,286	334	58	15	T	
Front Chief †		Bhs	1999	157,863	311,224	334	58	15	T	
Front Commander †		Bhs	1999	157,863	311,168	334	58	15	T	
Front Commodore †		Lbr	2000	159,397	298,620	333	60	15	T	ex Stena Commodore-01
Front Crown †		Bhs	1999	157,863	311,176	334	58	15	T	ex Front President-99
Front Eagle †		Bhs	2002	160,904	309,064	333	58	-	T	I/a Moseagle
Front Melody †		Lbr	2001	79,525	150,500	272	46	14	T	
Front Symphony †		Lbr	2001	79,525	150,500	272	46	14	T	
Front Tina †		Lbr	2000	159,463	298,824	333	60	16	T	
Front Warrior †		Bhs	1998	79,669	153,181	269	46	14	T	
Gertrud Salamon ‡		Pan	2000	38,888	74,078	225	32	14	B	ex Far Eastern Media-01
Golden Victory		Mhl	1999	159,423	300,155	333	60	15	T	
Hong Kong Star ‡		Mhl	1998	17,285	22,148	175	27	20	CC	ex Cape Norman-03, Tiger Breeze-02, Cape Norman-01, Sea-Land Europe-99, Maersk Ankara-99, Cape Norman-98
Kiowa Spirit ††		Bhs	1999	62,619	113,334	253	44	14	T	ex Bona Valiant-99
Koa Spirit ††		Bhs	1999	62,619	113,334	253	44	14	T	ex Bona Verity-99
Mercury Glory **		Pan	2001	157,831	298,990	332	58	15	T	
MOL Brasilia ‡		Lbr	1992	10,396	12,854	147	24	17	CC	ex Cala Porlamar-03, Cape Horn I-02, Otway-99, Maersk Davao-99, Cape Horn I-98, Eagle Star-98, Cape Horn I-97, Maersk La Paz-96, Cape Horn-94, TSL Gallant-94, Cape Horn-92
MSC Arabia		Mlt	1972	14,453	21,834	171	23	16	CC	Zim Odessa I-04, Heung-A Carmen-98, Leeward-96, Lizard-85, Neckar Express-84, Freienfels-80, Aristarchos-75
MSC Himalaya		Mlt	1978	27,297	33,621	228	29	19	CC	ex Himalaya-02, MSC Himalaya-02, Evge-01, Smart River-99, YS Prosperity-92, Oriental Premier-86, Oriental Expert-83 (len-83)
MSC Sharjah		Mlt	1972	14,453	21,876	171	23	16	CC	ex Zim Constantza I-04, Heung-A Grace-98, Grace-98, Carmen Carina-95, Biscay-86, Fulda Express-84, Frankenfels-80, Aristandros-74
MSC Socotra		Lbr	1980	35,065	43,070	246	32	23	CC	ex Astoria Bridge-03, Transworld Bridge-99
Neptune Glory **		Pan	1998	156,716	299,127	332	58	15	T	
Cape Scott ‡		Lbr	1997	10,197	13,623	151	24	18	CC	ex P&O Nedlloyd Thekwini-06, Cape Scott-02, Independent Leader-99, I/a Cape Scott
Pluto Glory **		Pan	2001	157,831	298,911	332	58	15	T	
Stena Venture		Hkg	2002	39,272	70,392	229	32	15	T	I/a Sanko Venture
TS Hongkong ‡		Lbr	1996	10,917	13,623	151	24	18	CC	ex Cape Spencer-03, Fanal Merchant-00, Grafton-99, Cape Spencer-99
TS Osaka ‡		Lbr	1997	10,925	13,741	151	24	18	CC	ex Cape Sorrell-03, Independent Concept-99, Cape Sorrell-97

*German KG investment fund with vessels chartered back to previous owners including * Torm Pool, ** Pacific Star (until 2015), † Frontline Ltd., Bermuda, †† Teekay Shipping Corp., Canada q.v. or § Exmar NV, Belgium q.v.*
‡ managed by Hanse Bereederungs GmbH, Germany q.v. Also see managed vessels under F. Laeisz Schiffahrts GmbH & Co

Polish Ocean Lines (Polskie Linie Oceaniczne)　　Poland
Chinese-Polish Joint Stock Shipping Co (Chinsko-Polskie Towarzystwo Okretowe SA)
Funnel: *Cream with cream 'C' and white 'P' on broad red band, narrow black top.*
Hull: *Grey with white 'CHIPOLBROK', green boot-topping.*

Name	Eng	Flag	Year	GRT	DWT	Loa	Bm	Kts	Type	Former names
B. Prus		Cyp	1979	16,869	24,400	171	25	17	Co	ex Concordia Sun-87, Hoegh Sun-84, Costa Mediterranea-83, Concordia Sun-82
Carnival		Mlt	1977	18,772	27,739	171	26	17	Co	ex Cai Lun-91, Willine Tysla-86, Tysla-82
Ceynowa		Mlt	1982	14,056	15,622	157	24	16	C	
Chipolbrok Moon		Hkg	2004	24,167	30,460	200	28	19	Co	
Chipolbrok Sun		Cyp	2004	24,336	30,396	200	28	19	Co	
Chong Ming		Chn	1993	18,177	22,109	170	28	16	Co	
Chopin		Cyp	1988	13,930	18,144	159	23	15	Co	
Ever Happy		Mlt	1977	18,846	27,817	171	26	17	Co	ex Da Yu-91, Hoegh Cape-86, Tsu-85, Barber Tsu-84, Tsu-81, Thalatta-77
Hua Tuo		Chn	1983	14,163	15,753	155	23	16	C	
Jan Dlugosz		Cyp	1984	15,246	15,622	157	25	16	C	
Jia Xing		Chn	1992	18,177	22,109	170	28	16	Co	ex Bao Zheng-92
Leopold Staff		Cyp	2004	24,167	30,469	200	28	19	Co	
Li Bai		Chn	1988	13,843	18,114	159	23	15	Co	
Lu Ban		Chn	1981	14,169	16,152	155	23	16	C	
Lu Xun		Chn	1988	13,843	18,144	159	23	15	Co	

Name	Eng	Flag	Year	GRT	DWT	Loa	Bm	Kts	Type	Former names
Moniuszko		Mlt	1989	13,938	18,144	159	23	15	Co	
Norwid		Mlt	1998	18,202	22,258	170	28	16	Co	
Pokoj		Cyp	1977	18,846	27,937	171	26	17	Co	ex Terrier-86, Hoegh Carrier-86, Terrier-85, Barber Terrier-84, Terrier-81
Szymanowski		Cyp	1991	18,184	22,313	170	28	16	Co	
Taixing		Hkg	1997	18,207	22,271	170	28	16	Co	
Wieniawski		Mlt	1992	18,208	22,130	170	28	16	Co	
Wladyslaw Orkan		Cyp	2003	24,336	30,435	200	28	19	Co	
Yong Xing		Mlt	1998	18,207	22,309	170	28	16	Co	

Polish Steamship Co (Polska Zegluga Morska) Poland

Funnel: *Black with red band between two narrow yellow bands, and shield with white letters 'PZM' and trident.*
Hull: *Black, blue, grey or (§) yellow, some with white 'POLSTREAM', red boot-topping.*

Name	Eng	Flag	Year	GRT	DWT	Loa	Bm	Kts	Type	Former names
Alexander **		Cyp	1990	11,572	13,864	149	22	16	Co	ex Golden Trader-03, Quarry Bay-01, Venus-99, Unisierra-98, Radom-93
Armia Krajowa ‡		Vut	1991	41,266	73,505	229	32	14	D	
Armia Ludowa		Lbr	1987	21,458	33,640	195	25	15	B	
Bataliony Chlopskie		Lbr	1988	21,460	33,618	195	25	14	B	
Daria		Cyp	1995	25,190	41,260	186	30	14	B	ex Taria-95
Danuta		Lbr	1983	24,681	41,796	192	30	14	B	ex Lake St. Clair-03, Elegance-96, Star Elegance-89, Elegance-87, I/a West Monnis
Delia		Cyp	1997	25,206	41,185	186	30	14	B	
Diana		Cyp	1997	25,206	41,425	186	30	14	B	
Dorine		Cyp	1998	25,065	41,488	186	30	14	B	
Gardno		Mhl	1980	11,632	16,753	159	22	14	B	ex Kopalnia Miechowice-93
General Dabrowski		Pan	1982	23,427	38,591	198	28	15	B	ex Lake Mead-03, General Dabrowski-92
General Grot-Rowecki		Mlt	1985	23,409	38,490	199	28	14	B	
Huta Zgoda		Pan	1974	9,117	14,176	146	21	15	B	
Ignacy Daszynski		Mlt	1988	21,437	33,639	195	25	14	B	
Irma		Cyp	2000	21,387	34,948	200	24	15	B	
Iryda		Cyp	1999	21,387	34,939	200	24	14	B	
Isa		Cyp	1999	21,387	34,939	200	24	14	B	
Isadora		Cyp	1999	21,387	34,948	200	24	14	B	
Isolda		Cyp	1999	21,959	34,949	200	24	14	B	
Jamno		Pan	1980	11,632	16,813	159	22	14	B	ex Kopalnia Gottwald-93
Kaliope		Bhs	1995	11,542	16,888	149	23	14	Tm	ex Fjordnes-97
Kopalnia Borynia		Mlt	1989	8,893	11,899	144	19	14	B	
Kopalnia Halemba		Mlt	1990	8,897	11,715	144	19	14	B	
Kopalnia Rydultowy		Mlt	1990	8,897	11,702	144	19	14	B	
Kopalnia Sosnowiec		Pan	1974	9,117	14,179	146	21	15	B	
Kopalnia Zofiowka		Pan	1975	9,117	14,176	147	21	15	B	
Kujawy		Bhs	2005	24,109	37,965	190	29	14	B	
Legiony Polskie ‡		Vut	1991	41,237	73,505	229	32	14	B	
Maciej Rataj		Mlt	1985	21,531	33,750	199	25	15	B	
Magdalena **		Mlt	1988	11,574	13,864	149	22	16	Co	ex Lodz II-00, Pineseas Venture-97, Lodz II-95
Major Hubal		Mlt	1985	21,531	33,725	199	25	15	B	
Mamry II		Mhl	1979	11,676	16,653	159	22	15	B	ex Mamry-04, Kopalnia Siemianowice-93
Mazury		Bhs	2005	24,109	38,056	190	29	14	B	
Mitrope		Mlt	1999	11,530	15,718	149	23	13	T	
Nida		Bhs	1993	9,815	13,759	143	21	14	B	ex Nidanes-99, I/a Nida
Nogat		Cyp	1999	11,848	17,064	149	23	13	B	
Odra		Bhs	1992	9,818	13,790	143	21	14	B	ex Odranes-99, I/a Odra
Oksywie *		Pol	1987	21,460	33,580	195	25	14	B	ex Wladyslaw Gomulka-91
Orla		Mlt	1999	11,848	17,064	149	23	14	B	
Orleta Lwowskie ‡		Vut	1991	41,238	73,505	229	32	14	B	
Penelope		Bhs	1996	11,829	15,329	149	23	14	T	
Pilica		Mlt	1999	11,540	17,064	149	23	14	B	
Podhale		Bhs	2005	24,109	38,056	190	29		B	
Polska Walczaca ‡		Vut	1992	41,220	73,505	229	32	13	B	
Pomorze Zachodnie		Pol	1985	16,696	26,696	180	23	14	B	
Powstaniec Listopadowy		Mlt	1985	21,531	33,767	199	25	15	B	
Powstaniec Styczniowy		Mlt	1986	21,531	33,780	195	25	14	B	
Reduta Ordona		Mlt	1978	20,357	33,490	198	24	15	B	ex Feliks Dzierzynski-90
Rega		Bhs	1995	11,542	16,880	149	23	14	C	ex Fossnes-02
Rodlo		Mlt	1985	21,531	33,742	199	25	15	B	
Rolnik		Pan	1975	9,117	14,176	146	21	15	B	

Name	Eng	Flag	Year	GRT	DWT	Loa	Bm	Kts	Type	Former names
Ros		Mhl	1980	11,676	16,693	159	22	14	B	ex Kopalnia Myslowice-93
Solidarnosc ‡		Vut	1991	41,252	73,470	229	32	14	B	
Stanislaw Kulczynski		Mlt	1988	21,456	33,627	195	25	14	B	
Szare Szeregi ‡		Vut	1991	41,191	73,505	229	32	14	B	
Talty		Pan	1979	11,676	16,728	159	22	14	B	ex Kopalnia Szombierki-93
Uniwersytet Slaski		Mlt	1979	20,357	33,470	198	24	16	B	
Wadag II		Pan	1980	11,632	16,753	159	22	15	B	ex Wadag-04, Kopalnia Siersza-93
Walka Mlodych		Mlt	1978	20,357	33,485	198	24	15	B	
Warmia		Bhs	2006	24,109	38,056	190	29		B	
Warta		Bhs	1992	9,815	13,756	144	21	12	B	ex Wartanes-99
Wigry		Mhl	1979	11,676	16,653	159	22	14	B	ex Kopalnia Jastrzebie-93
Wisla		Vut	1992	9,815	13,770	143	21	13	B	ex Wislanes-99
Ziemia Chelminska		Pol	1984	16,699	26,642	180	23	14	B	
Ziemia Cieszynska		Mhl	1992	17,464	26,264	180	23	14	B	ex Lake Carling-03, Ziemia Cieszynska-93
Ziemia Gnieznienska		Pol	1985	16,696	26,696	180	23	14	B	
Ziemia Gornoslaska		Mhl	1990	17,427	26,209	180	23	14	B	ex Lake Charles-03, Ziemia Gornoslaska-91
Ziemia Lodzka		Mhl	1992	17,458	26,264	180	23	14	B	ex Lake Champlain-03, Ziemia Lodzka-92
Ziemia Suwalska		Pol	1984	16,696	26,605	180	23	14	B	
Ziemia Tarnowska		Pol	1985	16,705	26,678	180	23	14	B	
Ziemia Zamojska		Pol	1984	16,696	26,605	180	23	14	B	

newbuildings - four further 24,100 grt 37,700 dwt bulk carriers for 2008-9 delivery.
Owned or managed by Polstream Oceantramp Ltd, * by Polish Shipping Company (Zegluga Polska Spolka Akcyjna) or ** Euroafrica Linie Zeglugowe. ‡ on long-term charter from Dansk Investeringsfond or K/S Difko companies, Denmark.

PowerGen plc UK

Funnel: Red with white 'e-on', black top.
Hull: Black with red boot-topping.

Name	Eng	Flag	Year	GRT	DWT	Loa	Bm	Kts	Type	Former names
Lord Hinton		Gbr	1986	14,201	22,447	155	25	12	B	
Sir Charles Parsons		Gbr	1985	14,201	22,530	155	25	12	B	

managed by Meridian Marine Management Ltd for E.On UK plc.

KG Projex-Schiffahrts GmbH & Co Germany

Funnel: White lower half and dark blue upper part with white 'PX' between narrow pale blue wavy bands or charterers colours.
Hull: Blue with pale blue wavy bands on bows, red boot-topping.

Name	Eng	Flag	Year	GRT	DWT	Loa	Bm	Kts	Type	Former names
Champion		Gbr	1998	23,897	30,416	188	30	21	CC	ex Lykes Falcon-02, CSAV Rimac-00, Mediterraneo-99, Champion-98
Clan Amazonas		Atg	1996	23,897	30,447	188	30	20	CC	ex Glory-05, Cap Vincent-01, Glory-00, Crowley Americas-99, Glory-99, Pacifico-98
CSAV California		Atg	1992	9,600	12,583	150	23	17	CC	ex MSC Atlas-05, OPDR Gran Canaria-02, City of Istanbul-01, Major-98, Saudi Buraydah-98, Sea-Land Colombia-97, Maersk Bogota-94, I/a Major
CSCL Barcelona		Atg	2001	30,024	36,019	208	32	22	CC	ex Bonny-01
CSCL Fos		Atg	2001	30,024	35,977	208	32	22	CC	I/a Bosun
CSCL Genoa		Atg	2001	30,026	36,189	208	32	22	CC	ex Bravo-01
CSCL Jakarta		Atg	2001	30,024	35,980	208	32	22	CC	I/a Bella
CSCL Kelang		Atg	2001	30,024	36,003	208	32	22	CC	I/a Chief
CSCL Napoli		Atg	2002	30,024	35,971	208	32	22	CC	I/a Mentor
Genoa Senator		Atg	1997	23,897	30,502	188	30	20	CC	ex Safmarine Letaba-05, Primus-02, CSAV Guayas-99, Primus-99, Sea Parana-99, Primus-97
Grand		Atg	1992	9,601	12,583	150	22	17	CC	ex P&O Nedlloyd Chania-05, Grand-03, OPDR Tenerife-02, Armada Sprinter-01, Maersk Douala-99, Maersk Recife-96, Sea-Land Salvador-95, Ankara-94
Harmony		Atg	1994	16,927	21,480	168	27	19	CC	ex MSC Fado-03, P&O Nedlloyd Beirut-02, DNOL Beirut-99, UB Tiger-98, Beirut-97, Contship Egypt-95, Harmony-94
Kota Perkasa		Hkg	2004	30,024	36,000	208	32	22	CC	ex Mate-04
Lykes Racer		Atg	1994	16,915	21,478	168	27	19	CC	ex Triumph-04, P&O Nedlloyd Everest-03, Triumph-01, P&O Nedlloyd Lagos-99, Nedlloyd Lagos-98, Nedlloyd Rio-97, I/a Triumph
Master I		Gbr	1997	23,897	30,416	188	30	21	CC	ex P&O Nedlloyd Brunel-06, Master I-03, Master-02, CMA CGM Paris-02, Lykes Kestrel-01, MOL Europe-00, Maersk Miami-99, I/a Master

Ray Shipping. GLOBAL LEADER (on charter to NYK). *Phil Kempsey*

Restis Group (Enterprises Shipping). LOUIS PASTEUR. *Hans Kraijenbosch*

Name	Eng	Flag	Year	GRT	DWT	Loa	Bm	Kts	Type	Former names
Noble		Atg	1992	9,601	12,583	150	23	17	CC	ex Maersk Asia Tertio-95, Noble-94, Kairo-92
Trophy		Atg	1990	24,495	31,584	182	31	18	CC	ex Choyang Trader-98, Asian Senator-97, I/a Trophy

newbuildings: two 27,300 grt container ships (Ulysses and Hermes) on order for 2006 delivery.

Ray Shipping Israel

Funnel: Green with large yellow 'R', narrow black top.
Hull: Blue with dark green upperworks, red boot-topping.

Name	Eng	Flag	Year	GRT	DWT	Loa	Bm	Kts	Type	Former names
Amber Arrow		Bhs	2004	57,718	21,120	200	32	20	V	
Crystal Ray †		Bhs	2000	57,772	21,400	200	32	20	V	
Diamond Ray †		Mlt	1979	45,571	17,714	190	32	18	V	ex Honshu I-99, Zama-94, Zama Maru-90
Galaxy Leader *		Bhs	2002	48,710	17,127	189	32	20	V	
Global Leader		Bhs	2002	48,710	17,125	189	32	20	V	
Golden Ray II		Lbr	1985	47,343	16,178	190	32	19	V	ex Tepozteco II-02, Nissan Bluebird-94
Hual Africa		Bhs	2004	57,718	21,300	200	32	20	V	
Hual America		Bhs	2003	57,718	21,182	200	32	20	V	
Ivory Arrow		Bhs	2004	57,718	21,300	200	32	20	V	
Jade Arrow		Bhs	1993	47,367	12,271	180	32	18	V	ex Blue Ridge Highway-01
Jasper Arrow		Bhs	2005	57,692	21,040	200	32	20	V	
Lapis Arrow		Bhs	2006	40,500	-	-	-	-	V	
Morning Calm †		Bhs	2004	57,962	21,005	200	32	20	V	I/a Opal Ray
Morning Champion †		Bhs	2005	57,692	21,106	200	32	20	V	
Morning Courier †		Bhs	2005	57,692	21,053	200	32	20	V	
Morning Crown †		Bhs	2005	57,692	21,052	200	32	20	V	
Onyx Arrow		Bhs	2005	57,700	21,000	200	32	20	V	
Pearl Ray †		Lbr	1980	45,376	14,837	190	32	18	V	ex San Marcos-01, Oppama-91, Oppama Maru-90
Platinium Ray †		Bhs	2000	57,772	21,000	200	32	20	V	
Ruby Ray †		Lbr	1978	30,256	10,555	180	28	18	V	ex Lerma-96, Nissan Silvia-84
Sapphire Ray †		Pan	1985	38,874	13,019	184	31	18	V	ex Eternal Sailor-01, Hyundai No. 101-96
St. Angelo		Pan	1973	25,312	10,587	188	23	17	V	ex Arno-03, Dyvi Skagerak-94, Hual Skagerak-83, I/a Dyvi Skagerak
Talia		Bhs	2006	57,700	21,000	200	32	-	V	
Topaz Ray †		Pan	1985	38,874	12,595	184	31	18	V	ex Eternal Trader-01, Hyundai No. 102-96
Veracruz I *		Pan	1977	30,259	10,535	180	28	18	V	ex Veracruz-02, Guanajuato-01, President-86
Vittoriosa										
Yohjin		Pan	1983	29,933	11,662	164	28	18	V	ex Nosac Yohjin-99, Yohjin-95, I/a Arafura Breeze

newbuildings: six 57,700 grt, four 40,500 grt and two 24,500 grt vehicle carriers and two 49,550 grt Lpg tankers for 2006-7 delivery.
Managed by Ray Car Carriers or Stamco Ship Management Co. Ltd. Greece
* on charter to NYK and † believed to be on charter to Eukor Car Carriers Inc. (under Wallenius-Wilhelmsen), but not confirmed.

Schiffahrtskontor Rendsburg GmbH Germany

Funnel: Blue or charterers colours.
Hull: Black or green with red boot-topping.

Name	Eng	Flag	Year	GRT	DWT	Loa	Bm	Kts	Type	Former names
Cala Paradiso		Deu	1998	23,986	30,259	188	30	21	CC	ex DAL Karoo-04, Westerhamm-02, Actor-01, Westerhamm-99
CSAV Mexico **		Deu	2002	30,047	35,768	207	32	22	CC	ex Westerland-05, Alianca Hamburgo-03
Maersk Dartmouth *		Lbr	2005	54,592	64,660	294	32	23	CC	
Maersk Novazzano *		Lbr	1997	23,896	30,600	188	30	21	CC	ex P&O Nedlloyd Horizon-05, Westerems-05, ANL Addax-03, Westerems-02, Lykes Voyager-01, Westerems-98, Maersk Cordoba-98, Westerems-97
Tuscany Bridge *		Atg	1997	23,896	30,291	188	30	21	CC	ex Westerburg-03, Lykes Achiever-01, Westerburg-98, Maersk La Plata-98, Westerburg-97
Westerdeich *		Lbr	1994	15,908	22,343	168	27	19	CC	ex Indamex Liberty-03, Westerdeich-02, Indamex Washington-02, Kota Serika-00, Zim Santos-99, Westerdeich-99, Zim Santos-96, Westerdeich-96, Maersk Rio Grande-96, TSL Gallant-96, Westerdeich-94
Westerhever *		Lbr	1994	15,908	22,340	168	27	20	CC	ex P&O Nedlloyd Coleridge-04, Westerhever-03, Maersk Durban-99, Westerhever-98, Maersk Rio Grande-97, CCNI Atacama-96, Westerhever-94
Westermoor *		Lbr	2001	30,047	35,653	208	32	22	CC	

Name	Eng	Flag	Year	GRT	DWT	Loa	Bm	Kts	Type	Former names
Westermuhlen *		Lbr	1993	14,961	20,140	167	25	17	CC	ex Cala Pinar del Rio-04, Norasia Chicago-01, CSAV New York-00, Westermuhlen-00, Nedlloyd Singapore-96, Westermuhlen-93

newbuildings: one 30,123 grt and two 32,322 grt (Westertal) container ships on order from Polish builder for 2006 delivery.
* managed for Reederei Hans Peterson & Sohne GmbH or ** Mar-Con GmbH & Co. KG., both Germany.

Reederei Karl Schluter GmbH & Co KG/Germany

Funnel: Blue with blue 'N' on broad white band, plain black or charterers colours.
Hull: Various charterers colours.

Name	Eng	Flag	Year	GRT	DWT	Loa	Bm	Kts	Type	Former names
Atlantic Castle		Atg	2001	16,807	24,765	176	23	14	B	ex Cedar-03
Cosco Norfolk		Cyp	1994	35,944	43,025	240	32	21	CC	ex Choyang Phoenix-01, Ville de Lyra-97, Northern Trust-94
Federal Mackinac *		Atg	2004	18,825	27,785	185	24	-	B	
Federal Margaree *		Deu	2005	18,825	25,781	185	24	-	B	
Indamex Colorado		Cyp	1995	36,606	45,217	245	32	23	CC	ex Northern Dignity-04, Ville de Gemina-02, Ming Gemina-01, Ville de Gemina-98, Northern Dignity-95
MSC China		Atg	1996	29,115	40,114	196	32	22	CC	ex Ming Fidelity-00, Hyundai Fidelity-98, Northern Valour-96
MSC Manaus		Atg	1990	24,344	31,552	182	31	18	CC	ex Kota Salam-02, German S-01, City of Haifa-01, CMA Dalian-00, German S-98, German Senator-98
MSC Rio Plata		Atg	1997	29,115	40,080	196	32	22	CC	ex Northern Vitality-02, Ming Trusty-01, Hyundai Trusty-98, I/a Northern Vitality
MSC Salvador		Atg	1997	29,115	40,080	196	32	22	CC	ex Safmarine Everest-02, CMBT Everest-01, I/a Northern Victory
MSC Uruguay		Atg	1996	29,115	40,087	196	32	22	CC	ex Northern Virtue-01, Hyundai Majesty-99, Northern Virtue-96
Northern Fortune		Atg	1991	30,509	30,685	203	31	19	CC	ex Canmar Trader-03, Northern Fortune-02, Zim Ashdod I-01, OOCL Dragon-01, CMA Kawasaki-00, Northern Fortune-98, Zim Ravenna-98, Northern Fortune-97, Zim Brisbane-97, Valencia Senator-95, Northern Fortune-94, A. Abraham-94
Northern Harmony		Atg	1994	19,819	20,252	174	27	18	CC	ex City of Tunis-05, Northern Harmony-94
Theodor Storm		Cyp	2004	28,270	33,282	213	32	23	CC	
Thomas Mann		Cyp	2003	28,270	33,282	213	32	23	CC	

newbuildings: eleven further containerships between 1700 and 5000 teu including Charles Dickens, Ernest Hemingway(for charter to Maersk) also William Shakespeare, Mark Twain (43,100 dwt) and Matthias Claudius (18,405 grt) for 2006-8 delivery.
* chartered to Fednav q.v.

Restis Group Greece

Enterprises Shipping & Trading SA/Greece

Funnel: Light grey with black top.
Hull: Black or red with red boot-topping.

Name	Eng	Flag	Year	GRT	DWT	Loa	Bm	Kts	Type	Former names
African Cobra		Bhs	1986	15,847	26,648	167	26	14	B	ex Nerano-05, Emerald 10-97, Emerald Sea-93, Nerano-88
African Impala		Bhs	1997	15,888	24,111	160	26	14	B	ex Sea Maestro-05
African Jaguar		Bhs	1996	16,041	26,477	169	26	14	B	ex Handy Roseland-05
African Kalahari		Bhs	1986	16,582	27,652	166	27	14	B	ex Handy Ruby-05, Sunrise Ruby-94, Ticao Sampaguita-90, Glory Star-89, I/a Sanko Star
African Karoo		Bhs	1986	16,582	27,652	166	27	14	B	ex Handy Emerald-05, Handy Torm-98, Handy Emerald-95, Pacific Emerald-94, Luzon Sampaguita-90, Glory Spirit-89, I/a Sanko Spirit
African Leopard		Bhs	1996	16,041	26,467	169	26	14	B	ex Pacific Mattsu-05
African Lion		Bhs	1995	16,041	26,300	169	26	14	B	ex Handy Gunner-05
African Oryx		Bhs	1997	15,888	24,110	160	26	14	B	ex Gangga Nagara-05
African Protea		Bhs	1997	15,888	24,111	160	26	14	B	ex Sea Maiden-05
African Puma		Bhs	1997	16,041	26,412	169	26	14	B	ex Pacific Selesa-05, I/a Selesa
African Python		Bhs	1985	15,933	26,587	167	26	14	B	ex Handy Islander-05, Citrus Island-95
African Shark		Bhs	1985	18,987	32,772	177	27	13	B	ex Handy Trader-05, J. Suda-94, Gransol-89, Albasol-88
African Wildcat		Bhs	1997	16,041	26,391	169	26	14	B	ex Marquisa-05
African Zebra		Bhs	1985	23,207	38,623	190	28	14	B	ex Handy Tiger-05, Brave Venture-94
Antwerp Max		Iom	1998	38,489	73,144	225	32	14	B	ex Bunga Saga Lima-05

Name	Eng	Flag	Year	GRT	DWT	Loa	Bm	Kts	Type	Former names
Bay Ranger		Bhs	1995	24,550	43,125	185	31	14	B	ex Bunga Melor Dua-05
Bergen Max		Iom	1994	39,012	72,338	225	32	14	B	ex Bunga Saga Tiga-05
Bremen Max		Iom	1993	39,012	73,503	225	32	14	B	ex Bunga Saga Satu-05
Brugge Max		Iom	1998	38,489	73,056	225	32	14	B	ex Bunga Saga Enam-05
Celigny		Gbr	1991	77,090	149,507	270	43	13	B	ex Wah Shan-02, Donau Ore-96, Wah Shan-94
Channel Ranger		Bhs	1995	24,550	43,108	185	31	14	B	ex Bunga Melor Tiga-05
Constantia		Bhs	1996	83,658	171,039	289	45	14	B	ex Cape Mercury-00, First Mercury-99
Coral Ranger		Bhs	1994	25,498	43,189	185	31	14	B	ex Bunga Orkid Tiga-05
Delta Ranger		Bhs	1995	24,550	43,108	185	31	14	B	ex Bunga Melor Empat-05
Elbe Max		Iom	1999	38,972	73,548	225	32	14	B	ex Bunga Saga 10-05
Energy Century		Iom	2003	41,397	70,470	228	32	-	T	
Energy Challenger		Iom	2005	42,011	70,675	228	32	-	T	
Energy Champion		Iom	2005	42,011	70,681	228	32	-	T	
Energy Chancellor		Iom	2005	42,011	70,558	228	32	-	T	
Energy Commander		Iom	2004	42,011	70,691	228	32	-	T	
Energy Conqueror		Iom	2004	42,011	70,616	228	32	-	T	
Energy Pioneer		Iom	2004	30,008	51,224	183	32	-	T	
Energy Power		Iom	2004	30,008	51,383	183	32	-	T	
Energy Pride		Iom	2004	30,008	51,318	183	32	-	T	
Energy Protector		Iom	2004	30,008	51,314	183	32	-	T	
Energy Ranger		Iom	1996	26,330	45,950	190	32	14	B	ex Energy Saver-02, Cape Infanta-02
Energy Skier		Iom	2005	81,345	159,089	274	48	-	T	
Energy Sprinter		Iom	2005	81,345	159,089	274	48	-	T	
Ferosa *		Vct	1992	90,991	171,800	298	46	13	B	
Force Ranger		Iom	1996	26,330	45,950	189	32	14	B	ex Cape Agulhas-02
Ghent Max		Iom	1998	38,489	73,220	225	32	14	B	ex Bunga Saga Tujuh-05
Glorius		Iom	2004	87,720	171,314	289	45	14	B	
Gulf Ranger		Bhs	1994	25,498	43,246	185	31	15	B	ex Bunga Orkid Satu-05
Hamburg Max		Iom	1994	39,012	72,338	225	32	14	B	ex Bunga Saga Empat-05
Iron Baron		Iom	1999	88,385	169,981	289	45	14	B	ex Philippe LD-04
Iron King		Iom	1996	81,155	161,167	280	45	14	B	ex Kalahari-02
Iron Prince		Iom	1995	82,830	163,554	284	45	14	B	ex Lowlands Trassey-03
Iron Queen		Iom	1996	81,155	161,183	280	43	14	B	ex Karoo-02
Island Ranger		Bhs	1994	24,550	42,427	185	31	14	B	ex Bunga Melor Satu-05
Lake Ranger		Bhs	1994	25,498	43,246	185	31	15	B	ex Bunga Orkid Dua-05
Louis Pasteur		Bhs	1996	9,330	9,000	138	22	21	R	ex Mont Blanc-96
Miden Max		Iom	1993	39,012	74,696	225	32	14	B	ex Bunga Saga Dua-05
Ntabeni		Pan	1984	25,005	37,425	183	30	15	Bp	ex Recife-96, Tellus-88
Ocean Ranger		Bhs	1995	25,498	43,246	185	31	15	B	ex Bunga Orkid Empat-05
Olympius		Iom	2004	87,720	171,314	289	45	14	B	
Ostende Max		Iom	1998	38,489	73,207	225	32	14	B	ex Bunga Saga Lapan-05
Padova		Bhs	1983	7,983	8,471	148	20	18	R	ex Hectoras-02, Hellenic-96, Chiquita Hellenic-92, Kurashima Maru-91
Pierre Doux		Bhs	1995	9,438	9,357	138	22	20	R	
Power Ranger		Iom	1996	26,330	45,946	189	32	14	B	ex Cape Recife-02
Ravenna		Bhs	1982	7,902	8,824	137	21	17	R	ex Hellas-02, Stevens-96
Roma		Bhs	1983	8,245	9,399	137	21	19	R	ex Helvetia-02, Hermes-96, Roma Universal-95, Chiquita Roma-93, Konvall-90
SA Altius		Bhs	2001	87,542	171,480	289	45	14	B	
SA Fortius		Bhs	2001	87,542	171,509	289	45	14	B	
Saldanha *		Iom	1995	90,312	172,173	296	46	13	B	
Salerno		Bhs	1981	12,167	12,545	146	25	21	R	ex Skater-02, Tundra Skater-91, Hilco Skater-88
Sea Ranger		Mys	1995	25,498	43,246	185	31	15	B	ex Bunga Orkid Lima-05
Steel Glory		Bhs	1984	23,536	39,345	181	31	14	B	ex Sea Mariner-02, Sanko Coral-91
Steel Might		Bhs	1985	22,132	39,132	181	31	15	B	ex Sea Trader-01, La Suerte-91
Storm Ranger		Bhs	1995	26,071	45,744	190	31	14	B	ex Lorenzina-03, Brilliance-00
Victorius		Iom	2004	87,720	171,314	289	45	14	B	

newbuildings: Twelve 30,900 grt bulk carriers (including Harmony, Melody, Rhapsody, Symphony) for 2006-7 delivery.
* owned by SafOre (formed jointly with Iscor, South Africa). Company also operates chartered bulk carriers as SwissMarine.

Rickmers Reederei GmbH & Cie KG   Germany

Funnel: Black with houseflag (white 'R' on red over green) on broad white band, or charterers colours.
Hull: Black, pale blue or green with red boot-topping.

Name	Eng	Flag	Year	GRT	DWT	Loa	Bm	Kts	Type	Former names
Aenne Rickmers		Lbr	1998	26,131	30,781	196	30	19	CC	ex CP Rome-06, Contship Rome-05, I/a Aenne Rickmers

Restis Group (Enterprises Shipping). SALERNO. *Hans Kraijenbosch*

Reederei Bertram Rickmers. MARFRET NORMANDIE. *J. M. Kakebeeke*

Reederei Bertram Rickmers. RICKMERS CHENNAI. *J. M. Kakebeeke*

Name	Eng	Flag	Year	GRT	DWT	Loa	Bm	Kts	Type	Former names
Alice Rickmers		Lbr	1998	26,131	30,726	196	30	20	CC	ex Direct Kea-04, CMA CGM Cezanne-01, CGM Cezanne-99, l/a Alice Rickmers
Andreas		Lbr	1998	26,131	30,723	196	30	20	CC	ex CGM Renoir-01, l/a Andreas Rickmers
APL Kobe		Mhl	2004	21,932	24,200	196	28	-	CC	ex Nina Rickmers-04
APL Mumbai		Mhl	2003	21,932	24,277	196	28	-	CC	ex Saylemoon Rickmers-04
Asta Rickmers ‡		Mhl	2001	14,278	15,315	159	26	21	CC	ex Hub Racer-01, Asta Rickmers-01
Camilla Rickmers		Mhl	1996	16,801	23,045	184	25	19	CC	ex CSAV Livorno-00, Camilla Rickmers-00, CCNI Anakena-98, Camilla Rickmers-96
CCNI Amadeo		Lbr	1999	22,817	35,230	171	31	17	CC	ex CCNI Austral-05, CSAV Genova-03, Lykes Challenger-00, l/a Marie Rickmers
CCNI Anakena ‡		Deu	1998	28,148	44,575	185	32	15	Co	l/a Valdermosa
CCNI Ancud ‡		Deu	1998	28,148	44,575	185	32	15	Co	ex CSAV Valencia-03, CCNI Ancud-01
CCNI Angol ‡		Deu	1998	28,148	46,376	185	32	15	Co	l/a Valdivia
CCNI Aviles ‡		Lbr	1999	22,817	35,466	171	31	16	Co	ex CCNI Antofagasta-05, CSAV Barcelona-03, CCNI Antofagasta-02, CSAV Barcelona-02, CCNI Antofagasta-01, Contship Mexico-01, CCNI Antofagasta-99
CCNI Busan		Mhl	1996	24,046	32,482	174	31	19	CC	ex Ghana Star I-04, Hamburgo-02, P&O Nedlloyd Ottawa-01, Superba Bridge-00, CCNI Aysen-00, Maersk Montevideo-98, CCNI Aysen-96
CCNI Chagres ‡		Lbr	1997	28,148	45,070	185	32	15	Co	ex Anna Rickmers-98
CCNI Potrerillos ‡		Lbr	1997	28,148	45,070	185	32	15	Co	l/a Lara Rickmers
CCNI Vancouver		Mhl	1996	24,046	32,482	174	31	19	CC	ex Togo Star-04, Santiago-02, CCNI Chiloe-00, Maersk Curitiba-98, CCNI Chiloe-96
Clipper Emperor		Mhl	2000	38,878	74,381	225	32	14	B	ex Pacemperor-03
CMA CGM Anapurna		Deu	2006	17,000	19,500	196	28	-	CC	l/a Jacob Rickmers
CMA CGM Everest		Mhl	2006	17,000	19,500	196	28	-	CC	l/a John Rickmers
CMA CGM Licorne		Lbr	1998	16,801	23,028	185	25	19	CC	ex Fiona Rickmers-04, Libra Barcelona-03, Fiona Rickmers-02, La Hispaniola-02, Zim Soa Paulo I-01, Paranagua-99, l/a Fiona Rickmers
CMA CGM Paulista		Mhl	1997	16,801	22,900	184	25	19	CC	ex Madeleine Rickmers-05, Sagittarius Challenger-01, Madeleine Rickmers-97
CMA CGM Samba		Deu	1997	10,743	14,191	163	23	17	CC	ex Mabel Rickmers-05, Kribi-98, l/a Mabel Rickmers
CMA CGM St. Laurent †		Mhl	1998	10,752	14,086	163	22	16	CC	ex Laurita-02, Melbridge Pearl-99, Laurita Rickmers-98
CMA CGM St. Martin †		Mhl	1998	10,752	14,040	163	22	16	CC	ex CGM Basse-Terre-01, Lilly Rickmers-98
CP London		Lbr	1997	26,131	30,781	195	30	20	CC	ex Contship London-05, Alexandra Rickmers-97
CP Tui		Lbr	1998	26,131	30,721	196	30	20	CC	ex Direct Tui-05, Contship Washington-02, Albert l/a Rickmers
CSAV Atlanta		Lbr	1998	26,131	30,730	196	30	20	CC	l/a Clasen Rickmers
CSAV Manzanillo		Atg	1996	16,800	22,900	184	25	19	CC	ex Pacific Challenger-01, Christa Rickmers-99, CCNI Arauco-98, Christa Rickmers-96
CSAV Maresias		Mhl	1996	16,801	23,028	185	25	19	CC	ex Delmas Cartier-04, Etha Rickmers-02, CSAV Tokyo-02, Zim Vancouver-01, Etha Rickmers-99, CCNI Antarctico-99, Panamerican-97, CCNI Antartico-96, Etha Rickmers-96
Deike Rickmers		Deu	1996	16,801	23,100	184	25	19	CC	ex Libra Rio Grande-05, Deike Rickmers-04, P&O Nedlloyd Kowie-03, Deike Rickmers-01, CSAV Genova-00, Deike Rickmers-00, Scorpio Challenger-99, Deike Rickmers-97, Panatlantic-97, l/a Deike Rickmers
Delmas Baudin ‡		Mhl	1997	24,053	28,352	205	27	20	CC	ex CSAV Itajai-04, Johan Rickmers-03, APL Chile-02, Sea Cougar-99, l/a Conti Oakland
Delmas Portugal		Deu	1992	9,601	12,583	150	22	17	CC	ex CMA CGM Karibu-05, Delmas Marula-05, New Orient-04, R.C.Rickmers-99, Nedlloyd Caldera-98, Sea-Land Mexico-95, TSL Bold-94, R.C.Rickmers-92
Denderah Rickmers		Lbr	1997	16,801	22,900	184	25	19	CC	ex Norasia Bavaria-05, CSAV Busan-03, Zim Seattle-01, Pictor Challenger-99, Denderah Rickmers-97
Dorothea Rickmers		Lbr	1998	16,801	23,027	184	25	19	CC	ex WAL Ulanga-03, Dorothea Rickmers-01
Elisabeth Rickmers †		Atg	1995	16,801	23,190	185	25	19	CC	ex Delmas Joinville-03, Elisabeth Rickmers-03, Pacific Discovery-01, Elisabeth Rickmers-99, CSAV Santos-97, l/a Elisabeth Rickmers
Ernst Rickmers		Mhl	2002	14,278	15,313	159	26	21	CC	ex Turkon America-03, Ernst Rickmers-02
Helene Rickmers †		Mhl	1998	16,801	23,106	184	25	19	CC	ex Lykes Crusader-02, Helene Rickmers-01, CCNI Arica-01, Helene Rickmers-98

Name	Eng	Flag	Year	GRT	DWT	Loa	Bm	Kts	Type	Former names
Henry Rickmers		Deu	2005	32,322	39,300	211	32	-	CC	
Hyundai No. 103		Pan	1986	40,772	12,893	184	31	18	V	
Ital Fastosa		Mhl	2006	36,000	43,100	239	32	24	CC	
Ital Festosa		Mhl	2006	36,000	43,100	239	32	24	CC	
Maersk Daesan		Lbr	2005	54,214	68,017	294	32	23	CC	
Maersk Davao		Lbr	2005	54,214	68,187	294	32	23	CC	
Maersk Dhaka		Lbr	2005	54,214	68,187	294	32	23	CC	
Maersk Djibouti		Lbr	2004	54,214	68,282	294	32	23	CC	
Maersk Douala		Lbr	2004	54,214	68,187	294	32	23	CC	
Maersk Durban		Deu	2004	54,214	68,187	294	32	23	CC	
Marfret Normandie		Lux	1993	10,778	14,069	163	22	17	CC	ex Maria Rickmers-02, Melbridge Palm-01, Maria Rickmers-98, Karawa-98, Maria Rickmers-97, Karawa-96, Maria Rickmers-95, CCNI Guayas-94, I/a Maria Rickmers
Marfret Provence		Lux	1998	26,131	30,725	196	30	19	CC	ex CGM Matisse-98, Andre Rickmers-98
Maruba Tango ‡		Mhl	1997	24,053	28,366	205	27	20	CC	ex Felicitas Rickmers-05, Sea Jaguar-02, Conti Jacksonville-97
MSC Florida		Mhl	2005	51,364	57,000	286	32	25	CC	ex Maya Rickmers-05
Norasia Valparaiso		Lbr	2002	51,364	58,341	286	32	25	CC	ex Cathrine Rickmers-02
OOCL Achievement		Mhl	2000	14,278	15,299	159	26	21	CC	ex Carla Rickmers-04
OOCL Advance ‡		Mhl	2001	14,278	15,273	159	26	21	CC	ex Jock Rickmers-04, APL Magnolia-01, I/a Jock Rickmers
P&O Nedlloyd Mahe		Lbr	1998	11,925	14,381	150	23	18	CC	ex Marine Rickmers-02, Fanal Mariner-01, Marine Rickmers-99
Patricia Rickmers †		Lbr	1998	26,131	30,781	196	30	19	CC	ex Contship Auckland-05, I/a Patricia Rickmers
Paul Rickmers		Lux	1993	10,733	14,191	163	22	17	CC	ex P&O Nedlloyd Amazonas-05, Paul Rickmers-05, MSC Caribbean-03, Paul Rickmers-02, Kamina-97, Zim Argentina-96, Paul Rickmers-94
Rickmer Rickmers		Atg	1995	16,800	22,900	185	25	19	CC	ex Norasia Sindh-04, Rickmer Rickmers-03, Columbus Hong Kong-02, Sassandra Challenger-01, Rickmer Rickmers-00, CSAV Rosario-98, Rickmer Rickmers-95
Rickmers Chennai *		Cyp	1979	17,128	22,267	178	27	18	C	ex Leon-04, Nacional Vitoria-96, Sonora-94, Gina Luisa-82
Rickmers Dalian *		Cyp	1979	17,128	22,378	178	27	18	Co	ex Bibi-04
Rickmers Genoa		Lbr	2004	23,119	29,900	193	28	19	Co/hl	
Rickmers Hamburg †		Mhl	2002	23,119	29,980	193	28	19	Co/hl	
Rickmers Jakarta †		Mhl	2004	23,119	29,750	193	28	19	Co/hl	ex Genoa-03
Rickmers Mumbai *		Cyp	1979	17,128	22,229	178	27	19	C	ex Merida-04, Silvia Sofia-07
Rickmers New Orleans		Mhl	2003	23,119	30,095	193	28	19	Co/hl	
Rickmers Seoul		Mhl	2003	23,119	30,151	193	28	19	Co/hl	
Rickmers Singapore †		Mhl	2002	23,119	30,018	193	28	19	Co/hl	
Rithi Bhum		Deu	2004	21,932	24,200	196	28	22	CC	ex Jacky Rickmers-04
Robert Rickmers ‡		Mhl	2003	16,802	23,063	185	25	198	CC	ex E.R. Stettin-03
Sandy Rickmers ‡		Cyp	2002	14,290	14,901	159	26	22	CC	I/a Mirko Rickmers
Satha Bhum		Deu	2004	21,932	24,219	196	28	22	CC	ex Moni Rickmers-04
Sea Puma ‡		Mhl	1998	26,125	30,738	196	30	19	CC	ex Crowley Lion-01, CSAV Boston-99, I/a Willi Rickmers
Sean Rickmers		Mhl	1999	16,986	21,184	168	27	20	CC	ex Kindia-04, Indamex Kindia-03, Kindia-02
Tete Rickmers		Mhl	2000	14,278	15,317	158	26	21	CC	
Zim Caribe IV		Mhl	1997	10,743	14,099	163	22	17	CC	ex Sophie Delmas-98, Mai Rickmers-97
Zim Mexico III		Atg	1993	10,778	14,120	163	22	17	CC	ex Peter Rickmers-99, Kaiama-99, Peter Rickmers-94
Zim Sao Paulo II		Mhl	1997	16,801	22,900	185	25	19	CC	ex Ursula Rickmers-01

newbuildings: twenty 41,500 grt, five 36,000 grt, one 35,600 grt, two 32,300 grt and four further 17,000 grt container ships for 2006-8 delivery.
* operated by subsidiary Rickmers-Linie (Cyprus) Ltd. (managed by Technomar Shipping Inc., Greece) and § owned by Hans Carl Rickners.
** managed by Carimar, Cuba, † by Columbus Shipmanagement GmbH, Germany, ‡ by Uniteam Marine Shipping GmbH (see under Roth)

Rigel Schiffahrts GmbH & Co KG   Germany

Funnel: Blue with black 'R' on six-pointed white star on black-edged red disc on narrower white band.
Hull: Blue with red boot-topping.

Name	Eng	Flag	Year	GRT	DWT	Loa	Bm	Kts	Type	Former names
Alsterstern		Iom	1994	11,426	17,080	161	23	15	T	
Donaustern		Iom	1995	11,426	17,078	161	23	14	T	
Geestestern		Iom	2004	26,634	37,188	186	31	15	T	
Havelstern		Iom	1994	11,423	17,080	161	23	14	T	

Name	Eng	Flag	Year	GRT	DWT	Loa	Bm	Kts	Type	Former names
Huntestern		Iom	2004	26,634	37,178	186	31	15	T	
Isarstern		Iom	1995	11,426	17,078	161	23	14	T	
Leinestern		Iom	2005	26,634	37,082	186	31	15	T	
Rheinstern		Iom	1993	11,423	17,080	161	23	14	T	
Rhonestern		Iom	2000	14,400	21,871	162	27	15	T	
Themsestern		Iom	2000	14,400	21,871	162	27	15	T	
Travestern		Iom	1993	11,423	17,080	161	23	15	T	
Weichselstern		Iom	1999	14,331	21,950	162	27	15	T	
Wolgastern		Iom	1999	14,331	21,950	162	27	15	T	

newbuildings: one further 26,634 grt 37,300 dwt tanker for 2007 delivery.

KG Reederei Roth GmbH & Co   Germany

Funnel: Blue with white symbol.
Hull: Black with red boot-topping.

Name	Eng	Flag	Year	GRT	DWT	Loa	Bm	Kts	Type	Former names
Bulk Asia		Lbr	2001	87,590	170,578	289	45	14	B	
Bulk Europe		Lbr	2001	87,590	169,770	289	45	14	B	
Clipper Monarch *		Mhl	2000	38,878	74,381	225	32	14	B	ex Pacmonarch-04
Greta R		Mmr	1989	37,519	68,772	225	32	14	B	ex Achilles-03
Monte Pelmo		Mmr	2000	38,684	72,917	225	32	15	B	ex Monte Carlo-01
Pro Asia		Cyp	1979	14,539	19,786	165	23	16	Co	ex Heron-94, Zim New Orleans-89, Tema Star-80
Sea Master **		Mmr	1985	14,159	23,743	160	24	14	B	ex Sun Master-91
Silver One		Pan	1999	38,684	72,917	224	32	15	B	ex Silverstone-03
Ulla R		Lbr	1989	25,766	43,665	186	30	14	B	ex Edip Karahasan-04, Star Barbara-95, KME Barbara-94, Lucky Giant-93, I/a Soarer Yoga
Vogebulker		Lbr	1999	86,192	169,168	289	45	14	B	ex Heng Shan-04

* owned by subsidiary Uniteam Marine Shipping GmbH or ** Uniteam Marine Ltd., Cyprus.

Ernst Russ GmbH & Co KG   Germany

Funnel: Black, red 'ER' bordered by narrow red bands or charterers colours.
Hull: Black or grey with red boot-topping.

Name	Eng	Flag	Year	GRT	DWT	Loa	Bm	Kts	Type	Former names
CSAV San Antonio		Lbr	1996	16,801	23,043	185	25	19	CC	ex Helene Russ-05, WAL Urundi-04, Helene Russ-01, CMA Rotterdam-00, Helene Russ-99, CSAV Rio de Janeiro-98, I/a Helene Russ
Feng		Cyp	1985	12,863	20,333	164	22	13	B	ex Jian Feng Ling-97
Mercosul Pescada		Lbr	1996	16,800	22,984	184	25	19	CC	ex Sofia Russ-01, CSAV Vancouver-00, Sofia Russ-00, Cielo del Venezuela-99, Sofia Russ-99, CSAV Rungue-98, Sofia Russ-96

Also operates large ro-ro vessels in European coastal trades.

Saga Forest Carriers International AS   Norway

Funnel : Black with white outlined dark blue and turquoise 'S' on dark blue above turquoise bands.
Hull : Orange or grey with black 'SAGA', red boot-topping.

Name	Eng	Flag	Year	GRT	DWT	Loa	Bm	Kts	Type	Former names
Saga Adventure †		Hkg	2005	29,758	46,627	199	32	15	BC	
Saga Andorinha ‡		Iom	1998	29,729	47,027	199	31	15	BC	ex Andorinha-01
Saga Beija-Flor †		Hkg	1997	29,729	47,029	199	31	14	BC	ex Beija-Flor-03
Saga Crest		Hkg	1994	29,381	47,069	199	31	15	BC	
Saga Horizon †		Hkg	1995	29,381	47,016	199	31	15	BC	
Saga Jandaia ‡		Hkg	1998	29,729	47,016	199	31	15	BC	ex Jandaia-01
Saga Marlin *		Bhs	1977	30,931	45,065	201	31	15	BC	ex Hoegh Marlin-04, Star Marlin-91, Hoegh Marlin-87
Saga Mascot *		Bhs	1977	30,931	45,063	201	31	15	BC	ex Hoegh Mascot-05, Mascot-03, Hoegh Mascot-94, Star Mascot-89, Hoegh Mascot-87
Saga Merchant *		Bhs	1977	30,987	44,895	201	31	15	BC	ex Hoegh Merchant-04, Star Merchant-93, Westwood Merchant-90, Hoegh Merchant-83
Saga Merit *		Bhs	1977	30,987	44,926	201	31	15	BC	ex Hoegh Merit-05, Star Merit-95, Hoegh Merit-94, Star Merit-94, Westwood Merit-90, Hoegh Merit-83
Saga Minerva *		Nis	1979	30,995	44,016	201	31	15	BC	ex Hoegh Minerva-05, Max Oldendorff-03, Hoegh Minerva-01, Star Minerva-89, Hoegh Minerva-87
Saga Miranda *		Nis	1979	30,995	44,016	201	31	15	BC	ex Hoegh Miranda-05, August Oldendorff-03, Hoegh Mirande-01, Star Miranda-89, Hoegh Mirande-87

Rigel Schiffs. ALSTERSTERN. *C. Lous*

Ernst Russ. CSAV SAN ANTONIO (on charter to CSAV). *Vandriessche Guido*

Samskip HF (Ost-West-Handel). ARGENTA. *F. de Vries*

Name	Eng	Flag	Year	GRT	DWT	Loa	Bm	Kts	Type	Former names
Saga Monal *		Bhs	1996	36,463	49,755	200	32	16	BC	ex Hoegh Monal-04, Saga Challenger-02
Saga Morus *		Bhs	1997	36,463	56,801	200	32	16	BC	ex Hoegh Morus-04
Saga Musketeer *		Bhs	1977	30,987	44,895	201	31	15	BC	ex Hoegh Musketeer-04, Star Musketeer-94, Westwood Musketeer-90, Hoegh Musketeer-83
Saga Sky †		Hkg	1996	29,381	47,034	199	31	15	BC	
Saga Spray §		Hkg	1994	29,381	47,029	199	31	15	BC	
Saga Tide		Hkg	1991	29,235	57,471	199	31	15	BC	
Saga Tucano †		Hkg	1998	29,729	47,032	199	31	14	BC	ex Tucano-01
Saga Viking ‡		Hkg	2002	29,867	46,500	199	31	14	BC	
Saga Voyager †		Hkg	2001	29,872	46,882	199	31	14	BC	
Saga Wave §		Hkg	1991	29,235	47,062	199	31	15	BC	
Saga Wind †		Hkg	1994	29,381	47,053	199	31	15	BC	

newbuildings: eight further 'Adventure' class for 2007-8 delivery.
Owned by Hesnes Group, Norway with(§) NYK and Leif Hoegh also having interests in the Saga Pool.
* managed by SMT Shipmanagement, Cyprus, † by Patt Manfield or ‡ by Anglo-Eastern Ship Management Ltd., Hong Kong (China)

Samskip HF   Iceland
Ost-West-Handel und Schiffahrt GmbH/Germany

Funnel: *White or black with red band.*
Hull: *Red, white or blue with red boot-topping.*

Name	Eng	Flag	Year	GRT	DWT	Loa	Bm	Kts	Type	Former names
Alyona		Vct	1981	32,226	22,447	205	31	22	Ro	ex Euroshipping Three-96, Smolensk-95
Argenta		Vct	1979	7,098	8,072	145	19	19	R	ex Argo-05, Sakura Rex-02, Sakura Reefer-96
Aurika		Vct	1979	7,246	8,873	141	20	20	R	ex Erato-05, Athenian Rex-03, Cap Ortegal-96, Royal Lily-89
Baltic Cliff		Mlt	1985	7,949	10,168	134	20	18	R	ex Firenze-02, Bretagne-02, C.R. Dieppe-93, Italian Reefer-88, l/a Extreluz
Baltic Cloud		Mlt	1985	7,949	10,168	134	20	18	R	ex Venizia-02, Brest-02, C.R. Alicante-93, Iberian Reefer-88, l/a Extresol
Baltic Meridian		Vct	1980	10,424	9,852	151	22	22	R	ex Swan Lagoon-03, Pocahontas-93, Isla Plaza-86, Pocahontas-84
Baltic Snow		Mlt	1979	11,243	12,570	144	24	21	R	ex Canadian Star-01, Canadian Reefer-01
Baltic Wave		Vct	1976	10,012	11,092	156	21	24	R	ex Almeda Star-01, Harlech-88, Arran-84, Almeda Star-84
Baltic Wind		Vct	1975	10,012	11,093	156	21	24	R	ex Avelona Star-01, Hornsound-90, Avelona Star-90, Castle Peak-88, Avelona Star-84
Crystal Crown		Mlt	1986	12,485	11,330	153	22	18	R	ex Hamburg Trader-04, Reutershagen-93
Crystal Rose		Mlt	1983	9,057	9,339	149	21	19	R	ex Reefer Prince-05, Reefer Princess-97, Lingo-94, Kiwi-87
Eisha		Vct	1975	6,916	9,147	141	18	22	R	ex Vista I-00, Argolic-99, Magellanic-96, Bagno Esmeraldas-94, Theodor Korner-90
Electra		Mlt	1985	9,096	11,464	149	22	17	R	ex Elektra-01, Astra-96, Astraia-94, Colombian Reefer-93, Cacilia B-86
Ice Bell		Vct	1976	10,012	11,093	156	21	24	R	ex Avila Star-03, Almeria Star-90, Perth-88, Almeria Star-84
Nordic Bay		Vct	1980	7,142	9,344	144	18	22	R	ex Kalypso-04, Curacao Reefer-03, Isla Pinta-95, Rio Babahoya-88
Nordic Cape		Vct	1979	7,142	9,344	144	18	22	R	Kirki-04, Balboa Reefer-03, Isla Fernandina-95, Rio Esmeraldas-89
Nordic Ice		Vct	1981	7,142	9,888	144	18	21	R	ex Armonia-03, Reno-02, Orenoco Reefer-99, Isla Isabela-95, Paquisha-89, l/a Rio Palora
Nordic Star		Vct	1980	7,142	9,300	144	18	22	R	ex Ariadne-03, Lilia I-02, Malicia-99, Malibu Reefer-99, Isla Genovesa-95, Rio Chone-88
Pietari Dream		Atg	1981	10,651	9,835	151	22	20	R	ex Mahone Bay-04, Avocado-99, Racisce-97
Pietari Flame		Vct	1978	10,853	10,988	161	23	21	R	ex Swan River-04, R.P. Jamaica-88, California Maru-87
Pietari Frost		Vct	1979	10,853	10,988	161	23	21	R	ex Swan Bay-04, Caribbean Maru-89
Pietari Glory		Vct	1979	10,153	9,996	168	23	21	R	ex Norman Star-04, EW Andes-94, Humboldt Rex No.2-89, Humboldt Rex-89
Pietari Great		Vct	1979	10,153	9,996	168	23	21	R	ex Saxon Star-04, EW Eiger-94, Tasman Rex-89
Santa Marina		Vct	1978	8,507	9,566	150	21	20	R	ex Disko Bay-05, Thistle-93, Paracale-93, Astoria-92, Asama-89, Asama Maru-86

Name	Eng	Flag	Year	GRT	DWT	Loa	Bm	Kts	Type	Former names

The Sanko Steamship Co Ltd

Japan

Funnel: Light green with two red rings around red disc on broad white band.
Hull: Light green with white 'SANKO LINE', red boot-topping.

Name	Eng	Flag	Year	GRT	DWT	Loa	Bm	Kts	Type	Former names
Ansac Asia *	Lbr	1998	19,882	33,945	178	28	14	B	
Crystal Mermaid	Jpn	1990	42,465	49,618	224	36	16	Lpg	
Gas Diana **	Lbr	2000	46,021	49,999	230	37	16	Lpg	
Gas Leo *	Lbr	1990	44,493	50,357	230	37	16	Lpg	
Gas Scorpio	Lbr	1995	44,546	49,679	230	37	16	Lpg	
Gas Taurus **	Lbr	2001	46,021	48,500	230	37	16	Lpg	
Iron Fortune *	Pan	2005	88,494	177,477	289	45	-	B	
Oval Nova *	Lbr	1993	44,549	50,357	230	37	16	Lpg	
Pacific Century *	Lbr	1991	44,493	50,357	230	37	15	Lpg	
Sanko Ability	Lbr	2002	50,199	83,657	239	38	14	T	
Sanko Advance	Lbr	2002	50,199	83,657	239	38	14	T	
Sanko Amity	Lbr	2002	50,199	84,999	239	38	14	T	
Sanko Blossom *	Pan	2005	56,172	105,699	239	42	-	T	
Sanko Breeze	Pan	2005	56,172	105,721	239	42	-	T	
Sanko Dynasty	Pan	1999	57,331	106,644	241	42	14	T	ex Pacific Libra-03
Sanko Eagle	Lbr	1997	18,108	27,868	169	27	14	B	ex Aqua Crystal-03, Alpha Cosmos-01
Sanko Eternal *	Lbr	1996	18,108	27,917	169	27	14	C	ex Aomori Willow-04
Sanko Falcon §	Lbr	1996	26,058	45,674	186	30	14	B	ex Seagull Hachinohe-04
Sanko Galaxy	Lbr	2005	29,372	52,980	189	32	-	B	
Sanko Glory	Lbr	2005	29,372	52,980	189	32	-	B	
Sanko Oasis	Pan	1995	81,058	161,192	280	45	14	T	
Sanko Phoenix *	Lbr	1997	27,011	46,610	189	31	14	B	ex Asian Phoenix-05
Sanko Quality	Lbr	1994	52,498	95,628	247	42	14	T	
Sanko Rally †	Lbr	1994	25,676	42,529	185	31	15	B	
Sanko Ranger	Vut	1995	25,676	42,529	185	31	14	B	
Sanko Rejoice †	Lbr	1994	25,676	42,529	185	31	15	B	
Sanko Robust *	Lbr	1995	25,676	42,529	185	31	15	B	
Sanko Rose *	Lbr	1995	25,676	42,529	185	31	14	B	
Sanko Royal §	Lbr	1995	25,676	42,529	185	31	15	B	
Sanko Sincere	Jpn	1998	29,688	50,655	195	32	15	C	
Sanko Spark *	Hkg	1996	77,211	150,961	274	45	14	B	ex World Spark-04
Sanko Spring	Lbr	1998	29,688	50,655	195	32	15	C	
Sanko Stream	Lbr	1998	29,688	50,655	195	32	15	C	
Sanko Summit	Lbr	1999	29,688	50,655	195	32	15	C	
Sanko Supreme *	Lbr	1999	29,688	50,655	195	32	15	C	
Sanko Unity	Pan	2000	159,577	298,920	333	60	15	T	

newbuildings - two 43,200 grt, one 19,900 grt bulk carriers and three 46,000 grt tankers on order for 2006-8 delivery.
* managed by Sanko Ship Management Co. Ltd. or ** by Anglo-Eastern Shipmanagement (Singapore) Pte. Ltd., both Japan, † by Executive Ship Management, Singapore, ‡ by Temm Maritime Co. Ltd., Japan or § by Eurasia International (Schulte Group) q.v.

Saudi Arabian Oil Co

Saudi Arabia

Vela International Marine Ltd/UAE

Funnel: Plain blue or blue with white 'VELA' below two narrow white bands (top of 'V' merged with lower band).
Hull: Light grey or blue with red boot-topping.

Name	Eng	Flag	Year	GRT	DWT	Loa	Bm	Kts	Type	Former names
Al Bahah	Sau	1998	28,519	47,204	183	32	15	T	ex Gansu-99
Al Bali Star	Lbr	1994	162,181	291,435	333	58	14	T	
Al Mahad	Sau	1982	29,240	48,530	177	32	14	T	ex World Crane-83
Al Safaniya	Sau	1982	29,240	48,582	177	32	14	T	ex World Athenian-83
Aldebaran Star	Lbr	2003	60,387	115,999	248	43	-	T	
Alnasl Star	Lbr	2005	32,083	49,000	200	32	-	T	
Alphard Star	Lbr	1995	159,222	301,858	333	56	14	T	
Altair Star	Lbr	2004	32,083	46,000	200	32	14	T	
Aries Star	Lbr	2003	164,292	316,478	333	60	15	T	
Capricorn Star	Lbr	2003	164,292	316,507	333	60	15	T	
Carina Star	Lbr	1994	159,766	305,668	332	58	14	T	
Gemini Star	Lbr	1995	159,222	301,862	333	56	14	T	
Hamal Star	Lbr	1994	158,680	301,550	332	58	14	T	
Hydra Star	Lbr	1994	159,766	305,846	332	58	14	T	
Leo Star	Lbr	2002	164,292	317,000	333	60	15	T	
Libra Star	Lbr	1993	162,181	291,435	333	58	14	T	
Markab Star	Lbr	1994	158,680	301,569	332	58	14	T	
Mars Glory	Lbr	2000	157,831	299,089	332	58	15	T	

Sanko Steamship. SANKO RALLY. *Hans Kraijenbosch*

Sanko Steamship. SANKO UNITY. *Hans Kraijenbosch*

Schoeller Holdings (Columbia). CAPE BAKER. *Hans Kraijenbosch*

Schoeller Holdings (Columbia). RICKMERS TOKYO (on charter to Rickmers). *J. M. Kakebeeke*

The Schulte Group. NDS PROVIDER (on charter to Nile Dutch Shipping). *J. M. Kakebeeke*

The Schulte Group. ANGELICA SCHULTE (in Sanko charter colours). *Hans Kraijenbosch*

Name	Eng	Flag	Year	GRT	DWT	Loa	Bm	Kts	Type	Former names
Mirfak Star		Lbr	1994	158,680	301,542	332	58	14	T	
Orion Star		Lbr	1994	159,766	305,783	332	58	14	T	
Pherkad Star		Lbr	1995	158,680	301,569	332	58	14	T	
Phoenix Star		Lbr	1993	162,181	291,435	333	58	14	T	
Pisces Star		Lbr	2002	164,292	316,808	333	60	15	T	
Polaris Star		Lbr	1994	158,680	301,591	332	58	14	T	
Shaula Star		Lbr	1994	158,680	301,591	332	58	14	T	
Shaybah		Pan	1998	28,519	47,185	183	32	15	T	ex Gantu-99
Suhail Star		Lbr	1994	159,222	301,862	333	56	14	T	
Venus Glory		Lbr	2000	157,831	299,089	332	58	15	T	

newbuildings - two 25,000 grt 49,000 dwt tankers for 2006 delivery.

Schepers & Co   Germany

Funnel: Black with black 'S' on red diamond on white square, black top.
Hull: Dark blue with red boot-topping.

Name	Eng	Flag	Year	GRT	DWT	Loa	Bm	Kts	Type	Former names
Calaparana		Atg	1996	18,166	26,337	179	28	19	CC	ex Jan S-04, Helene Delmas-01, SCL Zaandam-00, P&O Nedlloyd Zaandam-99, CMBT Africa-97, Morecombe Bay-97, CMBT Africa-96, I/a Jan S
CMA CGM Brasilia		Deu	2004	25,630	33,390	207	30	-	CC	ex Julius S-04
Conrad S		Atg	2006	9,966	14,450	150	23	18	CC	
Constantin S		Atg	2006	27,227	33,216	200	32	22	CC	
CSAV Peru		Deu	1998	25,624	33,914	207	30	21	CC	ex NYK Esperanza-03, Laura S-02, Lykes Innovator-01, TMM Manzanillo-00, Laura S-99, I/a Thea S
CSAV Rio Petrohue		Atg	2002	25,630	33,500	207	30	22	CC	ex Safmarine Kei-04, Thea S-02
CSAV Shenzhen		Atg	2003	27,227	33,232	200	32	22	CC	ex Jandavid S-03
CSAV Tianjin		Deu	2005	25,414	33,796	207	30	-	CC	ex Jula S-05
Heinrich S		Deu	1998	25,624	33,914	207	30	20	CC	ex Zim Singapore I-02, I/a Heinrich S
Inga S		Atg	1995	11,964	14,464	150	23	18	CC	
Karin S		Atg	2006	11,960	14,450	150	23	18	CC	
Libra Salvador		Atg	2002	25,370	33,742	207	30	22	CC	ex NYK Passion-05, Montemar Salvador-04, NYK Passion-03, Montemar Salvador-03, I/a Harald S
Lykes Commodore		Atg	1995	11,964	14,454	150	23	18	CC	ex MSC Panama-04, Katrin S-03, Santa Paula-97, Katrin S-95
Maersk Nantes		Deu	1997	25,361	33,976	207	30	21	CC	ex Michaela S-04, Contship Spirit-03, Michaela S-97
Maersk Nassau		Atg	2003	27,227	33,216	200	32	22	CC	ex Torge S-04, Superior Container-03
Norasia Everest		Atg	2001	35,645	42,211	220	32	22	CC	ex APL Venezuela-04, I/a Carolina, I/dn Camilla
Sakura		Atg	1995	11,964	14,454	150	23	18	CC	ex Bernhard S-04, MOL Manaus-02, Bernhard S-01
Syms Hunshan *		Atg	2005	9,957	14,464	150	23	18	CC	ex Maren S-05
Valparaiso Express		Deu	1997	25,361	33,936	207	30	21	CC	ex P&O Nedlloyd Pantanal-05, Kerstin S-97
Zim Buenos Aires		Atg	1995	16,316	23,130	164	28	18	CC	ex Libra Buenos Aires-99, Marlene S-97

newbuildings: one 27,200 grt 33,200 dwt (Helene S) and four 36,000 grt 43,200 dwt (Adelheid S, Tim S) container ships for 2006-7 delivery.
* owned by H. Schepers.

Schoeller Holdings Ltd   Cyprus

Columbia Shipmanagement Ltd/Cyprus

Funnel: Buff with blue 'CSM' on red band or charterers colours.
Hull: Green or red with red boot-topping.

Name	Eng	Flag	Year	GRT	DWT	Loa	Bm	Kts	Type	Former names
Brunhilde Salamon ***		Mhl	2001	39,126	75,940	225	32	14	B	ex Lake Camellia-04
Cape Akrotiri **		Cyp	1998	57,148	105,176	244	42	15	T	ex Nordgulf-04
Cape Ancona **		Cyp	1998	57,148	105,337	244	42	15	T	ex Nordlight-04
Cape Aspro **		Cyp	1998	57,148	105,337	244	42	15	T	ex Nordisle-04
Cape Avila **		Cyp	1998	57,148	105,337	244	42	15	T	ex Nordocean-04
Cape Baker **		Mhl	2002	84,586	164,487	274	50	-	T	ex Decathlon-03
Cape Balboa **		Mhl	2002	84,586	164,236	274	50	-	T	ex Pentathlon-03
Cape Bari **		Mhl	2005	81,076	159,186	274	48	-	T	
Cape Bastia **		Mhl	2005	81,076	159,156	274	48	-	M	
Cape Bata **		Mhl	2003	81,310	160,289	274	48	-	T	
Cape Bauld		Mhl	2004	29,327	46,700	183	27	14	M	
Cape Beale		Mhl	2005	25,108	40,327	176	31	-	T	
Cape Bille **		Mhl	2003	25,108	35,089	176	31	14	T	

Name	Eng	Flag	Year	GRT	DWT	Loa	Bm	Kts	Type	Former names
Cape Bird **		Mhl	2003	25,108	35,070	176	31	14	T	
Cape Blanc		Lbr	1998	21,165	33,540	179	25	14	T	
Cape Bon **		Mhl	2003	25,108	35,089	176	31	14	T	
Cape Bonny **		Mhl	2005	81,085	159,152	274	48	-	M	
Cape Bowen **		Mhl	2003	81,310	159,988	274	48	-	T	
Cape Bradley		Mhl	2004	25,108	35,159	176	31	-	T	ex J. Shartava-05
Cape Brasilia		Mhl	2006	25,108	40,327	-	-	-	T	
Cape Brindisi **		Mhl	2006	81,076	159,195	274	48	15	T	
Cape Bruny **		Mhl	2004	25,108	35,096	176	31	14	T	
Cape Falcon		Mhl	2003	14,308	16,421	155	25	-	CC	
Cape Norviega *		Mhl	1998	17,609	24,116	183	28	18	CC	ex Justice Container-03
CCNI Hong Kong **		Mhl	2002	23,132	30,396	193	28	19	Co	ex Cape Denison-04
CCNI Shanghai **		Mhl	2002	23,132	30,537	193	28	19	Co	ex Cape Don-04
CMA CGM Jefferson		Mhl	2006	27,786	37,800	222	30	22	CC	ex Cape Molloni-06
Cosco Dammam **		Mhl	2005	27,786	37,825	222	30	-	CC	ex Cape Moreton-05
Cosco Melbourne		Mhl	2005	27,786	37,883	222	30	-	CC	
Fedor ***		Mhl	2003	41,397	70,156	228	32	-	T	ex Nidia-04
Coldon Iolo **		Mhl	2001	23,132	30,537	193	28	19	Co	ex Cape Darby 04
Ibn Battotah		Cyp	1993	10,837	15,566	158	23	17	Co	ex Cape Ann-04, Silver Dawn-03, Maersk Melbourne-98, Silver Dawn-98, Mumbai Bay-97, Silver Dawn-96, Universal Bahana-96
Meridian Lion ***		Mhl	1997	156,880	300,349	330	58	15	T	
Rickmers Antwerp *		Mhl	2003	23,119	29,912	193	28	19	Co/hl	ex Cape Dart-02
Rickmers Shanghai *		Mhl	2003	23,119	30,000	193	28	19	Co/hl	
Rickmers Tokyo *		Mhl	2002	23,119	30,000	193	28	19	Co/hl	ex Cape Delgardo-02
SKS Senne *		Mhl	2003	81,270	159,385	274	48	15	T	
SKS Sinni *		Nis	2003	81,270	159,367	274	48	15	T	
SKS Sira *		Mhl	2002	81,270	159,453	274	48	15	T	
SKS Saluda *		Nis	2003	81,270	160,000	274	50	15	T	
Voyager ***		Mhl	2002	79,525	149,991	272	46	15	T	
YM Dammam *		Mhl	1998	17,609	23,752	183	28	19	CC	ex Cape Negro-04, Norasia Malabar-04, Cape Negro-03, Ace Container-03

newbuildings: six 42,000 grt, six 28,400 grt and nine 14-15,000 grt container ships for 2006-8 delivery.
Managed by Columbia Shipmanagement Ltd., Cyprus, except * by Columbia Shipmanagement (Deutschland) GmbH for ** 40% owned Konig & Cie KG, *** for Salamon AG or † for Knohr & Burchard GmbH, all Germany.

Hanse Bereederungs GmbH & Co KG/Germany

Name	Eng	Flag	Year	GRT	DWT	Loa	Bm	Kts	Type	Former names
Bruno Salamon ‡		Pan	1998	38,431	73,965	225	32	14	B	ex DS Excellent-01, Ever Excellent-01
C. Bright		Pan	1997	159,422	309,636	333	58	14	T	
Cape Arago		Cyp	1992	10,837	15,566	158	23	17	Co	ex Silver Sky-03, Maersk Singapore-98, Silver Sky-98, Global Bahana-96
Capr Bacton		MHL	2004	25,103	35,156	176	31	-	T	ex Celebes Wind-05, Chabua Amiredjibi-05
Cape Banks *		Deu	1997	21,162	33,540	179	25	14	T	ex Chembulk Hong Kong-02, Cape Banks-97
Cape Bear *		Deu	1997	21,165	33,540	179	25	14	T	ex Chembulk Vancouver-02, Cape Bear-97
Cape Benat		Lbr	1998	21,165	33,540	179	25	14	T	
Cape Conway		Cyp	1985	17,280	22,312	170	27	17	Co	ex Delmas Tourville-02, C.D.Pointe Noire-91, C.R.Pointe Noire-90
Cape Preston		Cyp	1983	17,210	22,351	170	27	17	Co	ex Delmas Bougainville-01, C.D.Douala-91, C.R.Douala-90
Cape Santiago *		Mhl	2002	14,241	18,402	159	24	18	CC	ex MSC Yaounde-03, Cape Santiago-02
Cape York		Cyp	1983	17,210	22,351	170	27	17	Co	ex Delmas Durville-02, Griffin Star-98, Australia Current-98, Delmas Joinville-96, C.D.Abidjan-91, C.R.Abidjan-90
Dover Strait **		Mhl	2002	14,241	18,402	159	24	19	CC	ex Cape Serrat-04, MOL Sahara-02, Cape Serrat-02
Ever Shining ‡		Pan	1999	39,052	74,345	225	32	14	B	
Hambisa		Mhl	1997	28,027	44,549	183	32	14	T	
Maria Salamon †		Pan	2001	38,888	74,117	225	32	14	B	ex Far Eastern Glory-01
Sunset Bay		Lbr	1998	17,285	22,339	175	29	20	CC	ex Ningbo Star-05, Cape Nati-03, Tiger Island-02, Cape Nati-02, Sea-Land Mediterranean-99
Willi Salamon †		Lbr	2000	38,888	74,005	225	32	14	B	ex Far Eastern Harvest-01
YM Da Nang		Mhl	2003	14,308	16,435	155	25	18	CC	ex TS Yokohama-04, Cape Fox-03
YM Genova II		Lbr	1998	17,285	22,800	175	27	20	CC	ex Cape North-04, Tiger Pearl-03, Cape North-01, Maersk Skagen-99, I/a Cape North
YM Subic		Mhl	2003	14,308	16,584	155	25	18	CC	ex Cape Ferro-05
YM Taichung		Mhl	2003	14,308	16,400	155	25	18	CC	ex Cape Frio-05

Subsidiary with vessels managed by Columbia Shipmanagement Ltd., Cyprus, * by Columbia Shipmanagement (Deutschland) GmbH, ** by C. Rehder, † by D-S Schiffahrt GmbH or ‡ by First Steamship (Germany) GmbH, all Germany

The Schulte Group

Germany

Funnel: *Dark grey with broad light blue band containing red disc with light blue 'SL' within large 'H'.*
Hull: *Dark grey with red boot-topping.*

Name	Eng	Flag	Year	GRT	DWT	Loa	Bm	Kts	Type	Former names
Annabelle Schulte †		Cyp	2002	27,093	34,638	210	30	22	CC	ex P&O Nedlloyf Barossa Valley-05, P&O Nedlloyd Barossa-02, I/a Kynouria
Antje Schulte ***		Atg	1997	15,929	22,015	168	27	21	CC	ex Alianca Rotterdam-01, Antje Schulte-00, CGM Mascareignes-99, CGM Santos Dumont II-99, Alianca America-98, CSAV Reloncav-98, Antje Schulte-97
Bahama Spirit *		Vut	1995	26,792	46,606	188	32	14	Bu	ex Freeport Miner-00, San Pietro-99 (conv B-00)
Cap Agulhas †		Cyp	2005	18,334	23,579	175	27	20	CC	ex Lambert Schulte-05
Cap Arnauti †		Cyp	2004	18,334	23,579	175	27	20	CC	ex Philipp Schulte-04
Cap Rojo ‡		Cyp	1997	16,281	22,352	179	25	19	CC	ex Henriette Schulte-05, P&O Nedlloyd Lome-03, Fesco Voyager-02, Henriette Schulte-00, CSAV Brasilia-98, Henriette Schulte-97
CMA CGM Papagayo *		Cyp	1994	14,619	20,275	166	25	-	CC	ex Bernhard Schulte-04, Tema Star II-00 Bernhard Schulte-99, Maersk Paita-98, TMM Tuxpan-97, Calapedra-96, Contship Tahiti-95, Bernhard Schulte-94
CMA CGM Wallaby *		Bmu	1998	16,281	22,330	179	25	19	CC	ex Hans Schulte-02, Cabo Creus-01, Hans Schulte-98
Crete §§		Pan	1988	25,060	40,553	176	32	15	T	ex Greta-05, Captain Martin-02
Denise C *		Cym	1999	26,862	46,700	188	32	14	B	ex Greyhawk-00
Donata Schulte ‡		Cyp	2001	26,582	34,717	210	30	22	CC	
Doubtless §		Lbr	1991	28,223	47,083	183	32	14	T	ex Izmaylovo-04
Eos §§		Pan	1993	54,827	99,440	244	46	16	T	
Esther Schulte ‡		Cyp	2001	26,582	33,871	210	30	22	CC	ex P&O Nedlloyd Altiplano-05, Esther Schulte-02, I/a Marianne Schulte
Evadia §§		Cyp	1986	16,282	27,325	170	23	15	T	ex Cielo di Barents-04, Maersk Barents-02, Edzard-97, Maersk Barents-97, Robert Maersk-97
Fabian Schulte ***		Atg	1997	15,929	22,015	168	27	21	CC	ex Maersk Cabello-98, Fabian Schulte-97
Flawless §		Lbr	1991	79,718	154,970	274	44	14	T	ex Tromso Confidence-04
Immanuel Kant §		Nis	1983	12,240	16,228	159	21	15	Lpg	
Hero §§		Pan	1994	54,827	99,489	244	46	16	T	
Icaro §§		Pan	1993	54,827	99,438	244	46	16	T	
Johann Schulte **		Iom	1997	15,180	17,914	155	23	16	Lpg	
Libra Ecuador ‡		Cyp	1997	16,281	22,361	192	25	19	CC	ex Helen Schulte-03, Direct Kiwi-03, Helen Schulte-99, Libra Houston-98, Helen Schulte-97
Maersk Vienna †		Cyp	2000	17,167	21,152	169	27	18	CC	ex Direct Eagle-04, Spica-00
MOL Faithful *		Gib	1996	10,730	14,148	163	22	17	CC	ex Sophie Schulte-05, Marfret Guyane-03, Sophie Schulte-03, CMA CGM Oyapock-02, X-press Annapurna-01, Sophie Schulte-00
MSC Rebecca *		Pan	1997	37,879	42,926	243	32	22	CC	ex Grand Concord-97
NDS Prodigy †		Cyp	1985	22,211	17,773	182	28	20	Ro	ex Silkeborg-98, Hudson-97, Yuriy Maksaryov-96
NDS Progress †		Cyp	1979	22,211	17,872	181	28	20	Ro	ex Atlantic Hope-97, Skulptor Zalkalns-95
NDS Prominence ††		Vct	1982	22,211	17,773	181	28	20	Ro	ex Atlantic Herald-03, NDS Prominence-03, Atlantic Herald-97, Georgiy Pyasetskiy-95
NDS Prospector ††		Atg	1981	32,068	22,447	204	31	22	Ro	ex Laura-04, Laura Delmas-02, Jolly Celeste-00, Katsina-99, Anatoily Vasilyev-97
NDS Provider †		Cyp	1979	22,186	17,665	182	28	20	Ro	ex Global Wind-98, Nikolay Cherkasov-96
Nereo §§		Pan	1993	54,827	99,355	244	46	16	T	
New Oji Pioneer		Phl	1994	38,844	42,730	200	32	14	Bw	
Parnaso §§		Pan	1993	54,827	99,371	244	46	16	T	
Proteo §§		Pan	1993	54,827	99,392	244	46	16	T	
Relentless §		Cyp	1993	28,223	47,070	183	32	14	T	ex Polyanka-04
Restless		Cyp	1991	27,829	47,083	183	32	14	T	ex Fili-04
Sabrewing §§		Pan	2004	29,647	49,323	186	32	14	T	
Santa Elena §§		Lbr	1986	28,017	50,600	183	32	14	T	ex Sanmar Sentinel-05, Torm Gunhild-96
Sea Alfa †		Cyp	2005	18,327	23,395	176	27	-	CC	
Sea Beta †		Cyp	2005	18,344	23,579	176	27	-	CC	
SJN Lopez *		Mhl	1984	19,882	33,264	180	28	15	B	ex Starly-05, Aurora Emerald-04, Pionero-94, Sawako-88
SJN Orcas *		Mhl	1984	19,340	33,024	175	27	14	B	ex Angelina F-05, Aurora Opal-04, Sanko Heart-94
Sovereign §§		Cyp	1992	28,223	47,083	183	32	14	T	ex Presnya-04
Spotless §		Lbr	1991	28,223	47,083	183	32	14	T	ex Arbat-04

Seatrade Groningen. CALA PICCOLA. *J. M. Kakebeeke*

Seatrade Groningen. COMOROS STREAM. *J. M. Kakebeeke*

Seatrade Groningen. ELVIRA. *Hans Kraijenbosch*

Name	Eng	Flag	Year	GRT	DWT	Loa	Bm	Kts	Type	Former names
Taxiarchis †		Lbr	1987	45,140	81,351	229	32	13	T	ex Bro Selma-05, United Selma-00, OT Selma-92, Osco Bellona-89
Teseo §		Pan	1993	54,827	99,477	244	46	16	T	
Thomas C *		Cym	1999	26,862	46,500	188	32	14	B	ex White Eagle-00
Transporter †		Sgp	1983	22,587	39,738	174	32	14	T	ex Bow Transporter-06, Owl Transporter-92, Atlas Transporter-84
Tycho Brahe †		Nis	1982	12,183	16,225	159	21	14	Lpg	
Vanguard §§		Cyp	1992	28,223	47,059	183	32	14	T	ex Ostankino-04
Weser Stahl *		Cyp	1999	28,564	47,257	192	32	12	Bu	
Wilhelm Schulte **		Iom	1997	15,180	17,900	155	23	16	Lpg	
World Swan		Phl	1995	39,023	46,799	200	32	14	Bw	
Zeus §§		Pan	1992	54,827	99,450	244	46	16	T	I/a Catatumbo

newbuildings: two 22,181 grt tankers for 2006 delivery.

*Owned by subsidiaries * Atlantic Marine Ltd Partnership, Bermuda, ** Dorchester Maritime Ltd, Isle of Man, *** Reimarus Schiffahrtskantor GmbH & Co KG (managed by Bus Shipmanagement GmbH) Germany, † Hanseatic Shipping Co Ltd or ‡ Navigo Shipmanagement Co., both Cyprus. †† managed by Hanseatic Shipping Co Ltd for Nile Dutch Africa Line, Netherlands or § Top Tankers or §§ other owners.*

Reederei Bernhard Schulte/Germany

Name	Eng	Flag	Year	GRT	DWT	Loa	Bm	Kts	Type	Former names
Abram Schulte *		Cyp	2004	41,503	72,663	228	32	14	T	I/a Penyu Pulan
Angelica Schulte *		Lbr	2005	56,163	106,433	243	42	-	T	
ANL Emblem *		Cyp	2002	35,589	40,995	232	32	22	CC	ex CMA CGM Gauguin-04, Arnold Schulte-02
Anna Schulte *		Lbr	2001	26,626	34,717	210	30	22	CC	ex P&O Nedlloyd Andes-05, P&O Nedlloyd Rose-01, I/a Anna Schulte
Caecilia Schulte *		Lbr	1995	10,749	14,148	163	22	17	CC	ex CGM Cayenne-02, Caecilia Schulte-99, Atika Delmas-98, CMBT Antarctica-98, Caecilia Schulte-96
Cap Maleas		Cyp	2005	18,334	23,679	175	27	20	CC	ex Konrad Schulte-05, I/a Lambert Schulte
Christiane Schulte *		Lbr	2001	26,582	33,871	210	30	22	CC	ex Elisabeth Schulte 01
City of Hamburg †		Hkg	1990	24,495	31,627	182	31	18	CC	ex Astrid Schulte-03, Ibn Al Kadi-98, American Senator-97, Choyang Green-97, American Senator 95
CMA CGM Chardin *		Cyp	2002	35,589	40,995	232	32	22	CC	ex Friedrich Schulte-02, CMA CGM Gauguin-02, I/a Friedrich Schulte
CMA CGM Claudel *		Lbr	2002	27,093	34,662	210	30	22	CC	ex Claudel-02, I/a Alexandria, I/dn Auguste Schulte
CMA CGM Oyapock *		Lbr	1994	14,619	20,275	166	25	17	CC	ex Karthago-04, Renate Schulte-01, Libra Houston-97, Renate Schulte-96, Europa Express-95, Renate Schulte-94
Elisabeth Schulte †		Hkg	2001	26,718	34,717	210	30	21	CC	I/a Esther Schulte
Elise Schulte ‡		Hkg	1999	56,239	106,122	241	42	14	T	ex Ammon-04
Everhard Schulte ‡		Hkg	2004	40,000	75,000	225	32	-	T	
Henrika Schulte *		Lbr	2001	26,718	33,871	210	30	22	CC	ex P&O Nedlloyd Atacama-05, I/a Henrika Schulte
Judith Schulte *		Lbr	1993	9,602	12,577	150	23	17	CC	ex P&O Nedlloyd Curacao-05, Judith Schulte-98, Maersk Conakry-98, Fas Lattaquie-96, Judith Schulte-96, Libra Barcelona-95, Judith Schulte-95, TSL Gallant-94, Judith Schulte-94
Kadriah II ‡		Mys	1988	18,023	29,998	167	27	14	T	ex Severn-03, Valiant Express-97
Kasper Schulte *		Cyp	2004	41,503	72,718	225	32	14	T	I/a Penyu Hijau
Libra Houston *		Lbr	2001	26,582	34,662	210	30	21	CC	ex Caroline Schulte-02, Thekla Schulte-01
Lissy Schulte *		Lbr	1995	16,800	23,001	185	25	20	CC	ex P&O Nedlloyd Takoradi-04, Lissy Schulte-01, CSAV Rubens-98, Lissy Schulte-95
Maersk Rhone *		Iom	1999	22,181	35,000	171	27	14	T	ex Rita Maersk-03
Marianne Schulte *		Lbr	2001	26,718	34,643	210	30	21	CC	ex P&O Nedlloyd Acapulco-05, I/a Marianne Schulte
Pacific Prosperity †		Pan	1998	90,876	179,385	290	47	14	B	ex Dyna Mercury-02
Rudolf Schulte ‡		Hkg	2004	42,432	75,000	225	32	16	T	
Susanne Schulte *		Lbr	2001	26,626	34,717	210	30	22	CC	ex P&O Nedlloyd Aconcagua-05, I/a Susanne Schulte
Thekla Schulte *		Lbr	2001	26,718	34,677	210	30	22	CC	ex P&O Nedlloyd Antisana-05, Thekla Schulte-01, I/a Caroline Schulte

newbuildings: four 27,000 grt container ships for 2006 delivery.

*Associated company with vessels owned by subsidiaries * Vorsetzen Bereederungs und Schiffahrtskontor GmbH & Co. KG, Germany, † Eurasia International (China) Ltd., Hong Kong or ‡ Eurasia International (Singapore) Pte Ltd, Singapore, the latter two companies also managing numerous vessels for other owners.*

Reederei Thomas Schulte GmbH/Germany

Name	Eng	Flag	Year	GRT	DWT	Loa	Bm	Kts	Type	Former names
Ariake		Cyp	2005	28,592	39,383	222	30	22	CC	I/a Sarah Schulte
CSAV Rotterdam		Cyp	2005	18,334	23,351	176	28		CC	I/a Maximilian Schulte, I/dn Laura Schulte

Name	Eng	Flag	Year	GRT	DWT	Loa	Bm	Kts	Type	Former names
Helena Schulte		Cyp	2006	35,697	41,500	231	32	23	CC	
Lisa Schulte		Cyp	2006	35,697	41,500	231	32	23	CC	
Maersk Nanhai		Cyp	2005	25,406	33,900	207	30	-	CC	ex P&O Nedlloyd Savannah-05, l/a Julia Schulte
Maersk Navia		Cyp	2005	25,406	33,900	207	30	-	CC	ex P&O Nedlloyd Mariana-05, l/a Antonia Schulte
Maersk Neuchatel		Cyp	2005	25,674	33,651	207	30	-	CC	ex Natalie Schulte-05
Maersk Neustadt		Cyp	2005	25,674	33,594	207	30	-	CC	ex Isabelle Schulte-05
Maersk Varna		Cyp	2004	18,334	23,579	175	27	20	CC	ex Laura Schulte-04, l/a Maximilian Schulte, l/dn Konrad Schulte
Maria Schulte		Cyp	2006	35,697	41,500	231	32	23	CC	
Marie Schulte		Atg	2001	16,803	22,900	185	25	20	CC	
NYK Floresta		Cyp	2005	25,406	33,900	208	30	-	CC	ex Victoria Schulte-05
Patricia Schulte		Cyp	2006	27,779	39,400	222	30	22	CC	
Safmarine Pakistan		Cyp	1998	15,929	22,020	169	27	21	CC	ex Francisca Schulte-03, Maersk San Jose-99, l/a Francisca Schulte
Tatiana Schulte		Cyp	2005	27,779	39,400	222	30	22	CC	

newbuildings: three further 35,700 grt container ship on order for 2006-7 delivery, including Philippa Schulte.

Seatrade Groningen BV   Netherlands

Funnel: *Blue with white 'S' and blue 'G' symbol on orange square.*
Hull: *White with blue 'Seatrade', red boot-topping.*

Name	Eng	Flag	Year	GRT	DWT	Loa	Bm	Kts	Type	Former names
Aconcagua Bay		Pan	1992	9,074	11,581	149	21	19	R	ex United Ice-06, Aconcagua-02
Agulhas Stream **		Ant	1998	9,298	11,048	150	22	20	R	
Arctic Mermaid ‡‡		Lbr	1992	9,829	10,461	142	23	19	R	ex Maud-04, Coral Mermaid-01
Ariake Reefer ##		Vct	1980	7,099	8,076	145	19	19	R	ex Ariake Star-, Ariake Reefer-94
Atlantic Hope ##		Pan	1984	7,777	8,494	142	20	18	R	ex Magellan Rex-96
Atlantic Mermaid ‡‡		Pan	1992	9,829	10,464	142	23	19	R	
Badrinath †		Lbr	1987	7,286	7,337	145	20	19	R	ex Vermont Universal-05, Fortune Reefer-96
Barents Bay §		Vct	1984	7,726	8,549	139	21	17	R	ex Chiricana-00, Juvante-87
Benguela Stream		Nld	1998	9,298	11,016	150	22	20	R	
Bristol Bay §		Pan	1984	7,736	8,556	139	21	17	R	ex Sun Alex-05, Punente-99
Buzzard Bay		Ant	1992	10,381	10,621	150	23	20	R	ex French Bay-04, Royal Star-99, Chiquita Honshu-94, Royal Star-92
Cala Palma		Ita	2000	13,400	13,492	174	24	21	R	
Cala Pedra		Ita	2000	13,346	11,502	175	24	21	R	
Cala Pevero *		Ant	1990	8,962	6,704	138	21	18	R	
Cala Piana *		Ant	1992	9,008	6,708	138	21	21	R	
Cala Piccola *		Ant	1991	8,984	6,703	138	21	18	R	
Cala Pino		Ita	1999	13,346	13,492	174	24	21	R	
Cala Portese *		Ant	1990	8,962	6,708	138	21	18	R	
Cala Pula		Ita	1999	13,346	13,492	174	24	21	R	
Cape Gris Nez		Mlt	1990	6,419	6,794	121	19	18	R	ex Minnesota-06, Blue Reefer-99, Blue Sky-94
Cape Vincente		Atg	1991	6,419	6,494	120	19	17	R	
Caribbean Mermaid		Bhs	1993	9,829	10,464	142	23	19	R	ex Northern Mermaid-04, Caribbean Mermaid-02
Changuinola Bay		Bhs	1988	8,487	9,727	141	21	-	R	ex Sun Rosie-06, Cap Changuinola-00
Cloudy Bay		Mlt	1984	10,325	11,779	152	22	21	R	ex Astro Bright-01, Nordenham-97
Cold Stream *		Ant	1994	8,414	10,066	140	22	19	R	l/a Prince of Streams
Comoros Stream		Nld	2000	11,382	12,906	155	24	21	R	
Condor Bay		Pan	1990	10,405	10,742	150	23	20	R	ex Ivory Nina-03, Ivory Cape-01
Cool Express		Nld	1994	5,471	7,480	126	16	18	R	
DAL East London		Ita	1996	16,803	22,878	184	25	19	CC	ex Wiking-04, CSAV Tianjin-01, Pacific Champion-01, Capricorn Challenger-99, Wiking-97
Discovery Bay		Bhs	1997	8,924	10,100	142	22	21	R	
Eagle Bay		Ant	1992	10,402	10,621	150	23	20	R	ex Ivory Eagle-03
Eastern Bay		Pan	1997	8,917	9,662	143	22	19	R	ex Eastern Express-05, l/a Frost Express
Elsebeth		Nld	1998	10,519	10,327	152	23	21	R	
Elvira		Nld	2000	10,532	10,309	152	23	21	R	
Emerald		Nld	2000	10,532	10,346	152	23	21	R	
Esmeralda		Nld	1999	10,532	10,358	152	23	21	R	
Everest Bay		Pan	1989	8,739	9,692	141	21	12	R	ex United Cold-06, E.W. Everest-02
Falcon Bay		Ant	1993	10,374	10,532	150	23	20	R	ex Ivory Falcon-02
Fortuna Bay		Ant	1993	10,203	11,585	145	22	19	R	ex Fortune Bay-03, Uruguayan Reefer-99
Fuji Reefer ##		Bhs	1979	7,095	8,084	145	19	19	R	ex Fuji Star-06, Fuji Reefer-93

Name	Eng	Flag	Year	GRT	DWT	Loa	Bm	Kts	Type	Former names
Hawk Bay		Ant	1992	10,381	10,603	150	23	20	R	ex Roman Bay-04, Roman Star-99, Chiquita Sulu-94
Hope Bay **		Ant	1996	8,396	9,639	143	22	20	R	
Izumo Bay §		Vct	1984	9,273	10,644	150	21	19	R	ex UB Libra-02, Libra-96, Izumo Reefer-95
Kailash †		Lbr	1988	8,487	9,734	141	21	19	R	ex Cap Triunfo-04
Kashima Bay §		Cym	1984	9,273	10,647	150	21	19	R	ex UB Gemini-02, Gemini-96, Kashima Reefer-95
Kasuga Bay §		Cym	1984	9,274	10,647	150	21	19	R	ex Arimao Universal-02, Kasuga Bay-95
Kedarnath †		Lbr	1986	7,286	7,348	145	20	19	R	ex Virginia Universal-05, Wealth Reefer-96
Klipper Stream ‡		Nld	1998	9,305	10,936	150	22	21	R	
Lombok Strait		Nld	2002	13,700	13,512	167	25	22	R	ex Leopard Max-02
Luzon Strait		Nld	2002	13,700	14,413	167	25	22	R	ex Tiger Max-02
Magic		Nld	1989	5,103	6,116	136	16	20	R	
Magnific		Nld	1992	5,103	6,116	136	16	20	R	
Majestic		Nld	1988	5,089	6,105	136	16	20	R	
Maveric		Nld	1993	5,103	6,105	136	16	20	R	
Missouri		Mlt	1990	6,419	6,794	121	19	18	R	ex Blue Frost-99, Blue Ice-95
Music		Nld	1990	5,103	6,116	136	16	20	R	
Mystic **		Ant	1988	5,089	6,105	136	16	20	R	
Nagoya Bay §		Vct	1983	9,755	12,181	150	22	18	R	ex Actric Dawn-00, Cap Frio-95, Oceanic Trader-93, Ocean Pride-92, I/a Ocean Bride
Pacific		Nld	1996	5,918	8,500	134	16	16	R	
Pacific Mermaid ‡‡		Pan	1992	9,820	10,466	142	23	19	R	
Pioneer Bay		Pan	1982	7,748	8,678	142	20	17	R	ex Pioneer Express-05, Pioneer Reefer-93, Rehmannia-88, Raffia Universal-86
Polarlight		Pan	1998	11,417	10,447	154	24	21	R	ex Polarlicht-04
Polarsteam		Nld	1999	11,417	10,449	154	24	21	R	ex Polarstern-03
Prince of Seas		Nld	1993	6,363	7,387	120	19	17	R	
Prince of Sounds		Pan	1993	7,534	8,053	136	20	19	R	ex Santiago I-04, Santiago-01
Prince of Streams		Ant	1993	7,533	8,384	137	20	18	R	ex Wilmington-02
Prince of Tides *		Bhs	1993	7,329	5,360	134	21	19	R	
Prince of Waves *		Bhs	1993	7,329	8,039	134	21	19	R	
Royal Bay §		Vct	1979	9,038	9,118	151	21	20	R	ex Royal Reefer-96, Barrios-84
Royal Cooler §		Vct	1979	9,020	9,101	151	21	20	R	ex African Queen-96, Turbo-89
Royal Klipper ‡		Nld	2000	11,382	12,906	155	24	21	R	ex Equator Stream-00
Royal Reefer §		Vct	1979	9,018	9,125	151	21	20	R	ex African Princess-96, Hawaii-89
Runaway Bay		Bhs	1992	9,070	11,579	149	21	17	R	ex Sun Maria-05, Diamond Reefer-98, Hudson Rex-95
Santa Catharina		Bhs	2000	8,597	9,259	143	22	19	R	I/a Santa Lucia II
Santa Lucia		Nld	1999	8,507	9,566	143	22	20	R	I/a Santa Lucia II
Santa Maria		Ant	1999	8,507	9,566	143	22	20	R	I/a Santa Maria III
Southern Bay		Pan	1997	8,879	9,609	143	22	19	R	ex Southern Express-05
Spring Bear		Bhs	1984	12,615	9,472	152	24	19	R	ex Spring Dream-85
Spring Bob		Nld	1984	12,111	10,098	151	24	19	R	ex Spring Blossom-85
Spring Bok		Nld	1984	12,113	10,113	151	24	18	R	ex Spring Bee-02, Spring Bird-84
Spring Deli		Ant	1984	12,783	9,891	152	24	18	R	ex Spring Delight-03
Spring Dragon §		Vct	1984	12,783	9,906	152	24	18	R	ex Spring Dream-98, Spring Desire-89
Spring Panda		Nld	1984	12,111	10,140	151	24	19	R	ex Spring Ballad-85, Spring Blossom-84
Spring Tiger		Nld	1984	12,340	10,110	148	24	19	R	ex Spring Breeze-90
Storm Bay		Vct	1983	10,325	11,720	152	22	21	R	ex Atlantic Dawn-01, Nienburg-95
Sun Beauty §		Lbr	1983	6,136	6,666	138	19	17	R	ex Thorhild—04, EW Aspen-96, Sea Beauty-88
Sun Claudia		Bhs	1983	7,741	8,538	139	21	18	R	ex Levante-98
Tama Hope		Bhs	1986	6,579	7,690	146	19	18	R	ex Lamitan-93, Tama Hope-92
Tama Star		Bhs	1987	6,579	7,685	146	19	18	R	ex Bulan-93, Tama Star-92
Tasman Bay §		Pan	1989	6,545	7,168	146	19	18	R	ex Kowhai-04
Timor Stream		Pan	1998	9,307	11,013	150	22	20	R	ex Stream Express-05
Tokyo Bay ##		Mlt	1978	7,111	8,078	145	19	19	R	ex Tokyo Reefer-94
United Cool		Pan	1990	8,739	9,692	141	21	21	R	ex E.W. Whitney-02
Yasaka Bay §		Cym	1983	9,273	10,647	150	21	19	R	ex Pasadena Universal-02, Yasaka Bay-95

newbuildings: three 9,966 grt refrigerated cargo/container vessels on order for 2006 delivery.
The company took over United Reefers in July 2005 and also owns or charters about 56 smaller refrigerated vessels.
*Owned/managed by subsidiaries * Dammers Shipmanagement NV, Netherlands Antilles or ** Triton Schiffahrts GmbH, Germany.*
Chartered from † Amer Shipping Ltd., Cyprus, ‡ Jaczon BV, Netherlands, ‡‡ Elmira Shipping & Trading SA, § Roswell Navigation Corp., both Greece or # by Lomar Shipping Ltd., UK or ## from various other owners.
Also see vessels chartered from F. Laeisz Schiffahrts GmbH and Thein & Heyenga GmbH, both Germany

Shell-Royal Dutch Group. HAUSTRUM. *Hans Kraijenbosch*

Solvang ASA. CLIPPER HARALD. *Hans Kraijenbosch*

OAO 'Sovcomflot'. PETROVSK. *Phil Kempsey*

Name	Eng	Flag	Year	GRT	DWT	Loa	Bm	Kts	Type	Former names

Shell-Royal Dutch Group

UK

Shell International Trading & Shipping Co Ltd/UK

Funnel: *Yellow with narrow black top.*
Hull: *Red, black or grey with red or blue boot-topping.*

Name	Eng	Flag	Year	GRT	DWT	Loa	Bm	Kts	Type	Former names
Estrella Atlantica ‡	Arg	1982	13,826	28,750	183	29	15	T	ex Humberto Beghin-95
Estrella Austral ‡	Arg	1984	28,259	45,718	197	32	14	T	ex Feosa Ambassador 2-88
Estrella Pampeana ‡	Arg	1981	37,685	57,741	229	32	14	T	ex Zenatia-96, Oak River-88, Salena-81
Ficus §	Iom	2001	27,539	44,881	183	32	16	T	I/a Elka Angelique
Fulgur §	Iom	2001	27,539	44,787	183	32	16	T	I/a Elka Eleftheria
Fusus §	Iom	2001	27,542	44,788	183	32	16	T	ex Elka Nikolas-01
Haminea *	Iom	1994	28,277	46,878	183	32	14	T	
Hastula *	Iom	1993	28,277	46,842	183	32	14	T	
Hatasia *	Iom	1994	28,277	46,851	183	32	14	T	
Haustrum *	Iom	1994	28,277	46,801	183	32	14	T	
Helix †	Aus	1997	28,810	46,186	183	32	14	T	
Nivosa	Aus	1984	72,609	136,115	265	46	14	T	

newbuilding: one 67,300 dwt tanker on order.
*Owned by * by Premier Product Tankers Group, Norway, † by Shell Co. of Australia Ltd., or ‡ by Shell Compania Argentina de Petroleo SA.*
§ managed for European Navigation Inc., Greece.
Also see chartered vessels under Frontline, Moller and Viken Ship Management (A/S J. Ludwig Mowinckels Rederi).
The Company also has interests in 22 Lng tankers operated by Australian LNG Ship Operating Co. Pty. Ltd., (formed jointly with BHP Petroleum Pty. Ltd.), by Brunei Shell Tankers Sendirian Berhad (formed jointly with Government of The State of Brunei) and by Nigeria LNG Ltd., Nigeria (formed jointly with Nigerian National Petroleum, Corp. (60%), Agip International BV (10%) and TotalFinaElf (10%)).

Solvang ASA

Norway

Funnel: *Brown with blue 'CS' on broad white band.*
Hull: *Brown with red boot-topping.*

Name	Eng	Flag	Year	GRT	DWT	Loa	Bm	Kts	Type	Former names
Clipper Harald	Nis	1999	10,692	13,779	146	21	17	Lpg	
Clipper Lady	Nis	1978	32,853	40,605	217	32	17	Lpg	ex Reynosa-99
Clipper Moon	Nis	2003	35,012	44,872	205	32	16	Lpg	
Clipper Posh	Nis	1983	34,384	46,316	216	32		Lpg	ex Nejma-04, Eupen-95, Petrogas II-86, Eupen-84
Clipper Skagen	Nis	1989	11,822	16,137	158	21	15	Lpg	ex Havkatt-97, Gaz Horizon-94, Sigulda-93
Clipper Sky	Nis	2004	35,158	44,617	205	32	16	Lpg	
Clipper Star	Nis	2003	34,970	44,807	205	32	16	Lpg	
Clipper Sun	Nis	1978	16,340	16,663	170	24	17	Lpg	ex Nuevo Laredo-00, Sydfonn-79
Cypress Trail *	Nis	1988	42,447	12,763	184	31	18	V	

newbuilding: two 18,100 grt Lpg tankers due for 2007 delivery.
** on charter to Eukor Car Carriers Inc. (see under Wallenius-Wilhelmsen)*

OAO 'Sovcomflot'

Russia

Funnel: *Light grey or white with blue 'S' symbol on white above pale blue over red horizontal banded rectangle (some variations)*
Hull: *Black or red with red boot-topping.*

Name	Eng	Flag	Year	GRT	DWT	Loa	Bm	Kts	Type	Former names
Anichkov Bridge	Lbr	2003	27,829	47,843	183	32	14	T	
Azov Sea	Lbr	1998	27,526	47,363	182	32	15	T	
Barents Sea	Lbr	1997	27,526	47,431	182	32	15	T	
Bering Sea	Lbr	1998	27,526	47,431	182	32	15	T	
Camberley	Lbr	2006	23,000	26,500	-	-	-	Lpg	
East Siberian Sea	Lbr	1998	27,526	47,358	182	32	15	T	
Hermitage Bridge	Lbr	2003	28,000	47,842	183	32	14	T	
Invincible	Cyp	1992	28,223	47,083	183	32	14	T	ex Sokolniki-04
Kara Sea	Lbr	1998	27,526	47,343	182	32	15	T	
Laptev Sea	Lbr	1998	27,526	47,314	182	32	15	T	
Ligovsky Prospect	Lbr	2003	62,586	115,000	250	44	15	T	
Moscow Sea	Lbr	1998	27,526	47,363	182	32	15	T	
Narodny Bridge	Lbr	2003	27,829	47,791	183	32	14	T	
Nevskiy Prospect	Lbr	2003	62,586	114,598	250	44	15	T	
Okhotsk Sea	Lbr	1999	27,526	47,363	182	32	15	T	
Okhta Bridge	Lbr	2004	27,829	47,000	182	32	14	T	
Petrodvorets	Lbr	1999	59,731	105,692	248	43	15	T	ex Astro Saturn-01
Petrokrepost	Lbr	1999	59,731	98,039	248	43	15	T	ex Astro Maria-01
Petropavlovsk	Lbr	2002	57,683	106,532	241	42	15	T	
Petrovsk	Lbr	2004	57,683	105,900	241	42	15	T	
Petrozavodsk	Lbr	2003	57,683	106,449	241	42	15	T	
Romea Champion	Lbr	1992	79,718	154,970	274	44	14	T	ex Tromso Champion-92

Name	Eng	Flag	Year	GRT	DWT	Loa	Bm	Kts	Type	Former names
SCF Aldan		Lbr	2005	81,076	159,200	274	48	15	T	
SCF Altai		Lbr	2001	81,085	159,169	274	48	15	T	
SCF Baltica		Lbr	2005	65,293	117,050	250	44	15	M	
SCF Byrranga		Lbr	2005	81,076	159,200	274	48	15	T	
SCF Caucasus		Lbr	2002	81,085	159,173	274	48	15	T	
SCF Khibiny		Lbr	2002	81,085	159,156	274	48	15	T	
SCF Sayan		Lbr	2002	81,085	159,184	274	48	15	T	
SCF Ural		Lbr	2002	81,085	159,169	274	48	15	T	
SCF Valdai		Lbr	2003	81,085	159,313	274	48	15	T	
Stena Contender		Lbr	2003	62,586	104,707	250	44	15	T	ex Liteyny Prospect-04
Teatralny Bridge		Lbr	2006	27,725	47,300	183	32	14	T	
Torgovy Bridge		Lbr	2005	27,725	47,363	183	32	14	T	
Tower Bridge		Lbr	2004	27,725	47,363	183	32	14	T	
Troitskiy Bridge		Lbr	2003	27,725	41,158	183	32	14	T	
Tropic Brilliance		Lbr	1992	79,718	154,970	274	44	14	T	ex Tromso Brilliance-92
Tuchkov Bridge		Lbr	2004	27,500	47,000	183	32	14	T	
Victor Konetsky		Lbr	2005	60,434	101,018	247	42	-	T	
Victorious		Lbr	1991	28,223	47,083	183	32	14	T	ex Nagatino-04
Yuri Senkevich		Lbr	2005	60,434	100,971	247	42	-	T	

newbuildings: four 82,250, four 28,500 grt tankers, two 23,000 grt Lpg and two 95,800 grt Lng tankers for 2006-7 delivery.
Managed by Unicom Management Services (Cyprus) Ltd. formed jointly with V.Ships Switzerland SA.
See also Hanjin Shipping Co. Ltd (Senator Line)

Spar Shipping AS   Norway

Funnel: *White.*
Hull: *Black with red boot-topping.*

Name		Flag	Year	GRT	DWT	Loa	Bm	Kts	Type	Former names
Spar Capella		Nis	1990	38,337	70,424	230	32	15	B	ex Maersk Tukang-00
Spar Carina		Nis	1990	38,337	70,424	230	32	15	B	ex Maersk Taikung-01
Spar Cetus		Nis	1998	25,982	45,725	186	30	15	B	ex Golden Protea-02
Spar Corona		Nis	1990	38,337	70,424	230	32	15	B	ex Maersk Tanjong-02
Spar Eight		Nis	1982	22,300	36,227	190	28	14	B	ex Negros Victory-95, Orchid II-91
Spar Emerald		Nis	1987	20,766	34,970	177	30	14	B	ex Mockingbird-97
Spar Jade *		Nis	1985	18,011	30,674	180	23	14	B	ex Federal Aalesund-97, Fiona Mary-93
Spar Leo		Nis	1989	36,074	65,850	226	32	13	B	ex Alianthos-04, CS Elegant-99,
										Rubin Elegant-94, Young Senator-92
Spar Lupus		Nis	1998	26,400	45,146	186	30	15	B	ex Golden Aloe-02
Spar Lynx		Nis	2005	32,474	53,565	190	32	-	B	
Spar Lyra		Nis	2005	32,474	53,565	190	32	-	B	
Spar Neptun		Nis	1994	36,559	70,101	225	32	15	B	ex Apollon-04, Gran Trader-99
Spar Opal *		Nis	1984	16,861	28,214	178	23	14	B	ex Matane-97, Federal Matane-97,
										Consensus Atlantic-92, Lake Shidaka-91
Spar Orion		Nis	1996	26,449	47,639	190	31	14	B	ex Western Orion-01
Spar Ruby *		Nis	1985	16,775	28,259	178	23	14	B	ex Solveig-00, Manila Bellona-98, Liberty Sky-96,
										Astral Neptune-90
Spar Sirius		Nis	1996	25,968	45,402	186	30	14	B	ex Western Transporter-01
Spar Taurus		Nis	2005	32,474	53,000	190	32	-	B	
Spar Three		Nis	1982	22,235	35,941	190	28	14	B	ex Diwata-90, Berta-87, Mino Maru-85
Spar Topaz		Nis	1987	22,155	38,455	181	31	14	B	ex Azteca 1-96
Spar Two		Pan	1982	22,258	35,971	180	28	14	B	ex Menina Barbara-93
Spar Vega		Nis	1995	38,779	73,350	225	32	14	B	ex Doric Herald-04
Spar Virgo		Nis	2005	32,474	53,000	190	32	-	B	

newbuildings: two further 32,400 grt 53,000 dwt bulk carriers for 2005/6 delivery from Chinese builder.
* chartered-out to Fednav Ltd. q.v.

Spliethoff's Bevrachtingskantoor BV   Netherlands

Funnel: *Orange with black 'S' on diagonally quartered white/red/orange/blue flag*
Hull: *Brown with white line above green boot-topping*

Name		Flag	Year	GRT	DWT	Loa	Bm	Kts	Type	Former names
Saimagracht		Nld	2004	16,639	21,250	168	25	19	Co	
Sampogracht		Nld	2004	16,639	21,250	168	25	19	Co	
Scheldegracht		Nld	2000	16,639	21,250	168	25	19	Co	
Schippersgracht		Ant	2000	16,641	21,402	168	25	19	Co	
Singelgracht		Nld	2000	16,641	21,402	168	25	19	Co	
Slotergracht		Nld	2000	16,641	21,402	168	25	19	Co	
Sluisgracht		Nld	2001	16,639	21,250	170	25	19	Co	
Snoekgracht		Nld	2000	16,641	21,400	168	25	19	Co	

Spliethoff's Bevrachtingskantor. SLUISGRACHT. *N. Kemps*

Spliethoff's (BigLift Shipping). DA HUA. *N. Kemps*

Star Reefers. AVILA STAR. *Hans Kraijenbosch*

Star Reefers. CARIBBEAN STAR. *Hans Kraijenbosch*

Stena AB. STENA CONTENDER. *Hans Kraijenbosch*

Stolt-Nielsen Group. STOLT MARKLAND. *N. Kemps*

Name	Eng	Flag	Year	GRT	DWT	Loa	Bm	Kts	Type	Former names
Spaarnegracht		Nld	2000	16,641	21,402	168	25	19	Co	
Spiegelgracht		Nld	2000	16,641	21,400	168	25	19	Co	
Spuigracht		Nld	2001	16,639	21,349	172	25	19	Co	
Stadiongracht		Nld	2000	15,500	21,250	168	25	19	Co	
Statengracht		Nld	2004	16,639	21,250	173	26	19	Co	
Suomigracht		Nld	2004	16,639	21,250	168	25	19	Co	

newbuildings: five 24,800 grt ro-ro vessels on order for 2006-7 delivery.
Also owns and manages numerous smaller vessels.

BigLift Shipping BV

Funnel: *Orange with black 'BigLift' or blue mammoth design.*
Hull: *Yellow with black 'BigLift' or blue mammoth design and 'MAMMOET', red boot-topping.*

Name	Eng	Flag	Year	GRT	DWT	Loa	Bm	Kts	Type	Former names
Da Fu **		Pan	1998	14,021	16,957	153	23	15	HL	
Da Hua **		Pan	1998	14,021	16,957	153	23	15	HL	
Da Qiang **		Pan	1998	14,021	16,957	153	23	15	HL	
Da Zhong **		Pan	1998	14,021	16,957	153	23	15	HL	
Enchanter *		Pan	1998	10,990	16,069	138	23	15	HL	ex Sailer Jupiter-98
Envoyager *		Sgp	1985	15,350	21,183	153	27	15	HL	ex Alps Maru-91
Happy Buccaneer	(2)	Nld	1984	16,341	13,740	146	28	15	HL	
Happy Ranger		Nld	1997	10,990	15,065	138	23	16	HL	
Happy River		Nld	1997	10,990	16,516	138	23	16	HL	
Happy Rover		Nld	1997	10,990	15,593	138	23	16	HL	

** owned by Pool member Mitsui OSK Lines Ltd (managed by New Asian Shipping Co. Ltd, Hong Kong) q.v. or ** by Guangzhou Ocean Shipping (COSCO), China.*

Star Reefers AS   Norway

Funnel: *White with red edged blue 5-pointed star, narrow blue band beneath red top.*
Hull: *Lilac grey, corn or blue with blue waterline over red boot-topping.*

Name	Eng	Flag	Year	GRT	DWT	Loa	Bm	Kts	Type	Former names
Afric Star *		Bhs	1990	11,590	12,683	159	24	18	R	ex Tundra Consumer-04, Del Monte Consumer-00
Almeda Star *		Bhs	1990	11,658	12,714	159	24	20	R	ex Tundra King-05, Del Monte Pride-91
Andalusia Star *		Bhs	1991	11,658	12,714	159	24	20	R	ex Tundra Princess-05, Del Monte Spirit-91
Argentina Star *		Lbr	1992	10,629	10,588	150	23	21	R	ex Polar Argentina-05, Horntide-98, Polar Argentina-98, Gordian-95
Avelona Star *		Bhs	1991	11,658	12,714	159	24	20	R	ex Tundra Queen-05, Del Monte Quality-91
Avila Star *		Bhs	1990	11,590	12,519	159	24	18	R	ex Tundra Trader-04, Del Monte Trader-99
Auckland Star ‡		Bhs	1985	10,691	11,434	151	22	19	R	ex Horncliff-89, Auckland Star-87
Brasil Star *		Lbr	1992	10,629	10,588	150	23	21	R	ex Polar Brasil-05, Hornstream-98, Polar Brasil-98, Numerian-95
Canterbury Star ‡		Bhs	1986	10,291	11,434	151	22	19	R	
Cape Town Star ‡		Bhs	1993	10,614	10,629	150	23	21	R	ex Caribbean Reef-03, Hornbreeze-98, Geestcrest-95, Hornbreeze-95, Caribbean Universal-94
Caribbean Star *		Pan	1997	11,435	10,362	154	24	20	R	ex Hornsea-00, Caribbean Star-98
Chaiten		Bhs	1988	13,312	12,838	152	24	18	R	
Chile Star *		Lbr	1993	10,629	10,620	150	23	21	R	ex Polar Chile-05, Trajan-96
Chiquita Brenda ***		Bmu	1993	8,665	11,973	151	20	20	R	ex Brenda-00, Chiquita Brenda-97, Chiquita Joy-93
Chiquita Joy ***		Bmu	1994	8,665	11,793	151	20	22	R	ex Joy-00, Chiquita Joy-97
Colombian Star †		Pan	1998	11,733	10,371	154	24	21	R	
Costa Rican Star *		Pan	1998	11,435	10,350	154	24	21	R	ex Hornwind-02, Costa Rican Star-98
Cote d'Ivoirian Star †		Pan	1998	11,733	11,000	154	24	21	R	
Durban Star ‡		Bhs	1993	10,614	10,629	150	23	20	R	ex Coral Reef-03, Horncloud-98, Geesttide-95, Horncloud-94, Coral Universal-94
Ecuador Star *		Lbr	1992	10,629	10,452	150	23	21	R	ex Polar Ecuador-05, Justinian-96
English Star ‡		Bhs	1986	10,291	11,434	151	22	19	R	ex Hornsea-89, English Star-87
Honduras Star *		Lbr	1992	10,629	10,593	150	23	21	R	ex Polar Colombia-05, Appian-95
Napier Star ***		Bmu	1994	8,665	11,822	151	20	19	R	ex Chiquita Elke-03, Elke-00, Chiquita Elke-97
Nelson Star ***		Bmu	1993	8,665	11,830	151	20	22	R	ex Chiquita Jean-03, Jean-00, Chiquita Jean-97
Regal Star *		Pan	1993	10,375	10,520	150	23	20	R	ex Tauu-96, Hornstrait-95, Chiquita Tauu-94
Regulus		Pan	1993	10,374	10,545	150	23	20	R	ex Regent Star-05, Nauru-00, Hornsound-95, Chiquita Nauru-94
Scottish Star ‡		Bhs	1985	10,291	13,058	151	22	19	R	
Solent Star †		Pan	2001	10,804	9,709	150	23	21	R	
Southampton Star †		Pan	1999	10,804	9,709	150	23	21	R	
Swan Chacabuco †		Bhs	1990	13,099	12,974	152	24	18	R	ex Chacabuco-97

Name	Eng	Flag	Year	GRT	DWT	Loa	Bm	Kts	Type	Former names
Tauranga Star ***		Bmu	1992	7,944	10,963	141	20	20	R	ex Chiquita Frances-02, France-00, Chiquita Frances-98
Trojan Star ‡		Bhs	1984	9,417	11,660	146	21	22	R	ex Walter Jacob-96, Cap Palmas-94, Walter Jacob-93, Bremerhaven-89, Walter Jacob-84
Tudor Star ‡		Bhs	1983	9,417	11,805	146	21	22	R	ex Helene Jacob-96, Saxon Star-94, Helene Jacob-93, Blumenthal-88, Helene Jacob-84
Uruguay Star *		Lbr	1993	10,629	10,593	150	23	21	R	ex Polar Uruguay-05, Hadrian-96
Valparaiso Star *		Bhs	1989	8,945	9,867	141	22	20	R	ex Harvester-04, Del Monte Harvester-99
Viking Star †		Bhs	1991	7,239	9,157	138	19	19	R	ex Consensus Reefer-05, Schoener-97, Hornwave-92, Schoener-92
Wellington Star ***		Bhs	1992	7,944	11,103	141	20	21	R	ex Bothnian Reefer-03

*Vessels managed by IUM Shipmanagement AS, * by Fleet Management Ltd., Hong Kong (China), by ** Dobson Fleet Management, Cyprus or by *** DFM Poland, by ‡ Teekay Marine Services q.v. † chartered from various other owners.*

Stena AB   Sweden

Funnel: White 'S' on wide red band separated from black top and base by narrow white bands.
Hull: Black, grey or blue with 'Stena Bulk', red boot-topping.

Name	Eng	Flag	Year	GRT	DWT	Loa	Bm	Kts	Type	Former names
Stena Alexita **	(2)	Nor	1998	76,826	127,466	263	46	15	T	
Stena Arctica		Swe	2005	65,293	117,099	250	44	-	T	
Stena Commander †		Ita	2003	41,000	72,365	229	32	15	T	ex Blue Dolphin-03, Stena Comanche-03, Blue Dolphin-03
Stena Companion		Lbr	2004	43,000	72,637	229	32	15	T	
Stena Compatriot		Lbr	2004	43,000	72,000	229	32	15	T	
Stena Concept		Bmu	2005	27,357	47,171	183	32	14	T	
Stena Conductor †		Pan	2003	58,100	107,198	247	42	14	T	
Stena Confidence		Bhs	2003	58,118	107,215	247	42	14	T	I/a Island Courage
Stena Conqueror †		Ita	2003	27,335	47,323	183	32	14	T	I/a Hellenica
Stena Conquest †		Ita	2003	27,335	47,136	183	32	14	T	ex Hispanica-03
Stena Contender		Lbr	2003	62,586	104,707	250	44	-	T	ex Liteyny Prospect-04
Stena Contest		Bmu	2005	27,335	47,288	183	32	14	T	
Stena Italica †		Ira	2004	27,355	47,288	183	32	14	T	
Stena Paris (2)		Bmu	2005	36,064	65,125	290	40	-	T	
Stena Provence		Swe	2006	36,000	65,000	290	40	-	T	
Stena Sirita **	(2)	Nor	1999	76,836	127,466	263	46	15	T	
Stena Victory *		Bmu	2001	163,761	312,679	335	70	16	T	
Stena Vision *		Bmu	2001	163,761	312,679	335	70	16	T	

newbuildings: two 113,600 dwt, four 72,000 dwt and two further 49,000 dwt shallow draft tankers on order.
* owned by associated Concordia Maritime AB, subsidiary Universe Tankships (Delaware) LLC which has six 49,000 dwt tankers on order.
** jointly owned with Ugland Marine Services AS and operated by Ugland Nordic Shipping ASA (under Teekay). † chartered from other owners.

Stolt-Nielsen Transportation Group BV   Netherlands

Funnel: White with large white 'S' on red square, narrow black top.
Hull: Yellow with black 'STOLT TANKERS', red or pink boot-topping.

Name	Eng	Flag	Year	GRT	DWT	Loa	Bm	Kts	Type	Former names
Stolt Achievement	(me)	Cym	1999	25,427	37,000	177	31	16	T	
Stolt Aquamarine		Cym	1986	23,964	38,746	177	32	15	T	
Stolt Avance		Lbr	1977	14,857	23,648	171	24	16	T	
Stolt Avenir		Lbr	1978	14,857	23,275	171	24	16	T	
Stolt Capability	(me)	Lbr	1998	24,625	37,042	177	31	16	T	
Stolt Concept	(me)	Cym	1999	24,495	37,236	177	31	16	T	
Stolt Condor		Lbr	1979	21,043	37,200	177	30	16	T	ex Stolt Okpo-79
Stolt Confidence	(me)	Cym	1996	24,625	37,015	177	31	16	T	
Stolt Creativity	(me)	Lbr	1997	24,625	37,271	177	31	16	T	
Stolt Eagle		Lbr	1980	21,043	37,067	177	30	16	T	ex Stolt Ulsan-80
Stolt Efficiency	(me)	Cym	1998	24,625	37,271	177	31	16	T	
Stolt Effort	(me)	Cym	1999	24,495	37,155	177	31	16	T	
Stolt Emerald		Cym	1986	23,964	38,719	177	32	15	T	
Stolt Excellence		Lbr	1979	20,157	31,379	177	27	16	T	
Stolt Falcon		Lbr	1978	21,043	37,201	174	30	15	T	ex Stolt Seoul-79
Stolt Guardian		Lbr	1983	22,904	39,723	175	32	13	T	ex Stolt Uskok-92, Maasuskok-89, Uskok-86, Iver Swift-85, Jo Swift-84, Iver Swift-84
Stolt Hawk		Lbr	1978	21,043	37,080	177	30	16	T	ex Stolt Inchon-79
Stolt Helluland		Cym	1990	18,994	31,454	175	30	15	T	
Stolt Heron		Lbr	1979	21,287	37,200	177	30	16	T	ex Stolt Yosu-79
Stolt Hill		Lbr	1992	22,620	40,159	176	32	14	T	ex Montana Star-06, Star Sapphire-02
Stolt Innovation	(me)	Cym	1996	24,625	37,015	177	31	16	T	

Name	Eng	Flag	Year	GRT	DWT	Loa	Bm	Kts	Type	Former names
Stolt Inspiration	(me)	Cym	1997	24,625	37,205	177	31	16	T	
Stolt Integrity		Lbr	1977	20,157	32,057	177	27	18	T	
Stolt Invention	(me)	Lbr	1998	24,625	37,271	177	31	16	T	
Stolt Jade		Cym	1986	23,964	38,746	177	32	15	T	
Stolt Loyalty		Lbr	1978	20,157	32,091	177	27	17	T	
Stolt Markland		Cym	1991	18,994	31,433	175	30	15	T	
Stolt Nanami *		Pan	2003	11,549	19,932	143	24	14	T	
Stolt Osprey		Lbr	1978	21,287	37,080	177	30	15	T	ex Stolt Busan-80
Stolt Peak		Lbr	1991	22,620	40,077	176	32	14	T	ex Montana Blue-06, Blue Sapphire-02
Stolt Perseverance	(me)	Cym	2000	25,196	37,059	177	31	16	T	
Stolt Pride		Lbr	1976	20,013	31,942	177	27	17	T	
Stolt Protector		Lbr	1983	22,587	39,782	174	32	14	T	ex Stolt Exporter-92, Exporter-88, Atlas Exporter-83
Stolt Sapphire		Lbr	1986	23,964	38,746	177	32	15	T	
Stolt Sea	(me)	Cym	1999	14,742	22,198	163	24	15	T	
Stolt Sincerity		Lbr	1976	20,013	31,943	177	27	17	T	
Stolt Span	(me)	Lbr	1998	14,775	22,273	163	24	15	T	
Stolt Spray	(me)	Cym	2000	14,180	22,460	163	24	15	T	
Stolt Stream	(me)	Cym	2000	14,180	22,199	163	24	15	T	
Stolt Sun	(me)	Cym	2000	14,152	22,460	163	24	15	T	
Stolt Surf	(me)	Cym	2000	14,180	22,460	163	24	15	T	
Stolt Tenacity		Lbr	1978	20,157	32,093	177	27	17	T	
Stolt Topaz		Cym	1986	23,964	38,818	177	32	15	T	
Stolt Valor **		Hkg	2004	15,600	25,100	159	26	-	T	
Stolt Vestland		Cym	1992	19,034	31,494	175	30	15	T	
Stolt Viking	(me)	Cym	2001	16,754	26,707	166	27	15	T	ex Isola Blu-05, I/a Isola Verde
Stolt Vinland		Cym	1992	19,034	31,434	175	30	15	T	

newbuildings: two 24,000 grt tankers for 2007-8 delivery.
* owned by V. Ships (Asia) Pte. Ltd. or ** by Central Marine Co. Ltd., Japan

Suisse-Atlantique Soc de Navigation Maritime SA   Switzerland

Funnel: *Black with red diagonal cross and two stars on yellow houseflag interrupting two yellow bands.*
Hull: *Grey with red boot-topping.*

Name		Flag	Year	GRT	DWT	Loa	Bm	Kts	Type	Former names
Celerina		Che	1999	39,161	73,035	225	32	14	B	
Corviglia		Che	1999	39,161	73,035	225	32	14	B	
Engiadina		Che	2002	27,779	40,878	222	30	22	CC	ex Norasia Engiadina-03, Engiadina-02
General Guisan		Che	1999	39,161	73,035	225	32	14	B	
Lausanne		Che	2003	27,779	40,878	222	30	22	CC	
Maersk Juan		Che	2005	27,779	39,384	221	30	23	CC	ex Jaun-05
Maersk Jenaz		Che	2005	27,779	39,384	221	30	23	CC	ex Jenaz-05
Moleson		Che	1998	38,289	73,018	225	32	14	B	
Norasia Sils		Che	2003	27,779	40,878	221	30	22	CC	ex Sils-03
Nyon		Bhs	1999	39,161	73,035	225	32	14	B	

John Swire & Sons Ltd   UK

The China Navigation Co Ltd/Hong Kong (China)

Funnel: *Black with houseflag.*
Hull: *Black with red, grey or pink boot-topping.*

Name		Flag	Year	GRT	DWT	Loa	Bm	Kts	Type	Former names
Chekiang		Hkg	1991	18,391	23,271	185	28	18	Co	ex Atlantic Challenger-99
Erawan		Iom	1982	35,716	64,643	225	32	13	B	ex Camarina-99, Starfest-95, Yamashiro Maru-90
Erradale *		Hkg	1994	82,701	163,554	284	44	15	B	
Indotrans Celebes		Lbr	1984	30,150	41,600	198	32	16	BC	ex Albert Oldendorff-04, Hoegh Dyke-01
Indotrans Flores		Lbr	1984	30,150	41,600	198	32	16	BC	ex Ingrid Oldendorff-04, Hoegh Drake-01
Indotrans Java		Lbr	1984	30,150	41,600	198	32	16	BC	ex Gitta Oldendorff-04, Hoegh Dene-01
Indotrans Makassar		Lbr	1984	30,061	41,600	198	32	16	BC	ex Edward Oldendorff-04, Hoegh Duke-01
Kwangtung		Hkg	1985	17,527	21,725	182	27	17	Co	ex CGM Kwangtung-95, Kwangtung-94, Woermann Africa-92, Kwangtung-92, Presidente Jose Pardo-89
Pacific Adventurer		Hkg	1991	18,391	23,737	185	28	18	Co	ex Changsha-05, Pacific Challenger-99
Tasman Endeavour		Cyp	1994	18,451	23,000	185	28	19	Co	ex Caribbean Challenger-03
Tasman Provider		Cyp	1994	18,451	23,683	185	28	19	Co	ex Meridian Challenger-03, Delmas Forbin-02, Meridian Challenger-00

* formerly owned, now on bareboat charter until 2009

Stolt-Nielsen Group. STOLT VALOR. *N. Kemps*

T&E Ship Management. SITAVERA. *N. Kemps*

Teekay Shipping. AXEL SPIRIT. *Hans Kraijenbosch*

Name	Eng	Flag	Year	GRT	DWT	Loa	Bm	Kts	Type	Former names
Bank Line/UK										
Boularibank	Iom	1984	18,663	22,911	174	25	17	Ro	ex Teignbank-06, Nikel-95
Gazellebank	Iom	1983	18,663	22,911	174	25	17	Ro	ex Foylebank-06, Tiksi-95
Mahinabank	Iom	1983	18,663	22,911	174	25	17	Ro	ex Speybank-06, Okha-95
Tikeibank	Iom	1983	18,663	22,911	174	25	17	Ro	ex Arunbank-06, Bratsk-95

Chartered from Andrew Weir Shipping Ltd., UK.

T&E Ship Management Alliance (TESMA) Norway

Funnel: *Black with blue and white diagonally divided shield on broad red band or owners colours.*
Hull: *Grey or brown with red boot-topping.*

Name	Eng	Flag	Year	GRT	DWT	Loa	Bm	Kts	Type	Former names
Difko Chaser *	Nis	1990	43,398	84,040	223	32	15	T	ex Northsea Chaser-01, Burwain Adriatic-95, Zafra-95
Difko Hanne *	Nis	1987	43,733	83,970	229	32	14	T	ex Sitalene-01, Burwain Nordic-95, Nordkap-92
Difko Susanne *	Nis	1989	43,398	84,040	229	32	15	T	ex Northsea Bellows-01, Burwain Arctic-95, Zidona-94
F. Elephant	Pan	1989	143,941	275,984	322	56	14	T	ex World Prospect-04
Marlin *	Mhl	1987	43,733	83,870	229	32	14	T	ex Difko Birtha-05, Sitalouise-01, Burwain Baltic-95, Nordfarer-92
Northsea Anvil *	Dis	1990	43,733	83,790	229	32	15	T	ex Zaphon-95
Samco †	Bhs	1989	142,647	255,087	322	56	14	T	ex Fina Samco-91
Samco America †	Fra	2003	160,889	318,778	333	60	16	T	
Samco Asia †	Mhl	2003	160,889	318,000	333	60	16	T	
Samco Scandinavia †	Mhl	2004	160,000	305,000	333	60	16	T	
Sara Viking *	Nis	1990	43,398	84,040	229	32	14	T	ex Torm Sita-01, Bona Bay-96, Golar Perth-93
Selandia	Dis	1996	30,928	48,800	200	31	14	B	ex Star Selandia-98, Selandia-96
Sigana **	Pan	1985	24,943	42,842	190	30	14	B	ex Spring Gannet-98, Sanko Gannet-86
Sitria **	Bhs	1985	25,221	41,876	187	29	15	B	ex Falstria-97, Star Falstria-96, Falstria-94, FP Clipper-94
Sivega **	Lbr	1985	24,111	41,081	185	30	14	B	ex Spring Vega-98, Sanko Vega-86
Sitacamilla *	Nis	1987	43,406	59,999	229	32	14	T	ex Burwain Pacific-95, Chrisholm-92
Sitakathrine *	Lbr	1986	43,733	83,970	229	32	14	T	ex Burwain Atlantic-95, Nordflex-91
Sitamarie *	Nor	1988	43,406	83,962	229	32	14	T	ex Burwain Scandic-96, Fredholm-91
Sitamia *	Nis	1988	43,414	84,040	229	32	13	T	ex Petrobulk Mars-97
Sitavera *	Lbr	1989	43,414	84,040	229	32	13	T	ex Petrobulk Jupiter-97

newbuildings:
Joint management company following ending of joint ownership company by two families.
*Managed for various owners including * Tesma Denmark AS, Denmark or † Saudi Maritime Holding Co., Saudi Arabia.*

Tschudi Shipping Co AS

Funnel: *As 'TESMA' or blue with eight-pointed white snowflake.*
Hull: *Grey or brown with red boot-topping.*

Name	Eng	Flag	Year	GRT	DWT	Loa	Bm	Kts	Type	Former names
Frea	Irl	2003	11,360	16,484	159	23	-	T	ex Julia-03, I/a Julia V
Nina	Irl	2004	11,400	16,500	159	23	-	T	
Safmarine Houston *	Est	1999	10,069	12,126	137	22	16	Co	ex Harjumaa-03, Didon-02, Harjumaa-99
Safmarine Onne *	Est	1995	10,069	12,126	137	22	16	Co	ex Sakala-03
Sibohelle ‡	Nis	1993	45,593	83,155	247	32	13	Obo	
Sibotessa ‡‡	Nis	1992	41,189	75,075	229	32	14	Obo	ex Vitessa-95

* owned by 100% controlled Estonian Shipping Co. (ESCO).
‡ on long-term bareboat charter from Dansk Investeringsfond or DMK Leasing A/S, Denmark and ‡‡ jointly operated.

Camillo Eitzen & Co AS

Funnel: *Red with white 'E' inside blue 'C' or * white with broad blue band beneath broad black top, some with 'ESO' below band.*
Hull: *Black or red with white 'EITZEN' or 'EITZEN CHEMICAL', red boot-topping.*

Name	Eng	Flag	Year	GRT	DWT	Loa	Bm	Kts	Type	Former names
Sibeia	Nis	1981	50,764	88,726	229	42	15	T	ex Gorbeia-95, Ambra Grey-93, Viking Osprey-89
Siboelf ‡	Nis	1993	41,189	75,075	229	32	14	Obo	
Sibonina ‡	Nis	1993	45,593	83,155	247	32	14	Obo	

‡ on long-term bareboat charter from Dansk Investeringsfond or DMK Leasing A/S, Denmark.

Teekay Shipping Corporation Bahamas

Funnel: *White with blue edged red 'TK' symbol, narrow black top.*
Hull: *Black with red boot-topping.*

Name	Eng	Flag	Year	GRT	DWT	Loa	Bm	Kts	Type	Former names
Aegean Leader Ø	Pan	1993	47,171	13,157	180	32	18	V	ex Ocean Beluga-99, Mercury Diamond-96
Aegean Spirit †	Bhs	2002	62,247	112,668	250	44	15	T	
African Spirit	Bhs	2003	79,668	151,736	269	46	-	T	

Name	Eng	Flag	Year	GRT	DWT	Loa	Bm	Kts	Type	Former names
Algeciras Spirit		Cni	2000	83,724	160,240	274	48	15	T	ex Nuria Tapias-04
Americas Spirit		Bhs	2003	63,213	111,920	256	45	-	T	I/dn Limerick Spirit
Asian Spirit		Bhs	2004	79,668	151,693	269	46	-	T	
Australian Spirit		Bhs	2004	63,213	111,942	256	45	-	T	
Avalon Spirit		Can	1998	57,925	107,181	236	42	-	T	ex Nassau Spirit-02
Axel Spirit		Bhs	2004	62,929	115,392	250	44	-	T	
Barrington **		Aus	1989	21,718	33,239	181	27	14	T	ex Australia Sky-96
Basker Spirit		Bhs	1992	56,020	97,069	241	41	14	T	ex Navion Basker-05, Nordic Yukon-05, Wilma Yukon-01, Wilomi Yukon-96
Catalunya Spirit	(st)	Cni	2003	90,942	72,204	284	43	19	Lng	ex Inigo Tapias-04
Chios Spirit †		Bhs	2002	62,247	112,679	250	44	-	T	ex Golden Star-02
Columbia Spirit		Bhs	1988	49,279	84,841	234	44	15	T	ex Bona Skipper-99, Ocean Explorer-94
Delos **		Aus	2004	25,124	37,000	176	31	-	T	
Erik Spirit		Bhs	2005	63,500	114,750	296	46	-	T	
Esther Spirit		Bhs	2004	62,929	115,444	250	44	-	T	
European Spirit		Bhs	2003	79,668	151,848	269	46	-	T	ex Cork Spirit-03
Everest Spirit		Bhs	2004	62,845	115,048	250	44	-	T	
Falster Spirit		Bhs	1995	52,875	95,317	244	42	14	T	ex Bona Rover-99, Vendonna-96
Fountain Spirit		Nis	1982	44,834	78,488	243	32	14	Obo	ex Teekay Fountain-03, Bona Fountain-99, Hoegh Fountain-92
Fuji Spirit		Bhs	2003	57,664	106,360	241	42	-	T	
Galicia Spirit		Cni	2004	94,822	76,500	280	43	19	Lng	
Goonyella Trader **		Lbr	1996	85,437	170,873	289	45	14	B	
Gotland Spirit		Bhs	1995	52,875	95,317	244	42	14	T	ex Bona Rider-99, Venessa-96
Hamane Spirit		Bhs	1997	57,463	105,203	245	41	14	T	
Helga Spirit		Bhs	2005	62,929	115,444	250	44	-	T	
Hispania Spirit		Cni	2004	94,822	79,363	280	43	19	Lng	ex Fernando Tapias-04
Hudson Spirit		Bhs	1988	49,279	84,841	234	44	15	T	ex Bona Spinner-99, Ocean Navigator-94
Ionian Spirit †		Bhs	2002	62,247	112,664	250	44	15	T	
Iron Yandi **		Aus	1996	82,306	109,960	289	46	14	B	
Kanata Spirit		Bhs	1999	62,685	113,021	249	44	14	T	
Kareela Spirit		Bhs	1999	62,685	113,021	249	44	14	T	
Karratha Spirit **		Aus	1988	59,289	106,671	257	43	14	T	ex Pioneer Spirit-02
Kilimanjaro Spirit		Bhs	2004	62,845	115,048	250	44	-	T	
Koyagi Spirit		Bhs	1989	52,787	95,983	232	42	15	T	
Kyeema Spirit		Bhs	1999	62,619	113,357	253	44	14	T	I/a Bona Vigour
Kyushu Spirit		Bhs	1991	53,988	95,562	233	42	14	T	
Leyte Spirit		Bhs	1992	57,440	98,744	245	41	14	T	
Lotus		Bhs	1991	57,450	100,314	245	41	14	T	ex Palmstar Lotus-05
Luzon Spirit		Bhs	1992	57,448	98,629	245	41	14	T	
Madrid Spirit	(st)	Cni	2004	90,835	77,213	284	43	19	Lng	ex Ivan Tapias-04
Matterhorn Spirit		Bhs	2005	63,694	114,834	254	44	-	T	
Mayon Spirit		Bhs	1992	57,448	98,507	245	41	14	T	
Nobel Foam		Bhs	1981	45,777	78,532	243	32	14	Obo	ex Foam Spirit-04, Teekay Foam-03, Bona Foam-99, Hoegh Foam-92
Nobel Fortuna		Nis	1982	45,777	78,532	243	32	14	Obo	ex Fortuna Spirit-04, Teekay Fortuna-03, Bona Fortuna-99, Hoegh Fortuna-92, Ambia Fortuna-89, Hoegh Fortuna-86
Nobel Forum		Bhs	1983	45,777	78,394	243	32	14	Obo	ex Forum Spirit-04, Teekay Forum-03, Bona Forum-99, Hoegh Forum-92
Nordic Spirit §		Bhs	2001	83,120	152,292	274	48	15	T	ex Storviken-02
Ocean Princess ‡		Bhs	1981	46,801	82,462	247	32	15	Obo	ex Bona Falcon-97, Hoegh Falcon-92
Oinoussian Spirit †		Bhs	2002	62,247	112,661	250	44	15	T	I/a Golden Sea
Orchid		Bhs	1989	57,450	100,047	245	41	14	T	ex Palmstar Orchid-05
Orkney Spirit		Bhs	1993	55,864	106,233	244	42	14	T	ex Bona Spray-99
Pacific Spirit		Bhs	1988	59,289	106,661	244	43	14	T	
Pacific Triangle **		Lbr	2000	100,330	184,744	300	50	14	B	
Palmerston **		Aus	1990	26,162	36,701	179	32	14	T	ex Ampol TVA-96
Palmstar Cherry		Bhs	1990	57,450	100,024	245	41	14	T	
Palmstar Rose		Bhs	1990	57,450	100,202	245	41	14	T	
Palmstar Thistle		Bhs	1991	57,450	100,047	245	41	14	T	
Poppy		Bhs	1990	57,450	100,031	245	41	14	T	ex Palmstar Poppy-05
Poul Spirit		Bhs	1995	57,463	105,351	245	41	14	T	
Rainier Spirit		Bhs	2005	62,877	114,880	250	44	-	T	
Sabine Spirit		Bhs	1989	49,279	84,841	234	44	15	T	ex Bona Shimmer-99, Ocean Leader-94
Samar Spirit **		Bhs	1992	57,448	98,640	245	41	14	T	
Saraji Trader **		Lbr	1997	85,616	169,907	289	45	14	B	

Name	Eng	Flag	Year	GRT	DWT	Loa	Bm	Kts	Type	Former names
Seahawk Freighter ‡		Mhl	1982	45,067	75,395	243	32	15	Obo	ex Freighter Spirit-04, Teekay Freighter-03, Bona Freighter-99, Hoegh Freighter-92, Siboseven-89
Sebarok Spirit		Bhs	1993	52,508	95,649	247	42	14	T	
Seletar Spirit		Bhs	1988	57,764	94,998	247	42	14	T	ex Pacific Mercury-98
Semakau Spirit		Bhs	1988	52,484	97,172	247	42	14	T	ex Nissos Amorgos-96, Seto Breeze-95
Senang Spirit		Bhs	1994	52,508	95,649	247	42	14	T	
Sentosa Spirit		Bhs	1989	52,500	97,159	247	42	14	T	
Seraya Spirit		Bhs	1992	52,507	97,119	247	42	14	T	
Shetland Spirit		Bhs	1994	55,864	106,263	244	42	14	T	ex Bona Sailor-99
Shilla Spirit		Bhs	1990	59,289	106,679	244	43	14	T	
Sotra Spirit		Bhs	1995	52,875	95,370	244	42	14	T	ex Bona Robin-99, Ventina-96
Stena Spirit		Bhs	2001	83,120	152,244	274	48	15	T	ex Erviken-01
Teide Spirit		Pmd	2004	83,594	159,426	274	48	15	T	
Tenerife Spirit		Cni	2000	83,724	160,373	274	48	15	T	ex Bosco Tapias-04
Toledo Spirit		Pmd	2005	83,724	159,342	274	48	-	T	
Torben Spirit		Bhs	1994	57,486	98,622	245	41	14	T	
Torres Spirit		Bhs	1990	54,963	96,144	242	42	14	T	ex Sanko Pioneer-97
Ulsan Spirit		Bhs	1990	59,289	106,679	244	43	14	T	
Vancouver Spirit		Bhs	1992	63,709	103,203	244	42	-	Obo	
Victoria Spirit		Bhs	1993	63,709	103,153	244	42	-	Obo	

newbuildings: twelve tankers on order between 76,000-115,000 dwt for 2006-8 delivery.
* owned by Teekay Shipping Ltd., Bahamas, ** by Teekay Shipping (Australia) Pty. Ltd, Australia or *** by Teekay Shipping (Japan) Ltd, Japan.
‡ managed by V.Ships Norway A/S, § by Viken Ship Management AS, Norway or † owned by Chartworld Shipping Corp., Greece.
Ø on charter to NYK q.v.   Also see Star Reefers AS

Teekay Marine Services/Norway

Funnel: *White with blue and red coloured/striped rectangle, black top.*
Hull: *Orange or dark blue with 'Navion' towards stern, red boot-topping.*

Name	Eng	Flag	Year	GRT	DWT	Loa	Bm	Kts	Type	Former names
Gulf Scandic **		Iom	1997	80,187	151,459	274	46	14	T	ex British Harrier-04
Navion Akarita ***		Bhs	1991	58,928	107,223	244	42	14	T	ex Nordic Akarita-05, Stena Akarita-02, Akarita-96
Navion Anglia	(2)	Nor	1999	72,449	126,749	265	43	15	T	
Navion Britannia	(2)	Nor	1998	72,110	124,821	265	43	15	T	
Navion Clipper ***		Bhs	1993	42,159	78,228	221	38	14	T	ex Polyclipper-98
Navion Fennia		Bhs	1992	50,907	96,058	241	40	14	T	ex Futura-03
Navion Hispania	(2)	Nor	1999	72,132	126,749	265	43	14	T	
Navion Oceania	(2)	Nor	1999	72,132	126,749	265	43	14	T	
Navion Saga ***		Bhs	1991	79,918	149,000	269	46	14	T	ex Polysaga-00
Navion Scandia	(2)	Nor	1998	72,132	126,749	265	43	14	T	
Navion Scotia		Nis	1993	52,348	95,029	238	42	14	T	ex Vinga-98
Nordic Discovery **		Nis	1998	79,669	153,328	269	46	14	T	ex Front Hunter-05
Nordic Fighter **		Nis	1998	79,669	153,328	269	46	14	T	ex Front Fighter-05
Nordic Freedom **		Bhs	2005	83,594	159,331	274	48	14	T	
Nordic Hawk **		Iom	1997	80,187	151,400	274	46	14	T	ex British Hawk-04
Nordic Hunter **		Iom	1997	80,100	151,400	274	46	14	T	ex British Hunter-04
Nordic Laurita		Nis	1981	42,575	68,139	244	32	15	T	ex Nordic Challenger-97, Houston Accord-89
Nordic Marita *		Cym	1999	58,117	103,894	246	42	14	T	
Nordic Rio		Bhs	2004	83,120	151,294	277	48	14	T	
Nordic Saturn **		Mhl	1998	81,565	157,331	274	48	14	T	ex Sabine-05
Nordic Savonita		Nis	1992	58,959	108,153	244	42	15	T	ex Stena Savonita-97, Savonita-94
Nordic Stavanger		Bhs	2003	80,691	148,729	277	46	14	T	
Nordic Svenita *		Bhs	1997	58,269	106,506	250	42	14	T	ex Svenner-98
Nordic Torinita *		Cym	1992	58,959	108,683	244	42	14	T	ex Torinita-96
Nordic Trym *		Nis	1987	45,104	80,745	229	32	14	T	ex Petrotrym-03, Primo-95, Osco Beduin-89
Petroatlantic ‡		Bhs	2003	54,865	92,968	235	42	14	T	
Petronordic ‡		Bhs	2002	54,885	92,995	234	42	14	T	
Petroskald *		Lbr	1982	23,174	39,750	174	32	14	T	ex Oktelia-86
Stena Natalita	(2)	Cym	2001	62,393	108,073	250	43	14	T	
Venture Spirit †		Hkg	2003	159,456	298,287	333	60	15	T	
Wilma Yangtze		Nis	1996	79,494	149,591	270	45	15	T	

98% owned except three owned jointly with Stena. * managed by IUM Shipmanagement AS, Norway
** owned by Nordic American Tanker Shipping Ltd. (managed by Scandic American Shipping, Bermuda) *** part owned by Overseas ShipholdingCorp and †
operated for Wah Kwong, Hong Kong. ‡ manged for PGS Production AS, Norway

Teekay Shipping. KOYAGI SPIRIT. *Hans Kraijenbosch*

Dampskib. Torm. TORM SIGNE. *N. Kemps*

Rederi AB Transatlantic. OSTRAND. *Hans Kraijenbosch*

Name	Eng	Flag	Year	GRT	DWT	Loa	Bm	Kts	Type	Former names

Thien & Heyenga GmbH   Germany

Funnel: Buff with houseflag (black over red with white 'T&H' over blue bands or charterers colours.
Hull: Black, grey, red or blue with red boot-topping.

Name	Eng	Flag	Year	GRT	DWT	Loa	Bm	Kts	Type	Former names
EWL Curacao	Deu	1998	9,528	12,920	146	23	20	CC	ex Stadt Dusseldorf-03, Sea-Land Guatemala-99, Stadt Dusseldorf-99
EWL Rotterdam	Deu	2003	9,528	13,760	148	23	20	CC	ex Tharos-03, I/a Stadt Bremen
Fas Gulf	Gib	1998	9,528	12,850	146	23	20	CC	ex Stadt Hamburg-03, Pelor-02, Stadt Hamburg-01, Cala Pilar-01, Stadt Hamburg-00
Glacier Bay *	Atg	1985	8,739	9,746	144	22	17	R	ex Cap Verde-95, Causewaybay-89, Cap Delgado-89
Green Costa Rica *	Atg	1991	7,743	7,726	131	20	19	R	ex Prince-06, Crystal Prince-04
Green Guatemala *	Bhs	1992	7,743	7,726	131	20	19	R	ex Primadonna-05, Crystal Primadonna-04
Green Honduras *	Lbr	1992	7,743	7,721	131	20	19	R	ex Pride-06, Crystal Pride-03
Hudson Bay *	Atg	1983	8,052	8,945	140	21	17	R	ex Kiwi-99, Central Reefer-95, Southern Laurel-90, Southern Universal-88
Melfi Halifax	Atg	1999	14,241	18,440	159	24	18	CC	ex MSC Ireland-04, Jork Venture-02, I/a Armin, I/d Stadt Schwerin
Melfi Havana	Atg	2003	9,528	12,920	146	23	20	CC	ex Alassa-03, I/a Stadt Flensburg
Melfi Italia II	Atg	2003	9,528	12,920	146	23	20	CC	ex Pirsos-03, I/a Stadt Rotenburg
New Confidence	Pan	2001	13,764	16,400	155	25	19	CC	I/a Stadt Lubeck
Nova Galicia *	Ant	1983	6,149	6,730	138	19	17	R	ex Sun Princess-96, Sun Field-94
Sable Bay *	Ant	1983	8,739	9,746	144	22	17	R	ex Santorini Rex-96, Cap Valiente-91, Cap Domingo-89
Seaboxer	Mlt	1994	16,749	24,024	183	28	19	CC	ex Nantai Venus-99
Stadt Berlin	Atg	1998	9,528	12,920	146	23	20	CC	ex Mekong Sapphire-01, Stadt Berlin-01
Stadt Emden	Atg	2002	9,528	12,920	146	23	20	CC	ex P&O Nedlloyd Araucania-05, MOL Rainbow-03, Lania-02, Stadt Emden-02
Stadt Munchen	Atg	1999	9,528	12,920	146	23	20	CC	ex P&O Nedlloyd Muisca-05, Stadt Munchen-03

newbuildings: two 34,800 grt (Stadt Aachen and Stadt Koeln), four 28,400 grt and four 17,000 grt container ships for 2006-7 delivery.
* chartered to Seatrade Groningen BV q.v.

Alfred C Toepfer KG Schiffahrts GmbH   Germany

Funnel: White with two narrow green bands above and below large green 'T' beneath black top, or charterers colours.
Hull: Black or green with red boot-topping.

Name	Eng	Flag	Year	GRT	DWT	Loa	Bm	Kts	Type	Former names
CP Achiever	Bmu	1987	40,439	40,870	270	32	20	CC	ex Lykes Achiever-05, Ming Pleasure-01
CP Hermosillo	Bmu	1986	40,447	40,744	270	32	20	CC	ex TMM Hermosillo-05, Ming Propitious-01
CP Jalisco	Bmu	1988	40,436	40,845	270	32	20	CC	ex TMM Jalisco-05, Ming Progress-01
MSC Lugano	Pan	1988	35,958	42,795	241	32	21	CC	ex CSCL Bremen-04, Choyang Success-01

Tonnevold Shipping AS   Norway

Funnel: Blue with broad white band or charterers colours.
Hull: White or charterers colours, red boot-topping.

Name	Eng	Flag	Year	GRT	DWT	Loa	Bm	Kts	Type	Former names
Maersk Rimini *	Bhs	1990	10,868	15,174	158	23	18	CC	ex Estestar-04, Safmarine Shebeli-03, Estestar-02, P&O Nedlloyd Kowie-01, Estestar-00, Kent Scout-00, Ulf Ritscher-98
Maersk Tacoma	Hkg	1982	37,238	44,142	241	32	24	CC	ex Luna Maersk-96, Newport Bay-92, Luna Maersk-91
Maersk Toledo	Iom	1985	43,332	53,325	270	32	22	CC	ex Lindo Maersk-00, Mc-Kinney Maersk-90
Maersk Trieste	Bhs	1983	43,332	53,310	270	32	24	CC	ex Leise Maersk-99, Regina Maersk-95
Thorbjorg	Pan	1993	7,313	8,045	134	21	19	R	ex Pentland Phoenix-05
Thordis	Pan	1982	6,070	6,348	146	18	17	R	ex Stork V-96, Suzuran-88
Thorgull	Bhs	1983	6,127	6,325	146	18	17	R	ex Reefer Penguin-96
Thorunn	Pan	1982	6,089	6,369	146	18	17	R	ex Calamo-96, Hamanasu-88

* managed by Anglo-Eastern UK Ltd.

A/S Dampskibsselskabet Torm   Denmark

Funnel: Black with blue 'T' on broad white band between two broad red bands.
Hull: Black or grey with red boot-topping.

Name	Eng	Flag	Year	GRT	DWT	Loa	Bm	Kts	Type	Former names
Potrero del Llano II ‡	Mex	1999	28,546	47,165	183	32	14	T	ex Torm Agnete-05, Zorca-04
Torm Alice	Dis	1995	28,628	47,629	183	32	14	T	
Torm Ann-Marie	Dis	1997	57,031	99,990	244	42	15	T	
Torm Anna	Dis	2004	42,432	75,000	225	32	14	T	

Name	Eng	Flag	Year	GRT	DWT	Loa	Bm	Kts	Type	Former names
Torm Anne ‡		Sgp	1999	28,932	45,507	180	32	14	T	
Torm Arawa ‡		Lbr	1997	18,108	29,096	175	26	14	B	
Torm Asia ‡		Sgp	1994	25,190	44,372	180	30	14	T	
Torm Baltic ‡		Sgp	1997	36,592	69,614	225	32	14	B	ex Navios Minerva-02
Torm Estrid		Dis	2004	42,432	74,999	225	32	14	T	
Torm Freya		Dis	2003	30,058	46,342	183	32	14	T	
Torm Gerd		Dis	2002	30,058	46,300	183	32	14	T	
Torm Gertrud		Dis	2002	30,058	46,362	183	32	14	T	
Torm Gotland		Dis	1995	28,628	47,629	183	32	14	T	
Torm Gudrun *		Lbr	2000	57,031	99,965	244	42	14	T	
Torm Gunhild		Dis	1999	28,909	45,457	181	32	14	T	
Torm Helene		Dis	1997	57,031	99,900	244	42	14	T	
Torm Helvig		Dis	2005	30,018	46,187	183	32	14	T	
Torm Herdis		Nis	1992	36,540	69,618	225	32	14	B	ex Santa Teresa-03, Navios Mariner-02
Torm Ingeborg		Nis	2003	57,095	99,900	244	42	14	T	
Torm Ismini		Dis	2004	42,432	74,999	228	32	15	T	
Torm Kristina *		Lbr	1999	57,080	105,002	244	42	14	T	
Torm Marina		Nis	1990	36,573	69,637	225	32	14	D	
Torm Marlene ‡		Sgp	1997	36,592	69,548	225	32	14	B	
Torm Marta		Pan	1997	36,592	69,638	225	32	14	B	
Torm Mary		Dis	2002	30,058	46,634	183	32	14	T	
Torm Pacific		Sgp	1997	18,108	29,071	175	26	14	B	
Torm Ragnhild		Lbr	2004	40,000	75,000	225	32	14	T	
Torm Rotna ‡		Sgp	2001	40,072	75,971	225	32	14	B	
Torm Sara ‡		Sgp	2003	41,690	72,718	228	32	15	T	ex Penyu Agar-05
Torm Signe		Sgp	2005	41,503	72,718	228	32	15	T	ex Penyu Siskl-05
Torm Sofia		Sgp	2005	41,503	72,650	228	32	15	T	ex Penyu Daun-05
Torm Tekla		Nis	1993	36,952	69,268	225	32	13	B	
Torm Thyra		Dis	2003	30,058	46,308	183	32	14	T	
Torm Tina ‡		Sgp	2001	40,030	75,966	225	32	14	B	
Torm Valborg		Nis	2003	57,095	99,900	244	42	14	T	
Torm Vita		Dis	2002	30,058	46,308	183	32	14	T	

newbuildings eight 61,000 grt 110,000 dwt tankers due for 2006-8 delivery from Chinese builders
30% owned by Beltest Shipping Co. Ltd.,, Cyprus and owns 32% of Dampskibsselskabet 'Norden' A/S, Denmark q.v..
* owned by Torm Shipping (Germany) GmbH, † by Torm Asia Ltd, Hong Kong or ‡ by Torm Singapore (Pte.) Ltd.
Torm Pool of product tankers comprises nearly 100 vessels.

Rederi AB Transatlantic   Sweden

Funnel: White with blue circular symbol on broad yellow band between narrow blue bands.
Hull: Grey or white with red boot-topping

Name	Eng	Flag	Year	GRT	DWT	Loa	Bm	Kts	Type	Former names
Ada Gorthon		Swe	1984	13,525	11,425	156	22	15	Ro	
Alida Gorthon		Swe	1977	12,750	14,240	141	22	15	B	
Anna Oden	(2)	Swe	1979	16,947	8,400	170	21	15	Ro	ex Southern Carrier-02, Tor Flandria-98, Anna Oden-88 (len-88)
Finnfighter		Swe	2001	18,286	15,092	159	26	17	Ro	
Finnpine		Swe	2002	18,286	14,100	159	26	17	Ro	
Finnwood		Swe	2002	18,286	15,092	159	26	17	Ro	
Ingrid Gorthon		Swe	1977	12,750	14,298	141	22	15	B	
Joh. Gorthon		Swe	1977	11,907	7,182	142	21	15	Ro	
Margit Gorthon		Bmu	1977	12,672	14,240	141	22	15	B	
Maria Gorthon		Swe	1984	13,533	11,491	156	22	15	Ro	
Obbola		Swe	1996	20,186	9,589	156	24	16	Ro	
Ortviken		Swe	1996	20,154	9,618	156	24	16	Ro	
Ostrand		Swe	1996	18,265	9,618	156	24	16	Ro	
Tofton		Nis	1980	12,409	14,883	159	21	16	C	ex Pokkinen-96
Viola Gorthon		Swe	1987	18,773	10,917	166	23	20	Ro	

newbuildings - three 25,000 grt 15,000 dwt ro-ro vessels on order for 2006 delivery from Finnish builder.
Formed by merger of Gorthon Lines and B&N Nordsjofrakt, part owned by Leif Hoegh & Co. ASA (49.98%) and all managed by Transatlantic Fleet Services AB
except ** owned by Dutch subsidiary BV Kustvaartbedrijf Moerman.

Transeste Schiffahrt GmbH   Germany

Funnel: Mainly in charterers colours.
Hull: Black, dark grey, blue or red with red boot-topping.

Name	Eng	Flag	Year	GRT	DWT	Loa	Bm	Kts	Type	Former names
Birte Ritscher **		Atg	1995	14,862	20,346	167	25	19	CC	ex Cala Piedad-02, Kaduna-00, TNX Express-98, Zim Argentina 2-98, CCNI Anakena-96, Birte Ritscher-95

Transeste Schiffahrt. NYK ESPIRITO (in charterers colours). *J. M. Kakebeeke*

TransPetrol Maritime. TENACITY. *C. Lous*

Trireme Vessel Management. BARRINGTON ISLAND. *Hans Kraijenbosch*

Tsakos Shipping & Trading. EURONIKE. *Hans Kraijenbosch*

United Arab Shipping Co. ASIR. *Hans Kraijenbosch*

United Thai Shipping. PATTAYA NAVEE. *J. M. Kakebeeke*

Name	Eng	Flag	Year	GRT	DWT	Loa	Bm	Kts	Type	Former names
Estetrader *		Atg	1993	14,953	20,140	167	25	18	CC	ex City of Oxford-03, Kent Courier-01, Seaboard Toronto-00, Keta-00, Wieland-98, Exporter-97, Red Sea Exporter-95, Wieland-94
Hanjin Dubai *		Atg	1999	25,705	33,843	208	30	22	CC	ex Trade Bravery-05, TPL Merchant-02, Lykes Crusader-01
Helle Ritscher		Atg	2006	17,350	22,200	179	28	21	CC	
MOL Satisfaction **		Atg	1999	25,705	33,750	208	30	22	CC	ex Trade Zale-05, TPL Eagle-02, TMM San Antonio-01, Jan Ritscher-99
Norasia Andes		Lbr	2004	35,881	42,300	220	32	22	CC	ex Anke Ritscher-04
Norasia Polaris		Lbr	2004	35,881	42,000	221	32	22	CC	ex Wieland-04
NYK Espirito		Deu	2001	25,705	33,795	208	30	22	CC	ex Sea Tiger-04, I/a Ulf Ritscher
Wotan		Deu	2001	25,703	33,795	208	30	22	CC	ex MSC Venezuela-03, I/a Wotan

newbuildings: one further 17,350 grt 22,200 dwt container ship due for 2006 delivery.
Managed for owning partner companies * Reederei Dietrich Tamke K.G. or ** Reederei Gerd Ritscher K.G., both Germany

TransPetrol Maritime Services NV   Belgium

Funnel: Black with white 'tp' above white vertical lines.
Hull: Black with grey or blue boot-topping.

		Flag	Year	GRT	DWT	Loa	Bm	Kts	Type	Former names
Affinity		Sgp	2005	42,661	73,741	228	32	15	T	
Endeavour		Sgp	2004	30,032	46,101	183	32	14	T	
Endurance		Sgp	1988	22,847	39,988	182	27	-	T	
Eternity		Sgp	1988	22,847	39,834	182	27	15	T	
Faith IV *		Sgp	1987	39,131	63,765	229	32	14	T	ex Argo Asia-93
Loyalty *		Pan	1985	43,363	75,992	229	32	15	T	ex A.C. Atom-93, Toluma-89
Perseverance		Sgp	2005	42,661	73,788	228	32	15	T	
Resolve		Sgp	2004	30,032	46,048	183	32	14	T	
Rowan		Bhs	1991	24,731	44,646	182	30	14	T	
Tenacity		Sgp	1996	53,371	87,240	228	42	15	T	
Trader		Sgp	1987	39,212	63,765	229	32	14	T	ex Ace Trader-97
Turmoil		Sgp	1988	22,487	39,872	186	27	14	T	
Venture		Sgp	1985	43,368	76,000	229	32	14	T	ex Wilanna-90

newbuildings: one 30,600 grt 45,800 dwt tanker on order for 2006 delivery.
* managed by International Tanker Management Holding Ltd., UAE.

Trireme Vessel Management NV   Belgium

Funnel: Dark blue with yellow 'EL' on red disc.
Hull: Orange with red boot-topping.

		Flag	Year	GRT	DWT	Loa	Bm	Kts	Type	Former names
Albemarle Island		Bhs	1993	14,061	14,160	179	25	21	R	
Arctic Ocean		Bhs	1989	10,829	10,303	151	22	22	R	
Atlantic Ocean		Bhs	1989	10,829	10,285	151	22	22	R	
Baltic Sea		Bhs	1973	6,892	9,072	141	18	22	R	ex Provincia del Guayas-95, Ciudad de Guayaquil-88, Lucky I-84, Lucky-84, Timur Girl-83, Hilco Girl-81, Golar Girl-77
Barrington Island		Bhs	1993	14,061	14,140	179	25	21	R	
Bering Sea		Bhs	1975	9,618	9,744	153	21	-	R	ex Punta Bianca-94
Celtic Sea		Bhs	1970	9,869	11,902	166	21	22	R	ex Provincia de los Rios-95, Indian Ocean-84, Nippon Reefer-78
Charles Island *		Bhs	1993	14,061	14,140	179	25	21	R	
Coral Sea		Bhs	1976	9,618	9,748	153	21	-	R	ex Punta Verde-94
Duncan Island *		Bhs	1993	14,061	14,140	179	25	21	R	
Hood Island *		Bhs	1994	14,601	14,140	179	25	21	R	
Indian Ocean		Bhs	1989	10,829	10,313	151	22	22	R	

* on long-term bareboat charter from Dansk Investeringsfond, Denmark.

Tsakos Shipping & Trading SA   Greece

Funnel: Yellow with red 'T' on broadwhite band edged with narrow blue bands.
Hull: Black with red boot-topping.

		Flag	Year	GRT	DWT	Loa	Bm	Kts	Type	Former names
Alaska *		Grc	2006	82,250	162,400	274	50	-	T	
Andes *		Grc	2003	39,085	68,439	229	32	14	T	
Antares *		Grc	2006	23,240	36,660	183	27	-	T	
Aramis		Lbr	1983	37,895	60,906	228	32	15	T	ex Hydra Mar-98, Caribbean Shoot II-90
Archangel *		Grc	2006	82,250	162,400	274	50	-	T	
Athens 2004 *		Grc	1998	57,925	107,181	247	42	14	T	

Name	Eng	Flag	Ycar	GRT	DWT	Loa	Bm	Kts	Type	Former names
Atlantida		Lbr	1980	53,944	87,542	243	42	14	T	ex Canadian Liberty-97, Columbia Liberty-85
Aztec *		Grc	2003	39,085	68,439	229	32	14	T	
Bregen *		Mlt	1989	38,792	68,160	243	32	15	T	
Crux *		Grc	1987	23,926	41,161	172	32	14	T	ex Neptune Crux-99
Dartagnan		Cyp	1984	36,706	61,762	229	32	14	T	ex Centaurus Mar-98, Fumi-90
Delphi *		Grc	2004	23,500	37,000	176	31	-	T	
Didimon *		Grc	2004	25,124	37,432	176	31	-	T	ex Dodoni-05
El Junior		Pan	1995	149,896	260,870	335	58	15	T	ex Tohzan-03
Eurochampion 2004 *		Grc	2005	85,431	164,000	274	50	-	T	
Euronike *		Grc	2005	85,431	164,000	274	50	-	T	
Hanjin Elizabeth		Pan	1992	50,792	62,723	290	32	24	CC	ex Hanjin Barcelona-05
Hanjin Irene		Pan	1994	50,792	62,742	290	32	24	CC	ex Hanjin Tokyo-05
Hesnes *		Mlt	1990	38,792	68,157	243	32	14	T	
Inca *		Grc	2003	39,085	68,439	229	32	14	T	
Irenes Logos		Pan	1995	18,716	24,370	194	28	20	CC	ex Ise-02
Irenes Myth		Cyp	1983	31,356	30,941	220	32	22	CC	ex Global Myth-02, Irenes Myth-97, California Triton-97, Japan Alliance-91
Irenes Rainbow		Grc	2006	27,779	39,000	222	30	23	CC	
Irenes Reliance		Grc	2005	28,592	39,396	222	30	23	CC	
Irenes Remedy		Grc	2005	28,592	39,382	222	30	23	CC	
Irenes Vigor		Cyp	1983	35,603	65,224	224	32	16	B	ex Global Vigor-02, Irenes Vigor-97, Oakby-97, Continental Reliance-92
Irenes Vision		Cyp	1982	76,055	145,177	273	43	13	B	ex Sabina-94, Shiraishi Maru-89
La Esperanza *		Pan	1993	158,475	299,700	344	56	14	T	ex Ehm Maersk-03, British Valour-02, Elisabeth Maersk-97
La Madrina *		Grc	1993	158,475	299,700	344	56	14	T	ex Maersk Estelle-04, Estelle Maersk-98
La Paz *		Pan	1995	158,475	299,700	344	56	14	T	ex Evelyn Maersk-03
La Prudencia		Grc	1992	158,475	298,900	344	56	14	T	ex Maersk Eleo-04, Eleo Maersk-98
Libra *		Grc	1988	23,926	41,161	172	32	14	T	ex NOL Libra-99, Neptune Libra-96
Marathon *		Grc	2003	58,127	107,181	247	42	14	T	
Maria Tsakos *		Grc	1998	57,925	107,181	247	42	14	T	
Maya *		Grc	2003	39,085	68,439	229	32	14	T	
Millennium *		Pan	1998	156,692	301,171	331	58	15	T	
MSC Brasilia		Grc	1986	35,598	43,270	241	32	21	CC	ex Kobe-02, Hanjin Kobe-02
MSC London		Cyp	1986	36,266	43,270	241	32	21	CC	ex Keelung-03, Hanjin Keelung-02
MSC Sardinia		Cyp	1986	36,270	42,880	241	32	22	CC	ex Hong Kong-03, Hanjin Hongkong-03
Oceanida		Cyp	1980	53,917	87,307	243	42	14	T	ex Rosby-99, Crosby-99, Mega Pilot-91, Bergen Pilot-89, Mega Pilot-88, Glorie-88
Olympia *		Cyp	1999	57,925	107,181	247	42	14	T	
Opal Queen *		Pan	2001	57,920	107,181	247	42	14	T	
Parthenon *		Grc	2003	58,157	107,081	247	42	14	T	
Porthos		Cyp	1981	37,758	65,779	228	32	14	T	ex Pegasus Erre-98, Loire-89, Fairfield Phoenix-86, Fairfield Venture-86
SCI Vijay		Lbr	1991	37,410	47,273	236	32	18	CC	ex Australia Bridge-06, Australian Endurance-96
Silia T *		Grc	2002	84,586	164,286	274	50	15	T	
Triathlon *		Grc	2002	84,586	164,445	274	50	14	T	
Vergina II *		Cyp	1991	53,569	96,709	247	42	14	T	ex Lark Lake-95
Victory III *		Ven	1990	38,798	68,157	243	32	15	T	ex Ryvingen-95

newbuildings: two 162,400 dwt (Arctic and Antarctic), two 105,000 dwt and five more 36,600 dwt (Arion, Andromeda, Aegeas, Byzantion and Bosporos)) tankers, one 73,800 dwt Lng tanker plus three 39,000 dwt (Irenes Resolve, Irenes Respect and Irenes Relief) container ships due for 2006/7 delivery
* managed by Tsakos Enegry Management Ltd. (TEN), Greece.
Reported to have agreed to purchase vessels operated by Western Petroleum qv.

Ugland Marine Services AS   Norway

Funnel: Yellow with white 'U' on broad red band below black top.
Hull: Grey, black or orange with black or white 'UGLAND', green or red boot-topping.

Name	Eng	Flag	Ycar	GRT	DWT	Loa	Bm	Kts	Type	Former names
Benarita		Nis	1984	23,594	40,688	183	30	14	B	ex Yuming-91, Sanko Elegance-91
Ellenita		Pan	1984	24,942	42,836	190	30	14	B	ex Golden Topaz-97, Samar Sampaguita-90, Diamond Azalea-89, New Azalea-87, Sanko Azalea-85
Evita		Nor	1989	72,120	126,352	260	46	14	T	
Fermita		Pan	2001	30,053	52,380	190	32	14	B	
Gerrita *		Nis	1990	60,866	112,046	243	43	14	T	ex Dicto-97, Dicto Knutsen-94
Jorita		Nis	1985	23,981	36,726	179	31	14	B	
Juanita *	(2)	Nor	1988	72,129	126,491	260	46	14	T	ex Lisita-89
Livanita		Pan	1997	26,044	45,426	186	30	15	B	

Name	Eng	Flag	Year	GRT	DWT	Loa	Bm	Kts	Type	Former names
Mattea †	(2)	Can	1997	76,216	126,380	272	46	15	T	
Rosita		Nis	2004	30,076	52,292	190	32	14	B	
Tamarita		Pan	2001	30,053	52,292	190	32	14	B	
Vinland †		Can	2000	76,567	125,827	272	46	14	T	

newbuildings: one 30,400 grt bulk carrier on order.
*Managed * for P/R Nordshuttle DA, Norway. † owned by Canship Ugland Ltd formed jointly with Canship Ltd. Also see Stena AB.*

United Arab Shipping Co (SAG)   Kuwait

Funnel: *Black, broad white band with red/purple bands above and black/green bands below black 6-spoked wheel containing black crossed anchors on blue centre disc.*
Hull: *Light grey with black 'UASC', green band over red boot-topping.*

Name	Flag	Year	GRT	DWT	Loa	Bm	Kts	Type	Former names
Abu Dhabi	Are	1998	48,154	49,844	277	32	24	CC	
Addiriyah	Sau	1979	20,526	24,272	183	27	17	CC	
Al Ihsa'a	Sau	1983	32,534	35,615	211	32	19	CC	
Al Manakh	Kwt	1983	32,534	35,615	211	32	19	CC	
Al Mariyah	Are	1983	32,534	35,615	211	32	19	CC	
Al Mirqab	Kwt	1983	32,534	35,615	211	32	19	CC	
Al Noof	Qat	1998	48,154	49,993	277	32	24	CC	
Al Wajba	Qat	1983	32,534	35,615	211	32	19	CC	
Al-Abdali	Kwt	1998	48,154	49,844	277	32	24	CC	
Al-Farahidi	Bhr	1998	48,154	50,004	277	32	24	CC	
Al-Mutanabbi	Bhr	1998	48,154	49,844	277	32	24	CC	
Al-Sabahia	Kwt	1998	48,154	49,848	277	32	24	CC	
Al-Wattyah	Kwt	1979	20,526	24,302	183	27	17	CC	
Asir	Sau	1998	48,154	49,856	277	32	24	CC	
Deira	Are	1998	48,154	49,993	277	32	24	CC	
Dubai	Are	1982	32,534	35,615	211	32	19	CC	
Fowairet	Qat	1998	48,154	49,993	277	32	24	CC	
Hammurabi	Kwt	1983	32,534	35,615	211	32	19	CC	ex Australian Advance-98, Hammurabi-86
Ibn Al Moataz	Sau	1977	15,455	23,618	175	24	16	C	
Ibn Bassam	Qat	1977	15,125	23,618	175	24	16	C	
Ibn Younus	Qat	1977	15,455	23,828	175	24	16	C	ex Trident Delta-90, Rickmers Shanghai-88, Ibn Younus-86
Jebel Ali	Are	1979	20,526	24,349	183	27	17	CC	
Khaled Ibn Al Waleed	Are	1983	32,534	35,615	211	32	19	CC	
Najran	Sau	1998	48,154	49,993	277	32	24	CC	
Qatari Ibn Al Fuja'a	Qat	1983	32,534	35,615	211	32	19	CC	ex Kota Selamat-02, Qatari Ibn Al Fuja'a-00

newbuildings: eight 76,000 dwt container ships on order for 2008 delivery from South Korean builder.
Formed jointly by The Government of The United Arab Emirates, The States of Bahrain, Kuwait and Qatar, The Kingdom of Saudi Arabia and The Republic of Iraq. See also The National Shipping Company of Saudi Arabia .

United Thai Shipping Corp Ltd   Thailand

Unithai Shipping Pte Ltd

Funnel: *Blue with broad white band containing separated red, blue and red shaped vertical bands.*
Hull: *Black with red boot-topping.*

Name	Flag	Year	GRT	DWT	Loa	Bm	Kts	Type	Former names
Chainat Navee	Tha	1978	15,938	20,258	157	25	15	HL	ex Dorinco-94, Malacca Maru-84
Korat Navee	Tha	1978	15,514	23,618	175	24	16	C	ex Trade Ever-94, Hickory-89, Christoffer Oldendorff-88, Theekar-87
Krabi Navee	Tha	1979	13,442	20,850	159	23	14	C	ex Caledonian Express-96, Crystal King-93, Twin Emerald-83
Pattaya Navee	Tha	1978	14,991	22,329	168	23	17	C	ex MC Jade-96, Vincenzia-89
Phayao Navee	Tha	1978	15,296	22,120	163	24	16	C	ex Far East Navee-95, Wakamizu Maru-87
Thai Bright *	Lbr	1984	18,723	26,140	169	26	16	BC	ex Candia-03, Cape York-01, Candia-99, Red Sea Encounter-92, Candia-91, Hanjin Candia-90, Candia-90, Red Sea Encounter-90, Lyme Bay-89, Candia-88
Thai Dawn *	Lbr	1985	18,722	26,140	169	26	16	BC	ex Caria-03, Victoria Bay-98, Caria-95, Santa Fe de Bogota-94, Caria-93, Lanka Abhaya-90, Norasia Caria-87, I/a Caria
Uthai Navee	Tha	1978	15,778	24,268	163	25	15	HL	ex Bosco VI-94, Trade Concord-92, Wakagiku Maru-87

Company 27% owned by Thailand government.
** managed for parent IMC Shipping Co. Pte. Ltd., Singapore and chartered to Gearbulk (see under Kristian Gerhard Jebsen AS)*

V Ships Group. BEBEDOURO. *Hans Kraijenbosch*

V Ships Group. YEOMAN BONTRUP. *F. de Vries*

F A Vinnen & Co. YM DUBAI (in charterers colours). *Hans Kraijenbosch*

215

Name	Eng	Flag	Year	GRT	DWT	Loa	Bm	Kts	Type	Former names

V Ships Group   Monaco

V Ships Monaco SAM

Funnel: *Yellow with blue 'V' or charterers colours.*
Hull: *Black or blue with green or red boot-topping.*

Name	Eng	Flag	Year	GRT	DWT	Loa	Bm	Kts	Type	Former names
African Sea		Pan	1985	15,893	17,850	174	23	15	Ro	ex Halifax-02, PCC Argos-99, Halifax-98, CSAV Rovno-96, Rovno-95
African Sky		Bhs	1986	15,893	17,850	172	23	17	Ro	ex Houston-02, Andrea S-97, Houston-97, Korsun-Shevchenkovskiy-96
African Sun		Pan	1985	15,893	17,850	174	23	15	Ro	ex Sunderland-02, PCC Buenos Aires-99, Sunderland-99, Global Atlantic-97, Brest-96
Battersea Bridge *		Bhs	1992	13,237	17,493	155	24	16	Co	ex Nordana Benefactor-99, Battersea Bridge-98, Zim Houston-97, Zim New York-96, Kapitan A.Krivobokov-92
Bebedouro		Lbr	1986	11,150	14,873	149	23	17	Tfj	
Chelsea Bridge		Nis	1987	47,249	51,466	220	38	16	Lpg	ex Berge Kobe-06, Co-op Sunrise-02
Euro Ace ‡		Pan	1999	38,530	73,976	225	32	-	B	ex Euro Trader-03
Euro Sea ‡		Mhl	2003	81,310	159,600	274	48	-	T	
Falcon Carrier		Pan	1992	39,036	68,960	226	32	14	T	ex United Will-04
Halifax		Mlt	1992	16,515	29,753	164	26	-	T	ex Stardust-99, Hawk-97, Maritime Prudence-94
Lion		Lbr	1985	26,113	46,100	172	32	14	T	ex Petrobulk Lion-96, Jahre Lion-86
Maersk Valletta		Gib	2002	17,189	22,308	179	28	21	CC	I/a Amadeus I
Maersk Vancouver		Gib	2001	17,189	22,200	179	28	21	CC	ex Aquarius-02
Maersk Venice		Gib	2002	17,189	22,308	179	28	21	CC	
Maersk Vigo		Gib	2002	17,189	22,308	179	28	21	CC	
NDS Promoter *		Bhs	1994	13,237	17,493	155	23	16	Co	ex Blackfriars Bridge-02, Libra Callao-99, Blackfriars Bridge-97, SEAL Madagascar-97, Kapitan A. Dotsenko-94
NDS Prosperity †		Bhs	1992	13,237	17,493	155	23	16	Co	ex Richmond Bridge-02, Lykes Victor-01, Richmond Bridge-00, Zim Mexico II-98, Libra Valparaiso-98, Kapitan V. Kiris-96, Zim Itajai-96, Kapitan V. Kiris-94, CMB Kiris-93, Kapitan V. Kiris-92
NDS Proteus *		Bhs	1993	13,237	17,493	155	23	16	Co	ex Westminster Bridge-03, Jolly Giada-03, Westminster Bridge-02, Zim Mexico 1-99, Westminster Bridge-97, Kapitan L. Golubev-97, Nedlloyd Cartagena-95, Kapitan L. Golubev-94
Puerto Cortes **	(2)	Bhs	1981	22,131	17,993	173	30	19	Ro	ex Kota Eagle-89, Contender Argent-87, Cavara-86, Contender Argent-84
Rip Hudner		Nis	1994	45,593	83,155	247	32	14	Obo	ex Sibonancy-05
Searose G		Nis	1994	45,493	83,155	247	32	14	Obo	ex Sibonata-05
Siboeva		Nis	1993	45,593	81,785	247	32	13	Obo	
Sibotura		Lbr	1992	41,189	74,928	229	32	14	Obo	ex Futura-96
Tower Bridge		Bhs	1991	42,286	49,345	224	36	16	Lpg	ex Berge Flanders-06, Flanders Gloria-03, Gloria-97
Yeoman Bank		Lbr	1982	24,870	38,997	205	27	15	Bu	ex Salmonpool-90
Yeoman Bontrup		Bhs	1991	55,695	96,725	250	38	15	Bu	ex Western Bridge-02
Yeoman Bridge		Bhs	1991	55,695	96,772	250	38	15	Bu	ex Eastern Bridge-00

*A small selection of the large number of vessels managed by V. Ships UK, by V.Ships Cyprus Ltd., by V.Ships Switzerland SA or V.Ships Greece Ltd, (formed jointly with LPL Shipping SA for various owners including ** for Sea Containers Services Ltd., UK, § for Gestion Maritime S.A.M., Monaco or †† for Morten Werring's Rederi, Norway*

F A Vinnen & Co (GmbH & Co)   Germany

Funnel: *Black with black 'M' on broad white band, white with blue 'V' or charterers colours.*
Hull: *Black with red boot-topping.*

Name	Eng	Flag	Year	GRT	DWT	Loa	Bm	Kts	Type	Former names
Kota Molek		Lbr	1996	15,929	22,026	168	27	21	CC	ex Merkur Cloud-04, Calapolos-02, I/a Merkur Cloud
Merkur Bay		Lbr	2002	30,047	35,770	208	32	22	CC	
Merkur Beach		Lbr	1996	16,800	22,900	185	26	19	CC	ex Delmas Charcot-03, Merkur Beach-02, MSC Quito-02, Merkur Beach-99, CSAV Rahue-98, I/a Merkur Beach
Merkur Bridge		Lbr	1993	9,597	12,575	150	22	17	CC	ex Sinar Banda-02, Kota Seri-01, Merkur Bridge-99, New Orient-99, Merkur Bridge-98, Ratana Ganya-97, TSL Bravo-96, Merkur Bridge-93

Name	Eng	Flag	Year	GRT	DWT	Loa	Bm	Kts	Type	Former names
Merkur Lake		Lbr	1994	9,600	12,574	150	23	18	CC	ex EWL Suriname-04, Merkur Lake-96, Libra Genova-95, Merkur Lake-95
Merkur Sea		Cyp	1984	16,430	21,888	166	27	18	CC	ex MSC Santiago-00, Merkur Sea-99, CSAV Ranco-98, City of Glasgow-97, Merkur Sea-93, CMB Merkur-91, Nedlloyd Himalaya-90, Merkur Sea-89, Dutch Senator-89, Ville d'Uranus-87, Merkur Sea-86
Merkur Sky		Lbr	1997	28,662	39,927	202	31	20	CC	ex MSC California-05, Merkur Sky-03, MSC Gauteng-02, Merkur Sky-02, MSC Sicily-01, Merkur Sky-99, Zim Piraeus-98, Merkur Sky-98
Merkur Star		Lbr	1996	29,181	39,528	203	31	19	CC	ex MSC Oman-03, Merkur Star-02, CMA CGM Seurat-02, Merkur Star-00, Houston Express-98, Merkur Star-96, I/a John Lykes
Safmarine Agulhas		Lbr	1995	16,800	22,900	185	25	19	CC	ex Merkur Delta-04, CSAV Salerno-01, Jolly Orca-00, CSAV Romeral-99, Merkur Delta-95
YM Dubai		Lbr	1998	15,929	22,026	168	27	21	CC	ex Merkur Tide-04, Calaparana-03, Merkur Tide-01, Atlantico-01, I/a Merkur Tide

Vroon BV   Netherlands

Funnel: *White with three wavy blue lines at base of blue 'V', narrow blue or black top or † white with blue 'LE', blue top*
Hull: *White, grey, black or red with red boot-topping.*

Name	Eng	Flag	Year	GRT	DWT	Loa	Bm	Kts	Type	Former names
Aegean Express		Pan	1997	15,095	18,581	169	27	18	CC	ex YM Bangkok-02, Kuo Ting-01
Arabian Express		Pan	1997	15,095	18,300	169	27	18	CC	ex Kuo Yang-03
Asian Dynasty		Phl	1999	55,719	21,224	200	32	20	V	
Belgian Express		Mhl	2000	16,960	21,373	169	27	20	CC	
Bermudian Express		Mhl	2000	16,850	21,548	169	27	20	CC	
Canadian Express		Lbr	1986	12,963	20,482	147	25	14	Co	ex Cape York-98, Canadian Express-97, ALS Express-96, Rickmers Dalian-91, Canadian Express-90, Waterfort-90, Canadian Express-90, Bavaria 89, Kriti Gold-88
Columbian Express		Pan	1986	12,963	20,479	147	25	14	Co	ex ALS Endeavour-01, Columbian Express-98, ALS Strength-97, Kriti Amber-88, ALS Strength-88, Kriti Amber-87
Eurasian Brilliance †		Phl	1985	26,746	9,763	159	28	17	V	ex Rubin Crest-94, Dairyu Maru-92
Eurasian Alliance †		Phl	1983	27,013	9,358	159	28	17	V	ex Daishun Maru-94
Eurasian Chariot †		Phl	1985	31,923	12,184	172	30	18	V	ex Eurasian Challenge-95, Ocean Cheer-94
Great Eastern *		Mhl	2005	23,356	37,515	183	27	14	T	
Iver Excel		Nld	1997	29,289	45,750	183	32	14	T	
Iver Experience		Nld	2000	29,289	45,500	183	32	15	T	
Iver Expert		Nld	1997	29,289	45,750	183	32	14	T	
Iver Exporter		Mhl	2000	29,289	45,500	183	32	15	T	
Libra Leader ‡		Pan	1998	57,674	22,734	200	32	19	V	
Merino Express		Nld	1978	25,756	12,711	176	27	17	L	ex Cormo Express-04, Mediterranean Highway-89
New England		Mhl	2005	23,356	37,000	183	27	14	T	
Nor'easter		Mhl	2005	23,356	37,000	183	27	14	T	
Scandinavian Express		Pan	2003	29,323	53,035	189	32	14	B	ex Anni Selmer-04
Scotian Express		Phl	1981	67,713	129,237	263	42	14	B	ex Ikaria-06, Thalassini Avra-97, Kepwave-86
Vega Spirit **		Pan	2001	15,016	22,820	153	25	13	T	ex Iver Spirit-05
Vega Spring **		Pan	2001	15,042	22,780	153	25	14	T	ex Iver Spring-05
Venice Express		Mhl	2001	16,850	21,579	169	27	20	CC	ex CP Success-06, Canmar Success-06, Brazilian Express-05
Young Liberty		Pan	1995	15,095	18,294	169	27	17	CC	ex Choyang Leader-01, Kuo Fah-95

newbuildings: three 29,200 grt 53,500 dwt and two 24,000 grt 37,000 dwt tankers for 2006-7 delivery.
Tankers and livestock carriers operated by wholly owned subsidiaries Iver Ships and Livestock Express respectively.
* managed by Norbulk Shipping, UK, ** by Fleet Management Ltd., Hong Kong (China) or † by Univan Ship Management Ltd., Hong Kong.
‡ chartered to NYK. Also see Eukor Car Carriers (Wallenius Wilhelmsen)

Wagenborg Shipping BV   Netherlands

Funnel: *Black with two narrow white bands.*
Hull: *Light grey with broad red band interrupted by white 'WAGENBORG' and diagonal white stripes, red or black boot-topping.*

Name	Eng	Flag	Year	GRT	DWT	Loa	Bm	Kts	Type	Former names
Amstelborg		Nld	2006	11,894	17,300	143	22	-	Co	
Nassauborg		Nld	2005	13,500	17,600	143	22	16	Co	
Prinsenborg		Nld	2003	13,340	16,615	143	22	16	Co	

Wallenius Wilhelmsen Logistics. MIGNON. *Phil Kempsey*

Wallenius Wilhelmsen Logistics. TOLEDO. *J. M. Kakebeeke*

Wallenius Wilhelmsen (Eukor). ASIAN PARADE. *Phil Kempsey*

Wan Hal Llnes. WAN HAI 301. *Hans Kraijenbosch*

Oskar Wehr KG. CSAV RIO BAKER. *Hans Kraijenbosch*

Western Petroleum. WESTERN ANTARCTIC. *Hans Kraijenbosch*

Name	Eng	Flag	Year	GRT	DWT	Loa	Bm	Kts	Type	Former names
Rhoneborg		Nld	1993	19,573	20,027	174	29	18	CC	ex MSC Java-03, European Express-02, Zim Australia-00, European Express-99, Freshwater Bay-96, European Express-94

newbuilding: five further 17,300 dwt cargo vessels for 2007-8 delivery (Arneborg, Amazoneborg, Asiaborg, Americaborg, Africaborg)
The company also operates large ro-ro vessels on northern European routes and numerous smaller vessels.

Wallenius Wilhelmsen Logistics Norway/Sweden

Funnel: *Yellow with yellow 'OW' on broad green band (Wallenius); black with two narrow light blue bands (Wilhelmsen); †† white with USA national flag and 'ARC' houseflag either side of black anchor, narrow black top.*
Hull: *Green with green 'Wallenius' or 'Wallenius Wilhelmsen' on white upperworks, green or red boot-topping; red, blue or black with red boot-topping (Wilhelmsen); †† blue with blue 'ARC' on white upperworks, red boot-topping.*

Name	Eng	Flag	Year	GRT	DWT	Loa	Bm	Kts	Type	Former names
Aegean Breeze †		Sgp	1983	27,876	12,527	164	28	18	V	
Arabian Breeze †		Sgp	1983	28,116	12,577	164	28	18	V	
Asian Breeze †		Sgp	1983	27,876	12,562	164	28	18	V	
Atlantic Breeze †		Sgp	1986	41,891	17,176	196	29	18	V	ex Bujin-91
Baltic Breeze †		Sgp	1983	28,116	12,466	164	28	18	V	
Boheme		Swe	1999	67,264	28,360	228	32	20	V	(len-05)
Carmen †		Sgp	1982	50,681	28,566	200	32	19	V	
Courage		Usa	1991	52,288	29,213	203	32	19	V	ex Aida-05
Don Carlos		Swe	1997	56,893	22,590	199	32	20	V	
Don Juan		Swe	1995	55,598	22,514	199	32	20	V	
Don Pasquale		Swe	1997	56,893	22,754	199	32	20	V	
Don Quijote		Swe	1998	56,893	14,927	199	32	20	V	
Elektra		Swe	1999	67,264	22,588	228	32	20	V	(len-05)
Falstaff		Swe	1985	51,858	28,529	200	32	20	V	
Figaro †		Sgp	1981	50,681	28,676	200	32	19	V	
Freedom ††		Usa	1997	49,821	19,884	190	32	19	V	ex Takamine-03
Honor		Usa	1996	49,821	19,844	190	32	19	V	ex Takasago-05
Independence ††		Usa	1978	47,089	17,406	195	32	19	V	ex Tellus-03, Nosac Ranger-96, Nosac Mascot-88, Nopal Mascot-84
Integrity		Usa	1992	52,479	29,152	203	32	20	V	ex Otello-05
Isolde		Swe	1985	51,071	28,396	200	32	19	V	
Liberty ††		Usa	1985	51,858	28,509	200	32	20	V	ex Faust-03
Madame Butterfly		Sgp	1981	50,681	28,689	200	32	19	V	
Manon		Swe	1999	67,264	14,863	228	32	20	V	(len-05)
Medea †		Sgp	1982	50,681	28,566	200	32	19	V	
Mignon		Swe	1999	67,264	28,127	228	32	20	V	(len-05)
Morning Glory †		Sgp	1978	45,037	15,406	196	32	20	V	ex Aniara-05, Avesta-83
Mosel Ace *		Pan	2000	37,237	12,761	177	31	19	V	
Pacific Breeze †		Sgp	1986	42,105	17,271	196	29	18	V	
Patriot ††		Usa	1987	47,219	15,680	190	32	18	V	ex Fidelio-03, Skaukar-94, Nosac Skaukar-92
Resolve ††		Usa	1994	49,443	20,082	190	32	19	V	ex Tanabata-03, Nosac Tanabata-96
Rigoletto		Swe	1977	43,487	17,197	192	32	21	V	
Tagus		Nis	1985	48,357	21,900	195	32	19	V	ex Nosac Express-96
Tai Shan **		Nis	1986	48,676	15,577	190	32	18	V	ex Nosac Tai Shan-96
Taiko		Nis	1984	66,532	43,986	262	32	21	Ro	ex Barber Hector-88
Takayama		Nis	1983	27,440	10,599	165	28	18	V	ex Nosac Takayama-96, Takayama-86
Talabot		Nis	1979	39,884	34,605	229	32	22	Ro	ex Barber Perseus-88
Talisman *		Nis	2000	67,140	38,500	241	32	20	Ro	
Tamerlane *		Nis	2001	67,140	38,500	241	32	20	Ro	
Tamesis *		Nis	2000	67,140	39,516	241	32	20	Ro	
Tampa		Nis	1984	66,532	44,013	262	32	21	Ro	ex Barber Tampa-89
Tampere		Nis	1979	40,542	35,098	229	32	22	Ro	ex Barber Nara-89
Tapiola		Nis	1978	39,535	33,702	229	32	21	Ro	ex Boogabilla-89
Tarago *		Nis	2000	67,140	39,516	241	32	20	Ro	
Taronga		Nis	1996	72,708	48,988	265	32	20	Ro	
Tasco		Nis	1985	48,393	22,067	195	32	19	V	ex Nosac Explorer-96, Nosac Tasco-89
Terrier		Nis	1982	47,947	17,863	194	32	19	V	ex Nosac Rover-96, Nosac Barbro-89, Nopal Barbro-84
Texas		Nis	1984	49,326	44,080	262	32	21	Ro	ex Barber Texas-89
Titus		Swe	1994	55,598	22,862	199	32	20	V	
Toba		Nis	1979	39,535	34,310	229	32	21	Ro	ex Barber Toba-89
Toledo		Gbr	2005	61,321	19,628	200	32	20	V	
Toronto		Gbr	2005	61,321	19,628	200	32	20	V	
Torrens		Gbr	2004	61,321	14,512	200	32	20	V	
Tosca †		Sgp	1978	45,037	15,350	196	32	20	V	

Name	Eng	Flag	Year	GRT	DWT	Loa	Bm	Kts	Type	Former names
Tourcoing		Nis	1978	39,535	33,719	229	32	21	Ro	
Traviata		Swe	1977	43,487	17,197	190	32	19	V	
Tristan		Swe	1985	51,071	28,536	200	32	19	V	
Turandot		Swe	1995	55,598	22,815	199	32	20	V	
Undine		Swe	2003	67,264	22,616	228	32	20	V	(len-06)
Verona *		Pan	2000	37,237	12,778	177	31	19	V	

newbuildings - 13 vehicle carriers on order for 2006-8 delivery including two sisters of Toledo.
*† owned by Wallenius Ship Management Pte. Ltd., Singapore or †† by subsidiary American Roll-on Roll-off Carrier (managed by Interocean American Shipping Corp.) both USA. * managed by Barber Shipmanagement Sendirian Berhad, Malaysia, ‡ by Wallenius Lines (Japan) Ltd.*
See also Paal Wilson & Co.

Eukor Car Carriers Inc/South Korea

Funnel: Cream with white curved cross on blue globe or owners colours.
Hull: Owners colours, some with 'EUKOR' on superstructure.

Name	Eng	Flag	Year	GRT	DWT	Loa	Bm	Kts	Type	Former names
Asian Captain *		Pan	1998	55,729	21,466	200	32	20	V	
Asian Chorus		Pan	1997	55,729	21,505	200	32	20	V	
Asian Empire		Pan	1998	55,729	21,485	200	32	20	V	
Asian Grace		Kor	1996	55,680	21,421	200	32	20	V	
Asian Legend		Pan	1996	55,680	21,421	200	32	20	V	
Asian Majesty		Pan	1999	55,729	21,483	228	32	20	V	(len. 06)
Asian Parade		Pan	1996	55,680	21,407	200	32	20	V	
Asian Sun		Pan	1995	44,891	13,292	185	31	18	V	
Asian Trust		Pan	2000	55,729	15,800	200	32	20	V	
Asian Venture		Pan	1995	44,891	13,241	185	31	18	V	
Asian Vision		Pan	1997	55,680	21,421	200	32	20	V	
Eternal Clipper		Pan	1980	23,107	10,803	164	25	17	V	ex Hyundai No.1-96
Eternal Mariner		Pan	1980	23,107	10,758	164	25	17	V	ex Hyundai No.2-96
Hyundai No. 201 *		Pan	1987	31,367	9,694	174	28	18	V	
Hyundai No. 202 *		Pan	1987	31,367	9,694	174	28	18	V	ex Tongala-99, Hyundai No.202-97, Nosac Clipper-93, Hyundai No.202-90
Hyundai No. 205 *		Pan	1987	42,247	12,706	184	31	19	V	ex Eurasian Beauty-93, Hyundai No.205-90
Hyundai No. 206 *		Pan	1987	42,247	12,706	184	31	18	V	ex Oriental Beauty-93, Hyundai No.206-90

Company owned by Walleniusrederierna AB (40%), Wilhelmsen ASA (40%), Hyundai Motor Group (10%) and Kia Motor Corp. (10%)
*Over 80 vessels operated, many on charter from * Eidseva Rederi ASA, Norway and from other owners including Cido Shipping, Ray Shipping, Vroon, Zodiac (Ofer Bros.) and Central Gulf Lines (International Shipholding Corp.).*

Wan Hai Lines Ltd   Taiwan

Funnel: Blue with large white 'W'.
Hull: Light grey with white outlined 'WAN HAI LINES' in red and blue lettering.

Name	Eng	Flag	Year	GRT	DWT	Loa	Bm	Kts	Type	Former names
Wan Hai 301		Sgp	2001	26,681	30,250	200	32	24	CC	
Wan Hai 302		Sgp	2002	26,681	30,234	200	32	24	CC	
Wan Hai 303		Sgp	2002	26,681	30,500	200	32	24	CC	
Wan Hai 305		Sgp	2002	26,681	30,246	200	32	24	CC	
Wan Hai 306		Sgp	2002	25,836	34,026	197	30	21	CC	
Wan Hai 307		Sgp	2002	25,836	34,026	197	30	21	CC	
Wan Hai 311		Sgp	2005	27,800	32,937	213	32	22	CC	
Wan Hai 312		Sgp	2006	27,800	33,000	213	32	22	CC	
Wan Hai 501		Sgp	2005	42,579	52,249	269	32	23	CC	
Wan Hai 502		Sgp	2005	42,579	52,146	269	32	23	CC	
Wan Hai 503		Sgp	2005	42,579	51,300	269	32	23	CC	
Wan Hai 505		Sgp	2005	42,579	51,300	269	32	23	CC	
Wan Hai 506		Sgp	2005	42,579	52,146	269	32	23	CC	

newbuildings: four 65,600 grt, nine 43,500 grt, four further 27,800 grt container ships for 2006-8 delivery.
Also owns 33 other 12-19,000 grt container ships operating mainly in the Far East.
Operates Far East-Europe container service jointly with Pacific International Lines q.v.;

Warwick & Esplen Ltd   UK

The Hadley Shipping Co Ltd

Funnel: Yellow with black 'HSC' inside white diamond, black top.
Hull: Black with red boot-topping.

Name	Eng	Flag	Year	GRT	DWT	Loa	Bm	Kts	Type	Former names
Corato		Iom	1989	36,042	64,293	217	32	14	B	ex Meridian Sky-99
Cumbria		Gbr	1994	35,886	69,043	225	32	14	B	ex Corona Brave-03
Cymbeline		Iom	2001	38,299	73,060	225	32	14	B	

Managed by Anglo-Eastern (UK) Ltd., UK.

Name	Eng	Flag	Year	GRT	DWT	Loa	Bm	Kts	Type	Former names

Oskar Wehr KG (GmbH & Co) Germany

Funnel: Black with blue 'W' in blue ring over two blue bands in centre and towards top of broad yellow band or charterers colours.
Hull: Blue or grey with diagonal stripes and blue or red boot-topping.

Name	Eng	Flag	Year	GRT	DWT	Loa	Bm	Kts	Type	Former names
Bremen Senator	Mhl	1997	16,801	23,051	184	25	20	CC	ex Wehr Ottensen-04, Indamex Nhava Sheva-02, Wehr Ottensen-01, CSAV Rio Grande-99, Wehr Ottensen-98
CSAV Rio Baker	Mhl	2002	25,630	33,767	207	30	21	CC	ex CCNI Arica-04, Wehr Alster-02
CSAV Rio Puelo	Mhl	2002	25,705	33,795	207	30	21	CC	ex CCNI Aysen-04, I/a Wehr Trave
CSAV Rio Tolten	Mhl	2002	25,703	33,795	208	30	21	CC	ex Wehr Havel-04
CSAV Rio Maule	Mhl	2002	25,705	33,793	208	30	21	CC	ex Columbus China-04, Wehr Warnow-02
CSAV Callao	Mhl	2001	25,703	33,795	203	30	22	CC	I/a Wehr Elbe
CSAV Hong Kong	Mhl	1998	16,801	22,983	184	25	19	CC	ex Wehr Muden-03, TMM Quetzal-01, CSAV Valencia-00, Crowley Express-00, CSAV Rimac-99, I/a Wehr Muden
CSAV Montreal	Mhl	1999	16,177	23,021	184	26	19	CC	ex Norasia Montreal-01, Illapel-00, I/a Wehr Blankensee
Delmas Mascareignes	Mhl	1999	16,802	23,028	185	25	19	CC	ex CMA CGM Bourgainville-04, Wehr Rissen-99
Elqui	Mhl	1999	16,177	23,026	184	26	19	CC	I/a Wehr Schulau
Frederike Selmar	Mhl	2004	30,012	52,483	190	32	14	B	
Frieda Selmar	Mhl	2004	31,218	55,718	190	32	14	B	
Helene Selmar	Mhl	2005	31,218	55,741	190	32	14	B	
Helga Selmer	Mhl	2004	27,913	50,326	190	32	14	B	
Ida Selmer	Mhl	2003	27,986	50,209	190	32	14	B	
Libra Chile	Mhl	2001	16,802	23,000	185	25	19	CC	I/a Wehr Nienstedten
Libra New York	Mhl	2001	25,703	33,795	203	30	22	CC	I/a Wehr Weser
Maersk Dellys	Mhl	2006	54,200	67,470	294	32	-	CC	ex Wehr Singapore-06
Maersk Derince	Mhl	2005	54,193	67,470	294	32	-	CC	ex Wehr Hongkong-06
Mimi Selmar	Mhl	2005	31,500	55,711	190	32	14	B	
NYK Estrela	Mhl	2002	25,624	33,739	208	30	21	CC	ex CSAV Rio Cochamo-05, Wehr Bille-04, CCNI Antartico-03, Wehr Bille-02
P&O Nedlloyd Yarra Valley	Mhl	2002	25,703	33,670	208	30	21	CC	ex Wehr Oste-03
Therese Selmar	Mhl	2006	31,500	56,000	190	32	14	B	
Wehr Altona	Mhl	1997	16,802	23,021	184	25	19	CC	ex Lykes Pathfinder-02, Norasia Yantian-01, CSAV Ningpo-00, Kota Sejarah-00, CSAV Rio de la Plata-99, I/a Wehr Altona
Wehr Flottbek	Lbr	1999	16,802	22,878	184	25	19	CC	ex Alianca Bahia-01, Wehr Flottbek-00
Wehr Loblenz	Mhl	1997	16,801	23,051	184	25	20	CC	ex P&O Nedlloyd Portbury-06, P&O Nedlloyd Calypso-04, Costa Rica-02, Wehr Koblenz-01, Panamerican-01, CSAV Rio Amazonas-99, I/a Wehr Koblenz

newbuilding: one 17,000 grt and one 25,360 grt container ships for 2006-7 delivery

Western Petroleum Group Switzerland

Funnel: White with black 'WP' logo between narrow red bands.
Hull: Black with red boot-topping.

Name	Eng	Flag	Year	GRT	DWT	Loa	Bm	Kts	Type	Former names
Western Antarctic	Bhs	2005	30,053	52,700	186	32	14	T	
Western Arctic	Bhs	2005	30,053	52,700	186	32	14	T	
Western Atlantic	Bhs	2005	30,053	52,700	186	32	14	T	
Western Baltic	Bhs	2005	30,053	52,700	186	32	14	T	
Western Icelandic	Bhs	2005	30,053	52,700	186	32	14	T	
Western Pacific	Bhs	2005	30,053	52,700	186	32	14	T	

newbuildings: three 62,400 grt 116,000 dwt Aframax tankers for 2006 delivery
Vessels reported sold to Tsakos Shipping & Trading SA.

Westfal-Larsen Management AS Norway

Funnel: Yellow with two narrow black bands, narrow black top
Hull: Dark blue or red with red boot-topping.

Name	Eng	Flag	Year	GRT	DWT	Loa	Bm	Kts	Type	Former names
Fossanger *	Nis	1988	22,637	40,264	171	32	14	T	ex Northern Wolf-89, Fort Wolf-88
Mauranger *	Lbr	1995	25,707	41,109	180	31	14	T	ex Bow Tribute-01
Moldanger *	Lbr	1997	25,707	40,845	180	31	14	T	ex Bow Triton-01

Westfal-Larsen. MOLDANGER. *C. Lous*

Westfal-Larsen (Star Shipping). STAR ISMENE. *Hans Kraijenbosch*

Yangming Marine. YM MARCH. *Hans Kraijenbosch*

Name	Eng	Flag	Year	GRT	DWT	Loa	Bm	Kts	Type	Former names
Nordanger		Nis	1992	43,635	59,421	220	34	16	Lpg	ex Baltic Flame-01

*Managed by Westfal-Larsen Management AS and * on charter to Team Tankers AS (see under Blystad Shipmanagement)*

Star Shipping AS/Norway

Funnel: *Yellow with two blue stars on white panel with blue top and bottom edges.*
Hull: *Blue or grey with red or blue boot-topping.*

Name	Eng	Flag	Year	GRT	DWT	Loa	Bm	Kts	Type	Former names
Star Alabama †		Nis	1985	20,916	30,204	169	27	15	BC	ex Hawaiian Rainbow-92
Star Altanger *		Sgp	1986	20,125	30,382	169	27	15	BC	ex Northern Dawn-96, Star New York-91, New York Rainbow-89
Star America †		Nis	1985	20,929	30,168	169	27	15	BC	ex Canadian Rainbow-91, Star Canadian-90, Canadian Rainbow-89
Star Atlantic †		Nis	1986	20,125	30,402	165	26	15	BC	ex Hoegh Mistral-03, Star Atlantic-03, Hoegh Mistral-03, Star Texas-90, Texas Rainbow-89
Star Austanger *		Nis	1985	20,915	30,173	169	27	15	BC	ex Anthony Rainbow-92
Star Davanger *		Sgp	1978	27,125	43,793	183	31	15	BC	ex Star Denver-89, Star Enterprise-85
Star Derby †		Nis	1979	27,104	43,700	183	31	15	BC	ex Star Carrier-85
Star Dieppe †		Nis	1977	27,104	43,082	183	31	15	BC	ex Star Shiraz-79, Star Dieppe-77
Star Djervanger *		Sgp	1978	27,743	43,051	183	31	15	BC	ex Star World-89
Star Dover †		Nis	1977	27,911	43,082	183	31	15	BC	ex Star Estahan-79, Star Dover-77
Star Drivanger *		Sgp	1978	27,735	43,052	183	31	15	BC	ex Star Hong Kong-92
Star Drottanger *		Sgp	1978	27,735	43,051	183	31	15	BC	ex Star Magnate-92
Star Eagle †		Nis	1981	24,479	39,749	180	29	15	BC	
Star Evanger *		Nis	1984	30,163	44,959	211	31	15	BC	ex Celestine-90, Birdie-89, Lily Star-87
Star Evviva †		Nis	1982	24,479	39,718	180	29	15	BC	
Star Florida †		Nis	1985	25,345	40,790	187	29	15	BC	
Star Fraser †		Nis	1985	25,345	40,840	187	29	15	BC	
Star Fuji †		Nis	1985	25,345	40,850	187	29	15	BC	
Star Geiranger		Nis	1986	27,972	43,131	200	29	15	BC	
Star Gran †		Nis	1986	27,192	43,759	198	29	16	BC	ex Triton-86
Star Grindanger		Nis	1986	27,972	43,131	201	29	15	BC	
Star Grip †		Nis	1986	27,192	43,712	198	29	16	BC	
Star Hansa †		Nis	1996	32,749	46,580	198	31	16	BC	
Star Hardanger *		Nis	1995	34,364	44,251	199	31	16	BC	
Star Harmonia †		Nis	1998	32,749	46,604	198	31	16	BC	
Star Heranger *		Nis	1995	34,363	44,251	199	31	16	BC	
Star Herdla †		Nis	1994	32,744	47,942	198	31	16	BC	
Star Hidra †		Nis	1994	32,749	46,547	198	31	16	BC	
Star Hosanger *		Nis	1995	34,363	44,251	199	31	16	BC	
Star Hoyanger *		Nis	1995	34,363	44,251	199	31	16	BC	
Star Ikebana *		Sgp	1999	30,840	39,751	185	31	16	BC	
Star Indiana *		Sgp	2000	30,745	39,760	185	31	16	BC	
Star Inventana *		Sgp	2000	30,745	39,789	185	31	16	BC	
Star Isfjord †		Nis	2000	29,898	41,749	185	31	16	BC	
Star Ismene †		Nis	1999	28,898	41,777	185	31	16	BC	
Star Isoldana *		Sgp	2000	30,745	39,465	185	31	16	BC	
Star Istind †		Nis	1999	29,898	41,749	185	31	16	BC	
Star Japan †		Nis	2004	32,844	46,387	198	31	16	BC	
Star Juventus †		Nis	2004	32,844	44,807	198	31	16	BC	
Star Langanger *		Sgp	1986	29,275	41,425	195	32	14	BC	ex Hawthorn Hill-89, Geliga-86
Star Leikanger *		Sgp	1986	29,275	41,409	195	32	14	BC	ex Maritime Wisdom-89, Wisteria Hill-87, Gemar-86
Star Okiana *		Sgp	2003	36,324	48,661	199	32	16	BC	
Star Optimana *		Sgp	2003	36,324	48,661	199	32	16	BC	
Star Osakana *		Sgp	2004	36,324	48,661	199	32	16	BC	
Star Oshimana *		Sgp	2003	36,324	48,661	199	32	16	BC	
Star Polaris ‡		Grc	1996	26,897	43,775	190	31	14	B	
Star Pollux ‡		Grc	1996	26,922	43,769	190	31	14	B	
Star Siranger *		Sgp	1991	11,878	17,012	149	23	14	BC	ex T.S.Adventure-93

newbuildings - two 33,100 grt open-hatch bulk carriers for 2006 delivery.
Star Shipping Pool is jointly owned by Westfal-Larsen (or subsidiary Masterbulk Pte. Ltd., Singapore) and † by Greig Shipping AS (or subsidiary Grieg Billabong A/S) both Norway. Also operates some chartered vessels including ‡ owned by Rethymnis & Kulukundis Ltd., UK.*

Anders Wilhelmsen & Co AS   Norway

Funnel: *Black with white 'W' on red/black divided diamond between two narrow red bands on broad white band.*
Hull: *Grey or red with red or grey boot-topping.*

Name	Eng	Flag	Year	GRT	DWT	Loa	Bm	Kts	Type	Former names
Nordic Voyager *		Nis	1996	79,494	149,775	270	45	15	T	ex Wilma Yantze-05

Name	Eng	Flag	Year	GRT	DWT	Loa	Bm	Kts	Type	Former names
Wilana		Nis	1997	79,494	149,706	270	45	15	T	
Wilmina		Nis	1997	79,388	149,775	270	45	15	T	

*Managed by Wilhelmsen Marine Services A/S and * operated by Nordic American Tanker Shipping (see under Teekay)*
See also Royal Caribbean International in Passenger Ship section.

Paal Wilson & Co AS

Norway

Funnel: *Blue with blue herringbone line on broad white band or charterers colours.*
Hull: *Red or * blue with white 'Jebsens', red boot-topping.*

	Eng	Flag	Year	GRT	DWT	Loa	Bm	Kts	Type	Former names
Takara		Nis	1986	48,547	15,546	190	32	18	V	ex Nosac Takara-96
Tancred		Nis	1987	48,676	15,577	190	32	18	V	ex Nosac Sea-96, Nosac Tancred-89
Trianon		Nis	1987	49,792	15,536	190	32	18	V	ex Nosac Star-96
Trimnes *		Pan	1990	14,145	17,309	150	24	13	Bu	ex Express-96
Trinidad		Nis	1987	49,750	15,528	190	32	18	V	ex Nosac Sky-96

newbuildings: nine 20,000 grt 33,500 dwt bulk carriers from Chinese builder for 2006-7 delivery.
*Owned by subsidiaries Actinor Shipping AS (operated by Wallenius Wilhelmsen Lines AB) or * by AJ Shipmanagement GmbH, Germany.*

Reederei Gebr Winter GmbH & Co KG

Germany

Funnel: *Mainly charterers colours*
Hull: *Grey, blue or red with red boot-topping.*

	Eng	Flag	Year	GRT	DWT	Loa	Bm	Kts	Type	Former names
Cala Piedad		Atg	1994	14,968	20,088	167	25	19	CC	ex Concord-03, Mercosul Pintado-03, Safmarine Emonti-02, Egoli Star I-01, Concord-99, Libra Santos-99, DG Concord-97, Concord-97, Victoria Bay-95, Concord-94
Classica		Deu	1998	23,897	30,241	188	30	21	CC	ex Safmarine Mtata-05, Maersk Dakar-04, Classica-02, Libra Buenos Aires-02, Classica-01, CMA Djakarta-00, Jolly Ocra-99, Classica-98
Commodore		Atg	2001	30,047	35,770	208	32	22	CC	ex MSC Andes-02, Commodore-01
Courier		Atg	1995	14,860	20,140	167	26	19	CC	ex Indamex Ganges-02, Libra Miami-00, Libra Buenos Aires-97, CSAV Rahue-96, Velma Lykes-95, l/a Courier
Maersk Pecem		Atg	2004	30,051	35,770	208	32	22	CC	ex Commander-04
Ocean		Atg	1996	12,029	14,587	157	24	19	CC	ex Cala Providencia-04, Ocean-02, Urundi-01, Ocean-99, Ankara-98, Ocean-97
Rothorn *		Atg	1996	12,029	14,507	157	24	10	CC	ex MOL Amazonas-02. Guatamala-01, Rothorn 98
Safmarine Gonubie		Deu	1998	23,897	30,258	188	30	21	CC	ex Libra Houston-02, TMM Veracruz-01, APL Atlantic-00, Columba-99, Maersk Genoa-98, l/a Columba
Shion		Deu	1996	12,029	14,643	157	24	18	CC	ex Caravelle-04, Cala Porlamar-04, Pellini-02, Caravelle-01, UB Puma-97, Caravelle-96
Weisshorn *		Atg	1996	12,029	14,643	157	24	19	CC	ex MSC Ghana-04, Weisshorn-02, DAL East London-01, Weisshorn-00, P&O Nedlloyd Maurtius-99, Weisshorn-98

newbuildings - four 17,000 grt container ships for 2008 delivery from German builder.
* owned by Contal Shipping Ltd., Switzerland.

Reederei Hermann Wulff

Germany

Funnel: *Mainly charterers colours*
Hull: *Grey with red boot-yopping.*

	Eng	Flag	Year	GRT	DWT	Loa	Bm	Kts	Type	Former names
CMA CGM Seagull		Lbr	2002	32,322	39,350	211	32	22	CC	ex P&O Nedlloyd Dammam-03, Antje-Helen Wulff-02
CSAV Rio Loa		Lbr	2002	32,284	39,600	211	32	22	CC	ex P&O Nedlloyd Dubai-04, Euro Max-02
CSAV Rio Maipo		Lbr	1999	32,222	39,128	211	32	22	CC	ex NYK Prosperity-04, Weserwolf-03, Columbia Bridge-01, Weserwolf-00
Guatemala		Deu	1996	14,473	18,355	159	24	18	CC	ex P&O Nedlloyd Mobasa-01, Steindeich-98
Hermann Wulff		Deu	2006	32,322	39,300	211	32	22	CC	
Ibn Khaldoun		Lbr	1999	32,221	39,340	211	32	21	CC	ex Aramac-06, Elbwolf-02, Ipex Equality-01, Elbwolf-99
Ilse Wulff		Lbr	1993	16,233	21,540	182	25	20	CC	ex Nigeria Star-03, Ilse Wulff-01, Direct Kookaburra-01, Isle Wulff-99, Maersk Pretoria-99, Maersk Pireaus-98, TSL Unity-98, Ilse Wulff-95, Contship Rotterdam-94, Ilse-93

Name	Eng	Flag	Year	GRT	DWT	Loa	Bm	Kts	Type	Former names
Inaba		Lbr	1993	16,233	21,540	182	25	20	CC	ex Hermann-04, P&O Nedlloyd Cotonou-03, Hermann-02, Direct Kea-01, MSC Cali-99, Hermann-99, Maersk Aarhus-98, Hermann-98, Sea Harmony-97, Hermann-96, CCNI Angol-96, Hermann-95, Contship New York-95, Hermann-93, Deppe Europe-93, Hermann-93
Maersk Diadem		Deu	2006	51,350	58,000	292	32	24	CC	ex Viktoria Wulff-06
Maersk Diadema		Deu	2005	51,350	58,000	292	32	24	CC	ex Charlotte Wulff-06
TS Kelang		Deu	1996	14,473	18,355	159	24	19	CC	ex ACX Primrose-04, Doris Wulff-03, Sakura-01, Norasia Montreal-00, Direct Jabiru-99, OOCL Amity-98, Doris Wulff-97, Nuova Ionia-96, Doris Wulff-96, Nuova Ionia-96, I/a Doris Wulff

newbuildings: three further 32,322 grt 39,300 dwt container ships for 2006-7 delivery from Polish builder.

Yangming Marine Transport Corp   Taiwan

Funnel: *Black with yellow band on broad red band interupted by white square containing black 'Y' within red outline.*
Hull: *Grey with red 'YANG MING LINE', red boot-topping.*

Name	Eng	Flag	Year	GRT	DWT	Loa	Bm	Kts	Type	Former names
Bamboo Bridge		Lbr	2001	64,005	68,615	275	40	26	CC	ex Jupiter Bridge-05, Ming Bamboo-02
Cypress Bridge		Lbr	2001	64,254	68,303	275	40	25	CC	ex Mercury Bridge-05, Ming Cypress-02
Glory Bridge		Lbr	1980	29,873	31,208	210	32	20	CC	ex Ocean Gulf-04, Gulf Bridge-03, Ming Glory-98
Giuseppe Rizzo		Lbr	2004	41,205	77,684	225	32	14	B	
Medi Taipei		Lbr	2003	39,727	76,633	225	32	14	B	
Ming Equality		Lbr	1996	36,559	70,252	225	32	14	B	ex Bel Ace-03
Pine Bridge		Lbr	2001	64,005	68,615	275	40	26	CC	ex Venus Bridge-05, Ming Pine-02
YM America		Lbr	1992	46,728	46,785	276	32	21	CC	ex Ming America-04
YM Asia		Lbr	1991	46,728	46,772	276	32	21	CC	ex Ming Asia-04
YM Champion		Lbr	1997	15,120	19,332	169	27	18	CC	ex Ming Champion-04
YM Comfort		Twn	1982	29,872	30,702	210	32	23	CC	ex Ming Comfort-04, Sentosa Bridge-04, Ming Comfort-03, Malacca Bridge-99, Ming Comfort-96
YM Container		Twn	1997	15,120	19,353	169	27	18	CC	ex Ming Container-04
YM Cosmos		Pan	2001	64,254	68,413	275	40	25	CC	ex Ming Cosmos-05
YM Cultivation		Twn	1996	35,905	69,163	225	32	14	B	ex Ming Cultivation-04, Bel Best-02
YM East		Twn	1995	46,697	45,995	276	32	21	CC	ex Ming East-05, Maersk Long Beach-96, Ming East-95
YM Energy		Lbr	1983	29,872	30,701	210	32	23	CC	ex Med Keelung-04, Ming Energy-93
YM Europe		Twn	1992	46,728	46,772	276	32	21	CC	ex Ming Europe-04
YM Fortune		Lbr	1983	29,872	30,669	210	32	23	CC	ex Kota Permas-04, Med Taichung-03, Maersk Dubai-96, Ming Fortune-94
YM Fountain		Lbr	2004	64,254	68,615	275	40	26	CC	
YM Galaxy		Lbr	1980	29,873	31,264	210	32	20	CC	ex Ocean Atlantic-04, Atlantic Bridge-02, Ming Galaxy-98
YM Great		Pan	2004	66,332	67,270	279	40	26	CC	
YM Green		Lbr	2001	64,254	68,413	275	40	26	CC	ex Ming Green-05
YM Harmony		Lbr	2005	15,167	19,104	169	27	-	CC	
YM Hawk		Lbr	2005	15,167	19,100	169	27	-	CC	
YM Heights		Lbr	2005	15,167	19,100	169	27	-	CC	
YM Horizon		Lbr	2005	15,167	16,965	169	27	-	CC	
YM Longevity		Twn	1983	29,872	30,646	210	32	23	CC	ex Ming Longevity-04, Gibraltar Bridge-98, Ming Longevity-96, Med Hong Kong-95, Maersk Jeddah-93, Ming Longevity-93
YM March		Pan	2004	66,332	67,270	279	40	25	CC	I/a Ming March
YM Moon		Lbr	1980	29,872	31,246	210	32	22	CC	ex Ocean Luna-04, Cosco Atlantic-02, Ming Moon-98
YM North		Lbr	1995	46,697	45,995	276	32	21	CC	ex Ming North-05
YM Ocean		Twn	1980	29,872	31,208	210	32	23	CC	ex Ming Ocean-04, Dover Bridge-98, Ming Ocean-96
YM Orchid		Pan	2000	64,254	68,303	275	40	26	CC	ex Ming Orchid-05
YM Plum		Pan	2000	64,254	68,413	275	40	26	CC	ex Ming Plum-05
YM Prominence		Lbr	1987	40,436	40,845	270	32	20	CC	ex Ming Prominence-04
YM Prosperity		Lbr	1988	40,415	40,845	270	32	20	CC	ex Med Taipei-04, Ville d'Hydra-95, Ming Prosperity-94
YM Rightness		Lbr	2004	41,400	77,684	225	32	14	B	
YM South		Twn	1995	46,697	45,995	276	32	21	CC	ex Ming South-05
YM Star		Lbr	1980	29,873	31,251	210	32	20	CC	ex Ocean Starlight-04, Starlight River-02, Ming Star-99
YM Success		Lbr	2004	64,254	68,615	275	40	25	CC	

Name	Eng	Flag	Year	GRT	DWT	Loa	Bm	Kts	Type	Former names
YM Sun		Lbr	1980	29,873	31,265	210	32	20	CC	ex Ocean Genius-04, Sun River-01, Ming Sun-98
YM Union		Twn	1997	15,120	19,338	169	27	18	CC	ex Ming Union-04
YM Victory		Lbr	1997	15,120	19,325	169	27	18	CC	ex Ming Victory-04
YM Virtue		Lbr	2003	39,749	73,840	225	32	14	B	ex Ming Virtue-05
YM Wealth		Lbr	2004	64,254	68,615	275	40	26	CC	
YM West		Lbr	1995	46,697	45,995	276	32	21	CC	ex Ming West-05, Maersk Singapore-96, Ming West-95
YM Zenith		Lbr	1996	46,697	45,995	276	32	21	CC	ex Ming Zenith-04

newbuildings - five 90,000 grt, four 88,600 grt, five 42,800 grt, twelve 15,700 grt container ships and a 42,000 grt bulk carrier for 2006-8 delivery.
Controlled by Government of Taiwan and also manages four tankers owned by associated Chinese Petroleum Corp.
See other chartered ships in index with 'YM' prefix.

Reederei Horst Zeppenfeld GmbH & Co KG Germany

Funnel: *Cream with black top.*
Hull: *Black with red boot-topping.*

Name	Eng	Flag	Year	GRT	DWT	Loa	Bm	Kts	Type	Former names
Cala Paestum		Lbr	2000	17,167	21,331	169	27	20	CC	ex YM Hakata-04, P&O Nedlloyd Canterbury-03, Mira-02
Merak		Sgp	2005	16,162	17,350	161	25	-	CC	
Mizar		Sgp	2005	16,162	17,350	161	25	-	CC	

newbuildings: two 16,162 grt 1180 teu container ships for 2008 delivery (to be named Algol and Alioth)
Managed by associated Reederei Navylloyd A.G., Switzerland.

Recent updates

Alpha Ship GmbH

Columbus W	renamed Cap Victor									
Saturn	renamed Delmas Anemone									

Bergshav Shipholding

Larvik	Bhs	2006	35,711	61,213	213	32	-	T

Hermann Buss

CP Canada	renamed Juist Trader

Cido Shipping

Name	Flag	Year	GRT	DWT	Loa	Bm	Kts	Type
Hyundai Harmony	Pan	2002	13,267	17,800	162	26	-	CC
Pos Jade	Hkg	2006	19,796	31,800	176	29	-	B
Pos Knight	Hkg	2006	19,800	31,800	176	29	-	B

CMA CGM

CMA CGM Kailas	Bhs	2006	21,971	24,000	196	28	-	CC

AP Moller-Maersk

Name	Flag	Year	GRT	DWT	Loa	Bm	Kts	Type
Georg Maersk	Dis	2006	97,900	115,700	367	43	25	CC
Maersk Gloucester	Dmk	2006	50,686	50,415	292	32	-	CC
Maersk Gosforth	Gbr	2006	50,686	50,415	292	32	-	CC
Maersk Greenock	Gbr	2006	50,686	50,415	292	32	-	CC
Maersk Guernsey	Dmk	2006	50,686	50,415	292	32	-	CC
Oriental Bay	renamed Maersk Montreal							
Peninsular Bay	renamed Maersk Madrid							

Chartered from Reederei Stefan Patjens

Name	Flag	Year	GRT	DWT	Loa	Bm	Kts	Type	
Maersk Drummond ‡	Lbr	2006	53,453	57,000	294	32	23	CC	I/a Serena
Maersk Drury ‡	Lbr	2006	53,453	57,000	294	32	23	CC	
Maersk Dryden ‡	Lbr	2006	53,453	57,000	294	32	23	CC	I/a Herma
Maersk Dubrovnik ‡	Lbr	2006	53,453	57,000	294	32	23	CC	

Schiffahrts Oltmann Verwaltung

Name	Flag	Year	GRT	DWT	Loa	Bm	Kts	Type
Maersk Dunbar	Lbr	2006	41,359	52,450	264	32	-	CC
Maersk Duncan	Lbr	2006	41,359	52,450	264	32	-	CC

Index

Name	Page	Name	Page	Name	Page
Atlantic Forest	90	Bangkok Express	144	Bermudian Express	217
Atlantic Fortune	152	Baniyas	101	Bernhard Oldendorff	160
Atlantic Hawk	110	Bantry	102	Bertina	113
Atlantic Hero	126	Barbarossa	116	Bertora	40
Atlantic Highway	100	Barbet Arrow	97	Beryl	168
Atlantic Hope	193	Barcelona Bridge	144	Betty Knutsen	102
Atlantic Liberty	126	Barcelona Express	85	Bijin	141
Atlantic Mermaid	193	Barents Bay	193	Bilbao Knutsen	102
Atlantic Ocean	212	Barents Sea	196	Bing He	48
Atlantic Prosperity	126	Barkald	102	Bio Bio	136
Atlantic Reefer	106	Barmbeck	102	Birka Princess	14
Atlantic Trader	45	Barranquilla	88	Birte Ritscher	209
Atlantica	68	Barrington Island	212	Black Marlin	68
Atlantida	213	Barrington	205	Black Prince	16
Atlantik Frigo	106	Basker Spirit	205	Black Sea	152
Atlas Highway	100	Bataliony Chlopskie	173	Black Watch	16
Atlas Mountains	153	Battersea Bridge	216	Blandine Delmas	50
Atlixco	124	Batu	32	Blue Dream	16
Attar	96	Bauhinia Bridge	100	Blue Hawk	141
Attila	68	Bauta	102	Blue Lady	20
Auckland Star	200	Bay Bridge	100	Blue Marlin	68
Auguste Oldendorff	160	Bay Ranger	178	Blue Master	112
Auk Arrow	97	Baynunah	32	Blue Moon	16
Aurelia	45	BBC India	37	Blue Sky	157
Aurika	184	BBC Korea	88	Bogdan	137
Aurora	10	BBC Russia	88	Boheme	220
Aurora	45	Beatanavis	49	Bonanza	104
Ausonia	14	Beatriz	160	Bonita	45
Australian Spirit	205	Beaumont	88	Bonn Express	83
Australis	47	Beauty River	48	Borg Arrow	97
Austyn Oldendorff	56	Bebedouro	216	Borga	134
Authentic	108	Belgian Express	217	Bosphoros Bridge	100
Avalon Spirit	205	Belgian Reefer	106	Boudicca	16
Avalon	45	Belgreeting	47	Boularibank	202
Avelona Star	200	Bellavia	66	Bourgogne	60
Avila Star	200	Bellona	141	Bow Americas	149
Avocet Arrow	97	Belmeken	137	Bow Andes	149
Axel Maersk	129	Belmonte	45	Bow Architect	149
Axel Spirit	205	Belnor	36	Bow Cardinal	149
Azalea Ace	124	Belo Horizonte	53	Bow Cecil	149
Azov Sea	196	Belsize Park	153	Bow Cedar	149
Aztec	213	Benarita	213	Bow Century	149
Azteca	92	Bengal Sea	152	Bow Chain	149
		Benguela Stream	193	Bow Cheetah	149
B. Prus	172	Berana	40	Bow Clipper	149
Baco-Liner 1	36	Berge Arctic	37	Bow Condor	149
Baco-Liner 2	36	Berge Arrow	37	Bow Eagle	149
Baco-Liner 3	36	Berge Atlantic	37	Bow Europe	149
Badrinath	193	Berge Bocton	37	Bow Fagus	149
Bahama Spirit	190	Berge Captain	37	Bow Faith	149
Bahamas Spirit	170	Berge Challenger	37	Bow Favour	149
Bahamian Express	32	Berge Clipper	37	Bow Fertility	149
Bakra	101	Berge Commander	37	Bow Fighter	149
Balder	101	Berge Danuta	37	Bow Firda	149
Balgarka	137	Berge Denise	37	Bow Flora	149
Bali Sea	90	Berge Eagle	37	Bow Flower	149
Balkan	137	Berge Everett	37	Bow Fortune	149
Ballangen	101	Berge Fjord	37	Bow Fraternity	149
Balsfjord	101	Berge Frost	37	Bow Heron	149
Baltic Action	92	Berge Hugin	37	Bow Hunter	149
Baltic Advance	92	Berge Munin	37	Bow Lady	149
Baltic Ambassador	92	Berge Nantes	38	Bow Lancer	149
Baltic Ambition	92	Berge Nice	38	Bow Leopard	149
Baltic Breeze	220	Berge Nord	38	Bow Lion	150
Baltic Captain I	92	Berge Odin	38	Bow Maasslot	150
Baltic Chief I	92	Berge Pacific	38	Bow Maasstad	150
Baltic Cliff	184	Berge Phoenix	38	Bow Maasstroom	150
Baltic Cloud	184	Berge Rachel	38	Bow Merkur	150
Baltic Commander I	92	Berge Racine	38	Bow Neptun	150
Baltic Highway	100	Berge Ragnhild	38	Bow Orion	150
Baltic Leader	141	Berge Saga	30	Bow Pacifico	150
Baltic Meridian	184	Berge Shan	38	Bow Panther	150
Baltic Sea	212	Berge Sisu	38	Bow Peace	150
Baltic Snow	184	Berge Spirit	38	Bow Petros	150
Baltic Sun II	92	Berge Stadt	38	Bow Pioneer	150
Baltic Swan	68	Berge Stahl	38	Bow Power	150
Baltic Wave	92	Berge Strand	38	Bow Pride	150
Baltic Wave	184	Berge Sund	38	Bow Prima	150
Baltic Wind	92	Berge Sword	38	Bow Prosper	150
Baltic Wind	184	Berge Vik	38	Bow Puma	150
Baltrum Trader	45	Bergeland	38	Bow Santos	150
Bamboo Bridge	226	Bergen Arrow	97	Bow Saturn	150
Banasol	101	Bergen Max	178	Bow Sky	150
Banastar	101	Bergitta	40	Bow Spring	150
Banda Sea	90	Bering Sea	196	Bow Star	150
Bandaisan	126	Bering Sea	212	Bow Summer	150
Bandar	101	Berlin Express	83	Bow Sun	150

Name	Page	Name	Page	Name	Page
Bow Viking	150	Bro Elizabeth	44	C.V. Stealth	114
Braemar	16	Bro Ellen	44	Cabo Creus	135
Brasil Express	83	Bro Elliot	44	Cabo Hellas	168
Brasil Star	200	Bro Etienne	44	Cabo Prior	88
Bravery Ace	124	Bro Premium	44	Cabo Sounion	168
Brazil Star	153	Bro Priority	44	Cadiz Carrier	66
Brazilian Reefer	106	Bro Promotion	44	Cadiz Knutsen	102
Brazos	164	Bro Provider	44	Caecilia Schulte	192
Braztrans I	61	Bro Sincero	44	Cala Palamos	157
Breeze Arrow	97	Bro Stella	44	Cala Palma	193
Bregen	213	Broadgate	153	Cala Palmira	45
Bregen	40	Brother Glory	153	Cala Paradiso	176
Bremen Express	83	Brugge Max	178	Cala Pedra	193
Bremen Max	178	Brugge Venture	60	Cala Pevero	193
Bremen Senator	222	Brunhilde Salamon	188	Cala Piana	193
Bremen	22	Bruno Salamon	189	Cala Piccola	193
Bridge Arrow	97	Brussels	60	Cala Piedad	225
Bright City	49	Bryggen	150	Cala Pilar	161
Bright Days	49	Buccleuch	153	Cala Pinar del Rio	161
Bright State	49	Bujin	141	Cala Pino	193
Brilliance of the Seas	18	Bulduri	105	Cala Pintada	66
Brilliant Ace	124	Bulgaria	137	Cala Portese	193
Bristol Bay	193	Bulk Africa	47	Cala Providencia	66
Britain Star	62	Bulk Asia	182	Cala Puebla	161
Britanis	47	Bulk Atlanta	47	Cala Pula	193
British Beech	41	Bulk Australia	47	Calapadria	32
British Chivalry	41	Bulk Cedar	47	Calaparana	188
British Cormorant	41	Bulk Europe	182	California Jupiter	141
British Courtesy	41	Bulk Fern	47	California Mercury	141
British Curlew	41	Bulk Leher	47	California Senator	146
British Cygnet	41	Bulkazores	47	Californian Highway	100
British Eagle	41	Bunga Anggerik	113	Calliroe Patronicola	165
British Endeavour	41	Bunga Bidara	113	Camberley	196
British Endurance	41	Bunga Cenderawasih	113	Camellia Ace	124
British Energy	41	Bunga Delima	113	Camilla Rickmers	180
British Engineer	41	Bunga Kantan Dua	113	Canada Senator	146
British Enterprise	41	Bunga Kantan Satu	113	Canadian Express	217
British Environment	41	Bunga Kantan Tiga	113	Canberra Express	84
British Esteem	41	Bunga Kasturi	113	Canelo Arrow	97
British Excellence	41	Bunga Kasturi Dua	113	Canmar Promise	157
British Experience	41	Bunga Kekaras	113	Canterbury Star	200
British Explorer	41	Bunga Kelana 3	113	Cap Agulhas	190
British Falcon	41	Bunga Kelana Dua	113	Cap Arnauti	190
British Fidelity	41	Bunga Kelana Empat	113	Cap Azul	108
British Gannet	41	Bunga Kelana Enam	113	Cap Blanco	152
British Harmony	41	Bunga Kelana Lima	113	Cap Bonavista	116
British Hawthorn	44	Bunga Kelana Satu	113	Cap Brett	152
British Hazel	44	Bunga Kelana Tudjuh	113	Cap Carmel	152
British Holly	44	Bunga Kenanga	113	Cap Cortes	116
British Innovator	44	Bunga Kenari	113	Cap Delgado	116
British Integrity	44	Bunga Kerayong	113	Cap Diamant	60
British Kestrel	44	Bunga Mawar	113	Cap Domingo	152
British Laurel	44	Bunga Melati Dua	113	Cap Doukato	88
British Liberty	44	Bunga Melati Empat	113	Cap Ferrato	146
British Loyalty	44	Bunga Melati Enam	113	Cap Finisterre	152
British Mallard	44	Bunga Melati Lima	113	Cap Frio	144
British Merchant	44	Bunga Melati Satu	113	Cap Georges	60
British Merlin	44	Bunga Melati Tiga	113	Cap Jean	60
British Oak	44	Bunga Melati Tudjuh	113	Cap Laurent	60
British Osprey	44	Bunga Pelangi Dua	113	Cap Leon	60
British Pioneer	44	Bunga Pelangi	113	Cap Lobos	108
British Pride	44	Bunga Raya Dua	113	Cap Maleas	192
British Progress	44	Bunga Raya Satu	113	Cap Matatula	33
British Purpose	44	Bunga Saga 9	113	Cap Melville	152
British Robin	44	Bunga Semarak	113	Cap Nelson	152
British Security	44	Bunga Seroja Satu	113	Cap Norte	68
British Serenity	44	Bunga Siantan	113	Cap Ortegal	116
British Swift	44	Bunga Tanjung	113	Cap Palmas	152
British Tenacity	44	Bunga Terasek	113	Cap Pierre	60
British Trader	44	Bunga Teratai 4	113	Cap Pilar	146
British Tranquility	44	Bunga Teratai Dua	113	Cap Polonia	152
British Unity	44	Bunga Teratai Tiga	113	Cap Reinga	116
British Vine	44	Bunga Teratai	113	Cap Roca	152
British Willow	44	Busan Express	144	Cap Rojo	190
Bro Albert	44	Bussewitz	104	Cap Romuald	60
Bro Alexandre	44	Buxcrown	146	Cap Salinas	144
Bro Anton	44	Buxfavourite	146	Cap San Antonio	152
Bro Arthur	44	Buxhill	146	Cap San Augustin	152
Bro Atland	44	Buxlagoon	146	Cap San Lorenzo	152
Bro Axel	44	Buxlink	146	Cap San Marco	152
Bro Caroline	44	Buxmaster	146	Cap San Nicolas	152
Bro Catherine	44	Buyihe	48	Cap San Raphael	152
Bro Cecile	44	Buzzard Bay	193	Cap Saray	88
Bro Charlotte	44			Cap Sunion	66
Bro Deliverer	44	C. Bright	189	Cap Trafalgar	152
Bro Designer	44	C. Columbus	22	Cap Van Diemen	33
Bro Edward	44	C.S. Stealth	114	Cap Verde	152

Name	No.		Name	No.		Name	No.
Hannover Express	84		Hellespont Prosperity	170		Houston	136
Hans Maersk	128		Hellespont Protector	170		HS Challenger	109
Hans Scholl	48		Hellespont Providence	170		HS Discoverer	109
Hansa Africa	109		Hellespont Tatina	170		HS Norma	109
Hansa Arendal	109		Hellespont Trader	170		HS Tosca	109
Hansa Bergen	109		Hellespont Trinity	170		Hua Tuo	172
Hansa Berlin	109		Hellespont Troope	170		Hua Yun He	49
Hansa Bremen	109		Helvetia	73		Hual Africa	176
Hansa Centaur	109		Hemina	38		Hual America	176
Hansa Century	109		Henning Maersk	128		Hual Asia	89
Hansa Commodore	109		Henriette Maersk	128		Hual Dubai	54
Hansa Greifswald	109		Henrika Schulte	192		Hual Durban	89
Hansa Kristiansand	109		Henry Hudson Bridge	100		Hual Paris	89
Hansa London	109		Henry Oldendorff	161		Hual Seoul	89
Hansa Lubeck	109		Henry Rickmers	181		Hual Tokyo	89
Hansa Narvik	109		Henry	65		Hual Trader	89
Hansa Rostock	109		Herakles	38		Hual Tramper	89
Hansa Stavange	109		Hercules Highway	100		Hual Transporter	89
Hansa Stockholm	109		Hermann Wulff	225		Hual Trapeze	89
Hansa Stralsund	109		Hermitage Bridge	196		Hual Trapper	89
Hansa Visby	109		Hero	190		Hual Treasure	89
Hanseatic	22		Heroic Ace	125		Hual Trekker	89
Happy Buccaneer	200		Hertford	32		Hual Trident	89
Happy Ranger	200		Hesnes	213		Hual Triumph	89
Happy River	200		Heythrop	154		Hudson Bay	208
Happy Rover	200		HHL Biscay	83		Hudson Leader	141
Harad	135		Hickory	90		Hudson Spirit	205
Harefield	97		High Challenge	65		Hudson	164
Harmen Oldendorff	161		High Courage	65		Hugo N	38
Harmony Ace	125		High Endeavour	65		Hugo Oldendorff	135
Harmony	174		High Endurance	65		Humber Bridge	100
Harriette N	38		High Energy	65		Humboldt Current	136
Hastula	196		High Harmony	65		Humboldt Express	84
Hatasia	196		High Light	65		Hume Highway	100
Hatsu Courage	148		High Performance	65		Iluntestern	182
Hatsu Crystal	148		High Power	65		Ilse Wulff	225
Hatsu Eagle	74		High Presence	65		Husum	69
Hatsu Elite	74		High Priority	65		Huta Zgoda	173
Hatsu Envoy	74		High Progress	65		Hyde Park	154
Hatsu Ethic	74		High Spirit	65		Hydra Star	185
Hatsu Excel	74		High Valor	65		Hyundai Admiral	154
Hatsu Pride	74		High Wind	65		Hyundai Advance	89
Hatsu Prima	74		Highgate	154		Hyundai Aquapia	89
Hatsu Shine	74		Hilda Knutsen	102		Hyundai Atlas	89
Hatsu Sigma	74		Hildegaard	112		Hyundai Banner	89
Hatsu Smart	74		Hille Oldendorff	161		Hyundai Baron	154
Hatsu Smile	74		Hilli	77		Hyundai Bridge	89
Haustrum	196		Hispania Spirit	205		Hyundai Challenger	62
Havdrott	38		Hispania	60		Hyundai Commodore	65
Havelstern	181		Hoechst Express	84		Hyundai Confidence	89
Havfrost	38		Hoegh Berlin	89		Hyundai Continental	89
Havfru	38		Hoegh Galleon	89		Hyundai Cosmos	89
Havglimt	38		Hoegh Gandria	89		Hyundai Cosmpia	89
Havis	38		Hoegh Oceania	54		Hyundai Discovery	154
Havkong	38		Hoegh Tracer	89		Hyundai Dominion	154
Havrim	38		Hoegh Transit	89		Hyundai Duke	65
Hawk Arrow	97		Hoegh Traveller	89		Hyundai Emperor	154
Hawk Bay	194		Hoegh Trinity	89		Hyundai Explorer	96
Hawk	75		Hoegh Trooper	89		Hyundai Fortune	90
Hawtah	135		Hoegh Tropicana	89		Hyundai Freedom	90
Headway	157		Hoegh Trotter	89		Hyundai Frontie	96
Heather Knutsen	102		Hoegh Trove	89		Hyundai Future	90
Hebridean Princess	26		Hoegh Trubadour	89		Hyundai Garnet	140
Hebridean Spirit	26		Hojin	141		Hyundai General	90
Hebris	38		Holiday Dream	16		Hyundai Glory	90
Hedda	38		Holiday	8		Hyundai Greenpia	90
Hedwig Oldendorff	161		Holland Maas Caraibes	69		Hyundai Highness	90
Heidelburg Express	84		Holsatia Express	154		Hyundai Highway	90
Heijin	141		Honduras Star	200		Hyundai Independence	154
Heinrich S	188		Hong Kong Express	84		Hyundai Innovator	96
Hekabe	157		Hong Kong Star	172		Hyundai Island	90
Helena Oldendorff	161		Hong Yun He	49		Hyundai Kingdom	154
Helena Schulte	193		Hongkong Senator	148		Hyundai Liberty	154
Helene Knutsen	102		Honor River	49		Hyundai National	154
Helene Maersk	128		Honor	220		Hyundai No. 103	181
Helene Rickmers	180		Hood Island	212		Hyundai No. 106	154
Helene Selmar	222		Hope Bay	194		Hyundai No. 107	154
Helga Selmer	222		Horizon	62		Hyundai No. 108	154
Helga Spirit	205		Horizon	164		Hyundai No. 109	154
Helga	38		Hornbay	66		Hyundai No. 201	221
Helice	38		Horncap	66		Hyundai No. 202	221
Helios	38		Horncliff	66		Hyundai No. 203	40
Helix	196		Hose Marti	105		Hyundai No. 205	221
Helle Ritscher	212		Houston Express	144		Hyundai No. 206	221
Hellespont Pride	170					Hyundai Oceania	90
Hellespont Progress	170					Hyundai Oceanpia	90
Hellespont Promise	170					Hyundai Olympia	90

Name	No.		Name	No.		Name	No.
Hyundai Patriot	154		Iran Baakeri	93		Iron Queen	178
Hyundai Pioneer	116		Iran Baghaei	93		Iron Yandi	205
Hyundai Power	90		Iran Bahonar	93		Irongate	154
Hyundai Progress	90		Iran Baluchestan	93		Iryda	173
Hyundai Prosperity	90		Iran Bayan	93		Isa	173
Hyundai Republic	154		Iran Beheshti	93		Isabel Knutsen	102
Hyundai Spirit	90		Iran Borhan	93		Isadora	173
Hyundai Sprinter	90		Iran Broojerdi	93		Isarstern	182
Hyundai Star	90		Iran Chamran	93		Isere	164
Hyundai Stride	90		Iran Dastghayb	93		ISI Olive	96
Hyundai Sun	90		Iran Deyanat	93		Island Escape	18
Hyundai Technopia	90		Iran Eghbal	93		Island Princess	10
Hyundai Universal	90		Iran Ehsan	93		Island Ranger	178
Hyundai Utopia	90		Iran Entekhab	93		Island Sky	24
Hyundai Vladivostok	90		Iran Eshraghi	93		Island Star	18
			Iran Esteghial	93		Isolda	173
Ibis Arrow	98		Iran Ghafari	93		Isolde	220
Ibn Al Moataz	214		Iran Ghazi	93		Ital Contessa	148
Ibn Bassam	214		Iran Gheyamat	93		Ital Fastosa	181
Ibn Battotah	189		Iran Ghodousi	93		Ital Festosa	181
Ibn Khaldoun	225		Iran Gilan	93		Ital Garland	75
Ibn Sina	148		Iran Golestan	93		Ital Universo	75
Ibn Younus	214		Iran Hamedan	93		Ivan Bogun	112
Ihra,l	98		Iran Hamzeh	93		Ivan Papanin	112
Ibuki	83		Iran Hesabi	93		Ivan Susanin	112
Ibukisan	126		Iran Hormozgan	93		Ivar Lauritzen	106
Icaro	190		Iran Ilam	93		Iver Excel	217
Ice Bell	184		Iran Isfahan	93		Iver Experience	217
Ida Selmer	222		Iran Jamal	93		Iver Expert	217
Igloo Moon	116		Iran Jomhuri	93		Iver Exporter	217
Igloo Star	116		Iran Kashani	93		Ivory Ace	106
Ignacy Daszynski	173		Iran Kerman	93		Ivory Arrow	176
Iguana	46		Iran Kermanshah	93		Ivory Dawn	106
Ikomasan	126		Iran Khorasan	93		Ivory Girl	106
Ilya Erenburg	145		Iran Khuzestan	93		Ivory Tirupati	106
Imagination	8		Iran Kordestan	93		Iwatesan	126
Immanuel Kant	190		Iran Lorestan	93		Izumo Bay	194
Imme Oldendorff	161		Iran Madani	93			
Inaba	226		Iran Mahallati	93		Jacamar	168
Inca	213		Iran Makin	93		Jade Arrow	176
Indamex Cauvery	143		Iran Matin	93		Jade Trader	45
Indamex Colorado	177		Iran Mazandaran	93		Jaeger Arrow	97
Indamex Delaware	92		Iran Meezan	93		Jag Anjali	80
Indamex Godavari	144		Iran Mobin	93		Jag Arnav	80
Independence	220		Iran Modares	93		Jag Arpan	80
Independence	20		Iran Mufateh	93		Jag Laadki	80
Independence	65		Iran Nabuvat	93		Jag Labh	80
Independent Action	69		Iran Navab	93		Jag Lakshya	80
Independent Endeavor	69		Iran Piroozi	93		Jag Lalit	80
Independent Pursuit	69		Iran Rajai	93		Jag Lamha	80
Independent Spirit	69		Iran Sadoughi	93		Jag Lata	80
Independent Trader	69		Iran Sadr	93		Jag Lavanya	80
Independent Venture	69		Iran Saeidi	93		Jag Laxmi	80
India Lotus	153		Iran Salam	93		Jag Leela	80
Indian Ocean	212		Iran Sarbaz	93		Jag Leena	80
Indiana Highway	100		Iran Sattari	93		Jag Leher	80
Indiga	112		Iran Seestan	93		Jag Lok	80
Indotrans Celebes	202		Iran Sepah	93		Jag Padma	80
Indotrans Flores	202		Iran Shahryar	96		Jag Pahel	80
Indotrans Java	202		Iran Shariat	96		Jag Palak	80
Indotrans Makassar	202		Iran Shariati	96		Jag Pankhi	80
Indra	105		Iran Sokan	96		Jag Pari	80
Infinity	18		Iran Tabatabaei	96		Jag Pavitra	80
Inga S	188		Iran Takhti	96		Jag Prachi	80
Inga	105		Iran Taleghani	96		Jag Pragdip	80
Ingeborg	164		Iran Tehran	96		Jag Pragati	80
Ingrid Gorthon	209		Iran Teyfouri	96		Jag Praja	80
Insignia	16		Iran Vahdat	96		Jag Pranam	80
Inspiration	8		Iran Vojdan	96		Jag Pratap	80
Integrity	220		Iran Yamin	96		Jag Prayog	80
Invicta	73		Iran Yasooj	96		Jag Preeti	80
Inviken	134		Iran Yazd	96		Jag Rahul	80
Invincible	196		Iran Zanjan	96		Jag Rani	80
Ioannis Zafirakis	110		Irenes Logos	213		Jag Ratna	80
Ionian Spirit	205		Irenes Myth	213		Jag Ravi	80
Ipanema	46		Irenes Rainbow	213		Jag Heena	80
Iran Abozar	92		Irenes Reliance	213		Jag Rishi	80
Iran Adi	92		Irenes Remedy	213		Jag Vayu	80
Iran Afzal	93		Irenes Vigor	213		Jag Vikas	80
Iran Akhavan	93		Irenes Vision	213		Jag Vikram	80
Iran Amanat	93		Irfon	154		Jag Viraj	80
Iran Ardebil	93		Iris Ace	125		Jakarta Express	85
Iran Ashrafi	93		Irma	173		Jakob Maersk	128
Iran Azadi	93		Iron Baron	178		James River Bridge	100
Iran Azarbayjan	93		Iron Fortune	185		Jamno	173
Iran Baabael	93		Iron King	178		Jan Dlugosz	172
			Iron Prince	178			

Name	Page
Janet	164
Jasmine Knutsen	102
Jasper Arrow	176
Jean LD	110
Jeanette	164
Jebel Ali	214
Jens Maersk	129
Jepperson Maersk	129
Jervis Bay	129
Jesper Maersk	128
Jessie Maersk	128
Jewel of the Seas	18
Jia Xing	172
Jill Jacob	96
Jin He	49
Jin Yun He	49
Jing Po He	49
Jingu Maru	141
Jinsei Maru	141
Jo Acer	150
Jo Ask	150
Jo Betula	150
Jo Birk	150
Jo Brevik	150
Jo Cedar	150
Jo Clipper	150
Jo Eik	150
Jo Gran	150
Jo Kashi	150
Jo Kiri	150
Jo Lind	150
Jo Lonn	150
Jo Oak	150
Jo Rogn	150
Jo Selje	150
Jo Sequoia	150
Jo Spruce	150
Jo Sycamore	150
Jo Sypress	150
Jobst Oldendorff	161
Joh. Gorthon	209
Johann Jacob	96
Johann Oldendorff	88
Johann Schulte	190
Johannes Maersk	129
Jolly	92
Jorgen Lauritzen	106
Jorita	213
Jorunn Knutsen	102
Josephine Maersk	129
Joviality	52
Joyous Age	52
Joyous Land	52
Joyous Society	52
Joyous World	52
Juanita	213
Judith Schulte	192
Julian N	38
Julie Delmas	58
Jumbo Javelin	98
Jupiter Diamond	141
Jurmo	140
Jurong Sea	52
Kadriah II	192
Kaga	141
Kaijin	141
Kailash	194
Kaimon	126
Kaimon II	126
Kaliningrad	110
Kaliope	173
Kaltene	105
Kaluga	145
Kamakura	141
Kamari	46
Kamenitza	137
Kamina	58
Kaminesan	126
Kanata Spirit	205
Kandalaksha	112
Kandilousa	72
Kansas	164
Kapitan Bochek	112
Kapitan Chukhchin	112
Kapitan Danilkin	112
Kapitan Georgi Georgiev	137
Kapitan Kudlay	112
Kapitan Nazarev	112
Kapitan Sviridov	112
Kapitan Vakula	112
Kapitan Vodenko	112
Kara Sea	196
Kareela Spirit	205
Karen Knutsen	102
Karen Maersk	129
Karin S	188
Karonga	73
Karratha Spirit	205
Kashima Bay	194
Kasper Schulte	192
Kassel	72
Kastelorizo	72
Kasuga Bay	194
Kate Maersk	129
Katja	112
Katori	126
Katrine Maersk	129
Katsuragi	141
Kazan	145
Kazimah	104
KCL Bardu	102
KCL Barracuda	102
Kedarnath	194
Keefan	104
Kemeri	105
Kemira Gas	61
Kenai	168
Kent Pioneer	161
Kent Timber	161
Kentucky Highway	100
Kenwood Park	154
Keoyang Majesty	82
Keoyang Noble	82
Keoyang Orient	82
Kerel	92
Kersaint	32
Kestrel Arrow	97
Kestrel I	153
Kestrel	75
Khaled Ibn Al Waleed	214
Khannur	77
Khatanga	112
Khirurg Vishnevskiy	145
Khudozhnik Moor	145
Kiani Satu	90
Kildare	154
Kilimanjaro Spirit	205
Kim Jacob	96
Kingsway	157
Kiowa Spirit	172
Kirsten Maersk	129
Kitano	141
Kite Arrow	98
Kitty Knutsen	102
Kiwi Arrow	98
Kiwi Auckland	89
Klements Gotvalds	105
Klipper Stream	194
Knock Adoon	162
Knock Allan	162
Knock Stocks	162
Knud Lauritzen	106
Knud Maersk	129
Koa Spirit	172
Kobe Express	84
Kodiak	168
Koh Jin	141
Kola	112
Kolguyev	112
Kolka	105
Kom	137
Kometik	48
Kopalnia Borynia	173
Kopalnia Halemba	173
Kopalnia Rydultowy	173
Kopalnia Sosnowiec	173
Kopalnia Zofiowka	173
Korat Navee	214
Kota Ekspres	83
Kota Ganteng	170
Kota Gemar	170
Kota Gembira	170
Kota Gunawan	170
Kota Kado	170
Kota Kamil	170
Kota Kaya	170
Kota Merdesa	33
Kota Mesra	33
Kota Molek	216
Kota Pahlawan	104
Kota Pekarang	143
Kota Pelangi	104
Kota Pemimpin	143
Kota Perkasa	174
Kota Permai	143
Kota Pertama	148
Kota Pusaka	104
Koyagi Spirit	205
Koznitsa	137
Krabi Navee	214
Krasnodar	145
Kristin Knutsen	102
Kristina Regina	26
Krymsk	145
Kuala Lumpur Express	62
Kuban	145
Kuiseb	57
Kujawy	173
Kuldiga	105
Kumasi	58
Kurzeme	106
Kuzma Minin	112
Kwangtung	202
Kyeema Spirit	205
Kyla	46
Kyoto Express	84
Kyushu Spirit	205
Kyushu Star	154
La Esperanza	213
La Forge	136
La Jolla	46
La Madrina	213
La Paz	213
La Prudencia	213
Lacerta	46
Lady Korcula	106
Lady Racisce	106
Lahore Express	85
Lake Erie	76
Lake Michigan	76
Lake Ontario	76
Lake Phoenix	154
Lake Ranger	178
Lake Superior	76
Lanikai	46
Lapis Arrow	176
Laptev Sea	196
Lars Maersk	129
Latgale	106
Laura Delmas	58
Laura Maersk	129
Lauren	164
Lausanne	202
Laust Maersk	129
Le Diamant	24
Le Levant	24
Leblon	152
Leda Maersk	129
Leda Trader	45
Leeds Castle	136
Legend of the Seas	18
Legiony Polskie	173
Leinestern	182
Leisure World	28
Leo Leader	141
Leo Star	185
Leonid Sobolyev	145
Leonid Utesov	145
Leopold Oldendorff	57
Leopold Staff	172
Leverkusen Express	84
Lexa Maersk	129
Leyte Spirit	205
Li Bai	172
Liao He	49
Liberty Ace	125
Liberty of the Seas	18
Liberty	220
Libra Ecuador	190
Libra	213
Libra Buenos Aires	164
Libra Chile	222
Libra Corcovado	162
Libra Houston	192
Libra Ipanema	69
Libra Leader	217
Libra New York	222
Libra Niteroi	162
Libra Patagonia	162
Libra Rio	69
Libra Salvador	188
Libra Santa Catarina	88
Libra Santos	69
Libra Star	185
Lica Maersk	129
Lielupe	106
Ligovsky Prospect	196
Liguria	62
Lili Marleen	26
Liliana Dimitrova	137
Lily Oldendorff	161
Lily	152
Limari	69
Lina	153
Linda Oldendorff	46
Lindavia	66
Linden Pride	141
Ling Yun He	49
Lion	216
Lions Gate Bridge	100
Lircay	69
Lisa Schulte	193
Lisbon Express	85
Lissy Schulte	192
Lista	134
Lita	110
Livanita	213
Livano Express	85
LNG Benue	38
LNG Enugu	38
LNG Oyo	38
LNG River Orashi	38
Loa	69
Loch Rannoch	133
Lofoten	28
Logos Hope	26
Logos II	26
Loire	164
Lombok Strait	194
London Express	84
London Senator	148
London Star	48
London Tower	154
Long Beach Bridge	100
Longavi	69
Lontue	69
Lord Hinton	174
Los Angeles Express	144
Los Roques	96
Lotus	205
Louis Pasteur	178
Lovina	46
Lowlands Beilun	61
Lowlands Brilliance	61
Lowlands Comfort	61
Lowlands Ghent	61
Lowlands Grace	61
Lowlands Longevity	61
Lowlands Maine	61
Lowlands Mimosa	61
Lowlands Nello	61
Lowlands Orchid	61
Lowlands Patrasche	61
Lowlands Phoenix	61
Lowlands Prosperity	61
Lowlands Saguenay	61
Lowlands Sumida	61
Lowlands Sunrise	61
Lowlands Trader	61
Loyalty	212
LT Cortesia	148
LT Genova	75
LT Glamour	75
LT Going	75
LT Grace	75
LT Greet	75
LT Lloydiana	75
LT Trieste	75
LT Ulysses	74
LT Unica	75
LT Unicorn	74
LT Usodimare	75
Lu Ban	172
Lu He	49
Lu Xun	172
Luan He	49
Lucas Oldendorff	161
Lucie Delmas	58
Lucky Transporter	154
Lucy Oldendorff	161
Ludolf Oldendorff	161
Ludwigshafen Express	84
Luetjenburg	144
Luise Oldendorff	105
Luna Maersk	129
Luni Castle	136
Luo Ba He	49
Luo He	49
Luxembourg	60
Luzon Spirit	205
Luzon Strait	194
Lydia Oldendorff	114
Lykes Commodore	188
Lykes Osprey	85
Lykes Racer	174
Lyra Leader	141
Lyra Pioneer	88
Lyubov Orlova	28
Maasdam	8
Maciej Rataj	173
Mackinac Bridge	100
Madagascar	28
Madame Butterfly	220
Madison Maersk	129
Madison	164
Madrid Spirit	205
Maersk Aberdeen	129
Maersk Ahram	129
Maersk Alabama	129
Maersk Alaska	133
Maersk Antwerp	129
Maersk Arizona	133
Maersk Arkansas	129
Maersk Arun	129
Maersk Athens	109
Maersk Atlantic	129
Maersk Auckland	109
Maersk Avon	129
Maersk Barcelona	136
Maersk Barry	133
Maersk Belawan	136
Maersk Brisbane	136
Maersk Carolina	129
Maersk Cloud	133
Maersk Constantia	65
Maersk Constellation	133
Maersk Crest	133
Maersk Curlew	128
Maersk Dabou	164
Maersk Daesan	181
Maersk Dale	85
Maersk Dallas	143
Maersk Dalton	129
Maersk Damascus	158
Maersk Dammam	83
Maersk Dampier	109
Maersk Danbury	109
Maersk Danville	164
Maersk Darlington	129
Maersk Darmstadt	109
Maersk Dartford	129
Maersk Dartmouth	176
Maersk Darwin	154
Maersk Dauphin	129
Maersk Davao	181
Maersk Davenport	109
Maersk Dayton	84
Maersk Decartur	158
Maersk Delano	129
Maersk Dellys	222
Maersk Delmont	129
Maersk Denia	158
Maersk Denton	158
Maersk Denver	143
Maersk Derby	33
Maersk Derince	222
Maersk Detroit	158
Maersk Deva	33
Maersk Dexter	85
Maersk Dhaka	181
Maersk Diadem	226
Maersk Diadema	226
Maersk Dieppe	158
Maersk Djibouti	181
Maersk Doha	154
Maersk Dolores	158
Maersk Dominica	158
Maersk Donegal	158
Maersk Dortmund	109
Maersk Douala	181
Maersk Douglas	158
Maersk Dresden	109
Maersk Driscoll	158
Maersk Dublin	83
Maersk Duffield	158
Maersk Duisburg	109
Maersk Dunafare	158
Maersk Dundee	154
Maersk Dunedin	158
Maersk Durban	181
Maersk Durham	158
Maersk Fuji	45
Maersk Fukuoka	45
Maersk Gairloch	129
Maersk Garonne	129
Maersk Gateshead	130
Maersk Georgia	133
Maersk Gironde	130
Maersk Greenock	128
Maersk Holyhead	128
Maersk Hong Kong	33
Maersk Humber	133
Maersk Ipanema	158
Maersk Itajai	33
Maersk Itaqui	36
Maersk Itea	36
Maersk Jenaz	202
Maersk Jewel	133
Maersk Juan	202
Maersk Kalamata	62
Maersk Kalmar	129
Maersk Kampala	130
Maersk Karachi	130
Maersk Kiel	130
Maersk Kimi	130
Maersk Kingston	130
Maersk Kithira	130
Maersk Kolkata	62
Maersk Kyrenia	130
Maersk Malacca	130
Maersk Malaga	109
Maersk Mandraki	62
Maersk Marseille	109
Maersk Merlion	130
Maersk Miami	130
Maersk Missouri	130
Maersk Mykonos	62
Maersk Naantali	88
Maersk Nairn	130
Maersk Nanhai	193
Maersk Nantes	188
Maersk Napier	143
Maersk Naples	135
Maersk Nara	130
Maersk Narbonne	135
Maersk Narvik	135
Maersk Nashville	135
Maersk Nassau	188
Maersk Navia	193
Maersk Neuchatel	193
Maersk Neustadt	193
Maersk New Orleans	143

Name	No.	Name	No.	Name	No.	Name	No.	Name	No.	Name	No.
Maersk Newark	143	Maersk Wave	133	Marlene Green	56	Meynell	154	MOL Faithful	190	Mount Adamello	88
Maersk Newcastle	143	Maersk Welkin	133	Marlin	204	Mi Yun He	49	MOL Fortune	125	Mount Fuji	88
Maersk Newport	88	Maersk Willow	133	Marmara Sea	153	Miden Max	178	MOL Glory	125	Mount McKinney	88
Maersk Nolanville	130	Maersk Wind	133	Marne	164	Midjur	137	MOL Golden Wattle	125	Mount Olympus	88
Maersk Nordenham	88	Magas	110	Mars Glory	185	Midnatsol	28	MOL Horizon	58	Mount Rainier	88
Maersk Norfolk	143	Magdalena	173	Mars	33	Midnight Sun	126	MOL Ingenuity	125	Mount Robson	88
Maersk Nottingham	130	Magdalena Green	56	Marshal Bagramyan	145	Mighty Servant 1	68	MOL Initiative	125	Mozu Arrow	98
Maersk Novazzano	176	Magdalena Oldendorff	161	Marshal Chu(y)kov	145	Mighty Servant 3	68	MOL Innovation	140	MS Simon	48
Maersk Palermo	130	Magic Sky	54	Marshal Vasilyevskiy	145	Mignon	220	MOL Integrity	125	MS Sophie	48
Maersk Patras	130	Magic Wave	54	Martorell	125	Mikhail Kutuzov	112	MOL Liberty	125	MSC Adele	116
Maersk Pecem	225	Magic Wind	54	Maruba Cathay	45	Mikhail Strekalovskiy	112	MOL Maas	125	MSC Adriana	116
Maersk Pelepas	128	Magic	194	Maruba Tango	181	Milin Kamak	137	MOL Miracle	125	MSC Agata	116
Maersk Pembroke	130	Magleby Maersk	130	Maruba Trader	45	Millennium	213	MOL Paramount	125	MSC Alabama	62
Maersk Penang	130	Magnavia	66	Marvellous	36	Millennium Explorer	126	MOL Performance	125	MSC Alessia	148
Maersk Perth	128	Magnific	194	Marvelous Ace	125	Millennium	18	MOL Precision	125	MSC Alexa	116
Maersk Peterhead	83	Magpie	32	Mass Enterprise	52	Milos	41	MOL Pride	125	MSC Alexandra	116
Maersk Petersburg	83	Mahinabank	204	Mass Glory	52	Mimi Selmar	222	MOL Priority	125	MSC Alice	116
Maersk Phoenix	133	Maikop	110	Mass Prosperity	52	Min He	49	MOL Progress	125	MSC Alpana	117
Maersk Phuket	130	Majestic Maersk	130	Master I	174	Mina Oldendorff	161	MOL Promise	125	MSC Alyssa	117
Maersk Pireaus	109	Majestic Unity	168	Mastera	140	Mindanao	77	MOL Rainbow	58	MSC America	117
Maersk Pittsburg	83	Majestic	108	Mathilde Maersk	130	Mineral Antwerpen	60	MOL Renaissance	164	MSC Amsterdam	33
Maersk Plymouth	128	Majestic	194	Matilde	105	Mineral Azalea	60	MOL Satisfaction	212	MSC Amy	117
Maersk Pointer	133	Majesty of the Seas	18	Matira	46	Mineral Beijing	60	MOL Solution	125	MSC Anahita	117
Maersk Portland	83	Major Hubal	173	Matjam	133	Mineral Belgium	60	MOL Thames *	125	MSC Anastasia	117
Maersk Princess	128	Majori	106	Mattea	214	Mineral China	60	MOL Triumph	125	MSC Andalucia II	153
Maersk Pristine	133	Makiri Green	56	Matterhorn Spirit	205	Mineral Kyoto	101	MOL Velocity	140	MSC Angela	117
Maersk Radiant	133	Makronissos	72	Mauranger	222	Mineral Noble	60	MOL Vision	140	MSC Aniello	117
Maersk Ramsey	133	Malaga Carrier	66	Maveric	194	Mineral Oak	60	MOL Wellington	125	MSC Annamaria	117
Maersk Rapier	133	Malyovitza	137	Max Jacob	96	Mineral Poterne	60	MOL Wisdom	125	MSC Annick	117
Maersk Ras Laffan	128	Mamry II	173	Max Oldendorff	161	Mineral Shanghai	60	MOL Wish	148	MSC Ans	117
Maersk Ravenna	98	Manasota	46	Maxim Gorkiy	16	Mineral Sines	60	Molda	134	MSC Antonia	117
Maersk Regent	133	Mandarin Arrow	98	May Oldendorff	161	Mineral Tianjin	60	Moldanger	222	MSC Antwerp	62
Maersk Rhine	48	Manhattan Bridge	101	Maya	213	Mineral Viking	60	Moleson	202	MSC Arabia	172
Maersk Rhode Island	133	Manon	220	Mayon Spirit	205	Minerva Alexandra	124	Mombasa Star	153	MSC Ariane	117
Maersk Rhone	192	Maple Ace II	125	Mayview Maersk	130	Minerva Alice	124	Mona Century	125	MSC Armonia	14
Maersk Richmond	133	Mapocho	61	Mazury	173	Minerva Anna	124	Mona Liberty	125	MSC Asli	117
Maersk Riga	48	Mar	106	Mc-Kinney Maersk	130	Minerva Astra	124	Mona Linden	126	MSC Atlantic	117
Maersk Rimini	208	Mara	96	MCT Alioth	83	Minerva Concert	124	Mona Lisa	26	MSC Augusta	117
Maersk Rio Grande	98	Maracas Bay	126	MCT Almak	83	Minerva Eleonora	124	Monarch of the Seas	18	MSC Aurora	117
Maersk Rosario	98	Marathon	213	MCT Altair	83	Minerva Ellie	124	Monchegorsk	112	MSC Austria	62
Maersk Rostock	98	Marble	77	MCT Arcturus	83	Minerva Emma	124	Moniuszko	173	MSC Ayala	117
Maersk Rosyth	133	Marble Highway	101	MCT Matterhorn	83	Minerva Grace	124	Monte Cervantes	152	MSC Barbara	117
Maersk Rotterdam	98	Marco Polo	22	Meandros	110	Minerva Helen	124	Monte Olivia	152	MSC Basel	105
Maersk Rouen	48	Mare Adriaticum	83	Med Carrara	136	Minerva II	12	Monte Pascoal	152	MSC Beijing	158
Maersk Rugen	48	Mare Balticum	83	Med Lerici	136	Minerva Iris	124	Monte Pelmo	182	MSC Belem	33
Maersk Rye	133	Mare Doricum	83	Med Riva	136	Minerva Joanna	124	Monte Rosa	152	MSC Benedetta	117
Maersk Sana	130	Mare Gallicum	83	Med Salvador	136	Minerva Julie	124	Monte Sarmiento	152	MSC Bilboa	69
Maersk Santana	130	Mare Hibernum	83	Medea	220	Minerva Libra	124	Montebello	164	MSC Boston	36
Maersk Sarnia	130	Mare Phoenicium	83	Modi Dubai	65	Minerva Lisa	124	Montego	46	MSC Brasilia	213
Maersk Scotland	128	Maren Maersk	130	Medi Taipci	226	Minerva Maya	124	Montemar Europa	72	MSC Brianna	117
Maersk Sea	133	Marfret Caraibes	148	Medi Tokyo	65	Minerva Nike	124	Monterey	14	MSC Bruxelles	158
Maersk Seville	130	Marfret Douce France	114	Mediterranean Highway	101	Minerva Nounou	124	Monteverde	45	MSC Busan	158
Maersk Sheerness	130	Marfret Normandie	181	Mediterranean	75	Minerva Rita	124	Montreux	32	MSC Caitlin	117
Maersk Sidney	130	Marfret Provence	181	Medusa	116	Minerva Roxanne	124	Moorgate	154	MSC Camille	117
Maersk Stralsund	144	Margara	96	Megalonissos	72	Minerva Zen	124	Morning Ace	54	MSC Canberra	117
Maersk Sun	133	Margaretha Green	37	MegaStar Aries	20	Minerva Zenia	124	Morning Breeze	54	MSC Carina	117
Maersk Tacoma	208	Margit Gorthon	209	MegaStar Taurus	20	Minerva Zoe	124	Morning Calm	176	MSC Carla	117
Maersk Taiki	133	Margrethe Maersk	130	Mekong Spirit	83	Ming Equality	226	Morning Champion	176	MSC Carmen	117
Maersk Taiyo	133	Maria A. Angelicoussi	36	Melbourne Highway	101	Minna	69	Morning Charm	54	MSC Carole	117
Maersk Tampa	96	Maria A. Angelicoussis	48	Melbourne Star I	148	Mirfak Star	188	Morning Cloud	154	MSC Carolina	117
Maersk Tangier	83	Maria C	65	Melfi Halifax	208	Missouri	194	Morning Courier	176	MSC Charleston	158
Maersk Taranaki	130	Maria Gorthon	209	Melfi Havana	208	Mitrope	173	Morning Crown	176	MSC Chelsea	117
Maersk Teal	133	Maria Knutsen	102	Melfi Italia II	208	Modern Chance	54	Morning Glory	220	MSC Chiara	117
Maersk Tide	133	Maria Salamon	189	Melide	32	Modern Express	54	Morning Ivy	54	MSC Chicago	158
Maersk Toba	62	Maria Schulte	193	Melody	14	Modern Link	54	Morning Light	54	MSC Chile	105
Maersk Tokyo	62	Maria Tsakos	213	Mercosul Palometa	158	Modern Peak	54	Morning Melody	141	MSC China	177
Maersk Toledo	208	Marianne Schulte	192	Mercosul Pescada	182	MOL Accord	109	Morning Mercator	89	MSC Chitra	117
Maersk Toyama	62	Maribella	47	Mercure	106	MOL Advantage	125	Morning Meridian	89	MSC Christina	164
Maersk Trieste	208	Marichristina	47	Mercury Ace	125	MOL Americas	69	Morning Noble	101	MSC Claudia	117
Maersk Vaasa	109	Marie Delmas	58	Mercury Glory	172	MOL Brasilia	172	Morning Power	54	MSC Clorinda	117
Maersk Valencia	143	Marie Maersk	130	Mercury	18	MOL Bravery	125	Morning Prince	54	MSC Corinna	117
Maersk Valletta	216	Marie Schulte	193	Meridian Lion	189	MOL Caledon	158	Morning Queen	54	MSC Corsica	117
Maersk Valparaiso	33	Marielle Bolten	41	Merino Express	217	MOL Callao	125	Morning Rise	54	MSC Cristiana	117
Maersk Vancouver	62	Marietta	47	Merkur Bay	216	MOL Columbus	125	Morning Rose	89	MSC Daniela	118
Maersk Varna	193	Marijeannie	47	Merkur Beach	216	MOL Confidence	125	Morning Saga	54	MSC Deborah	118
Maersk Venice	216	Marine Phoenix	154	Merkur Bridge	216	MOL Cullinan	158	Morning Sapphire	101	MSC Deila	118
Maersk Ventspils	109	Marine Reliance	54	Merkur Lake	217	MOL Discovery	125	Morning Sun	54	MSC Delhi	144
Maersk Vera Cruz	69	Mariner of the Seas	18	Merkur Sea	217	MOL Efficiency	125	Moscow	145	MSC Denisse	118
Maersk Verona	143	Marinicki	47	Merkur Sky	217	MOL Elbe	125	Moscow Kremlin	145	MSC Didem	118
Maersk Victoria	69	Marinus Green	56	Merkur Star	217	MOL Encore	125	Moscow River	145	MSC Diego	118
Maersk Vienna	190	Marion Green	37	Merkur	33	MOL Endeavor	125	Moscow Sea	196	MSC Don Giovanni	118
Maersk Vigo	216	Marissa Green	56	Merlin Arrow	98	MOL Endurance	125	Moscow Stars	145	MSC Donata	109
Maersk Vilnius	109	Marivia	66	Methane Princess	77	MOL Enterprise	125	Moscow University	145	MSC Dymphna	118
Maersk Virginia	130	Marivic	47	Methania	61	MOL Eternity	125	Mosel Ace	220	MSC Edith	118
Maersk Volos	109	Markab Star	185	Mette Maersk	130	MOL Excellence	125	Mosel N	40	MSC Edna	118
Maersk Voshod	109	Mark-C	46	Mexican Reefer	106	MOL Expeditor	125	Moselle	164	MSC Ela	118
Maersk Vungtau	130							MOL Express	125	Mostoles	46	MSC Elena	118

Ship	No.	Ship	No.	Ship	No.	Ship	No.
MSC Eleni	118	MSC Manu	121	MSC Sonia	122	NDS Promoter	216
MSC Eleonora	118	MSC Mara	121	MSC Sophie	122	NDS Prospector	190
MSC Eliana	118	MSC Maracaibo	114	MSC Stefania	122	NDS Prosperity	216
MSC Emilia S	118	MSC Maria Laura	121	MSC Stella	122	NDS Proteus	216
MSC Emma	118	MSC Maria Pia	121	MSC Sudan	64	NDS Provider	190
MSC Erminia	118	MSC Maria	121	MSC Suez	122	Neches	164
MSC Esthi	118	MSC Marianna	121	MSC Sukaiyna	122	Nedlloyd Adelaide	130
MSC Eyra	118	MSC Marina	121	MSC Susanna	122	Nedlloyd Adriana	130
MSC Fabienne	118	MSC Marta	121	MSC Tasmania	122	Nedlloyd Africa	130
MSC Fantasia	14	MSC Martina	121	MSC Teresa	122	Nedlloyd America	130
MSC Federica	118	MSC Marylena	121	MSC Texas	148	Nedlloyd Asia	130
MSC Fiorenza	118	MSC Matilde	121	MSC Tina	122	Nedlloyd Barentsz	130
MSC Flaminia	148	MSC Maureen	121	MSC Tokyo	158	Nedlloyd Clarence	130
MSC Florentina	118	MSC Maya	121	MSC Tomoko	122	Nedlloyd Clement	130
MSC Floriana	118	MSC Mediterranean	121	MSC Toronto	158	Nedlloyd Colombo	130
MSC Florida	181	MSC Mee May	121	MSC Toulouse	114	Nedlloyd de Liefde	130
MSC Francesca	118	MSC Melissa	121	MSC Trinidad	122	Nedlloyd Drake	132
MSC Gabriella	118	MSC Mexico	62	MSC Tuscany	64	Nedlloyd Dubai	132
MSC Geneva	148	MSC Mia Summer	121	MSC Ulsan	164	Nedlloyd Europa	132
MSC Germany	62	MSC Michaela	121	MSC Uruguay	177	Nedlloyd Evita	132
MSC Gianna	118	MSC Michele	121	MSC Valencia	69	Nedlloyd Honshu	132
MSC Giorgia	118	MSC Mirella	121	MSC Valeria	122	Nedlloyd Houston	132
MSC Giovanna	118	MSC Monica	121	MSC Vanessa	124	Nedlloyd Hudson	132
MSC Giulia	118	MSC Musica	14	MSC Venice	64	Nedlloyd Juliana	132
MSC Grace	118	MSC Namibia	62	MSC Veronique	124	Nedlloyd Marita	132
MSC Greece	33	MSC Napoli	156	MSC Vittoria	124	Nedlloyd Maxima	132
MSC Hailey	118	MSC Natalia	121	MSC Viviana	124	Nedlloyd Mercator	132
MSC Heidi	118	MSC Nederland	121	MSC Washington	64	Nedlloyd Muscat	132
MSC Himalaya	172	MSC Nerissa	121	MSC Yokohama	64	Nedlloyd Nina	132
MSC Hina	118	MSC New York	36	MSC Yorkshire	69	Nedlloyd Oceania	132
MSC Hobart	143	MSC Nicole	121	MSC Zrin	124	Nedlloyd Tasman	132
MSC Ilaria	118	MSC Nilgun	121	MSC Zurich	33	Nedlloyd Teslin	132
MSC Ilona	148	MSC Noa	121	Mulungisi	156	Nedlloyd Valentina	132
MSC Imma	120	MSC Normandie	121	Mumbai Express	83	Nele Maersk	132
MSC Immacolata	120	MSC Nuria	121	Murmansk	110	Nelson Star	200
MSC India	120	MSC Olga	121	Music	194	Neptune	168
MSC Ines	120	MSC Opera	14	Myrto	47	Neptune Ace	126
MSC Ingrid	120	MSC Orchestra	14	Mystic	194	Neptune Glory	172
MSC Insa	120	MSC Ornella	121			Neptune Voyager	48
MSC Iris	120	MSC Palermo	105	Nada V	141	Nereo	190
MSC Jade	120	MSC Pamela	121	Nagoya Bay	194	Neste	140
MSC Japan	62	MSC Paola	121	Najran	214	Netadola	46
MSC Jasmine	120	MSC Parana	96	Namur	60	Netsanet	73
MSC Java	114	MSC Paris	69	Nandu Arrow	98	Nevskiy Prospect	196
MSC Jeanne	120	MSC Patricia	122	Naparima	126	New Ace	168
MSC Jemima	120	MSC Peggy	122	Napier Star	200	New Alliance	168
MSC Jenny	120	MSC Perle	122	Nara	157	New Amber	168
MSC Jessica	120	MSC Peru	96	Nariva	126	New Ambition	168
MSC Jilhan	120	MSC Pilar	122	Narodny Bridge	196	New Amity	168
MSC Joanna	120	MSC Poesia	14	Nassauborg	217	New Argosy	168
MSC Johannesburg	158	MSC Poh Lin	122	Natalie Bolten	41	New Assurance	168
MSC Jordan	120	MSC Queensland	144	National Geographic		New Century	168
MSC Judith	120	MSC Rachele	122	Endeavour	26	New Confidence	208
MSC Katherine Ann	120	MSC Rafaela	122	Natura	140	New Delhi Express	85
MSC Katie	120	MSC Rania	122	Nautica	16	New Dynamic	140
MSC Katrina	120	MSC Rebecca	190	Navigator of the Seas	18	New England	217
MSC Kerry	120	MSC Regina	122	Navion Akarita	206	New Flamenco	24
MSC Korea	62	MSC Rio Plata	177	Navion Anglia	206	New Fortuner	168
MSC Krittika	156	MSC Rita	122	Navion Britannia	206	New Nada	141
MSC Lara	120	MSC Roberta	122	Navion Clipper	206	New Oji Pioneer	190
MSC Laura	120	MSC Romania II	62	Navion Europa	102	New Orleans Express	85
MSC Lauren	120	MSC Rosa M	122	Navion Fennia	206	New Spirit	168
MSC Laurence	120	MSC Rosalba	122	Navion Hispania	206	New Valor	168
MSC Lausanne	148	MSC Rossella	122	Navion Norvegia	102	New Venture	168
MSC Lea	120	MSC Sabrina	122	Navion Oceania	206	New Victory	168
MSC Leanne	120	MSC Salvador	177	Navion Saga	206	New Vitality	168
MSC Leila	120	MSC Samantha	122	Navion Scandia	206	New York Express	64
MSC Levina	120	MSC Samia	122	Navion Scotia	206	Newforest	156
MSC Lieselotte	120	MSC Sandra	122	Navix Astral	77	Newport Bridge	101
MSC Linzie	120	MSC Santhya	122	Navix Azalea	126	Nexø Maersk	132
MSC Lirica	14	MSC Sardinia	213	Naxihe	49	Nichihiko	126
MSC Lisa	120	MSC Sariska	122	Naxos	41	Nichinori	126
MSC London	213	MSC Scandinavia	83	NCC Arar	135	Nichioh	126
MSC Lorena	120	MSC Selin	122	NCC Asir	135	Nichiryu	126
MSC Loretta	120	MSC Selma	122	NCC Baha	135	Nichiwa	126
MSC Lucia	120	MSC Seranata	14	NCC Hijaz	135	Nicolai Maersk	132
MSC Lucy	121	MSC Serena	64	NCC Jizan	135	Nicolas Delmas	58
MSC Ludovica	121	MSC Shanghai	158	NCC Jubail	135	Nicoline Maersk	132
MSC Lugano	208	MSC Shannon	122	NCC Madinah	135	Nida	173
MSC Luisa	121	MSC Sharjah	172	NCC Mekka	135	Niels Maersk	128
MSC Madeleine	121	MSC Shaula	122	NCC Najd	135	Nile	37
MSC Maeva	121	MSC Sheila	122	NCC Riyad	135	Nina	204
MSC Magali	121	MSC Sicily	64	NCC Tihama	135	Nippon	141
MSC Malin	121	MSC Silvana	122	NCC Yamamah	135	Nippon Highway	101
MSC Manaus	177	MSC Sinfonia	14	NDS Prodigy	190	Nippon Maru	14
MSC Mandy	121	MSC Socotra	172	NDS Progress	190	Nisha	81
				NDS Prominence	190	Nivosa	196

Ship	No.	Ship	No.
Noa	156	Nordstrength	162
Nobel Foam	205	Nordsun	162
Nobel Fortuna	205	Nordsund	145
Nobel Forum	205	Nordtrave	162
Noble	176	Nordvenus	162
Noemi	96	Nordwelle	162
Nogat	173	Nordweser	162
Nona	116	Norfolk Express	84
Noordam	8	Norilsk	112
Nor'easter	217	Norman Lady	89
Nora Maersk	128	Normandie Bridge	101
Norasia Alps	109	Norna	37
Norasia Alya	69	Norsea	37
Norasia Andes	212	North Sea	153
Norasia Atlas	69	North Sea Producer	133
Norasia Atria	143	North Star	108
Norasia Balkans	69	Northern Delight	148
Norasia Bellatrix	156	Northern Divinity	144
Norasia Enterprise	69	Northern Faith	149
Norasia Everest	188	Northern Felicity	149
Norasia Hamburg	65	Northern Fortune	177
Norasia Integra	143	Northern Happiness	149
Norasia Makalu	69	Northern Harmony	177
Norasia Polaris	212	Northern Reliance	149
Norasia Rigel	32	Northgate	156
Norasia Sils	202	Northsea Anvil	204
Norasia Tegesos	92	Northumberland	156
Norasia Telamon	92	Northwest Swan	48
Norasia Valparaiso	181	Norwegian Crown	20
Nord Sound	88	Norwegian Dawn	20
Nord Spirit	41	Norwegian Dream	20
Nord Stream	144	Norwegian Jewel	20
Nord Sun	126	Norwegian Majesty	20
Nordamerika	92	Norwegian Spirit	20
Nordanger	224	Norwegian Star	20
Nordasia	144	Norwegian Sun	20
Nordatlantic	144	Norwegian Wind	20
Nordbeach	162	Norwegian Gem	20
Nordbright	144	Norweigian Pearl	20
Nordeagle	162	Norwid	173
Nordelbe	162	Noto	37
Nordems	162	Nova Galicia	208
Nordenergy	162	Ntabeni	178
Nordeuropa	144	Nuri	37
Nordglimt	144	NYK Andromeda	141
Nordholt	126	NYK Antares	141
Nordic Bay	184	NYK Aphrodite	141
Nordic Cape	184	NYK Apollo	141
Nordic Discovery	206	NYK Aquarius	141
Nordic Fighter	206	NYK Argus	141
Nordic Freedom	206	NYK Artemis	141
Nordic Hawk	206	NYK Athena	141
Nordic Hunter	206	NYK Atlas	141
Nordic Ice	184	NYK Canopus	142
Nordic Laurita	206	NYK Castor	142
Nordic Marita	206	NYK Espirito	212
Nordic Rio	206	NYK Estrela	222
Nordic Saturn	206	NYK Floresta	193
Nordic Savonita	206	NYK Kai	142
Nordic Spirit	205	NYK Leo	142
Nordic Sta	184	NYK Libra	142
Nordic Stavanger	206	NYK Loadstar	142
Nordic Svenita	206	NYK Lynx	142
Nordic Torinita	206	NYK Lyra	142
Nordic Trym	206	NYK Pegasus	142
Nordic Voyager	224	NYK Phoenix	142
Nordkapp	28	NYK Prestige	110
Nordmark	162	NYK Procyon	142
Nordmars	162	NYK Sirius	142
Nordmerkur	162	NYK Springtide	142
Nordmillennium	162	NYK Starlight	142
Nordmoritz	162	Nyon	202
Nordmosel	162	Nysa	37
Nordneptune	162	Nysted Maersk	128
Nordnes	64		
Nordnorge	28	Obbola	209
Nordpacific	145	Ocana	77
Nordpower	162	Ocean	225
Nordrhine	162	Ocean Ace	126
Nordscot	32	Ocean Ceres	142
Nordseas	162	Ocean Crystal	46
Nordsky	162	Ocean Highway	101
Nordstar	162	Ocean Majesty	28
Nordstjemen	145	Ocean Monarch	28
Nordstjernen	28	Ocean Preface	33
Nordstrand	162	Ocean Prelate	33
		Ocean Prelude	33

Name	Page
Restless	190
Reunion	64
Rhapsody of the Seas	18
Rhapsody	14
Rhein Bridge	101
Rhein	98
Rheinstern	182
Rhine Forest	92
Rhine	164
Rhone	98
Rhone	164
Rhoneborg	220
Rhonestern	182
Rialto Bridge	149
Ribe Maersk	128
Richard Maersk	128
Richmond Park	156
Rickmer Rickmers	181
Rickmers Antwerp	189
Rickmers Chennai	181
Rickmers Dalian	181
Rickmers Genoa	181
Rickmers Hamburg	181
Rickmers Jakarta	181
Rickmers Mumbai	181
Rickmers New Orleans	181
Rickmers Seoul	181
Rickmers Shanghai	189
Rickmers Singapore	181
Rickmers Tokyo	189
Riga	106
Rigoletto	220
Rila	137
Rio Adour	135
Rio Ardeche	135
Rio Blanco	61
Rio Branco	135
Rio Bueno	61
Rio Enco	61
Rio Grande	135
Rio Lawrence	135
Rio Negro	135
Rio Rubio	135
Rio Stora	135
Rio Susa	135
Rip Hudner	216
Rita D'Amato	65
Rita Knutsen	102
Rita Maersk	128
Rithi Bhum	181
River Elegance	49
River Mas	64
River Phoenix	156
River Wisdom	49
Robert Maersk	128
Robert Rickmers	181
Roberto C	65
Robin	32
Rodina	137
Rodlo	173
Rodopi	137
Rojen	137
Rokia Delmas	58
Rokkosan	128
Roland Delmas	58
Rolnik	173
Roma	178
Romantic	108
Romea Champion	196
Romoe Maersk	128
Ropazi	106
Ros	174
Rosa Delmas	58
Rosa Maersk	128
Rosario	161
Rosetta	164
Rosita	214
Rossel Current	136
Rothorn	225
Rotterdam Express	84
Rotterdam	8
Rousse	137
Rowan	212
Roxanne	161
Roy Maersk	128
Royal Bay	194

Name	Page
Royal Clipper	20
Royal Cooler	194
Royal Klipper	194
Royal Reefer	194
Royal Star	30
Rubens	136
Ruby Express	126
Ruby III	128
Ruby Ray	176
Ruby	164
Rudolf Schulte	192
Ruhr N	40
Runaway Bay	194
Rundale	106
Rutland	156
Ryndam	8
Ryujin	142
Ryuohsan	128
S.A. Helderberg	66
S.A. Sederberg	66
S.A. Winterberg	66
S/R American Progress	75
S/R Baytown	75
S/R Columbia Bay	75
S/R Hinchinbrook	75
S/R Long Beach	75
S/R Wilmington	75
SA Altius	178
SA Fortius	178
Saar N	40
Sable Bay	208
Sabrewing	190
Sacramento	164
Saetta	46
Safaniyah	135
Safmarine Agulhas	217
Safmarine Amazon	33
Safmarine Antwerp	64
Safmarine Asia	134
Safmarine Basilea	134
Safmarine Cameroun	134
Safmarine Concord	134
Safmarine Cotonou	134
Safmarine Cunene	143
Safmarine Europe	134
Safmarine Gonubie	225
Safmarine Himalaya	64
Safmarine Houston	204
Safmarine Ibhayi	134
Safmarine Igoli	64
Safmarine Ikapa	134
Safmarine Illovo	32
Safmarine Kuramo	134
Safmarine Leman	134
Safmarine Mbashe	69
Safmarine Memling	33
Safmarine Mgeni	69
Safmarine Mono	32
Safmarine Nimba	134
Safmarine Nokwanda	134
Safmarine Nolizwe	134
Safmarine Nomazwe	134
Safmarine Onne	204
Safmarine Oranje	134
Safmarine Pakistan	193
Safmarine Tugela	66
Safmarine Zambezi	143
Safwa	135
Saga Adventure	182
Saga Andorinha	182
Saga Beija-Flor	182
Saga Crest	182
Saga Horizon	182
Saga Jandaia	182
Saga Marlin	182
Saga Mascot	182
Saga Merchant	182
Saga Merit	182
Saga Minerva	182
Saga Miranda	182
Saga Monal	184
Saga Morus	184
Saga Musketeer	184
Saga Rose	20
Saga Ruby	20

Name	Page
Saga Sky	184
Saga Spray	184
Saga Tide	184
Saga Tucano	184
Saga Viking	184
Saga Voyager	184
Saga Wave	184
Saga Wind	184
Sagittarius Leader	142
Saigon Express	85
Saimagracht	197
Saint Petersburg	110
Saint Roch	58
Sakar	137
Sakura	188
Sala	37
Salamina	72
Salamis Glory	28
Saldanha	178
Salerno	178
Sallie Knutsen	102
Sally Maersk	132
Salusnavis	52
Samar Spirit	205
Samburga	106
Samco	204
Samco America	204
Samco Asia	204
Samco Scandinavia	204
Samothraki	72
Sampogracht	197
San Clemente	158
San Cristobal	158
San Felipe	158
San Fernando	158
San Francisco Express	144
San Francisco	158
San Jacinto	164
San Lorenzo	158
San Pedro Bridge	149
Sanaga	73
Sandnes	64
Sandra Azul	156
Sandra Blanca	156
Sandviken	134
Sandy Rickmers	181
Sanko Ability	185
Sanko Advance	185
Sanko Amity	185
Sanko Blossom	185
Sanko Brave	124
Sanko Breeze	185
Sanko Bright	124
Sanko Dynasty	185
Sanko Eagle	185
Sanko Eternal	185
Sanko Falcon	185
Sanko Galaxy	185
Sanko Glory	185
Sanko Oasis	185
Sanko Phoenix	185
Sanko Quality	185
Sanko Rally	185
Sanko Ranger	185
Sanko Rejoice	185
Sanko Robust	185
Sanko Rose	185
Sanko Royal	185
Sanko Sincere	185
Sanko Spark	185
Sanko Spring	185
Sanko Stream	185
Sanko Summit	185
Sanko Supreme	185
Sanko Unity	185
Santa Adrian	158
Santa Alexandra	158
Santa Alin	160
Santa Ana	96
Santa Annabella	160
Santa Arabella	160
Santa Barbara	156
Santa Carlotta	160
Santa Carolina	160
Santa Catalina	160
Santa Catharina	194

Name	Page
Santa Celina	160
Santa Cristina	160
Santa Cruz	156
Santa Elena	190
Santa Esmeralda	46
Santa Fabiola	160
Santa Federica	160
Santa Felicita	160
Santa Fiorenza	160
Santa Francesca	160
Santa Giovanna	160
Santa Giulietta	160
Santa Lucia	194
Santa Maddalena	160
Santa Maria	194
Santa Marina	184
Santa Markela	46
Santa Monica	156
Santa Monica	160
Santa Victoria	46
Santiago Express	84
Santorin II	41
Santos Star	88
Saone	164
Sapphire Ace	126
Sapphire Highway	101
Sapphire Princess	12
Sapphire Ray	176
Sapphire	14
Sara Viking	204
Saracen Star	54
Saraji Trader	205
Sarasota	46
Saratov	110
Sarpen	112
Satha Bhum	181
Satsuma	142
Sattar	96
Saturn	33
Saudi Abha	135
Saudi Diriyah	135
Saudi Hofuf	135
Saudi Tabuk	135
Savannah Express	144
Savannah	157
Savoie	60
Saxonia	32
Scandinavian Express	217
Scandinavian Highway	101
Scandinavian Reefer	106
SCF Aldan	197
SCF Altai	197
SCF Baltica	197
SCF Byrranga	197
SCF Caucasus	197
SCF Khibiny	197
SCF Sayan	197
SCF Ural	197
SCF Valdai	197
Scheldegracht	197
Schippersgracht	197
SCI Mahima	153
SCI Vijay	213
Scotian Express	217
Scottish Star	200
Sea Alfa	190
Sea Beta	190
Sea Bright	116
Sea Cloud II	22
Sea Cloud	22
Sea Crane	52
Sea Gloria	52
Sea Grace	52
Sea Master	182
Sea Navigator	92
Sea Phoenix	156
Sea Princess	12
Sea Puma	181
Sea Ranger	178
Seabass	88
Seabourn Legend	10
Seabourn Pride	10
Seabourn Spirit	10
Seaboxer	208
Seaconger	88

Name	Page
Seadevil	88
SeaDream I	28
SeaDream II	28
Seagate	156
Seahake	88
Seahawk Freighter	206
Sea-Land Achiever	133
Sea-Land Atlantic	133
Sea-Land Champion	132
Sea-Land Charger	133
Sea-Land Comet	133
Sea-Land Commitment	133
Sea-Land Defender	128
Sea-Land Developer	133
Sea-Land Eagle	132
Sea-Land Endurance	128
Sea-Land Explorer	133
Sea-Land Express	133
Sea-Land Florida	134
Sea-Land Freedom	132
Sealand Illinois	64
Sea-Land Independence	133
Sea-Land Innovator	133
Sea-Land Integrity	134
Sea-Land Intrepid	132
Sea-Land Liberator	134
Sea-Land Lightning	132
Sea-Land Mariner	132
Sea-Land Mercury	132
Sea-Land Meteor	132
Sealand Michigan	64
Sea-Land Motivator	134
Sealand New York	64
Sea-Land Patriot	134
Sea-Land Performance	134
Sea-Land Pride	132
Sea-Land Quality	134
Sea-Land Racer	132
Sea-Land Value	132
Sea-Land Voyager	134
Sealand Washington	64
Sealing	88
Seamullet	88
Sean Rickmers	181
Searadiance	52
Searay	88
Searose G	216
Seashark	88
Seaturbot	88
Sebarok Spirit	206
Sebu	37
Segovia Carrie	66
Seijin	142
Seine	165
Selandia	204
Selene Trader	128
Seletar Spirit	206
Selinda	73
Semakau Spirit	206
Senang Spirit	206
Senatore	96
Sensation	8
Sentinel	62
Sentosa Spirit	206
Seraya Spirit	206
Serenade of the Seas	18
Serenade	14
Sergey Lemesh(y)ev	145
Serifopoulo	72
Serifos	72
Seven Sea Mariner	16
Seven Seas Highway	101
Seven Seas Navigator	16
Seven Seas Voyager	18
SG Enterprise	38
SG Prosperity	38
Sha He	49
Shan He	49
Shanghai Bridge	101
Shanghai Express	84
Shanghai Highway	101
Shanghai Star I	114
Sharifa 3	47
Shaula Star	188

Name	Page
Shaybah	188
Shenandoah Highway	101
Shetland Spirit	206
Shetland	156
Shibumi	46
Shilla Spirit	206
Shing Star	101
Shinoussa	72
Shion	225
Shipka	137
Sibeia	204
Siboelf	204
Siboeva	216
Sibohelle	204
Siboninat	204
Sibotessa	204
Sibotura	216
Sibulk Premier	88
Sicilia	92
Sidsel Knutsen	102
Sierra Express	64
Sigana	204
Sigrun Bolten	41
Silia T	213
Silver Cloud	20
Silver One	182
Silver Shadow	20
Silver Whisper	20
Silver Wind	20
Silverfjord	113
Silvergate	156
Silvia	32
Sinar Toba	156
Sine Maersk	132
Sinfonia	101
Singapore Express	64
Singelgracht	197
Sinotrans Dalian	144
Sinotrans Qingdao	144
Sinotrans Shanghai	144
Sinotrans Tianjin	144
Sinotrans Tokyo	92
Sir Charles Parsons	174
Siri Knutsen	102
Sirius	77
Sirius Highway	101
Sirius Leader	142
Sirius	33
Siskin Arrow	98
Sitacamilla	204
Sitakathrine	204
Sitamarie	204
Sitamia	204
Sitavera	204
Sitria	204
Sivega	204
SJN Lopez	190
SJN Orcas	190
Skagen Maersk	132
Skauboard	96
Skaubryn	97
Skaugran	97
Skier Star	108
Skiropoula	72
Skopelos	72
SKS Mersey	97
SKS Mosel	97
SKS Saluda	189
SKS Senne	189
SKS Sinni	189
SKS Sira	189
SKS Tagus	97
SKS Tana	97
SKS Tanaro	97
SKS Tiete	97
SKS Torrens	97
SKS Trent	97
SKS Trinity	97
SKS Tugela	97
SKS Tweed	97
SKS Tyne	97
Skulptors Tomskis	106
Sky L	34
Sky Wonder	16
Skyros	41
Slavianka	137
Slotergracht	197

Name	Page	Name	Page
Sluisgracht	197	Stadt Emden	208
Snoekgracht	197	Stadt Munchen	208
Snowdon	156	Stafford	156
Sofia III	66	Stanislaw Kulczynski	174
Sofia	137	Star Alabama	224
Sofie Maersk	132	Star Altanger	224
Sol do Brasil	152	Star America	224
Solar Wing	126	Star Atlantic	224
Solent Star	200	Star Austanger	224
Solidarnosc	174	Star Clipper	20
Solstice	18	Star Davanger	224
Somerset	156	Star Derby	224
Somjin	165	Star Dieppe	224
Song He	49	Star Djervanger	224
Song Yun He	49	Star Dover	224
Songa Abra	40	Star Drivanger	224
Songa Ancora	40	Star Drottanger	224
Songa Anette	40	Star Eagle	224
Songa Arctic	45	Star Evanger	224
Songa Eva	40	Star Evviva	224
Songa Maya	40	Star Florida	224
Sonoma	46	Star Flyer	20
Sophia Britannia	64	Star Fraser	224
Sophie Oldendorff	161	Star Fuji	224
Sorø Maersk	132	Star Geiranger	224
Soro	37	Star Gran	224
Sorokaletiye Pobedy	145	Star Grindanger	224
Sotka	140	Star Grip	224
Sotra Spirit	206	Star Hansa	224
Southampton Star	200	Star Hardanger	224
Southern Bay	194	Star Harmonia	224
Southern Harvest	108	Star Heranger	224
Southgate	156	Star Herdla	224
Sovereign Maersk	132	Star Hidra	224
Sovereign of the Seas	18	Star Hosanger	224
Sovereign Unity	169	Star Hoyanger	224
Sovereign	190	Star Ikebana	224
Spaarnegracht	200	Star Indiana	224
Spar Capella	197	Star Inventana	224
Spar Carina	197	Star Isfjord	224
Spar Cetus	107	Star Ismene	224
Spar Corona	197	Star Isoldana	224
Spar Eight	197	Star Istind	224
Spar Emerald	197	Star Japan	224
Spar Jade	197	Star Juventus	224
Spar Leo	197	Star Langanger	224
Spar Lupus	197	Star Leikanger	224
Spar Lynx	197	Star Ohio	48
Spar Lyra	197	Star Okiana	224
Spar Neptun	197	Star Optimana	224
Spar Opal	197	Star Osakana	224
Spar Orion	197	Star Oshimana	221
Spar Ruby	197	Star Pisces	20
Spar Sirius	197	Star Polaris	224
Spar Taurus	197	Star Pollux	224
Spar Three	197	Star Princess	12
Spar Topaz	197	Star Siranger	224
Spar Two	197	Starway	157
Spar Vega	197	Statendam	8
Spar Virgo	197	Statengracht	200
Spiegelgracht	200	Stavronisi	72
Spiri	145	Steel Glory	178
Spirit of Adventure	20	Steel Might	178
Spirit of Oceanus	24	Stellar Voyager	48
Splendid Ace	126	Stellenbosch	113
Splendid Harvest	108	Stemnitsa	124
Splendour of the Seas	18	Stena Alexita	201
Splittnes	64	Stena Arctica	201
Sporades	72	Stena Commander	201
Spotless	190	Stena Companion	201
Spring Bear	194	Stena Compatriot	201
Spring Bob	194	Stena Concept	201
Spring Bok	194	Stena Concord	145
Spring Deli	194	Stena Conductor	201
Spring Dragon	194	Stena Confidence	201
Spring Panda	194	Stena Conqueror	201
Spring Tiger	194	Stena Conquest	201
Springwood	156	Stena Consul	145
Spruce Arrow	98	Stena Contender	197
Spuigracht	200	Stena Contender	201
St. Angelo	176	Stena Contest	201
St. Jacobi	48	Stena Arctica	201
St. Katharinen	32	Stena Natalita	206
St. Lucia	108	Stena Paris	201
St. Petri	48	Stena Provence	201
Stadiongracht	200	Stena Sirita	201
Stadt Berlin	208	Stena Spirit	206

Name	Page	Name	Page
Stena Venture	172	SuperStar Virgo	20
Stena Victory	201	Supreme Harvest	108
Stena Vision	201	Surfer Rosa	124
Steven N	38	Surrey	156
Stolt Achievement	201	Susan Maersk	132
Stolt Aquamarine	201	Susanne Schulte	192
Stolt Avance	201	Sussex	156
Stolt Avenir	201	Suva	37
Stolt Capability	201	Svend Maersk	132
Stolt Concept	201	Svendborg Maersk	132
Stolt Condor	201	Svilen Russev	137
Stolt Confidence	201	Swakop	73
Stolt Creativity	201	Swan	68
Stolt Dorset	40	Swan Arrow	98
Stolt Eagle	201	Swan Chacabuco	200
Stolt Efficiency	201	Swift	68
Stolt Effort	201	Swift Arrow	98
Stolt Emerald	201	Sydney Express	85
Stolt Excellence	201	Sylt	37
Stolt Falcon	201	Symphonic	108
Stolt Guardian	201	Syms Hunshan	188
Stolt Hawk	201	Synnove Knutsen	102
Stolt Helluland	201	Szare Szeregi	174
Stolt Hill	201	Szymanowski	173
Stolt Innovation	201		
Stolt Inspiration	202	Taganrog	145
Stolt Integrity	202	Tagus	220
Stolt Invention	202	Tahitian Princess	12
Stolt Jade	202	Tai He	49
Stolt Kent	40	Tai Shan	220
Stolt Loyalty	202	Taiko	220
Stolt Markland	202	Taixing	173
Stolt Nanami	202	Taizan	142
Stolt Osprey	202	Tajima	142
Stolt Peak	202	Takachiho II	142
Stolt Perseverance	202	Takamar	170
Stolt Pride	202	Takara	225
Stolt Protector	202	Takasago Maru	142
Stolt Sapphire	202	Takase	128
Stolt Sea	202	Takasuzu	142
Stolt Sincerity	202	Takayama	220
Stolt Span	202	Talabot	220
Stolt Spray	202	Talia	176
Stolt Stream	202	Talisman	220
Stolt Sun	202	Talty	174
Stolt Surf	202	Tama Hope	194
Stolt Tenacity	202	Tama Star	194
Stolt Topaz	202	Taman	145
Stolt Valor	202	Tamar	165
Stolt Vestland	202	Tamara	46
Stolt Viking	202	Tamarita	214
Stolt Vinland	202	Tambov	145
Stonegate	156	Tamerlane	220
Stones	64	Tamesis	220
Storm Bay	194	Tampa	220
Storm Ranger	178	Tampere	220
Storviken	134	Tanabe	170
Stove Campbell	36	Tancred	225
Stove Trader	36	Tanea	134
Stove Tradition	36	Taos	37
Stove Transport	36	Tapatio	48
Strait Mas	64	Tapiola	220
Striggla	46	Tarago	220
Strymon	110	Taronga	220
Stuttgart Express	84	Tasco	220
Suez Canal Bridge	101	Tåsinge Maersk	132
Suffolk	156	Tasman Adventurer	161
Suhail Star	188	Tasman Bay	194
Summer Bay	108	Tasman Challenger	114
Summer Flower	108	Tasman Discoverer	161
Summer Meadow	108	Tasman Endeavour	202
Summer Phoenix	156	Tasman Provider	202
Summer Wind	108	Tasman Trader	32
Summit	18	Tateyama	142
Sun Ace	126	Tatiana Schulte	193
Sun Beauty	194	Taunton	156
Sun Claudia	194	Tauranga Star	201
Sun Princess	12	Taurus	136
Sun Suma	98	Taxiarchis	192
Sunset Bay	189	Teal Arrow	98
Suomigracht	200	Teal	68
Super Adventure	36	Team Actinia	40
Super Challenge	37	Team Anatas	40
Super Servant 3	68	Team Anemonia	40
Super Servant 4	68	Team Aniara	40
SuperStar Gemini	20	Team Anja	40
SuperStar Libra	20	Team Jupiter	40

Name	Page	Name	Page
Team Leopard	40	Tokachi	142
Team Mars	40	Toki Arrow	98
Team Merkur	40	Tokyo Bay	194
Team Neptun	40	Tokyo Express	84
Team Panther	40	Toledo Spirit	206
Team Saturn	40	Toledo	220
Team Tiger	40	Tolteca	92
Teatralny Bridge	197	Tomsk	145
Teen	96	Tonga	46
Teide Spirit	206	Topaz Ace	54
Tempera	140	Topaz Ray	176
Temryuk	145	Topaz	108
Tenacity	212	Torben Maersk	132
Tenerife Spirit	206	Torben Spirit	206
Teng He	49	Tordis Knutsen	102
Teng Yun He	49	Torgovy Bridge	197
Tenryu	142	Torill Knutsen	102
Tern Arrow	98	Torinia	134
Tern	68	Torm Alice	208
Terrier	220	Torm Anna	208
Tervi	140	Torm Anne	209
Teseo	192	Torm Ann-Marie	208
Tete Rickmers	181	Torm Arawa	209
Tevere	165	Torm Asia	209
Texas Gal	161	Torm Baltic	209
Texas Highway	101	Torm Estrid	209
Texas	220	Torm Freya	209
Thai Bright	214	Torm Gerd	209
Thai Dawn	214	Torm Gertrud	209
Thames	165	Torm Gotland	209
The Calypso	14	Torm Gudrun	209
The Emerald	22	Torm Gunhild	209
The Topaz	28	Torm Helene	209
The World	28	Torm Helvig	209
Thekla Schulte	192	Torm Herdis	209
Themsestern	182	Torm Ingeborg	209
Theodor Oldendorff	161	Torm Ismini	209
Theodor Storm	177	Torm Kristina	209
Therese Selmar	222	Torm Marina	209
Thetis	47	Torm Marlene	209
Thies Maersk	132	Torm Marta	209
Thomas C	192	Torm Mary	209
Thomas Maersk	132	Torm Pacific	209
Thomas Mann	177	Torm Ragnhild	209
Thomson Celebration	22	Torm Rotna	209
Thomson Destiny	22	Torm Sara	209
Thomson Spirit	22	Torm Signe	209
Thorbjorg	208	Torm Sofia	209
Thordis	208	Torm Tekla	209
Thorgull	208	Torm Thyra	209
Thornbury	112	Torm Tina	209
Thorsriver	97	Torm Valborg	209
Thorstream	97	Torm Vita	209
Thorunn	208	Toronto	220
Thuringia Express	156	Torrens	220
Thurø Maersk	132	Torres Spirit	206
TI Africa	169	Tosca	220
TI Asia	60	Toucan Arrow	98
TI Creation	60	Touraine	61
TI Europe	60	Tourcoing	221
TI Guardian	60	Tove Knutsen	102
TI Hellas	60	Tove Maersk	132
TI Oceania	169	Tower Bridge	197
TI Topaz	60	Tower Bridge	101
Tian Fu Hai	52	Tower Bridge	216
Tian Li Hai	52	Trade Rainbow	164
Tian Yang Hai	52	Trader	212
Tianjing Highway	101	Trans Atlantic	48
Tigani	46	Trans Ocean	48
Tiger Island	160	Trans Pacific	48
Tiger Sky	144	Transporter	192
Tikeibank	204	Transshelf	68
Tikhoretsk	145	Trapezitsa	137
Tikhvin	145	Trave Trader	45
Tim Buck	112	Travestern	182
Timashevsk	145	Traviata	221
Timor Stream	194	Trein Maersk	132
Tineke	156	Trianon	225
Tinglev Maersk	132	Triathlon	213
Tinos	41	Trigger	54
Titus	220	Trimnes	225
Tiwai Maru	98	Trinidad	225
TMM Hidalgo	104	Trinity	165
Toba	220	Tristan	221
Tobias Maersk	132	Triton Highway	101
Tofton	209	Triton Reefer	108
Tohdoh	142		